THOMSON LEARNING

CERTIFIED BUSINESS MANAGER

CBM Examination Preparation Guide

Helping Business Specialists Become Business Generalists

P3

volume five
theory for integrated areas

APBM
ASSOCIATION OF PROFESSIONALS
IN BUSINESS MANAGEMENT

CBM

THOMSON
SOUTH-WESTERN

Australia · Canada · Mexico · Singapore · Spain · United Kingdom · United States

THOMSON

SOUTH-WESTERN

Certified Business Manager (CBM) Examination Preparation Guide
Part 3, Volume 5: Theory for Integrated Areas

VP/Editorial Director:
Jack W. Calhoun

VP/Executive Publisher:
Dave Shaut

Sr. Acquisition Editor:
Scott Person

Developmental Editor:
Sara Froelicher

Sr. Production Editor:
Deanna Quinn

Marketing Manager:
Mark Linton

Manufacturing Coordinator:
Charlene Taylor

Internal Designer:
Chris Miller

Cover Designer:
Chris Miller

Production House and Compositor:
Carlisle Publisher Services

Printer:
West Group

COPYRIGHT © 2004
by South-Western, a division of Thomson Learning. Thomson Learning™ is a trademark used herein under license.

Printed in the United States of America
1 2 3 4 5 06 05 04 03

For more information
contact South-Western,
5191 Natorp Boulevard,
Mason, Ohio 45040.
Or you can visit our Internet site at:
http://www.swlearning.com

ALL RIGHTS RESERVED.
No part of this work covered by the copyright hereon may be reproduced or used in any form or by any means–graphic, electronic, or mechanical, including photocopying, recording, taping, Web distribution or information storage and retrieval systems–without the written permission of the publisher.

For permission to use material from this text or product, contact us by
Tel (800) 730-2214
Fax (800) 730-2215
http://www.thomsonrights.com

Library of Congress Control Number: 2003095412

ISBN 0-324-20011-0

Contents

Preface vii

Section I. Understanding Of Business Concepts 1

Module 100	General Management and Organization	2
Module 200	Operations Management	44
Module 300	Marketing Management	56
Module 400	Quality and Process Management	71
Module 500	Human Resources Management	79
Module 600	Accounting	89
Module 700	Finance	107
Module 800	Information Technology	135
Module 900	Corporate Control and Governance	150
Module 1000	International Business	157

Section II. Application Of Business Concepts 169

Application 1	Strategic Management Analysis	171
Application 2	Marketing Management Analysis	172
Application 3	Leverage Analysis	173
Application 4	Supply Chain Management Analysis	175
Application 5	Pricing Analysis	177
Application 6	Capital Budget Analysis	179

Application 7	Mergers, Acquisitions, and Business Valuation Analysis	180
Application 8	Production Planning Analysis	183
Application 9	Process Analysis	184
Application 10	Advertising Analysis	186
Application 11	Manufacturing Management Analysis	187
Application 12	Value Analysis	189
Application 13	Manufacturing Operations Analysis	190
Application 14	Retail Management Analysis	194
Application 15	Service Management Analysis	200
Application 16	Cost Analysis	202
Application 17	Corporate Performance Analysis	204
Application 18	Financial Management Analysis	205
Application 19	International Trade and Financing Analysis	208
Application 20	Project Management Analysis	210
Application 21	Economic Analysis	211
Application 22	Cash Flow Analysis	212
Application 23	Fraud Analysis	213
Application 24	Quality Analysis	214
Application 25	Sensitivity and Scenario Analysis	217
Application 26	Divisional Performance Analysis	218
Application 27	Organizational and General Management Analysis	220
Application 28	Human Resource Management Analysis	226
Application 29	Logistics Analysis	227
Application 30	New Product Development and Product Management Analysis	230

Application 31	Sales Analysis	232
Application 32	Risk Analysis	233
Application 33	Decision Analysis	237
Application 34	Operating Budget Analysis	238
Application 35	Cost-Volume-Profit Analysis	240
Application 36	Control Analysis	241
Application 37	Customer Analysis	243
Application 38	Quantitative and Qualitative Analysis	244
Application 39	Productivity Analysis	248
Application 40	Competitive Analysis	249

Mathematical Tables — 251

Glossary — G-1

Endnotes — E-1

Subject Index — I-1

Preface

Helping Business Specialists Become Business Generalists

Here is the best source to help streamline your CBM Exam preparation efforts.

The *Certified Business Manager (CBM) Examination Preparation Guide: Part 3, Volume 5: Theory for Integrated Areas* is one of a six-volume series developed solely to help you prepare for the CBM Exam. Designed with flexibility in mind, each guide can be used either in a self-study or group-study environment. Third-party review course providers such as professional associations, universities, and private organizations can also use this series to conduct review classes for CBM Exam candidates.

Developed by the best minds in the business management field, this series is a compilation of information from subject matter experts who are highly trained and experienced in the business management field. For a complete listing of these experts, see the acknowledgements section.

The goal of the CBM program is to help business specialists become business generalists. The CBM is to a business manager as the CPA is to an accountant, as the PE is to an engineer, and as the CFA is to an investment and financial analyst.

The CBM Exam consists of three parts:

Part 1: Core Areas

Part 2: Functional Areas

Part 3: Integrated Areas

Designed specifically with these three parts in mind, this Study Guide series addresses all of these parts to make exam preparation both comprehensive and as easy as possible.

Part 1, Volume 1: Theory for Core Areas
Part 1, Volume 2: Practice for Core Areas
Part 2, Volume 3: Theory for Functional Areas
Part 2, Volume 4: Practice for Functional Areas
Part 3, Volume 5: Theory for Integrated Areas
Part 3, Volume 6: Practice for Integrated Areas

Each part requires two volumes to study from: Theory and Practice Guides. Theory Guides (Volumes 1, 3, and 5) cover the subject matter as defined in the Common Body of Knowledge for Business (CBKB), which is the basis for the CBM Exam. The CBKB is a blend of undergraduate and graduate studies in business spread over ten modules. Practice Guides (Volumes 2, 4, and 6) contain multiple-choice questions, answers, and explanations in line with the CBKB. The three-part CBM Exam contains multiple-choice questions only.

The best way to study the Theory Guides is to review the module glossary prior to reading the corresponding text. Due to the comprehensive nature of the Theory Guides, the CBM practitioner can also use them as desk reference resources. The best way to study the Practice Guides is to self-test the questions prior to reading the study questions, answers, and explanations. When reading the Theory and Practice Guides together, read the Theory Guides first followed by the Practice Guides.

Parts 1 and 2 of the CBM Exam focus on ten modules, learning one module at a time in a discrete manner. These modules include general management, operations, marketing, quality and process management, human resources, accounting, finance, information technology, control and governance, and international business. Part 3 of the CBM Exam focuses on integration of these modules, providing "how-to" approaches, and showing "big picture" perspectives. While Parts 1 and 2 emphasize the understanding of business concepts, Part 3 emphasizes the application of business concepts. Due to the integrated nature of Part 3, the CBM candidate is expected to refer to all six volumes offered in the preparation guide series when studying for the Part 3 Exam. Passing the Part 3 Exam improves the analytical and technical skills, enhances the cross-functional knowledge of business, and sharpens the problem-solving and decision-making skills of a business manager.

The CBM program is sponsored and administered by the Association of Professionals in Business Management (APBM) who can be reached at the following address.

> Association of Professionals in Business Management
> 4929 Wilshire Boulevard, Suite 930, Los Angeles, California, 90010-3835 USA
> Phone: 323-936-6757   Fax: 323-936-6171
> email: Info@cbmexam.com   Website: www.cbmexam.com

Questions related to application materials, eligibility requirements, examination sites and dates, fees, and other administrative matters should be directed to *info@cbmexam.com* or visit *www.cbmexam.com*.

To purchase this series, or individual guides, contact either South-Western, a division of Thomson Learning, *www.swlearning.com/cbm.html*, *www.cbmexam.com*, or SRV Professional Publications *www.srvbooks.com*. Volume purchases can be made through South-Western for university, corporate, government, and professional association purchases by contacting *www.swlearning.com/cbm.html* or 1-800-842-3636.

Acknowledgments

A special thanks to the following South-Western authors for allowing the use of their information in developing comprehensive and high-quality study guides to prepare for the CBM Exam.

General Management and Organization, Module 100

Management by Daft, 6th edition, © 2003, ISBN 0-030-35138-3.
Essentials of Organization Theory and Design by Daft, 2nd edition, © 2001, ISBN 0-324-02097-X.
Successful Project Management by Gido/Clements, 2nd edition, © 2003, ISBN 0-324-07168-X.
Essentials of Business Law and the Legal Environment by Mann/Roberts, 7th edition, © 2001, ISBN 0-324-04052-0.
Quantitative Methods for Business by Anderson/Sweeney/Williams, 8th edition, © 2001, ISBN 0-324-04499-2.
Fundamentals of Managerial Economics by Hirschey, 7th edition, © 3002, ISBN 0-324-18331-3.

Operations Management, Module 200

Production and Inventory Management by Fogarty/Blackstone/Hoffmann, 2nd edition, © 1991, ISBN 0-538-07461-2.
Successful Service Operations Management by Metters et al, © 2003, ISBN 0-324-13556-4.
Purchasing and Supply Chain Management by Monczka et al, 2nd edition, © 2002, ISBN 0-324-02315-4.
231 terms in Glossary from *APICS Dictionary*, 10th Edition, © 2002 by APICS—The Educational Society for Resource Management, Alexandria, Virginia, USA. Reprinted with permission.

Marketing Management, Module 300

Marketing: Best Practices by Hoffman et al, 2nd edition, © 2003, ISBN 0-030-34999-0.
Essentials of Business Law and the Legal Environment by Mann/Roberts, 7th edition, © 2001, ISBN 0-324-04052-0.
Fundamentals of Managerial Economics by Hirschey, 7th edition, © 2003, ISBN 0-324-18331-3.

Quality and Process Management, Module 400

Management and the Control of Quality by Evans/Lindsay, 5th edition, © 2002, ISBN 0-324-06680-5.
Successful Service Operations Management by Metters et al, © 2003, ISBN 0-324-13556-4.
Glossary from the *Certified Quality Manager Handbook* by Duke Okes and Russell T. Westcott (eds), 2nd Edition. © 2001 by ASQ Quality Press, Milwaukee, Wisconsin, USA. Reprinted with permission.

Human Resources Management, Module 500

Human Resources Management by Mathis/Jackson, 10th edition, © 2003 ISBN 0-324-07151-5.

Accounting, Module 600

Financial and Managerial Accounting by Warren/Reeve/Fess, 7th edition, © 2002, 0-324-02540-8.
International Accounting by Iqbal, 2nd edition, © 2002, 0-324-02350-2.

Finance, Module 700

Essentials of Managerial Finance by Besley/Brigham, 12th edition, © 2000, 0-030-25872-3.
International Financial Management by Madura, 7th edition, © 2003, 0-324-16551-X.
Short-Term Financial Management by Maness/Zietlow, 2nd edition, © 2002, 0-030-31513-1.

Information Technology, Module 800

Management Information Systems by Oz, 3rd edition, © 2002, 0-619-06250-9.

Corporate Control and Governance, Module 900

Fraud Examination by Albrecht, 1st edition, © 2003, 0-324-16296-0.
Business and Society by Carroll/Buchholtz, 5th edition, © 2003, 0-324-11495-8.
Risk Management and Insurance by Trieschmann, 11th edition, © 2001, 0-324-01663-8.

International Business, Module 1000

International Economics by Carbaugh, 8th edition, © 2002, 0-324-05589-7.
International Business by Czinkota, 6th edition, © 2003, 0-324-17660-0.
Essentials of Business Law and the Legal Environment by Mann/Roberts, 7th edition, © 2001, 0-324-04052-0.
International Management by Rodrigues, 2nd edition, © 2001, 0-324-04150-0.
International Business Law and Its Environment by Schaffer/Earle/Agusti, 5th edition, © 2002, 0-324-06098-X.

Additional Books

The Management of Business Logistics by Coyle/Bardi/Langley, 6th edition, © 1996, 0-314-06507-5.
Operations Management by Gaither/Frazier, 9th edition, © 2002, 0-324-06685-6 (test bank only).
Retailing by Dunne/Lusch/Griffith, 4th edition, © 2002, 0-030-32696-6.
Corporate Finance: A Focused Approach by Ehrhardt/Brigham, © 2003, 0-324-18035-7.
Marketing Strategy by Ferrell. et al, 2nd edition, © 2002, ISBN 0-030-32103-4.
Managerial Accounting by Jackson and Sawyers, © 2001, ISBN 0-030-21092-5.

About South-Western (A part of The THOMSON Corporation)

South-Western, a part of The Thomson Corporation, is the leading educational provider of business and economics materials worldwide. South-Western offers the most extensive selection of business education products and services on the market today for higher education, secondary education, as well as corporate and retail business environments. Integrating the latest technologies with many of its products, South-Western also delivers interactive learning solutions that engage learners, enhance retention, and provide results.

The Professional Portfolio

South-Western is pleased to add the *CBM Examination Preparation Guide* to its Professional Portfolio. This rapidly expanding, topic-specific collection includes corporate strategy, business and technology, finance, global business, marketing, and other significant business titles.

SECTION I

Understanding of Business Concepts

Module 100
General Management and Organization, 2

Module 200
Operations Management, 44

Module 300
Marketing Management, 56

Module 400
Quality and Process Management, 71

Module 500
Human Resources Management, 79

Module 600
Accounting, 89

Module 700
Finance, 107

Module 800
Information Technology, 135

Module 900
Corporate Control and Governance, 150

Module 1000
International Business, 157

General Management and Organization

Section 101. Corporate Strategies

Summaries and Conclusions

Strategic management begins with an evaluation of the organization's current mission, goals, and strategy. This evaluation is followed by situation analysis (called *strengths, weaknesses, opportunities, and threats* (SWOT) *analysis*), which examines opportunities and threats in the external environment as well as strengths and weaknesses within the organization. Situation analysis leads to the formulation of explicit strategic plans, which then must be implemented.

Strategy formulation takes place at three levels: corporate, business, and functional. Corporate grand strategies include growth, stability, retrenchment, and global. One framework for accomplishing them is the Boston Consulting Group (BCG) matrix. An approach to business-level strategy is Porter's competitive forces and strategies. The Internet is having a profound impact on the competitive environment, and managers should consider this when analyzing the five competitive forces and formulating business strategies. An alternative approach to strategic thought emphasizes cooperation rather than competition. Partnership strategies include preferred supplier arrangements, strategic business partnering, joint ventures, and mergers and acquisitions. Most of today's companies choose a mix of competitive and partnership strategies. Once business strategies have been formulated, functional strategies for supporting them can be developed.

Even the most creative strategies have no value if they cannot be translated into action. Managers implement a strategy by aligning all parts of the organization to be in congruence with the new strategy. Four areas that managers focus on for strategy implementation are leadership, structural design, information and control systems, and human resources.

Coca-Cola's CEO Douglas Daft has made several strategic moves to try to get the company back on top. Although Coke continues to use primarily a globalization strategy, Daft recognizes the growing need to be more responsive to the heterogeneity of international markets. Therefore, he is gradually shifting toward a transnational strategy. Whereas the company once sought unity in its marketing and advertising strategies, for example, it is now giving bottlers both in the United States and abroad a free hand to tailor promotions to local events and activities. Daft is pushing global managers to think outside the conventional boundaries and come up with ideas for everything from new products to new ways to gather market research. New products include calcium-fortified waters, vitamin-enriched drinks, and new products for international markets such as an Asian tea and a coffee drink. Partnerships are an important part of Coke's new business-level strategy. Coke hopes to attain synergy through a 50–50 joint venture with Procter & Gamble (P&G) by marrying Coke's distribution muscle with P&G's successful juice and snack brands. A similar partnership with Nestlé will develop new coffee and tea drinks for the global market. A deal with Warner Bros. allows Coke to co-market with the film *Harry Potter and the Sorcerer's Stone* around the world. And plans are in the works to create an "incubator" project that will provide office space and seed money to start-ups with innovative ideas that could benefit the giant corporation. The partnership approach is new for Coke, which has long been seen as an insular company bent on doing it all. According to Marketing Director Stephen C. Jones, Daft realizes that "there are too many changes now for us to have all the answers."[1]

Section 105. Management and Organization

Summaries and Conclusions

Nature of Management

High performance requires the efficient and effective use of organizational resources through the four management functions of planning, organizing, leading, and controlling. To perform the four functions, managers need three skills—conceptual, human, and technical. Conceptual skills are more important at the top of the hierarchy; human skills are important at all levels; and technical skills are most important for first-line managers.

Two major characteristics of managerial work are that (1) managerial activities involve variety, fragmentation, and brevity; and (2) managers perform a great deal of work at an unrelenting pace. Managers are expected to perform activities associated with ten roles: the informational roles of monitor, disseminator, and spokesperson; the interpersonal roles of figurehead, leader, and liaison; and the decisional roles of entrepreneur, disturbance handler, resource allocator, and negotiator.

These management characteristics apply to small businesses, entrepreneurial start-ups, and not-for-profit organizations just as they do to large corporations. In addition, they are being applied in a new workplace and a rapidly changing world. In the new workplace, work is free-flowing and flexible to encourage speed and adaptation, and empowered employees are expected to seize opportunities and solve problems. The workplace is organized around networks rather than vertical hierarchies, and work is often virtual. These changing characteristics have resulted from forces such as advances in technology and e-business, globalization, increased diversity, and a growing emphasis on change and speed over stability and efficiency. Managers need new skills and competencies in this new environment. Leadership is dispersed and empowering. Customer relationships are critical, and most work is done by teams that work directly with customers. In the new workplace, managers focus on building relationships with customers, partners, and suppliers. In addition, they strive to build learning capability throughout the organization. An emerging need is for leadership during crises and unexpected events. Managers in crisis situations should stay calm, be visible, put people before business, tell the truth, and know when to get back to business.

An excellent example of a leader during a crisis is Kenneth Chenault who is the chairman and CEO of American Express Company. Even though he was stuck in Salt Lake City during the Sept. 11, 2001 terrorists crisis in New York, Chenault took control, gathering information, talking with managers back at headquarters hourly, and taking steps to ensure the safety of employees. "He was there, and he was in the middle of it," said one manager. From the moment the crisis began, Chenault remained calm, steady, and focused, dealing with personal losses, refusing to complain about his company's problems, listening to employees and sharing their grief, taking care of customers, doing favors for other companies, and getting the company back to business as quickly as possible. Every decision he made was guided by concern for employees and customer service. After ordering the evacuation, he directed the call center to track down each and every employee. Then he turned to customers, helping 560,000 stranded American Express cardholders get home, waiving delinquent fees on late payments, and increasing credit limits if customers needed it.

When he returned to New York, Chenault gathered his employees together at the Paramount Theater, where he expressed his own despair, anger, and sadness and gave employees a chance to do the same. At the end, he told them, "I represent the best company and the best people in the world. In fact, you are my strength, and I love you." Thus began the long healing process, during which Chenault continued to be a highly visible leader. In his visits to the various temporary offices, he exchanged hugs and handshakes, tears and laughter. When President Bush visited New York, Chenault was there, stressing the need for greater airport security, joining with New York Mayor Rudolph Giuliani and Governor George Pataki to ask for more aid, and meeting with other business leaders to support the president's plan for economic recovery. During all this time, Chenault was also studying his company's financial problems and how to help the organization survive this extremely difficult period in its history. "If you're the leader, you've got to feel you're the person where the decisions rest," he says. "This is no time for excuses."[2]

Management Theories and Perspectives

New approaches are needed to manage learning organizations and the digital workplace. An understanding of the evolution of management helps current and future managers understand where we are now and continue to progress toward better management.

The three major perspectives on management that have evolved since the late 1800s are the classical perspective, the humanistic perspective, and the management science perspective. Each perspective has several specialized subfields. Recent extensions of management perspectives include systems theory, the contingency view, and total quality management. The most recent thinking about organizations has been brought about by the shift to a new workplace. Many managers are redesigning their companies toward the learning organization, which fully engages all employees in identifying and solving problems. The learning organization is characterized by a team-based structure, empowered employees, and open information. The learning organization represents a substantial departure from the traditional management hierarchy.

The shift to a learning organization goes hand-in-hand with today's transition to a technology-driven workplace. Ideas, information, and relationships are becoming more important than production machinery and physical assets, which requires new approaches to management. E-commerce is burgeoning as more economic activity takes place over digital computer networks rather than in physical space. Two specific management tools that support the digital workplace are enterprise resource planning and knowledge management. Both require managers to think in new ways about the role of employees in the organization. Managers value employees for their ability to think, build relationships, and share knowledge, which is quite different from the scientific management perspective of a century ago.

One almost century-old organization that is thriving as a technology-driven workplace is Cementos Mexicanos (Cemex). To help the organization compete in a rapidly changing, complex environment, managers looked for both technological and management innovations. A core element of the new approach is the company's complex information technology infrastructure, which includes a global positioning satellite system and on-board computers in all delivery trucks that are continuously fed with streams of day-to-day data on customer orders, production schedules, traffic problems, weather conditions, and so forth. Even more important are changes in how managers and employees think about and do their work. All drivers and dispatchers attended weekly secondary education classes for two years. Regular training in quality, customer service, and computer skills continues, with Cemex devoting at least 8 percent of total work time to employee training and development. Strict and demanding work rules have been abolished so that workers have more discretion and responsibility for identifying and solving problems.

As a result, Cemex trucks now operate as self-organizing business units, run by well-trained employees who think like businesspeople. The three-hour delivery window has been reduced to 20 minutes, and managers believe a goal of 10 minutes is within reach. According to Francisco Perez, operations manager at Cemex in Guadalajara, "They used to think of themselves as drivers. But anyone can deliver concrete. Now our people know that they're delivering a service that the competition cannot deliver." Cemex has transformed the industry by combining extensive networking technology with a new management approach that taps into the mindpower of everyone in the company. People at Cemex are constantly learning—on the job, in training classes, and through visits to other organizations. As a result, the company has a startling capacity to anticipate customer needs, solve problems, and innovate quickly.[3]

Section 110. Planning and Organizing

Summaries and Conclusions

Planning

Organizational planning involves defining goals and developing a plan with which to achieve them. An organization exists for a single, overriding purpose known as its mission—the basis for strategic goals and plans. Goals within the organization are defined in a hierarchical fashion, beginning with strategic goals followed by tactical and operational goals. Plans are defined similarly, with strategic, tactical, and operational plans used to achieve the goals. Other goal concepts include characteristics of effective goals and goal-setting behavior.

Several types of plans include strategic, tactical, operational, single-use, standing, and contingency plans, as well as management by objectives. A special type of contingency planning is crisis-management planning, which involves the stages of prevention, preparation, and containment. The Europa Hotel provides an example of crisis-management planning. The Europa, like most major hotels, has long had clear procedures for evacuation and dealing with disasters, and the hotel has a good record of getting people out fast. Amazingly, no one has ever been killed by a bomb at the Europa. Because the Europa has had so much experience dealing with crises, managers and employees have become ever alert to even the smallest signals that something is amiss, so they have been able to take quick action and prevent even greater damage or loss of life. The Europa is highly skilled at handling the containment stage of crisis. After one bomb ripped a huge hole in the side of the hotel and injured 13 people, everyone was back to work as usual by lunchtime. Hotel manager John Toner uses every crisis as a way to learn more, be better prepared, and make the company better and stronger. He believes the tendency to immediately look for ways to cut costs and lay people off following a crisis is dangerous. "I don't look for cost savings. I don't look at the bottom line—it'll look after itself," he says. Instead, Toner focuses on taking care of employees and guests and finding ways to make the business better. Because of that attention, hotel staff and guests have remained resolutely loyal to the Europa.[4]

In the past, planning was almost always done entirely by top managers, by consultants, or by central planning departments. In the new workplace, planning is decentralized and people throughout the organization are involved in establishing dynamic plans that can meet fast-changing needs from the environment. Some guidelines for planning in the new workplace include starting with a powerful mission, setting stretch goals, creating a culture that encourages learning, designing new roles for planning staff, and using temporary task forces that may include outside stakeholders. In the new workplace, employees on the front lines may constantly be adapting plans to meet new needs. However, top managers are still responsible for providing a guiding mission and a solid framework for planning and goal setting.

Organizing

Fundamental characteristics of organization structure include work specialization, chain of command, authority and responsibility, span of management, and centralization and decentralization. These dimensions of organization represent the vertical hierarchy and indicate how authority and responsibility are distributed along the hierarchy.

The other major concept is departmentalization, which describes how organization employees are grouped. Three traditional approaches are functional, divisional, and matrix; contemporary approaches are team and network structures. The most recent trend in organizing is the virtual approach. The functional approach groups employees by common skills and tasks. The opposite structure is divisional, which groups people by organizational output such that each division has a mix of functional skills and tasks. The matrix structure uses two chains of command simultaneously, and some employees have two bosses. The two chains of command in a domestic organization typically are functional and product division, and, for international firms, the two chains of command typically are product and geographic regions. The team approach uses permanent teams and cross-functional teams to achieve better coordination and employee commitment than is possible with a pure functional structure. The network approach means that a firm concentrates on what it does best and subcontracts other functions to separate organizations that are connected to the headquarters electronically. The virtual approach brings together a group of specialists to complete a specific project, and the group disbands when objectives are met. Each organization form has advantages and disadvantages and can be used by managers to meet the needs of the competitive situation. In addition, managers adjust elements of the vertical structure, such as the degree of centralization or decentralization, to meet changing needs.

At ConAgra Foods, a new CEO found that the highly decentralized divisional structure was causing problems. Although he is keeping a divisional structure, Bruce Rohde is revising it to increase the focus on the customer. His broad plan, named Operation Overdrive, calls for closing inefficient distribution centers and plants and reorganizing the dozens of separate units and product groups into three main divisions: food service (restaurants); retail (grocery stores); and agricultural products. By focusing the new structure on customers rather than product groups, Rohde hopes to get everyone working together to provide better service. Rohde has also centralized decision-making. Managers of the separate companies will no longer have full authority to run their companies as they see fit. They now have specific goals directed from the top that include sharing customers, knowledge, and products across company lines. Rohde is requiring, for example, that ConAgra's companies buy materials from each other rather than outside suppliers. If managers find this is not cost effective, they are required to explain why directly to the top. In addition, Rohde has centralized computing and accounting systems rather than having the many separate companies using their own systems. He believes this stronger centralized control is needed to help the company through its current crisis. So far, ConAgra's restructuring seems to be having positive effects. The stock has bounced back from a five-year low and the company has been reporting higher sales and earnings since Rohde began the reorganization.[5]

Section 120. Directing and Leading

Summaries and Conclusions

Leadership Traits

The early research on leadership focused on personal traits such as intelligence, energy, and appearance. Later, research attention shifted to leadership behaviors that are appropriate to the organizational situation. Behavioral approaches dominated the early work in this area; consideration and initiating structure were suggested as behaviors that lead work groups toward high performance. The Ohio State University and the University of Michigan studies and the leadership grid are in this category. The Ohio State study identified two major behaviors, called *consideration* and *initiating structures*. The University of Michigan study focused on employee-centered leaders and job-centered leaders. The leadership grid (Blake and Mouton grid) is a two-dimensional (people and production) construct that builds on the work of the Ohio State and Michigan studies. Each axis on the grid is a 9-point scale, with 1 meaning "low concern" and 9 meaning "high concern." Team management (9,9) is the most effective style and is recommended for managers because organization members work together to accomplish tasks. Country club management (1,9) occurs when primary emphasis is given to people rather than to work outputs. Authority-compliance management (9,1) occurs when efficiency in operations is the dominant orientation. Middle-of-the-road management (5,5) reflects a moderate amount of concern for both people and production. Impoverished management (1,1) means the absence of a management philosophy, where managers exert little effort toward interpersonal relationships or work accomplishment.

Management and leadership reflect two different sets of qualities and skills that frequently overlap within a single individual. Leader qualities include vision, creativity, inspiration, innovation, initiate the ability to change, and personal power. Manager qualities include persistence, analytical skills, problem-solving abilities, authoritativeness, and position power. Personal power includes expert power and referent power. Position power includes legitimate power, reward power, and coercive power. Leadership traits involve six categories of personal characteristics: (1) physical characteristics such as energy and physical stamina; (2) intelligence and ability characteristics such as knowledge, judgment, and decisiveness; (3) personality characteristics such as honesty and integrity, enthusiasm, and self-confidence; (4) social characteristics such as cooperativeness, tact, diplomacy, and interpersonal skills; (5) work-related characteristics such as achievement drive and the desire to excel; and (6) social characteristics such as education and mobility.

Leadership Concepts

Contingency approaches include Fiedler's theory, Hersey and Blanchard's situational theory, the path-goal model, and the substitutes-for-leadership concept. The Fiedler approach matches the leader's style with the situation most favorable to his or her success. By diagnosing leadership style and the organizational situation, the correct fit can be arranged. The leadership situation can be analyzed in terms of three elements: the quality of leader-member relationships, task structure, and position power. The Hersey and Blanchard situational theory links the leader's behavioral style with the task readiness of subordinates. The path-goal theory specifies that the leader's responsibility is to increase subordinate's motivation by clarifying the behaviors necessary for task accomplishment and rewards. The substitutes-for-leadership concept suggests that situational variables can be so powerful that they actually substitute for or neutralize the need for leadership.

Leadership concepts have evolved from the transactional approach to charismatic and transformational leadership behaviors. Charismatic and visionary leadership is the ability to articulate a vision and motivate followers to make it a reality. Transformational leadership extends charismatic qualities to guide and foster dramatic organizational change.

Four significant leadership concepts for the new workplace are Level 5 leadership, women's ways of leading, virtual leadership, and servant leadership. Level 5 leaders are characterized by personal humility combined with ambition to build a great organization that will continue to thrive beyond the leader's direct influence. Women's approach to leadership may be particularly suited to today's workplace because it emphasizes relationships and helping others develop to their highest potential. However, men as well as women can develop the characteristics associated with women's style of leadership, called *interactive leadership*. Managers in today's workplace also need to learn how to lead employees who may be working in a virtual environment and have little or no face-to-face contact with the leader. They may become servant leaders who facilitate the growth, goals, and development of others to liberate their best qualities in pursuing the organization's mission. In all of these new ways of leading, managers rely more on personal power than on position power.

As an example, Michael Abrashoff, the commander of the U.S. Navy destroyer U.S.S. Benfold, wanted to create an organization where people were so engaged and enthused about their work that they would willingly give their best. To do so meant casting aside the long Navy tradition of relying on formal position power and authority. To unleash the creativity and know-how of everyone, Abrashoff led with vision and values instead of command and control. Rather than issuing orders from the top, he started listening to ideas from below. Even though he admits that listening does not come easily to him, he made a commitment to treat every encounter with every person on the ship as the most important thing in the world at that particular moment. He also made an effort to get to know each and every sailor as an individual. When the Benfold's sailors saw that Abrashoff was sincere, they responded with energy, enthusiasm, and commitment. Good ideas that came from the bottom up were implemented immediately, and many of them have now become standard throughout the U.S. Navy. Abrashoff also began delegating responsibility so that people could learn and grow. "If all you do is give orders, then all you get are order takers," he said. Abrashoff wanted to develop strong leaders at all levels and to help people understand that they were the ones who made the ship successful. Under Abrashoff's leadership, the Benfold set all-time records for performance and retention. However, neither Abrashoff nor the crew are worried about what will happen when the captain moves on. "This crew ... [knows] what results they get when they play an active role," Abrashoff says. "And they now have the courage to raise their hands and get heard. That's almost irreversible."[6] Abrashoff illustrates characteristics of both interactive and servant leadership, as well as the potential to become a Level 5 leader.

Section 130. Controlling and Measuring

Summaries and Conclusions

Organizational Control

Organizational control is the systematic process through which managers regulate organizational activities to meet planned goals and standards of performance. The focus of the control system may include feedforward control to prevent problems, concurrent control to monitor ongoing activities, and feedback control to evaluate past performance. Well-designed control systems include four key steps: establish standards, measure performance, compare performance to standards, and make corrections as necessary.

Budgeting is one of the most commonly used forms of managerial control. Managers might use expense budgets, revenue budgets, cash budgets, and capital budgets, for example. Other financial controls include use of the balance sheet and income statement, and financial analysis of these documents.

Organizational Measurement

The philosophy of controlling has shifted to reflect changes in leadership methods. Traditional bureaucratic controls emphasize establishing rules and procedures, then monitoring employee behavior to make sure the rules and procedures have been followed. With decentralized control, employees assume responsibility for monitoring their own performance.

Besides monitoring financial results, organizations control the quality of their goods and services. They might do this by adopting total quality management (TQM) techniques such as quality circles, benchmarking, six sigma, reduced cycle time, and continuous improvement.

Recent trends in control include the use of international quality standards (ISO 9000), economic value-added (EVA) and market value-added (MVA) systems, and activity-based costing. Other important aspects of control in the new workplace are open-book management and use of the balanced scorecard.

The story of Samaritan Medical Center demonstrates the importance of control. A new top management team was facing a crisis because costs had been spiraling out of control, and Samaritan had lost money for fourteen of the past fifteen years. One of the first decisions the new team made was to monitor Samaritan's productivity with an eye toward lowering staff costs while maintaining quality of care. They first evaluated what data they needed and then established ideal standards, such as the most efficient and desirable number of employee hours per day per patient or per procedure.

Top managers implemented a type of activity-based costing to be sure all costs were accounted for and assigned where they belonged so they could get an accurate picture of what was going on. Because of the nature of hospital work, where people provide many different services in many different departments, costs are often overlooked or misplaced in traditional accounting procedures. Samaritan then fed the data into a basic accounting spreadsheet and compared it to industry benchmarks and to the data of other similar-sized operations. With these data analyzed, managers were able to establish high-performance yet attainable standards that would give department heads solid reference points for allocating staff and budgeting financial resources. Each department's progress was tracked on a graph that compared results to benchmarks, so people could note their success over the course of the year. Managers were able to take corrective action as needed by reassigning staff, revising patient-flow procedures, or, in some cases, revising targets if a department consistently overreached its goals. The financial turnaround that resulted from the improved control process was stunning. Within only a few months, Samaritan had reduced personnel for a savings of $2.5 million, without a decrease in service. A couple of years later, the organization was posting solid year-end profits. In addition, enhanced control and a revitalized bottom line led to a fresh spirit of teamwork and organizational vitality at Samaritan.[7]

Section 140. Motivating and Communicating

Summaries and Conclusions

Motivation

The content theories of motivation focus on the nature of underlying employee needs. Maslow's hierarchy of needs, Alderfer's ERG theory, Herzberg's two-factor theory, and McClelland's acquired needs theory all suggest that people are motivated to meet a range of needs.

Maslow's hierarchy of needs theory proposes that humans are motivated by multiple needs and that these needs exist in a hierarchical order: (1) physiological needs (lower), (2) safety needs, (3) belonging needs, (4) esteem needs, (5) self-actualization needs (higher). Alderfer's ERG theory proposes three categories of needs: existence, relatedness, and growth. Herzberg's two-factor theory proposes two factors: hygiene factors (areas of dissatisfaction) and motivators (areas of satisfaction). Hygiene factors involve the presence or absence of job dissatisfiers, including working conditions, pay and security, company policies, supervisors, and interpersonal relationships. Motivating factors influence job satisfaction based on fulfillment of high-level needs such as achievement, recognition, responsibility, work itself, and opportunity for personal growth. McClelland's acquired needs theory proposes that certain types of needs are acquired during the individual's lifetime. These needs include need for achievement, need for affiliation, and need for power.

Process theories examine how people go about selecting rewards with which to meet needs. Equity theory asserts that people compare their contributions and outcomes with others' and are motivated to maintain a feeling of equity. Expectancy theory suggests that people calculate the probability of achieving certain outcomes. Managers can increase motivation by treating employees fairly and by clarifying employee paths toward meeting their needs. Still another motivational approach is reinforcement theory, which says that employees learn to behave in certain ways based on the availability of reinforcements. Reinforcement tools include positive reinforcement, avoidance learning, punishment, and extinction.

The application of motivational ideas is illustrated in job design and other motivational programs. Job design approaches include job simplification, job rotation, job enlargement, job enrichment, and the job characteristics model. Managers can change the structure of work to meet employees' high-level needs. The recent trend toward empowerment motivates by giving employees more information and authority to make decisions in their work while connecting compensation to results. Empowerment is the delegation of power or authority to subordinates in an organization. Managers create the environment that determines employee motivation. One way to measure the factors that determine whether people are engaged and motivated at work is the Q12, a list of twelve questions about the day-to-day realities of a person's job. Other motivational programs include pay for performance, gain sharing, employee stock ownership plans (ESOPs), lump-sum bonuses, pay for knowledge, flexible work schedules, and team-based compensation.

A highly successful application of motivational ideas occurred for factory workers at Sandstrom Products. As an example, Leo Henkelman was an alienated mill operator considering quitting. When top management empowered workers by implementing open-book management, Henkelman was given the opportunity to take on more responsibility, learn new skills, and make improvements. He learned his own strengths and limitations in the process. While serving as a temporary plant manager, he found that delegation was not his strength—*doing* was. When a technician job opened up in the lab, he applied. Although he lacked the educational background normally required, the lab director gave him a chance. Now, using his experience, Henkelman guides the manufacturing process from beginning to end, working with customers to develop new products and refine old ones. As his skills and responsibilities have increased, so has his pay, thanks to a proficiency pay system that bases his pay on his skills and accomplishments and a gain-sharing plan that allows him to share in the company's profits. By trusting and empowering workers, Sandstrom has given them a reason to care about the company and the knowledge and power to make personal contributions to organizational performance. Results were staggering, as Sandstrom rebounded from a loss of $100,000 to earnings of almost $800,000 two years later.[8]

Communication

Communication takes up 80 percent of a manager's time. Communication is a process of encoding an idea into a message, which is sent through a channel and decoded by a receiver. Communication among people can be affected by communication channels, nonverbal communication, and listening skills. Important aspects of management communication include persuasion and influence. Managers use communication to sell people on the vision for the organization and to influence them to behave in such a way as to accomplish the vision. To influence others, managers connect with people on an emotional level by using symbols, metaphors, and stories to communicate their messages.

At the organizational level, managers are concerned with managing formal communications in a downward, upward, and horizontal direction. Informal communications also are important, especially management by wandering around and the grapevine. Moreover, research shows that communication structures in teams and departments should reflect the underlying tasks. Open communication, dialogue, and feedback and learning are important communication mechanisms in the new workplace.

Finally, several barriers to communication were described. These barriers can be overcome by active listening, selecting appropriate channels, engaging in management by walking around (MBWA), encouraging dialogue, developing a climate of trust, using formal channels, designing the correct structure to fit communication needs, and using feedback for learning.

At Childress Buick/Kia Company, Rusty Childress used a variety of tools to harness employee brainpower and break down communication barriers. Customers as well as employees were frustrated and dissatisfied, and Rusty knew the company needed to open the lines of communication fast to remain competitive in the volatile car dealership business. A new employee manual emphasizing the importance of active listening skills, together with a seven-week orientation program, refocused organizational efforts on service through communication. Upward as well as downward communications were strengthened with regular meetings such as "Donuts and Dialogue," town-hall-style get-togethers for all employees, and "Take 5" meetings between a manager and five employees to brainstorm about problems or opportunities. Committees were set up to encourage cross-functional communication and understanding. In addition, a monthly newsletter, employee mailboxes, a computer-based "Suggestion Connection," a telephone hot line, and a weekly e-mail update were implemented to keep information flowing across departmental lines to assure better and faster customer service. Today, information flows throughout the company in all directions, and an employee-run team is charged with continuous improvement in internal communications. Childress's customer service indexes are regularly above 95 percent for overall customer satisfaction, and employee turnover is among the lowest in the industry. The company boasts a wall full of "Best in Class" awards from General Motors, and Childress regularly hosts visitors from other organizations that use the dealership as a benchmark for customer service.[9]

Section 150. Problem Solving and Decision Making

Summaries and Conclusions

The study of decision making is important because it describes how managers make successful strategic and operational decisions. Managers must confront many types of decisions, including programmed and nonprogrammed, and these decisions differ according to the amount of risk, uncertainty, and ambiguity in the environment.

Three decision-making approaches are the classical model, the administrative model, and the political model. The classical model explains how managers should make decisions so as to maximize economic efficiency. The administrative model describes how managers actually make nonprogrammed, uncertain decisions with skills that include intuition. The political model relates to making nonprogrammed decisions when conditions are uncertain, information is limited and ambiguous, and there is conflict among managers about what goals to pursue or what course of action to take. Managers have to engage in discussion and coalition building to reach agreement for decisions.

Decision making should involve six basic steps: problem recognition, diagnosis of causes, development of alternatives, choice of an alternative, implementation of the alternative, and feedback and evaluation. Problem recognition at Encyclopaedia Britannica, Inc., was easy: the venerable old company was about to go under. In diagnosing the causes, new owners determined that a major factor was an ossified management culture dominated by book salesmen, leading to years of squabbling over new product development and thus hindering the move into electronic media. One of the first decisions Jacob Safra (an owner of the company) made was to bring in a new management team. The team then considered various alternatives for reviving the faltering company. The first decisions were to rush out a revamped, lower-cost CD-ROM package, targeted particularly to schools, and to launch the Britannica.com Web site, which allows users to call up encyclopedia entries online, as well as get a list of links to other Web sites related to the topic. Top executives also decided to create a separate digital media division to focus on new product development for the digital world. Managers in this new division quickly focused on the wireless Web as the route to the future. After evaluating alternatives for how to establish Britannica as the wireless Web's brand-name information source, they decided not to go it alone, but to create alliances with wireless carriers and license Britannica's content to other Web sites. Impressed with Britannica's content, companies have so far been glad to establish partnerships. These decisions have helped the company cross the bridge to the digital era, but so far the wireless Web has not proven to be much of a money-maker. Managers are in the process of evaluation to determine what new decisions need to be made.

Another factor affecting decision making is the manager's personal decision style. The four major decision styles are directive, analytical, conceptual, and behavioral. Managers can use the Vroom-Jago model to determine when a decision calls for group participation. Involving others in decision making contributes to individual and organizational learning, which is critical in today's fast-paced environment. In the new workplace, decisions often have to be made quickly and with limited information. To improve the effectiveness of decision making in fast-moving organizations, managers use the following guidelines: learn, do not punish; know when to bail; practice the five whys; build collective intuition; and engage in constructive conflict.

Section 160. Business Policy and Ethics

Summaries and Conclusions

Business Policy

Business policy, along with budgets, is a part of strategy execution and implementation in that the policy supports the strategy. Business policies can be established either at high level (for example, ethical behavior and pollution control) or low level (for example, employee compensation and training). Similar to business strategy, business policy can be both proactive and reactive. Business strategy precedes business policy, while business ethics succeeds business policy.

Business Ethics

Ethics is the study of what is right or good for human beings. *Business ethics* is the study of what is right and good in a business setting.

ETHICAL THEORIES
- *Ethical fundamentalism* posits that individuals look to a central authority or set of rules to guide them in ethical decision making.
- *Ethical relativism* asserts that actions must be judged by what individuals subjectively feel is right or wrong for themselves.
- *Situational ethics* contends that one must judge a person's actions by first putting oneself in the actor's situation.
- *Utilitarianism* teaches that moral actions are those that produce the greatest net pleasure compared with net pain.
  - *Act utilitarianism* assesses each separate act according to whether it maximizes pleasure over pain.
  - *Rule utilitarianism* supports rules that on balance produce the greatest pleasure for society.
  - *Cost-benefit analysis* quantifies the benefits and costs of alternatives.
- *Deontology* holds that actions must be judged by their motives and means as well as their results.

- *Social ethics theories* focus on a person's obligations to other members in society and on the individual's rights and obligations within society.
  - *Social egalitarians* believe that society should provide all its members with equal amounts of goods and services regardless of their relative contributions.
  - *Distributive justice* stresses equality of opportunity rather than results.
  - *Libertarians* stress market outcomes as the basis for distributing society's rewards.
- Other Theories
  - *Intuitionism* asserts that a rational person possesses inherent power to assess the correctness of actions.
  - *Good person* theory holds that individuals should seek out and emulate good role models.

ETHICAL STANDARDS IN BUSINESS Kohlberg's stages of moral development comprise a widely accepted model for choosing an ethical system. Because a corporation is a statutorily created entity, it is not clear whether it should be held morally responsible.

ETHICAL RESPONSIBILITIES OF BUSINESS Governmental regulation of business has been necessary because all the conditions for perfect competition have not been satisfied and free competition cannot by itself achieve other societal objectives. Because vast amounts of wealth and power have become concentrated in a small number of corporations, the need has arisen for these corporations to be controlled by a small group of corporate officers.

Arguments Against Social Responsibility
- *Profitability* Because corporations are artificial entities established for profit-making activities, their only social obligation should be to return as much money as possible to shareholders.
- *Unfairness* Whenever corporations engage in social activities, such as supporting the arts or education, they divert funds rightfully belonging to shareholders and/or employees to unrelated third parties.
- *Accountability* A corporation is subject to less public accountability than public bodies are.
- *Expertise* Although a corporation may have a high level of expertise in selling its goods and services, there is absolutely no guarantee that any promotion of social activities will be carried on with the same degree of competence.

Arguments in Favor of Social Responsibility
- *The social contract* Because society allows for the creation of corporations and gives them special rights, including a grant of limited liability, corporations owe a responsibility to society.
- *Less government regulation* By taking a more proactive role in addressing society's problems, corporations create a climate of trust and respect that has the effect of reducing government regulation.
- *Long-run profits* Corporate involvement in social causes creates goodwill, which simply makes good business sense.

Ethical Decisions

Ethics and social responsibility are hot topics for today's managers. The ethical domain of behavior pertains to values of right and wrong. Ethical decisions and behavior are typically guided by a value system. Four value-based approaches that serve as criteria for ethical decision making are utilitarian, individualism, moral rights, and justice. For an individual manager, the ability to make correct ethical choices will depend on both individual and organizational characteristics. An important individual characteristic is level of moral development. Corporate culture is an organizational characteristic that influences ethical behavior.

Corporate social responsibility concerns a company's values in relation to society. How can organizations be good corporate citizens? The model for evaluating social performance uses four criteria: economic, legal, ethical, and discretionary. Evaluating corporate social behavior often requires assessing its impact on organizational stakeholders. One issue of growing concern is environmental responsibility. Organizations may take a legal, market, stakeholder, or activist approach to addressing environmental concerns.

Ethical organizations are supported by three pillars: ethical individuals, ethical leadership, and organizational structures and systems, including codes of ethics, ethics committees, chief ethics officers, training programs, and mechanisms to protect whistle-blowers. Companies that are ethical and socially responsible perform as well as—and often better than—those that are not socially responsible. However, changes in the workplace are raising new ethical issues for managers and organizations, such as ethical use of technology for monitoring employees, trust among business partners, and the privacy of individuals on the Internet.

Returning to our management challenge, there are no easy right-or-wrong answers to drug companies' dilemma. Protecting intellectual property rights (drug patents) is a legitimate right of organizations, and drug companies would argue that it is also a responsibility to their employees and shareholders, as well as customers. Managers who take a utilitarian approach to ethics, for example, might argue that protecting their patents ultimately provides the most good for the most people, since patents are the foundation of research and development of new drugs. However, those who take a justice approach might argue that this decision does not take into account the concept of justice toward the unfortunate victims of AIDS in poor countries. In response to bad publicity and public outcry over the South Africa dispute, companies are taking some action, going beyond purely economic and legal responsibilities to take ethical issues into consideration. One response to social demands is to reduce the prices of AIDS drugs to Africa and other developing areas of the world. Merck, for example, says it will make no profit from the AIDS drugs it sells in developing countries. Officials with Doctors Without Borders welcomed the announcement, but warned that it might still leave drugs out of the reach of many poor AIDS sufferers in the developing world.[10] Most activists would like to see drug companies take an additional step toward *discretionary responsibility* by ensuring that anyone who needs HIV and AIDS medicines has access to them.

Section 165. Business and Government

Summaries and Conclusions

Government rules, regulations, and tax policy play a key role in shaping competitive forces. By understanding the rationale for government involvement in the market economy, a better appreciation of the part played by business is gained.

- From an economic efficiency standpoint, a given mode of regulation or government control is desirable to the extent that benefits exceed costs. In terms of efficiency, the question is whether market competition by itself is adequate or if government regulation is desirable. Equity, or fairness, criteria must also be carefully weighed when social considerations bear on the regulatory decision-making process.
- Market failure is the failure of market institutions to sustain socially desirable activities or to eliminate undesirable ones. Failure by market structure occurs in markets with too few buyers and sellers for effective competition. Failure by incentive occurs when some important benefits or costs of production and consumption are not reflected in industry prices. Differences between private and social costs or benefits are called *externalities*. For example, air pollution is a type of negative externality.
- Competitive markets are also attractive because they are consistent with basic democratic principles. Preservation of consumer choice or consumer sovereignty is an important feature of competitive markets. A second social purpose of regulatory intervention is to limit concentration of economic and political power.
- Property rights give firms the prerogative to limit use by others of specific land, plant and equipment, and other assets. The establishment and maintenance of private property rights are essential to the workings of a competitive market. With patents, government grants an exclusive property right to produce, use, or sell an invention or innovation for a limited period (twenty years in the United States for utility and plant patents). These valuable grants of legal monopoly power are intended to stimulate research and development. The tort system includes a body of law designed to provide a mechanism for victims of accidents and injury to receive just compensation for their loss. These laws create an incentive for firms and other parties to act responsibly in commerce.
- Government also responds to positive externalities by providing subsidies to private business firms. Subsidy policy can be direct or indirect, like government construction and highway maintenance grants that benefit the trucking industry. Tradable emissions permits are a new and controversial form of government subsidy that give firms the property right to pollute and to sell that right to others if they wish. Whereas subsidy policy gives firms positive incentives for desirable performance, tax policy contains penalties, or negative subsidies, designed to limit undesirable performance. Tax policy includes both regular tax payments and fines or penalties that may be assessed intermittently.
- Operating controls are regulations or standards that limit undesirable behavior by compelling certain actions while prohibiting others. The question of who pays for such regulation is seldom answered by simply referring to the point of tax collection, or point of tax incidence. The economic cost of regulation, or the tax burden, is often passed on to customers or suppliers.

- In some industries, average costs decline as output expands. The term *natural monopoly* describes this situation, because monopoly is a direct result of the superior efficiency of a single large producer. In such circumstances, the process of regulation is expensive in terms of administrative costs, lost operating efficiency, and the misallocation of scarce resources. Contributing to these costs is the problem of regulatory lag, or delay between the time a change in regulation is appropriate and the date it becomes effective.
- Antitrust laws are designed to promote competition and prevent unwarranted monopoly. These laws seek to improve economic efficiency by enhancing consumer sovereignty and the impartiality of resource allocation while limiting concentrations in both economic and political power.
- According to horizontal merger guidelines, mergers resulting in relatively unconcentrated markets or that result in a modest increase in market concentration are not likely to have adverse competitive effects and ordinarily will be approved. Mergers producing a large increase in market concentration, particularly those in already highly concentrated markets, are likely to create or enhance market power and would generally not be approved.
- The added value that new users add to network goods and services is called a *network externality*. Networks became a recent concern in antitrust policy because the Clinton Justice Department feared that if inferior networks got a decisive lead in "installed base" among consumers, switching costs might be sufficient to keep customers from switching to a superior standard. Switching costs might also constitute a barrier to entry in the industry and enable network monopolists to tie or bundle a second product in such a way as to foreclose competition in that secondary market.
- Tobin's q ratio is defined as the ratio of the market value of the firm relative to the replacement cost of tangible assets. Nobel laureate James Tobin conceived of this measure as an indicator of pending capital investment. According to Tobin, when high profits cause market values to greatly exceed replacement costs, firms have powerful incentives to expand, and capital investment should boom. Conversely, when low profits cause market values to fall below replacement costs, firms will shrink, and capital investment can be expected to wither. More recently, economists have used Tobin's q ratio as an indicator of above-normal or monopoly profits. However, given the growing importance of intangible capital in our economy, it becomes misleading to infer a simple increase in monopoly profits following an increase in Tobin's q over time.
- The capture theory of economic regulation says that the power of the state to prohibit or compel and to take or give money is often manipulated to selectively help or hurt a vast number of industries. Because of this, regulation may be actively sought by an industry. Capture theory contrasts sharply with the more traditional public interest theory view of regulation as a government-imposed means of private-market control.
- State and federal regulators have begun to address the high costs of regulation through new methods of incentive-based regulation, whereby both companies and their customers benefit through enhanced efficiency.
- In recognition that the regulatory process can sometimes harm rather than help consumer interests, a deregulation movement has sprung up and has grown to impressive dimensions. Similarly, the unnecessary costs of other forms of regulation dictate that regulatory reform is likely to remain a significant social concern.

Government regulation of the market economy is a natural by-product of public concern that unrestricted market competition has the potential to harm economic performance. As the benefits and costs of government/business interaction become better understood, the potential grows for a more constructive approach to government regulation.

Securities Regulation—Securities Act of 1933

- *Definition of security.* A security is any note, stock, bond, pre-organization subscription, or investment contract. An *investment contract* is any investment of money or property made in expectation of receiving a financial return solely from the efforts of others.
- *Registration of securities—disclosure requirements.* Disclosure of accurate material information is required in all public offerings of nonexempt securities unless the offering is an exempt transaction. Integrated disclosure and shelf registrations are permitted for certain qualified issuers.
- *Exempt securities.* These are securities not subject to the registration requirements of the 1933 Act. Types of exempt securities include short-term commercial paper, municipal bonds, and certain insurance policies and annuity contracts.
- *Exempt transactions for issuers.* This term is defined as the issuance of securities not subject to the registration requirements of the 1933 Act. Types of exempt transactions include limited offers under Regulation D and Section 4(6), Regulation A, and intrastate issues.

- *Exempt transactions for nonissuers.* This term refers to resales by persons other than the issuer that are exempted from the registration requirements of the 1933 Act. Types of exempt transactions include Rule 144 and Regulation A.
- *Liability.* Unregistered Sales Section 12(a)(1) imposes absolute civil liability; there are no defenses. False Registration Statements Section 11 imposes liability on the issuer, all persons who signed the statement, every director or partner, experts who prepared or certified any part of the statement, and all underwriters; defendants other than issuer may assert the defense of due diligence.

    Antifraud Provisions Section 12(a)(2) imposes liability upon the seller to the immediate purchaser, provided the purchaser did not know of the untruth or omission; but the seller is not liable if he or she did not know, and in the exercise of reasonable care could not have known, of the untrue statement or omission. Section 17(a) broadly prohibits fraud in the sale of securities. Willful violations are subject to a fine of not more than $10,000 and/or imprisonment of not more than five years.

Securities Regulation—Securities Exchange Act of 1934

- *Disclosure.* Registration and periodic reporting requirements apply to all regulated, publicly held companies and include one-time registration as well as annual, quarterly, and monthly reports.
- *Proxy Solicitations.* A *proxy* is a signed writing by a shareholder authorizing a named person to vote her or his stock at a specified meeting of shareholders. Proxy disclosure statements are required when proxies are solicited or an issuer submits a matter to a shareholder vote.
- *Tender Offers.* A *tender offer* is a general invitation to shareholders to purchase their shares at a specified price for a specified time. A *disclosure requirement* is a statement disclosing specified information that must be filed with the SEC and furnished to each offeree. The Foreign Corrupt Practices Act imposes internal control requirements on companies with securities registered under the 1934 Act.
- *Liability.* Misleading Statements in Reports Section 18 imposes civil liability for any false or misleading statement made in a registration or report filed with the SEC. Short-Swing Profits Section 16(b) imposes liability on certain insiders (directors, officers, and shareholders owning more than 10 percent of the stock of a corporation) for all profits made on sales and purchases within six months of each other, with any recovery going to the issuer. Antifraud Provision Rule 10b-5 makes it unlawful to (1) employ any device, scheme, or artifice to defraud; (2) make any untrue statement of a material fact; (3) omit to state a material fact; or (4) engage in any act that operates as a fraud.
    - *Requisites of Rule 10b-5* Recovery require (1) a misstatement or omission, (2) materiality, (3) scienter (intentional and knowing conduct), (4) reliance, and (5) connection with the purchase or sale of a security.
    - *Insider trading* "Insiders" are liable under Rule 10b-5 for failing to disclose material, nonpublic information before trading on the information.
- Express insider trading liability is imposed on any person who sells or buys a security while in possession of inside information. Civil penalties for inside trading may be imposed on inside traders in an amount up to three times the gains they made or losses they avoided. Any person who distributes a false or misleading proxy statement is liable to injured investors.
- Fraudulent Tender Offers Section 14(e) imposes civil liability for false and material statements or omissions or fraudulent, deceptive, or manipulative practices in connection with any tender offer. The Antibribery Provision of FCPA prohibits bribery and violations can result in fines and imprisonment. Individuals who willfully violate the 1934 Act are subject to a fine of not more than $1 million and/or imprisonment of not more than ten years.

Trade Secrets, Copyrights, and Patents

TRADE SECRETS A *trade secret* is commercially valuable, secret information. The owner of a trade secret may obtain damages or injunctive relief when the secret is misappropriated (wrongfully used) by an employee or a competitor. Federal law imposes criminal penalties for the theft of trade secrets.

TYPES OF TRADE SYMBOLS
- A *trademark* is a distinctive symbol, word, or design on a good that is used to identify the manufacturer.
- A *service mark* is a distinctive symbol, word, or design that is used to identify a provider's services.

- A *certification mark* is a distinctive symbol, word, or design used with goods or services to certify specific characteristics.
- A *collective mark* is a distinctive symbol used to indicate membership in an organization.

To be registered and thus protected by the Lanham Act, a mark must be distinctive and not immoral, deceptive, or scandalous. *Infringement* occurs when a person without authorization uses a substantially indistinguishable mark that is likely to cause confusion, mistake, or deception. The Lanham Act provides the following remedies for infringement: injunctive relief, profits, damages, destruction of infringing articles, costs, and, in exceptional cases, attorneys' fees.

TRADE NAMES A *trade name* is any name used to identify a business, vocation, or occupation. A trade name may not be registered under the Lanham Act, but infringement is prohibited. Damages and injunctions are available if infringement occurs.

COPYRIGHTS A *copyright* is an exclusive right, usually for the author's life plus seventy years, to original works of authorship. Registration is not required, but provides additional remedies for infringement. Copyright protection provides the exclusive right to (1) reproduce the copyrighted work, (2) prepare derivative works based on the work, (3) distribute copies of the work, and (4) perform or display the work publicly. The author of the copyrighted work is usually the owner of the copyright, which may be transferred in whole or in part.

Infringement occurs when someone exercises the copyright owner's rights without authorization. If infringement occurs after registration, the following remedies are available: (1) injunction, (2) impoundment and possible destruction of infringing articles, (3) actual damages plus profits or statutory damages, (4) costs, and (5) criminal penalties.

PATENTS A *patent* is the exclusive right to an invention for twenty years from the date of application for utility and plant patents, and fourteen years from grant for design patents. To be patentable, the invention must be (1) novel, (2) useful, and (3) not obvious. Patents are issued upon application to and after examination by the U.S. Patent and Trademark Office. Infringement occurs when anyone without permission makes, uses, or sells a patented invention. Remedies for infringement of a patent are (1) injunctive relief, (2) damages, (3) treble damages, when appropriate, (4) attorneys' fees, and (5) costs.

Labor Law and Employment Law

LABOR LAW The purpose of labor law is to provide the general framework in which management and labor negotiate terms of employment. The Norris–La Guardia Act established as U.S. policy the full freedom of labor to form labor unions without employer interference and withdrew from the federal courts the power to issue injunctions in nonviolent labor disputes (any controversy concerning terms or conditions of employment or union representation).

The National Labor Relations Act declares it a federally protected right of employees to unionize and to bargain collectively. The Act identifies five unfair labor practices by an employer. The National Labor Relations Board (NLRB) was created to administer these rights.

The Labor-Management Relations Act identifies seven unfair labor practices by a union. The Act prohibits *closed-shop agreements* that mandates that an employer can hire only union members. The Act also allows *union shops* where an employer can hire nonunion members, but the employee must join the union.

The Labor-Management Reporting and Disclosure Act is aimed at eliminating corruption in labor unions.

EMPLOYMENT LAW The Equal Pay Act prohibits an employer from discriminating between employees on the basis of gender by paying unequal wages for the same work. The Civil Rights Act of 1964 prohibits employment discrimination on the basis of race, color, gender, religion, or national origin.

- The *Equal Employment Opportunity Commission (EEOC)* is the enforcement agency for the Act.
- *Affirmative action* is the active recruitment of a designated group of applicants.
- Discrimination prohibited by the Act includes (1) using proscribed criteria to produce disparate treatment, (2) engaging in nondiscriminatory conduct that perpetuates past discrimination, and (3) adopting neutral rules that have a disparate impact.
- *Reverse discrimination* is affirmative action that directs an employer to consider an individual's race or gender when hiring or promoting for the purpose of remedying underrepresentation of that race or gender in traditionally segregated jobs.

- *Sexual harassment* is an illegal form of sexual discrimination that includes unwelcome sexual advances, requests for sexual favors, and other verbal or physical conduct of a sexual nature.
- The consideration of *comparable worth* demands equal pay for jobs that are of equal value to the employer.

Executive order prohibits discrimination by federal contractors on the basis of race, color, gender, religion, or national origin on any work the contractors perform during the period of the federal contract.

The Age Discrimination in Employment Act (ADEA) prohibits discrimination on the basis of age in hiring, firing, or compensating. In addition, several federal acts, including the Americans with Disabilities Act (ADA), provide assistance to people with disabilities in obtaining rehabilitation training, access to public facilities, and employment.

EMPLOYEE PROTECTION
- *Employee termination at will.* Under the common law, a contract of employment for other than a definite term is terminable at will by either party.
- *Statutory limitations.* These have been enacted by the federal government and some states.
- *Judicial limitations.* These are based on contract law, tort law, or public policy.
- *Limitations:* Several limitations are imposed by union contract.

The Occupational Safety and Health Act (OSHA) was enacted to ensure workers a safe and healthful work environment.

EMPLOYEE PRIVACY
- *Drug and alcohol testing.* Some states either prohibit such tests or prescribe certain scientific and procedural safeguards.
- *Lie detector tests.* Federal statute prohibits private employers from requiring employees or prospective employees to take such tests.

EMPLOYEE BENEFITS
Workers' Compensation is awarded to an employee who is injured in the course of his or her employment. Through *Social Security* measures, the government provides economic assistance to disabled or retired employees and their dependents. *Unemployment compensation* is awarded to workers who have lost their jobs and cannot find other employment. The *Fair Labor Standards Act* regulates the employment of child labor outside of agriculture. The *Worker Adjustment and Retraining Notification (WARN) Act* is a federal statute that requires an employer to provide sixty days' advance notice of a plant closing or mass layoff. The *Family and Medical Leave Act of 1993* requires some employers to grant employees leave for serious health conditions or certain other events.

Antitrust Laws

SHERMAN ANTITRUST ACT
Section 1 of this Act (Restraint of Trade) prohibits contracts, combinations, and conspiracies that restrain trade.

- The *rule of reason* is the standard that balances the anticompetitive effects against the procompetitive effects of the restraint.
- *Per se violations* are conclusively presumed unreasonable and therefore illegal.
- *Horizontal restraints* relate to agreements among competitors.
- *Vertical restraints* relate to agreements among parties at different levels in the chain of distribution.

Application of Section 1
- *Price fixing* is an agreement with the purpose or effect of inhibiting price competition; both horizontal and minimum vertical agreements are per se illegal, while maximum vertical price fixing is judged by the rule of reason.
- *Market allocation* refers to the division of markets by customer type, geography, or products; horizontal agreements are per se illegal, while vertical agreements are judged by the rule of reason standard.
- A *boycott* is an agreement among competitors not to deal with a supplier or customer; boycotts are per se illegal.
- A *tying arrangement* conditions the sale of a desired product (tying product) on the buyer's purchasing a second product (tied product); such arrangements are per se illegal if the seller has considerable power in the tying product or affects a more than insubstantial amount of interstate commerce in the tied product.

Section 2 of the Act (Monopolies) prohibits monopolization, attempts to monopolize, and conspiracies to monopolize.

- Monopolization requires market power (the ability to control or exclude others from the marketplace) plus either the unfair attainment of the power or the abuse of such power.
- The *attempt to monopolize* is the specific intent to monopolize, plus a dangerous probability of success.
- Conspiracies to monopolize are not allowed.

SANCTIONS

- Treble damages (three times actual loss)
- Criminal penalties

CLAYTON ACT

- *Tying arrangements* are prohibited if they create a monopoly or may substantially lessen competition.
- The term *exclusive dealing* refers to arrangements by which a party has sole right to a market; exclusive dealing is prohibited if it tends to create a monopoly or may substantially lessen competition.
- A *merger* is prohibited if it tends to create a monopoly or may substantially lessen competition.
  - *Horizontal merger* occurs when one company acquires a competing company.
  - *Vertical merger* occurs when a company acquires one of its suppliers or customers.
  - A *conglomerate merger* occurs when a company acquires another that is not a competitor, customer, or supplier. Sanctions include treble damages.

ROBINSON-PATMAN ACT

- *Price discrimination.* The Act prohibits buyers from inducing or sellers from giving different prices to buyers of commodities of similar grade and quality.
- *Injury.* A plaintiff may prove injury to competitors of the seller (primary-line injury), to competitors of other buyers (secondary-line injury), or to purchasers from other secondary-line sellers (tertiary-line injury).
- *Defenses.* These include (1) cost justification, (2) meeting competition, and (3) functional discounts.
- *Sanctions.* These include civil (treble damages), and criminal in limited situations.

FEDERAL TRADE COMMISSION (FTC) ACT The purpose of this Act is to prevent unfair methods of competition and unfair or deceptive practices. Sanctions may be brought by the FTC, not by private individuals.

Environment Law

COMMON LAW ACTIONS FOR ENVIRONMENTAL CHANGE Nuisance is of two types: Private nuisance and public nuisance. *Private nuisance* is substantial and unreasonable interference with the use and enjoyment of a person's land. *Public nuisance* is interference with the health, safety, or comfort of the public.

Trespass is an invasion of land that interferes with the right of exclusive possession of the property. *Strict liability for abnormally dangerous activities* is liability without fault for an individual who engages in an unduly dangerous activity in an inappropriate location.

NATIONAL ENVIRONMENTAL POLICY ACT (NEPA) The purpose of NEPA is to establish environmental protection as a goal of federal policy. The Council on Environmental Quality is a three-member advisory group that makes recommendations to the president on environmental matters. An *environmental impact statement* (EIS) is a detailed statement concerning the environmental impact of a proposed federal action.

- The scope of NEPA applies to a broad range of activities, including direct action by a federal agency as well as any action by a federal agency that permits action by other parties that will affect the quality of the environment.
- Content in the EIS must contain, among other items, a detailed statement of the environmental impact of the proposed action, any adverse environmental effects that cannot be avoided, and alternative proposals.

CLEAN AIR ACT
- The purpose of the Act is to control and reduce air pollution.
- Several provisions relate to existing sources.
  - *National Ambient Air Quality Standards (NAAQSs).* The EPA administrator must establish NAAQSs for air pollutants that endanger the public health and welfare.
  - *State Implementation Plan.* Each state must submit a plan for each NAAQS detailing how the state will implement and maintain the standard.
- *New stationary sources.* Owner/operator must employ the best technological system of continuous emission reduction that has been adequately demonstrated.
- *New vehicles.* Extensive emission standards are established.
- *Hazardous air pollutants.* In order to protect the public health, the EPA administrator must establish for hazardous air pollutants standards that provide ample safety margins.
- *Acid rain.* Standards are established to protect against acid rain (precipitation that contains high levels of sulfuric or nitric acid).

CLEAN WATER ACT
- The purpose of the Act is to protect against water pollution.
- *Point sources.* The Act established the National Pollutant Discharge Elimination System (NPDES), a permit system, to control the amount of pollutants that may be discharged by a point source into U.S. waters.
- *Nonpoint sources.* The Act requires the states to use the best management practices to control water runoff from agricultural and urban areas.
- The Federal Insecticide, Fungicide, and Rodenticide Act (FIFRA) regulates the sale and distribution of pesticides.
- The Toxic Substances Control Act (TSCA) provides a comprehensive scheme for regulation of toxic substances.
- The Resource Conservation and Recovery Act (RCRA) provides a comprehensive scheme for treatment of solid waste, particularly hazardous waste.
- *Superfund.* The Comprehensive Environmental Response, Compensation and Liability Act (CERCLA) establishes (1) a national contingency plan for responding to releases of hazardous substances, and (2) a trust fund to pay for removal and cleanup of hazardous waste.

INTERNATIONAL PROTECTION OF THE OZONE LAYER   The *Montreal Protocol* is a treaty by which countries agreed to cut production of chlorofluorocarbons (CFCs) by 50 percent. The *Kyoto Protocol* relates to resolution of greenhouse gases.

Section 169. Business Law and Management

Summaries and Conclusions

Contract Law

LAW OF CONTRACTS
- Definition of *contract:* A binding agreement that the courts will enforce.
- *Common law.* Most contracts are primarily governed by state common law, including contracts involving employment, services, insurance, real property (land and anything attached to it), patents, and copyrights.
- The Uniform Commercial Code (UCC) Article 2 of the UCC governs the sales of goods.
- *Sale* is the transfer of title from seller to buyer.
- *Goods* are tangible personal property. (*Personal property* is all property other than an interest in land.)

REQUIREMENTS OF A CONTRACT
- *Mutual assent.* The parties to a contract must manifest by words or conduct that they have agreed to enter into a contract.

- *Consideration.* Each party to a contract must intentionally exchange a legal benefit or incur a legal detriment as an inducement to the other party to make a return exchange.
- *Legality of object.* The purpose of a contract must not be criminal, tortious, or otherwise against public policy.
- *Capacity.* The parties to a contract must have contractual capacity.

CLASSIFICATION OF CONTRACTS

Express and Implied Contracts
- *Implied in fact contract.* Contract where the agreement of the parties is inferred from their conduct.
- *Express contract.* An agreement that is stated in words either orally or in writing.

Bilateral and Unilateral Contracts
- *Bilateral contract.* Contract in which both parties exchange promises.
- *Unilateral contract.* Contract in which only one party makes a promise.

Valid, Void, Voidable, and Unenforceable Contracts
- *Valid contract.* One that meets all of the requirements of a binding contract.
- *Void contract.* No contract at all; without legal effect.
- *Voidable contract.* Contract capable of being made void.
- *Unenforceable contract.* Contract for the breach of which the law provides no remedy.

Executed and Executory Contracts
- *Executed contract.* Contract that has been fully performed by all of the parties.
- *Executory contract.* Contract that has yet to be fully performed.

Promissory estoppel is the doctrine enforcing noncontractual promises where there has been justifiable reliance on the promise and justice requires the enforcement of the promise. A *quasi-contract* is an obligation not based upon contract that is imposed by law to avoid injustice; it is also called an *implied in law contract*.

Section 170. Economics and Management

Summaries and Conclusions

Basic Economic Concepts

Effective managerial decision making is the process of finding the best solution to a given problem. Both the methodology and tools of managerial economics play an important role in this process.

- The decision alternative that produces a result most consistent with managerial objectives is the optimal decision.
- Tables are the simplest and most direct form for listing economic data. When these data are displayed electronically in the format of an accounting income statement or balance sheet, the tables are referred to as *spreadsheets*. In many instances, a simple graph or visual representation of the data can provide valuable insight. In other instances, complex economic relations are written using an equation, or an analytical expression of functional relationships.
- The value of a dependent variable in an equation depends on the size of the variable(s) to the right of the equal sign, which is called an *independent variable*. Values of independent variables are determined outside or independently of the functional relation expressed by the equation.
- A marginal relation is the change in the dependent variable caused by a one-unit change in an independent variable. Marginal revenue is the change in total revenue associated with a one-unit change in output; marginal cost is the change in total cost following a one-unit change in output; and marginal profit is the change in total profit due to a one-unit change in output.
- In graphic analysis, slope is a measure of the steepness of a line and is defined as the increase (or decrease) in height per unit of movement along the horizontal axis. An inflection point reveals a point of maximum or minimum slope.

- Marginal revenue equals marginal cost at the point of profit maximization, as long as total profit is falling as output expands from that point. The break-even point identifies an output quantity at which total profit is zero. Marginal revenue equals zero at the point of revenue maximization, as long as total revenue is falling beyond that point. Average cost minimization occurs when marginal and average costs are equal and average cost is increasing as output expands.
- The incremental concept is often used as the practical equivalent of marginal analysis. Incremental change is the total change resulting from a decision. Incremental profit is the profit gain or loss associated with a given managerial decision.
- Basic economic relations provide the underlying framework for the analysis of all profit, revenue, and cost relations.

Economic Forecasting

Managerial decision making is often based on forecasts of future events. Several techniques for economic forecasting include qualitative analysis, trend analysis and projection, econometric models, and input-output methods.

- Qualitative analysis is an intuitive judgmental approach to forecasting that is useful when based on unbiased, informed opinion. The personal insight method is one in which an informed individual uses personal or organizational experience as a basis for developing future expectations. The panel consensus method relies on the informed opinion of several individuals. In the Delphi method, responses from a panel of experts are analyzed by an independent party to elicit a consensus opinion.
- Survey techniques that skillfully use interviews or mailed questionnaires constitute another important forecasting tool, especially for short-term projections.
- Trend analysis involves characterizing the historical pattern of an economic variable and then projecting or forecasting its future path based on past experience. A secular trend is the long-run pattern of increase or decrease in economic data. Cyclical fluctuation describes the rhythmic variation in economic series that is due to a pattern of expansion or contraction in the overall economy. Seasonal variation, or seasonality, is a rhythmic annual pattern in sales or profits caused by weather, habit, or social custom. Irregular or random influences are unpredictable shocks to the economic system and the pace of economic activity caused by wars, strikes, natural catastrophes, and so on.
- A simple linear trend analysis assumes a constant period-by-period unit change in an important economic variable over time. Growth trend analysis assumes a constant period-by-period percentage change in an important economic variable over time.
- Macroeconomic forecasting involves predicting the pace of economic activity, employment, or interest rates at the international, national, or regional level. Microeconomic forecasting involves predicting economic performance (for example, profitability) at the industry, firm, or plant level.
- The business cycle is the rhythmic pattern of contraction and expansion observed in the overall economy. Economic indicators are series of data that successfully describe the pattern of projected, current, or past economic activity. A composite index is a weighted average of leading, coincident, or lagging economic indicators. An economic recession is a significant decline in activity spread across the economy that lasts more than a few months. Recessions are visible in terms of falling industrial production, declining real income, shrinking wholesale-retail, and rising unemployment. An economic expansion exhibits rising economic activity.
- Exponential smoothing (or "averaging") techniques are among the most widely used forecasting methods. In two-parameter (Holt) exponential smoothing, the data are assumed to consist of fluctuations about a level that is changing with some constant or slowly drifting linear trend. The three-parameter (Winters) exponential smoothing method extends the two-parameter technique by including a smoothed multiplicative seasonal index to account for the seasonal behavior of the forecast series.
- Econometric methods use economic theory and mathematical and statistical tools to forecast economic relations. Identities are economic relations that are true by definition. Behavioral equations are hypothesized economic relations that are estimated by using econometric methods.
- Forecast reliability, or predictive consistency, must be accurately judged in order to assess the degree of confidence that should be placed in economic forecasts. A given forecast model is often estimated by using a test group of data and evaluated by using forecast group data. No forecasting assignment is complete until reliability has been quantified and evaluated. The sample mean forecast error is one useful measure of predictive capability.

The appropriate technique to apply in a given forecasting situation depends on such factors as the distance into the future being forecast, the lead time available, the accuracy required, the quality of data available for analysis, and the nature of the economic relations involved in the forecasting problem.

Market Structure Analysis

Market structure analysis begins with the study of perfect competition and monopoly. Competition is said to be perfect when producers offer what buyers want at prices just sufficient to cover the marginal cost of output. Monopoly is socially less desirable given its tendency for underproduction, high prices, and excess profits.

- *Market structure* describes the competitive environment in the market for any good or service. A *market* consists of all firms and individuals willing and able to buy or sell a particular product. This includes firms and individuals currently engaged in buying and selling a particular product, as well as potential entrants. A *potential entrant* is an individual or firm posing a sufficiently credible threat of market entry to affect the price/output decisions of incumbent firms.
- *Perfect competition* is a market structure characterized by a large number of buyers and sellers of essentially the same product, where each market participant's transactions are so small that they have no influence on the market price of the product. Individual buyers and sellers are price takers. Such firms take market prices as given and devise their production strategies accordingly.
- Monopoly is a market structure characterized by a single seller of a highly differentiated product. Monopoly firms are price makers that exercise significant control over market prices.
- A *barrier to entry* is any factor or industry characteristic that creates an advantage for incumbents over new arrivals. A *barrier to mobility* is any factor or industry characteristic that creates an advantage for large leading firms over smaller nonleading rivals. A *barrier to exit* is any restriction on the ability of incumbents to redeploy assets from one industry or line of business to another.
- *Monopsony* exists when a single firm is the sole buyer of a desired product or input.
- A natural monopoly occurs when the market-clearing price, where $P = MC$, occurs at a point at which long-run average costs are still declining.
- Underproduction results when a monopoly curtails output to a level at which the value of resources employed, as measured by the marginal cost of production, is less than the social benefit derived, where social benefit is measured by the price customers are willing to pay for additional output.
- *Countervailing power* is an economic influence that creates a closer balance between previously unequal sellers and buyers.
- Business profit rates are best measured by the accounting rate of return on stockholders' equity measure. *Return on equity* (ROE) is defined as net income divided by the book value of stockholders' equity, where stockholders' equity is the book value of total assets minus total liabilities. High ROE is derived from some combination of high profit margins, quick total asset turnover, and high leverage or a high rate of total assets to stockholders' equity. Business profits are also sometimes measured by the return on assets, defined as net income divided by the book value of total assets. Although ROA is a useful alternative indicator of the basic profitability of a business, it fails to account for the effects of financial leverage decisions on firm performance.
- Business profit rates often display a phenomenon known as *reversion to the mean*. Over time, entry into highly profitable industries tends to cause above-normal profits to regress toward the mean, just as bankruptcy and exit allow the below-normal profits of depressed industries to rise toward the mean.
- The nature of competition determines the suitability of managerial decisions and the speed with which they must be made. Survival of the fittest translates into success for the most able, and extinction of the least capable. *Competitive strategy* is the search for a favorable competitive position in an industry or line of business.
- In perfectly competitive industries, above-normal returns sometimes reflect economic luck, or temporary good fortune due to unexpected changes in industry demand or cost conditions. In other instances, above-normal returns in perfectly competitive industries reflect economic rents, or profits due to uniquely productive inputs. Another important source of above-normal profits in perfectly competitive industries is *disequilibrium profits*. These are above-normal returns that can be earned in the time interval between when a favorable influence on industry demand or cost conditions first transpires and the time when competitor reactions finally develop. *Disequilibrium losses* are below-normal returns that can be suffered in the time interval that often exists between when an unfavorable influence on industry demand or cost conditions first transpires and the time when exit or downsizing finally occurs.

- Only new and unique products or services have the potential to create monopoly profits. In many instances, these above-normal profits reflect the successful exploitation of a *market niche,* a segment of a market that can be successfully exploited through the special capabilities of a given firm or individual.

Many real-world markets do, in fact, closely approximate the perfectly competitive ideal, but elements of monopoly are often encountered. As a result, these market structure concepts often provide a valuable guide to managerial decision making.

Competitive Theories and Strategies

The study of market structure is extended to monopolistic competition and oligopoly. These models describe the behavior of competitors in imperfectly competitive markets across a broad spectrum of our economy in which both price competition and a wide variety of methods of nonprice competition are observed.

- Monopolistic competition is similar to perfect competition in that it entails vigorous price competition among a large number of firms and individuals. The major difference is that consumers perceive important differences among the products offered by monopolistically competitive firms, whereas the output of perfectly competitive firms is homogeneous.
- In an industry characterized by oligopoly, only a few large rivals are responsible for the bulk of industry output. High to very high barriers to entry are typical, and the price/output decisions of firms are interrelated in the sense that direct reactions from rivals can be expected. This "competition among the few" involves a wide variety of price and nonprice methods of rivalry.
- A group of competitors operating under a formal overt agreement is called a *cartel.* If an informal covert agreement is reached, the firms are said to be operating *in collusion.* Both practices are generally illegal in the United States. However, cartels are legal in many parts of the world, and multinational corporations (MNCs) often become involved with them in foreign markets.
- Price leadership results when one firm establishes itself as the industry leader and all other firms accept its pricing policy. This leadership may result from the size and strength of the leading firm, from cost efficiency, or as a result of the recognized ability of the leader to forecast market conditions accurately and to establish prices that produce satisfactory profits for all firms in the industry. Under a second type of price leadership, barometric price leadership, the price leader is not necessarily the largest or dominant firm in the industry. The price leader must only be accurate in reading the prevailing industry view of the need for price adjustment.
- An often-noted characteristic of oligopoly markets is "sticky" prices. Once a general price level has been established, whether through cartel agreement or some less formal arrangement, it tends to remain fixed for an extended period. Such rigid prices are often explained by what is referred to as the "kinked demand curve" theory of oligopoly prices. A kinked demand curve is a firm demand curve that has different slopes for price increases versus price decreases.
- *Game theory* is a general framework to help decision making when firm payoffs depend on actions taken by other firms. In a simultaneous-move game, each decision maker makes choices without specific knowledge of competitor counter moves. In a sequential-move game, decision makers make their move after observing competitor moves. In a one-shot game, the underlying interaction between competitors occurs only once; in a repeat game, there is an ongoing interaction between competitors.
- The so-called "Prisoner's Dilemma" is a classic conflict-of-interest situation. A dominant strategy gives the best result for either party regardless of the action taken by the other. A secure strategy guarantees the best possible outcome given the worst possible scenario. In a Nash equilibrium, neither player can improve its own payoff by unilaterally changing its own strategy. In a Nash bargaining game, two competitors or players "bargain" over some item of value. When competitors interact on a continuous basis, they are said to be involved in repeat games. Like any written guarantee or insurance policy, repeat transactions in the marketplace give consumers confidence that they will get what they pay for.
- The economic census provides a comprehensive statistical profile of the national economy.
- Concentration ratios measure the percentage market share held by (concentrated in) a group of top firms. When concentration ratios are low, industries tend to be made up of many firms, and competition tends to be vigorous. When concentration ratios are high, leading firms dominate and sometimes have the potential for pricing flexibility and economic profits. The Herfindahl Hirschmann Index (HHI) is a measure of competitor size inequality that reflects size differences among both large and small firms. Calculated in percentage terms, the HHI is the sum of the squared market shares for all industry competitors.

- An effective competitive strategy in imperfectly competitive markets must be founded on the firm's competitive advantage. *Competitive advantage* is the unique or rare ability to create, distribute, or service products valued by customers. It is the business-world analog to what economists call *comparative advantage,* or when one nation or region of the country is better suited to the production of one product than to the production of some other product.

Public and private sources offer valuable service through their regular collection and publication of market structure data on the number and size distribution of competitors, market size, growth, capital intensity, investment, and so on. All of this information is useful to the process of managerial decision making and provides a useful starting point for the development of successful competitive strategy.

Section 175. Organizational Behavior and Culture

Summaries and Conclusions

Organizational Behavior

The principles of organizational behavior describe how people as individuals and groups behave and affect the performance of the organization as a whole. *Attitudes* are evaluations that predispose people to behave in certain ways. Desirable work-related attitudes include job satisfaction and organizational commitment. Conflicts among attitudes create a state of cognitive dissonance, which people try to alleviate by shifting attitudes or behaviors. Attitudes affect people's perceptions and vice versa. Individuals often "see" things in different ways. The perceptual process includes perceptual selectivity and perceptual organization. Perceptual distortions, such as stereotyping, the halo effect, projection, and perceptual defense, are errors in judgment that can arise from inaccuracies in the perceptual process. *Attributions* are judgments that individuals make about whether a person's behavior was caused by internal or external factors.

Another area of interest is *personality,* the set of characteristics that underlie a relatively stable pattern of behavior. One way to think about personality is the "Big Five" personality traits of extroversion, agreeableness, conscientiousness, emotional stability, and openness to experience. Some important work-related attitudes and behaviors influenced by personality are locus of control, authoritarianism, Machiavellianism, and problem-solving styles. Four problem-solving styles are sensation-thinking, intuitive-thinking, sensation-feeling, and intuitive-feeling. Managers want to find a good person-job fit by ensuring that a person's personality, attitudes, skills, and abilities match the requirements of the job and the organizational environment.

New insight into personality has been gained through research in the area of emotional intelligence (EQ). Emotional intelligence includes the components of self-awareness, managing emotions, motivating oneself, empathy, and social skill. High emotional intelligence has been found to be important for success in a wide range of jobs and is particularly important for managers. EQ is not an in-born personality characteristic, but can be learned and developed.

As an example, Vinita Gupta needed to strengthen her emotional intelligence, particularly in the areas of self-awareness, empathy, and social skill, to improve morale and create a more positive work environment at Quick Eagle Networks. Gupta hired a corporate coach to help her learn more about herself and manage the personality characteristics and behaviors that could be contributing to decreased performance and higher turnover at Quick Eagle. Gupta worked on a series of exercises to help develop greater empathy and improve her social skills, including coaching employees, being more open and less defensive, and using humor to create a lighter atmosphere. Whereas before she rarely paused to speak to—or sometimes even glance at—anyone when she arrived at the office, she now makes a point of greeting people upon arrival, introducing herself to employees she has never met, and having lunch with colleagues. Gupta has learned that she cannot change some of her personality characteristics—for example, she will never score high on extroversion. However, she has learned to manage her attitudes and behaviors to make Quick Eagle a more pleasant, comfortable place to work. Employees have noticed that the atmosphere is lighter, and people are no longer afraid to speak up in meetings or if they have a concern. Turnover has decreased by 20 percent from a year earlier.[11]

Even though people's personalities may be relatively stable, individuals, like Vinita Gupta, can learn new behaviors. *Learning* refers to a change in behavior or performance that occurs as a result of experience. The learning process goes through a four-stage cycle, and individual learning styles differ. Four learning styles are Diverger, Assimilator, Converger, and Accommodator. Rapid changes in today's marketplace create a need for ongoing learning. They may also create greater stress for many of today's workers. *Stress* is a person's response to a stimulus that places a demand on that person. The causes of work stress include task demands, physical demands, role demands, and interpersonal demands. Individuals and organizations can alleviate the negative effects of stress by engaging in a variety of techniques for stress management.

Organizational Environments

Events in the external environment are considered important influences on organizational behavior and performance. The external environment consists of two layers: the task environment and the general environment. The task environment includes customers, competitors, suppliers, and the labor market. The general environment includes technological, sociocultural, economic, legal-political, and international dimensions. Management techniques for helping the organization adapt to the environment include boundary-spanning roles, interorganizational partnerships, and mergers and joint ventures.

Even companies in relatively simple, stable industries may face significant challenges from the external environment, As an example, managers at Gerber and its parent company, Norvartis AG, responded quickly to activists' allegation that Gerber baby food contained ingredients that could be harmful. While maintaining their stand that genetically altered products are not dangerous, Gerber is dropping some of its existing corn and soybean suppliers in favor of ones that produce crops that are not genetically altered. Plans for labeling changes to indicate if some products may contain minuscule amounts of genetically altered ingredients are being discussed. Gerber's rapid response was made at considerable cost and inconvenience, but managers knew the repercussions of ignoring this threat from the environment could be much more expensive in the long run. "I have got to listen to my customers," says Al Piergallini, president and CEO of Novartis's U.S. consumer health operations. "If there is an issue, or even an inkling of an issue, I am going to make amends." To keep in touch with this growing environmental issue, Gerber is consulting with various non-Greenpeace-affiliated environmentalists and consumer groups. Managers want to anticipate future problems from the external environment and be ready with a rapid response.[12]

One internal organizational factor that enabled Gerber to respond so quickly is the company's adaptive culture. Corporate culture is a major element of the internal organizational environment and includes the key values, beliefs, understandings, and norms that organization members share. Organizational activities that illustrate corporate culture include symbols, stories, heroes, slogans, and ceremonies. For the organization to be effective, corporate culture should be aligned with the needs of the external environment.

Organizational Culture

Four types of culture are adaptability, achievement, clan, and bureaucratic. Strong cultures are effective when they enable an organization to adapt to changes in the external environment. Shared cultural values are important for binding people together in today's changing workplace where employees may be dispersed. Managers are putting greater emphasis on selection and socialization of employees so that employees fit the cultural values of the organization. In addition, cultural leaders strengthen or change corporate culture by (1) communicating a compelling vision to employees and (2) reinforcing the vision through day-to-day activities, work procedures, and reward systems.

Section 180. Organizational Structure and Change Management

Summaries and Conclusions

Organizational Structure

As organizations grow, they add new departments, functions, and hierarchical levels. A major problem confronting management is how to tie the whole organization together. Structural characteristics such as chain of command, work specialization, and departmentalization are valuable organization concepts, but often are not sufficient to coordinate far-flung departments. Horizontal coordination mechanisms provide coordination across departments and include reengineering, task forces, teams, and project managers.

There is an increasing shift toward more horizontal versus vertical structures, which reflects the trend toward greater employee involvement and participation. At the apex of this movement is a type of organization called *the learning organization*. The learning organization is characterized by a horizontal structure, open information, decentralized decision making, empowered employees, and a strong, adaptive culture. Contingency factors of strategy, environment, production technology, and departmental interdependence influence the correct structural approach. When a firm's strategy is to differentiate the firm's product from competitors, a flexible structural approach using teams, decentralization, and empowered employees is appropriate. When environmental uncertainty is high, horizontal coordination is important, and the organization should have a looser, flexible structure, such as in a learning organization.

Other factors that influence structure are technology and interdependence. For manufacturing firms, small-batch production, continuous process production, and flexible manufacturing technologies tend to be structured loosely, whereas a tighter vertical structure is appropriate for mass production. Service technologies are people oriented, and firms are located geographically close to dispersed customers. In general, services have more flexible, horizontal structures, with decentralized decision making. Similarly, organizations based on new digital technology are typically horizontally structured and highly decentralized. Digital connections enable and encourage the free flow of information and work activities among various organizational participants, which might include customers, partners, and other outsiders, as well as employees.

Finally, workflow interdependence also determines the form of structure. An organization with a low level of interdependence can be controlled mainly with the vertical chain of command and standardization of procedures, rules, and regulations. When interdependence is high, such as for new-product introductions, then horizontal coordination mechanisms such as unscheduled meetings, teams, and project managers are required, or the organization may place the interdependent groups into separate, self-contained units. A high level of workflow interdependence means that departments must constantly exchange information and resources. A low level of workflow interdependence means that departments do their work independently and have little need for interaction, coordination, or exchange of materials.

Three types of interdependence that influence organization structure include pooled interdependence, sequential interdependence, and reciprocal interdependence. In the pooled form (for example, bank), chain of command, standardization of procedures, and rules and regulations are required to function. In the sequential form (for example, assembly line), plans and schedules, scheduled meetings, and liaison roles are needed to function. In the reciprocal form (for example, hospital), unscheduled meetings, teams, task forces, and project managers are needed to function.

At Motorola, a lack of horizontal communication and collaboration was turning the company once admired around the world into a has-been. Galvin, chairman of Motorola, worked with other top managers to initiate a complete overhaul of the company and transform Motorola into a new kind of organization that could adapt to the rapid changes of the digital era. To increase horizontal communication and collaboration, they combined all of the 30 different units that make cell phone, wireless equipment, satellite, and cable modem products into one large communications division. Managers are paid based on their ability to work collaboratively to give customers easy-to-use ways to stay tapped into the Internet, whether it be via cell phone, pager, modem, or something no one has yet invented. Furthermore, two horizontal coordination units were put in place: one charged with coordinating all the communication businesses to meet customer needs and the second charged with coordinating Internet strategies across all of Motorola's operations. Galvin's primary goal was to break down the intensely competitive culture that had developed within Motorola and replace it with one in which everyone puts the good of the whole above their individual business units.

After putting the new structure in place, managers began to work on external relationships. Motorola has developed strategic alliances with some of the most important players in the Internet world, including Cisco Systems, Yahoo!, America Online, and Amazon.com. In addition, the company is bringing major customers into the information network so they can also help shape the strategic direction Motorola will take. Motorola's shift to a more flexible, horizontal structure reflects its strategy of differentiating itself with innovative, Net-ready wireless products, the need to respond to rapid environmental changes, and the complexity and fast pace of digital technology. So far, the results of the shift have been dramatic. Motorola was able to bring out innovative phones embedded with Web browsers ahead of competitors, and customers are impressed with the quality and technological sophistication of the new equipment.[13] The increased horizontal communication and collaboration, both within the company and with outside organizations, have made Motorola mighty once again.

Change Management

Change is inevitable in organizations. *Organizational change* is defined as the adoption of a new idea or behavior by an organization. One of the most dramatic elements of change for today's organizations is the shift to a technology-driven workplace and an emphasis on information and relationships. Current trends such as e-business require profound changes in the organization and may be associated with a shift to the learning organization, which embraces continuous learning and change. Managers should think of change as having four elements: the forces for change, the perceived need for change, the initiation of change, and the implementation of change. Forces for change can originate either within or outside the firm, and managers are responsible for monitoring events that may require a planned organizational response.

Techniques for initiating changes include designing the organization for creativity, encouraging idea champions (change agents), establishing new-venture team and fund, using a skunkwork group, and idea incubators. A skunkwork group is a small, informal, highly autonomous, and often secretive group that focuses on breakthrough ideas for the business.

The final step is implementation. Force-field analysis is one technique for diagnosing barriers, which often can be removed. Force-field analysis defines driving forces and restraining forces (barriers) to a proposed change. Managers also should draw on the implementation tactics of communication, education, participation, negotiation, coercion, or top management support.

There are four roles in organizational change: inventor, champion, sponsor, and critic. During implementation of change, resistance to change is common and should be expected. Reasons for resistance include self-interest, lack of understanding and trust, uncertainty, and different assessments and goals.

There are specific types of change. Technology changes are accomplished through a bottom-up approach that utilizes experts close to the technology. Successful new-product introduction requires horizontal linkage among marketing, research and development, manufacturing, and perhaps other departments or customers, partners, and suppliers. Structural changes tend to be initiated in a top-down fashion because upper managers are the administrative experts and champion these ideas for approval and implementation. Culture/people change pertains to the skills, behaviors, and attitudes of employees. Training and organizational development are important approaches to change people's mindset and corporate culture. The organizational development (OD) process entails three steps: unfreezing (diagnosis of the problem), the actual change (intervention), and refreezing (reinforcement of new attitudes and behaviors). Popular OD techniques include team building activities, survey feedback, and large-group interventions.

For example, Corning Inc., has successfully transformed itself numerous times over its 150-year history. However, in recent years, innovation has slowed and the company was making only small, incremental improvements in existing products. When Roger Ackerman took over, he wanted to spur the creation of radical new ideas and rapidly translate them into new products for the marketplace. Ackerman and his top executives made both cultural and structural changes to facilitate the creation and implementation of new ideas. They closed low-profit and low-growth businesses and used the money to finance growth in other parts of the company, such as the fast-growing area of fiber optics. In addition, they stripped out layers of management bureaucracy that separated technologists and engineers from top decision makers who controlled the distribution of resources, and they took steps to create a culture that encouraged creativity and the sharing of information and ideas across functions. Corning doubled R & D spending and sent teams working on specific new ideas to a skunkworks so they could be separated from the bureaucracy and distractions of the larger company. The company began encouraging and supporting idea champions, giving people the time and space needed to work on "slightly crazy ideas." For example, a rule that researchers spend 10 percent of their time on "Friday afternoon experiments" means scientists can work on projects their bosses know nothing about—or even projects that superiors have already pulled the plug on. An entire genomics business is being built on an idea that was officially killed by the head of research but was pursued in Friday afternoon experiments. Corning's new emphasis on collaboration and innovation has led to several breakthrough products. An amazing 84 percent of products sold in 2000 were introduced within the past four years.[14]

Teamwork

A *team* is a unit of two or more people who interact and coordinate their work to accomplish a specific goal. Although a team is a group of people, the two terms are not interchangeable. A manager, a teacher, or a coach can put together a group of people and never build a team. The team concept implies a sense of shared mission and collective responsibility. The factors that influence team effectiveness begin with the organizational context. These factors include structure, strategy, environment, culture, and reward and control systems. Within the context, managers define teams. Important team characteristics are the type of team (formal, self-directed, informal, virtual, or global), the team structure (size and roles), and the team composition (knowledge, skills, benefits, and costs).

Organizations use teams both to achieve coordination as part of the formal structure and to encourage employee involvement. Formal teams include vertical teams along the chain of command and horizontal teams such as cross-functional task forces and committees. Special-purpose teams are used for special, large-scale, creative organization projects. Employee involvement via teams is designed to bring low-level employees into decision processes to improve quality, efficiency, and satisfaction. Companies typically start with problem-solving teams, which may evolve into self-directed teams that take on responsibility for management activities. New approaches to teamwork include virtual teams and global teams. These teams may include contingent workers, customers, suppliers, and other outsiders. Although team members sometimes meet face to face, they use advanced information and telecommunications technology to accomplish much of their work.

For example, at Rowe Furniture, Charlene Pedrolie believed teamwork could be the answer for helping Rowe meet the challenges of a fast-paced, competitive environment. She eliminated most supervisory positions, cross-trained employees to perform the different tasks required to build a piece of furniture, and then asked front-line workers to form horizontal clusters, or cells, to design the new production system. Each group selected its own members from the various functional areas, then created the processes, schedules, and routines for a particular product line. The assembly line was a thing of the past. Five hundred workers who had been accustomed to standing in one place and having the furniture come to them were suddenly working in teams, wandering from one partially assembled piece to another, performing a variety of tasks. Every team had instant access to up-to-date information about order flows, output, productivity, and quality. The sense of personal control and responsibility eventually led to a dramatic change in workers, who began holding impromptu meetings to discuss problems, check each other's progress, or talk about new ideas and better ways of doing things. Productivity and quality shot through the roof. Before long, the factory was delivering custom-made pieces within a month. Only a few months later, that lead time had decreased to a mere 10 days.[15]

Team characteristics that can influence organizational effectiveness are size, cohesiveness, norms, and members' roles. There are four specific roles: the task specialist role, the socio-emotional role, the dual role, and the non-participator role. Most teams go through systematic stages of development: forming, storming, norming, performing, and adjourning. The forming stage is the stage in which orientation to and acquaintance of team members occurs. Storming is the stage in which individual personalities and roles, and resulting conflicts, emerge. Norming is the stage in which conflicts developed during the storming stage are resolved and team harmony and unity emerges. Performing is the stage in which members focus on problem solving and accomplishing the team's assigned task. Adjourning is the stage in which members prepare for the team's disbanding.

All teams experience some conflict because of scarce resources, ambiguous responsibilities, communication breakdown, personality clashes, power and status differences, and goal differences. Various styles to handle conflicts in teams include the competing style, the avoiding style, the compromising style, the accommodating style, and the collaborating style. Techniques for resolving these conflicts include superordinate goals, bargaining and negotiation, mediation, and communication. A superordinate goal is one that cannot be reached by a single party. Techniques for facilitating team communication to minimize conflict are to focus on facts, develop multiple alternatives, maintain a balance of power, and never force a consensus. The advantages of using teams include increased motivation, integration of diverse knowledge and skills, satisfaction of team members, and organizational responsiveness and flexibility. The potential costs of using teams are power realignment, free riding, coordination costs, and revising systems.

Section 190. Project Management

Summaries and Conclusions

Types of Project Organizations

The three most common structures used to organize people to work on projects are functional, project, and matrix. These structures are applicable to a large majority of businesses and not-for-profit organizations.

The functional organization structure is typically used in businesses that primarily sell and produce standard products and seldom conduct external projects. The focus is on the technical excellence and cost competitiveness of the company's products, as well as the importance of each functional component's contribution of expertise to the company's products. For projects, a multifunctional project team or task force is formed, with members selected from the appropriate subfunctions. In this structure, the project manager does not have complete authority over the project team, since administratively the members still work for their respective functional managers. If there is conflict among the team members, it usually works its way through the organization hierarchy to be resolved. A company with a functional organization structure may periodically form project task forces to work on internal projects, but will seldom perform projects involving external customers.

The project organization structure is used by companies that are working on multiple projects at any one time and do not produce standard products. People are hired to work on a specific project, and each project team is dedicated to only one project. When the project is completed, team members may be assigned to another project if they have the appropriate expertise. A full-time project manager has complete project and administrative authority over the project team. A project-type organization is well positioned to be highly responsive to the project objective and customer needs because each project team is strictly dedicated to only one project. From a company-wide viewpoint, a project-type organization can be cost-inefficient because of the duplication of resources or tasks on several concurrent projects. Also, there is little opportunity for members of different project teams to share knowledge or technical expertise. Project organization structures are found primarily in companies that are involved in very large projects with high dollar values and long time frames.

The matrix-type organization is kind of a hybrid—a mix of both the functional and project organization structures. It is appropriate for companies that are working on multiple projects at any one time and projects that vary in size and complexity. It provides the project and customer focus of the project structure while retaining the functional expertise of the functional structure. The project and functional components of the matrix structure each have their responsibilities in contributing jointly to the success of each project and the company. In addition, the matrix-type organization provides for effective utilization of company resources. The sharing of individuals' time among several projects results in effective utilization of resources and minimizes overall costs for each project and for the entire company. All of the individuals assigned to a given project comprise the project team, under the leadership of a project manager who integrates and unifies their efforts.

In the matrix structure, the project manager is the intermediary between the company and the customer. The project manager defines what has to be done, by when, and for how much money to meet the project objective and satisfy the customer. The project manager is responsible for leading the development of the project plan, establishing the project schedule and budget, and allocating specific tasks and budgets to various functional components of the company organization. Each functional manager is responsible for how the assigned work tasks will be accomplished and who will do each task.

The advantages of a functional organization structure are no duplication of activities and functional excellence. Disadvantages include insularity, slow response time, and lack of customer focus. The project organization structure has control over resources and responsiveness to customers as advantages. Cost-inefficiency and low level of knowledge transfer among projects are its disadvantages. The advantages of a matrix organization structure include efficient utilization of resources, functional expertise available to all projects, increased learning and knowledge transfer, improved communication, and customer focus. Its disadvantages are the dual reporting relationships and the need for a balance of power.

CRITICAL SUCCESS FACTORS
- In a matrix-type organization, it is important to delineate the project management responsibilities and the functional management responsibilities.
- When implementing a matrix organization structure, operating guidelines should be established to assure proper balance of power between project managers and functional managers.

Project Management Concepts

A *project* is an endeavor to accomplish a specific objective through a unique set of interrelated tasks and the effective utilization of resources. It has a clearly defined objective stated in terms of scope, schedule, and cost. The responsibility of the project manager is to make sure that the project objective is accomplished and that the work scope is completed in a quality manner, within budget, on time, and to the customer's satisfaction.

The first phase of the project life cycle involves the identification of a need, problem, or opportunity and can result in the customer's requesting proposals from individuals, a project team, or organizations (contractors) to address an identified need or solve a problem. The second phase of the project life cycle is the development of a proposed solution to the need or problem. This phase results in the submission of a proposal to the customer by one or more individuals or contractors or the project team. The third phase of the project life cycle is the implementation of the proposed solution. This phase, which is referred to as "performing the project," results in accomplishment of the project objective, leaving the customer satisfied that the work scope was completed in a quality manner, within budget, and on time. The final phase of the project life cycle is terminating the project, which includes evaluating the execution of the project in order to enhance work on future projects.

Project management involves a process of first establishing a plan and then implementing that plan to accomplish the project objective. This planning effort includes clearly defining objectives, dividing and subdividing the project scope into major "pieces" called *work packages,* defining the specific activities that need to be performed for each work package, graphically portraying the activities in the form of a network diagram, estimating how long each activity will take to complete, defining the types of resources and how many of each resource are needed for each activity, estimating the cost of each activity, and calculating a project schedule and budget.

Taking the time to develop a well-thought-out plan is critical to the successful accomplishment of any project. Once the project starts, project management involves monitoring the progress to ensure that everything is going according to plan. The key to effective project control is measuring actual progress and comparing it to planned progress on a timely and regular basis and taking corrective action immediately, if necessary.

The ultimate benefit of implementing project management techniques is having a satisfied customer—whether you are the customer of your own project or a business (contractor) being paid by a customer to perform a project. Completing the full project scope in a quality manner, on time, and within budget provides a great feeling of satisfaction to everyone involved in the project.

CRITICAL SUCCESS FACTORS
- Planning and communication are critical to successful project management. They prevent problems from occurring or minimize their impact on the achievement of the project objective when they do occur.
- Taking the time to develop a well-thought-out plan before the start of the project is critical to the successful accomplishment of any project.
- A project must have a well-defined objective—an expected result or product, defined in terms of scope, schedule, and cost, and agreed upon by the customer.
- Involving the customer as a partner in the successful outcome of the project through active participation during the project is essential.
- Achieving customer satisfaction requires ongoing communication with the customer to keep the customer informed and to determine whether expectations have changed.
- The key to effective project control is measuring actual progress and comparing it to planned progress on a timely and regular basis and taking corrective action immediately, if necessary.
- After the conclusion of a project, the project performance should be evaluated to learn what could be improved if a similar project were to be done in the future. Feedback should be obtained from the customer and the project team.

Customer Needs Identification

Needs identification is the initial phase of the project life cycle. The customer identifies a need, a problem, or an opportunity for a better way of doing something. The need and associated requirements are usually written down by the customer in a document called a *request for proposal* (RFP).

Before a request for proposal is prepared, the customer must clearly define the problem or need. This may mean gathering data about the magnitude of the problem. It is important that the customer try to quantify the problem so as to determine whether the expected benefits from implementing a solution outweigh the costs or consequences of conducting the project.

Situations may occur where several needs or opportunities have been identified, but there are limited funds or resources available to pursue all of them. Project selection involves evaluating and selecting various needs and opportunities, and then deciding which of those should move forward as a project to be implemented. The steps in project selection are: developing a set of criteria against which the opportunity will be evaluated, listing assumptions about each opportunity; gathering data and information about each opportunity, and evaluating each opportunity against the criteria. Having a well-understood evaluation process and a well-rounded evaluation and selection committee will increase the chances of making the best decision that will result in the greatest overall benefit.

The purpose of preparing a request for proposal is to state, comprehensively and in detail, what is required, from the customer's point of view, to address the identified need. A good RFP allows contractors or a project team to understand what the customer expects so that they can prepare a thorough proposal that will satisfy the customer's requirements at a realistic price.

RFPs may contain a statement of work; customer requirements for physical or operational parameters, such as size, quantity, color, weight, and speed; deliverables the customer expects the contractor to provide; a list of any customer-supplied items; any approvals required by the customer; the type of contract the customer intends to use; the payment terms; the required schedule for completion of the project; instructions for the format and content of the contractor proposals; the due date by which the customer expects potential contractors to submit proposals; and criteria by which the proposals will be evaluated.

Once the RFP has been prepared, the customer solicits proposals by notifying potential contractors that the RFP is available. Business customers and contractors consider the RFP/proposal process to be a competitive situation.

Customers should be careful not to provide one or more contractors with information that is not provided to all interested contractors.

Not all project life cycles include the preparation of a written request for proposal and subsequent proposals from contractors. Some endeavors move right from defining the need into the project phase of the life cycle.

CRITICAL SUCCESS FACTORS
- The need must be clearly defined before preparing a request for proposal (RFP).
- When selecting a project from among several needs or opportunities, the decision should be based on which project will provide the greatest overall benefits compared to its costs and possible consequences.
- Having a well-understood evaluation and selection process and a well-rounded committee will increase the chances of making the best project selection decision.
- A good RFP allows contractors or a project team to understand what the customer expects so they can prepare a thorough proposal that is responsive to the customer's needs and requirements.
- A request for proposal should include a statement of work, customer requirements, expected deliverables, and the criteria by which the customer will evaluate proposals.
- An RFP should provide instructions for the format and content of contractor proposals so the customer will be able to make a consistent and fair comparison and evaluation of all the proposals.
- Customers must be careful not to provide information to only some of the contractors because it would give these contractors an unfair competitive advantage in preparing their proposals.

Proposed Solution

The development of proposed solutions by interested contractors or by the customer's internal project team is the second phase of the project life cycle. This phase starts when the RFP becomes available at the conclusion of the needs identification phase and ends when an agreement is reached with the person, organization, or contractor selected to implement the proposed solution.

Contractors should develop relationships with potential customers long before they prepare requests for proposal. Contractors should maintain frequent contacts with past and current customers and initiate contacts with potential customers. During these contacts, contractors should help customers identify areas in which the customers might benefit from the implementation of projects that address needs, problems, or opportunities. These pre-RFP/proposal efforts are crucial to establishing the foundation for eventually winning a contract from the customer.

Because the development and preparation of a proposal takes time and money, contractors interested in submitting a proposal in response to an RFP must be realistic about the probability of being selected as the winning contractor. Evaluating whether to go forward with the preparation of a proposal is sometimes referred to as the "bid/no-bid decision." Some factors that a contractor might consider in making a bid/no-bid decision are the competition, the risk, its business mission, the ability to extend its capabilities, its reputation with the customer, the availability of customer funds, and the availability of resources for the proposal and the project.

It is important to remember that the proposal process is competitive and that the proposal is a selling document that should be written in a simple, concise manner. In the proposal the contractor must highlight the unique factors that differentiate it from competing contractors. The contractor proposal must also emphasize the benefits to the customer if the customer selects the contractor to perform the project. The customer will select the contractor that it expects will provide the best value.

Proposals are often organized into three sections: technical, management, and cost. The objective of the technical section of the contractor proposal is to convince the customer that the contractor understands the need or problem and can provide the least risky and most beneficial solution. The technical section should show an understanding of the problem, a proposed approach or solution, and the benefits to the customer. The objective of the management section of the contractor proposal is to convince the customer that the contractor can do the proposed work and achieve the intended results. The management section should contain a description of work tasks, a list of deliverables, a project schedule, a description of the organization of the project, a synopsis of related experience, and a list of any special equipment and facilities the contractor has. The objective of the cost section of the contractor proposal is to convince the customer that the contractor's price for the proposed project is realistic and reasonable. The cost section usually consists of tabulations of the contractor's estimated costs of such elements as labor, materials, subcontractors and consultants, equipment and facilities rental, travel, documentation, overhead, escalation, contingency, and a fee or profit.

When contractors prepare proposals, they are generally competing with other contractors to win a contract. Therefore, they must consider the reliability of the cost estimates, the risk, the value of the project to the contractor, the customer's budget, and the competition when determining the price for the proposed project.

Customers evaluate contractors' proposals in many different ways. Sometimes the technical and management proposals are evaluated first, without consideration of cost. Those proposals with the highest points on the technical/management review are then evaluated for their costs. The customer weighs the technical/management merit against the costs to determine which proposal offers the best value. Some of the criteria that might be used by customers in evaluating contractor proposals include compliance with the customer's statement of work, the contractor's understanding of the customer's problem or need, the soundness and practicality of the contractor's proposed solution to the project, the contractor's experience and success with similar projects, the experience of key individuals who will be assigned to work on the project, the contractor's ability to plan and control the project, the realism of the contractor's schedule, and the price.

Once the customer has selected the winning contractor, the contractor is informed that it is the winner, subject to successful negotiation of a contract. A contract is an agreement between the contractor, who agrees to provide a product or service (deliverables), and the customer, who agrees to pay the contractor a certain amount in return.

There are basically two types of contracts: fixed-price and cost-reimbursement. In a fixed-price contract, the customer and the contractor agree on a price for the proposed work. The price remains fixed unless the customer and the contractor agree on changes. This type of contract provides low risk for the customer and high risk for the contractor. In a cost-reimbursement contract, the customer agrees to pay the contractor for all actual costs (labor, materials, and so forth), regardless of amount, plus some agreed-upon profit. This type of contract provides high risk for the customer, since contractor costs can overrun the proposed price, and low risk for the contractor.

A contract may include miscellaneous provisions covering misrepresentation of costs, notice of cost overruns or schedule delays, approvals for any subcontractors, customer-furnished equipment or information, patent ownership, disclosure of proprietary information, international considerations, termination, terms of payment, bonuses or penalties, and procedures for making changes.

CRITICAL SUCCESS FACTORS
- Pre-RFP/proposal efforts are crucial to establishing the foundation for eventually winning a contract from the customer.
- Wise contractors do not wait until formal RFP solicitations are announced by customers before starting to develop proposals. Rather, they develop relationships with potential customers long before they prepare their RFPs.
- Working closely with a potential customer puts a contractor in a better position to be selected as the winning contractor. Contractors should learn as much as possible about the customer's needs, problems, and decision-making process during the pre-RFP/proposal marketing.
- Becoming familiar with the customer's needs, requirements, and expectations will help in preparing a more clearly focused proposal.
- Contractors should be realistic about the ability to prepare a quality proposal and about the probability of winning the contract. It is not enough to just prepare a proposal; rather, the proposal must be of sufficient quality to have a chance of winning.
- A proposal is a selling document, not a technical report. It should be written in a simple, concise manner and should use terminology with which the customer is familiar.
- In a proposal, it is important to highlight the unique factors that differentiate it from competitors' proposals.
- Proposals must be realistic. Proposals that promise too much or are overly optimistic may be unbelievable to customers, and raise doubt about whether the contractor understands what needs to be done or how to do it.
- When bidding on a fixed-price project, the contractor must develop accurate and complete cost estimates, and include sufficient contingency costs.

The Project

Performing, or doing, the project—implementing the proposed solution—is the third phase of the project life cycle. This phase starts after a contract or agreement is drawn up between the customer and the contractor or project team, and it ends when the project objective is accomplished and the customer is satisfied that the work has been completed in a quality manner, within budget, and on time.

This third phase has two parts: doing the detailed planning for the project and then implementing that plan to accomplish the project objective. It is necessary to develop a plan that shows how the project tasks will be accomplished within budget and on schedule. Planning determines what needs to be done, who will do it, how long it will take, and how much it will cost. The result of the planning effort is a baseline plan for performing the project. It is important that the people who will be involved in performing the project also participate in planning the work. Participation builds commitment. Once a plan has been established, the project team, led by the project manager, implements the plan.

While the project work is being performed by the project team, it is necessary to monitor progress to ensure that everything is going according to plan. The project control process involves regularly gathering data on project performance, comparing actual performance to planned performance, and taking corrective actions if actual performance is behind planned performance. Project management is a proactive approach to controlling a project, to ensure that the project objective is achieved even when things do not go according to plan.

The fourth and final phase of the project life cycle is terminating the project. It starts after the project work has been completed. The purpose of this phase is to learn from the experience gained on the project in order to improve performance on future projects. Post-project evaluation activities include both individual meetings with team members and a group meeting with the project team. It is also important to meet with the customer to assess the level of customer satisfaction and determine whether the project provided the customer with the anticipated benefits. Projects may be terminated before completion for various reasons. They may be terminated by the customer because of dissatisfaction. This can result in a financial loss and tarnish the reputation of the contractor or organization performing the project. One way to avoid early termination due to customer dissatisfaction is to monitor the level of customer satisfaction continually throughout the project and take corrective action at the first hint of any dissatisfaction.

CRITICAL SUCCESS FACTORS
- It is important to develop a plan before the start of the project. Taking the time to develop a well-thought-out plan is critical to the successful accomplishment of the project.
- Participation builds commitment. The people who will be involved in performing the project must participate in planning the work.
- The contractor schedules regular, face-to-face meetings with the customer, regularly asking about the level of satisfaction with the progress of the project and keeping the customer informed about the project status and potential problems in a timely manner.
- The key to effective project control is measuring actual progress and comparing it to planned progress on a timely and regular basis and taking corrective action immediately, if necessary.
- After the conclusion of a project, the project performance should be evaluated to learn what could be improved if a similar project were to be done in the future. Feedback should be obtained from the customer and the project team.

Project Planning

Planning is the systematic arrangement of tasks to accomplish an objective. The plan lays out what needs to be accomplished and how it is to be accomplished. The plan becomes a benchmark against which actual progress can be compared; then, if deviations occur, corrective action can be taken.

The first step in the planning process is to define the project objective—the expected result or end product. The project objective is usually defined in terms of scope, schedule, and cost. The objective must be clearly defined and agreed upon by the customer and the organization or contractor that will perform the project.

Once the project objective has been defined, the next step is to determine which work elements, or activities, need to be performed to accomplish it. This requires developing a list of all the activities.

The work breakdown structure (WBS) breaks a project down into manageable pieces, or items, to help ensure that all of the work elements needed to complete the project work scope are identified. It is a hierarchical tree of end items that will be accomplished or produced by the project team during the project. It usually indicates the organization or individual responsible for each work item.

A responsibility matrix is often developed to display, in tabular format, the individuals responsible for accomplishing the work items in the WBS. This is a useful tool because it emphasizes who is responsible for each work item and shows each individual's role in supporting the overall project.

Finally, network planning is a technique that is helpful in planning, scheduling, and controlling projects that consist of many interrelated activities. In addition, it is also useful for communicating information about projects. There are several different network plan formats that can be used; the two most popular are activity-in-the-box (AIB) and activity-on-the-arrow (AOA).

In the AIB, each activity is represented by a box in the network diagram, and the description of the activity is written within the box. In the AOA format, each activity is represented by an arrow in the network diagram, and the activity description is written above the arrow.

After a list of activities has been created, a network diagram can be prepared. When deciding on the sequence in which the activities should be drawn to show their logical precedential relationship to one another, planners must determine (1) which activities must be finished immediately before a given activity can be started, (2) which activities can be done concurrently, and (3) which activities cannot be started until prior activities are finished.

Project planning is a critical activity in developing an information system (IS). A project management planning tool, or methodology, called the *systems development life cycle* (SDLC) is often used to help plan, execute, and control IS development projects. The SDLC consists of a set of phases or steps: problem definition, system analysis, system design, system development, system testing, and system implementation. All of these need to be completed over the course of a development project.

Numerous project management software packages are available to help project managers plan, track, and control projects in a completely interactive way.

CRITICAL SUCCESS FACTORS
- It is important to develop a plan before the start of the project. Taking the time to develop a well-thought-out plan is critical to the successful accomplishment of any project.
- Participation builds commitment. By participating in the planning of the work, individuals will become committed to accomplishing it according to the plan.
- The project objective must be clear, attainable, specific, measurable, and agreed upon by the customer and the organization that will perform the project.

Project Scheduling

After a plan is developed for a project, the next step is to develop a project schedule. The first step in this process is to estimate how long each activity will take, from the time it is started until the time it is finished. It is a good practice to have the person who will be responsible for an activity estimate its duration; however, with larger projects, this is often not possible.

An activity's duration estimate must be based on the quantity of resources expected to be used on the activity. The estimate should be aggressive, yet realistic. A consistent time base, such as hours or days or weeks, should be used for all the activity duration estimates.

The earliest start (ES) and earliest finish (EF) times and the latest start (LS) and latest finish (LF) times can be calculated for each activity. The ES and EF times are calculated by working forward through the network. The earliest start time for an activity is calculated on the basis of the project's estimated start time and the duration estimates for preceding activities. The earliest finish time for an activity is calculated by adding the activity's duration estimate to the activity's earliest start time. The earliest start time for a particular activity must be the same as or later than the latest of all the earliest finish times of all the activities leading directly into that particular activity.

The LS and LF times are calculated by working backward through the network. The latest finish time for an activity is calculated on the basis of the project's required completion time and the duration estimates for succeeding activities. The latest start time is calculated by subtracting the activity's duration estimate from the activity's latest finish time. The latest finish time for a particular activity must be the same as or earlier than the earliest of all the latest start times of all the activities emerging directly from that particular activity.

The total slack for a particular path through the network is common to and shared among all activities on that path. If it is positive, it represents the maximum amount of time that the activities on a particular path can be delayed without jeopardizing completion of the project by the required time. If total slack is negative, it represents the amount of time that the activities on that path must be accelerated in order to complete the project by the required time. If it is zero, the activities on that path do not need to be accelerated, but cannot be delayed. The critical path is the longest (most time-consuming) path of activities in the network diagram and represents a series of activities that cannot be postponed without delaying the entire project.

Scheduling the development of an information system is a challenging process. Unfortunately, such scheduling is often done in a haphazard manner, and thus a large percentage of IS projects are finished much later than originally promised. One of the most important factors in effective scheduling is arriving at activity duration estimates that are as realistic as possible. The project manager should be aware of the common problems that often push IS development projects beyond their scheduled completion dates. Project management software packages can help with the scheduling process.

CRITICAL SUCCESS FACTORS
- The person who will be responsible for performing the activity should make the duration estimate for that activity. This generates commitment from the person.
- An activity's duration estimate must be based on the quantity of resources expected to be used on the activity.
- Activity duration estimates should be aggressive yet realistic.
- Activities should not be longer in estimated duration than the time intervals at which the actual progress will be reviewed and compared to planned progress.

Project Control

Once a project actually starts, it is necessary to monitor progress to ensure that everything is going according to schedule. This involves measuring actual progress and comparing it to the schedule. If at any time during the project it is determined that the project is behind schedule, corrective action must be taken to get back on schedule. The key to effective project control is to measure actual progress and compare it to planned progress on a timely and regular basis and to take necessary corrective action immediately. Based on actual progress and on consideration of other changes that may occur, it is possible to calculate an updated project schedule regularly and forecast whether the project will finish ahead of or behind its required completion time.

A regular reporting period should be established for comparing actual progress with planned progress. Reporting may be daily, weekly, biweekly, or monthly, depending on the complexity or overall duration of the project. During each reporting period, two kinds of data or information need to be collected: data on actual performance and information on any changes to the project scope, schedule, or budget.

The project control process continues throughout the project. In general, the shorter the reporting period, the better the chances of identifying problems early and taking effective corrective actions. If a project gets too far out of control, it may be difficult to achieve the project objective without sacrificing the scope, budget, schedule, or quality.

Throughout a project, some activities will be completed on time, some will be finished ahead of schedule, and others will be finished later than scheduled. Actual progress—whether faster or slower than planned—will have an effect on the schedule of the remaining, uncompleted activities of the project. Specifically, the actual finish times (AFs) of completed activities will determine the earliest start and earliest finish times for the remaining activities in the network diagram, as well as the total slack.

Throughout a project, changes may occur that have an impact on the schedule. These changes might be initiated by the customer or the project team, or they might be the result of an unanticipated occurrence. Any type of change—whether initiated by the customer, the contractor, the project manager, a team member, or an unanticipated event—will require a modification to the plan in terms of scope, budget, and/or schedule. When such changes are agreed upon, a new baseline plan is established and used as the benchmark against which actual project performance will be compared.

Once data have been collected on the actual finish times of completed activities and the effects of any project changes, an updated project schedule can be calculated.

Project control involves four steps: analyzing the schedule to determine which areas may need corrective action, deciding what specific corrective actions should be taken, revising the plan to incorporate the chosen corrective actions, and recalculating the schedule to evaluate the effects of the planned corrective actions. Corrective actions that will eliminate the negative slack from the project schedule must be identified. These corrective actions must reduce the duration estimates for activities on the negative-slack paths. When analyzing a path of activities that has negative slack, you should focus on two kinds of activities: activities that are near term and activities that have long duration estimates.

There are various approaches to reducing the duration estimates of activities. These include applying more resources to speed up an activity, assigning individuals with greater expertise or more experience to work on the activity, reducing the scope or requirements for the activity, and increasing productivity through improved methods or technology.

CRITICAL SUCCESS FACTORS
- Project management involves a proactive approach to controlling a project to ensure that the project objective is achieved even when things do not go according to plan.
- Once the project starts, it is important to monitor progress to ensure that everything is going according to plan.

- The key to effective project control is measuring actual progress and comparing it to planned progress on a timely basis and taking corrective action immediately, if necessary.
- The key to effective schedule control is to address any paths with negative or deteriorating slack values aggressively as soon as they are identified. A concentrated effort to accelerate project progress must be applied to these paths. The amount of negative slack should determine the priority for applying these concentrated efforts.
- When attempting to reduce the duration of a path of activities that has negative slack, focus on activities that are near term and on activities that have long duration estimates.
- Addressing schedule problems early will minimize the negative impact on cost and scope. If a project falls too far behind, getting it back on schedule becomes more difficult, and usually requires spending more money or reducing the scope or quality.
- If corrective actions are necessary, decisions must be made regarding a trade-off of time, cost, and scope.
- Use the time-cost trade-off methodology to reduce the project duration incrementally for the smallest associated increase in incremental cost.
- A regular reporting period should be established for comparing actual progress to planned progress.
- The shorter the reporting period, the better the chances of identifying problems early and taking corrective actions.
- During each reporting period, data on actual performance and information on changes to the project scope, schedule, and budget need to be collected in a timely manner and used to calculate an updated schedule and budget.

Resource Considerations

Resources can include people, equipment, machines, tools, facilities, and space. Among the people may be many different types, such as painters, designers, cooks, computer programmers, and assembly workers.

The consideration of resources adds another dimension (beyond the element of time) to planning and scheduling. In many projects, the amounts of the various types of resources available to perform the project activities are limited. Several activities may require the same resources at the same time, and there may not be sufficient resources available to satisfy all the demands. If sufficient resources are not available, some activities may have to be rescheduled for a later time when resources are available for them.

One way to consider resources is to take them into account when drawing the logical relationships among activities in the network diagram. In addition to showing the technical constraints among activities, the network logic can also take into account resource constraints. The sequence of activities can be drawn to reflect the limited availability of a number of resources. If resources are to be considered in planning, it is necessary to indicate the amounts and types of resources needed to perform each activity. For this reason, a resource profile is often developed.

Resource leveling, or smoothing, is a method for developing a schedule that attempts to minimize the fluctuations in requirements for resources. This method levels resources so that they are applied as uniformly as possible without extending the project schedule beyond the required completion time. Resource leveling attempts to establish a schedule in which resource use is made as level as possible without extending the project beyond the required completion time. In resource leveling, the required project completion time is fixed, and the resources are varied in an attempt to eliminate fluctuation.

Resource-limited scheduling is a method for developing the shortest schedule when the number or amount of available resources is fixed. This method is appropriate when the resources available for the project are limited and these resource limits cannot be exceeded. This method will extend the project completion time if necessary in order to keep within the resource limits. It is an iterative method in which resources are allocated to activities based on the least slack. The steps are repeated until all resource constraints have been satisfied. In resource-limited scheduling, the resources are fixed, and the project completion time is varied (extended) in order not to exceed the resource limits. Exhibit 100.1

Exhibit 100.1 *Fixed Variable Elements for Resource Leveling and Resource-Limited Scheduling*

	Fixed	**Variable**
Resource Leveling	Project Required Completion Time	Resources
Resources-Limited Scheduling	Resources	Project Required Completion Time

shows the differences between resource leveling and resource-limited scheduling. For a large project that requires many different resources, each of which has a different limit of availability, resource-limited scheduling can get very complicated. Various project management software packages are available that will assist with this process.

CRITICAL SUCCESS FACTORS
- Resources can constrain the project schedule since the amounts of various types of resources available to perform the project activities may be limited.
- If resources are to be considered in planning, it is necessary to estimate the amounts and types of resources needed to perform each activity.
- If sufficient resources are not available, some activities may have to be rescheduled for a later time when resources become available to perform the activities.
- Resource leveling, or smoothing, is a method for developing a schedule that attempts to minimize the fluctuations in requirements for resources. It levels resources so that they are applied as uniformly as possible without extending the project schedule beyond the required completion time.
- Resource-limited scheduling is a method for developing the shortest schedule when the number or amount of resources is fixed. It will extend the project completion time if necessary in order to keep within the resource limits.

Cost Planning and Performance

Project costs are estimated when a proposal is prepared for the project. Once a decision is made to go forward with the proposed project, it is necessary to prepare a budget, or plan, for how and when funds will be spent over the duration of the project. Once the project starts, it is important to monitor actual costs and work performance to ensure that everything is within budget. Several parameters should be monitored at regular intervals during the project: cumulative actual amount spent since the start of the project, cumulative earned value of the work performed since the start of the project, and cumulative budgeted amount planned to be spent, based on the project schedule, from the start of the project.

Cost planning starts with the proposal for the project. The cost section of a proposal may consist of tabulations of the contractor's estimated costs for such elements as labor, materials, subcontractors and consultants, equipment and facilities rental, and travel. In addition, the proposal might also include an amount for contingencies to cover unplanned expenses.

The project budgeting process involves two steps. First, the project cost estimate is allocated to the various work packages in the project work breakdown structure. Second, the budget for each work package is distributed over the duration of the work package so that it is possible to determine how much of its budget should have been spent at any point in time.

Allocating total project costs for the various elements, such as labor, materials, and subcontractors, to the appropriate work packages in the work breakdown structure will establish a total budgeted cost (TBC) for each work package. Once a total budgeted cost has been established for each work package, the second step in the project budgeting process is to distribute each TBC over the duration of its work package in order to determine how much of the budget should have been spent at any point in time. This amount is calculated by adding up the budgeted costs for each time period up to that point in time. This total amount, known as the cumulative budgeted cost (CBC), will be used in analyzing the cost performance of the project. The CBC for the entire project or each work package provides a baseline against which actual cost and work performance can be compared at any time during the project.

Once the project starts, it is necessary to keep track of actual cost and committed cost so that they can be compared to the CBC. In addition, it is also necessary to monitor the earned value of the work that has been performed. Determining the earned value involves collecting data on the percent complete for each work package and then converting this percentage to a dollar amount by multiplying the TBC of the work package by the percent complete. This figure can then be compared to the cumulative budgeted cost and the cumulative actual cost.

After this has been done, the project cost performance can be analyzed by looking at the total budgeted cost, the cumulative budgeted cost, the cumulative actual cost, and the cumulative earned value. They are used to determine whether the project is being performed within budget and whether the value of the work performed is in line with the actual cost.

Another indicator of cost performance is the cost performance index (CPI), which is a measure of the cost efficiency with which the project is being performed. The CPI is calculated by dividing the cumulative earned value by the cumulative actual cost. Another indicator of cost performance is cost variance (CV), which is the difference between the cumulative earned value of the work performed and the cumulative actual cost.

Based on analysis of actual cost performance throughout the project, it is possible to forecast what the total costs will be at the completion of the project or work package. There are three different methods for determining the forecasted cost at completion (FCAC). The first method assumes that the work to be performed on the remaining portion of the project or work package will be done at the same rate of efficiency as the work performed so far. The second method assumes that, regardless of the efficiency rate the project or work package has experienced in the past, the work to be performed on the remaining portion of the project or work package will be done according to budget. The third method for determining the forecasted cost at completion is to reestimate the costs for all the remaining work to be performed and then add this reestimate to the cumulative actual cost.

The key to effective cost control is to analyze cost performance on a regular and timely basis. It is crucial that cost variances and inefficiencies be identified early so that corrective action can be taken before the situation gets worse. Cost control involves analyzing cost performance to determine which work packages may require corrective action, deciding what specific corrective action should be taken, and revising the project plan (including time and cost estimates) to incorporate the planned corrective action.

It is important to manage the cash flow on a project. Managing cash flow involves making sure that sufficient payments are received from the customer in time so that enough money is available to cover the costs of performing the project (employee payroll, charges for materials, invoices from subcontractors, and travel expenses, for example). The key to managing cash flow is to ensure that cash comes in faster than it goes out.

CRITICAL SUCCESS FACTORS

- Cost planning starts with the proposal for the project, at which time project costs are estimated.
- The person who will be responsible for the costs associated with the work should make the cost estimates. This will generate commitment from the person.
- Cost estimates should be aggressive yet realistic.
- Once the project starts, it is important to monitor actual costs and work performance to ensure that everything is within budget.
- A system should be set up to collect, on a regular and timely basis, data on costs actually expended and committed, and the earned value (percent complete) of the work performed, so they can be compared to the cumulative budgeted cost (CBC).
- If at any time during the project it is determined that the project is overrunning the budget, or the value of the work performed is not keeping up with the actual amount of costs expended, corrective action must be taken immediately.
- It is important to use the cumulative budgeted cost (CBC), rather than the total budgeted cost (TBC), as the standard against which cumulative actual cost (CAC) is compared. It would be misleading to compare the actual costs expended to the total budgeted cost, since cost performance will always look good as long as actual costs are below the TBC.
- To permit a realistic comparison of cumulative actual cost to cumulative budgeted cost, portions of the committed costs should be assigned to actual costs while the associated work is in progress.
- The earned value of the work actually performed is a key parameter that must be determined and reported throughout the project.
- For each reporting period, the percent complete data should be obtained from the person responsible for the work. It is important that the person make an honest assessment of the work performed relative to the entire work scope.
- One way to prevent inflated percent complete estimates is to keep the work packages or activities small in terms of scope and duration. It is important that the person estimating the percent complete assess not only how much work has been performed, but also what work remains to be done.
- The key to effective cost control is to analyze cost performance on a timely and regular basis. Early identification of cost variances (CV) allows corrective actions to be taken before the situation gets worse.
- For analyzing cost performance, it is important that all the data collected be as current as possible and be based on the same reporting period.
- Trends in the cost performance index (CPI) should be monitored carefully. If the CPI goes below 1.0, or gradually gets smaller, corrective action should be taken.
- As part of the regular cost performance analysis, the estimated cost at completion (ECA) should be calculated.
- The key to effective cost control is to address work packages or activities with negative cost variances and cost inefficiencies aggressively as soon as they are identified. A concentrated effort must be applied to these areas. The amount of negative cost variance should determine the priority for applying these concentrated efforts.

- When attempting to reduce negative cost variances, focus on activities that will be performed in the near term and on activities that have a large cost estimate.
- Addressing cost problems early will have less impact on scope and schedule. Once costs get out of control, getting back within budget becomes more difficult and is likely to require reducing the project scope or extending the project schedule.
- The key to managing cash flow is to ensure that cash comes in faster than it goes out.
- It is desirable to receive payments (cash inflow) from the customer as early as possible, and to delay making payments (cash outflow) to suppliers or subcontractors as long as possible.

The Project Manager

It is the responsibility of the project manager to make sure that the customer is satisfied that the work scope is completed in a quality manner, within budget, and on time. The project manager has primary responsibility for providing leadership in planning, organizing, and controlling the work effort to accomplish the project objective. In terms of planning, the project manager has to clearly define the project objective and reach agreement with the customer on this objective. In terms of organizing, the project manager must secure the appropriate resources to perform the work. In terms of controlling, the project manager needs to track actual progress and compare it with planned progress.

The project manager is a key player in the success of a project and needs to possess a set of skills that will help the project team succeed. The project manager should (1) be a good leader who inspires the people assigned to the project to work as a team to implement the plan and achieve the project objective successfully; (2) be committed to the training and development of the people working on the project; (3) be an effective communicator who interacts regularly with the project team, as well as with any subcontractors, the customer, and her or his own company's upper management; and (4) have good interpersonal skills. It is important that the project manager develop a relationship with each person on the project team and effectively use his or her interpersonal skills to try to influence the thinking and actions of others. An effective project manager can handle stress and has a good sense of humor. In addition, he or she is a good problem solver. Although it is easier to identify problems than to solve them, good problem solving starts with the early identification of a problem or potential problem. Good project managers also manage their time well.

These essential skills can be developed through experience, by seeking out feedback from others, by conducting a self-evaluation and learning from one's own mistakes, by interviewing effective project managers, by participating in training programs, by joining organizations, through reading, and through involvement with volunteer organizations in which these skills can be tested.

Project managers need to be good delegators. Delegation involves empowering the project team to achieve the project objective and empowering each team member to accomplish the expected results for her or his area of responsibility. It is the act of allowing individuals to carry out assigned tasks successfully.

One other important component of the project manager's job is managing and controlling changes in order to minimize any negative impact on the successful accomplishment of the project objective. In order to do this successfully, the project manager should, at the beginning of the project, establish procedures regarding how changes will be documented and authorized.

CRITICAL SUCCESS FACTORS
- Successful project managers accept responsibility for making sure the customer is satisfied and the work scope is completed in a quality manner, within budget, and on time.
- The project manager needs to be proactive in planning, communicating, and providing leadership to the project team to accomplish the project objective.
- The project manager needs to inspire the project team to succeed and to win the confidence of the customer.
- By involving the project team in developing the project plan, the project manager ensures a more comprehensive plan and gains the commitment of the team to achieve the plan.
- Successful project managers are proactive in addressing problems. They do not take a "let's wait and see how things work out" approach.
- The project manager needs to have a project management information system that distinguishes accomplishments from busyness.
- Effective project managers have strong leadership ability, the ability to develop people, excellent communication skills, good interpersonal skills, the ability to handle stress, problem-solving skills, and time-management skills.

- Successful project management requires a participative and consultative leadership style in which the project manager provides guidance and coaching to the project team. The effective project manager does not tell people how to do their jobs.
- Project managers show they value the contributions of team members when they seek advice and suggestions from them.
- Project managers can foster motivation through recognition. People want to feel they are making a contribution and need to be recognized. Positive reinforcement helps stimulate desired behavior; behavior that is recognized or rewarded gets repeated.
- The effective project manager does not monopolize, seek the spotlight, or try to take credit for the work of others.
- Capable project managers are optimistic and have high, yet realistic, expectations for themselves and each person on the project team.
- Projects should be fun. Project managers should enjoy their work and encourage the same positive attitude on the part of the project team members. The project manager should set a positive example for the team in terms of expected behavior.
- A good project manager provides opportunities for learning and development by encouraging team members to take the initiative, take risks, and make decisions. Rather than create a fear of failure, the project manager realizes that mistakes are part of the learning and growth experience.
- Good project managers spend more time listening than talking. They listen to the needs expressed by the customer and the ideas and concerns expressed by the project team.
- Communication by project managers needs to be timely, honest, and unambiguous.
- The project manager should create an atmosphere that fosters timely and open communication without fear of reprisal, and must be understanding of differing viewpoints.
- When unforeseen events cause turmoil on a project, effective project managers remain composed and do not panic.
- To make effective use of their time, project managers need to have self-discipline, be able to prioritize, and be willing to delegate.
- At the start of a project, the project manager needs to establish procedures for how changes will be documented and authorized.

The Project Team

A team is a group of individuals working interdependently to achieve a common goal. Teamwork is the cooperative effort by members of a team to achieve that common goal. The effectiveness—or lack thereof—of the project team can make the difference between project success and project failure.

Project teams evolve through various stages of development. Forming, the initial stage of the team development process, involves the transition from individual to team member. During this stage, individuals on the team begin to get acquainted. During the storming stage, conflict emerges and tension increases. Motivation and morale are low. Members may even resist team formation. However, after struggling through the storming stage, the team moves into the norming stage of development. Relationships among team members and between the team and the project manager have become settled, and interpersonal conflicts have been resolved for the most part. The fourth and final stage of team development and growth is the performing stage. In this stage, the team is highly committed and eager to achieve the project objective. The members feel a sense of unity.

Characteristics often associated with effective project teams include a clear understanding of the project objective, clear expectations of each person's role and responsibilities, a results orientation, a high degree of cooperation and collaboration, and a high level of trust. Barriers to team effectiveness include unclear goals, unclear definition of roles and responsibilities, lack of project structure, lack of commitment, poor communication, poor leadership, turnover of project team members, and dysfunctional behavior.

Team building—developing a group of individuals to accomplish the project objective—is an ongoing process. It is the responsibility of both the project manager and the project team. Socializing among team members supports team building. To facilitate socializing, team members can request that they be physically located in one office area for the duration of the project and they can participate in social events.

Conflict on projects is inevitable. During a project, conflict can emerge from a variety of situations. It can involve members of the project team, the project manager, and even the customer. Sources of potential conflict on projects include differences of opinion on how the work should be done, how much work should be done, at what level of quality the work should be done, who should be assigned to work on which tasks, the sequence in which the work should be done, how long the work should take, and how much the work should cost. Conflict can also arise because of prejudices or differences in individuals' values and attitudes.

Conflict is not just for the project manager to resolve; conflict among team members should be handled by the individuals involved. Dealt with properly, conflict can be beneficial because it causes problems to surface and be addressed.

It is unusual for a team to complete a project without encountering some problems along the way. A good nine-step problem-solving approach is to (1) develop a problem statement, (2) identify potential causes of the problem, (3) gather data and verify the most likely causes, (4) identify possible solutions, (5) evaluate the alternative solutions, (6) determine the best solution, (7) revise the project plan, (8) implement the solution, and (9) determine whether the problem has been solved. Brainstorming is a technique used in problem solving in which all members of a group contribute spontaneous ideas. In brainstorming, the quantity of ideas generated is more important than the quality of the ideas.

Good time management is essential for a high-performance project team. To manage their time effectively, team members should identify weekly goals, make a to-do list for each day, focus on accomplishing the daily to-do list, control interruptions, learn to say no to activities that do not move them closer to their goals, make effective use of waiting time, handle paperwork only once, and reward themselves for accomplishing their goals.

CRITICAL SUCCESS FACTORS
- Project success requires an effective project team. Although plans and project management techniques are necessary, it is the people—the project manager and project team—who are the key to project success.
- Putting a group of people together to work on a project does not create a team. Helping these individuals develop and grow into a cohesive, effective team takes effort on the part of the project manager and each member of the project team.
- Characteristics of effective project teams include a clear understanding of the project objective, clear expectations of each person's roles and responsibilities, a results orientation, a high degree of cooperation and collaboration, and a high level of trust.
- Each member of the project team needs to help create and foster a positive project environment.
- Effective team members have high expectations for themselves. They plan, control, and feel accountable for their individual work efforts.
- Members of effective teams have open, frank, and timely communication. They readily share information, ideas, and feelings. They provide constructive feedback to each other.
- Effective team members go beyond just doing their assigned tasks; they act as a resource for each other.
- The project manager and the project team need to acknowledge openly that conflict is bound to occur during the performance of the project and reach consensus on how it should be handled.
- Effective project teams resolve conflict through constructive and timely feedback and positive confrontation of the issues. Conflict is not suppressed; rather, it is seen as normal and as an opportunity for growth.
- Handled properly, conflict can be beneficial. It causes problems to surface and be addressed. It stimulates discussion and requires individuals to clarify their views. It can foster creativity and enhance problem solving.
- Conflict is not just for the project manager to handle and resolve; conflict between team members should be handled by the individuals involved.
- Each person must approach the conflict with a constructive attitude and a willingness to work in good faith with others to resolve the issues.
- To effectively manage their time, team members should establish weekly goals and make a daily to-do list.

Project Communication and Documentation

Project communication takes various forms, including personal communication, meetings, presentations, reports, and project documentation. Communication can be face to face or use some medium, including telephones, voice mail, e-mail, video conferencing, or groupware. It can be formal or informal. Personal communication can be either oral or written. Oral communication can be face to face or via telephone. Information can be communicated in a more accurate and timely manner through oral communication. Such communication provides a forum for discussion, clarification, understanding, and immediate feedback. Body language and tone are important elements in oral communication. Body language and customs reflective of cultural diversity must be considered in communications. Oral communication should be straightforward, unambiguous, free of technical jargon, and not offensive. Asking for or providing feedback enhances understanding.

Personal written communication is generally carried out through internal memos or external letters. Such means can be used to communicate effectively with a large group of people, but should not be used for trivial matters. Written communications should be clear and concise and should be used mostly to inform, confirm, and request.

Listening is an important part of making communication effective. Failure to listen can cause a breakdown in communication. Common barriers to effective listening include pretending to listen, distractions, bias and closed-mindedness, impatience, and jumping to conclusions. Listening skills can be improved by focusing on the person talking, engaging in active listening, asking questions, and not interrupting.

Project meetings are another forum for project communication. The three most common types of project meetings are status review, problem-solving, and technical design review meetings. The purposes of a status review meeting are to inform, identify problems, and establish action items. Items often covered include accomplishments since the previous meeting; cost, schedule, and work scope—status, trends, forecasts, and variances; corrective actions; opportunities for improvement; and action item assignment. Problem-solving meetings are called when problems or potential problems arise. They should be used to develop a problem statement, identify potential causes, gather data, identify and evaluate possible solutions, determine the best solution, revise the plan, implement the solution, and evaluate it. Technical design review meetings are for projects that include a design phase. They often include a preliminary design review meeting, in which the customer reviews the initial conceptual design, and a final design review meeting, in which the customer reviews completed, detailed design documents. These meetings are a mechanism for gaining customer approval before proceeding with the remainder of the project effort.

Before any meeting, the purpose of the meeting and the people who need to participate should be determined, an agenda should be drawn up and distributed, materials should be prepared, and room arrangements should be made. The actual meeting should start on time, notes should be taken, and the agenda should be reviewed. The meeting leader should facilitate, not dominate, the meeting. After the meeting, decision and action items should be published and distributed.

Project managers and team members are often called on to give formal presentations. In preparing for the presentation, it is important to determine the purpose of the presentation, find out about the target audience, make an outline, develop notes and visual aids, make copies of handout materials, and practice. Presenters should start by telling the audience what they are going to tell them, then tell it to them, then summarize the presentation by telling them what they told them. The presentation should be clear, simple, and interesting, and should conclude within the allotted time.

Written reports are often required during a project. The two most common types of project reports are progress reports and final reports. Progress reports often cover accomplishments since the prior report, the current project status, any potential problems that have been identified and corrective actions that are planned, and goals that should be accomplished during the next reporting period. Final reports provide a summary of the project and often include items such as the customer's original need, the original project objective and requirements, benefits resulting from the project, a description of the project, and a list of deliverables produced. All reports should be clear and concise and written as one would speak. They should be written to address what is of interest to the readers, not the writer.

Throughout a project, many types of documents may be created, such as manuals or drawings. They may need to be revised as a result of changes made by the customer or the project team. Early in the project, agreement should be reached regarding how changes will be documented and authorized.

CRITICAL SUCCESS FACTORS

- Effective and frequent personal communication is crucial to successful project management.
- A high degree of face-to-face communication is important early in the project to foster team building, develop good working relationships, and establish mutual expectations.
- Body language and customs reflective of cultural diversity must be considered in communications.
- One should be careful not to use remarks, words, or phrases that can be construed to be sexist, racist, prejudicial, or offensive.
- The heart of communication is understanding—not only to be understood, but to understand. Half of making communication effective is listening. Failure to listen can cause a breakdown in communication.
- Communication should be straightforward, unambiguous, free of technical jargon, and not offensive.
- Achieving customer satisfaction requires ongoing communication with the customer to keep her or him informed and to determine whether expectations have changed. Project managers should regularly ask the customer about the level of satisfaction with the progress of the project.

- Project managers should keep the customer and project team informed of the project status and potential problems in a timely manner.
- Project status meetings should be held on a regular basis. The project team should discuss meeting guidelines at a project team meeting at the beginning of the project so everyone understands what behavior is expected during such meetings.
- One should not confuse busyness and activity with accomplishment when communicating project progress.
- Reports must be written to address what is of interest to the reader, not what is of interest to the person writing the report.
- Reports should be concise. Format, organization, appearance, readability, and content are equally important.
- Early in the project, agreement should be reached regarding how changes will be authorized and documented.
- When documents are updated, they should immediately be distributed to all team members whose work will be affected.

Section 195. Quantitative Techniques and Management

Summaries and Conclusions

Uses of Quantitative Methods in Business

Quantitative methods can be used to help managers make better decisions. The focus is on the decision-making process and on the role of quantitative analysis in that process. The difference between the model and the situation or managerial problem it represents is an important point. Mathematical models are abstractions of real-world situations and, as such, cannot capture all the aspects of the real situation. However, if a model can capture the major relevant aspects of the problem and can then provide a solution recommendation, it can be a valuable aid to decision making.

One of the characteristics of quantitative analysis that will become increasingly apparent is the search for a best solution to the problem. In carrying out the quantitative analysis, we shall be attempting to develop procedures for finding the "best" or optimal solution.

Decision Analysis

Decision analysis can be used to determine a recommended decision alternative or an optimal decision strategy when a decision maker is faced with an uncertain and risk-filled pattern of future events. The goal of decision analysis is to identify the best decision alternative or the optimal decision strategy given information about the uncertain events and the possible consequences or payoffs. The uncertain future events are called *chance events* and the outcomes of the chance events are called *states of nature*.

Influence diagrams, payoff tables, and decision trees could be used to structure a decision problem and describe the relationships among the decisions, the chance events, and the consequences. Three approaches to decision making without probabilities include the optimistic approach, the conservative approach, and the minimax regret approach. When probability assessments are provided for the states of nature, the expected value approach can be used to identify the recommended decision alternative or decision strategy.

In cases where sample information about the chance events is available, a sequence of decisions has to be made. First we must decide whether to obtain the sample information.

If the answer to this decision is yes, an optimal decision strategy based on the specific sample information must be developed. In this situation, decision trees and the expected value approach can be used to determine the optimal decision strategy.

Even though the expected value approach can be used to obtain a recommended decision alternative or optimal decision strategy, the payoff that actually occurs will usually have a value different from the expected value. A risk profile provides a probability distribution for the possible payoffs and can assist the decision maker in assessing the risks associated with different decision alternatives. Finally, sensitivity analysis can be conducted to determine the effect changes in the probabilities for the states of nature and changes in the values of the payoffs have on the recommended decision alternative.

Decision analysis has been widely used in practice. Ohio Edison used decision analysis to select equipment that helped the company meet emission standards. Oglethorpe Power Corporation (OPC) used decision analysis to decide whether to invest in a major transmission system between Georgia and Florida.

In the OPC problem formulation step, three decisions were identified: (1) deciding whether to build a transmission line from Georgia to Florida, (2) deciding whether to upgrade existing transmission facilities, and (3) deciding who would control the new facilities. OPC was faced with five chance events: (1) construction costs, (2) competition, (3) demand in Florida, (4) OPC's share of the operation, and (5) pricing. The consequence or payoff was measured in terms of dollars saved. The influence diagram for the problem had three decision nodes, five chance nodes, a consequence node, and several intermediate nodes that described intermediate calculations. The decision tree for the problem had more than 8,000 paths from the starting node to the terminal branches.

An expected value analysis of the decision tree provided an optimal decision strategy for OPC. However, the risk profile for the optimal decision strategy showed that the recommended strategy was very risky and had a significant probability of increasing OPC's cost rather than providing savings.

The risk analysis led to the conclusion that more information about the competition was needed in order to reduce OPC's risk. Sensitivity analysis involving various probabilities and payoffs showed that the value of the optimal decision strategy was stable over a reasonable range of input values. The final recommendation from the decision analysis was that OPC should begin negotiations with Florida Power Corporation concerning the building of the new transmission line.

Utility in Decision Making

Expected utility can be used in decision situations in which an analysis based on expected monetary value would not lead to the best decision. Unlike monetary value, utility is a measure of the total worth of a consequence resulting from the choice of a decision alternative and the occurrence of a chance event. As such, utility takes into account the decision maker's attitude toward the profit, loss, and risk associated with a consequence. We can show how the use of utility analysis can lead to decision recommendations that differ from those based on expected monetary value.

Admittedly, a decision maker's utility can be difficult to measure. However, we can show a step-by-step procedure that can be used to determine a decision maker's utility for any payoff value. Using the decision maker's evaluation of a lottery involving only the best and worst payoffs, the procedure provides a method whereby each entry in the payoff table can be converted to a utility value. Then expected utility can be used to select the best decision alternative.

Even with utility as a measure of worth, we can demonstrate how the analysis for a conservative, or risk-avoiding, decision maker could lead to decision recommendations different from those of a risk taker. When the decision maker is risk neutral, we showed that the recommendations using expected utility are identical to the recommendations using expected monetary value.

Simulation

Simulation is a method for learning about a real system by experimenting with a model that represents the system. Simulation is frequently used for the following reasons.

- It can be used for a wide variety of practical problems.
- The simulation approach is relatively easy to explain and understand. As a result, management confidence is increased, and acceptance of results is more easily obtained.
- Spreadsheet packages now provide another alternative for model implementation, and third-party vendors have developed add-ins that expand the capabilities of the spreadsheet packages.
- Computer software developers have produced simulation packages that make it easier to develop and implement simulation models for more complex problems.

Simulation can be used for risk analysis by analyzing a situation involving the development of a new product. It can be used to select an inventory replenishment level that would provide both a good profit and a good customer service level. A simulation model for the bank ATM waiting line system is an example of a dynamic simulation model in which the state of the system changes or evolves over time.

An approach was to develop a simulation model that contained both controllable inputs and probabilistic inputs. Procedures were developed for randomly generating values for the probabilistic inputs, and a flowchart was developed to show the sequence of logical and mathematical operations that describe the steps of the simulation process. Simulation results were obtained by running the simulation for a suitable number of trials or length of time. Simulation results were obtained and conclusions were drawn about the operation of the real system.

Section 199. International Issues

Summaries and Conclusions

International Management

Successful companies are expanding their business overseas and successfully competing with foreign companies on their home turf. Business in the global arena involves special risks and difficulties because of complicated economic, legal-political, and sociocultural forces. Moreover, the global environment changes rapidly, as illustrated by the emergence of the European Union, the North American Free Trade Agreement (NAFTA), and the shift in Eastern Europe to democratic forms of government. Major alternatives for serving foreign markets are exporting, licensing, franchising, and direct investing through joint ventures or wholly owned subsidiaries.

International markets provide many opportunities but are also fraught with difficulty, as Wal-Mart discovered. The company has revised its merchandising and changed some of its tactics to better suit local cultures in Brazil and China. In Brazil, for example, it has scaled back the size of stores and moved to midsize cities where competition is less fierce. Wal-Mart is trying to work with local partners who can help the company translate its business cross-culturally. Despite problems, the company is opening more stores in both Brazil and Argentina. Bob Martin, Wal-Mart's head of international operations, believes the international market is worth the risks. "The market is ripe and wide open for us."[16]

Much of the growth in international business has been carried out by large businesses called *multinational corporations* (MNCs). These large companies exist in an almost borderless world, encouraging the free flow of ideas, products, manufacturing, and marketing among countries to achieve the greatest efficiencies. Managers in MNCs as well as those in much smaller companies doing business internationally face many challenges. Managers often experience culture shock when transferred to foreign countries. They must learn to be sensitive to cultural differences and tailor their management style to the culture. For managers and organizations in an increasingly borderless world, learning across borders is critical.

Operations Management

Section 201. Operations Strategies

Summaries and Conclusions

Purchasing and Supply Chain Management

Several points are clear regarding the role of purchasing in formulating sourcing strategies. The first is that purchasing must contribute to the formulation of corporate strategy by becoming an active participant in this process. Too many companies make decisions that profoundly affect their supply base while leaving purchasing personnel outside the decision-making process. The second point is that purchasing must become organized around critical commodities with dedicated personnel managing these commodities. Ideally, other functions such as engineering and production should also participate in the commodity strategy development process. The third major point involves the different types of purchasing strategies being developed by companies. Companies are increasingly shifting their attention from strategies such as supply-base optimization, purchase volume leverage, and total quality management (TQM), and are focusing on long-term supplier relationships, early involvement of suppliers in new-product development, supplier development, and total cost of ownership. The final point is that all of this does not take place quickly. Strategic management is essentially a change process that evolves over time.

Section 215. Just-in-Time Operations

Summaries and Conclusions

Just-in-time (JIT) presentations often employ the analogy of a stream when describing proper inventory management. Well-managed systems achieve a flow of inventory from raw material to the customer like a smooth river, unimpeded by shoals of scrap or machine breakdown or other problems.

Gradual progress has been achieved by emphasizing continuous improvement, reduced inventories, expanded roles for hourly workers, fewer levels of management, longer term relationships with customers and suppliers, and an emphasis on providing value to the customer. Many American firms are once again at or near world-class status. We should remember, however, that complacency is the principal barrier to maintaining world-class status. We must adopt the philosophy of Kaizen: continuous improvement. The Japanese underscore the urgency of maintaining competitiveness with a phrase taught to every schoolchild: "Export or die!" In yesterday's world, "export or die" was a truism for any island economy. In today's global village, "export or die" is a truism for all economies.

Section 220. Product Demand Management and Forecasting

Summaries and Conclusions

Demand Management

Individual item management concerns when to order (the order release) and how many to order (the lot size). The dependent demand-independent demand dichotomy is the major determinant of the appropriateness of the different models for a given item. Lot sizing decision rules are based on models that minimize the sum of carrying and preparation costs. Order point decision rules are predicated on a customer service level objective. A timely and accurate information processing system is required to implement these decision rules.

Demand Forecasting

Forecasting techniques are classified as qualitative, involving primarily judgment, and quantitative, involving primarily historical data and mathematical models. Quantitative techniques use both intrinsic data, data pertaining to the item to be forecast, and extrinsic data. All quantitative forecasting methods involve the implicit assumption that the near future will be similar to the recent past. To be reliable, all quantitative forecasting techniques require accurate data. Insuring accurate data requires that the data be monitored carefully to eliminate data input error and to adjust for one-time occurrences, such as special promotions.

The study of a set of data describing demand over time is called *time series analysis*. Three common techniques of time series analysis are moving averages, exponential smoothing, and time series decomposition. Time series decomposition is the most accurate of the three, but there is often too little data to permit decomposition. Winters' three-factor model, the most complex exponential smoothing application, is a good compromise whenever seasonal variation in demand exists but there is insufficient data to use time series decomposition.

All forecasts are subject to error, even when the model used for the forecast is properly defined. Production and inventory managers require an estimate of the average forecast error to determine appropriate levels of safety stock and other precautionary measures. The most frequently used measure of forecast error is the mean absolute deviation (MAD), the average of the absolute values of the forecasts minus the actual demands.

Section 230. Physical Supply Chain Management

Summaries and Conclusions

Strategic Supply Chain

Every purchasing professional is expected to play a major role in reducing supply chain-related costs. Because strategic cost management is such an important factor in today's purchasing environment, purchasing professionals have developed an assortment of tools, techniques, and approaches for managing the procurement and sourcing process. These tools, techniques, and approaches illustrate how purchasing managers can contribute to meeting an organization's goals and objectives through strategic cost management.

The focus is on supply chain management and some of the important issues that must be considered as organizations form closer relationships with other supply chain partners and begin to link information systems. Some of these activities involve specific disciplines, such as legal or transportation support, while others relate to the development of purchasing information systems and business-to-business electronic commerce. Organizations must also have a rigorous and relevant performance measurement system to track ongoing processes and make decisions regarding planned future changes. They are, however, integral stepping-stones to effective supply chain management.

Managing Supply Chain Inventory

The dollars committed to inventory represent a major investment in most organizations. Like any investment, inventory must be managed to ensure that it provides an adequate return. Supply chain managers, including purchasing, play an important role in the management of inventory investment. The goal is to create an awareness of the function of inventory, the operational problems that tempt firms to increase inventory levels, and some of the major approaches used to manage inventory investment. While inventory is technically an asset, it directly affects an organization's financial performance.

The following analogy is a useful way to envision the role of inventory investment. Inventory is the water in a river while operational problems are rocks piled along the river's bottom. One approach makes sure boats can safely pass (that is, keep the business running) by raising the water level (inventory) until the rocks (operational problems) are comfortably covered by water. Because the rocks are covered, boats can pass without fear, even though the cost to pass may be far too high. A second approach requires lowering the water (for example, reducing inventory safety stock levels) until the rocks are exposed one by one. As a rock becomes exposed, an effort is made to permanently remove the rock (the operational problem). In the long run, which approach will be the most cost effective—the approach that covers problems with inventory or the one that permanently eliminates problems one by one? Purchasing and supply chain professionals are responsible in managing the flow of physical inventory from suppliers. Throughout this flow, one will encounter problems along the way, so it is important to remember the river analogy and the correct ways to manage and control inventory.

Performance Measures

A purchasing and supply chain performance measurement and evaluation system should directly support corporate goals and objectives. A measurement system that directs behavior and activity away from those goals and objectives is counterproductive and can cause greater harm than good.

A need exists to create measurement systems that are responsive to change. Firms will also increasingly require measures that focus on end results rather than on specific activities. Emphasis will increasingly shift from efficiency measures to effectiveness measures. In addition, executive management must have the ability to distinguish between good and poor purchasing practices and results. A well-developed performance measurement and evaluation system can help provide this distinction.

Section 235. Manufacturing Planning and Scheduling

Summaries and Conclusions

Manufacturing Planning

Facility planning, resource planning, aggregate capacity planning, and production planning are all elements of long-range planning. Each encompasses the degree of detail appropriate to its planning horizon and to the organization's environment and objectives. Capacity planning at all levels in the capacity planning hierarchy is connected to measures of product and service outputs. These measures usually are stated in both physical and monetary units. In fact, both the required new capacity resources (facilities, equipment, labor, and information) and required material inputs must be converted to financial terms for the financial planning management system. Capacity planning at all levels should focus on critical resources (bottlenecks) that may be processing centers, engineering, or systems programmers.

Aggregate planning decisions are inherent to facility planning, resource planning, and master production planning. Although most organizations do not use mathematical aggregate planning models, they do recognize the aggregate planning problem and make decisions concerning it.

The aggregate capacity planning challenge can be met by attempting to alter demand, by managing supply through control of production output and inventories, or a combination of the two. The chase and level production strategies are at the opposite ends of the spectrum of aggregate capacity planning strategies. The costs of carrying inventory to meet future demand peaks and the cost of changing output rates are the two major costs affecting the management of supply in the aggregate planning decision.

Sensitivity analysis should be performed on the aggregate capacity plan to evaluate the effects of changes in costs or demand. This analysis can be used to develop contingency plans to deal with the situation when actual parameters differ substantially from projected parameters.

As time unfolds and the plan is implemented, control must take place. This requires that actual inventory, shipments, and costs be compared to the plan and that corrective action be taken as required. The following are some of the principles found.

- The production plan should be consistent with and support the sales plan, the financial play, and the business plan.
- Aggregate plans, including the aggregate production plan, are not static. They should be reviewed at least quarterly to determine that marketing, finance, and production are operating as a team with the same game plan.
- The more accurate and reliable the resource and production planning, the fewer the difficulties that will occur in master scheduling.
- Available capacity should be based on the actual (demonstrated) output of the key work centers.
- Control begins in the planning process by comparing the planned resource requirements to the estimated available requirements.

Master Production Schedule

Although the preparation and maintenance of all the elements of the master schedule may be complex in some situations, the principles and concepts are not. The master production schedule (MPS) is a vital link in the operations planning and control system due to its links (interfaces) with many other activities and systems in manufacturing, marketing, and engineering (product and process design). The items on the MPS, in particular their level in the bill of materials (BOM), should be consistent with the organization's competitive strategy. The efficacy of the master scheduling process and the MPS requires an accurate and reliable capacity planning system.

The master scheduler plays a key role in the master scheduling function. This individual plays a key role in marketing and manufacturing working to the same plan.

Available-to-promise (ATP) information is very useful for responding to customer requests for delivery. Planned on hand (POH) data is very helpful in indicating when the MPS is inadequate or will result in excessive inventory.

If actual production is consistently below the planned MPS, it suggests that actual capacity is less than the "capacity available" used in creating the MPS. And if actual orders completed in each period consistently differ substantially from those in the MPS, it suggests that the priority plan established by the MPS is not being followed throughout the system or that the MPS is not being controlled (revised) as unplanned changes in material, equipment, or personnel occur.

Section 240. Manufacturing Capacity Management

Summaries and Conclusions

Capacity Management Approaches

Three approaches to rough-cut capacity planning have been examined. The least detailed, the capacity planning using overall factors (CPOF) approach, is quickly computed but is insensitive to shifts in product mix. A second approach, bill of labor, involves multiplying two matrices: the bill of labor and the master production schedule. This approach picks up shifts in product mix, but does not consider lead-time offsets. The third approach, resource profile, takes lead-time offsets into account. Both the bill of labor approach and the resource profile approach implicitly assume a lot-for-lot policy for setting lot sizes. If some other technique, such as economic order quantity or the Silver-Meal algorithm, is used, then either approach is a very rough estimate. For that reason, the bill of labor approach is recommended because it is easily implemented on a microcomputer and is just as accurate as the more cumbersome resource profile approach. In any event, rough-cut capacity plans (RCCP) should be used only to determine if sufficient capacity exists over broad time frames such as a month or a quarter. Drum-buffer-rope is an emerging procedure that eliminates the need for iteration found in all three RCCP approaches. It is presently used by a small but growing number of corporations.

Capacity Requirements Planning

Note that capacity requirements planning (CRP) uses more information than RCCP but still produces only an estimate of the timing and quantity of capacity needed. CRP is a deterministic technique. To the extent that jobs wait in queue longer than expected, machines break down, jobs are completed in a sequence other than planned, and so on, reality deviates from CRP. Because queue control is such an important aspect of managing capacity within an MRP system, recognizing the random nature of queue lengths is extremely important.

Section 245. Inventory Management

Summaries and Conclusions

Whether inventory is an asset used to accomplish the objectives of an organization or a liability depends on its management, both conditions may exist in the same firm at the same time. The primary function of inventory is to decouple customer demand and production capacity. Functionally, inventory can be divided into anticipation, lot size, transportation, and fluctuation inventories and service parts. Each serves as a buffer between demand and production in a particular type of situation. However, in some instances inventory may be used to compensate for ineffective management.

Inventory management performance is measured in terms of customer service and inventory investment. There are many measures of customer service, and backorder service is an important component of any measure. Measuring customer service by multiple methods is a good idea in any situation. The availability of data, the effect of decisions on the measured results, and the relationship of the measured results to profit and productivity influence the selection of customer service measures.

Inventory investment is measured in both an absolute and a relative manner. An absolute value—$1 million, for example—serves as an upper limit constraint on inventory while an inventory turnover ratio measures inventory investment in relation to the cost of goods sold. Both types of measures should be employed in most situations.

ABC analysis, based on Pareto's Principle of the Vital Few and Trivial Many divides items into ranked categories on the basis of monetary value, scarcity, and other factors influencing the desired degree of control. Different control procedures are established for the different classes.

Inventory costs are easier to describe than they are to calculate. Preparation costs, carrying costs, stockout costs, and capacity-related costs affect inventory management decisions. Capacity-related costs are associated with medium-range aggregate type decisions more than with individual item decisions. Cost calculations should include opportunity costs as well as direct costs, while sunk costs should be excluded.

Determination of inventory classifications, performance measures, and costing procedures should precede aggregate, intermediate, and individual item inventory management decisions.

Section 250. Materials Management

Summaries and Conclusions

A closed-loop material requirements planning (MRP) system has four major advantages over the traditional order point system in the management of dependent demand items. These advantages include (1) the correspondence of MRP orders to actual demand requirements, (2) the recognition by MRP of vertical and horizontal dependencies among items, (3) the proactive planning and forward visibility of MRP, and (4) the ability of closed-loop MRP to integrate materials and capacity planning and control consistency while maintaining the progress of orders and capacity in the production facility. Implementing MRP requires a timely information processing system, a valid MPS, and the ability to manage change and priorities.

Section 255. Purchasing Management

Summaries and Conclusions

The Purchasing Process

Topics in purchasing include an overview of purchasing and the purchasing process, including the objectives of a world-class purchasing function, purchasing's span of control, the purchasing cycle, and the documents used to manage the purchasing process. These topics provide the foundation from which to introduce the tools, techniques, and strategies used by purchasing organizations in a competitive market.

There are many different categories of purchases. In addition to buying production material and items, purchasing can be responsible for buying transportation, services, packing supplies, maintenance, repair and operating (MRO) items, capital equipment, and even the corporate jet! There is no one system or approach that applies to all purchase situations.

Purchases can vary according to type, importance, impact on quality, time frame for delivery, and dollar volume. We rarely find purchasing personnel who are experts in all the different types of purchases, which is why so many purchasing departments have specialized personnel. These personnel all have one thing in common, however: the opportunity to manage large amounts of resources through the purchasing process.

Purchasing and Supply Chain Organization

As customer requirements continue to become more demanding, organizations must become better at responding to change. New markets, rapid advances in communications, and shortages of skilled labor are forcing one of the most fundamental reorganizations since the multidivisional corporation became standard in the 1950s. Senior managers are struggling to adapt their organizations to the twenty-first century business world that is rapidly taking shape. Thriving in the fast-paced environment requires a new kind of company and a new kind of leader. Organizations across many industries seem to be converging on a common management model to run their organizations, which relies on Western-style accounting and financial controls, yet stresses collaboration between groups and across organizations.

As it relates to purchasing and supply chain management, the organizational model for the twenty-first century has certain characteristics.

- Flattened hierarchies for faster decision making and freer flow of ideas
- Joint ventures and alliances with key suppliers and other supply chain members
- Cross-functional teams to pursue new opportunities and ensure cross-fertilization of ideas
- Global sourcing to capture the benefits from the world's best suppliers
- Greater decentralization of buying activity with centralized coordination of major spending categories
- Corporate cultures that nurture innovation, challenge assumptions, and seek new ideas
- Open information channels, with electronic mail, the Internet, intranets, and information technology systems that make information widely available throughout the supply chain
- Diversified management, which rotates younger managers around the world for three-month to two-year assignments

As organizations continue to make changes, purchasing managers must learn to acquire new skills, become more flexible, and continually improve their capabilities.

The twenty-first century will undoubtedly be full of uncertainty and risk. While rapid change frightens many purchasing managers, it is also exhilarating to be on the frontier of these changes. The next several decades will require the successful purchasing manager to be a supply chain risk and relationship manager rather than someone who reactively buys goods and services.

Purchasing Policies and Procedures

Understanding policies and procedures is essential for understanding how organizations operate and work. Policy is based on the idea that guidelines are documented and applicable to all the internal and external relations of an organization. A policy prescribes methods of accomplishment in terms broad enough for decision makers to exercise discretion while allowing employees to render judgment on an issue.[17] Well-formulated policies and procedures support efficient, effective, and consistent purchasing operations. On the other hand, policies and procedures that are out of date, require unnecessary action, or do not address current issues or topics will not support effective purchasing operations.

Relationship of Purchasing With Others

Purchasing needs to develop closer relations with internal and external groups. To accomplish this, purchasing professionals must develop a working knowledge of the principles of engineering, manufacturing, cost-based accounting, quality assurance, and team dynamics. The days when purchasing operated in a confined area with an occasional visit to a supplier are over.

Firms are using the team approach to streamline and improve the product development process. This directly affects firms that rely on innovative new products for their continued success. Purchasing has a key role to play on these teams. Their role involves helping to select suppliers for inclusion in the process, advising engineering personnel of suppliers' capabilities, and helping to negotiate contracts once the product team has selected a supplier. Purchasing also acts as a liaison throughout this process, in facilitating supplier participation at team meetings and helping to resolve conflicts between the supplier and the team when they occur. Purchasing may also be involved in developing a target price for the supplier to aim at while planning the component/system, and helping the supplier to analyze costs and identify ways of meeting this target price. Finally, purchasing may also be involved in developing nondisclosure and confidentiality agreements in cases where technology sharing occurs.

Part of the increased interaction between purchasing and other functions is due to the need to compete in an environment driven by reduced product cycle times. Purchasing supports this effort by developing closer internal and external relationships and by participating on cross-functional teams. Those interested in a purchasing profession should learn as much as they can about what it takes to compete in today's markets, including expanding their knowledge about the team approach as well as understanding how firms compete on cost, quality, and time. The need to interact effectively with different groups plays a major role in how well purchasing can accomplish its tasks.

Insourcing or Outsourcing

The insourcing or outsourcing decision is important to the economic success of an organization because the decision determines the firm's economic boundaries and its competitive character. The insourcing or outsourcing decision process has historically been conducted without a true strategic perspective. Typically, decisions were based on the purely economic issues of price, quality, and quantity of goods. Several factors will increasingly influence future insourcing or outsourcing decisions. Purchasing, operations, and technology managers will need to work together closely to identify activities where there is a distinctive competence. They must also identify those activities best performed by external sources. Managers must obtain clear insights into the relative long- and short-term economics associated with insourcing or outsourcing decisions, particularly from a total-cost perspective. Finally, organizations must conduct more accurate assessments of the technologies that are crucial to future success.

Supplier Evaluation, Selection, and Measurement

One of the most important functions of business is the evaluation, selection, and continuous measurement of suppliers. Performing these activities well establishes the foundation upon which to further develop and improve supplier performance. In his book *Purchasing in the 21st Century,* John Schorr maintains that a buyer should look for certain characteristics when evaluating and selecting suppliers.[18]

- A good supplier will build quality into the product, aiming for zero-defect production.
- Delivery performance is a key measure of a good supplier. This involves a willingness to make short and frequent deliveries to point-of-use areas within a purchaser's facility, along with a willingness to package items according to a purchaser's specifications.
- A good supplier will demonstrate responsiveness to a purchaser's needs by ensuring that qualified and accessible people are in charge of servicing the purchaser's account.
- Long lead times are the enemy of all businesses; a good supplier will work with a purchaser to reduce lead times as much as possible.
- A good supplier willingly provides a purchaser with information regarding capability and workload.
- The best suppliers create the future rather than fear its coming. Look for suppliers on the cutting edge of technology.
- A leading-edge supplier reinvests part of its profits in R&D; a good supplier takes a long-term view and is willing to spend for tomorrow.
- Good suppliers can meet the stringent financial stability criteria used when evaluating potential new customers for credit.

A focus on selecting only the best suppliers possible will make a major contribution to the competitiveness of the entire organization. The ability to make this contribution requires careful evaluation, selection, and continuous measurement of the suppliers that provide the goods and services that help satisfy the needs of an organization's final customers.

Supplier Quality Management

Improving supplier quality involves much more than providing clear specifications and maintaining open communication. The purchasing and sourcing process can effectively improve supplier quality practices and set a standard for excellence. Supplier quality excellence can be achieved through a number of approaches.

- Being a good customer
- Providing feedback
- Measuring performance and eliminating poor suppliers
- Certifying and rewarding performance
- Setting targets and helping suppliers reach their goals

In order to reach these goals, purchasing must have people who understand the principles and tools of total quality management and can effectively work with suppliers to ensure that zero supplier defects is the norm rather than the exception.

Creating a World-Class Supply Base

Managing and improving supplier performance is a primary purchasing and business function. Supplier management and development have become the new model of purchasing behavior. No longer does a buyer simply purchase parts from the lowest price source. The activities that best describe today's purchaser include planning, coordinating, managing, developing, and improving the performance capabilities of the supply base. For many items, purchasers no longer buy parts from suppliers; they manage supplier capabilities.

Purchasing must select and manage a proper mix of suppliers. To accomplish this, managers must have the proper resources for supplier management, including a supplier performance measurement system, contracts with preferred suppliers, and a wide range of supplier development resources. A well-supported supplier management program helps maximize the contribution received from suppliers.

Section 258. Electronic Procurement

Summaries and Conclusions

Purchasing must expand its use of information technology to increase both individual and functional performance. The use of Web-based applications, enterprise resource planning (ERP) systems, and decision support systems can help professional buyers shift attention from routine to strategic tasks. For example, systems that support the making of better supplier selection decisions—one of a firm's most strategic tasks—can reduce or eliminate future supply base problems. Also, a system that monitors supplier performance can provide timely visibility concerning potential supply problems. Ordering and implementing new ERP systems requires planning and work. The final decision about a system usually represents a long-term commitment to selected features and equipment. Purchasing professionals must identify systems that meet current operating requirements with the capability to meet future needs. Progressive purchasing functions should always be looking five years ahead to identify system trends, operating requirements, and systems applications. For purchasing to contribute to a firm's performance objectives, it must have the resources and ability to develop world-class information systems supported by leading-edge technology.

Section 260. Logistical Management

Summaries and Conclusions

Logistics and transportation are exciting and dynamic parts of supply chain management. A study by Ernst and Young titled "Corporate Profitability and Logistics: Innovative Guidelines for Executives" concluded that firms should follow some basic principles for logistics and transportation success. Because purchasing plays a greater role in transportation management, the conclusions of this study directly affect purchasing professionals. The study maintains that a number of principles underlie world-class logistics and transportation performance.

- Link logistic and transportation activities directly to corporate strategy.
- Organize logistics and transportation activities under a single executive-level position.
- Expand and use the power of information and information-processing technology within logistics and transportation.
- Form partnerships and alliances with external parties throughout the supply chain.
- Focus on financial performance by treating some logistical and transportation activities as cost or profit centers.
- Combine transportation volumes on a company-wide basis to realize increased purchase leverage and control.
- Measure logistics and transportation performance to sustain superior performance.

One topic that is critical to transportation and logistics management is the role of information technology. Systems such as electronic data interchange (EDI), electronic funds transfer (EFT), automatic identification, bar coding, global positioning systems, material tracking through the Internet, and automated materials handling are the technological enablers that support an integrated logistics system.

Managing a transportation system presents opportunities and challenges. An integrated logistics system can help firms gain or maintain industry leadership in terms of customer service and time-based competition. As global sourcing and global trade continues to increase, integrated logistics systems will become necessary in order to compete.

Purchasing's involvement, although fairly recent by historical standards, will continue to grow. Excellent opportunities exist for the purchasing professional to make major contributions in this important but often overlooked area.

Section 265. Service Strategy

Summaries and Conclusions

Over the years, the service sector has assumed a preeminent position in the U.S. economy. Both in overall employment and in trade with other countries, it far outdistances other sectors of the economy. This change did not take place in a vacuum. It is theorized that concurrently with the rise of the service economy came the "postindustrial society." In this new society, different values and desires from consumers have accompanied the rise of the service sector and have changed the emphasis of management.

Physically, much of this economic change took place through the operations function. The enhanced productivity of agriculture means that only 2 percent of U.S. workforce is required for this sector, which previously employed more than 80 percent. Likewise in manufacturing, the ever-increasing variety of goods is produced by fewer and fewer laborers. The challenge of effectively using the operations function of the service sector is therefore laid before us.

The four elements of the strategic service vision are (1) the focus on a target market, (2) the determination of a service concept, (3) the development of an operating strategy, and (4) the implementation of a service delivery system.

Capacity planning for many service firms can be far more difficult than for manufacturers. Manufacturers can set capacity by looking at long-run average demand. For many service firms, however, long-run averages become somewhat meaningless when capacity must be available and react to general seasonality, daily demand variations, and time-of-day demand fluctuations.

Four strategies for service capacity include (1) Provide: ensure sufficient capacity at all times; (2) Match: change capacity as needed; (3) Influence: alter demand patterns to fit firm capacity; and (4) Control: maximize capacity utilization.

To assist in crafting these four strategies, a host of specific tactics can be used to manage supply and demand. These tactics include: (1) plan for creative work schedules (for example, variable work hours), (2) increase customer participation, (3) allow for adjustable (surge) capacity, (4) share capacity, (5) partition demand, (6) offer price incentives and promotions for off-peak demand, (7) develop complementary services, and (8) implement yield-management techniques.

Managing for growth in services includes developing a "service life cycle" similar to the "product life cycle," industry roll-ups, and franchising. The five stages of the service life cycle are entrepreneurial, multisite rationalization, growth, maturity, and decline or regeneration.

The idea behind industry roll-up is to use publicly trades stock to buy up several small firms in a fragmented industry. When a roll-up succeeds, it is viewed as a way for small, independent operators to retain their local connections and personal touch while achieving economies of scale with the parent company. Examples include funeral homes, waste-management services, physicians, tow-truck operators, and direct marketing firms.

An alternative to the traditional internal funding of the growth stages is to franchise. Several operational problems arise with a franchised system. In a company-owned system, procedures, products, and channels of distribution can be changed at the discretion of management. Such is not the case with a franchised system. Flexibility is lost.

Advantages of franchising include self-financing, less risk, the provision of a career path for store owners, natural alignment of revenue maximizing incentives, and provision of marketing by the parent.

Disadvantages of franchising include limited income to the owner, difficulty in managerial control, difficulty in implementing operational change, limited marketing channels, and potential for brand shirking. In addition, special events are more difficult to plan and execute.

Several strategic decisions within franchise agreements can assist in creating a franchise system that succeeds. These decisions include passive ownership, master franchise agreements, fee structure, and geographic protection. The fee structure includes up-front (one-time) fees and royalties based on gross sales. Systems that focus more on up-front fees are more highly associated with failing. The systems lack the ability to monitor free-riders or brand shirkers.

MODULE 200. OPERATIONS MANAGEMENT

Section 270. Service Capacity Management

Summaries and Conclusions

Yield-management systems are used in a wide variety of industries that have limited capacity. Such systems can potentially make a significant difference in profitability for firms that use them well.

Three basic components of a yield-management system are overbooking, capacity allocation, and pricing. Quantitative methods can help to solve problems with overbooking and capacity allocation. However, a practical answer to the pricing problem still remains out of reach. Examples can be used to show how the environment of a yield-management system, with customer classes and capacity restrictions, can turn normal pricing decisions around.

Finally, a yield-management system is not just a computer program. It is a system that must be implemented with flesh-and-blood employees and customers. These human elements of the system must be attended to carefully because poor employee or customer education as to the limits and nature of such a system may lead to its circumvention in a variety of ways.

Section 275. Waiting Time Management in Services

Summaries and Conclusions

The waiting line problem is an important one for many services. It often forms the basis of the customer service quality judgment. Further, it is a problem that is inherently nonlinear and, therefore, difficult for managers to understand. Thoughtful, hard-working managers who are responsible for hiring decisions but do not understand this material can find themselves chronically short staffed and not know why.

Waiting line systems are not simply numbers, however. Marketing and operations must jointly attack the problem both through number crunching and by attacking the psychological components of waiting. Appropriately setting customer expectations and responding to unspoken customer needs for reassurance can be just as effective as adding expensive capacity.

Many waiting line situations are too complex. For those systems, simulation, rather than plugging in formulas, is the best way to discover answers to managerial questions.

Section 278. Managing Service Experiences

Summaries and Conclusions

It is important to develop services with an experience focus in today's competitive market. The experience focus is applicable to both for-profit and not-for-profit industries. Pine and Gilmore state that experiences should be designed for people to pay admission for the experience element, too, not just the accompanying product.[19,20]

Section 280. Engineering and Operations

Summaries and Conclusions

Engineering is an integral part of operations; that is, product/manufacturing engineers design a product while manufacturing (operations) personnel produce it. To design products for low-cost manufacture requires close coordination and cooperation between product design engineers and process design engineers, which is called *concurrent* or *simultaneous engineering*. If a product cannot be produced at a cost that will allow a profit to be made, then it is a failure for the firm. Related activities that affect both engineering and operations include design for manufacturability, reusable engineering, tool engineering, and industrial engineering.

Section 285. Economics and Operations

Summaries and Conclusions

Economics and operations are closely related; that is, operations incur costs to produce goods or services. Major concepts include economies of scale, economies of scope, learning curve, and economic analysis.

Economies of scale are obtained by spreading the costs of production over a large quantity of products. Economies of scope are obtained by spreading the costs of production over a wide variety of products. These two concepts are distinct in that scale refers to size or numbers whereas scope refers to functions and activities.

The learning curve phenomenon is often characterized as a constant percentage decline in average costs as cumulative output increases. Scale economies relate to cost differences associated with different output levels along a single learning curve average cost. On the other hand, learning curves relate cost differences to total cumulative output.

Operations managers can use economic analysis to assess automation opportunities and new product alternatives. This includes estimation of production volume, costs, and profits for the new product. Examples of economic analysis include incremental or average costs, break-even analysis, operating leverage analysis, capital budgeting techniques, and financial ratio analysis.

Sections 286 and 295. Law, Ethics, and Purchasing

Summaries and Conclusions

The field of purchasing is dynamic and changing rapidly. When dealing with suppliers in contract negotiations, contract management, breach of contracts, potential damages, and patent or trade secret disputes, purchasing managers must be sure to stipulate the appropriate terms and conditions. Nevertheless, many legal disputes are being handled through discussions with suppliers instead of being referred to legal departments. Both purchasing managers and suppliers also generally prefer using negotiation as an alternative to court decisions. In either case, purchasing managers must be aware of the potential pitfalls implicit in standard legal terminology and must seek to prevent the occurrence of such disputes. An operational rule of thumb is "When in doubt, err on the side of prudence."

Section 290. Quantitative Techniques and Operations

Summaries and Conclusions

Operational issues and problems are big both in size and scope and therefore require quantitative techniques to solve them. Major application of these techniques include linear programming, inventory models, waiting-line models, simulation, sensitivity analysis, and operations demand and supply forecasting.

Section 299. International Issues

Summaries and Conclusions

International purchases for raw materials, components, finished goods, and services will continue to increase. Purchasing personnel at all levels must become familiar with the nuances of worldwide purchasing. Benefiting from worldwide sourcing requires the proper structure and systems, which often means having an executive with the vision to coordinate and integrate purchasing operations on a global basis. While most organizations prefer to purchase from suppliers who are geographically close, this is not always possible. Firms operating in competitive industries must purchase from the best sources worldwide.

Perhaps one of the biggest barriers to international sourcing involves the cultural differences that arise when doing business with other countries. For instance, the standard procedures for negotiation and contracting are distinctly different in Asia, Europe, and the United States. Dealing with these issues requires purchasing personnel and organizations to develop the skills and capabilities required to manage the international purchasing process.

Marketing Management

Section 301. Marketing Strategies

Summaries and Conclusions

- Markets came into being and trading developed as a result of the spontaneous economic combustion between resource scarcity, labor specialization, and consumption satiation.
- In essence, markets and marketing exist because of consumers' desire for a variety of ever-improving products and because of the impracticality and inefficiency of each individual developing distinct products for his or her personal use.
- Marketing is based on the principle that exchange adds value and marketing facilitates the exchange process by performing a variety of activities. The completion of these marketing activities facilitates the flow of products along the supply chain from producers to customers. In doing so, marketing can have profound societal implications and is often closely related to the success of political and economic systems.
- Effective and efficient markets and marketing practices can help everyone, including poorer countries. But there is a price to this success: Greater prosperity as a result of trading integration and superior marketing systems places strains on the earth's ecology.
- Fifty years ago, the study of marketing developed a more managerial emphasis on earning profits through customer satisfaction, which became known as the *marketing concept*. This gave birth to the field of consumer research, which has developed a reputation for scholarship that is the equal of other social sciences. It also led to a more managerial emphasis on segmenting the market, targeting and serving segments with specially designed products, and carefully designing a marketing mix.
- As an organizational process, marketing develops and implements the marketing mix, consisting of product, distribution (place), promotion, and pricing decisions and activities specifically tailored to meet the needs of intended target markets. Marketing mix elements help firms develop positioning strategies that differentiate their products and brands from competitive offerings.
- Because businesses do not operate in a vacuum, successful firms regularly modify their marketing mix decisions to adapt to the changing internal and external environment, particularly to new types and forms of competition.
- Macroenvironmental forces include sociocultural, technological, economic, competitive, and legal/political influences. The microenvironment is comprised of organizational objectives and resources. An important role of marketing is to prepare situation analyses and reports on changes in these market environments.

Sections 310 and 315. New Product Development and Product Management

Summaries and Conclusions

- Products are the lifeblood of every organization, whether they are goods, services, people, places, or ideas. In general, products can be classified either as consumer or business-to-business products. Consumer products include convenience, shopping, specialty, and unsought products that are characterized based on how the consumer views and shops for the product. Business-to-business products include installations, accessories, raw materials, component parts/materials, and supplies and are classified based on how the products will be used.

- Few companies are successful by relying on a single product. Marketing's role in successfully accomplishing new product development requires firms to continually (1) understand customer needs and problems, (2) match technological capabilities to solving those problems, and (3) move projects through the corporation and into the market. Unless all three tasks are performed well, product development is unlikely to be successful.

- Understanding customer needs requires performing qualitative market research and making the details of that research available to the development team. No one technique will easily provide a list of *all* customer needs. Actually being a customer best conveys tacit needs. Process-related needs are identified most easily by critically observing customers. In-depth interviewing is the most efficient means to obtain masses of detailed needs, but may not provide tacit and process-related information. Few projects can afford the time and expense of fully implementing all these processes. Development teams must use the most appropriate customer need-generating technique(s), given the informational requirements, budget, and time frame for their project.

- Effectively using technological capabilities to solve problems requires implementing a strategy for the new product development (NPD) program overall, strategies for each project, and a product development process. Commercializing new products consists of repeatable tasks and less repeatable tasks. Firms that use a formalized new product process to help complete the more repeatable tasks in a consistent manner tend to have greater NPD success. Formalized processes are personalized to meet the needs of each firm.

- Shepherding products through the firm requires implementing effective leadership, providing an organizational structure that allows projects to move forward efficiently, and developing mechanisms to maintain management support over the life of projects. Project leaders, champions, and process owners all have been used to lead projects effectively. NPD in firms is organized through two different structures, each providing better ways to organize depending on the "newness to the organization" of the project being developed. No one structure seems to be associated with consistently higher performance. A number of different influence strategies, both formal and informal and affecting both rational and political decision-making processes, are used to obtain and maintain management support for projects.

- Product mix decisions must be made regarding the width and depth of product lines to be marketed. Additional product decisions must be made in the areas of branding, packaging, and labeling.

- Once launched, marketing must manage profitability throughout the product life cycle by modifying marketing mix elements to achieve the objectives of different life cycle stages. The objective in the introduction stage is to make potential early adopters aware of the product and persuade them to try it. During growth, the objective is achieving maximum market share. Profitability is the primary objective during both maturity and decline.

- Still more product decisions must be made with regard to sustaining growth. Established products are the mainstay of most companies. But a company that depends solely on its current stable of products may be headed for trouble. Growth opportunities exist in the form of market penetration, market development, product development, and product-diversification strategies.

- Long-term corporate success depends upon executing new product development effectively and efficiently. Managing product development is one of the most complex tasks of the organization, in part, because of the cooperation needed between different departments. Marketing is crucial in achieving successful new product development and making product decisions.

Section 320. Advertising and Promotion

Summaries and Conclusions

- A brand and its attributes/benefits must be communicated to customers through marketing communications. In today's highly competitive and dynamic marketing world, effective communications are critical to a company's success. Marketing managers have considerable discretion in determining which marketing communications (MarCom) elements to use and how much relative emphasis each should receive. Various factors such as the target market, product life-cycle stage, objectives, competitive activity, budget, and nature of the product all affect the appropriate mix of MarCom elements.

- Whereas historically many marketing communication decisions were treated as rather disparate and managed by independent departments that failed to carefully coordinate their activities, there has been a trend toward integrated marketing communications (IMC). Some key elements of IMC are that all marketing communication decisions start with the customer, which reflects the adoption of an outside-in mentality versus an inside-out position that historically has dominated this field. Another fundamental feature is that all communication elements must achieve synergy, or speak with a single voice. The belief that successful marketing communications must build a relationship between the brand and the customer is another key IMC feature.

- Advertising is a critical component of marketing communications, especially in the United States, where annual expenditures are huge. The process of developing advertising strategy consists of the following major activities: setting objectives, formulating a budget, establishing a positioning statement, developing a message strategy, designing a media strategy, and assessing advertising effectiveness.

- Sales promotion—the use of any incentive by a manufacturer to induce the trade (wholesalers and retailers) and/or final consumers to buy a brand and to encourage the sales force to aggressively sell it—is another key MarCom element. Consumer promotions (such as coupons, cents-off deals, premiums, and sweepstakes) and trade-oriented promotions (primarily off-invoice allowances to wholesalers and retailers) constitute, on average, approximately three-fourths of businesses' MarCom budgets. Sales promotions are particularly useful for purposes of introducing new or revised products to the trade, obtaining trial purchases from consumers, and enhancing repeat purchasing. However, sales promotions cannot compensate for inadequate personal selling or advertising, give the trade or consumers any long-term reason for buying a brand, or permanently stop an established brand's declining sales trend.

- Public relations (PR) is that aspect of promotion management uniquely suited to fostering goodwill between a company and its various publics. Public relations involves interactions with multiple publics (for example, government, stockholders), but emphasis in this section is limited to the more narrow aspect of public relations involving an organization's interactions with customers. This marketing-oriented aspect of public relations is called *marketing PR,* or MPR for short.

- Marketing PR can be further delineated as involving either proactive or reactive public relations. Proactive MPR is another tool in addition to advertising and sales promotion for enhancing a brand's equity. Its major role is to disseminate information about brand introductions or revisions. Reactive MPR is undertaken as a result of external pressures and challenges brought by competitive actions, changes in consumer attitudes, changes in government policy, or other external influences. Reactive MPR typically deals with changes that have negative consequences for the organization, such as instances of product defects or failures.

- One of the fastest growing aspects of marketing and marketing communications is the practice of corporate sponsorships. Sponsorships take two forms: event sponsorships (such as athletic and entertainment events) and cause-oriented sponsorships. Event marketing is growing rapidly because it provides companies alternatives to the cluttered mass media, an ability to segment on a local or regional basis, and opportunities for reaching narrow lifestyle groups whose consumption behavior can be linked with the local event. Cause-related marketing, a form of corporate philanthropy with benefits accruing to the sponsoring company, is based on the idea that a company will contribute to a cause every time the customer undertakes some action. In addition to helping worthy causes, corporations satisfy their own tactical and strategic objectives when undertaking cause-related efforts. By supporting a deserving cause, a company can enhance its corporate or brand image, generate incremental sales, increase brand awareness, broaden its customer base, and reach new market segments.

- Communications at the point of purchase is another major growth area in marketing. This is due to the fact that point-of-purchase (P-O-P) materials provide a useful service for all participants in the marketing process. P-O-P communications also serve as the capstone for an integrated MarCom program.

Section 330. Pricing Strategies

Summaries and Conclusions

- We should understand the factors that influence the setting of base prices, and the key reasons underlying why base prices are adjusted over time.
- The natural starting point for pricing decisions is cost, and the cost-based methods of pricing seem to predominate in the marketplace. Yet, there are difficulties with such approaches, particularly when demand is uncertain.
- Pricing decisions must, then, take into account the relationship between price and demand. The transition from a cost-based approach to a more market-driven approach begins with a break-even analysis, which motivates the question, "Can we sell the number of units needed at this price to make the desired profit?" From here, estimates of a demand schedule provide important input into pricing decisions, as do consideration of the firm's strategic position, competitive prices, and legal and ethical considerations.
- It is also significant to remember that there are many reasons why firms change base prices over time. Prices change both because objectives change over the product life cycle, and because competitors likely change prices.
- We should be aware of the reasons for price flexing for both business users and household consumers. Some of these reasons for flexible pricing are due to traditional discounting and price promotional practices. We should not forget the impact of new technology and the Internet. They are providing the possibility of aligning conditions of supply and demand almost instantaneously, leading to near-customized, or at least very efficient, pricing.

Section 340. Consumer Behavior

Summaries and Conclusions

- A consumer is a person who is party to a transaction with the marketer. Consumer behavior determines how we select, purchase, and dispose products to satisfy our needs and wants. The three roles a consumer plays are those of the user, the payer, and the buyer.
- Whether they are users, payers, or buyers, consumers have needs and wants. A need is an unsatisfactory physical condition of the consumer that leads him or her to an action that will satisfy or fulfill that condition. A want is a desire to obtain more satisfaction than is absolutely necessary to improve an unsatisfactory condition.
- Some of the underlying processes that consumers use to make product and brand choices are perception, learning, motivation, and attitude formation. The characteristics of the stimulus or incoming information, the context, and consumers themselves all influence the perceptual process.
- Consumer learning is directed at acquiring a potential for future adaptive behavior. Consumer motivations explain why consumers buy, pay for, and use specific products. This topic is organized in terms of needs, emotions, and psychographics. *Needs* are felt deprivations of desired states. Maslow's hierarchy is a useful classification scheme of needs. Human emotions also play a significant role in motivating human behavior. Psychographics describe consumers' profile of needs, emotions, and resulting behaviors, and as such explain much of consumer behavior. Psychographics include self-concept, personal values, and lifestyles. An important type of psychographics is VALS (values and lifestyles).
- Attitudes are consumers' likes and dislikes toward various products and their predispositions to respond to (approach or avoid) them.
- Consumer decision making is a five-step process: (1) problem recognition, (2) information search, (3) alternative evaluation, (4) purchase, and (5) post-purchase evaluation. The consumer decision process begins with problem recognition. The problem recognition occurs due to an internal cue, which comes from one's motives being in a state of unfulfillment, or from external stimuli evoking these motives. Once problem recognition occurs, the consumer either (a) relies on prior knowledge and previously learned solutions, or (b) searches for new solutions through new information acquisition and its evaluation and integration.
- Evaluations of alternatives entail use of compensatory (trade-off) and noncompensatory (non-trade-off) decision models. The latter include conjunctive, disjunctive, lexicographic, and elimination-by-aspects models.

- The outcome of these evaluation processes is the identification of a preferred brand and the formation of purchase intent. Such purchase intent is then implemented by the actual purchase act, but the purchase act does not always occur as planned. Sometimes, substantial delays occur in purchase implementation, and other times, the brand actually bought is different from the one planned, because of stock-outs or new information at the time of purchase. In the post-purchase evaluation phase, the processes of decision confirmation, satisfaction/dissatisfaction, exit, complaining, and loyalty responses take place.
- In addition to making purchase decisions as individuals, consumers often make purchase decisions as members of households. These household decisions are complex because the user, payer, and buyer roles are often distributed among different household members. The family buying process is one in which different members of the family influence various stages of the decision process. Children influence parental choices of products that they use as well as those used only by parents.

Section 350. Marketing Research

Summaries and Conclusions

- Market research and analysis is a very broad area of discussion, covering many topics and techniques. It also explains why so much market research is contracted out by companies to research suppliers who, like advertising agencies, are specialists in their profession.
- Some people might argue that market research is only "research" when it involves complex scientific method and analysis borrowed from the social sciences and economics. But such research often costs tens of thousands of dollars, sometimes millions of dollars. In reality, how many firms undertake such research? Several hundred huge packaged-goods and service companies spend millions of dollars a year on market research, employing highly skilled researchers. A few thousand companies spend hundreds of thousands a year on marketing research, mainly using smaller market research firms whom they work with over many years. What sort of market research do the remaining hundreds of thousands of businesses undertake? Their managers spend a lot of time observing customers, competitors, and distributors firsthand. They are increasingly using secondary sources of information they obtain from the business press, government sources, or Web searches. The reason why we emphasize simple methods such as observing customers, competitors, and distributors is because these are the methods that all firms should use, but that few actually employ.
- Over the last 100 years, much has been learned about how to practice market research. The first general lesson that has been learned is that market research is about helping to improve managers' intuitive understanding of the behavior of customers, competitors, and distributors.
- The second lesson is that a firm should follow a systematic market research process. This process includes seven steps: (1) recognize problem, (2) meet and define problem and determine how to solve it, (3) search secondary data sources and own databases, (4) undertake quick-and-dirty primary research, (5) undertake thorough primary research, (6) analyze information, and (7) present findings. First gather, analyze, and discuss all the information that managers already have on hand from their own information systems, from their sales force, from secondary information, and from their own personal observation. A particular market research project needs to be defined in terms of the crucial questions that need to be answered. Ways of quickly and cheaply answering these questions need to be pursued, then a cost/benefit decision has to be made as to whether to pursue more expensive research. Millions of dollars were at stake in the decision by R. G. Barry Company to raise its slipper prices. For about $40,000 the company was able to assure management and its retail customers that it could raise its prices with little loss in sales. The research also provided other valuable information about product design and merchandising practices.
- The third lesson is that market research methods are evolving as new technologies are being used. Fifty years ago, computers did not exist, and all analyses had to be undertaken mechanically or by hand. Today, a personal computer can do sophisticated quantitative and qualitative analyses that were unheard of 30 years ago. Twenty years ago, scanner technology was invented and with it the ability to track company and competitor sales through specific distribution channels. Today, companies that specialize in Web-based market research are being invented. These companies may greatly increase the quality and decrease the cost of market research in the near future.

- The fourth and final lesson is that research needs to be reported in ways that make it easy for decision makers to understand what is going on. This is best achieved by developing digital files on consumer, competitor, and distributor behavior that can be readily consulted and analyzed, online, for changing patterns. These files can be used by marketing analysts and planners to provide heads-up situation reports for senior managers, sales management, research and development, and marketing planning. Companies with superior market research and analysis skills are able to change their thinking about the marketplace faster than their competition. Such fast insight and learning may give them more time to innovate, imitate, and avoid crisis management. A company with such superior decision-making skills has a clear competitive advantage over its rivals.

Section 355. Marketing Channels and Distribution

Summaries and Conclusions

- Marketing channels, the networks of organizations that create time, place, and possession utilities, allow hundreds of millions of customers to gain convenient access to a vast array of goods and services.
- As one of the four Ps of the marketing mix—product, price, promotion, and place—marketing channels' place is a key part of any firm's marketing strategy.
- Channel structure is the form or shape taken by the marketing channel, and consists of three dimensions: (1) length, (2) intensity, and (3) types of intermediaries.
- Channel structure is determined by three major factors: (1) the distribution tasks that need to be performed, (2) the economics of performing the distribution tasks, and (3) management's desire for control of the channel.
- Marketing channels create five flows: (1) product flow, (2) negotiation flow, (3) ownership flow, (4) information flow, and (5) promotion flow. All of these flows need to be managed to achieve effective and efficient marketing channels.
- Marketing channels are social systems as well as economic systems, so power and conflict play an important role.
- Marketing channel management consists of analyzing, planning, organizing, and controlling a firm's marketing channels. Six areas are involved: (1) formulating channel strategy, (2) designing channel structure, (3) selecting channel members, (4) motivating channel members, (5) coordinating channel strategy, and (6) evaluating channel member performance.
- The planning, implementation, and control of the physical flows of materials and final goods from points of production to points of use is referred to as *logistics, physical distribution* (PD), or *supply chain management*.
- A logistics system consists of six major components: (1) transportation, (2) materials handling, (3) order processing, (4) inventory control, (5) warehousing, and (6) packaging.
- Logistics managers need to employ the systems concept to understand the relationships among the components and the total cost approach to determine and account for all of the costs of the logistical systems.

Section 360. Electronic Commerce and Marketing

Summaries and Conclusions

- Electronic commerce includes all the activities of a firm that use the Internet to aid in the exchange of products.
- As fast as the Internet is expanding, the number and type of Internet sites is increasing. Sites can be classified into four major categories: company/brand sites, service sites, selling sites, and information sites. These sites are obviously not mutually exclusive and collectively exhaustive.
- The growth of the Internet required three separate developments in order for it to become an efficient marketing tool. First, businesses had to develop their electronic commerce intranets and extranets that connect to the Internet. Second, network server growth, allowing fast connection, was necessary. Finally, consumers (either at work or at home) had to have access to the Internet.

- E-commerce expanded on the Internet primarily because of four major areas of improvement to business practices: reduced costs, inventory reduction, improved customer service, and market/product development opportunities.
- Web sites make money through the use of advertising, subscriptions, product vending, and intermediary commissions. Many Web sites utilize a combination of these strategies.
- E-marketing can aid a company's overall marketing effort in a number of ways. First, e-marketing allows a company/brand to increase its brand equity in the marketplace. Second, e-marketing allows marketers to develop a prospective customer into a buying customer. Third, e-marketing can improve customer service by allowing customers to serve themselves when and where they choose. The fourth benefit to marketers is information transfer. Traditionally, marketers gathered information via expensive focus groups, mail surveys, telephone surveys, and personal interviews. The Web offers a mechanism for companies to collect similar information at a fraction of the cost.
- Although there are numerous advantages for companies using e-marketing, there are two major drawbacks at this time: a limited target audience and consumers' resistance to change. Both of these are likely to change as the Internet diffuses throughout our society.
- The digital revolution is here and will have similar effects as any revolution would have on a society. A mere ten years ago the Internet thrust itself upon society. As this innovation permeates society, it becomes increasingly important for businesses to make the Internet an integral component of their marketing strategy.

Section 365. Ethics and Marketing

Summaries and Conclusions

- Marketing has a social responsibility to be efficient and effective, to behave decently and obey the law, and to help market worthy social causes.
- As marketers respond to the marketing environment, they must do so in a manner that reflects their concern for the welfare of others. This has been termed the *social contract*.
- A "free market" does not mean that suppliers and customers are free to do whatever they like, whenever they like. What it means is that they are free to pursue their own self-interests, but they are also free to suffer the economic and moral consequences of such behavior. For instance, competition forces sellers to serve the interests of customers. It is in the self-interest of a firm to serve the interests of the consumer and others who help the firm achieve its goals.
- The paradox of free markets is that sellers are free to blindly and naively pursue their own self-interest at the expense of customers and facilitators, but if they do so, they will very soon no longer have customers or any help from anyone else. Consequently, it is simply not true, as claimed by Adam Smith 225 years ago and by the influential *Economist* magazine today, that the unfettered pursuit of self-interest can be justified within the free-market, capitalist system because it collectively serves the public good.
- Ethical, lawful behavior, particularly honesty, is required to make markets work efficiently and to keep them from failing. Marketers must not cheat and steal because, when this becomes the norm, markets collapse and marketing ceases. Failed economies such as those that exist in Africa today provide ample evidence of the consequences of unethical and unlawful business practices.
- Marketers' decisions as to what to offer the marketplace and how to offer it also have an impact on the prevailing values and ethics of a society. Some products and marketing practices are ethically questionable. This heavy responsibility cannot be simply shrugged off. The enlightened leadership that marketing planners are expected to display is most put to the test when they are faced with ethical dilemmas created by conflicts of interests among customers, employees, and owners. How they choose to resolve such dilemmas tells them a lot about themselves.
- Many of the criticisms of marketing that are popular among modern socialists simply have no basis in fact, reflecting instead the ideological prejudices of the critics. The collapse of the corrupt and hopelessly inefficient communist systems has not muted the shrillness of the critics of the capitalist market. It also has not increased their insights. Despite the unreasonableness of much of the criticism of marketing, the fact is that the world faces several potential "tragedy of the commons" effects on clean air, fresh water, trees, fish, participatory democracy, and young women's self-esteem. All functions of a firm, including marketing, have to be sensitive to such effects.

- Ethics in marketing gives rise to more questions than definitive answers. Like any marketing skill, the skill of behaving ethically and socially responsibly develops with practice—the practice of asking the right questions, answering them honestly, and resolving dilemmas by balancing short- and long-term interests.

Section 370. Economics and Marketing

Summaries and Conclusions

Supply and Demand

The forces of supply and demand establish the prices and quantities observed in the markets for all goods and services. A fundamental understanding of demand and supply concepts is essential to the successful operation of any economic organization.

- Demand is the quantity of a good or service that customers are willing and able to purchase under a given set of economic conditions. Direct demand is the demand for products that directly satisfy consumer desires. The value or worth of a good or service—its utility—is the prime determinant of direct demand. The demand for all inputs is derived demand and determined by the profitability of using various inputs to produce output.
- The market demand function for a product is a statement of the relation between the aggregate quantity demanded and all factors that affect this quantity. The demand curve expresses the relation between the price charged for a product and the quantity demanded, holding constant the effects of all other variables.
- A change in the quantity demanded is a movement along a single demand curve. A shift in demand, or shift from one demand curve to another, reflects a change in one or more of the nonprice variables in the product demand function.
- The term *supply* refers to the quantity of a good or service that producers are willing and able to sell under a given set of conditions. The market supply function for a product is a statement of the relation between the quantity supplied and all factors affecting that quantity. A supply curve expresses the relation between the price charged and the quantity supplied, holding constant the effects of all other variables.
- Movements along a supply curve reflect change in the quantity supplied. A shift in supply, or a switch from one supply curve to another, indicates a change in one or more of the nonprice variables in the product supply function.
- A market is in equilibrium when the quantity demanded and the quantity supplied are in perfect balance at a given price. *Surplus* describes a condition of excess supply. Shortage is created when buyers demand more of a product at a given price than producers are willing to supply. The market equilibrium price just clears the market of all supplied product.

Demand Relations

Product demand is a critical determinant of profitability, and demand estimates are key considerations in virtually all managerial decisions. There are methods for quantifying and interpreting demand relations.

- *Elasticity* is the percentage change in a dependent variable, Y, resulting from a 1 percent change in the value of an independent variable, X. Point elasticity measures elasticity at a point on a function. *Arc elasticity* measures the average elasticity over a given range of a function.
- Factors such as price and advertising that are within the control of the firm are called *endogenous variables;* factors outside the control of the firm, such as consumer incomes, competitor prices, and the weather are called *exogenous variables*.
- The price elasticity of demand measures the responsiveness of the quantity demanded to changes in the price of the product, holding constant the values of all other variables in the demand function. With elastic demand, a price increase will lower total revenue and a decrease in price will raise total revenue. Unitary elasticity describes a situation in which the effect of a price change is exactly offset by the effect of a change in quantity demanded. Total revenue, the product of price times quantity, remains constant. With inelastic demand, a price

increase produces a less than proportionate decline in quantity demanded, so total revenue rises. Conversely, a price decrease produces less than a proportionate increase in quantity demanded, so total revenue falls.
- A direct relation between the price of one product and the demand for another holds for all substitutes. A price increase for a given product will increase demand for substitutes; a price decrease for a given product will decrease demand for substitutes. Goods that are inversely related in terms of price and quantity are known as *complements;* they are used together rather than in place of each other. The concept of cross-price elasticity is used to examine the responsiveness of demand for one product to changes in the price of another.
- The income elasticity of demand measures the responsiveness of demand to changes in income, holding constant the effect of all other variables that influence demand. For a limited number of inferior goods, individual consumer demand is thought to decline as income increases because consumers replace them with more desirable alternatives. Demand for such products is countercyclical, actually rising during recessions and falling during economic booms. More typical products, whose individual and aggregate demand is positively related to income, are defined as *normal goods*. Goods for which $0 < \epsilon_I < 1$ are often referred to as *noncyclical normal goods* because demand is relatively unaffected by changing income. For goods having $\epsilon_I > 1$, referred to as *cyclical normal goods*, demand is strongly affected by changing economic conditions.

Pricing Practices

There are several popular pricing practices. It becomes apparent that the methods commonly employed by successful firms reflect a careful appreciation of the use of marginal analysis to derive profit-maximizing prices.

- Many firms derive an optimal pricing policy using a technique called *markup pricing,* whereby prices are set to cover all direct costs plus a percentage markup for profit contribution. Flexible markup pricing practices that reflect differences in marginal costs and demand elasticities constitute an efficient method for ensuring that $MR=MC$.
- Markup on cost is the profit margin for an individual product or product line expressed as a percentage of unit cost. The numerator of this expression, called the *profit margin,* is the difference between price and cost. Markup on price is the profit margin for an individual product or product line expressed as a percentage of price, rather than unit cost.
- During peak periods, facilities are fully utilized. A firm has excess capacity during off-peak periods. Successful firms that employ markup pricing typically base prices on fully allocated costs under normal conditions but offer price discounts or accept lower margins during off-peak periods, when substantial excess capacity is available.
- The optimal markup-on-cost formula is $OMC^* = -1/(\epsilon_p + 1)$. The optimal markup-on-price formula is $OMP^* = -1/\epsilon_p$. Either formula can be used to derive profit-maximizing prices solely on the basis of marginal cost and price elasticity of demand information.
- Price discrimination occurs whenever different market segments are charged different price markups for the same product. A market segment is a division or fragment of the overall market with essentially different or unique demand or cost characteristics. Price discrimination is evident whenever identical customers are charged different prices, or when price differences are not proportional to cost differences. Through price discrimination, sellers are able to increase profits by appropriating the *consumers' surplus,* (or *customers' surplus*), which is the value of purchased goods and services above and beyond the amount paid to sellers.
- The extent to which a firm can engage in price discrimination is classified into three major categories. Under first-degree price discrimination, the firm extracts the maximum amount each customer is willing to pay for its products. Each unit is priced separately at the price indicated along each product demand curve. Second-degree price discrimination involves setting prices on the basis of the quantity purchased. Quantity discounts that lead to lower markups for large versus small customers are a common means for second-degree price discrimination. The most commonly observed form of price discrimination, third-degree price discrimination, results when a firm separates its customers into several classes and sets a different price for each customer class.
- Multiple-unit pricing strategies have also proved an effective means for extracting consumers' surplus for the benefit of producers. In general, a firm can enhance profits by using two-part pricing comprised of a per-unit fee equal to marginal cost, plus a fixed fee equal to the amount of consumers' surplus generated at that per-unit fee. If you have ever purchased a 12-pack of soft drinks, a year's supply of tax preparation services, or bought a "two-for-the-price-of-one" special, you have firsthand experience with the bundle pricing concept. As in the case of two-part pricing, the optimal level of output is determined by setting price equal to marginal cost and solving for quantity. Then, the optimal bundle price is a single lump sum amount equal to the total area under the demand curve at that point.

- A *by-product* is any output that is customarily produced as the direct result of an increase in the production of some other output. Profit maximization requires that marginal revenue be set equal to marginal cost for each by-product. Although the marginal costs of by-products produced in variable proportions can be determined, it is impossible to do so for by-products produced in fixed proportions. Common costs, or expenses that are necessary for manufacture of a joint product, cannot be allocated on any economically sound basis.
- A vertical relation is one where the output of one division or company is the input to another. Vertical integration occurs when a single company controls various links in the production chain from basic inputs to final output. Transfer pricing deals with the problem of pricing intermediate products transferred among divisions of vertically integrated firms. When transferred products cannot be sold in competitive external markets, the marginal cost of the transferring division is the optimal transfer price. When transferred products can be sold in perfectly competitive external markets, the external market price is the optimal transfer price. When transferred products can be sold in imperfectly competitive external markets, the optimal transfer price equates the marginal cost of the transferring division to the marginal revenue derived from the combined internal and external markets.

It has been shown that efficient pricing practices require a careful analysis of marginal revenues and marginal costs for each relevant product or product line. Rule-of-thumb pricing practices employed by successful firms can be reconciled with profit-maximizing behavior when the costs and benefits of pricing information are properly understood. These practices add tremendous value to the managerial decision-making process.

Section 375. Law and Marketing

Summaries and Conclusions

Federal Trade Commission

The purpose of the Federal Trade Commission (FTC) is to prevent unfair methods of competition and unfair or deceptive acts or practices.

STANDARDS
- *Unfairness* requires injury to be (1) substantial, (2) not outweighed by any countervailing benefit, and (3) unavoidable by reasonable consumer action.
- *Deception* is misrepresentation, omission, or practice that is likely to mislead the consumer acting reasonably in the circumstances.
- *Ad substantiation* requires advertisers to have a reasonable basis for their claims.

REMEDIES
- A *cease and desist order* is a command to stop doing the act in question.
- *Affirmative disclosure* requires an advertiser to include certain information in its ad so that the ad is not deceptive.
- *Corrective advertising* requires an advertiser to disclose that previous ads were deceptive.
- *Multiple product order* requires an advertiser to cease and desist from deceptive statements regarding all products it sells.

Consumer Health and Safety

The Consumer Product Safety Act is a federal statute enacted to do the following.
- Protect the public against unsafe products
- Assist consumers in evaluating products
- Develop uniform safety standards
- Promote safety research

Federal warranty protection applies to sellers of consumer goods who give written warranties.

- *Presale disclosure* requires terms of warranty to be simple and readily understood and to be made available before the sale.
- The *labeling requirement* requires the warrantor to inform consumers of their legal rights under a warranty (full or limited).
- The *disclaimer limitation* prohibits a written warranty from disclaiming any implied warranty.

State "Lemon Laws" are state laws that attempt to provide new car purchasers with rights similar to full warranties under Magnuson-Moss.

In certain instances a consumer is granted a brief period of time during which he or she may rescind (cancel) an otherwise binding obligation. This is known as the *consumer right of rescission*.

Consumer Credit Transactions

- Any credit transaction involving goods, services, or land for personal, household, or family purposes is referred to as a *consumer credit transaction*.
- *Access to the market* means discrimination is prohibited in extending credit on the basis of gender, marital status, race, color, religion, national origin, or age.
- *Disclosure requirements (Truth-in-Lending Act)*. This Act requires the creditor to provide certain information about contract terms, including APR (annual percentage rate), to the consumer before he or she formally incurs the obligation.
- *Contract terms* Statutory and judicial limitations that have been imposed on consumer obligations.
- *Credit Card Fraud Act.* This Act prohibits certain fraudulent practices and limits a card holder's liability for unauthorized use of a credit card to $50.
- The *Fair credit reporting* law requires that consumer credit reports are prohibited from containing inaccurate or obsolete information.

Creditors' Remedies

- *Wage assignments and garnishment.* Most states limit the amount that may be deducted from an individual's wages through either assignment or garnishment.
- *Security interest.* The seller may retain a security interest in goods sold or other collateral of the buyer, although some restrictions are imposed.
- *Debt collection practices.* Abusive, deceptive, and unfair practices by debt collectors in collecting consumer debts are prohibited by the Fair Debt Collection Practices Act.

Warranties

TYPES OF WARRANTIES
- *Warranty:* an obligation of the seller to the buyer (or lessor to lessee) concerning title, quality, characteristics, or condition of goods.
- *Warranty of title:* the obligation of a seller to convey the right of ownership without any lien. (In a lease, the warranty protects the lessee's right to possess and use the goods.)
- *Express warranty:* an affirmation of fact or promise about the goods, or a description, including a sample, of the goods, which becomes part of the basis of the bargain.
- *Implied warranty:* a contractual obligation, arising out of certain circumstances of the sale or lease, imposed by operation of law and not found in the language of the sales or lease contract.
- *Merchantability:* warranty by a merchant seller that the goods are reasonably fit for the ordinary purpose for which they are manufactured or sold, pass without objection in the trade under the contract description, and are of fair, average quality.

- *Fitness for particular purpose:* warranty by any seller that goods are reasonably fit for a particular purpose if, at the time of contracting, the seller had reason to know the buyer's particular purpose and that the buyer was relying on the seller's skill and judgment to furnish suitable goods.

OBSTACLES TO WARRANTY ACTION
- A *disclaimer of warranties* is a negation of a warranty.
- An *express warranty* is not usually possible to disclaim.
- A *warranty of title* may be excluded or modified by specific language or by certain circumstances, including judicial sale or a sale by a sheriff, executor, or foreclosing lien.
- In an *implied warranty of merchantability,* the disclaimer must mention "merchantability" and, in the case of a writing, must be conspicuous. (In a lease, the disclaimer must be in writing and conspicuous.)
- In an *implied warranty of fitness for a particular purpose,* the disclaimer must be in writing and conspicuous.
- In *other disclaimers of implied warranties,* the implied warranties of merchantability and fitness for a particular purpose may also be disclaimed (1) by expressions like "as is," "with all faults," or other similar language; (2) by course of dealing, course of performance, or usage of trade; or (3) as to defects an examination ought to have revealed where the buyer has examined the goods or where the buyer has refused to examine the goods.
- The *Magnuson-Moss Warranty Act,* federal legislation, protects purchasers of consumer goods by providing that warranty information be clear and useful and that a seller who makes a written warranty cannot disclaim any implied warranty.

The *limitation or modification of warranties* is permitted as long as it is not unconscionable.

Privity of Contract

Privity of contract is a contractual relationship between parties that was necessary at common law to maintain a lawsuit.

- *Horizontal privity* is the doctrine determining who benefits from a warranty and who therefore may bring a cause of action; the Code provides three alternatives.
- *Vertical privity* is the doctrine determining who in the chain of distribution is liable for a breach of warranty; the Code has not adopted a position on this.

If a buyer fails to notify a seller of any faults within a reasonable time, he or she is barred from any remedy against the seller.

Plaintiff's Conduct

- *Contributory negligence* is not a defense.
- *Voluntary assumption* of the risk is a defense.

Strict Liability in Tort

NATURE *General rule* imposes tort liability on merchant sellers for both personal injuries and property damage for selling a product in a defective condition unreasonably dangerous to the user or consumer.

DEFECTIVE CONDITION
- *Manufacturing defect.* By failing to meet its own manufacturing specifications, the product is not properly made.
- *Design defect.* The product, though made as designed, is dangerous because the design is inadequate.
- *Failure to warn.* Failure to provide adequate warning of possible danger or to provide appropriate directions for use of a product is prohibited.

If a product is *unreasonably dangerous,* it contains a danger beyond that which would be contemplated by the ordinary consumer.

OBSTACLES TO RECOVERY   *Contractual defenses* such as privity, disclaimers, and notice generally do not apply to tort liability.

PLAINTIFF'S CONDUCT
- *Contributory negligence* is not a defense in the majority of states.
- The rule of *comparative negligence* has been applied by most states to strict liability in tort.
- *Voluntary assumption of risk* is a defense.
- *Misuse or abuse of the product* is a defense.

Subsequent alteration holds that liability exists only if the product reaches the user or consumer without substantial change in the condition in which it is sold. The *statute of repose* limits the time period for which a manufacturer is liable for injury caused by its product.

Section 380. Market Segmentation and Target Markets

Summaries and Conclusions

- Successful firms must truly understand the markets they serve and match their marketing mix to the needs of the market. This process is called *target marketing*. A *market* is an individual, group of individuals, or organizations willing and able to purchase a firm's product. A market may be subdivided into any number of smaller markets, called *segments*. The number and the size of markets a firm may select for targeting can vary greatly, from mass market to one individual.
- The target marketing process is extremely important to businesses because it allows firms to identify and analyze their customers, develop tailored market mixes to meet customer needs, identify market demand, identify competition, increase operating efficiencies, improve product positioning, and identify opportunities. Despite these advantages, there are some disadvantages to target marketing. Most notably, some firms have targeted disadvantaged, poor, or uneducated consumers with illegal or unethical products; others have portrayed some market segments stereotypically and offensively, and in doing so both groups have created cynicism toward target marketing practices. These firms may have actually inhibited brand popularity and loyalty, and wasted money and effort.
- Nevertheless, the target marketing process is important and begins with: (1) identifying the total market; (2) determining the need for segmentation based on criteria for segmentation, strategic factors, and external factors; and (3) determining the bases for segmentation using demographic, geographic, psychographic, benefits sought, situation, and behavior (usage) descriptors. The firm must then collect segmentation data. These sources may be internal (from the company's database) or external (from research, other firms, or the government). The target marketing process continues with the following steps: (4) profiling each selected segment; (5) assessing potential profitability of each segment and selecting segments for targeting; (6) selecting the positioning strategy on the basis of price/quality, product attributes, product user, product usage, product class, competition, or symbols; (7) developing and implementing an appropriate marketing mix; and (8) monitoring, evaluating, and controlling the selection process.
- Firms that target other businesses can segment their markets using the same process. However, the bases for segmentation for business markets include demographics, operating characteristics, purchasing approaches, product use or usage situations, situational factors, and buyers' personal characteristics. Targeting global markets also requires the same target market selection process, but has slightly different segmentation descriptors. Along with the consumer markets segmentation descriptors, global segments should be profiled using economic, political/legal, and cultural factors.

Section 385. Services Marketing

Summaries and Conclusions

- Service consumers purchase a bundle of benefits that are provided by the service experience that is created for consumers. The four primary factors that influence the customer's service experience are the service providers, the servicescape, other customers, and the invisible organization and systems. Service firms that are able to effectively mold the customer's experience have mastered the means to develop "compelling experiences"—the latest competitive weapon in the war against service commoditization.
- The major differences between the marketing of goods and services are often attributed to four unique service characteristics: intangibility, inseparability, heterogeneity, and perishability. Of the four unique characteristics that distinguish goods from services, intangibility is the primary source from which the other three characteristics emerge.
- A goal for all marketers is to strive for customer satisfaction. Customers typically assess satisfaction by comparing expectations to perceptions. If perceptions meet or exceed expectations, then customers are satisfied. As such, customer satisfaction can be increased by lowering expectations or by enhancing perceptions. It is crucial to remember that this entire process of comparing expectations to perceptions takes place in the minds of customers. Hence, it is the *perceived* service that matters, not the *actual* service. One of the most recent business practices affecting customer satisfaction levels (both positively and negatively) is customer relationship management (CRM)—the process of identifying, attracting, differentiating, and retaining customers. CRM allows a firm to focus its efforts disproportionately on its most lucrative clients.
- Service quality can be examined in terms of gaps that exist between expectations and perceptions on the part of management, employees, and customers. The most important gap—the service gap—is between customers' expectations of service and their perception of the service actually delivered. Ultimately, the service gap is a function of the knowledge gap, the standards gap, the delivery gap, and the communications gap. As each of these gaps increases or decreases, the service gap responds in a similar manner.
- The value of retaining existing customers is critical in these days of saturated markets and rising marketing costs. In fact, some experts believe that customer retention has a more powerful effect on profits than market share, economies of scale, and core competencies commonly associated with competitive advantage. Firms that excel at customer retention maintain a proper perspective, remember customers between sales transactions, build trusting relationships with customers, monitor the service delivery process, ensure proper product installation, and train customers in how to use products that they have purchased. Customer service-oriented firms also are available when needed most, provide discretionary effort to assist customers, offer service guarantees, and anticipate needs for recovery.

Sections 390 and 395. Sales Administration, Management, and Ethics

Summaries and Conclusions

- Personal selling involves direct communication between the sales representative and the customer.
- Personal selling is one of the most important elements of the promotion mix and a critical element of marketing, but it is also the most expensive form of promotion a firm can undertake.
- Personal selling offers several advantages: salespersons can adapt their presentations to suit the needs of individual customers, immediate feedback from the customer can be responded to during sales presentations, and the effectiveness of personal selling can be more easily measured.

- Personal selling provides exciting and challenging career opportunities with a focus on relationship selling and the development of partnerships based on the long-term satisfaction of customers' needs.
- Personal selling occurs in different environments, and each environment determines which types of salespeople are utilized. The three environments in which personal selling may occur are telemarketing, over-the-counter selling, and field selling.
- Types of salespeople include inbound or outbound telemarketers, order getters, order takers, professional salespeople, national account managers, missionary salespeople, and support salespeople.
- The sales process is composed of prospecting, preapproach and planning, approaching the client, identifying client needs, presenting the product, handling objections, gaining commitment, and following up on and keeping promises.
- Sales management requires the skills of planning, directing, controlling, and implementing the personal selling function.
- Sales managers are responsible for many tasks, including recruiting, training, motivating, compensating, and evaluating the sales force, as well as organizing and allocating territories, and updating the sales force's technological capabilities.
- Sales managers must be aware of potential ethical issues with which the sales force may struggle, and set appropriate guidelines to prevent and control these issues.

Section 394. Quantitative Techniques and Marketing

Summaries and Conclusions

Linear programming techniques can be used in media selection and marketing research. Markov process models are used in analyzing market share (competitive analysis).[21]

Section 399. International Issues

Summaries and Conclusions

- International marketing offers new complexities, challenges, and opportunities to a firm.
- Managers need to understand and cope with a new set of macro-environmental variables, which consist of varying cultural dimensions, different socioeconomic levels, and divergent and sometimes even conflicting legal and political approaches.
- In investigating global market opportunities, the firm must first identify and screen markets internationally based on general country factors and firm-specific criteria. After identifying specific desirable markets, management must then choose between a concentrated or diversified expansion approach to these markets.
- The initiation of internationalization depends very heavily on managerial commitment to the international strategy and on the firm's motivation for going international. Initial modes of entry are typically exporting or importing and licensing and franchising, and are often assisted by intermediaries. Over time and with growing experience, firms then expand through direct foreign investment, joint ventures, or contract manufacturing.
- As a next step, the firm needs to adjust its marketing mix in order to be responsive to differences in market, product, or company characteristics.
- Finally, managerial processes as well as the organizational structure need to be reviewed and adjusted in order to enable the worldwide implementation of marketing programs.

Quality and Process Management

Section 401. Quality Strategies

Summaries and Conclusions

- Leadership is the ability to positively influence people and systems under one's authority to have a meaningful impact and achieve important results. Leaders create clear and visible quality values and integrate these into the organization's strategy.
- Although we often equate leadership with the executive level of an organization, leadership is critical for the organization as a whole, among teams, and for individuals in their daily work.
- Five core leadership skills are vision, empowerment, intuition, self-understanding, and value congruence. These skills help true leaders to promote and practice total quality by creating a customer-driven vision, setting high expectations, demonstrating personal involvement, integrating quality into daily management, and sustaining an environment for quality excellence.
- Essential practices for leadership include (1) creating a customer-focused strategic vision and clear, quality values that serve as a basis for business decisions; (2) sustaining a leadership system and environment for empowerment, innovation, and organizational learning; (3) setting high expectations and demonstrating substantial personal commitment and involvement in quality; (4) integrating quality values into daily leadership and management; (5) communicating extensively through the leadership structure and to all employees; and (6) integrating public responsibilities and community support into business practices.
- Leadership has been studied from at least five major perspectives: the trait approach, the behavioral view, the contingency approach, and the role approach. Some of the new and emerging theories include attributional, transactional, and emotional intelligence theories.
- The leadership system refers to how leadership is exercised throughout a company, including how key decisions are made, communicated, and carried out at all levels; mechanisms for leadership development; and guidance regarding behaviors and practices. An effective leadership system creates clear values, sets high expectations for performance and performance improvements, builds loyalties and teamwork, encourages initiative and risk taking, and subordinates organization to purpose and function.
- An important aspect of an organization's leadership is its responsibility to the public and its practice of good citizenship, including ethics and protection of public health, safety, and the environment.
- Strategy is the pattern of decisions that determines and reveals a company's goals, policies, and plans, and is determined through strategic planning. A focus on both customer-driven quality and operational performance excellence—as opposed to traditional financial and marketing goals—is essential to an effective strategy.
- Leading practices for effective strategic planning include active participation by top management, employees, and even customers or suppliers in the planning process; systematic planning systems for strategy development and deployment, including measurement, feedback, and review; gathering and analyzing a variety of data about external and internal factors; aligning short-term action plans with long-term strategic objectives and communicating them throughout the organization; and using measurements to track progress.
- Strategy development begins with determining the organization's mission, vision, and guiding principles; conducting an environmental assessment of customer and market requirements and expectations; evaluating the competitive environment; financial, societal, and other risks; and weighing human resource, operational, and supplier and partner capabilities. These aspects lead to strategies, strategic objectives, and action plans that set the direction for achieving the mission.
- *Deployment* refers to developing detailed action plans, defining resource requirements and performance measures, and aligning work unit, supplier, and partner plans with overall strategic objectives. Deploying strategy effectively is often done through a process called *hoshin kanri*. *Hoshin kanri* emphasizes organization-wide planning and

- setting of priorities, providing resources to meet objectives, and measuring performance as a basis for improving it. It is essentially a total quality approach to executing a strategy.
- The seven management and planning tools help managers to implement policy deployment and are useful in other areas of quality planning. These tools are the affinity diagram, interrelationship digraph, tree diagram, matrix diagram, matrix data analysis, process decision program chart, and arrow diagram.
- Common organizational structures are the line, line and staff, and matrix organization.
- Organizational structures for quality must reflect individual company differences and provide the flexibility and ability to change. Companies must understand that processes, rather than hierarchical reporting relationships, drive quality within the organization.
- Leadership and Strategic Planning are two of the seven categories of the Malcolm Baldrige National Quality Award Criteria for Performance Excellence. These categories address Organizational Leadership, Public Responsibility and Citizenship, Strategy Development, and Strategy Deployment.

Section 410. Quality Principles and Practices

Summaries and Conclusions

- *Quality assurance* refers to any action directed toward providing consumers with goods and services of appropriate quality. Although craftspeople were attentive to quality, the Industrial Revolution moved responsibility for quality away from the worker and into separate staff departments, which had the effect of making quality a technical, as opposed to managerial, function. This thinking carried through Western industry until about 1980.
- W. Edwards Deming and Joseph Juran taught techniques of quality control and management to the Japanese in the 1950s. Over the next twenty years, Japan made massive improvements in quality, while the quality of U.S. products increased at a much slower rate.
- Four significant influences brought about the "quality revolution" in the United States in the 1980s: (1) consumer pressure, (2) changes in technology, (3) outdated managerial thinking, and (4) loss of national competitiveness. Quality assumed an unprecedented level of importance in the United States. The quality movement has influenced not only product and service improvements, but the way in which organizations are managed.
- *Quality* is defined from many viewpoints, including transcendent quality, product- and value-based quality, fitness for use, and conformance to specifications.
- The official definition of *quality* is "the totality of features and characteristics of a product or service that bears on its ability to satisfy given needs." Most businesses today define it as "meeting or exceeding customer expectations."
- Customers include consumers, who ultimately use a product; external customers, who may be intermediaries between the producer and the consumer; and internal customers, who are the recipients of goods and services from suppliers within the producing firm.
- Total quality is a total, company-wide effort—through full involvement of the entire workforce and a focus on continuous improvement—that companies use to achieve customer satisfaction.
- Total quality is grounded in three core principles: (1) a focus on customers, (2) participation and teamwork, and (3) continuous improvement and learning.
- These principles are supported by an organizational infrastructure that includes customer relationship management, leadership and strategic planning, human resources management, process management, and data and information management, as well as a set of management practices and tools.
- *Competitive advantage* denotes a firm's ability to achieve market superiority over its competitors. Quality is a key source of competitive advantage, and studies have shown that quality is positively related to increased market share and profitability.
- Quality efforts have been criticized in the media as a passing fad and a flawed philosophy. However, a number of objective studies have shown that total quality principles are alive and well and that the benefits of TQ far outweigh its weaknesses.
- Quality begins at a personal level. The use of personal checklists is one way of reinforcing this idea and establishing positive values and ownership that pave the way for achieving a quality-oriented culture in an organization and in one's own life.

- Businesses should view quality at the organizational level, the process level, and the performer level. This perspective cuts across traditional functional boundaries and provides better information for achieving customer satisfaction.

Section 415. Quality Tools and Techniques

Summaries and Conclusions

- A *problem* is a deviation between what is actually happening and what should be happening. Problem solving is a highly creative effort at the heart of quality improvement that encompasses problem redefinition and analysis, idea generation, evaluation and selection of ideas, and implementation.
- The Deming cycle is a problem-solving methodology that consists of four elements: plan, do, study, and act (PDSA). It is based on management by fact and continuous improvement principles and has been the foundation of most Japanese quality improvement efforts.
- Juran's quality improvement approach is based on breakthrough: improvement that takes an organization to unprecedented levels of performance. Juran's breakthrough sequence consists of proof of the need, project identification, organization for breakthrough, the diagnostic journey, the remedial journey, and holding the gains.
- Crosby proposed a 14-step program for quality improvement based more on a managerial/behavioral approach than on the use of analytical tools.
- The creative problem-solving process consists of mess finding, fact finding, problem finding, idea finding, solution finding, and implementation. The emphasis on finding root causes and separating idea generation from evaluation of solutions distinguishes this approach from traditional problem-solving techniques.
- Six-Sigma represents a quality level of at most 3.4 defects per million opportunities. It is a way of measuring quality levels and a comprehensive methodology for breakthrough improvement that relies heavily on statistical and other analytical tools. Companies such as Motorola, General Electric, and Allied Signal have significant bottom-line results from Six-Sigma initiatives.
- The Seven Quality Control (QC) Tools for quality improvement are flowcharts, run charts and control charts, check sheets, histograms, Pareto diagrams, cause-and-effect diagrams, and scatter diagrams. These tools support quality improvement processes and problem-solving efforts.
- *Poka-yoke* is an approach to mistake-proofing a process by using simple, inexpensive devices or procedures to reduce inadvertent errors in performing work. Poka-yokes may be applied to both manufacturing and service delivery processes.

Section 420. Quality, Costs, and Profits

Summaries and Conclusions

- Measurement is the act of quantifying the performance dimensions of products, services, processes, and other business activities. Measures and indicators refer to the numerical information that results from measurement. Organizations need performance measures to drive strategies and organizational change, to manage resources, and to operate processes effectively and continuously improve.
- Data and information support control, diagnosis, and planning at the three levels of quality. Benefits include better knowledge of product and service quality, worker feedback, a basis for reward and recognition, a means of assessing progress, and reduced costs through better planning.
- Leading practices for information management include (1) developing a set of performance indicators that reflect customer requirements and key business drivers, (2) using comparative information and data to improve performance, (3) involving everyone and ensuring that information is widely visible throughout the organization, (4) ensuring that data are reliable and accessible, (5) using sound analytical methods that support strategic planning and daily decision making, and (6) continually refining information sources and practices.

- The balanced scorecard consists of four perspectives: financial, internal, customer, and innovation and learning perspectives. A good balanced scorecard contains both leading and lagging measures and links them through logical cause-and-effect relationships.
- The Baldrige criteria provides a slightly different view of a balanced scorecard, and focuses on five categories of performance measurements and indicators: customer, financial and market, human resource, supplier and partner, and organizational effectiveness measures. Although many specific measures and indicators can be defined in each category, the ones an organization chooses should be tied to those factors that make it competitive in its industry.
- Comparative and benchmark data on which to evaluate performance results are needed to gain an accurate assessment of performance. Such data can be acquired through third parties and benchmarking leading organizations, such as Baldrige winners.
- Performance measures and indicators used by senior leaders should be aligned with company strategy and be actionable. Process-level measures are derived through close examination of the processes that create products and services. Strategic and process measures should be aligned in order to drive strategic goals through the organization.
- Quality cost programs translate quality problems into the language of upper management: money. Through the use of quality cost information, management identifies opportunities for quality improvement. Quality cost information also aids in budgeting and cost control and serves as a scoreboard to evaluate an organization's success.
- Quality costs generally are categorized into prevention, appraisal, internal failure, and external failure costs. These costs are often expressed as indexes using labor, manufacturing cost, sales, or unit measurement bases. Pareto analysis identifies quality problems that account for a large percentage of costs and that, if solved, result in high returns on investment.
- Activity-based costing allocates overhead cost to the products and services that use them. This practice can capture many quality costs that traditional accounting systems are unable to capture, and provides more useful information for quality improvement.
- Some organizations measure the return on quality (ROQ) as a means of justifying quality expenditures and demonstrating their value to senior management.
- This approach requires statistical techniques to measure the effects of changes in customer satisfaction, loyalty, and other factors on profitability.
- Organizations must ensure that data are valid and reliable; that is, they measure what they are supposed to consistently, and that employees have access to the data they need to do their jobs. Effective analysis capabilities ensure that managers can understand the meaning of data, particularly cause and effect linkages between external lagging results and internal leading indicators.
- *Interlinking* is the quantitative modeling of cause-and-effect relationships between external and internal performance measures. Interlinking allows managers to determine objectively the effects of internal variables under their control upon external measures, and hence to make better managerial decisions.
- The Baldrige criteria address an organization's performance measurement system, focusing on how measures and indicators are selected and aligned, how comparative information and data are used, and how all information is analyzed and used to support senior executive review, organizational planning, and daily operations.

Section 425. Quality Models and Awards

Summaries and Conclusions

- W. Edwards Deming, Joseph Juran, and Philip Crosby are recognized as the top three international leaders of modern quality thinking. A. V. Feigenbaum, Kaoru Ishikawa, and Genichi Taguchi have also made significant contributions to modern quality-management practices.
- Deming's philosophy is based on improving products and services by reducing uncertainty and variation. Systems thinking, statistical understanding of variation, the theory of knowledge, and psychology are the foundation of his philosophy. He advocates a radical cultural change in organizations, which is embodied in his 14 Points.

- The Deming chain reaction states that quality improvement reduces cost, increases productivity, increases market share, and allows firms to stay in business and provide jobs.
- Joseph Juran's philosophy seeks to provide change within the current American management system. Quality is defined as fitness for use. The Quality Trilogy—planning, control, and improvement—provides a direction for quality assurance in organizations.
- Philip Crosby's approach to quality is summarized in his Absolutes of Quality Management and Basic Elements of Improvement. He places more emphasis on behavioral change rather than on the use of statistical techniques as advocated by Deming and Juran.
- A. V. Feigenbaum views quality as a strategic business tool and coined the phrase "total quality control." He promoted the importance of shifting quality responsibility to everyone in an organization and developing cost-of-quality approaches.
- Kaoru Ishikawa was instrumental in the Japanese quality movement, particularly in advocating a company-wide quality control approach, the use of employee teams, and the use of problem-solving tools for quality improvement.
- Genichi Taguchi explained the economic value of reducing variation around a target value in production and proposed new engineering approaches for product design focused on quality improvement.
- Managers need to understand the differences and similarities in the leading quality philosophies and develop a quality-management approach tailored to their organizations.
- The Deming Prize was established in 1951 to recognize companies that have achieved distinction through the application of company-wide quality-control approaches, supported by statistical methods and continuous improvement efforts.
- The Malcolm Baldrige National Quality Award recognizes U.S. companies that excel in quality-management practices and business results that achieve the highest levels of customer satisfaction. The Baldrige Award criteria define seven key practices in categories of leadership, strategic planning, customer and market focus, information and analysis, human resource focus, process management, and business results. The Baldrige Award has generated a phenomenal amount of interest, and many companies use its criteria as a basis for internal assessment of their quality systems. Many state and international award programs are patterned after the Baldrige Award.

Section 430. Quality and Environmental Standards

Summaries and Conclusions

Quality Standards

- ISO 9000 defines quality system standards, based on the premise that certain generic characteristics of management practices can be standardized, and that a well-designed, well-implemented, and carefully managed quality system provides confidence that the outputs will meet customer expectations and requirements. The eight principles that underlie the 2000 revision of the ISO 9000 standards align those standards more closely with the spirit of Baldrige's seven key practices and other international quality award frameworks that focus on performance excellence.
- The eight principles of ISO 9000 include (1) customer focus, (2) leadership, (3) involvement of people, (4) process approach, (5) systems approach to management, (6) continual improvement, (7) factual approach to decision making, and (8) mutually beneficial supplier relationships.
- The Baldrige Award criteria define seven key practices in categories of (1) leadership, (2) strategic planning, (3) customer and market focus, (4) information and analysis, (5) human resource focus, (6) process management, and (7) business results.

Environmental Standards

- The U.S. Environmental Agency (EPA) protects and enhances the environment today for future generations to the fullest extent possible under the laws enacted by the U.S. Congress. The agency's mission is to control and abate pollution in the areas of air, water, solid waste, pesticides, radiation, and toxic substances. Its mandate is to mount an integrated, coordinated attack on environmental pollution in cooperation with state and local governments.

- ISO 14000 is the international standard for environmental management. Environmental compliance should be a part of business strategy, not viewed as a "cost of doing business." The scope of the standard includes all the efforts to minimize waste and redesign manufacturing processes, products, and packaging to prevent pollution.

Section 440. Statistics and Quality Control

Summaries and Conclusions

Statistics contributes much to controlling the quality of products or services. In order to assure that business processes are continuously improved, data should be collected and analyzed on a continuing basis, with particular attention to variation in processes. The causes of variation are examined to determine whether they result from special circumstances ("special causes") or from recurring causes ("common causes"). Different strategies should be adopted to correct each occurrence. The immediate objectives of the analysis and measurement effort are to reduce rework, waste, and cycle-time and to improve cost-effectiveness and accuracy.

Section 450. Process-Management Practices

Summaries and Conclusions

- Process management involves design, control, and improvement of key business processes, which include design, production/delivery, support, and supplier/partnering processes. To apply process-management techniques, processes must be repeatable and measurable.
- Leading process-management practices include (1) translating customer requirements into product and service design requirements; (2) ensuring that quality is built into products using appropriate engineering and statistical tools; (3) effectively managing the product development process; (4) defining and documenting important production/delivery and support processes; (5) managing supplier and partnering relationships; (6) controlling quality and operational performance of all key business processes; (7) continuously improving processes using systematic problem-solving approaches; and (8) innovating to achieve breakthrough performance.
- The product-development process consists of idea generation, preliminary concept development, product/process development, full-scale production, product introduction, and market evaluation.
- Good product design relies on sound quality engineering to produce a functional design that meets customer requirements, and establishing specifications and tolerances for production or service delivery. The Taguchi loss function is a way of quantifying costs due to variation from a target specification and has been used to demonstrate the economic value of being on target.
- Improvements in cost and quality often result from simplifying designs and employing techniques such as design for manufacturability.
- Public responsibilities in the design process include product safety and environmental concerns, which have made design for environment (DFE) an important feature of products because it permits easy removal of components for recycling or repair and eliminates other environmental hazards.
- Concurrent, or simultaneous, engineering is an effective approach for managing the product development process by using multifunctional teams to help remove organizational barriers between departments and therefore reduce product development time.
- Customers, engineers, and designers speak different languages. Quality function deployment (QFD) is a technique used to carry the voice of the customer through the design and production process. The major planning document in QFD is called the *House of Quality*. It provides a planning structure for relating customers' needs to technical specifications and confirming that key specifications are identified and deployed throughout the subsequent production process.

- Flowcharts and backward chaining are useful tools for designing processes. A basic approach involves identifying the product or service, customers, suppliers, and process steps; mistake-proofing the process; and controlling and improving the process using measurements.
- In designing services, one must consider physical facilities, processes, and procedures; behavior; and professional judgment. Classification of services along dimensions of customer contact and interaction, labor intensity, and degree of customization directs attention to the proper balance of these design elements.
- *Control* is the continuing process of evaluating performance, comparing outputs to goals or standards, and taking corrective action when necessary. Any control system has three components: (1) a standard or goal, (2) a means of measuring accomplishment, and (3) comparison of actual results with the standard to provide feedback for corrective action.
- Strong customer-supplier relationships are based on recognizing the strategic importance of suppliers in accomplishing business objectives, developing win-win relationships through partnerships, and establishing trust through openness and honesty. Supplier certification systems are often used to manage supplier relationships.
- Process improvement has been approached in various ways, including work simplification, planned methods change, and more recently, *kaizen*. *Kaizen*, a Japanese term meaning "improvement," is a philosophy of quality improvement in all areas of business, using small, frequent, and gradual improvements over the long term.
- Stretch goals force an organization to think in a radically different way and to encourage breakthrough improvements. Benchmarking and reengineering often facilitate breakthrough thinking. *Benchmarking* is the search for best practices in any industry and *reengineering* is the fundamental rethinking and radical redesign of business processes to achieve dramatic improvements in performance. Both approaches complement continuous improvement efforts in a total quality (TQ) culture.

Section 455. Service Quality

Summaries and Conclusions

- As services constitute a larger and larger percentage of the economy, service quality becomes a competitive tool. Improving this quality, however, is more elusive as a result of the temporary nature of a service. As the TQM movement shifts to a focus on return on quality, customers set the parameters for quality service based on their needs.
- *Service quality* is often defined as the satisfaction of expectations based on a customer's need for the service. Customers' expectations can reflect their "expectations" of what might, could, should, or better not happen. Service quality definitions often do not reflect the perspectives of all the various stakeholders, however.
- SERVQUAL, also commonly known as the "Gaps model," conceptualizes service quality on the basis of the differences between customers' expectations with respect to five dimensions and their perceptions of what was actually delivered. When asked which of SERVQUAL's five dimensions (reliability, responsiveness, assurance, empathy, or tangibles) was most important, customers consistently chose reliability, the area where many service companies fail.
- Service design can greatly affect the quality of a service. Creating a service blueprint can identify where service failures may occur. Designing fail-safe techniques and poka-yoke devices into the service can often block mistakes before they become service defects.
- The cost of quality is often seen as an added expense in the design of additional features. It can also be seen as freedom from a service failure that can cost a company. Service quality generally pays off in the final analysis, because it creates loyal customers. Scientific study links quality with profits.
- Implementing quality service can include offering service guarantees and refunds. A good guarantee should be identified and clearly defined as part of the initial service design. Service recovery is another critical part of delivering quality service. All services experience moments of failure, and the response to that failure creates either a delighted customer or a lost customer. Organizations must, therefore, prepare carefully for their service recovery response.

Sections 460–492. Best Practices, Benchmarking, Business Process Reengineering, Improvement, Redesign, and Change Management

Summaries and Conclusions

- *Benchmarking* is defined as "measuring one's performance against that of best-in-class companies, determining how the best-in-class companies achieve those performance levels, and using the information as a basis to develop one's own company's targets, strategies, and implementation." The term *best practices* refers to approaches that produce exceptional results, are usually innovative in terms of the use of technology or human resources, and are recognized by customers or industry experts.
- *Business process reengineering* (BPR) has been defined as "the fundamental rethinking and radical redesign of business processes to achieve dramatic improvements in critical, contemporary measures of performance, such as cost, quality, service, and speed."
- *Business process improvement* (BPI) should be continuous, not discrete, and is an incremental change that may affect only a single task or segment of the organization. The concept of fundamental or radical change is the basis of the major difference between BPR and BPI. BPR focuses on radical change, while BPI promotes incremental change.
- The primary customer (external or internal) should be the driving force behind the redesign process. Once a process is redesigned, it must continually be monitored, reassessed, changed, and improved in order to meet changing demands of the organization.
- *Business process change management* focuses on the future, which requires a proactive approach in order to be effective. The change will be brought about by several factors such as change in the world economic situation, competition (both national and international), decline in revenues, loss of market share, reduction in budgets, or need to improve with better products and services.

Section 494. The Quality Organization

Summaries and Conclusions

- Companies adopt Total Quality (TQ) to react to competitive threats or take advantage of perceived opportunities. In most cases, threats have provided the incentive to act and change the company's culture. Successful adoption of TQ requires a readiness for change, sound practices and implementation strategies, and an effective organization.
- Gaining commitment for TQ from senior leadership is critical to success, but not easy. Successful strategies for selling the concept include aligning objectives with those of senior management and stakeholder goals, using quantitative arguments such as Return on Quality, developing sympathetic allies, and getting early "wins."
- A *corporate culture* is a company's value system and collection of guiding principles, and is often reflected in mission and vision statements as well as the management policies and actions that a company practices. The Core Values and Concepts from the Baldrige criteria are a useful summary of the culture defining a TQ organization.
- Changing the corporate culture is necessary if TQ is to take root in an organization. Change is easier when management has a clear vision, a focus on customers and continuous improvement, strong measurement, cross-functional orientation, and high employee morale. A clear understanding of the differences between TQ and traditional organizations helps define the cultural changes required.
- Organizations encounter numerous barriers to successful implementation. They need to recognize these barriers and avoid the common mistakes that stifle quality efforts, particularly the lack of alignment between components of the organizational system, and ignoring the financial impacts of TQ efforts.

- Designing an effective organizational infrastructure requires an understanding of best practices, a process-oriented quality assurance system, and a process for continuous evolution toward high-performance management practices. Most successful organizations have developed their own unique approaches to implementing TQ.
- Self-assessment provides a starting point to initiate a quality effort. Best practices depend on the level of performance. Low performers must stick to basics such as process simplification, training, and teamwork, while high performers can benefit from benchmarking world-class organizations and using more advanced approaches.
- All employees play a role in TQ implementation. Senior managers must lead the effort and provide resources; middle managers must act as change agents to ensure that strategic goals are met; and the workforce must take personal responsibility for making it happen. Unions must play a part in ensuring the welfare of the organization and work cooperatively with management.
- Quality must be viewed as a never-ending journey. Implementation takes time as well as effort, and organizations must not regard TQ approaches as quick fixes. Organizations must continue to learn and adapt to changing environments. Organizational learning is a key aspect of the Baldrige criteria; thus, it is not surprising that Baldrige winners have demonstrated continual improvement and the ability to change successfully.
- Knowledge management, particularly the sharing of internal best practices (called *internal benchmarking*), is critical to learning and improvement, yet rarely practiced effectively. Such sharing is inhibited by a variety of logistical, structural, and cultural hurdles.

Human Resources Management

Section 501. Human Resources Strategies

Summaries and Conclusions

- Human resource (HR) planning is tied to the broader process of strategic planning, and begins with identifying the philosophy and mission of the organization.
- Human resources can provide a core competency for the organization, which may represent unique capabilities of the organization.
- HR strategies are affected by the culture of the organization.
- Productivity at national, organizational, and individual levels is critical for organizational success.
- Service is critical to meeting customer expectations, and HR must support service through selection, training, and other activities.
- Different organizational strategies require different approaches to HR planning.
- HR planning involves analyzing and identifying the future needs for and availability of human resources for the organization. The HR unit has major responsibilities in HR planning, but managers must provide supportive information and input.
- When developing HR plans, it is important for managers to scan the external environment to identify the effects of governmental influences, economic conditions, geographic and competitive concerns, and workforce composition and patterns.
- Assessment of internal strengths and weaknesses as a part of HR planning requires that current jobs and employee capabilities be audited and organizational capabilities be inventoried.
- Information about past and present conditions is used to identify expected future conditions and forecast supply and demand for human resources. This process can be carried out with a variety of methods and for differing periods of time.

- Management of HR surpluses may require downsizing. Attrition, layoffs, early retirement, and outplacement are commonly used.
- HR departments must set goals and measure effectiveness.
- Primary researchers gather data directly on issues, whereas secondary researchers use research conducted by others and reported elsewhere.
- HR audits can be used to gather comprehensive information about how well HR activities in an organization are being performed.
- Benchmarking allows an organization to compare its practices against best practices in different organizations.
- A *human resource information system* (HRIS) is an integrated system designed to improve the efficiency with which HR data is compiled and to make HR records more useful as information sources.
- An HRIS offers a wide range of HR services, with payroll, benefits administration, and equal employment opportunity (EEO)/affirmative action tracking being the most prevalent.
- The growth of Web-based HRIS options means that training and security issues must be addressed.

Section 510. Employee Performance and Retention Management

Summaries and Conclusions

- Individual performance components include individual ability, effort expended, and organizational support.
- Motivation deals with the needs and desires of human behavior. Various theories of motivation have been developed.
- A psychological contract contains the unwritten expectations that employees and employers have about the nature of their work relationships. These contracts are changing, along with employee loyalty to employers.
- The interaction of individuals with their jobs affects both job satisfaction and organizational commitment.
- Absenteeism is expensive, but it can be controlled by discipline, positive reinforcement, or some combination of the two.
- Turnover is costly and can be classified in a number of different ways.
- Retention of employees is a major focus of HR efforts in organizations, as seen by use of retention measures and establishment of retention officers in some firms.
- The determinants of retention can be divided into five general categories, with the key organizational components being organizational values and culture, strategies and management, and job continuity and security.
- Organizational career opportunities are frequently cited as crucial to employee retention.
- Rewards must be relatively competitive and different based on performance to enhance employee retention.
- The jobs and work done by employees impact retention, particularly if individuals are properly selected, work flexibility exists, and work/life balancing programs are offered.
- Employee relationships with managers and co-workers are important in enhancing retention.
- Retention management should be seen as a process composed of measurement and assessment, interventions, and evaluation/follow-up.
- Turnover should be measured and its costs determined. Employee surveys and exit interviews aid assessing turnover.
- HR interventions to reduce turnover can include a number of different HR activities. The efforts of those interventions should be evaluated and appropriate follow-up made.

Section 530. Staffing, Development, and Employment Practices

Summaries and Conclusions

Jobs

- Work is organized into jobs for people to do. Workflow analysis and business process re-engineering are two approaches used to check how well this has been done.
- Job design is involved with developing jobs that people like to do. It may include simplification, rotation, enlargement, or enrichment.
- Designing jobs so that they incorporate skill variety, task identity and significance, autonomy, and feedback can make for jobs people are more likely to prefer.
- "Crafting" jobs is another way of allowing employees to participate in the design of their jobs, while using team design is another option.
- Job analysis is a systematic investigation of the tasks, duties, and responsibilities necessary to do a job.
- Task-based job analysis focuses on the tasks, duties, and responsibilities associated with jobs.
- The end products of job analysis are job descriptions, which identify the tasks, duties, and responsibilities in jobs, and job specifications, which list the knowledge, skills, and abilities (KSAs) needed to perform a job satisfactorily.
- Job analysis information is useful in most HR activities, such as human resource planning, recruiting and selection, compensation, training and development, performance appraisal, safety and health, and union relations.
- Legal compliance in HR must be based on job analysis. The Americans with Disabilities Act (ADA) has increased the importance of job analysis and its components.
- Behavioral factors, including creating a managerial straitjacket and employee anxieties, must be considered when conducting a job analysis.
- Methods of gathering job analysis information include observation, interviews, questionnaires, some specialized methods, and computer job analysis. In practice, a combination of methods is often used.
- The process of conducting a job analysis has the following steps.
  - Planning the job analysis
  - Preparing and communicating the job analysis
  - Conducting the job analysis
  - Developing job descriptions and job specifications
  - Maintaining and updating job descriptions and job specifications
- When writing job descriptions and job specifications, the essential job functions and KSAs should be described clearly.
- One approach to job analysis identifies competencies, which are the basic characteristics linked to the performance of individuals or teams.
- Once competencies have been identified, they can be used for HR selection, development, compensation, and performance management.

Recruiting

- Recruiting is the process of generating a pool of qualified applicants for organizational jobs through a series of activities.
- Recruiting must be viewed strategically, and discussions should be held about the relevant labor markets in which to recruit.

- The components of labor markets are labor force population, applicant population, and applicant pool.
- Labor markets can be categorized by geographic industry, occupations, and qualifications.
- A strategic approach to recruiting begins with human resource planning and decisions about organizational recruiting responsibilities.
- Employers must make decisions about organizational-based versus outsourcing of recruiting, such as flexible staffing.
- Efforts should be made to recruit a diverse workforce, including older workers, individuals with disabilities, women, and racial/ethnic minority individuals.
- The decision to use internal or external sources should consider both the advantages and disadvantages of each source.
- The most common methods of internal recruiting are job posting, current employee referrals, and re-recruiting former employees.
- Internet recruiting has grown in use through job boards and various Web sites.
- Internet recruiting can save costs and time, but also can generate more unqualified applicants and frequently may not reach certain groups of potential applicants.
- The most common external recruiting sources include colleges and universities, schools, labor unions, employment agencies, and media sources.
- Recruiting efforts should be evaluated to assess how effectively they are being performed.
- Recruiting evaluation typically includes examining the costs and benefits of various recruiting sources, tracking the time to fill openings, and evaluating applicant quality and quantity.

Selection and Placement

- *Selection* is a process that matches individuals and their qualifications to jobs in an organization.
- Placement of people increasingly considers both person-job fit and person-organization fit.
- Predictors linked to criteria are used to identify job applicants more likely than others to perform jobs successfully.
- The selection process—from applicant interest through pre-employment screening, application, testing interviewing, and background investigations—must be handled by trained, knowledgeable individuals.
- A growing number of employers use electronic pre-employment screening.
- Application forms must meet EEO guidelines and ask only for job-related information.
- Selection tests include ability, assessment centers, personality, honesty/integrity, and other more controversial types.
- Structured interviews, including behavioral and situational ones, are more effective and face fewer EEO compliance concerns than nondirective and unstructured interviews.
- Interviews can be conducted individually, by multiple individuals, and by video technology. Regardless of the method, effective interviewing questioning techniques should be used.
- Background investigations can be conducted in a variety of areas. However, care must be taken when either requesting or giving reference information to avoid potential legal concerns such as negligent hiring, libel, and slander.
- Medical examinations may be an appropriate part of the selection process for some employers, but only after a conditional job offer has been made.
- Drug testing has grown in use as a pre-employment screening device in spite of some problems and concerns associated with it.

Training

- *Training* is the learning process whereby people acquire capabilities to aid in the achievement of organizational goals.
- The integration of learning, training, and job performance enhances organizational competitiveness.
- Performance consulting compares desired and actual results in order to identify both needed training and non-training actions.
- A strategic approach to training links organizational strategies and HR planning to training efforts.
- The training process contains four phases: assessment, design, delivery, and evaluation.

- Assessment of training needs can be done using organizational, job/task, and individual analyses in order to set training objectives.
- Training design must consider learner readiness, the learning environment, legal issues, and training transfer.
- Basic learning considerations that guide training design should include trainees' ability and motivation to learn, and adult learning styles and concepts.
- Orientation as a kind of training is designed to help new employees learn about their jobs.
- Training can be delivered internally in the organization and done formally, informally, or on the job.
- External training delivery may include use of outside sources, including government training programs.
- E-learning is training conducted using the Internet or an intranet, and its development must consider both advantages and disadvantages.
- Common training methods available include cooperative programs, classroom and conference training, and distance learning.
- Various organizations are taking advantage of training that uses technology such as multimedia, video streaming, simulation, and virtual reality.
- Evaluation of training can be done at four levels: reaction, learning, behavior, and results.
- Training evaluation may include cost-benefit analyses, return on investment, and benchmarking.
- A pre-/post-measure with control group design is the most rigorous training evaluation design, but others can be used as well.

Careers and Development

- Career planning may focus on organizational needs, individual needs, or both.
- A person chooses a career based on interests, self-image, personality, social background, and other factors.
- A person's life is cyclical, as is his or her career. Putting the two together offers a useful perspective.
- Organizations are increasingly dealing with individuals who have hit career plateaus.
- Technical employees sometimes may be able to follow dual-career ladders.
- Dual-career couples increasingly require relocation assistance for the partners of transferring employees.
- Development differs from training because it focuses on less tangible aspects of performance, such as attitudes and values.
- Successful development requires top management support and an understanding of the relationship of development to other HR activities.
- Assessment centers provide valid methods of assessing management talent and development needs.
- Succession planning is a process that identifies how key employees are to be replaced.
- On-the-job development methods include coaching, committee assignments, job rotation, and assistant-to positions.
- Off-the-job development methods include classroom courses, human relations training, simulations, sabbatical leaves, and outdoor training.
- Through mentoring and modeling, younger managers can acquire the skills and know-how necessary to be successful. Mentoring follows a four-stage progression such as initiation, cultivation, separation, and redefinition. The last stage is an ongoing process.

Performance Management and Appraisal

- Performance management systems attempt to identify, encourage, measure, evaluate, improve, and reward employee performance.
- Performance provides the critical link between organizational strategies and results.
- Job criteria identify important job dimensions, such as teaching for a college professor, runs batted in for a major-league outfielder, or orders completed by a warehouse shipping worker.
- Relevance, contamination, and deficiency of criteria affect performance measurement.
- Appraising employee performance serves useful development and administrative purposes.
- Performance appraisal can be done either informally or systematically. Systematic appraisals usually are done annually.

- Appraisals can be conducted by superiors, employees, teams, outsiders, or a combination of raters. Employees also can conduct self-appraisals.
- Four types of appraisal methods are available: category rating, comparative, narrative, and behavioral/objective.
- Category rating methods, especially graphic rating scales and checklists, are widely used.
- Comparative methods include ranking and forced distribution.
- Narrative methods include the critical incident technique, the essay approach, and field review.
- Two behavioral/objectives methods of appraisal include behavioral rating approaches and management by objectives (MBO).
- Many performance appraisal problems are caused by rater errors, which can include varying standards, recency effect, rater bias, rating patterns (such as central tendency error), halo effect, contrast error, and others.
- The appraisal feedback interview is a vital part of any appraisal system.
- The reactions of both managers and employees must be considered as performance appraisals are done.
- Federal employment guidelines and numerous court decisions affect the design and use of the performance appraisal process. The absence of specific job-relatedness can create legal problems, as can subjectivity.
- Training appraisers and guarding against the tendency to reduce performance to a single number contribute to the effectiveness of a performance management system.

Section 540. Workforce Diversity Management

Summaries and Conclusions

- Diversity management is concerned with organizational efforts to ensure that all people are valued regardless of their differences.
- Efforts to value diversity can enhance organizational performance, aid in employee attraction and retention, encourage more varied decision making, and reduce discrimination.
- Diversity training has had limited success, possibly because it too often has focused on beliefs rather than behaviors.
- Affirmative action has been intensely litigated, and the debate continues today.
- Discrimination on the basis of race and national origin is illegal and employers must be prepared to deal with language issues and racial harassment as part of effectively managing racial/ethnic diversity.
- As more women have entered the workforce, sex/gender issues in equal employment have included discrimination in jobs and careers and sexual harassment, which takes two forms: (a) *quid pro quo,* and (b) hostile environment.
- Employers should develop policies on sexual harassment, have identifiable complaint procedures, train all employees on what constitutes sexual harassment, promptly investigate complaints, and take action when sexual harassment is found to have occurred.
- Aging of the U.S. workforce has led to more concerns about age discrimination, especially in the form of forced retirements and terminations.
- Employers are recognizing the value of attracting and retaining older workers through greater use of part-time work and phased retirement programs.
- Individuals with disabilities represent a significant number of current and potential employees; the definition of who is disabled has expanded in recent years.
- Employers are making reasonable accommodations for individuals with disabilities, including those with mental or life-threatening illnesses.
- Reasonable accommodation is a strategy that can be used to deal with the religious diversity of employees.
- Managing diversity means ensuring that individuals with differing lifestyles and sexual orientations are treated with respect at work.

Section 570. Employee Benefits and Compensation

Summaries and Conclusions

Employee Benefits

- Benefits provide additional compensation to employees as a reward for organizational membership.
- Because benefits generally are not taxed, they are highly desired by employees. The average employee now receives an amount equal to about 40 percent of his/her pay in benefit compensation.
- Strategic reasons for offering benefits include attracting and retaining employees, improving the company's image, and enhancing job satisfaction.
- The general types of benefits include security, retirement, health care, financial, social and recreational, family-oriented, and time off.
- An important distinction is made between mandated and voluntary benefits. Mandatory benefits are required by law.
- Three prominent security benefits are workers' compensation, unemployment compensation, and severance pay.
- Organizations that provide retirement-related benefits should develop policies on how to integrate Social Security benefits into employees' benefit plans.
- The pension area is a complex one, and it is governed by the Employee Retirement Income Security Act (ERISA) and other laws.
- Individual retirement accounts (IRAs), 401(k) plans, and Keogh plans are important individual options available for supplementing retirement benefits.
- Because health-care benefits are the most costly insurance-related benefits, employers are managing their health-care costs more aggressively.
- Various types of insurance, financial planning assistance, tuition aid, and other benefits that employers may offer enhance the appeal of the organization to employees.
- Family-related benefits include complying with the Family and Medical Leave Act (FMLA) of 1993 and offering both child-care and elder-care assistance.
- Holiday pay, vacation pay, and various leaves of absence are means of providing time-off benefits to employees.
- Because of the variety of benefit options available and the costs involved, employers need to develop systems to communicate these options and costs to their employees.
- Flexible benefits systems, which can be tailored to individual needs and situations, are increasing in popularity.

Compensation Strategies

- Compensation provided by an organization can come directly through base pay and variable pay and indirectly through benefits.
- Compensation responsibilities of both HR specialists and managers must be performed well. Compensation practices are closely related to organizational culture, philosophies, strategies, and objectives.
- A continuum of compensation philosophies exists, ranging from an entitlement-oriented philosophy to a performance-oriented philosophy.
- More companies are using competency-based pay, which focuses on individuals' capabilities.
- When designing and administering compensation programs, behavioral aspects must be considered. Equity, organizational justice, pay openness, and external equity are all important.
- The Fair Labor Standards Act (FLSA), as amended, is the major federal law that affects pay systems. It requires most organizations to pay a minimum wage and to comply with overtime provisions, including appropriately classifying employees as exempt or nonexempt and as independent contractors or employees.

- Other laws place restrictions on employers who have federal supply contracts or federal construction contracts, or on those employers who garnish employees' pay.
- Administration of a wage and salary system requires the development of pay policies that incorporate internal and external equity considerations.
- Job evaluation determines the relative worth of jobs. Several different evaluation methods exist, with the point method being the most widely used.
- Once the job evaluation process has been completed, pay survey data must be collected and a pay structure developed. An effective pay system requires that changes continue to be made as needed.
- Developing a pay structure includes grouping jobs into pay grades and establishing a pay range for each grade.
- Broadbanding, which uses fewer pay grades with wider ranges, provides greater career movement possibilities for employees and has grown in popularity.
- Individual pay must take into account employees' placement within pay grades. Problems involving "red circled" jobs, whose rates are above pay range, and "green circled" jobs, whose rates are below pay range, may be addressed in a number of different ways.
- Individual pay increases can be based on performance, cost-of-living adjustments, seniority, or a combination of approaches.
- Many organizations use seniority of employees and provide cost-of-living adjustments, but this negates a pay-for-performance approach.

Variable Pay and Executive Compensation

- Variable pay, traditionally called *incentives,* is additional compensation linked to individual, team (group), and/or organizational performance.
- Effective variable pay plans should recognize organizational culture and resources, be clear and understandable, be kept current, tie incentives to performance, recognize individual differences, and identify plan payments separate from base pay.
- Sales employees may have their compensation tied to their performance on a number of sales-related criteria. Sales compensation can be provided as salary only, commission only, or salary plus commissions or bonuses.
- Design of team (group) variable pay plans must consider how team incentives are to be distributed, the timing of the incentive payments, and how decisions are made about who receives how much of the variable payout.
- To overcome some problems associated with individual incentives, team (group) variable pay plans encourage and reward teamwork and group effort.
- One prominent organization-wide variable pay plan is gainsharing, which provides rewards based on greater-than-expected gains in profits and/or productivity.
- Profit-sharing plans set aside a part of the profits earned by organizations for distribution to employees.
- An employee stock ownership plan (ESOP) enables employees to gain ownership of the firm for which they work.
- Executive compensation must be viewed as a total package composed of salaries, bonuses, long-term performance-based incentives, benefits, and perquisites (perks).
- A compensation committee, which is a subgroup of the board of directors, has authority over executive compensation plans.
- Performance-based incentives often represent a significant portion of an executive's compensation package.

Section 580. Health, Safety, and Security

Summaries and Conclusions

- Health is a general state of physical, mental, and emotional well-being, while safety involves protecting the physical well-being of people.
- Security involves protection of employees and organizational facilities.

- Workers' compensation coverage is provided by employers to protect employees who suffer job-related injuries and illnesses.
- Both the Family Medical Leave Act (FMLA) and the Americans with Disabilities Act (ADA) affect employer health and safety policies and practices.
- The Fair Labor Standards Act (FLSA) limits the types of work that employees under the age of eighteen can perform.
- The Occupational Safety and Health Act (OSHA) states that employers have a general duty to provide safe and healthy working conditions.
- The OSHA enforcement standards have been established to aid in a number of areas, including hazard communications and others.
- Ergonomics looks at the physiological and physical demands of work and has grown in importance.
- OSHA requires employers to keep records on occupational illnesses and injuries, conducts inspections of workplaces, and can issue citations for several different levels of violations.
- Effective safety management requires integrating three different approaches: organizational, engineering, and individual.
- Developing safety policies, establishing safety committees, conducting safety training, and evaluating work areas for safety concerns are all part of comprehensive safety management efforts.
- Substance abuse, emotional/mental health concerns, workplace air quality, and smoking at work, among other common health issues, are growing concerns for organizations and employees.
- Health promotion efforts by employers are important and can occur at several levels.
- Employers have responded to health problems by establishing and supporting wellness programs and employee assistance programs (EAPs).
- Establishing and maintaining an organizational health culture continues to pay off for a number of employers.
- Security of workplaces has grown in importance, particularly in light of the increasing frequency in which workplace violence occurs.
- Employers can enhance security by conducting a security audit, controlling access to workplaces and computer systems, screening employees adequately, and providing security personnel.

Section 590. Law and Human Resources

Summaries and Conclusions

- Diversity is a broad concept that recognizes differences among people; equal employment opportunity (EEO) holds that individuals should have equal treatment in all employment-related actions.
- Affirmative action requires employers to identify problem areas in the employment of protected-class members and to set goals and take steps to overcome them, but concerns have been raised about "reverse discrimination."
- The 1964 Civil Rights Act, Title VII, was the first significant equal employment law. The Civil Rights Act of 1991 both altered and expanded on the 1964 provisions.
- Employers must be able to defend their management practices based on *bona fide* occupational qualifications (BFOQ), business necessity, and job relatedness.
- Disparate treatment occurs when protected-class members are treated differently from others, regardless of discriminatory intent.
- Disparate impact occurs when employment decisions work to the disadvantage of members of protected classes, regardless of discriminatory intent.
- Employers have the burden of proof once a *prima facie* case of discrimination has been shown, and they should take care to avoid retaliation against individuals who exercise their rights.
- Many employers are required to develop affirmative action plans (AAPs) that identify problem areas in the employment of protected-class members and initiate goals and steps to overcome those problems.
- Laws on sex/gender discrimination have addressed issues regarding pregnancy discrimination, unequal pay for similar jobs, and sexual harassment.

- The Americans with Disabilities Act (ADA) requires that most employers identify the essential functions of jobs and make reasonable accommodation for individuals with disabilities, unless undue hardship results.
- Age discrimination against persons over age forty is illegal, based on the Age Discrimination in Employment Acts.
- The Immigration Reform and Control Act (IRCA) identifies employment regulations affecting workers from other countries.
- A number of other concerns have been addressed by laws, including discrimination based on religion, genetic bias, appearance and weight, sexual orientation, and others.
- The Equal Employment Opportunity Commission (EEOC) and the Office of Federal Contract Compliance Programs (OFCCP) are the major federal equal employment enforcement agencies.
- The 1978 Uniform Guidelines on Employee Selection Procedures are used by enforcement agencies to examine recruiting, hiring, promotion, and many other employment practices. Two alternative compliance approaches are identified: (1) no disparate impact, and (2) job-related validation.
- Job-related validation requires that tests measure what they are supposed to measure (validity) in a consistent manner (reliability).
- Disparate impact can be determined through the use of the 4/5ths rule.
- One of the three types of validity, content-validity, uses a sample of the actual work to be performed.
- The two criterion-related strategies measure concurrent validity and predictive validity. Predictive validity involves a "before-the-fact" measure, whereas concurrent validity involves a comparison of tests and criteria measures available at the same time.
- Construct validity involves the relationship between a measure of an abstract characteristic, such as intelligence, and job performance.
- Implementation of equal employment opportunity requires appropriate record keeping, such as completing the annual report (EEO-1), and keeping applicant flow data.

Section 595. Ethics and Human Resources

Summaries and Conclusions

- HR management is concerned with formal systems in organizations to ensure the effective and efficient use of human talent to accomplish organizational goals.
- The need for HR management occurs in all organizations, but larger ones are more likely to have a specialized HR function.
- HR challenges faced by managers and organizations include economic and technological changes, workforce availability and quality concerns, demographics, and organizational restructuring.
- HR management activities can be grouped as follows: HR planning, equal employment opportunity compliance, staffing, HR development, compensation and benefits, health, safety and security, and employee and labor/management relations.
- HR management must perform four roles: administrative, employee advocate, operational, and strategic.
- It is important for HR management to be a strategic business contributor in organizations.
- Outsourcing is being utilized more frequently than in past years.
- Ethical behavior is crucial in HR management, and a number of HR ethical issues are regularly being faced by HR professionals.
- HR as a career field requires maintaining current knowledge in HR management.

Section 599. International Issues

Summaries and Conclusions

- Globalization of business continues to grow because of forces such as population changes, economic interdependence, regional alliances, and global communications capabilities.
- Organizations doing business internationally may evolve from organizations engaged in importing and exporting activities, to multinational enterprises, to global organizations.
- Legal, political, economic, and cultural factors influence global HR management.
- Culture consists of the societal forces that affect the values, beliefs, and actions of a distinct group of people.
- One scheme for classifying national cultures considers power distance, individualism, masculinity/femininity, uncertainty avoidance, and long-term orientation.
- Staffing global jobs can be done using expatriates, host-country nationals, and third-country nationals.
- Global assignments can be used for a number of reasons and for varying timeframes.
- The selection of global employees should consider cultural adjustment, organizational requirements, personal characteristics, communications skills, and personal/family factors.
- Once selected, the assignments of global employees must be managed through both effective expatriation and repatriation.
- Training and development for international employees focus on pre-departure orientation and training, continued employee development, and readjustment training for repatriates.
- Compensation practices for international employees are much more complex than those for domestic employees because many more factors must be considered.
- Global organizations must be concerned about the health, safety, and security of their employees.
- Labor-management relations vary from country to country.

Accounting

Sections 601 and 603. Accounting Strategies and Role of Accounting and Controller

Summaries and Conclusions

Accounting Strategies

The accounting function in a firm is a service activity. Its objective is to provide quantitative information, primarily financial in nature, about economic entities that is intended to be useful in making economic decisions. The economic decision makers, whether they are external or internal to a firm, must recognize that the information they receive from the accounting function of a firm constitute only a part of the information they need to make sound decisions. Examples of external decision makers include investors, creditors, and regulators. Examples of internal decision makers are managers, owners, and employees. Both types of decision makers are part of a firm's stakeholders.

The two primary qualities that distinguish useful accounting information are relevance and reliability. Secondary qualities of accounting information include comparability and consistency. "Earnings management" strategy can destroy the primary and secondary qualities of accounting information.

The challenge to accounting management, as well as to senior management of a firm, is to develop strategies to achieve the primary and secondary qualitative characteristics of useful accounting information. When accounting information has these qualitative characteristics, the firm can provide the useful and needed quantitative information to decision makers.

Role of Accounting and Controller

NATURE OF A BUSINESS   A business is an organization in which basic resources (inputs), such as materials and labor, are assembled and processed to provide goods or services (outputs) to customers. The objective of most businesses is to maximize profits. There are three different types of businesses that are operated for profit: manufacturing, merchandising, and service businesses.

A business is normally organized in one of three different forms: proprietorship, partnership, or corporation. A business stakeholder is a person or entity (such as an owner, manager, employee, customer, creditor, or the government) who has an interest in the economic performance of the business.

ROLE OF ACCOUNTING IN BUSINESS   Accounting is an information system that provides reports to stakeholders about the economic activities and condition of a business. Accounting is the "language of business."

IMPORTANCE OF BUSINESS ETHICS AND THE BASIC PRINCIPLES OF PROPER ETHICAL CONDUCT
Ethics are moral principles that guide the conduct of individuals. Proper ethical conduct implies a behavior that considers the impact of one's actions on society and others. Sound ethical principles include (1) avoiding small ethical lapses, (2) focusing on long-term reputation, and (3) being willing to suffer adverse personal consequences for holding to an ethical position.

THE PROFESSION OF ACCOUNTING   Accountants are engaged in either private accounting or public accounting. The two most common specialized fields of accounting are financial accounting and managerial accounting. Other fields include cost accounting, environmental accounting, tax accounting, accounting systems, international accounting, not-for-profit accounting, and social accounting.

DIFFERENCES BETWEEN MANAGERIAL AND FINANCIAL ACCOUNTING   Managerial accounting and financial accounting serve different needs and, as such, have different characteristics. Managerial accounting serves the reporting needs of managers in meeting strategic and operational goals. Managerial accounting is not bound by a set of generally accepted accounting principles, as is financial accounting.

As a result, the practice of managerial accounting is as diverse as are organizations. This additional complexity in understanding the structure of managerial accounting is offset by the degree of creativity that can be applied to managerial information needs.

ORGANIZATIONAL ROLE OF MANAGEMENT ACCOUNTANT, CONTROLLER   The financial function is generally a staff function of the organization. The chief accountant is often called the controller. The controller's function includes providing a variety of reports to support management decision making.

DEVELOPMENT OF ACCOUNTING PRINCIPLES AND RELATING THEM TO PRACTICE   Financial accountants follow generally accepted accounting principles (GAAP) in preparing reports so that stakeholders can compare one company to another. Accounting principles and concepts develop from research, accepted accounting practices, and pronouncements of authoritative bodies. Currently, the Financial Accounting Standards Board (FASB) is the authoritative body having the primary responsibility for developing accounting principles.

The business entity concept views the business as an entity separate from its owners, creditors, or other stakeholders. The business entity limits the economic data in the accounting system to that related directly to the activities of the business. The cost concept requires that properties and services bought by a business be recorded in terms of actual cost. The objectivity concept requires that accounting records and reports be based upon objective evidence. The unit of measure concept requires that economic data be recorded in dollars.

THE ACCOUNTING EQUATION   The resources owned by a business and the rights or claims to these resources may be stated in the form of an equation, as follows.

$$\text{Assets} = \text{Liabilities} + \text{Owner's Equity}$$

BUSINESS TRANSACTIONS All business transactions can be stated in terms of the change in one or more of the three elements of the accounting equation. That is, the effect of every transaction can be stated in terms of increases or decreases in one or more of these elements, while maintaining the equality between the two sides of the equation.

FINANCIAL STATEMENTS OF A CORPORATION The principal financial statements of a corporation are the income statement, the retained earnings statement, the balance sheet, and the statement of cash flows. The income statement reports a period's net income or net loss, which also appears on the retained earnings statement. The ending retained earnings reported on the retained earnings statement is also reported on the balance sheet. The ending cash balance is reported on the balance sheet and the statement of cash flows.

RATIO OF LIABILITIES TO STOCKHOLDERS' EQUITY The ratio of liabilities to stockholders' equity is useful in analyzing the ability of a business to pay its creditors. The lower the ratio, the better able the business is to withstand poor business conditions and still fully meet its obligations to creditors.

Sections 605 and 610. The Accounting Process and Assets, Liabilities, and Owner's Equity

Summaries and Conclusions

Accounting Cycle

FINANCIAL STATEMENTS The income statement is normally prepared directly from the work sheet. On the income statement, the expenses are normally presented in the order of size, from largest to smallest.

The basic form of the retained earnings statement is prepared by listing the beginning balance of retained earnings, adding net income during the period, and deducting the dividends.

Various sections and subsections are often used in preparing a balance sheet. Two common classes of assets are current assets and fixed assets. Cash and other assets that are normally expected to be converted to cash, sold, or used up within one year or less are called *current assets*. Property, plant, and equipment may be called *fixed assets* or *plant assets*. The cost, accumulated depreciation, and book value of each major type of fixed asset are normally reported on the balance sheet.

Two common classes of liabilities are current liabilities and long-term liabilities. Liabilities that will be due within a short time (usually one year or less) and that are to be paid out of current assets are called *current liabilities*. Liabilities that will not be due for a long time (usually more than one year) are called *long-term liabilities*.

The stockholders' claim against assets is presented below the liabilities section and added to the total liabilities. The total liabilities and total stockholders' equity must equal the total assets.

After closing entries have been posted to the ledger, the balance in the retained earnings account will agree with the amount reported on the retained earnings statement and balance sheet. In addition, the revenue, expense, and dividends accounts will have zero balances.

The last step of the accounting cycle is to prepare a post-closing trial balance. The purpose of the post-closing trial balance is to make sure that the ledger is in balance at the beginning of the next period.

SEVEN BASIC STEPS OF THE ACCOUNTING CYCLE The basic steps of the accounting cycle follow.

- Transactions are analyzed and recorded in a journal.
- Transactions are posted to the ledger.
- A trial balance is prepared, adjustment data are assembled, and the work sheet is completed.
- Financial statements are prepared.
- Adjusting entries are journalized and posted to the ledger.
- Closing entries are journalized and posted to the ledger.
- A post-closing trial balance is prepared.

FISCAL YEAR AND THE NATURAL BUSINESS YEAR The annual accounting period adopted by a business is known as its *fiscal year*. A corporation may adopt a fiscal year that ends when business activities have reached the lowest point in its annual operating cycle. Such a fiscal year is called the *natural business year*.

INTERPRETATION OF FINANCIAL SOLVENCY OF A BUSINESS The ability of a business to pay its debts is called *solvency*. Two financial measures for evaluating a business's short-term solvency are working capital and the current ratio. Working capital is the excess of the current assets of a business over its current liabilities. The current ratio is computed by dividing current assets by current liabilities. Some treat working capital as net working capital.

Statement of Cash Flows

PURPOSE OF THE STATEMENT OF CASH FLOWS The statement of cash flows reports useful information about a firm's ability to generate cash from operations, maintain and expand its operating capacity, meet its financial obligations, and pay dividends. This information assists investors, creditors, and others in assessing the firm's profit potential and its ability to pay its maturing debt. The statement of cash flows is also useful to managers in evaluating past operations and in planning future operating, investing, and financing activities.

TYPES OF CASH FLOW ACTIVITIES The statement of cash flows reports cash receipts and cash payments by three types of activities: operating activities, investing activities, and financing activities.

Cash flows from operating activities are cash flows from transactions that affect net income. There are two methods of reporting cash flows from operating activities: (1) the direct method, and (2) the indirect method.

Cash inflows from investing activities are cash flows from the sale of investments, fixed assets, and intangible assets. Cash outflows generally include payments to acquire investments, fixed assets, and intangible assets.

Cash inflows from financing activities include proceeds from issuing equity securities, such as preferred and common stock. Cash inflows also arise from issuing bonds, mortgage notes payable, and other long-term debt. Cash outflows from financing activities arise from paying cash dividends, purchasing treasury stock, and repaying amounts borrowed.

Investing and financing for a business may be affected by transactions that do not involve cash. The effect of such transactions should be reported in a separate schedule accompanying the statement of cash flows.

Because it may be misleading, cash flow per share is not reported in the statement of cash flows.

STATEMENT OF CASH FLOWS USING THE INDIRECT METHOD To prepare the statement of cash flows, changes in the noncash balance sheet accounts are analyzed. This logic relies on the fact that a change in any balance sheet account can be analyzed in terms of changes in the other balance sheet accounts. Thus, by analyzing the noncash balance sheet accounts, those activities that resulted in cash flows can be identified. Although the noncash balance sheet accounts may be analyzed in any order, it is usually more efficient to begin with retained earnings. Additional data are obtained by analyzing income statement accounts and supporting records.

STATEMENT OF CASH FLOWS USING THE DIRECT METHOD The direct method and the indirect method will report the same amount of cash flows from operating activities. Also, the manner of reporting cash flows from investing and financing activities is the same under both methods.

The methods differ in how the cash flows from operating activities data are obtained, analyzed, and reported. The direct method reports cash flows from operating activities by major classes of operating cash receipts and cash payments. The difference between the major classes of total operating cash receipts and total operating cash payments is the net cash flow from operating activities.

The data for reporting cash flows from operating activities by the direct method can be obtained by analyzing the cash flows related to the revenues and expenses reported on the income statement. The revenues and expenses are adjusted from the accrual basis of accounting to the cash basis for purposes of preparing the statement of cash flows.

When the direct method is used, a reconciliation of net income and net cash flow from operating activities is reported in a separate schedule. This schedule is similar to the cash flows from operating activities section of the statement of cash flows prepared using the indirect method.

INTERPRETATION OF FREE CASH FLOW Free cash flow is the amount of operating cash flow remaining after replacing current productive capacity and maintaining current dividends. Free cash flow is the amount of cash available to reduce debt, expand the business, or return to shareholders through increased dividends or treasury stock purchases.

Sections 620 and 665. Analysis and Use of Financial Statements and Reporting

Summaries and Conclusions

Basic Analytical Procedures

FINANCIAL STATEMENT ANALYTICAL PROCEDURES The analysis of percentage increases and decreases in related items in comparative financial statements is called *horizontal analysis*. The analysis of percentages of component parts to the total in a single statement is called *vertical analysis*. Financial statements in which all amounts are expressed in percentages for purposes of analysis are called *common-size statements*.

FINANCIAL STATEMENT ANALYSIS TO ASSESS THE SOLVENCY OF A BUSINESS The primary focus of financial statement analysis is the assessment of solvency and profitability. All users are interested in the ability of a business to pay its debts as they come due (solvency) and to earn income (profitability). Solvency analysis is normally assessed by examining the following balance sheet relationships: (1) current position analysis, (2) accounts receivable analysis, (3) inventory analysis, (4) the ratio of fixed assets to long-term liabilities, (5) the ratio of liabilities to stockholders' equity, and (6) the number of times interest charges are earned.

FINANCIAL STATEMENT ANALYSIS TO ASSESS THE PROFITABILITY OF A BUSINESS Profitability analysis focuses mainly on the relationship between operating results (income statement) and resources available (balance sheet). Major analyses used in assessing profitability include (1) the ratio of net sales to assets, (2) the rate earned on

Exhibit 600.1 *Summary of Basic Analytical Measures*

	Method of Computation	Use
Solvency measures:		
Working capital	Current assets − Current liabilities	
Current ratio	$\dfrac{\text{Current assets}}{\text{Current liabilities}}$	To indicate the ability to meet currently maturing obligations
Acid-test ratio	$\dfrac{\text{Quick assets}}{\text{Current liabilities}}$	To indicate instant debt-paying ability
Accounts receivable turnover	$\dfrac{\text{Net sales on account}}{\text{Average accounts receivable}}$	To assess the efficiency in collecting receivables and in the management of credit
Numbers of days' sales in receivables	$\dfrac{\text{Accounts receivable, end of year}}{\text{Average daily sales on account}}$	
Inventory turnover	$\dfrac{\text{Cost of goods sold}}{\text{Average inventory}}$	To assess the efficiency in the management of inventory
Number of days' sales in inventory	$\dfrac{\text{Inventory, end of year}}{\text{Average daily cost of goods sold}}$	
Ratio of fixed assets to long-term liabilities	$\dfrac{\text{Fixed assets (net)}}{\text{Long-term liabilities}}$	To indicate the margin of safety to long-term creditors
Ratio of liabilities to stockholders' equity	$\dfrac{\text{Total liabilities}}{\text{Total stockholders' equity}}$	To indicate the margin of safety to creditors
Number of times interest charges are earned	$\dfrac{\text{Income before income tax } + \text{ Interest expense}}{\text{Interest expense}}$	To assess the risk to debtholders in terms of number of times interest charges were earned

(continued)

Exhibit 600.1 *Continued*

	Method of Computation	Use
Profitability measures:		
Ratio of net sales to assets	$$\frac{\text{Net sales}}{\text{Average total assets (excluding long-term investments)}}$$	To assess the effectiveness in the use of assets
Rate earned on total assets	$$\frac{\text{Net income + Interest expense}}{\text{Average total assets}}$$	To assess the profitability of the assets
Rate earned on total stockholders' equity	$$\frac{\text{Net income}}{\text{Average total stockholders' equity}}$$	To assess the profitability of the investment by stockholders
Rate earned on common stockholders' equity	$$\frac{\text{Net income} - \text{Preferred dividends}}{\text{Average common stockholders' equity}}$$	To assess the profitability of the investment by common stockholders
Earnings per share on common stock	$$\frac{\text{Net income} - \text{Preferred dividends}}{\text{Shares of common stock outstanding}}$$	
Price-earnings ratio	$$\frac{\text{Market price per share of common stock}}{\text{Earnings per share of common stock}}$$	To indicate future earnings prospects, based on the relationship between market value of common stock and earnings
Dividends per share of common stock	$$\frac{\text{Dividends}}{\text{Shares of common stock outstanding}}$$	To indicate the extent to which earnings are being distributed to common stockholders
Dividend yield on common stock	$$\frac{\text{Dividends per share of common stock}}{\text{Market price per share of common stock}}$$	To indicate the rate of return to common stockholders in terms of dividends

total assets, (3) the rate earned on stockholders' equity, (4) the rate earned on common stockholders' equity, (5) earnings per share on common stock, (6) the price-earnings ratio, (7) dividends per share, and (8) dividend yield.

USES AND LIMITATIONS OF ANALYTICAL PROCEDURES In selecting and interpreting analytical procedures and measures, conditions peculiar to a business or its industry should be considered. For example, the type of industry, capital structure, and diversity of the business's operations affect the measures used. In addition, the influence of the general economic and business environment should be considered.

CONTENTS OF CORPORATE ANNUAL REPORTS Corporate annual reports normally include financial statements and the following sections: Financial Highlights, President's Letter to the Stockholders, Management Discussion and Analysis, Independent Auditors' Report, and Historical Summary.

Section 630. Cost Behavior, Control, and Decision Making

Summaries and Conclusions

Cost Concepts

CLASSIFICATION OF COSTS BY THEIR BEHAVIOR *Cost behavior* refers to the manner in which a cost changes as a related activity changes. Variable costs are costs that vary in total in proportion to changes in the level of activity.

Fixed costs are costs that remain the same in total dollar amount as the level of activity changes. A mixed cost has attributes of both a variable and a fixed cost.

CONTRIBUTION MARGIN, THE CONTRIBUTION MARGIN RATIO, AND THE UNIT CONTRIBUTION MARGIN

The contribution margin concept is useful in business planning because it gives insight into the profit potential of a firm. The contribution margin is the excess of sales revenues over variable costs. The contribution margin ratio is computed as follows.

$$\text{Contribution margin ratio} = (\text{unit selling price} - \text{unit variable cost})/\text{unit selling price}$$

The unit contribution margin is the excess of the unit selling price over the unit variable cost.

BREAK-EVEN POINT

The mathematical approach to cost-volume-profit analysis uses the unit contribution margin concept and the following equations to determine the break-even point and the volume necessary to achieve a target profit for a business.

$$\text{Break-even sales (units)} = \frac{\text{Fixed costs}}{\text{Unit contribution margin}}$$

$$\text{Break-even sales (units)} = \frac{\text{Fixed costs} + \text{Target profit}}{\text{Unit contribution margin}}$$

COST-VOLUME-PROFIT CHART AND A PROFIT-VOLUME CHART

A cost-volume-profit chart focuses on the relationships among costs, sales, and operating profit or loss. It can be used to determine the break-even point and the volume necessary to achieve a target profit. The profit-volume chart focuses on profits rather than on revenues and costs. It can be used to determine the break-even point and the volume necessary to achieve a target profit.

BREAK-EVEN POINT FOR A BUSINESS SELLING MORE THAN ONE PRODUCT

Calculating the break-even point for a business selling two or more products is based upon a specified sales mix. The sales mix is the relative distribution of sales among the various products sold by a business. Given the sales mix, the break-even point can be computed.

MARGIN OF SAFETY AND THE OPERATING LEVERAGE

The margin of safety as a percentage of current sales is computed as follows.

$$\text{Margin of safety} = \frac{\text{Sales} - \text{Sales at break-even point}}{\text{Sales}}$$

The margin of safety is useful in evaluating past operations and in planning future operations. For example, if the margin of safety is low, even a small decline in sales revenue will result in an operating loss. Operating leverage is computed as follows.

$$\text{Operating leverage} = \frac{\text{Contribution margin}}{\text{Income from operations}}$$

Operating leverage is useful in measuring the impact of changes in sales on income from operations without preparing formal income statements. For example, a high operating leverage indicates that a small increase in sales will yield a large percentage increase in income from operations.

ASSUMPTIONS UNDERLYING COST-VOLUME-PROFIT ANALYSIS

The primary assumptions underlying cost-volume-profit analysis are as follows.

- Total sales and total costs can be represented by straight lines.
- Within the relevant range of operating activity, the efficiency of operations does not change.
- Costs can be accurately divided into fixed and variable components.
- The sales mix is constant.
- There is no change in the inventory quantities during the period.

Section 640. Product and Service Costs

Summaries and Conclusions

Product and Service Costing Methods

DEFINITION OF MATERIALS, FACTORY LABOR, AND FACTORY OVERHEAD COSTS A manufacturer converts materials into a finished product by using machinery and labor. The cost of materials that are an integral part of the manufactured product is direct materials cost. The cost of wages of employees who are involved in converting materials into the manufactured product is direct labor cost. Costs other than direct materials and direct labor costs are factory overhead costs, including indirect materials and labor. Direct labor and factory overhead are termed *conversion costs*. Direct materials, direct labor, and factory overhead costs are associated with products and are called *product costs*.

ACCOUNTING SYSTEMS USED BY MANUFACTURING BUSINESSES A cost accounting system accumulates product costs. The cost accounting system is used by management to determine the proper product cost for inventory valuation on the financial statements, to support product pricing decisions, and to identify opportunities for cost reduction and improved production efficiency. The two primary cost accounting systems are job order and process cost systems.

JOURNAL ENTRIES FOR A JOB ORDER COST ACCOUNTING SYSTEM A job order cost system provides for a separate record of the cost of each particular quantity of product that passes through the factory. Direct materials, direct labor, and factory overhead costs are accumulated in a subsidiary cost ledger, in which each account is represented by a job cost sheet. Work-in-Process (WIP) is the controlling account for the cost ledger. As a job is finished, its costs are transferred to the finished goods ledger, for which Finished Goods is the controlling account.

JOB ORDER COST INFORMATION FOR DECISION MAKING Job order cost information can support pricing and cost analysis. Managers can use job cost information to identify unusual trends and areas for cost improvement.

FLOW OF COSTS FOR A SERVICE BUSINESS THAT USES A JOB ORDER COST ACCOUNTING SYSTEM For a service business, the cost of materials or supplies used is normally included as part of the overhead. The direct labor and overhead costs of rendering services are accumulated in a work-in-process account. When a job is completed and the client is billed, the costs are transferred to a cost-of-services account.

THE DIFFERENCE BETWEEN JOB ORDER COSTING AND PROCESS COSTING SYSTEMS The process cost system is best suited for industries that mass-produce identical units of a product that often have passed through a sequence of processes on a continuous basis. In process cost accounting, costs are charged to processing departments, and the cost of the finished unit is determined by dividing the total cost incurred in each process by the number of units produced.

PHYSICAL FLOWS AND COST FLOWS FOR A PROCESS MANUFACTURER Materials are introduced, converted, and passed from one department to the next department or to finished goods. The accumulated costs transferred from preceding departments and the costs of direct materials and direct labor incurred in each processing department are debited to the related work-in-process account in a process cost system. Each work-in-process account is also debited for the factory overhead applied.

ACCOUNTING FOR COMPLETED AND PARTIALLY COMPLETED UNITS UNDER THE FIRST-IN, FIRST-OUT (FIFO) METHOD Frequently, partially processed materials remain in various stages of production in a department at the end of a period. In this case, the manufacturing costs must be allocated between the units that have been completed and those that are only partially completed and remain within the department.

To allocate processing costs between the output completed and the inventory of goods within the department under FIFO, it is necessary to determine the number of equivalent units of production during the period for the beginning inventory, units started and completed currently, and the ending inventory.

COST OF PRODUCTION REPORT A cost of production report is prepared periodically for each processing department. It summarizes (1) the units for which the department is accountable and the disposition of those units, and (2) the production costs incurred by the department and the allocation of those costs. The report is used to control costs and improve the process.

USE OF COST OF PRODUCTION REPORTS FOR DECISION MAKING The cost of production report provides information for controlling and improving operations. Most cost of production reports include the detailed manufacturing costs incurred for completing production during the period. Analyzing trends in each of these costs over time can provide insights about process performance.

CONTRAST OF JUST-IN-TIME PROCESSING WITH CONVENTIONAL MANUFACTURING PRACTICES The just-in-time (JIT) processing philosophy focuses on reducing time, cost, and poor quality within the process. This is accomplished by combining process functions into work centers, assigning overhead services directly to the cells, involving the employees in process improvement efforts, eliminating wasteful activities, and reducing the amount of work in process inventory required to fulfill production targets.

Section 650. Operating Budgets and Performance Evaluation

Summaries and Conclusions

Operating Budgets

OBJECTIVES OF BUDGETING AND ITS IMPACT ON HUMAN BEHAVIOR Budgeting involves (1) establishing specific goals, (2) executing plans to achieve the goals, and (3) periodically comparing actual results with these goals. In addition, budget goals should be established to avoid problems in human behavior. Thus, budgets should not be set too tightly, too loosely, or with goal conflict.

BASIC ELEMENTS OF THE BUDGET PROCESS, THE TWO MAJOR TYPES OF BUDGETING, AND THE USE OF COMPUTERS IN BUDGETING The budget process is initiated by a budget committee. The annual estimates received by the budget committee should be carefully studied, analyzed, revised, and finally integrated together into the budget. Two major types of budgets are the static budget and the flexible budget. The static budget does not adjust with changes in activity, while the flexible budget does adjust with changes in activity. Computers can be useful in speeding up the budgetary process and in preparing timely budget performance reports. In addition, simulation models can be used to determine the impact of operating alternatives on various budgets.

MASTER BUDGET FOR A MANUFACTURING BUSINESS The master budget consists of the budgeted income statement and budgeted balance sheet. These two budgets are developed from detailed budgets that are described here.

BASIC INCOME STATEMENT BUDGETS FOR A MANUFACTURING BUSINESS The basic income statement budgets are the sales budget, production budget, direct materials purchases budget, direct labor cost budget, factory overhead cost budget, cost of goods sold budget, and selling and administrative expenses budget.

BALANCE SHEET BUDGETS FOR A MANUFACTURING BUSINESS Both the cash budget and the capital expenditures budget can be used in preparing the budgeted balance sheet. The cash budget consists of budgeted cash receipts and budgeted cash payments. The capital expenditures budget is an important tool for planning expenditures for fixed assets.

Performance Evaluation

ADVANTAGES AND DISADVANTAGES OF DECENTRALIZED OPERATIONS The advantages of decentralization may include better decisions by the managers closest to the operations, more time for top management to focus on strategic planning, training for managers, improved ability to serve customers and respond to their needs, and improved manager morale. The disadvantages of decentralization may include failure of the company to maximize profits because decisions made by one manager may affect other managers in such a way that the profitability of the entire company may suffer.

RESPONSIBILITY ACCOUNTING REPORT FOR A COST CENTER   Because managers of cost centers have responsibility and authority to make decisions regarding costs, responsibility accounting for cost centers focuses on costs. The primary accounting tools for planning and controlling costs for a cost center are budgets and budget performance reports.

RESPONSIBILITY ACCOUNTING REPORTS FOR A PROFIT CENTER   In preparing a profitability report for a profit center, operating expenses are subtracted from revenues in order to determine the income from operations before service department charges. Service department charges are then subtracted in order to determine the income from operations of the profit center.

INTERPRETATION OF RATE OF RETURN ON INVESTMENT, THE RESIDUAL INCOME, AND THE BALANCED SCORECARD FOR AN INVESTMENT CENTER   The rate of return on investment for an investment center is the income from operations divided by invested assets. The rate of return on investment may also be computed as the product of (1) the profit margin, and (2) the investment turnover. Residual income for an investment center is the excess of income from operations over a minimum amount of desired income from operations.

The balanced scorecard combines nonfinancial measures in order to help managers consider the underlying causes of financial performance and tradeoffs between short-term and long-term performance.

MARKET PRICE, NEGOTIATED PRICE, AND COST PRICE APPROACHES TO TRANSFER PRICING   Under the market price approach, the transfer price is the price at which the product or service transferred could be sold to outside buyers. Market price should be used when the supplier division is able to sell to outsiders and is operating at capacity.

Under the negotiated price approach, the managers of decentralized units agree (negotiate) among themselves as to the transfer price. Negotiated prices should be used when the supplier division is operating below capacity.

Under the cost price approach, cost is used as the basis for setting transfer prices. A variety of cost concepts may be used, such as total product cost per unit or variable product cost per unit. In addition, actual costs or standard (budgeted) costs may be used. The cost price approach should be used for supplier divisions that are organized as cost centers.

Section 660. Decision Making and Accounting

Summaries and Conclusions

Relevant Costs

DIFFERENTIAL ANALYSIS REPORT FOR DECISION MAKING   Differential analysis reports are useful for leasing or selling, discontinuing a segment or product, making or buying, replacing equipment, processing or selling, and accepting business at a special price. Each analysis focuses on the differential revenues and/or costs of the alternative courses of action.

SELLING PRICE OF A PRODUCT USING THE TOTAL COST, PRODUCT COST, AND VARIABLE COST CONCEPTS
The three cost concepts commonly used in applying the cost-plus approach to product pricing are summarized below.

Cost Concept	Covered in Cost Amount	Covered in Markup
Total cost	Total costs	Desired profit
Product cost	Total manufacturing costs	Desired profit + Total selling and administrative expenses
Variable cost	Total variable costs	Desired profit + Total fixed costs

The markup percentages used in applying each cost concept follow.
Total cost concept:

$$\text{Markup percentage} = \frac{\text{Desired profit}}{\text{Total costs}}$$

Product cost concept:

$$\text{Markup percentage} = \frac{\text{Desired profit} + \text{Total selling and administrative expenses}}{\text{Total manufacturing costs}}$$

Variable cost concept:

$$\text{Markup percentage} = \frac{\text{Desired profit} + \text{Total fixed costs}}{\text{Total variable costs}}$$

RELATIVE PROFITABILITY OF PRODUCTS IN BOTTLENECK PRODUCTION ENVIRONMENTS The profitability of a product in a bottleneck production environment may not be accurately shown in the contribution margin product report. Instead, the best measure of profitability is determined by dividing the contribution margin per unit by the bottleneck hours per unit. The resulting measure indicates the product's profitability per hour of bottleneck use. This information can be used to support product-pricing decisions.

Variable Costing and Absorption Costing Methods

INCOME REPORTING UNDER VARIABLE COSTING AND ABSORPTION COSTING Under absorption costing, direct materials, direct labor, and factory overhead become part of the cost of goods manufactured. Under variable costing, the cost of goods manufactured is composed of only variable costs—the direct materials, direct labor, and only those factory overhead costs that vary with the rate of production. The fixed factory overhead costs do not become a part of the cost of goods manufactured but are considered an expense of the period.

Deducting the variable cost of goods sold from sales in the variable costing income statement yields the manufacturing margin. Deducting the variable selling and administrative expenses from the manufacturing margin yields the contribution margin. Deducting the fixed costs from the contribution margin yields the income from operations.

The difference in the income reported under variable costing and absorption costing is summarized in the following table:

	Units manufactured
Equal units sold	Variable costing income equals absorption costing income.
Exceed units sold	Variable costing income is less than absorption costing income.
Less than units sold	Variable costing income is greater than absorption costing income.

INCOME ANALYSIS UNDER VARIABLE COSTING AND ABSORPTION COSTING Management should be aware of the effects of changes in inventory levels on income from operations reported under variable costing and absorption costing. If absorption costing is used, managers could misinterpret increases or decreases in income from operations due to changes in inventory levels to be the result of operating efficiencies or inefficiencies.

MANAGEMENT'S USE OF VARIABLE COSTING AND ABSORPTION COSTING FOR CONTROLLING COSTS, PRICING PRODUCTS, PLANNING PRODUCTION, ANALYZING MARKET SEGMENTS, AND ANALYZING CONTRIBUTION MARGINS Variable costing is especially useful at the operating level of management because the amount of variable manufacturing costs are controllable at this level. The fixed factory overhead costs are ordinarily controllable by a higher level of management.

In the short run, variable costing may be useful in establishing the selling price of a product. This price should be at least equal to the variable costs of making and selling the product. In the long run, however, absorption costing is useful in establishing selling prices because all costs must be covered and a reasonable amount of operating income must be earned.

Variable costing can make a significant contribution to management decision making in analyzing and evaluating market segments, such as territories, products, salespersons, and customers.

Contribution margin analysis is the systematic examination of differences between planned and actual contribution margins. These differences can be caused by (1) an increase or decrease in the amount of sales, or (2) an increase or decrease in the amount of variable costs. An increase or decrease in either element may in turn be due to (1) an increase or decrease in the number of units sold, or (2) an increase or decrease in the unit sales price or unit cost. The effect of these two factors on either sales or variable costs may be stated as follows.

- Quantity factor—the effect of a difference in the number of units sold, assuming no change in unit sales price or unit cost. The quantity factor is the difference between the actual quantity sold and the planned quantity sold, multiplied by the planned unit sales price or unit cost.

- Unit price or unit cost factor—the effect of a difference in unit sales price or unit cost on the number of units sold. The unit price or unit cost factor is the difference between the actual unit price or unit cost and the planned unit price or unit cost, multiplied by the actual quantity sold.

Section 670. Information Systems and Accounting

Summaries and Conclusions

Accounting Information Systems

THE ACCOUNTING SYSTEM AND ITS IMPLEMENTATION   An accounting system is the methods and procedures for collecting, classifying, summarizing, and reporting a business's financial information. The three steps through which an accounting system evolves are (1) analysis of information needs, (2) design of the system, and (3) implementation of the systems design.

Section 680. Control and Accounting

Summaries and Conclusions

Control Over Cash

OBJECTIVES AND ELEMENTS OF INTERNAL CONTROL   Internal control provides reasonable assurance that (1) assets are safeguarded and used for business purposes, (2) business information is accurate, and (3) laws and regulations are complied with. The five elements of internal control are the control environment, risk assessment, control procedures, monitoring, and information and communication.

THE NATURE OF CASH AND THE IMPORTANCE OF INTERNAL CONTROL OVER CASH   Cash includes coins, currency (paper money), checks, money orders, and money on deposit that is available for unrestricted withdrawal from banks and other financial institutions. Because of the ease with which money can be transferred, businesses should design and use controls that safeguard cash and authorize cash transactions.

BASIC PROCEDURES FOR ACHIEVING INTERNAL CONTROL OVER CASH RECEIPTS   One of the most important controls to protect cash received in over-the-counter sales is a cash register. A remittance advice is a preventive control for cash received through the mail. Separating the duties of handling cash and recording cash is also a preventive control.

VOUCHER SYSTEM   A voucher system is a set of procedures for authorizing and recording liabilities and cash payments. A voucher system uses vouchers, a file for unpaid vouchers, and a file for paid vouchers.

THE NATURE OF A BANK ACCOUNT AND ITS USE IN CONTROLLING CASH   The forms used with bank accounts include a signature card, deposit tickets, checks, and a record of checks drawn. Each month, the bank usually sends a bank statement to the depositor, summarizing all of the transactions for the month. The bank statement allows a business to compare the cash transactions recorded in the accounting records to those recorded by the bank.

BANK RECONCILIATION AND JOURNAL ENTRIES   The first section of the bank reconciliation begins with the cash balance according to the bank statement. This balance is adjusted for the depositor's changes in cash that do not appear on the bank statement and for any bank errors. The second section begins with the cash balance according to the depositor's records. This balance is adjusted for the bank's changes in cash that do not appear on the depositor's records and for any depositor errors. The adjusted balances for the two sections must be equal.

No entries are necessary on the depositor's records as a result of the information included in the first section of the bank reconciliation. However, the items in the second section must be journalized on the depositor's records.

ACCOUNTING FOR SMALL CASH TRANSACTIONS USING A PETTY CASH FUND   A petty cash fund may be used by a business to make small payments that occur frequently. The money in a petty cash fund is placed in the custody of a specific employee who authorizes payments from the fund. Periodically, or when the amount of money in the fund is depleted or reduced to a minimum amount, the fund is replenished.

PRESENTATION OF CASH ON THE BALANCE SHEET   Cash is listed as the first asset in the Current Assets section of the balance sheet. Companies that have invested excess cash in highly liquid investments usually report Cash and Cash Equivalents on the balance sheet.

INTERPRETATION OF RATIO OF CASH TO CURRENT LIABILITIES   A company that is in financial distress may have difficulty converting its receivables, inventory, and prepaid assets to cash on a timely basis. In these cases, the ratio of cash to current liabilities, called the *doomsday ratio,* may be useful in assessing the ability of creditors to collect what they are owed.

Control Over Receivables

COMMON CLASSIFICATIONS OF RECEIVABLES   The term *receivables* refers to all money claims against other entities, including people, business firms, and other organizations. They are normally classified as accounts receivable, notes receivable, or other receivables.

EXAMPLES OF INTERNAL CONTROL PROCEDURES THAT APPLY TO RECEIVABLES   The internal controls that apply to receivables include the separation of responsibilities for related functions. In this way, the work of one employee can serve as a check on the work of another employee.

THE NATURE OF AND THE ACCOUNTING FOR UNCOLLECTIBLE RECEIVABLES   The two methods of accounting for uncollectible receivables are the allowance method and the direct write-off method. The allowance method provides in advance for uncollectible receivables. The direct write-off method recognizes the expense only when the account is judged to be uncollectible.

JOURNAL ENTRIES FOR THE ALLOWANCE METHOD OF ACCOUNTING FOR UNCOLLECTIBLES AND ESTIMATION OF UNCOLLECTIBLE RECEIVABLES BASED ON SALES AND ON AN ANALYSIS OF RECEIVABLES   A year-end adjusting entry provides for (1) the reduction of the value of the receivables to the amount of cash expected to be realized from them in the future, and (2) the allocation to the current period of the expected expense resulting from such reduction. The adjusting entry debits Uncollectible Accounts Expense and credits Allowance for Doubtful Accounts. When an account is believed to be uncollectible, it is written off against the allowance account.

When the estimate of uncollectibles is based on the amount of sales for the fiscal period, the adjusting entry is made without regard to the balance of the allowance account. When the estimate of uncollectibles is based on the amount and the age of the receivable accounts at the end of the period, the adjusting entry is recorded so that the balance of the allowance account will equal the estimated uncollectibles at the end of the period.

The allowance account, which will have a credit balance after the adjusting entry has been posted, is a contra asset account. The uncollectible accounts expense is generally reported on the income statement as an administrative expense.

MODULE 600. ACCOUNTING

JOURNAL ENTRIES FOR THE DIRECT WRITE-OFF OF UNCOLLECTIBLE RECEIVABLES Under the direct write-off method, the entry to write off an account debits Uncollectible Accounts Expense and credits Accounts Receivable. Neither an allowance account nor an adjusting entry is needed at the end of the period.

THE NATURE AND CHARACTERISTICS OF PROMISSORY NOTES A note is a written promise to pay a sum of money on demand or at a definite time. Characteristics of notes that affect how they are recorded and reported include the due date, interest rate, and maturity value. The basic formula for computing interest on a note is: Principal × Rate × Time = Interest. The due date is the date a note is to be paid, and the period of time between the issuance date and the due date is normally stated in either days or months. The maturity value of a note is the sum of the face amount and the interest.

JOURNAL ENTRIES FOR NOTES RECEIVABLE TRANSACTIONS A note received in settlement of an account receivable is recorded as a debit to Notes Receivable and a credit to Accounts Receivable. When a note matures, Cash is debited, Notes Receivable is credited, and Interest Revenue is credited. If the maker of a note fails to pay the debt on the due date, the note is said to be dishonored. When the holder of a dishonored note has been paid by the endorser, the amount of the endorser's claim against the maker of the note is debited to an accounts receivable account.

PRESENTATION OF RECEIVABLES ON THE BALANCE SHEET All receivables that are expected to be realized in cash within a year are presented in the Current Assets section of the balance sheet. It is normal to list the assets in the order of their liquidity, which is the order in which they can be converted to cash in normal operations.

INTERPRETATION OF ACCOUNTS RECEIVABLE TURNOVER AND THE NUMBER OF DAYS' SALES IN RECEIVABLES The accounts receivable turnover is net sales on account divided by average accounts receivable. It measures how frequently accounts receivable are being converted into cash. The number of days' sales in receivables is the end-of-year accounts receivable divided by the average daily sales on account. It measures the length of time the accounts receivable have been outstanding.

Control Over Inventories

EXAMPLES OF INTERNAL CONTROL PROCEDURES THAT APPLY TO INVENTORIES Internal control procedures for inventories include those developed to protect the inventories from damage, employee theft, and customer theft. In addition, a physical inventory count should be taken periodically to detect shortages as well as to deter employee thefts.

IMPACT OF INVENTORY ERRORS ON FINANCIAL STATEMENTS Any errors in reporting inventory based upon the physical inventory will misstate the ending inventory, current assets, total assets, and stockholders' equity (retained earnings) on the balance sheet. In addition, the cost of goods sold, gross profit, and net income will be misstated on the income statement.

INVENTORY COST FLOW ASSUMPTIONS The three common cost flow assumptions used in business are the (1) first-in, first-out (FIFO) method, (2) last-in, first-out (LIFO) method, and (3) average cost method. Each method normally yields different amounts for the cost of merchandise sold and the ending merchandise inventory. Thus, the choice of a cost flow assumption directly affects the income statement and balance sheet.

COST OF INVENTORY UNDER THE PERPETUAL INVENTORY SYSTEM In a perpetual inventory system, the number of units and the cost of each type of merchandise are recorded in a subsidiary inventory ledger, with a separate account for each type of merchandise.

COST OF INVENTORY UNDER THE PERIODIC INVENTORY SYSTEM In a periodic inventory system, a physical inventory is taken to determine the cost of the inventory and the cost of merchandise sold.

USE OF THE THREE INVENTORY COSTING METHODS The three inventory costing methods will normally yield different amounts for (1) the ending inventory, (2) the cost of the merchandise sold for the period, and (3) the gross profit (and net income) for the period. During periods of inflation, the FIFO method yields the lowest amount for the cost of merchandise sold, the highest amount for gross profit (and net income), and the highest amount for the ending inventory. The LIFO method yields the opposite results. During periods of deflation, the preceding effects are reversed. The average cost method yields results that are between those of FIFO and LIFO.

VALUATION OF INVENTORY AT OTHER THAN COST, USING THE LOWER-OF-COST-OR-MARKET AND NET REALIZABLE VALUE CONCEPTS   If the market price of an item of inventory is lower than its cost, the lower market price is used to compute the value of the item. Market price is the cost to replace the merchandise on the inventory date. It is possible to apply the lower of cost or market to each item in the inventory, to major classes or categories, or to the inventory as a whole.

Merchandise that can be sold only at prices below cost should be valued at net realizable value, which is the estimated selling price less any direct cost of disposal.

BALANCE SHEET PRESENTATION OF MERCHANDISE INVENTORY   Merchandise inventory is usually presented in the Current Assets section of the balance sheet, following receivables. Both the method of determining the cost of the inventory (FIFO, LIFO, or average) and the method of valuing the inventory (cost or the lower of cost or market) should be shown.

COST OF INVENTORY, USING THE RETAIL METHOD AND THE GROSS PROFIT METHOD   In using the retail method to estimate inventory, the retail prices of all merchandise acquired are accumulated. The inventory at retail is determined by deducting sales for the period from the retail price of the goods that were available for sale during the period. The inventory at retail is then converted to cost on the basis of the ratio of cost to selling (retail) price for the merchandise available for sale.

In using the gross profit method to estimate inventory, the estimated gross profit is deducted from the sales to determine the estimated cost of merchandise sold. This amount is then deducted from the cost of merchandise available for sale to determine the estimated ending inventory.

INTERPRETATION OF THE INVENTORY TURNOVER RATIO AND THE NUMBER OF DAYS' SALES IN INVENTORY   The inventory turnover ratio, computed as the cost of merchandise sold divided by the average inventory, measures the relationship between the volume of goods (merchandise) sold and the amount of inventory carried during the period. The number of days' sales in inventory, computed as the ending inventory divided by the average daily cost of merchandise sold, measures the length of time it takes to acquire, sell, and replace the inventory.

Controls Over Fixed Assets and Intangible Assets

FIXED ASSETS AND ACCOUNTING   Fixed assets are long-term tangible and noncurrent assets that are owned by the business and are used in the normal operations of the business. Examples of fixed assets are equipment, buildings, and land. The initial cost of a fixed asset includes all amounts spent to get the asset in place and ready for use. For example, sales tax, freight, insurance in transit, and installation costs are all included in the cost of a fixed asset. As time passes, all fixed assets except land lose their ability to provide services. As a result, the cost of a fixed asset should be transferred to an expense account, in a systematic manner, during the asset's expected useful life. This periodic transfer of cost to expense is called *depreciation*.

DEPRECIATION ACCOUNTING FOR FIXED ASSETS   In computing depreciation, three factors need to be considered: (1) the fixed asset's initial cost, (2) the useful life of the asset, and (3) the residual value of the asset.

The straight-line method spreads the initial cost less the residual value equally over the useful life. The units-of-production method spreads the initial cost less the residual value equally over the units expected to be produced by the asset during its useful life. The declining-balance method is applied by multiplying the declining book value of the asset by twice the straight-line rate.

FIXED ASSET COSTS AS EITHER CAPITAL EXPENDITURES OR REVENUE EXPENDITURES   Costs for additions to fixed assets and other costs related to improving efficiency or capacity are classified as capital expenditures. Costs for additions to an asset and costs that add to the usefulness of the asset for more than one period (called *betterments*) are also classified as capital expenditures. Costs that increase the useful life of an asset beyond the original estimate are capital expenditures and are called *extraordinary repairs*. Expenditures that benefit only the current period or that maintain normal operating efficiency are debited to expense accounts and are classified as revenue expenditures.

MODULE 600. ACCOUNTING

JOURNAL ENTRIES FOR THE DISPOSAL OF FIXED ASSETS The journal entries to record disposals of fixed assets will vary. In all cases, however, any depreciation for the current period should be recorded, and the book value of the asset is then removed from the accounts. The entry to remove the book value from the accounts is a debit to the asset's accumulated depreciation account and a credit to the asset account for the cost of the asset. For assets retired from service, a loss may be recorded for any remaining book value of the asset.

When a fixed asset is sold, the book value is removed and the cash or other asset received is also recorded. If the selling price is more than the book value of the asset, the transaction results in a gain. If the selling price is less than the book value, there is a loss.

When a fixed asset is exchanged for another of similar nature, no gain is recognized on the exchange. The acquired asset's cost is adjusted for any gains. A loss on an exchange of similar assets is recorded.

LEASE AND ACCOUNTING RULES RELATED TO THE LEASING OF FIXED ASSETS A lease is a contract for the use of an asset for a period of time. A capital lease is accounted for as if the lessee has purchased the asset. The lease payments under an operating lease are accounted for as rent expense for the lessee.

INTERNAL CONTROLS OVER FIXED ASSETS Internal controls over fixed assets should include procedures for authorizing the purchase of assets. Once acquired, fixed assets should be safeguarded from theft, misuse, or damage. A physical inventory of fixed assets should be taken periodically.

DEPLETION ACCOUNTING FOR NATURAL RESOURCES The amount of periodic depletion is computed by multiplying the quantity of minerals extracted during the period by a depletion rate. The depletion rate is computed by dividing the cost of the mineral deposit by its estimated size. The entry to record depletion debits a depletion expense account and credits an accumulated depletion account.

AMORTIZATION ACCOUNTING FOR INTANGIBLE ASSETS Long-term assets that are without physical attributes but are used in the business are classified as intangible assets. Examples of intangible assets are patents, copyrights, trademarks, and goodwill. The initial cost of an intangible asset should be debited to an asset account. This cost should be written off, or amortized, over the years of the asset's expected usefulness by debiting an expense account and crediting the intangible asset account.

REPORTING OF DEPRECIATION EXPENSE The amount of depreciation expense and the method or methods used in computing depreciation should be disclosed in the financial statements. In addition, each major class of fixed assets should be disclosed, along with the related accumulated depreciation.

REPORTING OF INTANGIBLE ASSETS Intangible assets are usually presented in the balance sheet in a separate section immediately following fixed assets. Each major class of intangible assets should be disclosed at an amount net of the amortization recorded to date.

INTERPRETATION OF RATIO OF FIXED ASSETS TO LONG-TERM LIABILITIES The ratio of fixed assets to long-term liabilities is a solvency measure that indicates the margin of safety to creditors. It also provides an indication of the ability of a company to borrow additional funds on a long-term basis.

Controls Over Current Liabilities

EXAMPLES OF CURRENT LIABILITIES Current liabilities are obligations that are to be paid out of current assets and are due within a short time, usually within one year. Current liabilities arise from either (1) receiving goods or services prior to making payment, or (2) receiving payment prior to delivering goods or services.

JOURNAL ENTRIES FOR SHORT-TERM NOTES PAYABLE A note issued to a creditor to temporarily satisfy an account payable is recorded as a debit to Accounts Payable and a credit to Notes Payable. At the time the note is paid, Notes Payable and Interest Expense are debited and Cash is credited. Notes may also be issued to purchase merchandise or other assets or to borrow money from a bank. When a discounted note is issued, Interest Expense is debited for the interest deduction at the time of issuance, an asset account is debited for the proceeds, and Notes Payable is credited for the face value of the note. The face value and the maturity value of a discounted note are equal.

ACCOUNTING TREATMENT FOR CONTINGENT LIABILITIES AND PRODUCT WARRANTIES A contingent liability is a potential obligation that results from a past transaction but depends on a future event. If the contingent liability is both probable and estimable, the liability should be recorded. If the contingent liability is reasonably possible or is not estimable, it should be disclosed in the footnotes to the financial statements. An example of a recordable contingent liability is product warranties. If a company grants a warranty on a product, an estimated warranty expense and liability should be recorded in the period of the sale. The expense and the liability are recorded by debiting Product Warranty Expense and crediting Product Warranty Payable.

EMPLOYER LIABILITIES FOR PAYROLL, INCLUDING LIABILITIES ARISING FROM EMPLOYEE EARNINGS AND DEDUCTIONS FROM EARNINGS An employer's liability for payroll is calculated by determining employees' total earnings for a payroll period, including overtime pay. From this amount, employee deductions are subtracted to arrive at the net pay to be paid each employee. The employer's liabilities for employee deductions are recognized at the time the payroll is recorded. Most employers also incur liabilities for payroll taxes, such as Social Security tax, Medicare tax, federal unemployment compensation tax, and state unemployment compensation tax.

PAYROLL ACCOUNTING SYSTEMS THAT USE A PAYROLL REGISTER, EMPLOYEE EARNINGS RECORDS, AND A GENERAL JOURNAL The payroll register is used in assembling and summarizing the data needed for each payroll period. The data recorded in the payroll register include the number of hours worked and the earnings and deduction data for each employee. The payroll register also includes columns for accumulating total wages or salaries to be debited to the various expense accounts. It is supported by a detailed payroll record for each employee, called an *employee's earnings record*.

JOURNAL ENTRIES FOR EMPLOYEE FRINGE BENEFITS, INCLUDING VACATION PAY AND PENSIONS Fringe benefits are expenses of the period in which the employees earn the benefits. Fringe benefits are recorded by debiting an expense account and crediting a liability account. For example, the entry to record accrued vacation pay debits Vacation Pay Expense and credits Vacation Pay Payable.

QUICK RATIO TO ANALYZE THE ABILITY OF A BUSINESS TO PAY ITS CURRENT LIABILITIES The quick ratio or acid-test ratio is a measure of a business's ability to pay current liabilities within a short period of time. The quick ratio is quick assets divided by current liabilities. A quick ratio exceeding 1 is usually desirable.

Section 699. International Issues

Summaries and Conclusions

Cultural Influences on Accounting

- A study of cultural influences is the necessary first step in explaining the accounting system of a nation. The important environmental influences include the economic system, the political system, the legal system, the educational system, and religion.
- Environmental factors affect the development of global business strategy.
- International operations pose unique and complex challenges in the design of a control system.
- Problems encountered in the design of a global control system include diversity among nations with respect to culture and languages.
- The same control system may work well in one country but not in another due to cultural differences.
- Policy formulation in different countries should take into account organizational goals, cultural differences, business practices, and business ethics.
- A local staff can provide valuable input during the policy formulation process because of their knowledge of local culture.
- Top management's attitude and its leadership are critical factors in the cultivation of an ethical corporate culture that is essential for the long-term survival of an organization.

Accounting Measurement and Disclosures

- Financial reporting disclosures include many types of disclosures, and the trend is toward more disclosures.
- A corporation is held accountable to investors and creditors as well as society at large. The latter accountability arises from a corporation using scarce resources, and its ability to influence lifestyles and quality of life of parties other than capital providers.
- Several factors prompt corporations to make financial reporting disclosures. Corporations make required as well as voluntary disclosures.
- Total costs of disclosures include both monetary costs as well as nonmonetary costs.
- Disclosures in financial reports are directly affected by how economic transactions are recorded (measured).
- There is a diversity in the measurement process worldwide.
- Reserves are used for multiple purposes, including additional protection to creditors. They are part of a conservative accounting practice called the Prudence Concept. Laws in many countries (for example, Japan, France, and Italy) permit undervaluation of assets and overstatement of expenses and liabilities. Reserve categories include expense liability reserve, legal (statutory) reserve, general reserve, and revaluation reserve. These reserves are called equity reserves and appear in the stockholders' equity section of the balance sheet.
- The method of disclosure affects perceptions of users of financial reports.
- Lack of disclosure uniformity exists even when companies are using the same accounting standards.
- Different multinationals use different disclosure approaches ranging from compliance with base country requirements to preparation of secondary statements.
- Social impact disclosures are heavily influenced by societal concerns in a country, with human resource disclosures receiving the most attention.

Worldwide Disclosures Diversity and Harmonization

- Facilitation of international trade and investment requires accounting standards that are not country-specific.
- Harmonization of accounting standards improves the comparability of financial statements.
- Worldwide harmonization efforts consist of three levels: international, regional, and national.
- The International Accounting Standards Committee (IASC) is the leading organization in the efforts to harmonize accounting standards.
- The IASC standards cover measurement, recording, and disclosure issues dealing with the preparation of financial reports.
- The European Union (EU) is the leading trading bloc in the efforts to harmonize accounting standards among its member countries.
- The Fourth and Seventh EU Company Law Directives address the preparation and consolidation of financial statements, respectively.
- Canada, Mexico, and the United States are members of the North American Free Trade Agreement.
- National efforts to harmonize accounting standards should be encouraged. The ultimate success of worldwide harmonization efforts will depend on their acceptance by the setters of national accounting standards.
- The five countries selected for comparative analysis (Brazil, Germany, Japan, The Netherlands, and United States) have different environments. As a result, diversity in standard setting is a natural outcome.
- All of the five countries selected require the balance sheet and the income statement. The same is not true for the statement of funds/cash flow.
- The five countries examined have generally reached similar understandings on issues of going concern, accrual basis, and consistency in the application of accounting principles from one period to the next.
- Many countries have adopted International Accounting Standards (IAS) as their national standards. Others have used IASs to develop the national standards.

Auditing Issues for Global Operations

- Internal auditing and external auditing share a common objective: to determine the reliability of accounting information.

- The internal audit is performed to determine whether an organization's policies and procedures are being followed, and whether its assets are safeguarded and used efficiently.
- Factors contributing to the enhancement of internal auditing include audit committees, technological advances, reliance of external auditors on internal audit reports, and international operations.
- Policy formulation in different countries should take into account cultural differences, company goals, and business ethics.
- Top management's attitude and its leadership are critical factors in the cultivation of a healthy corporate culture for the long-term survival of an organization.
- Internal audit organizations can take various forms. While making a selection, the independence of internal auditors should be the uppermost consideration.
- The Foreign Corrupt Practices Act (FCPA), although a U.S. law, has worldwide impact.
- The Institute of Internal Auditors (IIA) is the most influential organization in the development of internal auditing standards in the world.
- The basic objective of the external audit is to determine if financial statements are properly prepared.
- External audits are performed differently in different countries because accounting and auditing standards differ among countries.
- Many public accounting firms provide external audit services throughout the world.
- The "true and fair view" concept has been adopted in the EU Fourth Directive.
- "Present fairly," as used in the United States, requires an independent auditor to use judgment on several issues.
- Many countries require statutory audits to determine whether financial statements are in compliance with applicable laws.
- Many countries have either successfully adopted the international federation of accountant (IFAC) audit standards or have changed national auditing standards to make them consistent with the IFAC standards.
- The IFAC, the International Organization of Securities Commissions (IOSCO), and the EU are among the most prominent organizations attempting to harmonize auditing standards in the world.

Finance

Sections 701 and 703. Finance Strategies and Role of Finance and Chief Financial Officer (CFO)

Summaries and Conclusions

- Finance consists of three interrelated areas: (1) financial markets and institutions, (2) investments, and (3) managerial finance.
- Managerial finance has undergone significant changes over time, but four issues have received the most emphasis in recent years: (1) inflation and its effects on interest rates, (2) deregulation of financial institutions, (3) a dramatic increase in technology, such as the use of telecommunications for transmitting information and the use of computers for analyzing the effects of alternative financial decisions, and (4) the increased importance of global financial markets and business operations.
- Financial managers are responsible for obtaining and using funds in a way that will maximize the value of their firms.
- The three main forms of business organization are the proprietorship, the partnership, and the corporation.
- Although each form of organization offers some advantages and disadvantages, most business is conducted by corporations because this organizational form maximizes most firms' values.
- The primary goal of management should be to maximize stockholders' wealth, and this means maximizing the price of the firm's stock. Further, actions that maximize stock prices also increase social welfare.

- An agency problem is a potential conflict of interest that can arise between (1) the owners of the firm and its management or (2) the stockholders and the creditors (debtholders).
- There are a number of ways to motivate managers to act in the best interests of stockholders, including (1) the threat of firing, (2) the threat of takeovers, and (3) properly structured managerial incentives.
- The price of the firm's stock depends on the firm's projected earnings per share, the timing of its earnings, the riskiness of the projected earnings, its use of debt, and its dividend policy.
- Non–U.S. firms generally have more concentrated ownership than U.S. firms. In some cases, firms in other countries are part of an industrial group, which is a network of firms with common ownership ties that provides the different functions required to manufacture and sell a product from start to finish. Examples of industrial groups include the *keiretsu* in Japan and the *chaebol* in Korea.
- International operations have become increasingly important to individual firms and to the national economy. A multinational corporation (MNC) is a firm that operates in two or more nations.
- Companies go "international" for five primary reasons: (1) to seek new markets, (2) to seek raw materials, (3) to seek new technology, (4) to seek production efficiency, and (5) to avoid trade barriers.
- Six major factors distinguish managerial finance as practiced by domestic firms from that of multinational corporations: (1) different currency denominations, (2) economic and legal ramifications, (3) languages, (4) cultural differences, (5) role of governments, and (6) political risk.
- Small businesses are quite important in the aggregate and there are many more in number than the large businesses.

Section 704. Working Capital Policy

Summaries and Conclusions

- There are relationships among working capital accounts, working capital policy, and alternative ways of financing current assets.
- *Working capital* refers to current assets, and *net working capital* is defined as current assets minus current liabilities. The term *working capital policy* refers to decisions related to the level of current assets and the way they are financed. Net working capital is also called working capital by some.
- Decisions affecting one working capital account will have an impact on other working capital accounts.
- Once the firm's operations have stabilized so that the inflows and the outflows into working capital accounts are the same, the account balance can be computed using the following equation.

$$\text{Account balance} = \begin{pmatrix} \text{Amount of} \\ \text{daily activity} \end{pmatrix} \times \begin{pmatrix} \text{Average life} \\ \text{of the account} \end{pmatrix}$$

- The inventory conversion period is the average length of time required to convert raw materials into finished goods and then to sell them.
- The receivables collection period is the average length of time required to convert the firm's receivables into cash, and it is equal to the day's sales outstanding (DSO).
- The payables deferral period is the average length of time between the purchase of raw materials and labor and when payment for them is made.
- The cash conversion cycle is the length of time between paying for purchases and receiving cash from the sale of finished goods. The cash conversion cycle is calculated as follows.

$$\begin{pmatrix} \text{Cash} \\ \text{conversion} \\ \text{cycle} \end{pmatrix} = \begin{pmatrix} \text{Inventory} \\ \text{conversion} \\ \text{period} \end{pmatrix} + \begin{pmatrix} \text{Receivables} \\ \text{collection} \\ \text{period} \end{pmatrix} - \begin{pmatrix} \text{Payables} \\ \text{deferral} \\ \text{period} \end{pmatrix}$$

- Under a relaxed current asset investment policy, a firm holds relatively large amounts of each type of current asset. Under a restricted current asset investment policy, the firm holds minimal amounts of these items.

- Permanent current assets are those current assets that the firm holds even during slack times, whereas temporary current assets are the additional current assets that are needed during seasonal or cyclical peaks. The methods used to finance permanent and temporary current assets constitute the firm's current asset financing policy.
- A moderate approach to current asset financing involves matching, to the extent possible, the maturities of assets and liabilities so that temporary current assets are financed with short-term, spontaneous debt and permanent current assets and fixed assets are financed with long-term debt or equity plus nonspontaneous debt. Under an aggressive approach, some permanent current assets and perhaps even some fixed assets are financed with short-term debt. A conservative approach would be to use long-term capital to finance all permanent assets and some of the temporary current assets.
- The advantages of short-term credit are (1) the speed with which short-term loans can be arranged, (2) increased flexibility, and (3) the fact that short-term interest rates are generally lower than long-term rates. The principal disadvantage of short-term credit is the extra risk that the borrower must bear because (1) the lender can demand payment on short notice, and (2) the cost of the loan will increase if interest rates rise.
- Multinational firms face a more complex task when managing working capital because business cultures, political environments, currencies, and so forth, differ among countries.
- Entrepreneurs often underestimate working capital needs because rapid growth is a greater "cash drain" than first expected—rapid growth might generate immediate paper profits, but cash profits generally do not begin until some later date.

Section 705. Managing Short-Term Assets

Summaries and Conclusions

Cash Management

- The primary goal of cash management is to reduce the amount of cash held to the minimum necessary to conduct business.
- The transactions balance is the cash necessary to conduct day-to-day business, whereas the precautionary balance is a cash reserve held to meet random, unforeseen needs. A compensating balance is a minimum checking account balance that a bank requires as compensation either for services provided or as part of a loan agreement. Firms also hold speculative balances, which allow them to take advantage of bargain purchases.
- Effective cash management encompasses the proper management of cash inflows and outflows, which entails (1) synchronizing cash flows, (2) using float, (3) accelerating collections, (4) determining where and when funds will be needed and ensuring that they are available at the right place at the right time, and (5) controlling disbursements.
- Disbursement float is the amount of funds associated with checks written by a firm that are still in process and hence have not yet been deducted by the bank from the appropriate account. Collections float is the amount of funds associated with checks written to the firm that have not been cleared and hence are not yet available for the firm's use. Net float is the difference between disbursement float and collections float, and it also is equal to the difference between the balance in the firm's checkbook and the balance on the bank's records. The larger the net float, the smaller the cash balances that must be maintained; so net float is good.
- Two techniques that can be used to speed up collections are (1) lockboxes and (2) preauthorized debits. Also, a concentration banking system consolidates cash into a centralized pool that can be managed more efficiently than a large number of individual accounts.
- Three techniques for controlling disbursements are (1) payables centralization, (2) zero-balance accounts, and (3) controlled disbursement accounts.
- Firms can reduce cash balances by holding marketable securities, which can be sold easily on short notice at close to their quoted market values. Marketable securities serve both as a substitute for cash and as a temporary investment for funds that will be needed in the near future. Safety is the primary consideration when selecting marketable securities.

- When a firm sells goods to a customer on credit, an account receivable is created.
- Firms can use an aging schedule and the day's sales outstanding (DSO) to help keep track of their receivables position and to help avoid an increase in bad debts.
- A firm's credit policy consists of four elements: (1) credit standards, (2) credit terms, (3) collection policy, and (4) monitoring receivables.
- A firm should change its credit policy only if the costs of doing so will be more than offset by the benefits.
- Inventory management involves determining how much inventory to hold, when to place orders, and how many units to order.
- Inventory can be grouped into three categories: (1) raw materials, (2) work-in-process, and (3) finished goods.
- The economic ordering quantity (EOQ) model is a formula for determining the order quantity that will minimize total inventory costs.

$$EOQ = \sqrt{\frac{2 \times O \times T}{C \times PP}}$$

Where O is the fixed cost per order, T is sales in units, C is the percentage cost of carrying inventory, and PP is the purchase price per unit.

- The reorder point is the inventory level at which new items must be ordered. Safety stocks are held to avoid shortages (1) if demand increases or (2) if shipping delays are encountered. If suppliers offer quantity discounts to purchase materials, it might be beneficial for the firm to order more than the EOQ amount.
- Firms use inventory control systems such as the red-line method, as well as computerized inventory control systems, to help them keep track of actual inventory levels and to ensure that inventory levels are adjusted as sales change. Just-in-time (JIT) systems and outsourcing are also used to hold down inventory costs and, simultaneously, to improve the production process.
- Multinational firms use techniques similar to purely domestic firms to manage short-term assets, but they face more complex situations due to differences in the business, economic, and legal environments of various countries.

Short-Term Investment Management

Short-term investment management is a challenging and rapidly changing area of financial management. The number of securities from which the investment manager can select and the stream of innovative new securities that must be evaluated present a unique opportunity to conduct risk-return analysis. Not only must individual security risks be appraised, but interdependencies and risk in a portfolio context must also be managed.

The investment manager begins the portfolio selection by considering the cash forecast, the company's financial position, and the investment policy. The investment policy limits the types of securities to be included and perhaps gives guidelines to follow in assembling the portfolio. This information is combined with an understanding of the company's posture on the total amount invested in cash and securities and the cash-securities mix. The Baumol, Miller-Orr, and Stone models may be consulted for help in determining how and to what extent funds should be reallocated from securities to cash. These models should be used only as part of a more comprehensive analysis of liquidity and current asset investment, so that shareholder wealth is maximized. The financial manager attempts to maximize the present value of cash flows, not merely to minimize the company's costs.

If the company decides to have an outside investment manager, the next step is selecting the manager(s) to be used. A common choice for such firms is to wire money to a money market mutual fund, which provides daily interest and immediate access to funds. If done internally, corporate personnel are faced with sifting through a set of potential securities to evaluate their risk and risk-return tradeoff. After doing individual security risk analysis, the manager should have a shorter list of potential investments, which are then reevaluated from a portfolio perspective. Regardless of whether decision making is done externally or internally, the results must be monitored and evaluated. The common benchmarks are U.S. Treasury bill rates, money market mutual fund rates, indexes, or synthetic composites.

Two types of investment strategies include passive and active investments. Passive strategies, such as the buy-and-hold strategy, typify the approach taken by many companies when investing surplus cash. Active strategies usually imply an interest rate forecast, but the analyst may be wrong more often than right unless the forecaster possesses special analytical ability or more rapid access to critical information. The predominant concerns for most managers are safety and liquidity, not yield. The possibility of yield enhancement may be viewed as too risky for the short-term securities portfolio.

Section 710. Managing Short-Term Financing

Summaries and Conclusions

Managing Short-Term Liabilities

- *Short-term credit* is defined as any liability originally scheduled for payment within one year. The four major sources of short-term credit are (1) accruals, (2) accounts payable, (3) bank loans, and (4) commercial paper.
- Accruals, which are continually recurring short-term liabilities, represent free, spontaneous credit.
- Accounts payable, or trade credit, is the largest category of short-term debt. This credit arises spontaneously as a result of purchases on credit. Firms should use all the free trade credit they can obtain, but they should use costly trade credit only if it is less expensive than other forms of short-term debt. Suppliers often offer discounts to customers who pay within a stated discount period. The following equation can be used to calculate the approximate percentage cost, on an annual basis, of not taking discounts.

$$\text{Approximate cost of forgoing a cash discount (\%)} = \frac{\text{Discount percent}}{100 - \text{Discount percent}} = \frac{360 \text{ days}}{\text{Total days net credit is available} - \text{Discount period}}$$

- Bank loans are an important source of short-term credit. Interest on bank loans might be quoted as simple interest, discount interest, or add-on interest. The effective rate on a discount or add-on loan always exceeds the quoted simple rate. In general, the effective cost of a bank loan can be computed as follows.

$$\text{Effective annual rate} = (1 + \text{Rate per period})^m - 1.0$$

where m is the number of borrowing (compounding) periods in one year (for example, if the loan is for one month, m equals 12). The rate per period can be computed using the following equation.

$$\text{Interest rate per period (cost)} = \frac{\text{Dollar cost of borrowing}}{\text{Amount of usable funds}}$$

- When a bank loan is approved, a promissory note is signed. It specifies (1) the amount borrowed, (2) the percentage interest rate, (3) the repayment schedule, (4) the collateral, and (5) any other conditions to which the parties have agreed.
- Banks sometimes require borrowers to maintain compensating balances, which are deposit requirements set at between 10 percent and 20 percent of the loan amount. Compensating balances generally increase the effective rate of interest on bank loans.
- A line of credit is an understanding between the bank and the borrower indicating the maximum amount of credit the bank will extend to the borrower.
- A revolving credit agreement is a formal, guaranteed line of credit that involves a commitment fee.
- Commercial paper is unsecured short-term debt issued by a large, financially strong corporation. Although the cost of commercial paper is lower than the cost of bank loans, commercial paper's maturity is limited to 270 days, and it can be used only by large firms with exceptionally strong credit ratings.
- Sometimes a borrower will find it necessary to borrow on a secured basis, in which case the borrower pledges assets such as real estate, securities, equipment, inventories, or accounts receivable as collateral for the loan.

- Accounts receivable financing involves either pledging or factoring receivables. Under a pledging arrangement, the lender not only gets a claim against the receivables, but also has recourse to the borrower. Factoring involves the purchase of accounts receivable by the lender, generally without recourse to the borrower.
- There are three primary methods of inventory financing. An inventory blanket lien gives the lender a lien against all of the borrower's inventories. A trust receipt is an instrument that acknowledges that goods are held in trust for the lender. Warehouse receipt financing is an arrangement under which the lender employs a third party to exercise control over the borrower's inventory and to act as the lender's agent.
- Pledging receivables is especially sensible for a small firm that has customers with better credit histories than the firm itself, as this allows the firm to take advantage of the strength of its customer base.
- For small firms with limited managerial resources and limited experience in monitoring and collecting credit accounts, factoring might be more than worth the cost. The small firm's comparative advantage is its ability to deliver a product; the factor's advantage is its ability to provide financial and credit services.

Short-Term Financing Alternatives

Short-term financing alternatives differ from spontaneous financing provided through trade credit and accruals. Financing sources are discretionary, the use of which must be explicitly sought.

The financial strategy should focus on the maturity decision. The question of managing the maturity structure of the firm's financing sources is difficult, but three different strategies to mitigate this difficulty include the aggressive strategy, the conservative strategy, and the moderate strategy.

Effective rate of interest can be calculated on two popular forms of short-term financing: a bank credit line and commercial paper. Commercial paper is a good example of non-bank financing and the inclusion of dealer spreads and commitment fees. The bank credit line financing source includes factors, such as compensating balances, that are not a part of commercial paper issues.

Short-term financing is an important component of maintaining the firm's liquidity. The financial manager should forecast the firm's cash position on a regular basis and then have in place contingency financing sources to handle forecasted as well as unexpected cash needs. Effective financing of the firm's short-term financing position impacts the firm's liquidity position and so ultimately affects its value.

Section 715. Managing Long-Term Financing

Summaries and Conclusions

Common Stock

- Stockholders' equity consists of the firm's common stock, paid-in capital (funds received in excess of the par value), and retained earnings (earnings not paid out as dividends).
- Book value per share is equal to stockholders' equity divided by the number of shares of stock outstanding. A stock's book value often is different from its par value and its market value.
- A proxy is a document that gives one person the power to act for another person, typically the power to vote shares of common stock. A proxy fight occurs when an outside group solicits stockholders' proxies in order to vote a new management team into office.
- Stockholders often have the right to purchase any additional shares sold by the firm. This right, called the *preemptive right*, protects the control of present stockholders and prevents dilution of the value of their stock.
- The major advantages of common stock financing are as follows: (1) there is no obligation to make fixed payments, (2) common stock never matures, (3) the use of common stock increases the creditworthiness of the firm, and (4) stock often can be sold on better terms than debt.
- The major disadvantages of common stock financing are (1) it extends voting privileges to new stockholders, (2) new stockholders share in the firm's profits, (3) the costs of stock financing are high, (4) using stock can raise the firm's cost of capital, and (5) dividends paid on common stock are not tax deductible.
- A closely held corporation is one that is owned by a few individuals who typically are associated with the firm's management. A publicly owned corporation is one that is owned by a relatively large number of individuals who are not actively involved in its management.

- Going public facilitates stockholder diversification, increases liquidity of the firm's stock, makes it easier for the firm to raise capital, and establishes a value for the firm. However, reporting costs are high, operating data must be disclosed, and public ownership might make it harder for management to maintain control of the firm.
- Security markets in the United States are regulated by the Securities and Exchange Commission (SEC).
- Financial instruments available in the international markets are similar to those issued in the United States. But most Americans invest in foreign companies through American Depository Receipts (ADRs), which are certificates that represent foreign stocks held in trust, generally by a bank, in the country where the company is located.
- Stock traded internationally generally is referred to as either *Euro stock* or *Yankee Stock*. Euro stock is traded in countries other than the country where the company is located, except the United States, where such stock is called *Yankee stock*.
- An investment banker assists in the issuing of securities by helping the firm determine the size of the issue and the type of securities to be used, by establishing the selling price, by selling the issue, and, in some cases, by maintaining an after-market for the stock.
- A small firm's stock sold in an initial public offering (IPO) often increases in price immediately after issue, with the largest price increases being associated with issues where uncertainties are greatest.

Long-Term Debt

- Term loans and bonds are long-term debt contracts under which a borrower agrees to make a series of interest and principal payments on specific dates to the lender. A term loan is generally sold to one lender (or a few), while a bond typically is offered to the public and sold to many different investors.
- There are many different types of bonds. They include mortgage bonds, debentures, convertibles, bonds with warrants, income bonds, putable bonds, and purchasing power (indexed) bonds. The return required on each type of bond is determined by the bond's riskiness.
- A bond's indenture is a legal document that spells out the rights of the bondholders and of the issuing corporation. A trustee is assigned to make sure that the terms of the indenture are carried out.
- A call provision gives the issuing corporation the right to redeem the bonds prior to maturity under specified terms, usually at a price greater than the maturity value (the difference is a call premium). A firm typically will call a bond and refund it if interest rates fall substantially.
- A sinking fund is a provision that requires the corporation to retire a portion of the bond issue each year. The purpose of the sinking fund is to provide for the orderly retirement of the issue.
- Some innovations in long-term financing that have occurred in the past few decades include zero coupon bonds, which pay no annual interest but are issued at a discount; floating rate debt, whose interest payments fluctuate with changes in the general level of interest rates; and junk bonds, which are high-risk, high-yield instruments issued by firms that use a great deal of financial leverage.
- Bonds are assigned ratings that reflect the probability of their going into default. The higher a bond's rating, the less risky it is considered, so the lower its interest rate.
- A firm's long-term financing decisions are influenced by its target capital structure, the maturity of its assets, current and forecasted interest rate levels, the firm's current and forecasted financial condition, restrictions in its existing debt contracts, and the suitability of its assets for use as collateral.
- Bankruptcy is an important consideration both to companies that issue debt and to investors, for it has a profound effect on all parties. Refunding, or paying off high-interest rate debt with new, lower-cost debt, also is an important consideration, because many firms that issued long-term debt in the early 1980s at rates of 12 percent or more now have an opportunity to refund this debt at a cost of about 9 percent or less.
- The Eurodebt market includes any debt sold in a country other than the one in whose currency the debt is denominated. Examples of Eurodebt are Eurobonds, Eurocredits, Euro-commercial paper, and Euronotes.

Alternative Financing Arrangements

- Alternative forms of long-term financing include (1) preferred stock, (2) leasing, and (3) option securities.
- Preferred stock is a hybrid security having some characteristics of debt and some of equity. Equity holders view preferred stock as being similar to debt because it has a claim on the firm's earnings ahead of the claim of the

common stockholders. Bondholders, however, view preferred stock as equity because debtholders have a prior claim on the firm's income and assets.
- The primary advantages of preferred stock to the issuer are (1) preferred dividends are limited, and (2) failure to pay them will not bankrupt the firm. The primary disadvantage to the issuer is that the cost of preferred stock is higher than that of debt because preferred dividend payments are not tax deductible.
- To the investor, preferred stock offers the advantage of more dependable income than common stock, and to a corporate investor, 70 percent of such dividends are not taxable. The principal disadvantages to the investor are that the returns are limited and the investor has no legally enforceable right to a dividend.
- Leasing is a means of obtaining the use of an asset without purchasing that asset. The three most important forms of leasing are (1) sale-and-leaseback arrangements, under which a firm sells an asset to another party and leases the asset back for a specified period under specific terms; (2) operating leases, under which the lessor both maintains and finances the asset; and (3) financial leases, under which the asset is fully amortized over the life of the lease, the lessor does not normally provide maintenance, and the lease is not cancelable.
- The decision to lease or buy an asset is made by comparing the financing costs of the two alternatives and choosing the financing method with the lower cost. All cash flows should be discounted at the after-tax cost of debt because lease analysis cash flows are relatively certain and are on an after-tax basis.
- An option is a contract that gives its holder the right to buy (or sell) an asset at some predetermined price within a specified period of time. Options features are used by firms to "sweeten" debt offerings.
- A warrant is an option issued by a firm that gives the holder the right to purchase a stated number of shares of stock at a specified price within a given period. A warrant will be exercised if it is about to expire and the stock price is above the exercise price.
- A convertible security is a bond or preferred stock that can be exchanged for common stock. When conversion occurs, debt or preferred stock is replaced with common stock, but no money changes hands. Conversion price is par value of a bond divided by the conversion ratio.
- The conversion of bonds or preferred stock by their holders does not provide additional funds to the company, but it does result in a lower debt ratio. The exercise of warrants does provide additional funds, which strengthens the firm's equity position, but it still leaves the debt or preferred stock on the balance sheet. Thus, low interest rate debt remains outstanding when warrants are exercised, but the firm loses this advantage when convertibles are converted.
- A leveraged buyout (LBO) is a transaction in which a firm's publicly owned stock is bought up in a mostly debt-financed tender offer, and a privately owned, highly leveraged firm results. Often, the firm's own management initiates the LBO.
- The reasons mergers take place include (1) synergy, (2) tax considerations, (3) low asset values, (4) diversification, and (5) ownership control. Mergers can be classified as horizontal, vertical, congeneric, or conglomerate.
- For the small firm, leasing offers three advantages: (1) cash is conserved, (2) managers' time is freed for other tasks, and (3) financing often can be obtained quickly and at a relatively low cost.

Valuation of Financial Assets

Corporate decisions should be analyzed in terms of how alternative courses of action are likely to affect the value of a firm. However, it is necessary to know how bond and stock prices are established before attempting to measure how a given decision will affect a specific firm's value.

- The value of any asset can be found by computing the present value of the cash flows the asset is expected to generate during its life.
- A bond is a long-term promissory note issued by a business or governmental unit. The firm receives the selling price of the bond in exchange for promising to make interest payments and to repay the principal on a specified future date.
- The value of a bond is found as the present value of an annuity (the interest payments) plus the present value of a lump sum (the principal). The bond is evaluated at the appropriate periodic interest rate over the number of periods for which interest payments are made.

- The equation used to find the value of a bond follows.

$$V_d = \sum_{t=1}^{N \times m} \frac{INT}{\left(1 + \frac{k_d}{m}\right)^t} + \frac{M}{\left(1 + \frac{k_d}{m}\right)^{N \times m}}$$

$$= INT\left(PVIFA_{\frac{k_d}{m}, N \times m}\right) + M\left(PVIF_{\frac{k_d}{m}, N \times m}\right)$$

  where INT is the dollar interest received each period, N represents the years to maturity, k_d is the required return on similar investments, and m equals the number of times interest is paid during the year.

- The return earned on a bond held to maturity is defined as the bond's yield to maturity (YTM).
- The longer the maturity of a bond, the more its price will change in response to a given change in interest rates; this is called *interest rate price risk*. Bonds with short maturities, however, expose the investor to high interest rate reinvestment risk, which is the risk that income will differ from what is expected because cash flows received from bonds will have to be reinvested at different interest rates.
- The value of a share of stock is calculated as the present value of the stream of dividends it is expected to provide in the future.
- A zero-growth stock is one whose future dividends are not expected to grow at all, while a nonconstant growth stock is one whose earnings and dividends are expected to grow at a rate different from the economy as a whole over some specified time period.
- Most preferred stocks are perpetuities, thus zero growth stocks, and the value of a share of such stocks is found as the dividend divided by the required rate of return:

$$P_0 = D/k_s$$

- The equation used to find the value of a constant, or normal, growth stock follows.

$$\hat{P}_0 = \hat{D}_1/(k_s - g).$$

- The expected total rate of return from a stock consists of an expected dividend yield plus an expected capital gains yield. For a constant growth firm, both the expected dividend yield and the expected capital gains yield are constant.
- The equation for $\hat{k}_s$, the expected rate of return on a constant growth stock, can be expressed as follows: $\hat{k}_s = \hat{D}_1/P_0 + g$.
- To find the present value of a nonconstant growth stock, (1) find the dividends expected during the nonconstant growth period; (2) find the price of the stock at the end of the nonconstant growth period; (3) discount the dividends and the projected price back to the present; and (4) sum these PVs to find the current expected value of the stock, $\hat{P}_0$.
- The Efficient Markets Hypothesis (EMH) holds that (1) stocks are always in equilibrium, and (2) it is impossible for an investor to consistently "beat the market." Therefore, according to the EMH, stocks always are fairly valued ($\hat{P}_0 = P_0$), the required return on a stock is equal to its expected return ($k_s = \hat{k}_s$), and all stocks' expected returns plot on the SML.
- Differences can and do exist between expected and actual returns in the stock and bond markets—only for short-term, risk-free assets are expected and actual (or realized) returns equal.
- Like a financial asset, the value of a real asset is computed as the present value of the cash flows the asset is expected to provide in the future.
- Determining the value of the stock of a small firm is the same as for larger companies with nonconstant growth, except small firms often do not pay dividends until later in their lives, which might be many years from the current period.

Section 720. Financial Forecasting, Planning, and Control

Summaries and Conclusions

Financial Planning and Control

- Corporations project their financial statements and determine their capital requirements. The business manager needs to evaluate the effects of changes in forecasts on the income of the firm.
- Financial planning involves making projections of sales, income, and assets based on alternative production and marketing strategies and then deciding how to meet the forecasted financial requirements.
- Financial control deals with the feedback and adjustment process that is required (1) to ensure that plans are followed or (2) to modify existing plans in response to changes in the operating environment.
- Management establishes a target balance sheet on the basis of ratio analysis.
- The projected, or pro forma, balance sheet method is used to forecast financial requirements.
- A firm can determine the amount of additional funds needed (AFN) by estimating the amount of new assets necessary to support the forecasted level of sales and then subtracting from that amount the spontaneous funds that will be generated from operations. The firm can then plan to raise the AFN through bank borrowing, by issuing securities, stocks or bonds or both.
- Operating break-even analysis is a method of determining the point at which sales will just cover operating costs, and it shows the magnitude of the firm's operating profits or losses if sales exceed or fall below that point.
- The operating break-even point is the sales volume at which total operating costs equal total revenues and operating income (earnings before interest and taxes, EBIT) equals zero. The equation used to compute the operating break-even point follows.

$$Q_{OpBe} = \frac{F}{P - V} = \frac{F}{\text{Contribution margin}}$$

where F is total fixed cost, V is variable cost/unit, P is selling price /unit.

- Operating leverage is a measure of the extent to which fixed costs are used in a firm's operations. A firm with a high percentage of fixed costs is said to have a high degree of operating leverage (DOL).
- The DOL shows how a change in sales will affect operating income. Whereas breakeven analysis emphasizes the volume of sales the firm needs to be profitable, the DOL measures how sensitive the firm's profits are to changes in the volume of sales. The equation used to calculate the DOL follows.

$$DOL_Q = \frac{Q(P - V)}{Q(P - V) - F}$$

where Q is quantity, F is total fixed cost, V is variable cost/unit, P is selling price /unit.

- Financial break-even analysis is a method of determining the point at which EBIT will just cover financing costs, and it shows the magnitude of the firm's earnings per share (EPS) if EBIT exceeds or falls below that point.
- The financial break-even point is the level of EBIT that produces EPS equal to zero. The equation used to compute the financial break-even point follows.

$$EBIT_{FinBE} = I + \frac{D_{ps}}{(1 - T)}$$

- Financial leverage is a measure of the extent to which fixed financial costs exist in a firm's operations. A firm with a high percentage of fixed financial costs is said to have a high degree of financial leverage (DFL).

- The DFL shows how a change in EBIT will affect EPS. The equation used to calculate the DFL follows.

$$\text{DFL} = \frac{\text{EBIT}}{\text{EBIT} - I} = \frac{\text{EBIT}}{\text{EBIT} - [\text{Financial BEP}]}$$

- Total (combined) leverage is a measure of the extent to which total fixed costs (operating and financial) exist in a firm's operations. A firm with a high percentage of total fixed costs is said to have a high degree of total leverage.
- The DTL shows how a change in sales will affect EPS. DTL = DOL × DFL. The equation used to calculate the DTL follows.

$$\text{DTL} = \frac{S - VC}{\text{EBIT} - I} = \frac{Q(P - V)}{Q(P - V) - F - I}$$

where S is selling price/unit, Q is quantity sold, VC is variable cost/unit, F is total fixed cost, I is interest cost.
- The forecasting and control functions require continuous attention to ensure that the goals of the firm are being met. Forecasting and control provide the foresight needed to implement adjustments to future operations so the firm moves in the intended direction and wealth maximization is achieved.

Cash Forecasting

Cash forecasts add value primarily by enabling the company to borrow less or extend investment maturities, resulting in higher investment yields. Even the existence of real-time order, shipment, or payment data does not eliminate the need to forecast. Two major cash forecasting intervals, monthly and daily, are available.

Section 725. Cost of Capital, Capital Structure, and Dividend Policy

Summaries and Conclusions

The Cost of Capital

- The cost of capital to be used in capital budgeting decisions is the weighted average of the various types of capital the firm uses, typically debt, preferred stock, and common equity.
- The component cost of debt is the after-tax cost of new debt. It is found by multiplying the cost of new debt by $(1 - T)$, where T is the firm's marginal tax rate: $k_{dT} = k_d(1 - T)$.
- The component cost of preferred stock is calculated as the preferred dividend divided by the net issuing price, where the net issuing price is the price the firm receives after deducting flotation costs: $k_{ps} = D_{ps}/[P(1 - F)] = D_{ps}/NP$.
- The cost of common equity is the cost of retained earnings as long as the firm has retained earnings, but the cost of equity becomes the cost of new common stock once the firm has exhausted its retained earnings.
- The cost of retained earnings is the rate of return required by stockholders on the firm's common stock, and it can be estimated using one of three methods: (1) the capital asset pricing method (CAPM) approach, (2) the bond-yield-plus-risk-premium approach, and (3) the dividend-yield-plus-growth-rate, or DCF, approach.
- To use the CAPM approach, (1) estimate the firm's beta, (2) multiply this beta by the market risk premium to determine the firm's risk premium, and (3) add the firm's risk premium to the risk-free rate to obtain the firm's cost of retained earnings:

$$k_s = k_{RF} + (k_M - k_{RF})\beta_s.$$

- The bond-yield-plus-risk-premium approach calls for adding a risk premium of from 3 to 5 percentage points to the firm's interest rate on long-term debt:

$$k_s = k_d + RP.$$

- To use the discounted cash flow (DCF) approach when constant growth exists, add the firm's expected growth rate to its expected dividend yield:

$$k_s = \hat{D}_1/P_0 + g$$

- The cost of new common equity is higher than the cost of retained earnings because the firm incurs flotation expenses to sell stock. To find the cost of new common equity, the stock price is first reduced by the flotation expense, then the dividend yield is calculated on the basis of the price the firm actually will receive, and finally the expected growth rate is added to this adjusted dividend yield:

$$k_e = \hat{D}_1/[P_0(1 - F)] + g$$

- Each firm has an optimal capital structure, defined as that mix of debt, preferred stock, and common equity that minimizes its weighted average cost of capital (WACC):

$$WACC = w_d k_{dT} + w_{ps} k_{ps} + w_e(k_s \text{ or } k_e)$$

- The marginal cost of capital (MCC) is defined as the cost of the last dollar of new capital that the firm raises. The MCC increases as the firm raises more and more capital during a given period. A graph of the MCC plotted against dollars raised is the MCC schedule.
- A break point occurs in the MCC schedule each time the cost of one of the capital components increases.
- The investment opportunity schedule (IOS) is a graph of the firm's investment opportunities, ranked in order of their internal rates of return (IRR).
- The MCC schedule is combined with the IOS schedule, and the intersection defines the corporate cost of capital, which is used to evaluate average-risk capital budgeting projects.
- Equity cost estimation techniques have serious limitations when applied to small firms, thus increasing the need for the small-business manager to use judgment.
- The average flotation cost for small firms is much greater than for large firms. As a result, a small firm would have to earn considerably more on the same project than a large firm. Also, the capital market demands higher returns on stocks of small firms than on otherwise similar stocks of large firms. This is called the *small-firm effect*.

Capital Structure

- A firm's optimal capital structure is that mix of debt and equity that maximizes the price of the firm's stock. At any point in time, the firm's management has a specific target capital structure in mind, presumably the optimal one, although this target might change over time.
- Several factors influence a firm's capital structure decisions. These factors include the firm's (1) business risk, (2) tax position, (3) need for financial flexibility, and (4) managerial conservatism or aggressiveness toward using debt.
- Business risk is the uncertainty associated with projections of a firm's future returns on equity. A firm will tend to have low business risk if the demand for its products is stable, if the prices of its inputs and products remain relatively constant, if it can adjust its prices freely when costs increase, and if a high percentage of its costs are variable and hence decrease as its output and sales decrease. Other things the same, the lower a firm's business risk, the higher its optimal debt/assets ratio.
- Financial leverage is the extent to which fixed-income securities (debt and preferred stock) are used in a firm's capital structure. Financial risk is the added risk to stockholders that results from financial leverage.
- The EPS indifference point is the level of sales at which EPS will be the same whether the firm uses debt or common stock financing. Equity financing will be better if the firm's sales end up below the EPS indifference point, whereas debt financing will be better at higher sales levels.
- The degree of operating leverage (DOL) shows how changes in sales affect operating income, whereas the degree of financial leverage (DFL) shows how changes in operating income affect earnings per share. The degree of total leverage (DTL) shows the percentage change in EPS resulting from a given percentage change in sales: DTL = DOL × DFL.

- Modigliani and Miller (MM) developed a trade off theory of capital structure, where debt is useful because interest is tax deductible, but debt brings with it costs associated with actual or potential bankruptcy. Under MM's theory, the optimal capital structure strikes a balance between the tax benefits of debt and the costs associated with bankruptcy.
- An alternative (or, really, complementary) theory of capital structure relates to the signals given to investors by a firm's decision to use debt or stock to raise new capital. The use of stock is a negative signal, while using debt is a positive or at least a neutral signal. Therefore, companies try to maintain a reserve borrowing capacity, and this means using less debt in "normal" times than the MM trade off theory would suggest.
- Capital structures vary widely around the world. It seems the primary reason for such variation is the risk associated with firms' operations and financing arrangements.

Although it is theoretically possible to determine the optimal capital structure, as a practical matter we cannot estimate this structure with precision. Accordingly, financial executives generally treat the optimal capital structure as a range—for example, 40 to 50 percent debt—rather than as a precise point, such as 45 percent. The above concepts can help managers understand the factors they should consider when they set the target capital structure ranges for their firms.

Dividend Policy

- Dividend policy involves the decision to pay out earnings versus retaining them for reinvestment in the firm, and dividend policy decisions can have either favorable or unfavorable effects on the price of a firm's stock.
- The optimal dividend policy is that policy that strikes the exact balance between current dividends and future growth that maximizes the price of the firm's stock.
- Miller and Modigliani (MM) developed the dividend irrelevance theory, which holds that a firm's dividend policy has no effect either on the value of its stock or on its cost of capital.
- Those who believe in dividend relevance suggest that a particular dividend policy might be preferred because dividends are considered less risky than potential capital gains, taxes must be paid on dividends received in the current period, while taxes on capital gains can be deferred until the stock is sold, and so on.
- Because empirical tests of the theories have been inconclusive, academicians simply cannot tell corporate managers precisely how a change in dividend policy will affect stock prices and capital costs. Thus, actually determining the optimal dividend policy is often a matter of judgment.
- Dividend policy should reflect the existence of the information content of dividends (signaling), the clientele effect, and the free cash flow effect. The information content, or signaling, hypothesis states that investors regard dividend changes as a signal of management's forecast of future earnings. According to the clientele effect, a firm will attract investors who like the firm's dividend policy. And the free cash flow effect suggests that firms with few capital budgeting opportunities and great amounts of cash should have higher dividend payout ratios if the value maximization goal is pursued.
- In practice, most firms try to follow a policy of paying a stable, predictable dividend. This policy provides investors with a stable, dependable income, and it also gives investors information about management's expectations for earnings growth through signaling effects.
- Other dividend policies used include (1) the residual dividend policy, in which dividends are paid out of earnings left over after the capital budget has been financed; (2) the constant payout ratio policy, in which a constant percentage of earnings is targeted to be paid out; and (3) the low-regular-dividend-plus-extras policy, in which the firm pays a constant, low dividend that can be maintained even in bad years and then pays an extra dividend in good years.
- A dividend reinvestment plan (DRIP) allows stockholders to have the company automatically use their dividends to purchase additional shares of the firm's stock. DRIPs are popular with investors who do not need current income because the plans allow stockholders to acquire additional shares without incurring normal brokerage fees.
- Other factors, such as legal constraints, investment opportunities, availability and cost of funds from other sources, and taxes, are considered by managers when they establish dividend policies.
- A stock split is an action taken by a firm to increase the number of shares outstanding. Normally, splits reduce the price per share in proportion to the increase in shares because splits merely divide the pie into smaller slices. A stock dividend is a dividend paid in additional shares of stock rather than in cash. Both stock dividends and splits are used to keep stock prices within an "optimal," or psychological, range.

- Dividend policies differ substantially among companies in different countries. All else equal, firms pay out greater relative amounts of earnings as dividends in countries that have measures that protect the rights of minority stockholders.
- Small, rapidly growing firms generally need to retain all their earnings and to obtain additional capital from outside sources to support growth. As the firm matures, its growth will slow down, and its need for funds will diminish. The market recognizes that new, profitable firms often grow so fast that they simply must issue common stock and that such issues indicate that the firm's managers anticipate extraordinarily good investment opportunities.

Section 735. Capital Budgeting

Summaries and Conclusions

Capital Budgeting Techniques

- Capital budgeting is the process of analyzing potential noncurrent and fixed asset investments. Capital budgeting decisions are probably the most important ones financial managers must make.
- The traditional payback period is the expected number of years required to recover a project's cost. The traditional payback method ignores cash flows beyond the payback period, and it does not consider the time value of money. The payback does, however, indicate a project's risk and liquidity because it shows how long the invested capital will be "at risk." It is used as a preliminary screening method.
- The discounted payback method is similar to the traditional payback method except that it discounts cash flows at the project's required rate of return. Like the traditional payback, it ignores cash flows beyond the discounted payback period.
- The net present value (NPV) method discounts all cash flows at the project's required rate of return and then sums those cash flows. The project is acceptable if this sum, called the *NPV*, is positive. The NPV method expresses results in absolute terms.
- The accounting rate of return (ARR) method is based on accounting data and is computed as the average annual profits after taxes divided by the initial cash outlay in the project. Drawbacks of the ARR method are that it does not consider the project's cash flows and that it ignores the time value of money.
- The profitability index (PI) method is a benefit/cost ratio and is computed as the present value of future net cash flows divided by the initial cash outlay in the project. As long as the PI is 1.00 or greater, the project is acceptable. For any given project, the NPV method and the PI method give the same accept-reject answer. The PI method expresses the results in relative terms.
- The internal rate of return (IRR) is defined as the discount rate that forces a project's NPV to equal zero. The project is acceptable if the IRR is greater than the project's required rate of return or hurdle rate.
- The NPV and IRR methods make the same accept/reject decisions for independent projects, but if projects are mutually exclusive, then ranking conflicts can arise. If conflicts arise, the NPV method generally should be used. The NPV and IRR methods are both superior to the payback, but NPV is generally the single best measure of a project's profitability because it incorporates the discounted cash flow technique (DCF).
- The NPV method assumes that cash flows can be reinvested at the firm's required rate of return, while the IRR method assumes reinvestment at the project's IRR. Because reinvestment at the required rate of return generally is a better (closer to the truth) assumption, the NPV is superior to the IRR.
- Sophisticated managers consider several of the project evaluation measures because different measures provide different types of information.
- The post-audit is a key element of capital budgeting. By comparing actual results with predicted results, and then determining why differences occurred, decision makers can improve both their operations and their forecasts of projects' outcomes.

- Small firms tend to use the payback method rather than a "sophisticated" method. This might be a rational decision because (1) the cost of a DCF analysis might outweigh the benefits for the project being considered, (2) the firm's required rate of return cannot be estimated accurately, or (3) the small business owner might be considering nonmonetary goals.

Project Cash Flows and Risks

- The most important, but also the most difficult, step in analyzing a capital budgeting project is estimating the incremental after-tax cash flows the project will produce.
- Net cash flows consist of net income plus depreciation. In determining incremental cash flows, opportunity costs (the cash flow forgone by using an asset) must be included, but sunk costs (cash outlays that have been made and that cannot be recouped) should not be included. Any externalities (effects of a project on other parts of the firm) should also be reflected in the analysis. In addition, inflation effects must be considered in project analysis. The best procedure is to build inflation directly into the cash flow estimates.
- Capital projects often require an additional investment in net working capital (NWC). An increase in NWC must be included in the Year 0 initial cash outlay and then shown as a cash inflow in the project's final (terminal) year.
- Replacement analysis is slightly different from that for expansion projects because the cash flows from the old asset must be considered in replacement decisions.
- A project's stand-alone risk is the risk the project would have if it were the firm's only asset and if the firm's stockholders held only that one stock. Stand-alone risk is measured by the variability of the asset's expected returns, and it is often used as a proxy for both beta and corporate risk because (1) beta and corporate risks are difficult to measure, and (2) the three types of risk are usually highly correlated.
- Within-firm, or corporate, risk reflects the effects of a project on the firm's risk, and it is measured by the project's effect on the firm's earnings variability. Stockholder diversification is not taken into account.
- Beta risk reflects the effects of a project on the risks borne by stockholders, assuming stockholders hold diversified portfolios. In theory, beta risk should be the most relevant type of risk.
- Corporate risk is important because it influences the firm's ability to use low-cost debt, to maintain smooth operations over time, and to avoid crises that might consume management's energy and disrupt employees, customers, suppliers, and the community.
- Sensitivity analysis is a technique that shows how much an output variable such as NPV will change in response to a given change in an input variable such as sales, other things held constant.
- Scenario analysis is a risk analysis technique in which the best- and worst-case NPVs are compared with the project's expected NPV. Base-case is in between the other two cases.
- Monte Carlo simulation is a risk-analysis technique in which a computer is used to simulate probable future events and thus to estimate the profitability distribution and riskiness of a project.
- The pure play method can be used to estimate betas for large projects or for divisions.
- The risk-adjusted discount rate is the rate used to evaluate a particular project. The discount rate is increased for projects that are riskier than the firm's average project, but is decreased for less risky projects.
- Capital rationing occurs when management places a constraint on the size of the firm's capital budget during a particular period. This rationing can be applied to a division, a project, or to the whole company.
- Investments in international capital projects expose the investing firm to exchange rate risk and political risk. The relevant cash flows in international capital budgeting are the dollar cash flows that can be turned over to the parent company.

Both the measurement of risk and its incorporation into capital budgeting involve judgment. It is possible to use a quantitative technique such as simulation as an aid to judgment, but in the final analysis the assessment of risk in capital budgeting is a subjective process.

Sections 745 and 775. Financial Markets, Instruments, and Institutions, and Economics and Finance

Summaries and Conclusions

- There are many different types of financial markets. Each market serves a different region or deals with a different type of security.
- Transfers of capital between borrowers and savers take place by (1) direct transfers of money and securities; (2) transfers through investment banking houses, which act as middlemen; and (3) transfers through financial intermediaries, which create new securities.
- The stock market is an especially important market because this is where stock prices (which are used to "grade" managers' performances) are established.
- There are two basic types of stock markets: the organized exchanges and the over-the-counter market.
- Capital is allocated through the price system—a price must be paid to "rent" money. Lenders charge interest on funds they lend, while equity investors receive dividends and capital gains in return for letting firms use their money.
- Four fundamental factors affect the cost of money: (1) production opportunities, (2) time preferences for consumption, (3) risk, and (4) inflation.
- The risk-free rate of interest, k_{RF}, is defined as the real risk-free rate, k^*, plus an inflation premium (IP): $k_{RF} = k^* + IP$.
- The nominal (or quoted) interest rate on a debt security, k, is composed of the real risk-free rate, k^*, plus premiums that reflect inflation (IP), default risk (DRP), liquidity (LP), and maturity risk (MRP):

$$k = k^* + IP + DRP + LP + MRP.$$

- If the real risk-free rate of interest and the various premiums were constant over time, interest rates in the economy would be stable. However, both the real rate and the premiums—especially the premium for expected inflation—do change over time, causing market interest rates to change. Also, Federal Reserve intervention to increase or decrease the money supply (as well as international currency flows) leads to fluctuations in interest rates.
- The relationship between the yields on securities and the securities' maturities is the term structure of interest rates, and the yield curve is a graph of this relationship.
- The yield curve is normally upward sloping—this is called a normal yield curve—but the curve can slope downward (an inverted yield curve) if the demand for short-term funds is relatively strong or if the rate of inflation is expected to decline.
- Interest rate levels have a profound effect on stock prices. Higher interest rates (1) slow down the economy, (2) increase interest expenses and thus lower corporate profits, and (3) cause investors to sell stocks and transfer funds to the bond market. Each of these factors tends to depress stock prices.
- The value of any asset depends on the stream of after-tax cash flows it produces. Tax rates and other aspects of our tax system are changed by U.S. Congress every year or so.
- In the United States, income tax rates are progressive—the higher one's income, the larger the percentage paid in taxes, up to a point.
- Assets such as stocks, bonds, and real estate are defined as capital assets. If a capital asset is sold for more than the purchase price, the profit is called a capital gain. If the capital asset is sold for a loss, it is called a capital loss.
- Interest income received by a corporation is taxed as ordinary income; however, 70 percent of the dividends received by one corporation from another is excluded from taxable income.
- Because interest paid by a corporation is a deductible expense while dividends are not, our tax system favors debt financing over equity financing.

- Ordinary corporate operating losses can be carried back to each of the preceding two years and carried over for the next twenty years to offset taxable income in those years.
- S corporations are small businesses that have the limited-liability benefits of the corporate form of organization yet obtain the benefits of being taxed as a partnership or a proprietorship.

Section 755. Financial Risk Management

Summaries and Conclusions

Financial Risk

- Risk should be measured in financial analysis because risk affects rates of return.
- Risk can be defined as the chance that some event other than expected will occur.
- Most rational investors hold portfolios of stocks, and they are more concerned with the risks of their portfolios than with the risks of individual stocks.
- The expected return on an investment is the mean value of its probability distribution of possible returns.
- The higher the probability that the actual return will be significantly different from the expected return, the greater the risk associated with owning an asset.
- The average investor is risk averse, which means that he or she must be compensated for holding risky securities; therefore, riskier securities must have higher expected returns than less risky securities.
- A stock's risk consists of (1) company-specific risk, which can be eliminated by diversification; plus (2) market, or beta, risk, which cannot be eliminated by diversification.
- The relevant risk of an individual security is its contribution to the riskiness of a well-diversified portfolio, which is the security's market risk. Because market risk cannot be eliminated by diversification, investors must be compensated for it.
- A stock's beta coefficient, β, is a measure of the stock's market risk. Beta measures the extent to which the stock's returns move with the market.
- A high-beta stock is more volatile than an average stock, while a low-beta stock is less volatile than an average stock. An average stock has $\beta = 1.0$.
- The beta of a portfolio is a weighted average of the betas of the individual securities in the portfolio.
- The Security Market Line (SML) equation shows the relationship between a security's risk and its required rate of return. The return required for any security j is equal to the risk-free rate plus the market risk premium times the security's beta: $k_j = k_{RF} + (k_M - k_{RF})\beta_j$.
- Even though the expected rate of return on a stock generally is equal to its required return, a number of things can happen to cause the required rate of return to change: (1) the risk-free rate can change because of changes in anticipated inflation, (2) a stock's beta can change, or (3) investors' aversion to risk can change.
- Security's rate of return affects its value. A firm's management can influence a stock's riskiness and hence its price.

Country's Risk

- The factors used by MNCs to measure a country's political risk include attitude of consumers toward purchasing locally produced goods, the host government's actions toward the MNC, the blockage of fund transfers, currency inconvertibility, war, bureaucracy, and corruption.
- These factors can increase the costs of international business.
- The factors used by MNCs to measure a country's financial risk are the country's interest rates, exchange rates, and inflation rates.
- The techniques typically used by MNCs to measure the country risk are the checklist approach, the Delphi technique, quantitative analysis, and inspection visits. Because no one technique covers all aspects of country risk, a combination of these techniques is commonly used. The measurement of country risk is essentially a weighted average of the political or financial factors that are perceived to comprise country risk. Each MNC has its own view as to the weights that should be assigned to each factor. Thus, the overall rating for a country may vary among MNCs.

- Once country risk is measured, it can be incorporated into a capital budgeting analysis by adjustment of the discount rate. The adjustment is somewhat arbitrary, however, and may lead to improper decision making. An alternative method of incorporating country risk analysis into capital budgeting is to explicitly account for each factor that affects country risk. For each possible form of risk, the MNC can recalculate the foreign project's net present value under the condition that the event (such as blocked funds, increased taxes, and so forth) occurs.

Section 770. Quantitative Techniques and Finance

Summaries and Conclusions

Financial decisions often involve situations in which someone pays money at one point in time and receives money at some other time. Dollars that are paid or received at two different points in time are different, and this difference is recognized and accounted for by time value of money (TVM) analysis.

- Compounding is the process of determining the future value (FV) of a cash flow or a series of cash flows. The compounded amount, or future value, is equal to the beginning amount plus the interest earned.

$$\text{Future value (single payment): } FV_n = PV(1 + i)^n = PV(FVIF_{i,n})$$

Example: *$924.56 compounded for two years at 4 percent:*
$$FV_2 = \$924.56(1.04)^2 = \$1,000$$

- Discounting is the process of finding the present value (PV) of a future cash flow or a series of cash flows; discounting is the reciprocal (inverse) of compounding.

$$\text{Present value (single payment): } PV = \frac{FV}{(1 + i)^n} = FV_n\left[\frac{1}{(1 + i)^n}\right] = FV_n(PVIF_{i,n})$$

Example: *$1,000 discounted back for two years at 4 percent:*
$$PV = \frac{\$1,000}{(1.04)^2} = \$1,000\left[\frac{1}{(1.04)^2}\right] = \$1,000(0.9246) = \$924.60$$

- An annuity is defined as a series of equal periodic payments (PMT) for a specified number of periods. Future value of an annuity:

$$FVA_n = PMT(1 + i)^0 + PMT(1 + i)^1 + \ldots + PMT(1 + i)^{n-1}$$

$$= PMT\sum_{t=1}^{n}(1 + i)^{n-t} = PMT\left[\frac{(1 + i)^n - 1}{i}\right] = PMT(FVIFA_{i,n})$$

Example: *FVA of three payments of $1,000 when i is 4 percent:*
$$FVA_3 = \$1,003(3.1216) = \$3,121.60$$

Present value of an annuity:

$$PVA_n = \frac{PMT}{(1 + i)^1} + \frac{PMT}{(1 + i)^2} + \ldots + \frac{PMT}{(1 + i)^n}$$

$$= PMT\sum_{t=1}^{n}\left[\frac{1}{(1 + i)^t}\right] = PMT\left[\frac{1 - \frac{1}{(1 + i)^n}}{i}\right] = PMT(PVIF_{i,n})$$

> **Example:** *PVA of three payments of $1,000 when i is 4 percent:*
>
> $$PVA_3 = \$1,000(2.7751) = \$2,775.10$$

- An annuity whose payments occur at the end of each period is called an ordinary annuity. The preceding formulas are for ordinary annuities.
- If each payment occurs at the beginning of the period rather than at the end, then we have an annuity due. The payments would be shown at Years 0, 1, and 2 rather than at Years 1, 2, and 3. The PV of each payment would be larger because each payment would be discounted back one year less; hence, the PV of the annuity would also be larger.
- Similarly, the FV of the annuity due would also be larger because each payment would be compounded for an extra year. The following formulas can be used to convert the PV and FV of an ordinary annuity to an annuity due.

$$PVA(DUE)_n = PMT\,[(PVIFA_{i,n}) \times (1+i)] = PMT\,[PVIFA(DUE)_{i,n}]$$

> **Example:** *PVA of three beginning-of-year payments of $1,000 when i is 4 percent:*
>
> $$PVA(DUE)_3 = \$1,000\,[(2.7751)(1.04)] = \$2,886.10$$
> $$FVA(DUE)_n = PMT\,[(FVIFA_{i,n}) \times (1+i)] = PMT\,[FVIFA(DUE)_{i,n}]$$

> **Example:** *FVA of three beginning-of-year payments of $1,000 when i is 4 percent:*
>
> $$FVA(DUE)_3 = \$1,000[(3.1216)(1.04)] = \$3,246.46$$

- If the cash flow time line was extended out forever so that the $1,000 payments went on forever, we would have a perpetuity whose value could be found as follows.

$$\text{Value of a perpetuity} = PVP = \frac{PMT}{i} = \frac{\$1,000}{0.04} = \$25,000$$

- If the cash flows were unequal, we could not use the annuity formulas. To find the PV or FV of an uneven cash flow series, find the PV or FV of each individual cash flow and then sum them. However, if some of the cash flows constitute an annuity, then the annuity formula can be used to calculate the present value of that part of the cash flow stream.
- Thus far in the summary we have assumed that payments are made and interest is earned at the end of each year, or annually. However, many contracts call for more frequent payments. For example, mortgages and auto loans call for monthly payments, and most bonds pay interest semiannually. Similarly, most banks compute interest daily. When compounding occurs more frequently than once a year, this fact must be recognized. First, the following formula is used to find an effective annual rate (EAR):

$$\text{Effective annual rate} = EAR = \left(1 + \frac{i_{SIMPLE}}{m}\right)^m - 1.0$$

For semiannual compounding, the effective annual rate is 4.04 percent:

$$\left(1 + \frac{0.04}{2}\right)^2 - 1.0 = (1.02)^2 - 1.0 = 1.0404 - 1.0 = 0.0404 = 4.04\%$$

- The general equation for finding the future value of a single payment for any number of compounding periods per year is

$$FV_n = PV\left(1 + \frac{i_{SIMPLE}}{m}\right)^{n \times m}$$

MODULE 700. FINANCE

where

i_{SIMPLE} = Quoted interest rate
m = Number of compounding periods per year
n = Number of years

- An amortized loan is one that is paid off in equal payments over a specified period. An amortization schedule shows how much of each payment constitutes interest, how much is used to repay the debt, and the remaining balance of the loan at each point in time.

Section 799. International Issues

Summaries and Conclusions

International Flow of Funds

- The key components of the balance of payments are the current account and the capital account. The current account is a broad measure of the country's international trade balance. The capital account is a measure of the country's long-term and short-term capital investments, including direct foreign investment and investment in securities (portfolio investment).
- A country's international trade flows are affected by inflation, national income, government restrictions, and exchange rates. High inflation, a high national income, low or no restrictions on imports, and a strong local currency tend to result in a strong demand for imports and a current account deficit. Although some countries attempt to correct current account deficits by reducing the value of their currencies, this strategy is not always successful.
- A country's international capital flows are affected by any factors that influence direct foreign investment or portfolio investment. Direct foreign investment tends to occur in those countries that have no restrictions and much potential for economic growth. Portfolio investment tends to occur in those countries where taxes are not excessive, where interest rates are high, and where the local currencies are not expected to weaken.

International Financial Markets

- The existence of market imperfections prevents markets from being completely integrated. Consequently, investors and creditors can attempt to capitalize on unique characteristics that make foreign markets more attractive than domestic markets. This motivates the international flow of funds and results in the development of international financial markets.
- The foreign exchange market allows currencies to be exchanged in order to facilitate international trade or financial transactions. Commercial banks serve as financial intermediaries in this market. They stand ready to exchange currencies on the spot or at a future point in time with the use of forward contracts.
- The Eurocurrency market is composed of several large banks that accept deposits and provide short-term loans in various currencies. This market is primarily used by governments and large corporations.
- The Eurocredit market is composed of the same commercial banks that serve the Eurocurrency market. These banks convert some of the deposits received into Eurocredit loans (for medium-term periods) to governments and large corporations.
- The Eurobond market facilitates international transfers of long-term credit, thereby enabling governments and large corporations to borrow funds from various countries. Eurobonds are underwritten by a multinational syndicate of investment banks and are placed in various countries.
- Just as the Eurocurrency, Eurocredit, and Eurobond markets enable firms to borrow funds in foreign countries, international stock markets enable firms to obtain equity financing in foreign countries. Thus, these markets have helped MNCs finance their international expansion.

Financing International Trade

- The common methods of payment for international trade are (1) prepayment (before goods are sent), (2) letters of credit, (3) drafts, (4) consignment, and (5) open account.
- The most popular methods of financing international trade are (1) accounts receivable financing, (2) factoring, (3) letters of credit, (4) banker's acceptances, (5) working capital financing, (6) medium-term capital goods financing (forfaiting), and (7) countertrade.
- The major agencies that facilitate international trade with export insurance and/or loan programs are (1) Export-Import Bank, (2) Private Export Funding Corporation, and (3) Overseas Private Investment Corporation.

Currency Derivatives

- A forward contract specifies a standard volume of a particular currency to be exchanged on a particular date. Such a contract can be purchased by a firm to hedge payables or sold by a firm to hedge receivables.
- A currency futures contract can be purchased by speculators who expect the currency to appreciate.
- Conversely, it can be sold by speculators who expect that currency to depreciate. If the currency depreciates, the value of the futures contract declines, allowing those speculators to benefit when they close out their positions.
- Futures contracts on a particular currency can be purchased by corporations that have payables in that currency and wish to hedge against the possible appreciation of that currency.
- Conversely, these contracts can be sold by corporations that have receivables in that currency and wish to hedge against the possible depreciation of that currency.
- Currency options are classified as call options or put options. Call options allow the right to purchase a specified currency at a specified exchange rate by a specified expiration date. Put options allow the right to sell a specified currency at a specified exchange rate by a specified expiration date.
- Call options on a specific currency can be purchased by speculators who expect that currency to appreciate. Put options on a specific currency can be purchased by speculators who expect that currency to depreciate.
- Currency call options are commonly purchased by corporations that have payables in a currency that is expected to appreciate. Currency put options are commonly purchased by corporations that have receivables in a currency that is expected to depreciate.

International Short-Term Financing

- Multinational corporations (MNCs) may use foreign financing to offset anticipated cash inflows in foreign currencies so that exposure to exchange rate risk will be minimized. Alternatively, some MNCs may use foreign financing in an attempt to reduce their financing costs. Foreign financing costs may be lower if the foreign interest rate is relatively low or if the foreign currency borrowed depreciates over the financing period.
- MNCs can determine whether to use foreign financing by estimating the effective financing rate for any foreign currency over the period in which financing will be needed. The expected effective financing rate is dependent on the quoted interest rate of the foreign currency and the forecasted percentage change in the currency's value over the financing period.
- When MNCs borrow a portfolio of currencies that have low interest rates, they can increase the probability of achieving relatively low financing costs if the currencies' values are not highly correlated.

International Cash Management

- Each subsidiary of an MNC can assess its cash flows by estimating expected cash inflows and outflows to forecast its balance in each currency. This will indicate whether it will have excess cash to invest or a cash deficiency. The MNC's parent may prefer to use a centralized perspective, in which the cash flow positions of all subsidiaries are consolidated. In this way, funds could be transferred among subsidiaries to accommodate cash deficiencies at particular subsidiaries.

- The common techniques to optimize cash flows are (1) accelerating cash inflows, (2) minimizing currency conversion costs, (3) managing blocked funds, and (4) implementing intersubsidiary cash transfers (netting).
- The efforts by MNCs to optimize cash flows are complicated by (1) company-related characteristics, (2) government restrictions, and (3) characteristics of banking systems.
- MNCs can possibly achieve higher returns when investing excess cash in foreign currencies that either have relatively high interest rates or may appreciate over the investment period. If the foreign currency depreciates over the investment period, however, this may offset any interest rate advantage of that currency.

International Long-Term Financing

- Some MNCs may consider long-term financing in foreign currencies to offset future cash inflows in those currencies and therefore reduce exposure to exchange rate risk. Other MNCs may consider long-term financing in foreign currencies to reduce financing costs. If a foreign interest rate is relatively low or the foreign currency borrowed depreciates over the financing period, long-term financing in that currency can result in low financing costs.
- An MNC can assess the feasibility of financing in foreign currencies by applying exchange rate forecasts to the periodic coupon payments and the principal payment. In this way, it determines the amount of its home currency that is necessary per period to cover the payments. The annual cost of financing can be estimated by determining the discount rate that equates the periodic payments on the foreign financing to the initial amount borrowed (as measured in the domestic currency). The discount rate derived from this exercise represents the annual cost of financing in the foreign currency, which can be compared to the cost of domestic financing. The cost of long-term financing in a foreign currency is dependent on the currency's exchange rate over the financing period and therefore is uncertain. Thus, the MNC will not automatically finance with a foreign currency that has a lower interest rate, as its exchange rate forecasts are subject to error. For this reason, the MNC may estimate the costs of foreign financing under various exchange rate scenarios over time.
- For bonds that have floating interest rates, the coupon payment to be paid to investors is uncertain. This creates another uncertain variable (along with exchange rates) in estimating the amount in the firm's domestic currency that is required per period to make the payments. This uncertainty can be accounted for by estimating the coupon payment amount necessary under various interest rate scenarios over time. Then, with the use of these estimates, the amount of the firm's domestic currency required to make the payments can be estimated, based on various exchange rate scenarios over time.

Exhibit 700.1 *Summary of Formulas or Equations as They Relate to Finance*

The Determinants of Market Interest Rates

$$k = k^* + IP + DRP + LP + MRP = k_{RF} + DRP + LP + MRP$$

$$k_{RF} = k^* + IP$$

$$IP_n = \frac{I_1 + I_2 + \ldots I_n}{n}$$

$$\text{Equivalent pretax yield on taxable investment} = \frac{\text{Yield on tax-free investment}}{1 - T}$$

Analysis of Financial Statements

$$\text{Current ratio} = \frac{\text{Current assets}}{\text{Current liabilities}}$$

$$\text{Quick, or acid test, ratio} = \frac{\text{Current assets} - \text{Inventories}}{\text{Current liabilities}}$$

$$\text{Inventory turnover ratio} = \frac{\text{Cost golds sold}}{\text{Inventories}}$$

$$\text{DSO} = \text{Days sales outstanding} = \frac{\text{Receivables}}{\text{Average sales per day}} = \frac{\text{Receivables}}{\text{Annual sales}/360}$$

$$\text{Fixed assets turnover ratio} = \frac{\text{Sales}}{\text{Net fixed assets}}$$

Exhibit 700.1 *Summary of Formulas or Equations as They Relate to Finance (continued)*

$$\text{Total assets turnover ratio} = \frac{\text{Sales}}{\text{Total assets}}$$

$$\text{Debt ratio} = \frac{\text{Total debt}}{\text{Total assets}}$$

$$\text{Times-interest-earned (TIE) ratio} = \frac{\text{EBIT}}{\text{Interest charges}}$$

$$\text{Fixed charge coverage ratio} = \frac{\text{EBIT} + \text{Lease payments}}{\text{Interest charges} + \text{Lease payments} + \left[\dfrac{\text{Sinking fund payments}}{(1 - \text{Tax rate})}\right]}$$

$$\text{Profit margin on sales} = \frac{\text{Net income}}{\text{Sales}}$$

$$\text{Return on total assets (ROA)} = \frac{\text{Net income}}{\text{Total assets}}$$

$$\text{ROA} = \left(\begin{array}{c}\text{Profit}\\ \text{margin}\end{array}\right)\left(\begin{array}{c}\text{Total assets}\\ \text{turnover}\end{array}\right) = \left(\frac{\text{Net income}}{\text{Sales}}\right)\left(\frac{\text{Sales}}{\text{Total assets}}\right)$$

$$\text{Return on common equity (ROE)} = \frac{\text{Net income available to common stockholders}}{\text{Common equity}}$$

$$\text{Price/earnings (P/E) ratio} = \frac{\text{Market price per share}}{\text{Earnings per share}}$$

$$\text{Earnings per share} = \frac{\text{Net income available to common stockholders}}{\text{Number of common shares outstanding}}$$

$$\text{Book value per share} = \frac{\text{Common equity}}{\text{Shares outstanding}}$$

$$\text{Market/book (M/B) ratio} = \frac{\text{Market price per share}}{\text{Book value per share}}$$

Financial Planning and Control

$$\text{Full capacity sales} = \frac{\text{Sales level}}{\text{Percentage of capacity used to generate sales level}}$$

$$TC = F + (V \times Q)$$

$$Q_{OpBE} = \frac{F}{P - V} = \frac{F}{\text{Contribution margin}}$$

$$S_{OpBE} = \frac{FC}{1 - \left(\dfrac{V}{P}\right)} = \frac{F}{\text{Gross profit margin}}$$

$$DOL = \frac{\left(\dfrac{\Delta \text{EBIT}}{\text{EBIT}}\right)}{\left(\dfrac{\Delta Q}{Q}\right)}$$

(continued)

MODULE 700. FINANCE

Exhibit 700.1 *Summary of Formulas or Equations as They Relate to Finance (continued)*

$$DOL_Q = \frac{Q(P-V)}{Q(P-V) - F}$$

$$DOL_S = \frac{S - VC}{S - VC - F} = \frac{\text{Gross profit}}{EBIT}$$

$$EBIT = (P \times Q) - (V \times Q) - F = Q(P - V) - F$$

$$EBIT_{FinBE} = I + \frac{D_{ps}}{(1 - T)}$$

$$DFL = \frac{\left(\frac{\Delta EPS}{EPS}\right)}{\left(\frac{\Delta EBIT}{EBIT}\right)}$$

$$DFL = \frac{EBIT}{EBIT - I}; \text{ if preferred stock} = 0$$

$$DFL = \frac{EBIT}{EBIT - [\text{Financial BEP}]}$$

$$DTL = DOL \times DFL = \frac{S - VC}{EBIT - I}; \text{ if preferred stock} = 0$$

$$DTL = \frac{\text{Gross profit}}{EBIT - [\text{Financial BEP}]}$$

Risk and Rates of Return

$$\text{Expected rate of return} = \hat{k} = \sum_{i=1}^{n} Pr_i k_i$$

$$\text{Variance} = \sigma^2 = \sum_{i=1}^{n} (k_i - \hat{k})^2 Pr_i$$

$$\text{Standard deviation} = \sigma = \sqrt{\sum_{i=1}^{n} (k_i - \hat{k})^2 Pr_i}$$

$$CV = \frac{\sigma}{\hat{k}}$$

$$\hat{k}_p = \sum_{j=1}^{N} w_j \hat{k}_j$$

$$\beta_p = \sum_{j=1}^{N} w_j \beta_j$$

$$SML = k_j = k_{RF} + (k_M - k_{RF})\beta_j = k_{RF} + (RP_M)\beta_j$$

$$\beta = \frac{Y_2 - Y_1}{X_2 - X_1} = \text{slope coefficient in } \bar{k}_{jt} = \alpha + \beta \bar{k}_{Mt} + \epsilon_t$$

The Time Value of Money

$$FV_n = PV(1 + i)^n = PV(FVIF_{i,n})$$

$$PV = FV_n \left[\frac{1}{(1 + i)^n}\right] = FV_n(PVIF_{i,n})$$

Exhibit 700.1 *Summary of Formulas or Equations as They Relate to Finance (continued)*

$$PVIF_{i,n} = \frac{1}{FVIF_{i,n}}$$

$$FVA_n = PMT(FVIFA_{i,n}) = PMT\left[\frac{(1+i)^n - 1}{i}\right]$$

$$FVA(DUE)_n = PMT[FVIFA(DUE)_{i,n}] = PMT(FVIFA_{i,n})(1+i)]$$

$$PVA_n = PMT(PVIFA_{i,n}) \simeq PMT\left[\frac{1 - \frac{1}{(1+i)^n}}{i}\right]$$

$$PVA(DUE)_n = PMT[PVIFA(DUE)_{i,n}] = PMT[(PVIFA_{i,n}(1+i)]$$

$$PVP = \frac{\text{Payment}}{\text{Interest rate}} = \frac{PMT}{i}$$

$$PV_{\text{Uneven stream}} = \sum_{j=1}^{n} CF_t \left[\frac{1}{(1+i)^t}\right] = \sum_{t=1}^{n} CF_t(PVIF_{i,t})$$

$$FV_{\text{Uneven stream}} = \sum_{t=1}^{n} CF_t(1+i)^{n-t} = \sum_{t=1}^{n} CF_t(FVIF_{i,n-t})$$

$$FV_n = PV\left(1 + \frac{i_{SIMPLE}}{m}\right)^{m \times n}$$

$$EAR = \text{Effective annual rate} = \left(1 + \frac{i_{SIMPLE}}{m}\right)^m - 1.0$$

$$\text{Period rate} = \frac{i_{SIMPLE}}{m}$$

$$i_{SIMPLE} = APR \text{ (Periodic rate)} \times (m)$$

$$FV_n = PV(e^{i \times n})$$

$$PV = FV_n(e^{-i \times n})$$

Asset Valuation Concepts

$$\text{Asset value} = V = \sum_{t=1}^{n} \frac{\hat{CF}_t}{(1+k)^t}$$

$$V_d = \sum_{t=1}^{n} \frac{INT}{(1+k_d)^t} + \frac{M}{(1+k_d)^n}$$
$$= INT(PVIFA_{kd,n}) + M(PVIF_{kd,n})$$

$$V_d = \sum_{t=1}^{2N} \frac{INT/2}{(1+k_d/2)^t} + \frac{M}{(1+k_d/2)^{2N}} = \frac{INT}{2}(PVIFA_{k_d/2,2N}) + M(PVIF_{k_d/2,2N})$$

$$\text{Approx. yield to maturity} = \frac{\left(INT + \frac{M - V_d}{N}\right)}{\left[\frac{2(V_d) + M}{3}\right]}$$

$$\text{Price of callable bond} = \sum_{t=1}^{N} \frac{INT}{(1+k_d)^t} + \frac{\text{Call price}}{(1+k_d)^{Nc}}$$

(continued)

MODULE 700. FINANCE

Exhibit 700.1 Summary of Formulas or Equations as They Relate to Finance (continued)

Value of stock $= V_s = \sum_{t=1}^{\infty} \dfrac{\hat{D}_1}{(1 + k_s)^t}$

Zero growth: $g = 0$; $P_0 = \dfrac{D}{k_s}$

Constant growth: $g_1 = g_2 = \ldots = g_\infty$; $P_0 = \dfrac{\hat{D}_1}{k - g} = \dfrac{D_0(1 + g)}{k - g}$

$\hat{k}_s = \dfrac{\hat{D}_1}{P_0} + g$

Capital gains yield $= \dfrac{(\text{Ending value}) - (\text{Beginning value})}{(\text{Beginning value})}$

Capital Budgeting Techniques

PB = Payback = Number of years before full recovery of original investment + $\left(\dfrac{\text{Unrecovered cost at start of full-recovery year}}{\text{Total cash flow during full-recovery year}} \right)$

$\text{NPV} = \hat{CF}_0 + \dfrac{\hat{CF}_1}{(1 + k)^1} + \dfrac{\hat{CF}_2}{(1 + k)^2} + \ldots + \dfrac{\hat{CF}_n}{(1 + k)^n}$

$= \sum_{t=0}^{n} \dfrac{\hat{CF}_t}{(1 + k)^t} = \hat{CF}_0 + \sum_{t=1}^{n} \hat{CF}_t(\text{PVIF}_{k,t}).$

IRR: $\hat{CF}_0 + \dfrac{\hat{CF}_1}{(1 + \text{IRR})^1} + \dfrac{\hat{CF}_2}{(1 + \text{IRR})^2} + \ldots + \dfrac{\hat{CF}_n}{(1 + \text{IRR})^n} = 0$

$\sum_{t=0}^{n} \dfrac{\hat{CF}_t}{(1 + \text{IRR})^t} = 0$

MIRR: PV Costs $= \sum_{t=0}^{n} \dfrac{\text{COF}_t}{(1 + k)^t} = \dfrac{\sum_{t=0}^{n} \text{CIF}_t(1 + k)^{n-t}}{(1 + \text{MIRR})^n} = \dfrac{TV}{(1 + \text{MIRR})^n}$

Project Cash Flows and Risks

Net cash flow = Net income + Depreciation

Incremental operating $CF_t = \Delta NI_t + \Delta Depr_t = (\Delta S_t - \Delta OC_t)(1 - T) + T(\Delta Depr_t)$

$E(\text{NPV}) = \sqrt{\sum_{i=1}^{n} Pr_i(\text{NPV}_i)}$

$\sigma_{\text{NPV}} = \sqrt{\sum_{i=1}^{n} Pr_i[\text{NPV}_i = E(\text{NPV})]^2}$

$\text{CV}_{\text{NPV}} = \dfrac{\sigma_{\text{NPV}}}{E(\text{NPV})}$

$k_{\text{proj}} = k_{RF} + (k_M - k_{RF})\beta_{\text{proj}}$

The Cost of Capital

After-tax component cost of debt $= k_{dT} = k_d(1 - T)$

Component cost of preferred stock $= k_{ps} = \dfrac{D_{ps}}{\text{NP}} = \dfrac{D_{ps}}{P_0 - \text{Flotation costs}}$

Exhibit 700.1 *Summary of Formulas or Equations as They Relate to Finance (continued)*

$$k_s = k_{RF} + RP = \frac{\hat{D}_1}{P_0} + g = \hat{k}_s$$

$$k_s = k_{RF} + (k_M - k_{RF})\beta_s$$

$$k_s = \text{Bond yield} + \text{Risk premium}$$

$$k_e = \frac{\hat{D}_1}{P_0(1-F)} + g = \frac{\hat{D}_1}{NP} + g$$

$$\text{WACC} = w_d k_{dT} + w_p k_p + w_s(k_s \text{ or } k_e)$$

$$BP = \frac{\text{Total amount of lower-cost capital of a given type}}{\text{Proportion of this type of capital in the capital structure}}$$

Capital Structure

$$\text{EPS} = \frac{(S - F - VC - I)(1 - T)}{\text{Shares outstanding}} = \frac{(\text{EBIT} - I)(1 - T)}{\text{Shares outstanding}}$$

$$\text{DOL}_Q = \frac{Q(P - V)}{Q(P - V) - F}$$

$$\text{DOL}_S = \frac{S - VC}{S - VC - F} = \frac{\text{Gross profit}}{\text{EBIT}}$$

$$\text{DFL} = \frac{\text{EBIT}}{\text{EBIT} - I}$$

$$\text{DTL} = \frac{Q(P - V)}{Q(P - V) - F - I} = \frac{S - VC}{S - VC - F - I} = \frac{\text{Gross profit}}{\text{EBIT} - I} = \text{DOL} \times \text{DFL}$$

$$\text{EPS}_1 = \text{EPS}_0[1 + (\text{DTL})(\%\Delta\text{Sales})]$$

Dividend Policy

$$\begin{pmatrix}\text{Dollars transferred from}\\ \text{retained earnings due to}\\ \text{stock dividend}\end{pmatrix} = \begin{pmatrix}\text{Number of}\\ \text{shares}\\ \text{outstanding}\end{pmatrix}\begin{pmatrix}\text{Stock}\\ \text{dividend as}\\ \text{a percent}\end{pmatrix}\begin{pmatrix}\text{Market}\\ \text{price of}\\ \text{the stock}\end{pmatrix}$$

Working Capital Policy

$$\begin{pmatrix}\text{Account}\\ \text{balance}\end{pmatrix} = \begin{pmatrix}\text{Amount of}\\ \text{daily activity}\end{pmatrix} \times \begin{pmatrix}\text{Average life}\\ \text{of the account}\end{pmatrix}$$

$$\begin{pmatrix}\text{Inventory}\\ \text{conversion period}\end{pmatrix} = \frac{\text{Inventory}}{\text{CGS}/360} \text{ where CGS is cost of goods sold}$$

$$\begin{pmatrix}\text{Receivables}\\ \text{collection period}\end{pmatrix} = \text{DSO} = \frac{\text{Receivables}}{\text{Sales}/360}$$

$$\begin{pmatrix}\text{Payables}\\ \text{deferral period}\end{pmatrix} = \text{DPO} = \frac{\text{Accounts payable}}{\text{CGS}/360}$$

$$\begin{pmatrix}\text{Cash conversion}\\ \text{cycle}\end{pmatrix} = \begin{pmatrix}\text{Inventory}\\ \text{conversion period}\end{pmatrix} + \begin{pmatrix}\text{Receivables}\\ \text{collection period}\end{pmatrix} - \begin{pmatrix}\text{Payables}\\ \text{deferral period}\end{pmatrix}$$

Managing Short-Term Assets

$$\text{Average daily sales} = \text{ADS} = \frac{\text{Annual sales}}{360} = \frac{(\text{Units sold})(\text{Sales price})}{360}$$

$$\text{Days sales outstanding} = \text{DSO} = \frac{\text{Receivables}}{\text{ADS}}$$

(continued)

Exhibit 700.1 *Summary of Formulas or Equations as They Relate to Finance (continued)*

Receivables investment = (DSO × ADS) × v where v is variable cost ratio

Cost of carrying receivables = [(DSO)(Sales/360)(v)](k_{AR}) where k_{AR} is opportunity cost of funds

Average inventory = $A = \dfrac{\text{Units per order}}{2} = \dfrac{Q}{2}$

Total carrying cost = TCC = $(C)(PP)(A) = (C)(PP)\left(\dfrac{Q}{2}\right)$

Total ordering cost = TOC = $O\left(\dfrac{T}{Q}\right)$

Total inventory cost = TIC = TCC + TOC
$$= (C)(PP)\left(\dfrac{Q}{2}\right) + O\left(\dfrac{T}{Q}\right)$$

Economic ordering quantity = EOQ = $\sqrt{\dfrac{2(O)(T)}{(C)(PP)}}$

Reorder point = (Lead time in weeks × Weekly usage)

Managing Short-Term Liabilities

Approximate cost of foregoing a cash discount (%) = $\dfrac{\text{Discount percent}}{100 - \text{Discount percent}} \times \dfrac{360 \text{ days}}{\text{Total days of credit available} - \text{Discount period}}$

Interest rate per period = $\dfrac{\text{Dollar cost of borrowing}}{\text{Amount of usable funds}}$

Effective annual rate = $\left[1 + \dfrac{i_{SIMPLE}}{m}\right]^m - 1.0 = [1 + \text{Interest rate per period}]^m - 1.0$

Annual percentage rate = APR = (Interest rate per period) × $(m) = i_{SIMPLE}$

Compensating balance requirement = CB = Principal amount × Compensating balance as a decimal

Usable funds if checking is $0 = (Principal amount) − CB = (Principal amount)(1 − %CB).

Required loan amount if checking is $0 = $\dfrac{\text{Amount of usable funds needed}}{1 - (\text{CB as a decimal})}$

Required loan amount if checking is $0 (Discount & Compensating balance) = $\dfrac{\text{Amount of usable funds needed}}{1 - \%CB - \left(\dfrac{i_{SIMPLE}}{m}\right)}$.

Required loan amount for a loan with a compensating balance requirement if checking balance is > $0 = $\dfrac{\text{Amount of usable funds needed} - \text{Checking account balance}}{1 - \%CB}$

Approximate period rate (Add-on) $\dfrac{\text{Interest}}{\left(\dfrac{\text{Amount received}}{2}\right)}$

Information Technology

Sections 801 and 830. Information Technology Strategies and Value Creation With IT

Summaries and Conclusions

Some information systems (ISs) have become strategic tools as a result of strategic planning; others have evolved into strategic tools. To compete in the market, executives need to define strategic goals and determine whether new or improved ISs can support these goals. No longer regarded as tools for mere automation of previously manual processes, information systems are competitive weapons. Rather than waiting complacently until a problem occurs, businesses actively look for opportunities to improve their position with information systems. An IS that wins an organization strategic advantage is called a *strategic information system* (SIS). To assure optimal utilization of IT for competitive advantage, top managers must participate in generating ideas and champion new, innovative uses of information systems. In recent years, many of these ideas involved using the Internet.

A company achieves strategic advantage by using strategy to maximize its strengths, resulting in a competitive advantage. Significant cost reduction enables a business to sell more units of its products or services while maintaining or increasing its profit margin. Raising barriers to potential entrants to the industry lets an organization maintain a sizable market share by developing systems that are prohibitively expensive for competitors to emulate. By establishing high switching costs, a business can make buying from competitors unattractive to clients. Developing totally new products and services can create an entirely new market for an organization. And if the organization cannot create new products or services, it can still enjoy competitive advantage by differentiating its products so that customers view them as better than a competitor's products.

Organizations also attain advantage by enhancing existing products or services. Many new services we enjoy are the fruits of alliances between companies: each contributes its own expertise to "package" services that entice customers with an overall value greater than that offered by the separate services individually.

Another approach to gaining strategic advantage is by locking in clients or suppliers, that is, by creating conditions that make dealing with competitors infeasible. In recent years, software firms pursued this strategy by creating standards, applications so widely used that they justify the purchase of complementary software.

Many of these initiatives to gain strategic advantage can be obtained by using an innovative SIS. While many SISs were not originally planned with strategy in mind, organizations do try to devise and develop SISs. Among the questions they need to ask are "Would an IS help implement a strategy in which we believe?", "Would better information help establish an advantage?", and "Can we develop an information system that would provide this information?" We proposed several steps for evaluating the potential for an SIS and for running meetings to generate ideas about an SIS. Sometimes, such sessions suggest ways to totally change a business process, which may start a reengineering effort. Reengineering is the process of designing a business process from scratch to achieve hundreds of percentage points in improvement rates. Almost always, reengineering involves implementing new ISs.

SISs can evolve from different initiatives. They may create an advantage through massive automation of a manual process, thus significantly cutting costs. They may provide a new service that was infeasible without information technology (IT). A new technology may provide an advantage. Some organizations obtain a strategic advantage by selling excess information obtained through daily operations (such as customer information collected by retail chains) to companies that can use that information in direct mail operations, for example. And some organizations use ISs to augment their services vertically by offering related services; realtors use this strategy when they offer financing and relocation information in addition to information about houses for sale.

In the software industry, creating standards often creates strategic advantage. A standard is an application used by a significant share of the users. To this end, many companies go as far as giving software away. When the standard has been established, the company enjoys a large sales volume of compatible and add-on software. Many have accused Microsoft, the software giant, of using unfair trade practices in trying to establish standards and squash competitors.

Many entrepreneurs who rushed to establish Web-based business thinking that the Web alone secured their strategic advantage soon found out that any business, offline or online, cannot succeed without a sound business model. The major challenge in online business is the difficulty of maintaining technological superiority, raising barriers to potential competitors, and establishing high switching costs for customers. This difficulty caused many companies that enjoyed brief competitive advantages to close their doors in the early 2000s.

Some ideas for SISs, such as Acumax, have been implemented successfully. Others, such as MortgagePower Plus, failed because of shortcuts and poor technical implementation. Good ideas must be carefully executed if a company is to seize opportunities.

Strategic advantages from information systems are usually short-lived because competitors quickly emulate the systems for their own benefit. Therefore, looking for new opportunities must be an ongoing process. Owners must develop new features to keep the system on the leading edge. But they also must be mindful of the bleeding edge, the high risks of being the first to use new technology with the hope of establishing a competitive advantage.

Section 805. Information Systems Planning

Summaries and Conclusions

Planning involves an attempt to control the development of future events. Business planning is the process of setting goals and objectives, making decisions pertaining to resources required to obtain the objectives, and determining the policies that are to govern the acquisition, use, and distribution of the resources.

There are several planning methods. Top-down planning focuses on organizational goals first and then on the needs of business units. Bottom-up planning assumes that the well-being of the organization depends on the well-being of the individual business units, and therefore concentrates on planning at the business unit level first. Critical success factors (CSF) planning lets executives define their critical success factors first, so that planning can be carried out to address the resources to support these factors. The top-down approach is goal-driven, while the bottom-up and CSF approaches are usually problem-driven.

The rapid proliferation of computers in the 1980s and 1990s convinced a growing number of organizations that they must plan their information systems to achieve success. Modern IS planning is integrated into the overall organizational strategic plan. There are several prerequisites for organizational IS planning. Top management must (1) recognize IT as an indispensable resource, (2) understand that IT is a complex resource that must be planned and controlled, (3) regard IT as owned by the entire organization and not just by the IS unit, (4) regard IT as a source for gaining strategic goals, and (5) view IT as a tool to control power.

The IS plan starts with a mission statement and a long-term vision. The planners then set goals and objectives. They outline the strategic plan for IS resources and the tactical steps to attain the strategic goals. Then they get down to the more specific details of operations: projects, priorities, staffing, purchasing of hardware and software, and funding. In the latter effort, the planners consider several factors: flexibility of the hardware and software in supporting a variety of business needs, compatibility of hardware and software, connectivity of equipment, and scalability.

Planning initiatives do not necessarily come only from IS managers but also from top management, line managers, and users. All may trigger discussions of needs that may result in the addition of new elements to the IS plan.

Experience shows that it often takes a champion to promote the approval and building of an IS. The champion is a high-ranking officer who commands sufficient political clout to include IS in planning and see to it that adequate resources are secured for its development. Often, it is not top management that needs to be convinced of the merits of a new IS but the users. They must accept the changes that will come with the new system. Systems analysts play an important role as agents of change, in addition to their technical performance as system developers.

IS professionals have a great impact on planning, building, and maintaining ISs. This puts great power in their hands. However, while many other professions have mandatory codes of ethics and professional standards, IS professionals do not. Therefore, IS professionals may not have clear guidelines regarding which party's interest to pursue when there is a conflict of obligations.

Sections 815, 870, and 880. Information Technology Risk Management, Security, Controls, and Contingency Plans

Summaries and Conclusions

The purpose of controls and security measures is to maintain the functionality of ISs, the confidentiality of information, the integrity and availability of data and computing resources, the uninterruptible availability of data resources and online operations, and compliance with security and privacy laws. Risks to ISs include risks to hardware, software, and telecommunications.

Risks to hardware include natural disasters, such as earthquakes, fires, floods, and power failures, as well as vandalism. Protective measures run the gamut from surge protectors to the maintenance of duplicate systems, which make ISs fault tolerant. Risks to applications and data include theft of information, data alteration, data destruction, defacement of Web sites, computer viruses and logic bombs, and nonmalicious mishaps such as forbidden downloading and installation of software. Risks to online operations include denial of service and spoofing.

To minimize disruption, organizations use controls. Controls include program robustness and constraints on data entry, periodic backup of software and data files, access controls, atomic transactions, and audit trails. Program robustness and data entry controls provide a clear and sound interface with the user. Menus and data limits ensure that the user enters data in a desired sequence and that the data are reasonable and do not deviate from preset ranges. Audit trails are built into an IS so that transactions can be traced to people, usage times, and authorization information. Access controls ensure that only authorized people can gain access to systems and files. In addition to passwords, access controls include biometrics. Atomic transactions ensure that transaction data are recorded properly in all the pertinent files to ensure integrity. Backup procedures minimize the risk of losing data if the original data are destroyed or altered.

As use of the Internet has increased, encryption schemes have been developed, which scramble messages into ciphertext at the sending end and descramble them into plaintext at the receiving end. Encryption is also used to authenticate the sender or recipient of a message, verifying that the user is indeed the party he or she claims to be and to keep messages secret.

To encrypt and decrypt messages the communicating parties must use a key. In symmetric encryption, both users use a private, secret key. In asymmetric key encryption, the parties use a combination of a public and a private key. The public-private key method does not require both parties to have an agreed-on secret key before the communication starts. To encrypt, the sender needs the recipient's public key; to decrypt, the recipient uses his or her private key. This system is a useful feature that lets consumers and organizations transact business confidentially on the Web. Secure hypertext transfer protocol (SHTTP) and secure socket layer (SSL) are encryption standards specially designed for the Web. They are embedded in Web browsers.

Organizations and individuals can obtain their own public and private keys from certificate authorities or from companies that provide public key applications, such as pretty good privacy (PGP).

New laws in the United States and other countries make electronic signatures legally valid in commercial transactions. Digital signatures are one type of electronic signature. They are created by using a recipient's public key to encrypt a message digest. Digital signatures are used in public key encryption to both authenticate the sender of a message and to verify that the message has not been changed after its launch. Certificate authorities issue digital certificates, which contain the certificate holder's public key and other information, such as the issue and expiration date of the certificate.

To protect resources that are linked to the Internet, organizations use firewalls, which are special software to control access to servers and their contents.

For advice on security measures, professionals can use standards such as the U.S. government's Orange Book or the International Standards Organization (ISO) standards. While protecting resources, access controls have the downside of slowing down employee work and interaction of Web visitors and customers with an organization's site.

In addition to taking steps to prevent disruption, organizations also need a recovery plan so that they can resume business as soon as possible after a disaster strikes. Many organizations have business recovery plans that are developed and periodically tested by a special committee. The plans identify mission-critical applications and prescribe steps that various departments should take in a disaster. Companies may also outsource their business recovery plans.

When considering how much to invest in security measures, organizations should evaluate the dollar amounts of the potential damage on one hand, and the cost of security on the other hand. The more that is spent on security, the smaller the potential loss. Organizations should spend the amount that brings the combined costs to a minimum.

Governments are obliged to protect citizens against crime and terrorism and therefore must be able to tap electronic communication of suspects. Such practices often collide with individuals' right to privacy.

Section 820. Managing Information and Technology

Summaries and Conclusions

Organizations are run by managers. The majority of organizations are structured in a pyramid model with several layers of management. Managers can be roughly classified into these levels: strategic (at the top of the organizational hierarchy), tactical (below top managers), and operational managers (below tactical). Managers at the three levels have different information needs, and typically use different types of information systems to satisfy these needs.

Senior managers make decisions that affect the entire organization, or large parts of it, in the long run. They use highly summarized information that is based on a wide data range, both in terms of the number of organizational units that the data cover, and the time span: long historic periods, and periods well into the future. They use both internal data and external data sources. Senior managers operate in highly unstructured environments. The typical information systems they use are executive information systems (EISs), decision support systems (DSSs), and, to a smaller extent, expert systems (ESs).

Middle managers receive strategic decisions as general directives within which they develop tactics to achieve specific objectives. The information they use is processed from data that cover narrower organizational units and shorter time spans. Their typical information systems consist of DSSs and ESs. Like top managers, they must make unstructured decisions.

Operational managers are responsible for daily operations. They make relatively simple decisions that affect only their departments in the short run. The information they need reflects transactions of their own small units and very narrow time spans. However, the information is very detailed and usually comes from more structured data, such as numbers and other factual information. Too much information can result in information overload, or the inability to comprehend the meaning of facts and figures. One way to avoid overload is to examine cases that fall outside certain parameters, called *management by exception*. Operational managers use transaction processing systems to generate reports. Much of their work involves monitoring, sometimes including electronic monitoring of employees, which may infringe on the employees' right to privacy.

Clerical and other workers typically carry out their supervisors' orders. They use transaction processing systems (TPS) to record transactions and satisfy queries from other employees, customers, and suppliers.

A major task of middle managers in the past was to screen information and pass it on to higher-level managers. Because information technology allows top managers to extract their information directly and conveniently, many organizations have reduced whole layers of middle management, resulting in a flatter organizational structure.

Effective information conveys a message with minimum necessity for interpretation. Many applications allow users to present information in the form that best suits their individual preferences: tabular or graphical. Innovative applications also provide online analytical processing (OLAP) multidimensional information and dynamic representation of time-dependent information.

Information systems have not escaped the influence of politics. On the contrary, because information is power, managers often do not use rational approaches to the development and control of ISs. Often, managers try to obtain power by controlling ISs beyond their real business need. Sometimes, they reject new ISs because the systems were "not invented here." Politics harm the effort to deliver and share information for the benefit of the organization as a whole.

Section 825. Decision Making and Information Technology

Summaries and Conclusions

Decision making is a major component of a manager's job. Whenever there is more than a single way to solve a problem, a decision must be made. The decision-making process comprises three major phases: intelligence, design, and choice. In the first phase, data are collected from which relevant information will be gleaned. In the design phase, the manager organizes the data into useful information, and uses models to analyze it and produce potential courses of action. In the final stage, the manager selects an alternative, that is, makes the decision.

Problems span a continuum between two extremes: structured and unstructured. A structured problem is one for whose solution there is a proven algorithm. Parameters are the data that are used as input in algorithms. Because programs can be written to solve structured problems, they are often called *programmable problems*. An unstructured problem is one for which there are multiple potential solutions. Between the two extremes we find semistructured problems, which are often dealt with by executives. Finding solutions to unstructured and semistructured problems requires expertise. Decision-support systems (DSSs) offer help in dealing with semistructured and unstructured problems.

Most DSSs have three components. The data management module gives the user access to databases from which relevant information can be retrieved. The model management module selects, or lets the user select, an appropriate model through which the data are analyzed. The dialog module serves as an interface between the user and the other two modules. It allows the user to enter queries and parameters, and then presents the result in an appropriate or selected form, such as tabular or graphical.

Personal DSSs serve individual users in their daily decision making. Group DSSs (GDSSs) are sometimes installed in special conference rooms. They promote brainstorming and decision making by groups of people. Some organizations place DSSs on intranets for access by employees from multiple sites. Intranet-based GDSSs enable employees to collaborate and reach decisions without having to sit in the same room.

DSSs provide a quick way to perform sensitivity analysis. The user can change one or several parameters in the model and answer "what if" questions, called *what if analysis*.

Executive information systems (EISs) are a special type of DSS that alleviate the information overload with which high-ranking executives are burdened. EISs select the most relevant data for analysis and present the results as ratios and charts that are easy to comprehend and use for decision making. Executives can also drill down through the data to find root causes of problems.

Because the development of a new DSS may be expensive, management should consider several factors before making a commitment. To what extent is the problem structured? Are the relevant data available in electronic form? How often do managers encounter the problem? How many employees will use the system? And, can the prospective users spare enough time to participate in the development effort? The involvement of the users in the development of the DSS is essential.

Powerful software tools such as electronic spreadsheets let users with little expertise in systems development create their own DSSs. They develop the systems on their own PCs and use them for their individual specific daily jobs, to save time and effort in decision making.

When the decisions to be made involve locations and routes, managers can use geographic information systems (GISs). GISs provide maps with icons and colors to represent population concentrations, potential natural resources, deployment of police forces, and other factors that have to do with locations and routes. A typical decision that a GIS could help make is where to build the new store of a retail chain.

Sections 835 and 840. Quality and Best Practices in Information Technology

Summaries and Conclusions

Quality in Information Technology

Similar to product quality in a manufacturing department, quality in IT products and services is important to survival of a firm. The objective is to "build" controls into the system before they are implemented instead of "adding on" such controls later. This measure is in keeping with a proactive management attitude.

Best Practices in Information Technology

There are three key functions critical to building a modern IT management infrastructure: (1) deciding to work differently; (2) directing resources toward high-value uses; and (3) supporting improvements with the right skills, roles, and responsibilities.

An IT investment management process is an integrated approach to managing IT investments that provides for the continuous identification, selection, control, life-cycle management, and evaluation of IT investments. This structured process provides a systematic method for organizations to minimize risks while maximizing the return on IT investments.

Section 845. Data and Knowledge Management

Summaries and Conclusions

Database Management

In their daily operations, organizations can collect vast amounts of data. These data are raw material for highly valuable information, but they are useless without tools to organize them, store them in an easily accessible manner, and manipulate them flexibly to produce that information. These functions are the great strength of databases—collections of interrelated data that, within an organization and sometimes between organizations, are shared by many units and contribute to productivity and efficiency. The database approach has several advantages over the more traditional file approach (which uses flat files): less data redundancy, application-data independence, greater data integrity, and a higher level of security. Database technology, which is a powerful tool for daily operations and decision making, has had a dramatic and far-reaching impact on our business and personal lives. Consumers can now access large organizational databases, rich with business and other information, via the Internet. From their online database, businesses offer textual and graphical information about their numerous products and services to anyone who can use a Web browser.

To understand how databases are built, you must first know the "data hierarchy." The smallest piece of data collected about an entity is a character. Several characters make up a field. Several fields make up a record. A collection of related records is a file. Databases usually contain several files, but the database approach can be applied to a single file.

The software tool that enables us to apply the database approach to managing data is called a *database management system* (DBMS). DBMSs allow managers and other users to construct databases, populate them with data, and manipulate the data. Most DBMSs come as part of 4GLs that can be used to develop applications that facilitate queries and produce reports. Usually, a DBMS supports one specific type of the three database models, or general logical structures of records in a database. In a hierarchical database, each entity value may have several entity values linked to it in what is called a *parent-child relationship*. This model affords only one-to-many relationships. The network model allows a child to have more than one parent, thereby allowing many-to-many relationships. In the relational model, the links among entities are maintained by the use of keys. Primary keys are unique identifiers. Composite keys are combinations of two or more fields that are used as a primary key. Foreign keys link one table to another within the database. The relational model is the most popular nowadays. Object-oriented databases afford the maintenance of data along with the applications that process them, and duplication of objects and their characteristics is called *inheritance*. Some vendors offer DBMSs that accommodate a combination of relational and object-oriented models, called *object-relational.*

To plan databases, designers need to lay out a diagram showing the relationships among the different entities, called an *entity relationship diagram*. Then they can move on to constructing a schema, which is the structure of all record structures of the entities, and the relationships among them. To construct a schema, the developer uses a data definition language (DDL). The DDL is also used to build the data dictionary, which is a repository of information about the data and their organization. To query the database, we use a data manipulation language (DML). Structured query language (SQL), a language that serves as DDL and DML, has been adopted as an international standard language for relational databases. Modern PC DBMSs provide intuitive interfaces with menus and icons that make the DDL and DML transparent to the users, for ease of operation.

Due to the drop in cost and the increasing power of microcomputers, organizations have moved from an architecture of a mainframe and terminals to a network consisting of a computer that is used as a server, with microcomputers as its clients. This change is a move from the traditional shared resource architecture to the newer client/server architecture. The latter affords more flexible utilization of data and applications and empowers workers to develop simple applications for their specific tasks.

To support management decision making, organizations maintain data warehouses or data marts. Building a data warehouse involves three phases: extraction, cleansing, and loading. One type of software for analysis of data warehouses is data mining software, which helps find useful, hidden patterns such as clients' purchasing patterns. Data-mining techniques help find relationships in data that managers might not think of, such as finding out that two products tend to be purchased together on a certain day of the week. To analyze data in warehouses, organizations often use online analytical processing (OLAP) applications.

The greater challenge for organizations is to capture and manage knowledge. Knowledge is either information we have about a subject or information about where to find such information. Knowledge management involves gathering, organizing, sharing, analyzing, and disseminating knowledge. Knowledge management may improve organizational performance.

The low price of efficient and effective database software exacerbates a societal problem of the information age: invasion of privacy. Because every transaction of an individual can be easily recorded and later combined with other personal data, it is inexpensive to produce whole dossiers on individual consumers. Commercial organizations insist that they need personal information to improve their products and services and to target their marketing only to interested consumers.

Knowledge Systems

Artificial intelligence (AI) scientists study methods to develop computer programs that mimic the human mind and behavior. The field consists of several subfields. Robotics engineers build robots that replace human laborers. In manufacturing, robots are used to carry out routine tasks such as the assembly and painting of cars. Both in manufacturing and in police work, computer-controlled machines replace human beings in dangerous assignments.

Robots that move in space must have vision. Artificial vision allows them to sense walls and obstacles and to recognize an object that they are to operate on. Artificial vision is also used in machines other than robots for sorting and identification.

Natural language processors (NLPs) are programs that recognize human commands. They rid computer-based system users of the need to learn programming or other rigid interfaces. Natural language processors must be able to recognize that one sentence may have different meanings in different contexts.

Expert systems (ES) are programs that simulate human expertise. Early attempts to create a program that would be a general problem solver failed. Over the past two decades, numerous ESs have been developed for use in engineering, medicine, chemistry, mineral exploration, and business.

Neural networks are programs built to solve problems while learning and refining their knowledge, mimicking what scientists believe is the way our own brains learn and act. The programs start with a base model. As the programs solve problems, human operators input the results of the programs' analysis in terms of "hits" or "misses." The program incorporates this new input into its knowledge base, thereby continually improving its performance.

The latest development in AI is intelligent agents, programs that carry out daily tasks on public networks such as the Internet (which involves sifting through and selecting data from massive amounts of information) that otherwise would have to be performed by human beings. For instance, intelligent agents can move inside a network and find desired literature or the best price of a product, answer electronic messages, pay debts through a credit charge, and carry out electronically many other mundane tasks. These "electronic butlers" save human beings time and serve us more efficiently than we can now serve ourselves in many respects, especially when using the Internet. The technology has also been integrated into supply chain management (SCM) applications for such purposes as detection of imminent delay of a supplier's parts shipment and finding where efficiency can be increased in a business process.

Of these subfields of AI, ESs have played the most important role in business. An ES is comprised of three parts: The knowledge base is a compilation of facts and beliefs, and the connections between them, garnered from one or more experts. The inference engine is code that combines user input with information in the knowledge base to find a solution to a problem. The dialog component allows the user to interact with the inference engine conveniently.

Although the majority of ESs have their knowledge base organized in the form of IF-THEN rules, there are other methods of representing knowledge. In one method, the knowledge is organized in frames that store attributes and values. There is a table for each object in the domain. In semantic nets, objects are represented as nodes, and relationships are the lines that connect the nodes. The relationships may be "has," "belongs to," "is," and so on.

Fuzzy logic is a theory that takes a completely different approach to knowledge representation. The theory recognizes that many of an expert's decisions are based on subjective linguistic variables, such as "low" risk, "moderate" risk, and "high" risk. A function is constructed to represent the possibility that an event, or entity, will fall into a category. The same event, or entity, may have a certain probability of falling into one category, while having another probability of falling into an adjacent category. Therefore, the boundaries of the categories, or sets, are "fuzzy." Fuzzy logic has been incorporated into expert systems in appliances, locomotives, managerial decision making, and many other areas.

Two parties are involved in the construction of an ES: the expert and the knowledge engineer. The knowledge engineer possesses questioning techniques and experience in translating the knowledge garnered from the expert into a computer program.

Early ESs were developed using special AI programming languages, such as LISP, Prolog, and KEE. Nowadays, ES shells are used to construct new ESs. An ES shell may be thought of as an ES that has been emptied of its knowledge. The shell prompts the builder to enter the antecedents (conditions or IF statements) and conclusions (THEN statements) of conditions. It transparently builds the knowledge base and the inference engine according to the information supplied by the builder.

ESs reach a solution in one of two ways: forward chaining or backward chaining. In forward chaining, the user inputs the parameters of the problem at hand, and the system uses the rules to produce the best outcome. Thus, this process is also called *result-driven*. Often, the user wishes to specify a desired goal and receive as output the conditions that would produce the result. The ES then performs backward chaining, which is referred to as *goal-driven*.

Like decision-support systems, ESs help make decisions in unstructured domains. But the investment is often great, because it involves the time of both highly paid domain experts and knowledge engineers. Therefore, certain conditions must exist to justify the investment in a new ES: the problems must not be trivial; the domain in which the ES operates should be highly unstructured; the problems should occur frequently; and an expert must be available for questioning.

ESs support managerial activities: planning, decision making, and diagnosis. Organizations use the systems to replace human trainers. An ES may provide knowledge that exceeds the expertise of a single expert. Once the expertise is captured in software, it may be cheaply replicated and disseminated throughout an organization. Unlike human experts, ESs can be made available at all times. All members of an organization using an ES can reach the same decisions under given conditions, so management achieves consistency in operations.

However, there are some limitations to the systems. Effective ESs can handle only narrow domains. They do not yet possess common sense, and despite the progress in neural nets, they are limited in their ability to learn.

ESs and other AI applications put expertise at the tips of our fingers and thus add to our quality of life. They make us more independent of human experts, but at the same time, they make us more dependent on software. When the software is defective, the damage done by the systems may be considerable. ESs pose a challenge to the legal system because individuals and organizations may be adversely affected by decisions provided by the systems.

Section 850. Systems Development and Acquisition

Summaries and Conclusions

Systems Development

The development of a new IS is triggered by an opportunity, a problem, or a directive. Modern systems development is regarded as a continuation of IS planning. Once a decision to develop is reached, a systems development life cycle (SDLC) process begins that consists of analysis, design, implementation, and support. Sometimes the effort is carried out not to create a new system, but to integrate several existing systems. The purpose of systems analysis is to determine what need the system will satisfy. Developers interview managers and prospective users to determine business needs. Three feasibility studies are performed: technical, economic, and operational. The technical feasibility study examines the technical state of the art to ensure that the hardware and software exist to build the system. In the economic feasibility study, the benefits of the system are weighed against its cost. The process will continue only if the benefits are expected to outweigh the costs. The operational feasibility study determines whether the system will fit the organizational culture and be used to full capacity. After these studies comes definition of the system requirements, in which users specify exactly what they need the system to do.

The system design consists of physical and logical arrangements of the system. Tools such as flowcharts and data flow diagrams are used to create a model of the system. Construction is the actual building of the system, consisting mainly of code writing. Walk-throughs and simulations are performed to ensure that the code will work well.

When the system is completed, it is implemented. Implementation includes training and conversion from the old system to the new system. Conversion can take place by one of several strategies: parallel, phased, cold turkey, or piloting. The system cycle does not end here, but continues in the form of support. The system is maintained to ensure operability without fault and satisfaction of changing business needs.

Prototyping is a popular alternative to the traditional systems development approach. The developer performs a quick needs assessment and develops a working model that is turned over to users for evaluation. The users express their criticism, and the developers implement the additional requirements. This process of refinement continues until the users are satisfied. Prototyping saves up to 85 percent of development time, and thus much of the cost, but it should be practiced only with relatively small, uncomplicated, unstructured, and uninterfaced ISs. However, prototyping is also used in the programming phase of practically any development of a new IS.

Systems developers often use computer-aided software engineering (CASE) tools to ease and expedite both design and construction of applications. CASE tools are special programs that help developers build data flow diagrams and flowcharts and plan data dictionaries and database schemas. The availability of increasingly sophisticated and user-friendly CASE tools has increased the popularity of prototyping.

Development of an IS is an effort that requires management of resources and activities. This undertaking is called *project management*. Effective project managers divide the effort into smaller modules that can be handled without interfering with the development of other modules. Project management staffs use tools such as Gantt and PERT charts to keep track of resources spent and milestones to be met. The goals of project management are to complete the project on time and within budget and to meet the requirements and expectations.

In recent years, a growing portion of the systems development effort has been assigned to users. In some cases, the effort is actually led by users, called *systems development led by users* (SDLU). This involvement increases their feeling of responsibility and ownership. However, the complexity of large projects makes it doubtful that the phenomenon will spread to large-scale ISs. Systems integration is often much more complicated than systems development because it requires IT professionals to make different applications to communicate with each other seamlessly. The complexity is multiplied when integrating ISs of several organizations that must work together over the Web.

The importance of meticulous IS development is accentuated when we examine mishaps caused by faulty systems. Utility companies, banks, and many other institutions rely heavily on ISs for their daily operations. Errors and mistakes ("Bugs") that were unnoticed in the development process may wreak havoc, cause financial damage, and in some cases cause death. Because of the great responsibility of IS professionals, the question of whether certification is needed has come up. If doctors, civil engineers, lawyers, and public accountants are subject to mandatory certification, many people argue, IS professionals should be, too.

Alternative Approaches to Systems Development

There are several alternatives to having applications developed in-house: outsourcing, purchasing ready-made software, or renting applications, using the services of an application service provider (ASP), maintaining an IS subsidiary, and user application development. Outsourcing is an organization's use of a separate company to handle all or part of its IS resources. Its advantages include (1) improving cost clarity and reducing license and maintenance fees; (2) freeing organizations to concentrate on their core businesses; (3) shortening the number of implementation cycles; (4) reducing personnel and fixed costs; (5) gaining access to highly qualified know-how; (6) receiving ongoing consulting as part of standard support; (7) decreasing investments in software tools and training; and (8) improving security.

The main disadvantage of outsourcing is the long-term loss of control over IS development and operations. When outsourcing, organizations that operate in a fast-changing environment can lose the flexibility to adapt their ISs to new business needs and opportunities. To avoid misunderstanding and disappointment, clients must sign detailed service level agreements with outsourcing vendors.

The first option organizations should explore before investing in a new IS is purchasing packaged software. Purchasing ready-to-use applications is significantly less expensive than developing software in-house.

Benchmarking, the codified comparison of performance measures between systems, is an important step in software selection as well as for ongoing evaluation after implementation. It ensures that the adopted application satisfies the organization's minimum requirements, such as access time to data and processing speed.

Renting software helps an organization avoid tying up large sums of money in applications that may be obsolete in just a few years. In recent years, using the services of an ASP has become popular. In addition to making applications available to an organization immediately via private or public communication networks, the client avoids the costs of storage hardware and large IT staffs. Both in renting and ASP services, the client pays monthly fees based on the type of application used and the number of users. Either way, the client does not have to make a long-term commitment of capital to software that may become obsolete in two or three years. The downsides of ASP services are the loss of control over the system, the potentially low speed of interaction, and the security risks associated with using an IS via a public network.

Large companies whose information needs are substantial have established large IS organizational units. Some have turned these units into independent IS service subsidiaries that offer their services to the market at large. These spin-offs allow the parent company to have access to readily available IS resources, while not having to absorb the cost of overhead and fluctuations in demand for IS services.

Several factors have encouraged organizations to let their users develop their own applications: the programming backlog (the build-up of programming requests awaiting attention by the IS department), the increasing use of PCs, the emergence of 4GLs and GUI tools, the popularity of prototyping, and the adoption of client/server systems. There are several advantages to user application development: a short lead time, good fit of application capabilities to business needs, good compliance with organizational culture, efficient utilization of computing resources, acquisition of skills by users, and the freeing of IS staff to deal with the more complex systems challenges. But there are also risks: poorly developed applications, undesirable islands of information and "private databases," duplications of effort, security problems, and poor documentation. Thus, end-user development of applications needs to be managed. IS managers should determine the applications that users should and should not develop and dictate the tools that should be used as well.

Well over half of America's office workers now have rich computer resources at the tips of their fingers. Often, employees do not know which activity is welcomed and which is not. If an organization lacks a clear policy, employees are not discouraged from abusing computers. This abuse is especially true when employees access Web sites that are objectionable to their employer or when employees use e-mail for purposes not intended by the employer. If no policy has been established, the simple rule is that employees should not use their computers for anything but work.

Sections 803 and 855. Managing Information Technology Resources and Role of IT and Chief Information Officer (CIO)

Summaries and Conclusions

Information system (IS) infrastructure refers to the hardware, software, telecommunications devices and lines, and other IS resources an organization owns. Organizations deploy their IS resources in various ways. The manner in which the resources are organized is often referred to as *IS architecture*. In a centralized architecture, the organization is served by a mainframe computer or several smaller computers centrally located. Workers use PCs and terminals to access data and applications that reside on these central computers. The main advantage of this arrangement is the tight control that management can retain over information resources.

In a decentralized architecture, business units, often geographically remote, have their own local area networks connecting PCs and terminals to a local larger computer. In extreme cases, the local resources are not connected to those of headquarters or other sites. Such an arrangement supports independent decision making regarding IS resources so that the resources can best fit local needs. In a distributed architecture, local resources are often connected to headquarters and other organization sites. While maintaining a measure of independent decision making for IS resources, each site can enjoy the resources of other sites. Management still maintains main control. Many organizations are now moving in this direction, using extranets to connect employees from all sites.

There are many ways to organize the IS staff. At one extreme is a central IS organization whereby all of the IS professionals report to the CIO or another person who is the highest IS authority. At the other extreme is functional IS organization, which places IS staff within an organization's business units. Central IS management usually includes a steering committee, whose members are drawn from key business units. Regardless of organization approaches, IS staff are responsible for systems implementation and maintenance, communications networks, research and development, data administration, and the information center. The information center coordinates and controls the purchasing of hardware and software and also provides training and support. The best information centers provide a single contact point, such as a help desk, from which calls for assistance are routed to the appropriate expert. Centralized IS management has several advantages: standardized hardware, common software, easier training, common reporting systems, effective planning of shared systems, efficient use of personnel, and the ability of management to maintain tight control of the company's ISs.

The decentralization of IS management has advantages as well, including a better fit of systems to particular needs of business units, timely response to requests by business units, encouragement of end-user computing, encouragement of innovation, and accommodation of decentralized management style.

Successful use of IS technology depends on understanding and collaboration between managers of business units and IS managers. IS managers must have a broad understanding of business activities. They are expected to respond promptly to the information needs of business units, use jargon-free language when dealing with their non–IS clients, explain what is and what is not possible with ISs, detail the resources that would be needed to implement and maintain a new IS, and designate personnel who will be responsible for resolving problems reported by the users.

IS managers expect business managers to project their future information needs, clearly explain the business processes that ISs should support, and thoroughly detail the features they desire in a new IS.

Companies sometimes treat IS services as an overhead cost, a general expense incurred as part of running the company. However, to encourage proper use of resources, organizations often implement charge-back systems, by which departments are charged for their use of IS resources. Successful charge-back systems make managers accountable for their use of IS resources. They let managers control IS use, and they provide timely usage reports, link the charges to the benefits of usage, and are congruent with general IS goals. In a charge-back system, IS departments often charge users for personnel hours, computer time, external storage space, the number of input and output operations on shared computers, and the amount of paper output.

IS professionals pursue various careers, including programmer/analyst, systems analyst, database administrator, telecommunications manager, Webmaster, chief information officer, chief technology officer, and chief knowledge officer. IS professionals typically serve as agents of change in their organizations to keep them competitive. The chief knowledge officer can be an integral part of creating a learning organization, one that continually improves its products and processes. In such organizations, the chief knowledge officer is often called the *chief learning officer*. Many IS professionals today elect to be independent consultants.

Section 860. Telecommunications and Networks

Summaries and Conclusions

In recent years, telecommunications technology has driven the major developments in the dissemination and use of information. Organizations are increasingly dependent on fast, reliable business data communications both internally and with other organizations. Thus, to succeed as a manager, one must understand the underlying technological developments and the ways in which telecommunications technology is used to facilitate business processes.

Telecommunications is communication over distance, primarily communication of digital data over distance. Telecommunications operates in three directional modes: simplex, in which only one party transmits and the other receives; half-duplex, in which each party can transmit or receive, but only one at a time; and full-duplex, in which both parties can both transmit and receive at the same time.

Bits represent data in data communications. Inside the computer and between a computer and its peripheral devices, data can be communicated using parallel transmission, in which all bits of a byte are transmitted at the same time through a bundle of parallel wires, with one bit traveling through each wire. Over a long distance, however, the bits must be transmitted so that one follows another, in a process called *serial transmission*.

Different media are said to have different capacities, meaning that they are capable of carrying different numbers of bits per second (bps) without garbling messages. To ensure correct data reception, transmission and reception must be synchronous. When special synchronization devices are employed, the transmission is said to be synchronous. When communication is synchronized without synchronization devices, the transmission is said to be asynchronous. Asynchronous transmission adds extra bits to each data byte to indicate the beginning and end of the byte and for error detection.

Data are transmitted between computers digitally as bits (in the form of 0s and 1s) represented in some form of two states, either using electrical impulses or bursts of light. However, in much of the world, telephone lines are still capable of transmitting only analog (continuous) signals, not digital (discrete) signals. And even though a significant portion of the telephone network in some countries is ready for digital transmission, the old copper wires connecting home and office telephone lines to the network do not accommodate such communication unless special technology is used. To transmit digital data using an analog line requires that the amplitude, frequency, or phase of the analog signal be modulated to represent equivalent digital communication.

This modulation is executed by a modem; its name is an abbreviation of modulator/demodulator. When the computer sends data, the modem modulates the digital signal into an analog signal. When the computer receives data, the modem accepts the modulated signal and de-modulates it into the original digital signal.

While often incorporating modems, multiplexers are more sophisticated devices that allow several computers to communicate with another computer via the same channel, thereby making the use of the channel more efficient.

Data are transmitted through guided and unguided media. Guided media include old telephone lines made of twisted pairs of copper wires, coaxial cables, and optical fibers. Microwave devices transmit data through air and outer space, which are unguided media.

When computers are connected locally within an office or a campus, we call the arrangement a *local area network* (LAN). When computers communicate over long distances, we call the network a *wide area network* (WAN). Both LANs and WANs can be organized in several physical layouts: star, ring, bus, tree, or a combination of these—all of which have strengths and weaknesses. Both LANs and WANs increasingly employ wireless technology, which significantly reduces the need for expensive wiring.

To ensure that a computer receives accurate messages, rules have been established to which all computers on a network must adhere. A set of rules that governs telecommunications is called a *protocol*. One rule is the form of switching, or the manner in which a message is communicated: in its entirety from the transmitting computer to the receiving computer (circuit switching) or divided into packets of bytes and transmitted via several nodes on the network (packet switching).

Telecommunications technology has changed the business environment. Businesspeople are now more mobile; they can use cellular phones not only for voice communication but also for data communications. Videoconferencing brings together managers who are thousands of miles apart. Voice mail allows businesspeople to record voice messages on computers; a person can receive his or her message without ever picking up a phone. Fax capability is now incorporated into modems and allows the communication of graphic information in addition to text.

Both organizations and individuals have a variety of choices when subscribing to networking services. They can choose among Integrated Services Data Networks (ISDN) lines, digital subscriber lines (DSL), coaxial cable lines, T1 and T3 lines, satellite links, fixed wireless service, and other options. These great advances in technology have noticeable social impacts. We are witnessing the emergence of the "virtual organization," an organization independent of a physical location, whose members do not commute but telecommute. Telecommuting has advantages, but it does not serve some basic human needs, like socializing, the short hallway chat during lunch break, and the clear separation between work and family obligations.

When an organization connects its information systems to public networks, it must protect them against risks of unauthorized access. Preventive measures such as backup, access controls, atomic transactions, data entry controls, and audit trail must be taken to provide adequate security.

Section 865. Business Information Systems

Summaries and Conclusions

Effectiveness is the degree to which a task is accomplished. The better a person performs a job, the more effective he or she is. Efficiency is measured as the ratio of output to input. The more output with the same input, or the less input for the same output used in a process, the more efficient the process. ISs can help companies attain more effective and efficient business processes. Productivity is the measure of people's efficiency. When people use ISs, their productivity increases.

ISs have been integrated into almost every functional business area. The earliest business ISs were implemented in accounting and payroll because of the routine and structured nature of accounting tasks. The systems automatically post transactions in the books and automate the generation of reports for management and for legal requirements.

Financial ISs help manage cash. Managers can track cash available for transactions, while ensuring that available money is invested in short- or long-term programs to yield the highest interest possible. Investment-related analysis ISs help build portfolios based on historical performance and other characteristics of securities.

ISs are an important tool in modern engineering processes. Computer-aided design (CAD) systems help engineers design new products and save and modify drawings electronically. Manufacturing ISs, especially materials requirement planning (MRP) and manufacturing resource planning (MRP II) systems, facilitate production scheduling and material requirement planning, and shorten lead time between idea and product. Manufacturing execution systems help pinpoint production bottlenecks.

Many of today's marketing and sales techniques would be impossible without ISs. For instance, database technology, programs that support the construction and manipulation of large pools of digital data, are instrumental in targeted marketing, which defines potential customers as narrowly as possible. Statistical models help market researchers find the best populations for new and existing products. The Web affords corporations an excellent opportunity to reach more shoppers and also serve customers better. Shoppers receive more information before they purchase and thus return fewer products. Customer service via the Web is available twenty-four hours per day, seven days per week, and saves the company labor hours and telephone expenses.

Staff selection and efficient record keeping have been improved, mainly thanks to human resource ISs. An increasing amount of recruiting is done via the Web. Managers often use evaluation software to help assess their subordinates' performance. Employees can use expert systems to choose health care and other benefits programs that best suit their situation.

Rather than use disparate ISs for business functions, many organizations opt to install a single system that encompasses all their business processes, or at least the major ones. They employ enterprise resource planning (ERP) systems to support their supply chain management, the series of main and supporting activities from order to delivery.

A work cycle, or simply cycle, is a series of sequential tasks performed to complete a product. Groupware helps workers in different locations communicate ideas, brainstorm, and work together as if they were sitting in the same room. The result is better ideas and shorter processes. Groupware also allows collaborative work and document tracking. It has helped shorten cycles of routine operations such as engineering jobs and publishing.

Section 875. Electronic Commerce and Information Technology

Summaries and Conclusions

The Internet is a huge network connecting millions of computers throughout the world. Its most exciting section is the World Wide Web (www or Web), which has elevated the network from a text-based medium to one that facilitates the communication of graphical and sound content as well. There are many business models, or the manner in which organizations generate income, on the Internet. The Internet's major communication lines are collectively called the *backbone;* Internet servers are linked to the backbone. People who access the Internet are often called *surfers,* and many of them typically gain their access through Internet service providers (ISPs). Each device linked to the Internet must have an Internet protocol (IP) number. An IP number is often associated with a domain name.

The Internet allows organizations and individuals to send and receive e-mail, transfer data files via File Transfer Protocol (FTP), access newsgroups, and communicate a wide variety of text, pictures, sounds, and animation. Internet relay chat (IRC), often known as *instant messaging,* enables people to chat in real time over the Internet.

Hypertext Transfer Protocol (HTTP) determines how files should be coded, transferred, and viewed on the Internet. The Web is defined by a common programming language, HTML (Hypertext Markup Language). Web users can use special applications called *browsers* to access different Web sites. They can also use special software called *plug-ins* to use voice and video on the Net. A home page is the first page that is displayed at a Web site. Web page editors help automate the design of pages. Small modules of Java code that execute within HTML are called *applets.* Java servlets enable individual computers to interact with the servers. Java, JavaScript, and ActiveX modules are often embedded in HTML code to enhance pages and provide advanced features. Extensible Markup Language (XML) is a more recent language that is used to characterize different types of information, making it possible to identify and use these types of information (such as phone numbers, addresses, and prices) for specific purposes. Common Gateway Interface (CGI) applications process data captured in forms and either store them for later use or respond to the user with requested information. Virtual Reality Modeling Language (VRML) is the standard for delivering three-dimensional interactive scenes on the Internet. Telephoning via the Web is expected to improve and reach the quality available with conventional telephone lines.

Intranets are the intra-organizational versions of the Internet. Many organizations have adopted Web technologies for use in building Web sites for internal use by their employees. The same technologies are also used to build extranets, which are networks connecting business partners. Usually, the development of new internal Web sites does not require a significant investment in additional hardware and telecommunications devices because these devices have already been installed for local area networks and corporate intersite communications.

When establishing a Web site, businesses have several options, each with its advantages and disadvantages: setting up their own server, contracting with an ISP, contracting with a Web portal, setting up an electronic storefront as part of a provider's cybermall, contracting with a Web hosting service, or establishing a virtual Web server or a sub-domain. If the business decides to hire the services of another party, it should consider several factors, such as the quality of the technical and content support, set-up fees, monthly fees, and the amount of disk space provided. Critical to a quick and dependable online business connection is load balancing, which transfers visitors from a busy server to a less busy one.

Electronic commerce, popularly called *e-commerce,* can be classified as business-to-business (B2B) or business-to-consumer (B2C). In the former, businesses use networks to trade with other businesses. In the latter, businesses advertise and sell goods and services to consumers via networks, mainly through the Web. The greater volume of e-commerce is conducted between businesses.

Business-to-business trading often relies on electronic data interchange (EDI), which traditionally has been conducted via private or leased networks and now is moving to the Internet. B2B includes exchanges and auction sites, which are also called *electronic marketplaces,* online business alliances, and application service providers (ASPs). B2C trading includes advertising, electronic retailing, auctions and reverse auctions, content selling, and stock trading. Local, state, and federal governments, too, have created Web sites to conduct business both with businesses and citizens. Surveys show greater numbers of older people, women, and lower income earners among Web surfers, and a spread of Internet use in developing countries. Businesses notice these demographic changes and try to respond accordingly. Many online businesses also use sophisticated customer relationship management (CRM) software to capture consumers' movement and preferences at their site and tailor services to the consumers' needs.

To be successful, an online business must target the right customers, own the customer's total experience, personalize the service, shorten the business cycle, let customers help themselves, and be proactive in seeking customers. Among the successful business models have been those that pursue niche retailing, those that sell hard-to-obtain information, and brick-and-mortar businesses that extended operations to the Web. With the proliferation of hand-held computers capable of wireless connection to the Internet, the next wave in B2C may be mobile commerce, popularly called *m-commerce.*

Free speech on the Internet has been a controversial issue for many years, especially because it is difficult for anyone to control what is communicated through the Internet. Many sites present materials that are acceptable in some cultures and by some people but not by others. For almost every corporate and political domain name, there is now an anti-domain site. Spamming has been the ire of many e-mail users, who are trying to stop it through legal means.

Section 899. International Issues

Summaries and Conclusions

Organizations find that sharing ISs benefits all participants in business activities. Increasingly, organizations are investing in inter-organizational information systems to facilitate business processes. Organizations operate in both vertical markets and horizontal markets. In vertical information interchange, which is exchange of information between buyers and sellers, companies such as Toys R Us and Kmart reduce costs by opening their ISs to suppliers, who then assume the cost of inventory control, while also making their own operations more efficient and effective. Horizontal information interchange occurs among companies in the same line of business. This practice is common in the banking industry, which shares databases of credit histories; the airline industry, which shares reservation information; and among realtors, who share data about available real estate. An increasing number of businesses use the Internet to exchange information vertically and horizontally.

Electronic data interchange (EDI) networks have been established by many businesses to support vertical interaction with their suppliers. EDI not only speeds up communication between organizations, but also saves money by reducing the number of paper documents and the costs involved in handling them. Use of electronic signatures now allows contractual transactions to take place online. Value-added network (VAN) EDI has existed for many years. The opening of the Internet for use by private businesses provides an excellent opportunity to implement EDI inexpensively. The network is already available to all, the interface is quite familiar to workers, training costs are low, and the Internet backbone provides high-speed communication. Web EDI does not afford nonrepudiation and is more susceptible to security risks. Web EDI relies on extensible markup language (XML), a standard similar to hypertext markup language (HTML), but whose tags indicate the content of data rather than how to display data.

In recent years, an increasing number of organizations have augmented their supply chain management systems (SCMS) to link with business suppliers and customers. The applications are often part of an ERP system and can be purchased ready-made.

As more and more companies use the Web for business, both B2C and B2B, they realize that they must accommodate non–English speaking audiences and tailor their sites to local preferences. They also must be carefully attuned to the cultural differences and payment preferences of different world regions.

The number of multinational corporations is growing, and so is the need for international ISs. However, implementation of international ISs faces some challenges. Linguistic, cultural, economic, and political interests may interfere in the flow of information across national borders, as can different standards and privacy laws.

One important issue that has not been resolved is the discrepancy between the laws governing the collection and manipulation of personal data in two economic powers, the United States and the European Union (EU), which have incompatible data privacy laws. This difference restricts the flow of personal data between the United States and the EU.

Several cases have demonstrated that the old legal approach of territorial jurisdiction is inadequate when so much information is communicated and so much business is conducted on the Internet. Issues such as free speech and consumer litigation of e-tailers (online retailers) have brought to light the need for an international legal reform for cyberspace.

Corporate Control and Governance

Sections 901, 910, and 920. Corporate Control Strategies, Control Models, and Best Practices in Control

Summaries and Conclusions

Corporate Control Strategies

Control strategies should be linked to business strategies in that controls and the control environment in an organization should facilitate the achievement of business objectives. Controls can be divided into three categories: management control, operational control, and internal control.

Management control is the process by which managers assure that resources are obtained and used effectively and efficiently in the accomplishment of the organization's objectives. Operational control is the process of assuring that specific tasks are carried out effectively and efficiently. The focus of operational control is on individual tasks or transactions. The scope of internal control is broad in nature in that it consists of (1) organizational structure that creates a division of responsibilities among employees, (2) management authorization of business transactions, (3) communication programs explaining the company's policies and standards to all employees, and (4) selection and training of qualified and competent managers. Management control encompasses both operational control and internal control.

Control Models

Several control models exist for effective functioning and continual improvement of internal control systems. These include the COSO model, the CoCo model, the Control Self-Assessment model, the Turnbull model, the King model, the KonTrag model, the COBIT model, and the CONCT model.

Best Practices in Control

The term *best practices* refers to approaches that produce exceptional results. Best practices in internal control should be explored and implemented in operations, marketing and sales, service, and financial and operational reporting.

Section 930. Corporate Fraud

Summaries and Conclusions

Fighting Fraud

Most organizations spend most of their fraud-fighting dollars investigating frauds once predication is present. Investigation is only one of four major activities related to fraud. Organizations that do not work proactively at fraud prevention and detection can find themselves frequently targets of fraud schemes, and the scams come at a greater cost. In addition, even when organizations successfully investigate fraud, they often merely terminate perpetrators rather than seek legal action because termination is "the easy way out." Unfortunately, organizations that only terminate or do not sanction perpetrators also experience more fraud than organizations who enforce strict prosecution policies. Perpetrators are often first-time offenders and may be respected employees, clients, vendors, or customers. If they are terminated, they usually do not tell even their families the reason for their termination. Because they do not suffer the humiliation that ensues when friends, family members, and other loved ones become aware of their crime, perpetrators often undertake fraudulent activities again when opportunities present themselves.

Organizations must decide how much fraud they are willing to tolerate. Although it is difficult to get accurate statistics, research indicates that money spent on proactive prevention and detection and rigorous, legal follow-up tends to reduce future occurrences of fraud.[22] One Fortune 500 company with approximately $25 million of known fraud annually decided to take proactive steps to reduce fraud. The company worked hard on prevention, including making a video that was shown periodically to train employees in fraud awareness (as well as awareness training in other undesirable activities, such as substance abuse, safety violations, and discrimination). The company also provided employees with cards that specified who they should contact if they saw any of these problems. A proactive code of conduct was developed, and every employee signed it each year. It also focused on detection methods, including computer search techniques and a fraud hotline. Finally, it developed a comprehensive fraud policy specifying how potential frauds would be investigated and what actions would be taken against fraud perpetrators. Its efforts paid large dividends, especially given the multiplier effect. In only a couple of years, known frauds in the organization totaled less than $1 million annually.

Fraud Against Organizations

Fraud against organizations include thefts of cash, thefts of inventory, and bribery. Organizations that understand the types of frauds that they are particularly vulnerable to can "customize" this taxonomy for their individual situation and thereby pinpoint where their risks are greatest. They can then take proactive steps to reduce and/or eliminate risks and begin to audit for frauds that may be occurring.

Financial Statement Fraud

Four areas must be examined in detecting financial statement fraud: (1) management and directors, (2) relationships with others, (3) the organization and its industry, and (4) financial results and operating characteristics. Perpetrators choose fraud schemes for their "ease to commit and conceal" more often than for any other reason. Most fraud symptoms, especially those that show up in the financial results and the organization's operating characteristics, are scheme-specific.

Examples of fraud types include understatement of liability frauds, overstatement of asset frauds, and inadequate disclosure frauds. Management needs to be aware of which symptoms indicate that fraud may be occurring, ways to search for fraud symptoms, and ways to determine whether observed symptoms are occurring because of fraud or because of some other reason.

Revenue and Inventory Frauds

Revenue and inventory frauds are closely related because revenues are generated by selling inventory. Inventory, by its nature, has physical characteristics that should be compared to ascertain whether the numbers reported on the financial statements match. This ensures that the reported inventory levels are realistic.

Liability, Asset, and Inadequate Disclosure Frauds

Looking for fraud is like hiking in a forest. Perpetrators stand camouflaged and motionless as they try to conceal themselves and their fraud. Many people walk right by deer or elk in the forest; they do not see the animal unless they look for movement, changes in color or shadows, or changes in shapes, or the animal is pointed out to them. Likewise, to discover fraud, we look for analytical symptoms (movements), accounting or documentary symptoms (changes in color), behavioral and lifestyle symptoms (changes in shapes), control symptoms (changes in shadows), and tips and complaints (the evidence that is pointed out).

Generally accepted accounting principles (GAAP) require that companies prepare their financial statements using accrual-based accounting. Because of accrual-based accounting, reconciling the difference between the cash a company is generating and its reported net income is sometimes difficult. Indeed, that is one of the major purposes of the statement of cash flows. Timing and other elements create differences between a company's cash flows and its accrual-based net income. Over the life of a firm, however, these timing and other differences should even out so that the cash generated is approximately equal to the net income that is reported.

One of the best overall fraud indicators we have found is to track the differences and trend between cash flows (only cash can pay debts and keep a company liquid) and reported net income. We track this difference using the following ratio.

$$\text{Income Reconciliation Ratio} = \frac{\text{Net Income} - \text{Cash Flow from Operations}}{\text{Total Assets}}$$

The numerator is the difference between reported net income (from the income statement) and cash flow from operations (from the statement of cash flows.) The denominator is total assets (from the balance sheet) and is used to standardize the numerator. Over time, this ratio should hover around zero, with some positive years and some negative years. Progressive deterioration in this ratio (measured by increasingly longer positive numbers) can often spell trouble and hint that financial statement fraud is occurring, with reported net income increasing and cash flows decreasing.

Section 940. Corporate Risk Management

Summaries and Conclusions

Fundamentals of Risk

- Risk is defined as uncertainty concerning loss.
- Risk creates an economic burden for society by raising the cost of certain goods and services and eliminating the provision of others.
- The cost of risk includes outlays to reduce risks, the opportunity cost of activities foregone due to risk considerations, expenses of strategies to finance potential losses, and the cost of unreimbursed losses.
- Pure risk exists when there is uncertainty as to whether loss will occur. Speculative risk exists when there is uncertainty about an event that could produce either a profit or a loss.
- Static risks are present in an unchanging, stable society. Dynamic risks are produced by changes in society.
- Subjective risk refers to the mental state of an individual.
- Objective risk, which is measurable, is the probable variation of actual from expected experience.
- There are many sources of risk. One way of classifying them is in relation to property, liability, life, health, loss of income, and financial exposures.
- Chance of loss is the long-term relative frequency of a loss due to a particular peril, or cause of loss. The degree of risk is the relative variation of actual from expected losses.
- A hazard is a condition that increases the chance of loss due to peril. Hazards can arise out of both physical conditions and the mental attitudes of individuals.
- Risk management is the process used to systematically manage exposures to pure risk. The four steps in the process are (1) identify risks, (2) evaluate risks, (3) select risk management techniques, and (4) implement and review decisions.
- Integrated or enterprise risk management is an emerging view that recognizes the importance of risk, regardless of its source, in affecting a firm's ability to realize its strategic objectives.

Risk Identification and Evaluation

- Loss exposure checklists, financial statement analysis, flowcharts, contract analysis, on-site inspections of property, and the statistical analysis of past losses can be helpful in identifying risk.
- After risks are identified, they should be evaluated regarding their expected frequency of occurrence, the probable severity of associated losses, the maximum probable loss, and the maximum possible loss. Risk mapping is one way to catalogue the wide variety of risks identified.
- A probability distribution is a mutually exclusive and collectively exhaustive list of all events that result from a chance process. Risk managers use both empirical and theoretical probability distributions of losses in evaluating identified risks.

- The mean, median, and mode are ways of measuring the center of a probability distribution.
- The variance, standard deviation, and coefficient of variation are important ways of measuring the variation of actual from expected experience.
- Three theoretical distributions that are especially useful for risk managers are the normal, binomial, and Poisson distributions.
- "Value at risk" analysis involves the construction of probability distributions of risks alone and in various combinations to obtain estimates of the risk of loss at various probability levels.
- The law of large numbers indicates that as the number of exposure units increases, the degree of risk decreases. And, given a constant number of exposure units, as the chance of loss increases, the degree of risk decreases.
- When the probability of loss is very small, a larger number of exposure units is needed to achieve the same degree of risk than when the probability of loss is large.

Risk Management Techniques

- Risk avoidance is a conscious decision not to be exposed to a particular risk of loss. It is not always feasible, and even when it is, it is often not desirable.
- Loss control involves actions to reduce the losses associated with particular risks. Some forms of loss control concentrate on reducing the frequency of losses, whereas others focus on reducing loss severity. Two special forms of severity reduction are separation and duplication.
- Heinrich's domino theory states that employee injuries take the final place in the following sequence: heredity and social environment, personal fault, an unsafe act or physical hazard, an accident, and the resultant injury.
- Another way of classifying loss control is whether it involves actions prior to a loss, concurrent with a loss, or after a loss occurs.
- Expected gains from an investment in loss control should at least equal the expected costs in order to justify the expenditure. But it is not necessarily easy to identify and quantify all potential costs and benefits.
- Risk transfer involves payment by the transferor to the transferee, who agrees to assume a risk that the transferor desires to escape. Risk retention involves the assumption of risk, and can be planned or unplanned. It can also be either funded or unfunded prior to a loss.
- Four types of funded retention possibilities are the use of credit, the establishment of a reserve fund, self-insurance, and captive insurers.
- Self-insurance involves prefunding of expected losses and a sufficiently large group of exposure units to enable accurate loss prediction.
- Large businesses can often use risk retention to a greater extent than can small firms, partly because of their more extensive financial resources. Other factors to consider are the ability to predict losses and the overall feasibility of the retention program.
- All else being the same, the greater the following, the greater is a firm's ability to use risk retention: assets, revenues, liquidity, revenues/net worth, and retained earnings. All else being the same, firms with lower debt-to-equity ratios are better able to use risk retention.
- Four types of noninsurance risk transfer methods are hold-harmless agreements, incorporation, diversification, and hedging.
- Three types of hold-harmless agreements are limited form, intermediate form, and broad form. Hold-harmless agreements may not be legally enforceable if the transferor is in a superior position to the transferee with respect to either bargaining power or knowledge of the factual situation.
- Risk management activities such as risk transfer add value to a publicly traded firm by efficiently allocating risk among the firm's claimholders, reducing bankruptcy costs, increasing the likelihood that obligations to debtholders are met, providing access to the real services of insurers, and reducing expected tax liabilities.

Implementing Risk Management Techniques

- Because of the dynamic nature of risks and the techniques for managing them, risk management decisions must be reviewed regularly.
- The steps for selecting among risk management techniques are (a) avoid risks if possible, (b) implement appropriate loss control measures, and (c) select the optimal mix of risk retention and risk transfer.

- Net present value (NPV) analysis can be useful in deciding how much money to spend on loss control. If the NPV of the cash flows is positive, expenditures are justified.
- "High" versus "low" loss frequency and severity classifications are useful in deciding on an appropriate mix of risk retention and risk transfer. Risk retention tends to be optimal when expected severity is low, especially if expected frequency is high.
- Risk transfer is appropriate when expected frequency is low but there is high potential severity. If losses have both high expected frequency and severity, a variety of risk transfer, risk retention, risk avoidance, and loss control may be necessary.
- Both capital budgeting and statistical analysis can be used to select the best mix of risk retention and risk transfer. This mix may be accomplished through the selection of a deductible and/or the establishment of a self-insurance fund.
- Self-insurance may provide some financial advantages to a firm because interest can be earned on funds that are not currently needed to pay for losses.
- Businesses considering self-insurance should analyze their ability to predict probable losses, maintain accurate loss records, administer the many details of the arrangement, and deal with large and unusual losses.
- Risk managers in businesses must learn how to work with a variety of persons, both inside and outside of their firms, in implementing appropriate risk management decisions.
- In addition to risk avoidance, control, retention, and transfer, two methods for reducing subjective risk are obtaining more information and group discussion.
- Enterprise risk management is changing the way firms approach the management of risk. The integration of risk management strategies across all categories of risk facing the firm is causing firms to utilize alternative risk transfer tools, such as blended risk contracts, multiple-trigger insurance policies, and securitization of risk.

Section 950. Corporate Citizenship and Accountability

Summaries and Conclusions

Important and related concepts include those of corporate citizenship, corporate social responsibility (CSR), responsiveness, and performance. The corporate social responsibility concept has a rich history. It has grown out of many diverse views and even today does not enjoy a consensus of definition. A four-part conceptualization broadly conceives CSR as encompassing economic, legal, ethical, and philanthropic components. The four parts were presented as part of the Pyramid of CSR.

The concern for corporate social responsibility has been expanded to include a concern for social responsiveness. The responsiveness focus suggests more of an action-oriented theme by which firms not only must address their basic obligations but also must decide on basic modes of responding to these obligations. A corporate social performance (CSP) model brought the responsibility and responsiveness dimensions together into a framework that also identified realms of social or stakeholder issues that must be considered. The identification of social issues has blossomed into a field now called *issues management* or *stakeholder management*.

The interest in corporate social responsibility extends beyond the academic community. On an annual basis, *Fortune* magazine polls executives on various dimensions of corporate performance; one major dimension is called "Social Responsibility." The Council on Economic Priorities published a landmark volume entitled *Rating America's Corporate Conscience,* which further heightened public interest in the social and ethical domains of business performance. A new organization, Business for Social Responsibility, promises to be on the cutting edge of CSR practice. Walker Information has investigated how the general consuming public regards social responsibility issues. The term *corporate citizenship* has arrived on the scene to embrace a host of socially conscious activities and practices on the part of businesses. This term has become quite popular in the business community.

Finally, the socially conscious or ethical investing movement seems to be flourishing. This indicates that there is a growing body of investors who are sensitive to business's social and ethical (as well as financial) performance. Studies of the relationship between social responsibility and economic performance do not yield consistent results, but social efforts are nevertheless expected and are of value to both the firm and the business community. In the final analysis, sound corporate social (stakeholder) performance is associated with a "multiple-bottom-line effect" in which a number of different stakeholder groups experience enhanced bottom lines.

Section 960. Corporate Public Policy and Affairs

Summaries and Conclusions

Corporate public policy is a firm's posture or stance regarding the public, social, or ethical aspects of stakeholders and corporate functioning. It is a part of strategic management, particularly enterprise-level strategy. Enterprise-level strategy is the broadest, overarching level of strategy, and its focus is on the role of the organization in society. The other strategy levels include the corporate, business, and functional levels.

The strategic management process entails six stages: (1) goal formulation, (2) strategy formulation, (3) strategy evaluation, (4) strategy implementation, (5) strategic control, and (6) environmental analysis. A concern for social, ethical, and public issues may be seen at each stage. The stage at which public issues are most addressed for planning purposes is the environmental analysis stage. Vital components of environmental analysis include scanning, monitoring, forecasting, and assessing. In the overall environmental analysis process, social, ethical, and public issues are considered along with economic, political, and technological factors.

Public affairs might be described as the management function that is responsible for monitoring and interpreting a corporation's noncommercial environment and managing its response to that environment. Public affairs is intimately linked to corporate public policy, environmental analysis, issues management, and crisis management. The major functions of public affairs departments today include government relations, political action, community involvement/responsibility, issues management, international public affairs, and corporate philanthropy. A major growth area is international public affairs.

In terms of public affairs strategy, a collaborative/problem-solving strategy has been shown to be more effective than one that is individualistic/adversarial. Research has shown that a firm's corporate social performance, as well as its industry legitimacy, viability, and economic performance, is a function of business exposure, top management's philosophy, external affairs strategy, and external affairs design. In addition to being viewed as a staff function, public affairs is important for operating managers. Four specific strategies for incorporating public affairs into operating managers' jobs are (1) make it relevant, (2) develop a sense of ownership, (3) make it easy, and (4) show how it can make a difference.

Section 970. Issues Management and Crisis Management

Summaries and Conclusions

Issues Management

Issues management and crisis management are two key approaches by which companies can plan for the turbulent stakeholder environment. Both these approaches are frequently found housed in a company's department of public affairs. Issues management is a process by which an organization identifies issues in the stakeholder environment, analyzes and prioritizes those issues in terms of their relevance to the organization, plans responses to the issues, and then evaluates and monitors the results. There are two approaches to issues management: the conventional approach and the strategic management approach. Issues management requires a knowledge of the changing mix of issues, the issues management process, the issues development process, and how companies might implement issues management in practice. Issues management serves as a bridge to crisis management.

Crisis Management

Crisis management, like issues management, is not a panacea for organizations. In spite of well-intended efforts by management, not all crises will be resolved in the company's favor. Nevertheless, being prepared for the inevitable makes sense, especially in today's world of instantaneous global communications and obsessive media coverage. Whether we are thinking about the long term, the intermediate term, or the short term, managers need to be prepared to handle crises. A crisis has a number of different stages, and managing crises requires a number of key steps in the process. These steps include identifying areas of vulnerability, developing a plan for dealing with threats, forming crisis teams, using crisis drills, and learning from experience. Crisis communication is critical for successful crisis management. When used in tandem, issues and crisis management can help managers fulfill their economic, legal, ethical, and philanthropic responsibilities to stakeholders.

Section 980. Corporate Ethics and Management Assurance

Summaries and Conclusions

Corporate Ethics

Business ethics has become a serious challenge for the business community over the past several decades. Polls indicate that the public does not have high regard for the ethics of managers. It is not easy to say whether business's ethics have declined or just seem to have done so because of increased media coverage and rising public expectations. Business ethics concerns the rightness, wrongness, and fairness of managerial behavior, and these are not easy judgments to make. Multiple norms compete to determine which standards business behavior should be compared with. The conventional approach to business ethics was introduced as an initial way in which managers might think about ethical judgments. One major problem with this approach is that it is not clear which standards or norms should be used, and thus the conventional approach is susceptible to ethical relativism. A Venn diagram can be an aid to making decisions when economics, law, and ethics expectations compete with each other. Four important ethics questions are (1) What really is? (2) What ought to be? (3) How can we get from what is to what ought to be? (4) What is our motivation in this transition?

Three models of management ethics are (1) immoral management, (2) moral management, and (3) amoral management. Amoral management is further classified into intentional and unintentional categories. There are two hypotheses about the presence of these three moral types in the management population and in individuals. A generally accepted view is that moral judgment develops according to the pattern described by Lawrence Kohlberg. His three levels of moral development are (1) preconventional, (2) conventional, and (3) postconventional, autonomous, or principled. Three answers to the question "Why do manager behave ethically?" include the following.

- Most of us want to avoid some punishment and receive some reward.
- Many of us want to be responsible to family, friends, or superiors.
- Very few of us want to do what is right or pursue some ideal principle, such as justice.

Some research, however, suggests that there are gender-based differences in the perspectives taken by men and by women as they perceive and deal with moral issues. Managers' ethics are affected by sources of values originating external to the organization and sources from within the organization. The latter category includes respect for the authority structure, loyalty, conformity, and a concern for financial performance and results. Finally, there are six elements in developing moral judgment. If the moral management model is to be realized, these six elements need to be developed. These six elements include (1) moral imagination, (2) moral identification and ordering, (3) moral evaluation, (4) tolerance of moral disagreement and ambiguity, (5) integration of managerial and moral competence, and (6) a sense of moral obligation.

Management Assurance

Management of an organization is responsible for preparing the financial statements and the external auditor is responsible for expressing an opinion on them. The fact that the auditor assists the management in the preparation of financial statements does not relieve management from their responsibility. Ultimately, management is responsible for all decisions concerning the form and content of the financial statements. In this regard, management should exercise legal and ethical responsibility in preparing financial statements. The auditor should maintain professional skepticism during the audit about management's assertions and assurances.

Section 990. Corporate Governance

Summaries and Conclusions

To remain legitimate, corporations must be governed according to the intended and legal pattern. Corporations were not always being governed the way they were intended to be, but the trends of the last decade indicate that there is good reason to be hopeful. Of course, problems remain. Runaway CEO compensation remains a concern, as is finding good candidates to fill vacant board seats. Overall, though, the corporate governance picture has improved. Of course, continual vigilance must be maintained if corporate governance is to fully realize its promise—being responsive to the needs of the range of individuals and groups who have a stake in the firm.

Section 999. International Issues

Summaries and Conclusions

Ethical dilemmas pose difficulties, in general, for businesses, and those arising in connection with doing business in foreign lands are among the most complex. The current period is characterized by an increasing antiglobalization sentiment, and the attacks on the World Trade Center have created an unstable global environment. A cursory examination of major issues that have arisen in global business ethics over the past several decades shows that they rank right up there with the most well-known news stories. The infant formula controversy, the Bhopal tragedy, corruption and bribery, concern about sweatshops, and the exploits of MNCs in Third World countries have all provided an opportunity for business critics to assail corporate ethics in the international sphere. These problems arise for a multiplicity of reasons, but differing cultures, value systems, forms of government, socioeconomic systems, and underhanded and ill-motivated business exploits have all been contributing factors.

The balancing of home and host country standards using Integrative Social Contracts Theory, global codes of conduct, the integration of ethical considerations into corporate strategy, the option of suspending activities, the use of ethical impact statements, and the adherence to international rights and moral guidelines offer some hope that global business can be better managed. Despite the recent terrorist attacks, current trends point to a growth in business activity in the transnational economy, and though there is some evidence of a backlash against globalization, these issues will become more rather than less important in the future. Indeed, it could easily be argued that business's greatest ethical challenges in the future will be at the global level, and especially in the developing countries.

International Business

Section 1001. Global Business Strategies

Summaries and Conclusions

Domestic business enterprises internationalize their operations in response to opportunities and threats generated by changes that have taken place in foreign markets. They develop international strategies to seize the opportunities or to combat the threats. To develop effective international strategies, managers must be totally familiar with the firm's external environment as well as with its internal resources and capabilities. If a firm does not possess the ability to manage international operations, it may have to form a partnership with a firm that does.

There are four types of international strategies: ethnocentric, multidomestic, global, and transnational. The international enterprise must establish strategic and tactical objectives in at least eight areas of organizational performance: market standing, innovations, productivity, physical and financial resources, profitability, manager performance and responsibility, worker performance and attitude, and social responsibility.

Section 1010. Forms of International Business and Marketing Strategies

Summaries and Conclusions

Forms of International Business

The business environment changed dramatically from the end of World War II to the 2000s. To be competitive in world markets today, the international manager or world trader needs to be familiar with economics, culture, politics, and law. Multinational firms have adopted business strategies that see the world—and profits—in global terms. Even small- and medium-sized manufacturing and service firms are important competitors in international markets, and will become even more important in the future.

The three basic forms of international business—trade, licensing, and investment—are methods of entering foreign markets. They are not mutually exclusive. One joint venture agreement, for instance, can have provisions for the building of a plant and the manufacture of goods, for the licensing of trademarks or patents to the joint venture for a determined period, and for the export or import of those products to other countries of distribution. The methods employed to enter a foreign market must be tailored to the type and size of firm, the nature of its product or service, and its experience and goals.

The process of managing an international business transaction is the process of managing risk. Nowhere is that risk greater than in the rapidly changing developing world, in Eastern Europe, or in the newly independent republics of the former Soviet Union. The economic and social problems in those regions make experience and caution a prerequisite to tapping the new opportunities that wait there. Through the study of international business law, one can better prepare to identify potential risks and problems and to plan business strategies accordingly.

International Marketing Strategies

When managers develop international product/service strategy, they must consider the self-reference criterion (SRC), which often leads one to assume that what sells at home will sell abroad in the same form—which usually is not true. Some products and services can be sold globally in standardized form, but most products and services must be customized to fit the varying needs of different societies. Managers must also consider that many products and services introduced into a society will not sell well right away; they must be diffused into the society over time.

The method of getting the product or service to foreign customers will vary from nation to nation. The fundamental approaches are exporting to it or manufacturing in it. Six approaches to manufacturing abroad include licensing, franchising, management contracts, joint ventures, contractual alliances, and wholly owned subsidiaries. Various factors influence international pricing strategy, such as the foreign government, monetary exchange, and the requirement for barter trade. Some international firms use pricing strategy to develop foreign markets; others are content to simply get some revenue from the foreign market. Some international firms use a transfer pricing approach to get around a country's high tax rate, currency restrictions, currency devaluations, and mandate to reduce prices and increase wages. Four types of barter trade are barter, compensation, switch, and counterpurchase.

Relative to promotion strategy, various factors influence international promotions, including the legal aspects of the country, language differences, and cultural diversity. Reasons that international promotional strategies sometimes fail include insufficient research, overstandardization, poor follow-up, narrow vision, and rigid implementation.

Section 1020. International Risks

Summaries and Conclusions

The political and legal environment in the home and host countries and the laws and agreements governing relationships among nations are important to the international business executive. Compliance is mandatory in order to do business successfully abroad. To avoid the problems that can result from changes in the political and legal environment, it is essential to anticipate changes and to develop strategies for coping with them. Whenever possible, the manager must avoid being taken by surprise and letting events control business decisions.

Governments affect international business through legislation and regulations, which can support or hinder business transactions. An example is when export sanctions or embargoes are imposed to enhance foreign policy objectives.

Similarly, export controls are used to preserve national security. Nations also regulate the international business behavior of firms by setting standards that relate to bribery and corruption, boycotts, and restraint of competition.

Through political actions such as expropriation, confiscation, or domestication, countries expose firms to international risk. Management therefore needs to be aware of the possibility of such risk and alert to new developments. Many private sector services are available to track international risk situations. In the event of a loss, firms may rely on insurance for political risk or they may seek redress in court. International legal action, however, may be quite slow and may compensate for only part of the loss.

Managers need to be aware that different countries have different laws. One clearly pronounced difference is between code law countries, where all possible legal rules are spelled out, and common law countries such as the United States, where the law is based on tradition, precedent, custom, and court cases.

Managers must also pay attention to international political relations, agreements, and treaties. Changes in relations or rules can mean major new opportunities and occasional threats to international business. Even though conflict in international business may sometimes lead to litigation, the manager needs to be aware of the alternative of arbitration, which may resolve the pending matter more quickly and at a lower cost.

Section 1030. Global Organization Structure and Control

Summaries and Conclusions

Organizational structures and control mechanisms are needed to operate in the international business field. The elements define relationships between the entities of the firm and provide the channels through which the relationships develop.

International firms can choose from a variety of organizational structures, ranging from a domestic organization that handles ad hoc export orders to a full-fledged global organization. The choice will depend heavily on the degree of internationalization of the firm, the diversity of international activities, and the relative importance of product, area, function, and customer variables in the process. A determining factor is also the degree to which headquarters wants to decide important issues concerning the whole corporation and the individual subsidiaries. Organizations that function effectively still need to be revisited periodically to ensure that they remain responsive to a changing environment. Some of the responsiveness is showing up not as structural changes, but rather in how the entities conduct their internal business.

In addition to organization, the control function takes on major importance for multinationals because of the high variability in performance resulting from divergent local environments and the need to reconcile local objectives with the corporate goal of synergism. While it is important to grant autonomy to country organizations so that they can be responsive to local market needs, it is of equal importance to ensure close cooperation among units to optimize corporate effectiveness.

Control can be exercised through bureaucratic means, which emphasize formal reporting and evaluation of benchmark data, or through cultural means, in which norms and values are understood by the individuals and entities that make up the corporation. U.S. firms typically rely more on bureaucratic controls, while MNCs from other countries frequently run operations abroad through informal means and rely less on stringent measures.

The implementation of controls requires great sensitivity to behavioral dimensions and the environment. The measurements used must be appropriate and reflective of actual performance rather than marketplace vagaries. Similarly, entities should be judged only on factors over which they have some degree of control.

Section 1040. International Trade and Investment

Summaries and Conclusions

The theory of international trade has changed drastically from that first put forward by Adam Smith. The classical theories of Adam Smith and David Ricardo focused on the abilities of countries to produce goods more cheaply than other countries. The earliest production and trade theories saw labor as the major factor expense that went into any product. If a country could pay that labor less, and if that labor could produce more physically than labor in other countries, the country might obtain an absolute or comparative advantage in trade.

Subsequent theoretical development led to a more detailed understanding of production and its costs. Factors of production are now believed to include labor (skilled and unskilled), capital, natural resources, and other potentially significant commodities that are difficult to reproduce or replace, such as energy. Technology, once assumed to be the same across all countries, is now seen as one of the premier driving forces in determining who holds the competitive edge or advantage. International trade is now seen as a complex combination of thousands of products, technologies, and firms that are constantly innovating to either keep up with or get ahead of the competition.

Modern trade theory has looked beyond production cost to analyze how the demands of the marketplace alter who trades with whom and which firms survive domestically and internationally. The abilities of firms to adapt to foreign markets, both in the demands and the competitors that form the foreign markets, have required much of international trade and investment theory to search out new and innovative approaches to what determines success and failure.

Finally, as world economies grew and the magnitude of world trade increased, the simplistic ideas that guided international trade and investment theory have had to grow with them. The choices that many firms face today require them to directly move their capital, technology, and know-how to countries that possess other unique factors or market advantages that will help them keep pace with market demands. Even then, world business conditions constitute changing fortunes.

Section 1050. International Payments

Summaries and Conclusions

The balance of payments (BOP) is the summary statement of all international transactions between one country and all other countries. The balance of payments is a flow statement, summarizing all the international transactions that occur across the geographic boundaries of the nation over a period of time, typically a year. Because of its use of double-entry bookkeeping, the BOP must always balance in theory, though in practice there are substantial imbalances as a result of statistical errors and misreporting of current account and capital/financial account flows.

The two major subaccounts of the balance of payments—the current account and the capital account—summarize the current trade and international capital flows of the country. Due to the double-entry bookkeeping method of accounting, the current account and capital account are always inverse on balance, one in surplus while the other experiences deficit. Although most nations strive for current account surpluses, it is not clear that a balance on current or capital account, or a surplus on current account, is either sustainable or desirable. The monitoring of the various subaccounts of a country's balance of payments activity is helpful to decision makers and policymakers at all levels of government and industry in detecting the underlying trends and movements of fundamental economic forces driving a country's international economic activity.

Section 1060. International Cultures and Protocols

Summaries and Conclusions

The communication process in an international/ cross-cultural context is difficult. How cross-cultural communicators (senders) construct ideas to be communicated is influenced by the receivers' culture. The same concepts will be perceived differently across cultures. Thus, what works in one culture will not necessarily work in another, and adaptations must be made. The words, gestures, symbols, idioms, jargon, and slang a sender uses to communicate an idea are also affected by the particular receivers' culture. Different societies use different languages and social behaviors to communicate. Therefore, for effective communication to take place, the appropriate adaptations must be made.

The means—written, oral, or nonverbal—of transmitting the message is also affected by the receivers' culture. Culturally, some people prefer oral communication and others prefer written communication. Some cultures prefer flamboyant, flashy presentations; other cultures are offended by such presentations. The cross-cultural communicator must use the means most fitted to the receivers' culture. In essence, the sender of the message must know and use the words, concepts, and behaviors that the receivers will understand, which means that, to be effective, a cross-cultural communicator must learn to be both a sender and a receiver.

It is interesting to note that how differing cultural views on time, material possessions, family roles, and relationships affect the ways one transacts business across societies. For example, in the United States, "time is money," but in many parts of the world, people value relationships more than time. Thus, the "hurry up" business approach used by Americans would not be effective in, for instance, Spain, where establishing a relationship is more important than "time equals money." Negotiating styles vary from culture to culture and from nation to nation. If a cross-cultural negotiator does not become familiar with and adapt to the style of the society where he or she is negotiating for business contracts, the consequence is likely to be failure. The manager needs to understand the issues related to strategic and tactical planning for international negotiations.

Section 1070. Economics and International Business

Summaries and Conclusions

Macroeconomic Policy

- International economic policy refers to various government activities that influence trade patterns among nations, including (1) monetary and fiscal policies, (2) exchange-rate adjustments, (3) tariff and nontariff trade barriers, (4) foreign-exchange controls and investment controls, and (5) export-promotion measures.
- Since the 1930s, nations have actively pursued internal balance (full employment without inflation) as a primary economic objective. Nations also consider external balance (BOP equilibrium) as an economic objective. A nation realizes overall balance when it attains internal balance and external balance.
- To achieve overall balance, nations implement expenditure-changing policies (monetary and fiscal policies), expenditure-switching policies (exchange-rate adjustments), and direct controls (price and wage controls).
- Although exchange-rate adjustments primarily influence a nation's BOP position, they have secondary impacts on the domestic economy. A nation with a BOP deficit and high unemployment could devalue its currency to resolve these problems; a nation with a BOP surplus and inflation could revalue its currency. Such policies are dependent upon the willingness of other nations to refrain from implementing offsetting exchange-rate adjustments. International economic-policy cooperation is thus essential when nations are economically interdependent.
- Under a fixed exchange-rate system, fiscal policy is successful in promoting internal balance, whereas monetary policy is unsuccessful. Under a floating exchange-rate system, monetary policy is successful in promoting internal balance, whereas fiscal policy is unsuccessful.

- Given a fixed exchange-rate system, in the short run, an expansionary monetary policy worsens the BOP position, and a contractionary monetary policy improves the BOP position. An expansionary fiscal policy leads to a worsening of the trade account and an improvement in the capital account; the impact on the overall BOP depends on the relative strength of these opposing forces.
- Policy agreement occurs when an economic policy helps eliminate internal disequilibrium and external disequilibrium, thus promoting overall balance for the nation. Policy conflict occurs when an economic policy helps eliminate one economic problem (such as internal disequilibrium), but aggravates another economic problem (such as external disequilibrium).
- Given a fixed exchange-rate system, for monetary policy the disequilibrium zones of unemployment-with-BOP-surplus and inflation with-BOP-deficit are zones of policy agreement. The disequilibrium zones of unemployment with-BOP-deficit and inflation-with-BOP-surplus are zones of policy conflict; a dilemma exists for monetary authorities concerning which objective to pursue. A combination of policies may be needed to resolve these economic problems.
- When a nation experiences inflation with unemployment, achieving overall balance involves three separate targets: BOP equilibrium, full employment, and price stability. Three policy instruments may be needed to achieve these targets.
- International economic-policy coordination is the attempt to significantly modify national policies in recognition of international economic interdependence. Nations regularly consult with each other in the context of the international monetary fund (IMF), organization for economic cooperation and development (OECD), Bank for International Settlements, and Group of Seven. The Smithsonian Agreement, Plaza Agreement, and Louvre Accord are examples of international economic-policy coordination.
- Several problems confront international economic-policy coordination: (1) different national economic objectives, (2) different national institutions, (3) different national political climates, (4) different phases in the business cycle. Moreover, there is no guarantee that governments can design and implement policies that are capable of achieving the intended results.

International Equilibrium

- Demand and supply conditions determine the basis for trade and the direction of trade. Demand also helps establish the international terms of trade—that is, the relative prices at which commodities are exchanged between nations.
- A community indifference curve depicts a nation's tastes or preferences. Community indifference curves illustrate the various combinations of two commodities that yield equal satisfaction to a nation. A higher indifference curve indicates more satisfaction. Community indifference curves are analogous to an individual's indifference curve. The slope of a community indifference curve at any point indicates the marginal rate of substitution between two goods in consumption. This shows the amount of one good a nation is willing to sacrifice in order to gain an additional unit of another good while still remaining on the same indifference curve.
- The introduction of community indifference curves into the trade model permits a restatement of the basis for trade and the gains from trade.
- In the absence of trade, a nation achieves equilibrium when its community indifference curve is tangent to its production possibilities schedule. The domestic relative commodity price is denoted by the common slope of these two curves at their point of tangency. When the relative commodity prices of two nations differ, a basis for mutually beneficial trade exists.
- A nation will benefit from trade when it is able to reach a higher indifference curve (level of satisfaction) than could be achieved without trade. Gains from trade will be maximized when a nation's post-trade consumption point is located where the international terms-of-trade line is tangent to a community indifference curve.
- Because Ricardian trade theory relied solely on supply analysis, it was not able to determine precisely the equilibrium terms of trade. This limitation was addressed by John Stuart Mill in his theory of reciprocal demand. This theory suggests that before the equilibrium terms of trade can be established, it is necessary to know both nations' demands for both products. The theory of reciprocal demand can be analyzed by means of offer curves, which illustrate the determination of the equilibrium terms of trade.
- The commodity terms of trade is often used to measure the direction of trade gains. It indicates the relationship between the prices a nation gets for its exports and the prices it pays for its imports over a given time period.

Tariff Trade Barriers

- Even though the free-trade argument has strong theoretical justifications, trade restrictions are widespread throughout the world. Trade barriers consist of tariff restrictions and nontariff trade barriers.
- There are several types of tariffs. A specific tariff represents a fixed amount of money per unit of the imported commodity. An ad valorem tariff is stated as a fixed percentage of the value of an imported commodity. A compound tariff combines a specific tariff with an ad valorem tariff.
- Concerning ad valorem tariffs, several procedures exist for the valuation of imports. The free-on-board (FOB) measure indicates a commodity's price as it leaves the exporting nation. The cost-insurance-freight (CIF) measure shows the product's value as it arrives at the port of entry.
- The effective tariff rate tends to differ from the nominal tariff rate when the domestic import-competing industry uses imported resources whose tariffs differ from those on the final commodity. Developing nations have traditionally argued that many advanced nations escalate the tariff structures on industrial commodities to yield an effective rate of protection several times the nominal rate.
- U.S. trade laws mitigate the effects of import duties by allowing U.S. importers to postpone and prorate over time their duty obligations by means of bonded warehouses and foreign trade zones.
- The welfare effects of a tariff can be measured by its protective effect, consumption effect, redistributive effect, revenue effect, and terms-of-trade effect.
- If a nation is small compared with the rest of the world, its welfare necessarily falls by the total amount of the protective effect plus the consumption effect if it levies a tariff on imports. If the importing nation is large relative to the world, the imposition of an import tariff may improve its international terms of trade by an amount that more than offsets the welfare losses associated with the consumption effect and the protective effect.
- Although tariffs may improve one nation's economic position, any gains generally come at the expense of other nations. Should tariff retaliations occur, the volume of international trade decreases, and world welfare suffers. Tariff liberalization is intended to promote freer markets so that the world can benefit from expanded trade volumes and international specialization of inputs.
- Tariffs are sometimes justified on the grounds that they (1) protect domestic employment and wages, (2) help create a level playing field for international trade, (3) equate the cost of imported products with the cost of domestic import competing products, (4) allow domestic industries to be insulated temporarily from foreign competition until they can grow and develop, or (5) protect industries necessary for national security.

NonTariff Trade Barriers

- With the decline in import tariffs in the past two decades, nontariff trade barriers have gained in importance as a measure of protection. Nontariff trade barriers include such practices as (1) import quotas, (2) orderly marketing agreements, (3) domestic content requirements, (4) subsidies, (5) antidumping regulations, (6) discriminatory government procurement practices, (7) social regulations, and (8) sea transport and freight restrictions.
- An import quota is a government-imposed limit on the quantity of a product that can be imported. Quotas are imposed on a global (worldwide) basis or a selective (individual country) basis. Although quotas have many of the same economic effects as tariffs, they tend to be more restrictive. A quota's revenue effect generally accrues to domestic importers or foreign exporters, depending on the degree of market power they possess. If government desired to capture the revenue effect, it could auction import quota licenses to the highest bidder in a competitive market.
- A tariff-rate quota is a two-tier tariff placed on an imported product. It permits a limited number of goods to be imported at a lower tariff rate, whereas any imports beyond this limit face a higher tariff. Of the revenue generated by a tariff-rate quota, some accrues to the domestic government as tariff revenue and the remainder is captured by producers as windfall profits.
- Orderly marketing agreements are market-sharing pacts negotiated by trading nations. They generally involve quotas on exports and imports. Proponents of orderly marketing agreements contend that they are less disruptive of international trade than unilaterally determined tariffs and quotas.
- Because an export quota is administered by the government of the exporting nation (supply-side restriction), its revenue effect tends to be captured by sellers of the exporting nation. For the importing nation, the quota's revenue effect is a welfare loss in addition to the protective and consumption effects.

- Domestic content requirements try to limit the practice of foreign sourcing and encourage the development of domestic industry. They typically stipulate the minimum percentage of a product's value that must be produced in the home country for that product to be sold there. Local content protection tends to impose welfare losses on the domestic economy in the form of higher production costs and higher-priced goods.
- Government subsidies are sometimes granted as a form of protection to domestic exporters and import-competing companies. They may take the form of direct cash bounties, tax concessions, credit extended at low interest rates, or special insurance arrangements. Direct production subsidies for import-competing producers tend to involve a smaller loss in economic welfare than do equivalent tariffs and quotas. The imposition of export subsidies results in a terms-of-trade effect and an export-revenue effect.
- International dumping occurs when a firm sells its product abroad at a price that is (1) less than average total cost, or (2) less than that charged to domestic buyers of the same product. Dumping can be sporadic, predatory, or persistent in nature. Idle productive capacity may be the reason behind dumping. Governments often impose stiff penalties against foreign commodities that are believed to be dumped in the home economy.
- Government rules and regulations in areas such as safety and technical standards and marketing requirements can have significant impacts on world trade patterns.

Exchange Rate Systems

- Most nations maintain neither completely fixed nor floating exchange rates. Contemporary exchange-rate systems generally embody some features of each of these standards.
- Small, developing nations often peg their currencies to a single currency or a currency basket. Pegging to a single currency is generally used by small nations whose trade and financial relationships are mainly with a single trading partner. Small nations with more than one major trading partner often peg their currencies to a basket of currencies.
- The special drawing right (SDR) is a currency basket composed of five currencies of International Monetary Fund (IMF) members. The basket-valuation technique attempts to make the SDR's value more stable than the foreign currency value of any single currency in the basket. Developing nations often choose to peg their exchange rates to the SDR.
- Under a fixed exchange-rate system, a government defines the official exchange rate for its currency. It then establishes an exchange stabilization fund, which buys and sells foreign currencies to prevent the market exchange rate from moving above or below the official rate.
- Under a fixed exchange-rate system, nations may officially devalue/revalue their currencies to restore trade equilibrium. The purpose of devaluation is to promote a depreciation in the home currency's exchange value, which helps reduce a trade deficit. The purpose of revaluation is to promote an appreciation in the home currency's exchange value, which helps reduce a trade surplus.
- Currency boards are a method of stabilizing exchange rates of developing countries. A currency board is a monetary authority that issues notes and coins convertible into a foreign currency at a fixed exchange rate. Usually, the fixed exchange rate is set by law, making changes to the exchange rate very costly for governments. The most vital contribution a currency board can make to exchange-rate stability is to impose discipline on the process of money creation. This results in greater stability on domestic prices which, in turn, stabilizes the value of the domestic currency.
- Rather than using a currency board to stabilize currency values, countries may dollarize their monetary systems. Dollarization occurs when residents of a country use the U.S. dollar alongside or instead of their own currency. Dollarization is seen as a way to protect a country's growth and prosperity from bouts of inflation and currency depreciation.
- Under floating exchange rates, market forces of supply and demand determine currency values. Among the major arguments for floating rates are (1) simplicity, (2) continuous adjustment, (3) independent domestic policies, and (4) reduced need for international reserves. Arguments against floating rates stress (1) disorderly exchange markets, (2) reckless financial policies on the part of governments, and (3) conduciveness to price inflation.

- The adjustable pegged exchange-rate system resulted from the Bretton Woods Agreement of 1944. The idea was to provide participating nations with stable but flexible exchange rates. In the short run, nations would use exchange stabilization funds to maintain fixed exchange rates; in the long run, currency devaluations and revaluations would be used to help reverse persistent payment imbalances.
- With the breakdown of the Bretton Woods system, the major industrial nations adopted a system of managed floating exchange rates. Under this system, central-bank intervention in the foreign-exchange market is intended to prevent disorderly market conditions in the short run. In the long run, exchange rates are permitted to float in accordance with changing supply and demand.
- To offset a depreciation in the home currency's exchange value, a central bank can (1) use its international reserves to purchase quantities of that currency on the foreign-exchange market; (2) initiate a contractionary monetary policy, which leads to higher domestic interest rates, increased investment inflows, and increased demand for the home currency. To offset an appreciation in the home currency's exchange value, a central bank can sell additional quantities of its currency on the foreign exchange market or initiate an expansionary monetary policy.
- Under a crawling-peg exchange-rate system, a nation makes frequent devaluations (or revaluations) of its currency to restore payments balance. Developing nations suffering from high inflation rates have been major users of this mechanism.
- Exchange controls are sometimes used by governments in an attempt to gain control of the balance of payments. To limit imports, the government may ration foreign exchange to domestic traders and investors. Multiple exchange rates are sometimes used in an attempt to ensure that only necessary goods will be imported.
- Nations such as Belgium have resorted to dual exchange rates to insulate the balance of payments from short-term capital movements while providing exchange-rate stability for commercial transactions.

Section 1075. International Banking

Summaries and Conclusions

- The purpose of international reserves is to permit nations to bridge the gap between monetary receipts and payments. Deficit nations can use international reserves to buy time in order to postpone adjustment measures.
- The demand for international reserves depends on two major factors: (1) the monetary value of international transactions, and (2) the size and duration of balance-of-payments disequilibriums.
- The need for international reserves tends to become less acute under a system of floating exchange rates than under a system of fixed rates. The more efficient the international adjustment mechanism and the greater the extent of international policy coordination, the smaller the need for international reserves.
- The supply of international reserves consists of owned and borrowed reserves. Among the major sources of reserves are (1) foreign currencies, (2) monetary gold stocks, (3) special drawing rights (SDRS), (4) international monetary fund (IMF) drawing positions, (5) the General Arrangements to Borrow, and (6) swap arrangements.
- When making international loans, bankers face credit risk, country risk, and currency risk.
- Among the indicators used to analyze a nation's external debt position are its debt-to-export ratio and debt service/export ratio.
- A nation experiencing debt-servicing difficulties has several options: (1) cease repayment on its debt, (2) service its debt at all costs, or (3) reschedule its debt. Debt rescheduling has been widely used by borrowing nations in recent years.
- A bank can reduce its exposure to developing nation debt through outright loan sales in the secondary market, debt buybacks, debt-for-debt swaps, and debt/equity swaps.
- Eurocurrencies are deposits, denominated and payable in dollars and other foreign currencies, in banks outside the United States. Dollar deposits located in banks outside the United States are called *Eurodollars,* and banks that conduct trading in markets for Eurocurrencies are known as *Eurobanks.*

Section 1080. Law and International Business

Summaries and Conclusions

The International Environment

- International law includes law that deals with the conduct and relations of nation-states and international organizations as well as some of their relations with persons. Such law is enforceable by the courts of a nation that has adopted the international law as domestic law.
- The International Court of Justice (ICJ) is a judicial branch of the United Nations having voluntary jurisdiction over nations.
- Regional trade communities include international organizations, conferences, and treaties focusing on business and trade regulations; the EU (European Union) is the most prominent of these.
- International treaties are agreements between or among independent nations, such as the General Agreement on Tariffs and Trade (GATT), now called the World Trade Organization (WTO).

Jurisdiction Over Actions of Foreign Governments

- Sovereign immunity is a foreign country's freedom from a host country's laws.
- The Act of State Doctrine is rule that a court should not question the validity of actions taken by a foreign government in its own country.

TAKING OF FOREIGN INVESTMENT PROPERTY

- *Expropriation* is governmental taking of foreign-owned property for a public purpose and with payment of just compensation.
- *Confiscation* is governmental taking of foreign-owned property without payment (or for a highly inadequate payment) or for a nonpublic purpose.

Transacting Business Abroad

- Flow of trade is controlled by trade barriers on imports and exports.
  - Tariff duty or tax is imposed on goods moving into or out of a country.
  - Nontariff barriers include quotas, bans, safety standards, and subsidies.
- Flow of labor is controlled through passport, visa, and immigration regulations.
- Flow of capital involves the International Monetary Fund (IMF), which facilitates the expansion and balanced growth of international trade, assists in eliminating foreign exchange restrictions, and smoothes the international balance of payments.
- International contracts involve additional issues beyond those in domestic contracts, such as differences in language, legal systems, and currency.
  - The U. N. Convention on Contracts for the International Sales of Goods (CISG) governs all contracts for international sales of goods between parties located in different nations that have ratified the CISG.
  - A *letter of credit* is a bank's promise to pay the seller, provided certain conditions are met; it is used to manage the payment risks in international trade.
- Antitrust laws of the United States apply to unfair methods of competition that have a direct, substantial, and reasonably foreseeable effect on the domestic, import, or export commerce of the United States.
- Securities regulation is applicable to foreign issuers who issue securities, or whose securities are sold in the secondary market in the United States. Issues must register these securities unless an exemption is available. The antifraud provisions apply where there is either *conduct* or *effects* in the United States relating to a violation of the federal securities laws.

- In order to obtain protection of intellectual property, the owner of an intellectual property right must comply with each country's requirements to obtain from that country whatever protection is available.
- The Foreign Corrupt Practices Act (FCPA) prohibits all U.S. companies from bribing foreign governmental or political officials.
- The United States laws such as the Title VII of the Civil Rights Act of 1964, the Americans with Disabilities Act, and the Age Discrimination in Employment Act apply to U.S. citizens employed in foreign countries by U.S.-owned or -controlled companies or subsidiaries.

Forms of Multinational Enterprises

- A multinational enterprise (MNE) is any business that engages in transactions involving the movement of goods, information, money, people, or services across national borders. Here MNE is the same as the MNC.
- The choice of form of MNE depends on a number of factors including financing considerations, tax consequences, and degree of control.
  - In *direct export sales,* the seller contracts directly with the buyer in the other country.
  - A *foreign agent,* a local agent in the host country, may be used to provide limited involvement for an MNE.
  - In a *distributorship,* the MNE sells to a foreign distributor who takes title to the merchandise.
  - A *licensing* MNE sells a foreign company the right to use technology or information.
  - In a *joint venture,* two independent businesses from different countries share profits, liabilities, and duties.
  - A *wholly owned subsidiary* enables an MNE to retain control and authority over all phases of operation.

Section 1090. Ethics and International Business

Summaries and Conclusions

Certain business practices, such as bribery, are viewed as unethical in some cultures but ethical in others. The practice of bribery and "payoffs" by numerous U.S. MNCs led to the passage of the Foreign Corrupt Practices Act (FCPA) of 1977. Managers of many MNCs have complained that the act, because it precluded them from bribing or "paying off" officials in foreign countries to obtain "favors," even if it was an acceptable practice in the country, put them at a competitive disadvantage with foreign competitors who were not bound by the act. Some international executives condone the concept of "cultural relativism," which holds that no culture's ethics are any better than any other's; that there are no international "rights" or "wrongs." However, the practice of cultural relativism often backfires. Some international executives condone the concept of "universalism," which holds that there should be a global yardstick by which to measure all moral issues. This approach often leads to a show of disrespect for valid cultural differences. The media often influence MNCs to reject cultural relativism and apply the concept of universalism. There is a large business ethics gap between the United States and other advanced nations; Americans are exposed to far more business misconduct issues than are people in other advanced countries.

Section 1099. International Issues

Summaries and Conclusions

International business is a complex and difficult activity, yet it affords many opportunities and challenges. Observing changes and analyzing how to best incorporate them in the international business mission is the most important task of the international manager. If the international environment were constant, there would be little challenge to international business. The frequent changes are precisely what make international business so fascinating and often highly profitable for those who are active in the field.

SECTION II

Application of Business Concepts

Application 1
Strategic Management Analysis, 171

Application 2
Marketing Management Analysis, 172

Application 3
Leverage Analysis, 173

Application 4
Supply Chain Management Analysis, 175

Application 5
Pricing Analysis, 177

Application 6
Capital Budget Analysis, 179

Application 7
Mergers, Acquisitions, and Business Valuation Analysis, 180

Application 8
Production Planning Analysis, 183

Application 9
Process Analysis, 184

Application 10
Advertising Analysis, 186

Application 11
Manufacturing Management Analysis, 187

Application 12
Value Analysis, 189

Application 13
Manufacturing Operations Analysis, 190

Application 14
Retail Management Analysis, 194

Application 15
Service Management Analysis, 200

Application 16
Cost Analysis, 202

Application 17
Corporate Performance Analysis, 204

Application 18
Financial Management Analysis, 205

Application 19
International Trade and Financing Analysis, 208

Application 20
Project Management Analysis, 210

Application 21
Economic Analysis, 211

Application 22
Cash Flow Analysis, 212

Application 23
Fraud Analysis, 213

Application 24
Quality Analysis, 214

Application 25
Sensitivity and Scenario Analysis, 217

Application 26
Divisional Performance Analysis, 218

Application 27
Organizational and General Management Analysis, 220

Application 28
Human Resource Management Analysis, 226

Application 29
Logistics Analysis, 227

Application 30
New Product Development and Product Management Analysis, 230

Application 31
Sales Analysis, 232

Application 32
Risk Analysis, 233

Application 33
Decision Analysis, 237

Application 34
Operating Budget Analysis, 238

Application 35
Cost-Volume-Profit Analysis, 240

Application 36
Control Analysis, 241

Application 37
Customer Analysis, 243

Application 38
Quantitative and Qualitative Analysis, 244

Application 39
Productivity Analysis, 248

Application 40
Competitive Analysis, 249

Strategic Management Analysis

This application is related to General Management and Organization (Module 100), and specifically to Section 101 (Corporate Strategies).

Strategic Analysis

A firm should develop strategies that focus on core competencies, develop synergy, and create value for customers. Control helps management achieve its planned goals. Strategy should change over time to fit environmental conditions.

Strategy formulation deals with goals and specific plans. The term *strategy implementation* refers to the use of managerial tools to direct resources toward the achievement of strategic goals. Strategy implementation is the most difficult and most important part of a company's strategic management.

Situation analysis includes analyzing strengths, weaknesses, opportunities, and threats (SWOT). Determination of strengths and weaknesses is the result of scanning internal environments. On the other hand, designation of opportunities and threats is a result of scanning external environments.

Gap analysis identifies the distance between a company's current condition and its desired condition.

Leadership is the primary key to successful implementation of a strategy. Leadership means using persuasion, motivating employees, and shaping culture and values to support the new strategy. Managers may make speeches to employees, build coalitions of people who support the new strategic direction, and persuade middle managers to go along with their vision for the company.

Michael E. Porter proposed five competitive forces: (1) potential new entrants, (2) threat of substitute products, (3) bargaining power of buyers, (4) bargaining power of suppliers, and (5) rivalry among competitors. He also suggested three competitive strategies: (1) differentiation, (2) cost leadership, and (3) focus. Using differentiation strategy, the organization seeks to distinguish its products or services from competitors'. Cost leadership strategy involves seeking efficient facilities, cutting costs, and using tight cost controls to be more efficient than competitors. Focus strategy emphasizes concentration on a specific regional market or buyer group.

Strategic Business Units

The Boston Consulting Group (BCG) matrix evaluates strategic business units (SBUs) with respect to the dimension of business growth rate and market share. The business growth rate pertains to how rapidly the entire industry is increasing. The market share defines whether a business unit has a larger or smaller share than competitors. The matrix has four quadrants or categories: stars (high growth rate and high market share), cash cows (low growth rate and high market share), question marks (high growth rate and low market share), and dogs (low growth rate and low market share).

Marketing Management Analysis

This application is related to Marketing Management (Module 300), and specifically to Sections 355 (Marketing Channels and Distribution) and 310 (New Product Development).

Marketing Channel Profitability Analysis

There are two methods of allocating expenses to marketing channels: the sales method and the activity method. The sales method allocates costs to the channel based on its sales, assuming that greater sales will produce higher net income. The activity method allocates expenses based on activities involved in a channel.

The following formulas are used in this application.

Sales − Cost of Goods Sold (COGS) = Gross Profit

Gross Profit − Expenses = Net Income

The activity method is more accurate than the sales method because of its focus on activities, which are better cost drivers.

Target Returns, Target Profits, and Target Costs

Companies set target profit margins by applying a target return-on-sales percent to the sales revenue from their product mix. This return-on-sales (ROS) ratio, in turn, is determined by several measures such as return-on-assets (ROA), return-on-equity (ROE), or economic value-added (EVA) that a company must earn to remain viable.

ROA = Asset Turnover × Profit Margin

Asset Turnover = Sales/Assets

Profit Margin = Profit/Sales

The target cost is determined by subtracting the target profit from the sales for each product, that is, sales minus target profit equals target cost.

Market-Share and Profit Margin Analysis

Senior management's goal is to increase the market share for its company. The marketing strategy is to increase the market share by increasing advertising efforts, increasing price, dropping small and unprofitable dealers, and enhancing product features. The financial criteria are to increase the profit margin on products.

Philip Kotler[23] recommends a useful way to analyze market-share movements in terms of four components: customer penetration, customer loyalty, customer selectivity, and price elasticity. The market share of a company is the product of these four components.

Price Response Analysis

Price response analysis is the study of the effects of price decreases and price increases on profits. Price response coefficients are usually collected from market research staff.

Generally, price and sales volume varies inversely. This means that higher prices should result in a small number of units sold, and vice versa. For example, a price response coefficient of −2.0 means that if price falls by 5 percent, sales would be expected to increase by 10 percent. Similarly, a price response coefficient of +1.5 means that if price falls by 6 percent, sales would be expected to decrease by 9 percent.

The contribution margin (CM) ratio measures the effect on income from operations of an increase or decrease in sales volume. Additional income or loss from operations due to price decrease or increase is computed as follows.

Additional Increase or Decrease in Net Income from Operations = Expected Price Decrease × Sales Response Coefficient × Current Net Sales × CM Ratio

Brand Management Analysis

According to Philip Kotler,[24] a brand can convey up to six levels of meaning: attributes, benefits, values, culture, personality, and user. Of these six, only values, culture, and personality are the most enduring meanings.

Brand equity is closely related to the number of customers who are devoted to a brand. Some brands have a higher degree of awareness, acceptability, and preference than others. Although brand equity is not shown in the balance sheet, income statement, or the statement of cash flows, it is reflected in the acquisition price of a company as a premium the brand commands in the market.

Brand dilution occurs when consumers no longer associate a brand with a specific product. It is closely related to brand extension, and it is a risk. Cobranding and dual branding occur when two or more well-known brands are combined in an offer (for example, Keebler cookies with M&M candies). Competitors benefit from brand dilution because the offering company has a weak position in the market. The more narrow its focus, the stronger the brand.

Leverage Analysis

This application is related to Finance (Module 700) and Accounting (Module 600), and specifically to Sections 720 (Financial Forecasting, Planning, and Control) and 630 (Cost Behavior, Control, and Decision Making).

Leverage

Leverage is of three types: operating, financial, and total. Leverage can be good or bad, depending on how it is used. Operating leverage is a measure of the extent to which fixed operating costs are used in a firm's operations. A firm with a high percentage of fixed operating costs is said to have a high degree of operating leverage (DOL). Similarly, financial leverage is a measure of the extent to which fixed financial costs (such as interest) exist in a firm's operations. A firm with a high percentage of fixed financial costs is said to have a high degree of financial leverage (DFL). Total leverage is the product of operating and financial leverages, that is, DTL = DOL × DFL, where DTL is the degree of total leverage.

Operating Leverage

One way to measure operating leverage is contribution margin (CM) divided by income from operations. The closer a firm's sales are to its operating break-even point, the greater its DOL (more risk). The farther a firm's sales are from its operating break-even point, the lower its DOL (less risk).

The lower the contribution margin, the less each product sold is able to help cover fixed operating costs, and the closer the firm is to its operating break-even point. Therefore, the higher the DOL for a particular firm, the closer that firm is to its operating break-even point, and the more sensitive its operating income is to change in sales volume. Greater sensitivity implies greater risk.

First, we need to compute the break-even point (BEP) in units, total CM, and income from operations for each alternative. The break-even point in units is calculated by dividing total fixed costs with the contribution margin per unit, which is selling price per unit minus variable cost per unit. Total contribution margin is computed by multiplying contribution per unit by sales units. Income from operations is calculated by subtracting total fixed costs from total contribution margin. Compute the DOL for each alternative by dividing total contribution margin by income from operations.

The following formulas will be useful in determining operating leverage.

Contribution Margin (CM) per Unit = Sales Price per Unit − Variable Cost per Unit
BEP in Units = Total Fixed Costs/CM per Unit
Total CM = CM per Unit × Production or Sales Volume in Units
Income from Operations = Total CM − Total Fixed Costs
DOL = Total CM/Income from Operations

Another way of measuring the DOL given fixed costs and operating cash flows follows.

DOL = 1 + (Fixed Costs/Operating Cash Flows)

When fixed costs, expressed as a percentage of operating cash flows, get smaller and smaller, the leverage effect decreases, and the DOL becomes smaller.

The effect of DOL is that cash flows will increase or decrease by the amount of change in sales percentage multiplied by DOL. For example, if Quarter 4 sales are planned to increase by 25 percent and the DOL is 1.68, the increase in cash flows is 42 percent, that is 25% × 1.68.

Financial Leverage

Financial leverage deals with the amount of debt and preferred stock in a company's capital structure. Capital structure consists of the amount of debt and equity. The higher the debt amount, the higher the financial leverage, keeping everything else constant. The more debt a firm has (as a percentage of assets), the greater its degree of financial leverage (DFL). Debt acts like a lever in the sense that using it can greatly magnify both gains and losses. The DFL can increase rewards to shareholders in terms of greater return on equity (ROE), but it can also increase financial distress or business failure. This is because debt incurs interest costs (financial costs), which are fixed financial obligations and at the same time are tax deductible. The company is paying for some of its interest costs while the tax authorities are paying for the remainder of the interest costs. The after-tax cost of debt is lower to the company. This is the effect of financial leverage. A company's financial risk is measured by the standard deviation of ROE. This risk is proportional to the amount of fixed-income securities such as debt or preferred stock used in a firm's capital structure.

Three specific ratios can help in determining a company's financial leverage. These include total debt ratio, which is (total assets − total equity)/total assets, times interest earned ratio, which is EBIT/interest, and cash coverage ratio, which is (EBIT + depreciation)/interest.

The following formulas can be used to calculate return on total assets (ROA), total asset turnover, return on equity (ROE), financial leverage, and return on net worth.

ROA = Profit Margin on Sales Percentage × Total Asset Turnover
Profit Margin on Sales = Net Income/Net Sales
Total Asset Turnover = Net Sales/Total Assets
Financial Leverage = Total Assets/Common Stock Outstanding or Stockholders' Equity or Total Liabilities/Total Assets and the result is divided into 1, or Total Assets/Net Worth
Return on Net Worth = ROA × Financial Leverage
ROA = Net Income/Total Assets × 100
Return on Equity (ROE) = Net Income Available to Common Stockholders/Common Stock Outstanding, multiplied by 100
ROE = ROA × Financial Leverage
Net Worth = Total Assets − Total Liabilities = Stockholders' Equity

The marketing manager can increase ROA by several ways, including increasing the profit margin by increasing sales or reducing costs, and increasing the asset turnover by increasing sales or reducing assets.

Total Leverage

Total leverage is the combined leverage of the operating and financial leverages: DTL = DOL × DFL. DTL has a multiplicative and magnifying effect on cash flows and net income. The current EPS will change by the amount of DTL for every 1 percent change in sales. That is, the new EPS resulting from a 10 percent increase in sales will increase by 10 percent of the DTL amount plus the current EPS. The equation is given below.

New EPS for a Firm = Current EPS × (1 + (% increase in sales × DTL)/100))

Supply Chain Management Analysis

This application is related to Operations Management (Module 200), and specifically to Sections 230 (Physical Supply Chain Management) and 255 (Purchasing Management).

Make or Buy Analysis

An important task for a supply chain specialist is to analyze make-or-buy alternatives. Relevant costs include direct materials, direct labor, and variable overhead. Allocated fixed overhead should be ignored because it is going to be incurred regardless. A company's fixed costs will not change, whether a part is made or bought, or whether a special order is accepted or not. Factors such as product quality, plant capacity, and demand patterns are considered in the make-or-buy decision.

When plant capacity is not fully utilized, it is good to accept a special order that covers all variable costs, ignore allocated fixed costs, and do not consider profits. This is applicable to short-term decision making only. When plant capacity is fully utilized, the special order has an opportunity cost, and it should recover all costs (both variable and fixed), including profits.

When buying a part from a vendor, a company is guaranteed only the price charged by the vendor. The buyer has no control, at least in the short term, over product quality, delivery, or support/service.

Cost Effectiveness Measures

Cost reduction efforts focus on changing the cost structure of a firm, that is, how many of the costs are fixed costs and how many are variable costs.

Cost avoidance represents the difference between a price paid and a potentially higher price that might have occurred if purchasing had not obtained the lower price through a specific effort or action. Cost changes (cost reduction, cost improvement, cost containment, or cost increase) represent an actual change from a prior period price, while cost avoidance refers to the amount that would have been paid minus the amount actually paid. Cost changes are tangible, while cost avoidance is intangible. Some people refer to cost avoidance as "soft money," "funny money," and "easy to manipulate." Assume that purchasing paid $5 per unit for an item in the past, but the supplier now quoted a price of $5.50 per unit. If the buyer negotiates a price of $5.25 per unit, then the buyer achieved a cost avoidance of $0.25 per unit ($5.50 − $5.25).

Inventory Investment

Financial management views inventory as a firm's assets, while supply chain management views it as a liability. Having low inventory results in reduced handling and carrying costs, which, in turn, improves the profit margin. This, in turn, improves the return on investment (ROI).

The following formulas are used in inventory investment.

Inventory Turnover Ratio = Sales/Inventories

Asset Turnover = Sales/Total Assets

ROI = Profit Margin × Asset Turnover

APPLICATION 4. SUPPLY CHAIN MANAGEMENT ANALYSIS

Purchasing Learning-Curve Analysis

Buyers are often involved in performing learning curve analysis with suppliers. A supplier may use a production process that historically may demonstrate an 80 percent learning curve; that is, as the production rate doubles, there is a 20 percent reduction in the average direct-labor hours required to produce a unit. Given this learning rate, a buyer hopes to capture the reduced labor requirements through a lower purchase price.

Supplier Base and Supplier Performance Analysis

The supplier base—that is, the number of suppliers—should be reduced by implementing partnership arrangements and alliances with suppliers. The number of suppliers in the marketplace is the most important factor between a single source and multiple sources. If there is only one supplier available for a component, the decision is obvious. Understanding who the other customers of the supplier are can help in assessing competitive strengths and weaknesses.

Reverse Price Analysis

A buyer can analyze a supplier's cost structure for a publicly traded company using publicly available information on overhead, material, and labor indexes. Some suppliers are not interested in sharing cost data with the buyer. In the absence of specific cost data, a supplier's overall cost structure must be estimated using a technique called *reverse price analysis*. This analysis will indicate whether the supplier is assigning costs to products in an appropriate manner, which will eventually reflect in the price paid by the buyer.

Vendor Analysis and Selection

Companies research available vendors (suppliers) for sourcing of raw materials, parts, and components. For each supplier, the weight of each factor is multiplied with the rating for that factor. The supplier with the highest score is chosen. Expected values can also be used in selecting vendors. Select the vendor with the highest expected value. Decision trees can also be used in the vendor selection process.

Vendor analysis should be conducted on a periodic basis or whenever there is a significant change in the weights assigned to the scoring factors. Price, quality, and service are important factors in selecting vendors.

Suppliers should be viewed as outside partners who can contribute to the long-term success of a buying firm. If suppliers are selected on the basis of price only, they will be switched continuously, which will destabilize the purchasing process.

Supplier Audits and Supplier Certification

Supplier auditing is an important first step in supplier certification programs. Usually, supplier audits focus on suppliers' production or service capabilities and quality and delivery programs. The scope of the audit should cover vendor management style, quality assurance programming, product and process design methods, materials management, product and process improvement opportunities, and policies and procedures for problem identification and corrective action. The audit cycle follows this general sequence: problem prevention, detection, correction, problem resolution, and follow-up.

There is less risk with certified suppliers than with noncertified suppliers due to their increased capabilities. The certification process verifies that a supplier meets or exceeds the requirements of a buyer. Certified suppliers are referred to as *world-class suppliers*. Some companies rely on standard industry certification such as ISO 9000. Others may have their own certification either in addition to or as a substitute for the ISO 9000.

Value Analysis, Value Engineering, and Purchasing

Companies can lose their market share if their prices and product costs are higher than their competitors. Value analysis and value engineering techniques can help in reducing product costs and prices, and can create competition in the industry.

The scope of value analysis includes examination of functions and costs to determine whether functions can be added, removed, substituted, or improved to reduce costs and to improve overall performance of the finished product. Here, value is related to a product's functions and costs.

Value analysis is most applicable to parts, raw materials, and components that have high unit cost and high annual usage. Because the product of high unit cost and high annual usage is significant in dollar amount, it makes sense to analyze these items for cost reduction.

Supplier Break-Even Analysis

Break-even analysis allows a buyer to anticipate a supplier's (seller's) pricing strategy during negotiation. Research indicates that a direct relationship exists between the amount of preparation that went into negotiation and negotiation effectiveness.

Buyers often perform the break-even analysis for a supplier. The intent is to estimate a supplier's expected profit or loss given fixed and variable costs. The buyer needs to collect total fixed costs, variable costs per unit, and target purchase price for each item under consideration. The break-even analysis assumes that variable costs fluctuate in a linear fashion with respect to volume. It ignores semi-variable costs, which include both fixed and variable costs. Sometimes the buyer may need to provide assistance in reducing costs at the supplier location.

The following formulas or equations can be used in the supplier break-even analysis.

Break-Even Point in Units = (Total Fixed Costs)/(Selling Price per Unit − Variable Cost per Unit)

Contribution Margin per Unit = Selling Price per Unit − Variable Cost per Unit

Net Income or Profit = Total Revenue − Total Variable Costs − Total Fixed Costs

Another way of computing profit is (sales units multiplied by contribution margin per unit) minus total fixed costs.

Pricing Analysis

This application is related to Marketing Management (Module 300) and Accounting (Module 600), and specifically to Sections 330 (Pricing Strategies) and 660 (Decision Making and Accounting).

Pricing Methods

The normal selling price of a product can be viewed as the target-selling price to be achieved in the long run. The basic approaches to setting this price follow.

- Market methods include demand-based methods and competition-based methods.
- Cost-plus methods include total cost concept, product cost concept, and variable cost concept.

Managers using the cost-plus methods price the product in order to achieve a target profit. Managers add to the cost an amount called a *markup*, so that all costs plus a profit are included in the selling price.

APPLICATION 5. PRICING ANALYSIS

Markup Percentage on Selling Price

Markup percentage on selling price is the profit margin for an individual product expressed as a percentage of the price. There are many variations in the markup percentage on selling price approach.

Markup % on Price = (Price − Cost)/Price
Price = (Total Unit Cost)/(1 − Markup %).
Total Unit Cost = Variable Cost per Unit + Fixed Cost per Unit
Target-Return Price = Unit Cost + (Desired Return % × Invested Capital)/Unit Sales

With the standard markup approach, the selling price = (unit cost)/(1 − markup %).

Markup Percentage on Cost

Markup percentage on cost is the profit margin for an individual product or product line expressed as a percentage of unit cost. The following formula can be used.

Markup % on Cost = (Price − Cost)/Cost

Interrelationships Between Price and Cost

The following relationships hold true between the markup percentage on price and the markup percentage on cost.

Markup % on Price = (Markup % on Cost)/(1 + Markup % on Cost)
Markup % on Cost = (Markup on % Price/(1 − Markup % on Price)

Transfer Pricing Methods

When a division of a company transfers its products or renders services to another division, a transfer price is used to charge for the products or services. Transfer prices should be set so that overall company income is increased when goods are transferred between divisions. Transfer prices may be used when decentralized units are organized as cost, profit, or investment centers.

There are three approaches to set transfer prices: the market price approach, the negotiated price approach, and the cost price approach.

The transfer price should be set at full cost if a division has no excess capacity to produce parts for its internal division. Alternatively, a negotiated price of cost plus a reasonable markup can be established. The negotiated price depends on the negotiating skills of the parties involved.

Determining Selling Price

Both marketers and accountants determine the selling price of a product for a variety of reasons.

Markup % on Cost = (Desired Profit + Total Fixed Costs)/Total Variable Costs
Selling Price = Cost + Markup % on Cost

Capital Budget Analysis

This application is related to Finance (Module 700), and specifically to Section 735 (Capital Budgeting).

Investment Evaluation Techniques

Many techniques are available to evaluate capital expenditure projects and their investments. These techniques include traditional payback, discounted payback, accounting rate of return, net present value (NPV), profitability index (PI), and internal rate of return (IRR).

The traditional payback period is initial cost or investment divided by annual savings or annual after-tax cash flows. Drawbacks of the traditional payback method are that it does not consider the time value of money and that it ignores the project's cash flows after the payback period.

The discounted payback period is similar to the traditional payback period except that it discounts cash flows at the project's required rate of return. A drawback of the discounted payback method is that it ignores the project's cash flows after the payback period. An advantage of this method is that it does consider the time value of money.

The accounting rate of return (ARR) method is based on accounting data and is computed as the average annual profits after taxes divided by the initial cash outlay in the project. This rate is then compared to the required rate of return to determine if a project should be accepted or rejected. Drawbacks of the ARR method are that it does not consider the project's cash flows and that it ignores the time value of money.

The net present value (NPV) method is total present value (PV) of cash inflows minus total present value of cash outflows. If the NPV is positive or zero, accept the project; otherwise, reject it. Select the project with the highest NPV, as it will increase shareholders' value.

First, we need to compute the operating cash inflows from the project. Next, we compute the present values of these cash flows using the discount rate (which is the cost of capital or weighted average cost of capital, WACC). Next, we compute the net present value as the difference between the present value of cash inflows and the initial investment or cost. We need to add the working capital investment in the last year because the same investment must be recovered. The following formulas are used in calculating the NPV.

Operating Cash Inflows = EBIT + Depreciation − Taxes

PV of Cash Inflows = Annual Cash Inflows After Taxes × PV Factor at Cost of Capital

NPV = PV of Cash Inflows − Initial Investment or Cost

The profitability index (PI) method is total present value of total cash inflows divided by total present value of cash outflows. If the PI ratio is equal to or greater than 1, accept the project; otherwise, reject it. Both NPV (expressed in absolute terms) and PI (expressed in relative terms) methods will yield the same results because they use the same data. The following formula can be used to compute the PI ratio.

PI Ratio = Present Value of Cash Inflows/Initial or Cost Investment

The net present value (NPV) method is superior of all other investment evaluation techniques available. The traditional payback period, the discounted payback period, and the accounting rate of return methods are inferior when compared to NPV. Both the traditional payback and the accounting rate of return methods do not consider the time value of money. Although the discounted payback method considers the time value of money, it does not consider full cash flows from a project.

To calculate the internal rate of return (IRR), we first need to compute the present value of annuity discount factor. This is initial cost or investment divided by the PV of cash inflows (for example, annual savings or annual incremental benefits). Then, the IRR percentage is found from the mathematical (interest) table for the corresponding present value of annuity discount factor. The following formula can be used to compute the IRR.

IRR = Initial Investment or Cost/Present Value of Cash Inflows

Capital Rationing and Capital Budgets

Capital rationing exists when management cannot raise enough funds to invest in all available good projects. Debt covenants can restrict raising additional capital. In theory, capital rationing should not exist, but it does exist in practice.

It is true that capital rationing cannot maximize shareholder value in the long run because the company is foregoing profitable investment projects that yield more than their required rate of return (that is, cost of capital). This is a difficult tradeoff that management of a firm often faces.

Project Risks and Capital Budgets

When two projects are mutually exclusive, we select the one with the largest NPV. When projects are independent, we select the one whose IRR exceeds the cost of capital.

If project risk is not considered in capital budgeting analysis, incorrect decisions are possible. When a project's risk is high, increase the cost of capital used to evaluate the project to reflect the higher risk of the project. High-risk projects can be handled by adjusting the discount rate upward for increasing risk.

Application 7

Mergers, Acquisitions, and Business Valuation Analysis

This application is related to Finance (Module 700), and specifically to Section 760 (Mergers, Acquisitions, and Business Valuations).

Merger and Acquisition Characteristics

Merger and acquisition analysis should be conducted in the same manner as capital budgeting analysis. That is, if the present value of the cash flows expected to result from the merger exceeds the price that must be paid for the company being acquired (target company), then the merger has a positive net present value (NPV) and the acquiring firm should proceed with the acquisition.

The target company in the merger and acquisition analysis should have high liquidity (solvency), low leverage, a low price/earnings (P/E) ratio, increasing cash flows, and high earnings power. The strategy of acquiring a firm with a low P/E ratio gives an illusion of growth in the combined firm's earnings per share (EPS).

There are several approaches to valuing a business. One such approach follows.

Total Value of a Firm = EBITDA × Earning Multiple

where EBITDA is earnings before interest, taxes, depreciation, and amortization combined.

Another approach to valuing the target company follows.

Value of the Target Company to the Acquiring Company = Value of the Target Company + Present Value of Synergy from the Acquisition

Present Value of Synergy = Incremental Cash Flows/Weighted Average Cost of Capital (WACC)

Return on Equity (ROE) = Net Income/Total Equity

Net Cash Flows = Cash Inflows − Investment

Another method focuses on the dividend growth model.

Present value without the acquisition using the perpetual dividend growth model

Present value with the acquisition using the perpetual dividend growth model

Difference in present value with and without the acquisition

If the difference is more than the acquisition price, the target company should be acquired

Another method focuses on valuing a business's operations. The following formula can be used to value business's operations when the same cash flows occur evenly per year.

Value of Operations = $FCF_n/(r - g)$

where FCF is free cash flows, r is WACC, g is the growth rate, and n is the number of periods.

The following formulas can be used to value business's operations when cash flows occur unevenly per year with a terminal value.

$HV_n = FCF_n(1 + g)/(r - g)$

where HV_n is the horizon or terminal value, FCF is free cash flows, r is WACC, g is the growth rate, and n is the number of periods.

Next, find the present value of the free cash flows and the horizon value to give the value of operation. The terminal value is added to the final year's cash flows.

The following formula can be used to determine the terminal value of a business when the cash flows occur evenly forever.

Horizon Value $(HV_n) = FCF_n/(r - g) = FCF_n(1 + g)/(r - g)$

where HV_n is horizon or terminal value, FCF is free cash flows, r is WACC, g is the growth rate, and n is the number of periods.

The following formulas can be used to estimate the stock price of the target company.

Total Market Value = Value of Operations + Value of Nonoperating Assets

Market Value of Equity = Total Market Value − Value of Debt (Notes Payable + Long-Term Debt + Preferred Stock)

Price per Share = Market Value of Equity/Number of Shares

Price-Earning Ratios and Business Valuations

Capitalization rate is the reciprocal of the price-earnings (P/E) ratio. Capitalization rate is also the reciprocal of the traditional payback period or discounted payback period. In a way, both the P/E ratio and the payback period are related to each other in terms of recovering initial investment. The P/E ratio indicates the amount an investor is willing to pay for a firm's earnings on a per-share basis. The payback period indicates how fast the initial investment can be recovered. While the traditional payback period does not consider the time value of money, the discounted payback period does.

The value based on the P/E ratio is net earnings multiplied by the P/E ratio, and the value based on discounted payback is net earnings multiplied by the discounted payback period.

Exchange Ratios and Earnings per Share

A dilution in earnings per share (EPS) occurs when the P/E ratio paid for the target Firm B exceeded the P/E ratio of the acquiring Firm A. The P/E ratio paid is computed by dividing the offer price per share by the EPS of the target firm. We need to compute the offer price that equates the P/E ratio of the acquiring firm (Firm A) and the EPS of the target firm (Firm B).

Net Present Values and Economic Values

The economic value (EV) method presents a clearer picture of the value created than does the net present value (NPV) method. The EV method eliminates economic distortion of a one-time full charge for the capital. It can be used to forecast valuation scenarios. The NPV method distorts the economic picture due to fluctuations in cash flows. Net cash flows are computed by adding the capital invested in each period to the cash flows for each period. These cash flows are then multiplied by present value (PV) discount factors to obtain the PV of net cash flows.

The economic value method considers the charge for use of the capital (capital cost), while the NPV method does not. EVs are obtained by adding the capital cost for each period to the cash flows for each period. These economic values are then multiplied by present value discount factors to obtain the present value of economic values.

Market Value and Competition

The market value of a company is determined as capital invested plus present value of current improvements plus the present value of future improvements. Shareholders require both current improvements completed and future improvements planned. The present value of future improvements is calculated as market value minus capital invested minus present value of current improvements.

Initial Public Offering Analysis

In the initial public offering (IPO) deal, managers of a private company want to take their company public for wider distribution of its stock and to tap into capital markets for funds. In the IPO deal, if the initial stock is priced below the true market value, the issuer's existing shareholders will experience an opportunity loss when they sell their shares for less than they are worth.

Underpricing is fairly common in IPOs, but not always guaranteed. Although IPOs have positive initial returns on an average, most of them have price drops. When the new issue is priced too low, the issue is often "oversubscribed." An investor's ability to make money in an IPO is directly related to his ability to purchase only the IPOs that are underpriced. Underpricing is a kind of insurance for the investment bank when it is sued by angry investors if it consistently overpriced securities. On an average, new investors will come out ahead with underpricing. Underpricing helps new shareholders and hurts existing ones because new shareholders can earn a higher return on the shares they buy.

Leveraged Buyout Analysis

A leverage buyout (LBO) means that a company's management is considering going private through an LBO deal. LBOs can be initiated in one of two ways. The firm's own managers can set up a new company whose equity comes from the managers themselves, plus some equity from pension funds and other institutions. This new company then arranges to borrow a large amount of money by selling bonds through an investment banking firm. With financing arranged, the management group then makes an offer to purchase all publicly owned shares through a tender offer.

Alternatively, a specialized LBO firm will identify a potential target company, go to the management, and suggest that an LBO deal be conducted. The following is the interrelationship between IPO and LBO.

IPO takes a private company public.
LBO takes a public company private.

We need to compute the annual earnings before interest and taxes (EBIT) that are needed to service the debt incurred to close the LBO deal. If the EBIT is not enough, either the debt has to be rearranged or the LBO deal should not proceed.

Production Planning Analysis

This application is related to Operations Management (Module 200), and specifically to Sections 235 (Manufacturing Planning and Scheduling) and 240 (Manufacturing Capacity Management).

Production Capacity Levels

The objective of the production plan is to provide sufficient finished goods by period to meet sales plan objectives while staying within financial and production capacity constraints. When demand varies from period to period, planning production to exceed demand in one period can provide inventory to fill excessive demand in a following period.

There are three approaches to managing the supply side of production: the level capacity strategy, the chase capacity approach, and the hybrid capacity approach. Chase strategy is also called the *matching demand approach*.

Using the level capacity approach, production capacity is held constant over the planning horizon. The difference between the constant production rate and the varying demand rate is made up by inventory, backlog, overtime, part-time labor, temporary workers, subcontracting, or outsourcing. Level capacity costs can include inventory carrying costs, which are calculated as average ending inventory multiplied by the carrying cost.

Using the matching demand approach, production capacity in each time period is varied to match the forecasted aggregate demand in that time period. Such an approach varies the level of the workforce in each time period by hiring new workers or laying off workers. It incurs hiring and rehiring costs. Matching demand costs can include employee hiring and firing costs.

Production Capacity Expansion

Production capacity can be expanded through additional operating shifts, overtime, subcontracting, and outsourcing. Costs for each alternative should be computed. The goal is to determine which department or operation is overloaded and then adjusting the capacity accordingly.

Master Production Schedule

The master production schedule (MPS) is the primary output of the master scheduling process. The MPS specifies the end items the organization anticipates manufacturing each period. End items are either final products or the items from which final assemblies (products) are made. Thus, the MPS is the plan for providing the supply to meet the demand.

Process Analysis

This application is related to Quality and Process Management (Module 400) and Information Technology (Module 800), and specifically to Sections 470 (Business Process Reengineering), 480 (Business Process Improvement), 440 (Statistics and Quality Control), and 830 (Value Creation with Information Technology).

Manufacturing Performance Measures

The senior management of a manufacturing company evaluates plant managers on both financial and nonfinancial performance measures. Examples of nonfinancial measures include total manufacturing cycle time, manufacturing cycle efficiency (MCE), and total throughput.

Total Manufacturing Cycle Time

Total manufacturing cycle time is a combination of value-added time and non-value-added time. The value-added time is called *process time* or *assembly time*, and the non-value-added time is the time spent in inspecting, waiting, and moving things around in the plant.

At this time, it is appropriate to introduce the term *cycle time*, since it has many meanings and definitions. Viewpoints are different for different functions of the business. Here are some viewpoints.

- From a manufacturing viewpoint, production cycle time is the time between two identical units being completed on a production line.
- From a marketing viewpoint, new product cycle time is the time it takes to get new products to market. It is the time from initial concept to market introduction of a new product (time-to-market). It can also be defined as the time from idea conception to idea commercialization.
- From an inventory management viewpoint, inventory cycle time is the length of time between the placing of two consecutive orders.
- From a logistics viewpoint, customer order cycle time is the time it takes from receiving the customer order to filling the order.
- From a finance viewpoint, payment cycle time is the time it takes from billing a customer to receiving payment from the customer.

A *cycle* is a complete set of elements or tasks included in an operation or a process. *Cycle time* is the number of steps or procedures necessary to complete those elements or tasks.

Manufacturing Cycle Efficiency

Manufacturing cycle efficiency (MCE) is calculated by dividing the total hours of value-added time in the production process by the total manufacturing cycle time in hours, where the latter includes both value-added and non-value-added times. As such, reducing the non-value-added time increases the MCE. The impact of changing the value-added time depends on the proportion of the value-added time to the non-value-added time. Process time or assembly time is a value-added activity.

Total Throughput

Total throughput is measured by dividing the number of good units produced by the total manufacturing cycle time. The throughout time (velocity of production) is process time plus inspection time plus move time plus queue time. Actual delivery cycle time is wait time plus throughput time plus shipping time.

Management should compare actual performance against the target to pinpoint areas requiring improvement. Two actions must be taken quickly: eliminating non-value-added activities and decreasing delivery cycle time. Elimination or reduction of non-value-added activities will increase the MCE. When the MCE is increased, it will decrease the throughput time also. MCE is value-added time divided by throughput time. The complement of MCE is non-value-added activities.

Manufacturing Balanced Scorecard

Similar to financially-oriented balanced scorecard, manufacturing-oriented balanced scorecard is useful to measure manufacturing management's performance. Some factors to consider include throughput time in days, delivery cycle time in days, value-added time in days, percent of on-time deliveries, and total production units.

The goal of manufacturing management should be to reach 100 percent of MCE. This can be achieved when all non-value-added activities have been eliminated and the process time is equal to the throughput time.

Business Process Reengineering

Business process reengineering (BPR) has been defined as the fundamental rethinking and radical redesign of business processes to achieve dramatic improvements in costs, quality, service, and speed. A fresh approach is required during process reengineering. Any business process that is slow, inadequate, inefficient, and ineffective should be subject to reengineering. One of the enablers of reengineering is information technology (IT) geared to helping achieve the goals of reengineering. Benchmarking is the process of measuring an organizational process against the best in the industry. Benchmarking should be undertaken prior to embarking on the BPR program.

Business Process Improvements

Business process improvement (BPI) should be continuous, not discrete, and involves incremental change that may affect only a single task or segment of the organization. BPI takes on small changes, not radical changes, and frequent interventions. It is similar to the *kaizen* approach in that it involves a slow and continuous process improvement.

Business Process Flows

Business processes transform inputs into outputs with the use of resources such as labor, capital, materials, and energy. Key process measures include throughput (R), average flow time (T), and average inventory (I), and the relationship between these measures is called Little's law.[25]

Inventory = Throughput × Average flow time = $I = R \times T$

Inventory can be decreased by reducing the batch sizes, throughput (average flow rate) can be increased by increasing the process capacity, and average flow time can be decreased by shortening critical activity times.

For a given level of throughput in any process, the only way to reduce the flow time is to reduce inventory and vice versa. Short flow times in production and short delivery processes reduce the inventory and its associated costs.

The inventory turnover ratio is expressed in two ways:

Inventory turnover ratio (ITR) is throughput divided by average inventory = ITR = R/I

Using Little's law, inventory turnover ratio is the inverse of average flow time = ITR = $1/T$.

The goal is to maintain a stable process. Uncertainties in flows have a major impact on the process performance, which can be controlled by safety inventory, safety capacity, safety time, and dynamic feedback control.

Management can take the following actions to improve business processes:

1. Increase the throughput and decrease the flow time
2. Decrease the inventory and decrease the flow time
3. Decrease the inventory and decrease the process cost

APPLICATION 9. PROCESS ANALYSIS

Process Capability Index

Process capability is a production process's ability to manufacture a product within the desired expectations of customers. The process capability index (PCI) must be equal to or greater than 1.00 to meet customer expectations. The PCI with less than 1.00 means it does not meet customer expectations. The PCI indicates whether a process is capable of meeting customer expectations. It is computed as follows.

PCI = (UL − LL)/[(6)(Standard Deviation of Process)]

Standard Deviation of Process = (UL−LL)/[(6)(PCI)]

where UL is upper limit and LL is lower limit.

Application 10

Advertising Analysis

This application is related to Marketing Management (Module 300), and specifically to Section 320 (Advertising and Promotion).

Advertising Reach and Exposure

Companies spend huge amounts of money on advertising, whether the medium is print, radio, television, or the Internet. Management should ensure that the company is getting an adequate return on the money spent on advertising.

According to Philip Kotler,[26] the total number of exposures (E) is the reach (R) times the average frequency (F). The weighted number of exposures for an advertisement is the reach (R) times the average frequency (F) times the average impact (I), that is, WE = $R \times F \times I$. The gross rating points (GRP) of a media schedule is the same as the total number of exposures, that is, GRP = $R \times F$.

Advertising Effectiveness

The advertising effectiveness ratio is calculated as actual share of market percentage divided by share of voice percentage. According to Philip Kotler,[27] an advertising effectiveness rating (ratio) of 100 means an effective level of advertising expenditure. A rating below 100 means a relatively ineffective advertising level; a level above 100 indicates a very effective advertising level.

Advertising Response Analysis

Keeping all other marketing mix elements constant, an increase in advertising budget should increase the sales volume. An advertising response coefficient of +0.3 means a proposed 50 percent increase in advertising expenditures will increase sales volume by 15 percent (that is, 50% × 0.3). The gross margin (GM) is net sales minus cost of goods sold. The formulas used in this area include the following.

Increase in Gross Margin Amount = Increase in Advertising Budget × Advertising Response Coefficient × Current Net Sales × GM Percentage

Impact of Marketing Public Relations on Sales

The major objective of a marketing public relations (MPR) function is to serve the marketing department in areas such as the launching of new products, the building of interest in a product category, and the repositioning of a mature market. A corporation spends money on an MPR communication campaign on a product, which increases its sales. Marketing management can estimate which part of a sales increase is due to MPR, and which is the result of additional advertising and sales promotion activities. Under this scenario, return on the MPR investment is contribution margin due to MPR divided by investment or cost.

Manufacturing Management Analysis

This application is related to Operations Management (Module 200) and Accounting (Module 600), and specifically to Sections 240 (Manufacturing Capacity and Management), 285 (Economics and Operations), and 660 (Decision Making and Accounting).

Theory of Constraints

The theory of constraints (TOC) is a manufacturing strategy that focuses on reducing the influence of bottlenecks in a manufacturing process. A production bottleneck (constraint) occurs at the point in the manufacturing process where the demand for the company's product exceeds the company's ability to produce the product.

First, we need to compute the contribution margin (CM) per bottleneck hour as CM per unit divided by bottleneck hours per unit. CM per unit is selling price per unit minus variable cost per unit. Then, we rank the products according to their profitability or the CM per bottleneck hour.

Plant Capacity and Bottlenecks

Manufacturing management's goal is to ensure that adequate production capacity is available all the time so that customer needs are serviced properly. For example, the capacity of a machine can be expressed in terms of the number of pounds per hour per machine. The goal is to locate the bottlenecks (limited resources) and remove them. An operation that has a lower capacity than what is needed can quickly become a bottleneck. Options to reduce bottlenecks include (1) increasing the capacity of the limited resource, (2) reducing the use of the limited resource in production, and (3) focusing on finished products that require less of the limited resource. CM analysis can help in deciding which products with resource constraints should be prioritized for production.

Machine Selection

Whenever a machine or part wears out, the company has to replace it with a new one to stay in operation. Manufacturing management considers several machines with different lives during the selection process.

To decide which machine to purchase, compute the equivalent annual costs (EACs) for all machines using the appropriate annuity factors. EAC is total present value of costs divided by the annuity factor. Based on the EAC analysis, the company should purchase the machine with the lowest EAC.

Plant Selection

A manufacturing company plans to open a new pharmaceutical plant. The company must choose one plant from among several with different capacities. Usually, large plants will require larger fixed costs. The plant with high fixed costs will have a high break-even point because it takes more sales to recover all fixed costs. The reverse is true with small plants.

If a plant has 100 percent of its capacity utilized, there is no safety or cushion for plant downtime, machine breakdowns, holidays, and other unforeseen conditions. A plant capacity utilization percent of 80 to 90 percent is desirable. The following formulas can be used in plant selection.

Plant's Break-Even Point (BEP) in Units = Total Sales Revenues = Total Fixed Costs + Total Variable Costs

Plant's Capacity Utilization = (Sales Demand/Available Production Capacity) × 100

Companies should select the plant with low BEP and high capacity utilization percentage.

Plant Close or Open Analysis

Manufacturing management looks for opening new plants and closing down existing plants that are not meeting requirements in terms of volume, profits, and cost goals. Sometimes, plants are too far from major suppliers and customers. To solve this problem, management needs to collect data on production costs, production and shipping volumes, annual plant capacity, and transportation costs from plant to suppliers or customers. A plant must be either closed or opened based on cost analysis and meeting customer requirements at the same time.

Standby Parts

Occasionally the demand for a part is more or less than its supply. Management studies the level of demand for standby parts for its most valuable and most frequently used parts. If a standby part is not available when needed, it costs money in terms of lost gross profit margin. An excess standby part costs money for storage and obsolescence costs. Management wants to know how much quantity to stock to meet the demand for the part.

We can solve this problem with a payoff table, where total cost of each demand level is computed after considering the lost gross profit margin and cost per part for an excess standby part and multiplying by the probability of each demand level. We need to select the demand level with the least total cost.

Production Learning-Curve Analysis

Manufacturing companies receive big contract orders to manufacture special products from major customers. The labor-hours required for a portion of the order will be known. Management wants to employ the learning-curve concept to estimate the learning rate for the remainder of the order. We need to compute the learning rate for each of the "doubles" of production units and then average them to get the approximate learning rate expressed in percentages.

Value Analysis

This application is related to Quality and Process Management (Module 400) and Information Technology (Module 800), and specifically to Sections 410 (Quality Principles and Practices), 470 (Business Process Reengineering), and 830 (Value Creation with Information Technology).

Value Analysis and Value Chain

Value Analysis

Value analysis is the organized study of an item's function as it relates to value and cost. The value of an item is defined as the function of the item divided by the cost of the item. There will be valued-added and non-value-added tasks in any function due to tasks that were neither changed nor challenged. The goal is to identify those tasks or activities that are not adding value to a function, product, or process. Value-engineering techniques can be implemented to identify non-value-added activities and streamline the business processes in order to improve their efficiency and effectiveness.

Assembling tasks, whether subassembly or final assembly, and process times are value-added activities of a manufactured product, while other activities are non-value-added activities. Examples of non-value-added activities from a customer's viewpoint include inspection time, move time, reporting time, governmental compliance time, storage time, wait time, and queue time.

Value Chain

The value chain of a manufacturing company includes all activities and departments from idea creation to idea commercialization. This includes research and development (R&D) to post-sale customer service. Discontinuing a product or department does not take away any value to a customer unless it was providing the value before.

The value chain is improved when delays, defects, waste, and inventories are eliminated in business processes. The goal is to make such processes lean, flexible, stable, and predictable. This requires elimination of sources of inefficiency, rigidity, and variability, and use of information technology (IT) to integrate business subprocesses.

Value Index and Value Engineering

The value index is a ratio of relative importance of a component to a customer to the total cost devoted to that component. Both numerator and denominator are expressed as percentages. The components with a value index of less than 1 are candidates for value engineering in terms of reducing costs. The components with a value index of more than 1 are candidates for value enhancement, since they need more investment to improve features important to customers.

Management wants to determine how to provide product functions at the lowest cost without reduction in required performance. Value engineering principles can help achieve these as well as cost goals.

- When the value index ratio for a component is less than 1, it is a candidate for cost reduction. Its costs are higher relative to its importance to customers.
- When the value index ratio for a component is more than 1, it is a candidate for value enhancement. Its relative importance to customers is more than its cost.

Cost Improvements and Business Process Reengineering

Both production engineers and quality engineers in conjunction with the accounting and manufacturing departments implement target costing methods through value engineering, activity-based costing methods, business process reengineering principles, and just-in-time inventory methods to address legacy costs. They redesign some product components while eliminating others. Management wants to determine the return on assets (ROA) invested in the cost improvement process. The following formulas can be used in this situation.

New Return on Sales (ROS) = New Net Income/New Sales

New Asset Turnover (AT) = New Sales/New Assets

New ROA = New Net Income/New Assets (Check: ROA = ROS × AT)

Although target price is determined by the market forces of supply and demand variables, management can control target cost through business process reengineering principles and value engineering techniques. The interrelationships between target price, target cost, and target profit are shown here.

Target Price = Target Cost + Target Profit

Application 13

Manufacturing Operations Analysis

This application is related to Operations Management (Module 200) and Accounting (Module 600), and specifically to Sections 235 (Manufacturing Planning and Scheduling), 245 (Inventory Management), 250 (Materials Management), 630 (Cost Behavior, Control, and Decision Making), and 660 (Decision Making and Accounting).

Cost Savings

Manufacturing operations expend significant amounts of resources (materials, machines, labor, money, energy) in manufacturing products. Changes in automation policies and competitive forces aided by technology changes can lead to testing different automation alternatives. Cost saving is one of the criteria for initiating automation projects. For example, a proposal might be to change from a job shop to a cellular manufacturing setting.

Under these conditions, both fixed costs and variable cost per unit along with production alternatives need to be considered. The alternative with maximum cost savings should be selected.

Manufacturing Make-or-Buy Analysis

In the make-or-buy analysis, management is deciding whether to buy a part or component from outside or to produce the part or component itself. Fixed costs, variable costs, and alternatives (buy or make, automated or manual) should be studied, and the alternative with the least cost should be selected.

Product Tree Structure

Product structure is the sequence of operations that components follow during their manufacture into a product. A typical product structure would show raw material converted into fabricated components, components put together to make subassemblies, subassemblies going into assemblies, and assemblies into finished product. A *product tree* is a graphical (or tree) representation of the bill of material with parent at the top and components at lower levels. The purpose of a product tree structure is to show the quantities required per each component and rolled up to the parent level. Later, these quantities are either manufactured or purchased.

Inventory Levels at Work Center

Inventories at a work center should be treated as an input and output analysis method. The purpose of this analysis is to determine whether a certain work center is receiving more work than planned. It is important to compare actual inputs to planned inputs, and actual outputs to planned outputs. Any differences should be highlighted for corrective action.

Production Job Scheduling

Jobs in a manufacturing plant must be processed in a particular sequence because of product design, operations routing rules, customer priorities, and resource needs. There are several job sequencing or dispatching rules that can help management in selecting jobs for processing. Some of these rules include first-come, first-served, shortest processing time, critical ratio, and least changeover cost.

According to the first-come, first-served (FCFS) rule, the next job to be produced is the one that arrived first among the waiting jobs. Flow time is calculated by adding the flow time for the preceding job and the production time for the present job.

According to the shortest processing time (SPT) rule, the next job to be produced is the one with the shortest processing time among the waiting jobs.

According to the critical ratio (CR) rule, the next job to be produced is the one with the least CR ratio, which is calculated as time to due date remaining by the expected elapsed time to finish the job. Other ways to compute the CR ratio are time remaining divided by work remaining, or time to promised delivery divided by production time. A ratio of 1.0 indicates the job is behind schedule, a ratio greater than 1.0 indicates the job is ahead of schedule, and a ratio of 1.0 indicates the job is on schedule.

The least changeover cost rule analyzes the total cost of making all of the machine changeovers between jobs. Jobs that follow and jobs that precede in a plant should be reviewed. Because job changeover costs can be significant, jobs should be sequenced properly to minimize total changeover costs.

In deciding which sequencing rule performs best for a group of waiting jobs, the following criteria can be applied: (1) average flow time, which is the average amount of time jobs spend in the plant, (2) average flow rate, which is the number of jobs in the system, or (3) total changeover costs.

Materials Scheduling

The objectives of the materials requirements planning (MRP) system are to improve customer service, reduce investment in inventory, and improve operating efficiency of a plant. Customer service is improved when the MRP system helps management in meeting promised delivery dates by shortening delivery times. Investment in inventory is reduced when the MRP system helps control the quantity and timing of deliveries of raw materials and parts to production operations, resulting in lower levels of inventory. Plant operating efficiency is improved when the MRP system helps management meet production commitments without increases in the number of employees and machines. More work is done with fewer resources.

The following rows are available in the MRP table.

- *Gross requirements* are dependent demand for a product taken from the master production schedule. This is what we need to produce in a given period.
- *Scheduled receipts* are orders placed on a manufacturer or a vendor and represent a commitment to make or buy. Data show the quantities ordered and when they are expected to be completed and available.
- *Available inventory* is projected number of units available after a manufacturing order has been released and subtracted. This inventory is not available for other orders.
- *Net requirements* are gross requirements minus scheduled receipts minus available inventory.

- *Planned order receipt* is the quantity planned to be received at a future date as a result of a planned order release. Planned order receipts differ from scheduled order receipts in that they have not been released.
- *Planned order release* is derived from planned order receipts by taking the planned receipt quantity and offsetting to the left by the appropriate lead time.

Note that the planned order release of the parent becomes the gross requirement of the component, following the product structure tree concept.

Work Center Performance Analysis

Plant performance indicators can help operations management in determining whether manufacturing resources are being utilized efficiently and effectively. The following formulas can aid in this effort.

Utilization % = (Hours Actually Worked ÷ Available Hours) × 100
Efficiency % = (Standard Hours of Work Produced ÷ Hours Actually Worked) × 100
Available (Rated or Calculated) Capacity = Available Time in Hours × Utilization % × Efficiency %
Measured (demonstrated) capacity is an average of previous production output.

Work Center Load Balancing Analysis

Load is the amount of planned wok scheduled for and actual work released to a facility, work center, or operation for a specific span of time, such as a day or week. Usually load is expressed in terms of standard hours of work or units of production.

Load balancing (leveling) is spreading work orders out in time or rescheduling operations so that the amount of work makes it more economical to produce in larger lots than are needed for immediate purposes.

Total load is release load plus planned load. Over- or under-capacity can occur, which is the difference between the total load and the available capacity. The term *over-capacity* means that the work center is overloaded, and the term *under-capacity* means that the work center is under-loaded.

Production Automation Alternatives

Break-even point analysis can help management in making a choice between a manual and a semi-automatic production process for a new product line. Again, both fixed costs and variable costs are considered for each alternative.

Cycle Counting of Inventories

Inventory is an asset of a company, and as such it must be accurate. Cycle counting is an inventory accuracy audit technique where inventory is counted on a cyclic schedule rather than once a year. A cycle inventory count is usually taken on a regular, defined basis. High-value and fast-moving items are counted more frequently, while low-value and slow-moving items are counted less frequently. The key purpose of cycle counting is to identify items in error, thus triggering research, identification, and elimination of the cause of the errors.

An ABC inventory classification system would help in prioritizing items for cycle counting. The ABC system can define the number of materials per class and the number of counts per material per year. The typical decision involves determining how many workers are needed to cycle count the inventory, how many inventory items they can count per day, how many hours they work, and the total costs.

Operations Lead-Times and Queuing Models

A manufacturing operation acts like a single channel, single phase queuing system. A company wants to reduce the operation's lead-time. Jobs arrive at operations at a specified rate and operations can process them at a certain rate. We need to balance arrival rates with process rates. Optimal rates can be determined using queuing models.

Kanban Containers

Kanban is a method of just-in-time (JIT) production that uses standard containers or lot sizes with a single card attached to each. It is a pull system, in which work centers signal with a card that they wish to withdraw parts from feeding operations or suppliers. Management is interested in reducing the number of containers and in increasing the efficiency rating.

Machine Setup Cost and Time

Making each different product in a manufacturing plant involves obtaining necessary materials, arranging specific equipment setups, filling out required papers, and charging proper time and materials to the right work order. Machine setup is a part of getting ready to produce another product. Each machine setup costs money because maintenance personnel and materials are involved in the changeover process. An economic order quantity (EOQ) model can be used to determine the amount of setup costs.

The necessary setup cost is computed as follows.

EOQ = Square Root of $[(2DS/C)(p/(p-d))]$
S = $[(C)(EOQ**2)/2D][(p-d)/p]$

where *D* is annual demand, *p* is daily production rate, *d* is daily demand, *C* is carrying cost per item,** 2 means raised to the power of 2, and *S* is setup cost.

The necessary setup time is computed as follows.

Setup Time = Setup Cost/Labor Rate

Service Levels and Lead Times

Service level is the probability that a stockout will not occur during lead time. It is a measure of satisfying demand through inventory or by the current production schedule in time to satisfy the customer's requested delivery dates and quantities. Management wants to provide a 95 percent or higher service level during lead time, and they want to determine how much safety stock is needed during lead time.

Order point (OP) is calculated from frequency distribution values after considering safety stock levels and knowing how long stockouts can occur. The safety stock (SS) level is computed as:

SS = OP − EDDLT

where EDDLT is expected demand during lead time (DDLT).

Demand During Lead Times

Management wants to determine demand during lead time so that stockouts will be limited. It can be assumed that demand during lead time is normally distributed based on past data. Another simplified assumption is that future use is accurately depicted by the historical DDLT. The decision requires computing the expected DDLT (EDDLT) for a material based on the average of all historical DDLT data. We need to add the computed EDDLT to safety stock (SS), so that order point (OP) is determined as follows.

OP = EDDLT + SS

Plant Layout

Space is a valuable resource and should be used very efficiently in both the plant and the office. Plant layout becomes even more important when building a new plant or new office. The layout can be mapped out using a block diagram

APPLICATION 13. MANUFACTURING OPERATIONS ANALYSIS

analysis. To solve the space problem, we need to know the expected movement of products between departments as well as the required area in square feet for each department. The following rules would help in this situation.

- Departments that have the highest amount of product movement between them should be located close to each other.
- Departments that have no product movement between them should be located at opposite ends of the building.

Production Cycle Time and Workstations

Manufacturing operations management is looking to improve the production line and plan to use the incremental utilization heuristic. They know the productive time per hour and the demand per hour. They have collected individual tasks, tasks that must immediately precede them, and the time to perform such tasks. The key requirement is to determine cycle time and the theoretical minimum number of workstations needed. The following formulas can help in this area.

- Cycle time is productive time in minutes per hour divided by demand per hour.
- The theoretical minimum number of workstations should equal (sum of tasks times per unit $\times$ demand per hour) divided by productive time in minutes per hour.

Preventive Maintenance Management

Preventive maintenance activities are performed to keep equipment in good working order and to prevent malfunctions before they occur. These activities include machine adjustments, lubrication, cleaning, parts replacements, painting, and needed repair and overhaul work.

For example, the repair rate for vehicles is number of vehicles repaired per week.

The average repair rate is $m = 1 + 1/ts$

Number of mechanics $= m \div$ vehicles per mechanic per week

where ts is average time in the system and is computed as $1/(\mu - \lambda)$.

Another maintenance measure is having enough standby machines. If a standby machine is not available when a breakdown occurs, there is a cost due to lost production time, overtime usage on the other machines, and emergency repair procedures. On the other hand, there is a cost for machines not in use due to storage and special handling expenses. There is a trade-off here.

The number of standby machines needed is calculated using the expected values and relative frequencies (probabilities) to minimize expected costs. A payoff table can be used to determine how many standby machines a company should maintain.

Retail Management Analysis

This application is related to Operations Management (Module 200) and Accounting (Module 600), and specifically to Sections 220 (Product Demand Management and Forecasting), 245 (Inventory Management), 250 (Materials Management), 660 (Decision Making and Accounting), and 680 (Control and Accounting).

Merchandise Pricing

Merchandise pricing decisions must be made in conjunction with other retail decisions. For example, the price of an item depends on lines of merchandise carried, location of the store, promotion, credit, customer services, and the store image the retailer wishes to convey, as well as legal constraints such as price discrimination laws.

The marketing department of a retail company studies the effects of different markups, costs, and selling prices to meet its profit and sales goals. Some formulas used in this effort include the following.

Selling Price = Cost/(100% − Markup %)

Cost + Markup Dollars = Selling Price

Percent Markup on Cost = (Selling Price − Cost)/Cost

Initial Markup Percentage = (Operating Expenses + Profits + Reductions)/(Net Sales + Reduction)

Maintained Markup Percentage = Initial Markup % − [(Reduction %) × (100% − Initial Markup %)]

Reduction Percentage = Amount of Reductions/Net Sales

The maintained markup, which is the difference between the actual selling price and the cost of that merchandise, is more important than the initial markup because it is the key to profitability.

Merchandise Planning

Buyers, working with senior management, are responsible for the dollar planning of merchandise requirements. Once planned sales for the period under consideration have been projected, buyers are then able to use any of the following methods for planning dollars invested in merchandise.

A retail company uses different merchandise planning systems for different departments and stores within the company. Beginning-of-month (BOM) inventory can be determined by five methods: (1) the basic stock method, (2) the percentage variation method, (3) the week's supply method, (4) the stock-to-sales ratio method, and (5) a combination of the preceding four.

- The basic stock method equals average stock minus average monthly sale.
- The percentage variation method is average stock for season multiplied by 0.5 [1 + (planned sales for the month/average monthly sales)].
- The week's supply method is average weekly sales times the number of weeks to be stocked.
- The stock-to-sales ratio method is stock-to-sales ratio times planned monthly sales.

The basic stock method will yield negative basic stock levels for each month when the annual inventory turnover rate is more than 6. The percentage variation, week's supply, and stock-to-sales ratio methods are good when the turnover rate is more than 6.

Merchandise Control

Control over the merchandise budget is exercised through the open-to-buy (OTB) approach. The OTB represents the dollar amount that a buyer can currently spend on merchandise without exceeding the planned amount of merchandise.

For example, the OTB amount for the month of February is calculated as follows.

Planned sales for February	$xxx
Plus planned reductions for February	xxx
Plus end of month (EOM) planned retail stock	xxx
Minus beginning of month (BOM) planned retail stock	xxx
Equals planned purchases at retail	xxx
Minus commitments at retail for delivery	xxx
Equals OTB amount	xxx

Some common buying errors in controlling merchandise include the following: (1) buying merchandise that is either priced too high or too low for the target market; (2) buying the wrong type of merchandise; (3) having too much or too little basic stock on hand; (4) buying from too many vendors; (5) failing to identify the season's hot items early enough in the season; and (6) simply repeating the original order, resulting in a limited selection.

APPLICATION 14. RETAIL MANAGEMENT ANALYSIS

Retail Inventory Valuation Methods

Two methods are commonly used for valuing a retailer's inventory: the cost method and the retail method. Most retailers today use the retail method of inventory valuation since it is the oldest and most useful. A third method, which is not as popular, is the lower of cost or market method. It is an inventory valuation method that reports inventory at the lower of its cost or current market value (or replacement cost, whichever is available).

The true ending book inventory value can be correctly calculated if there are no errors in recording beginning inventory, purchases, freight-in, markups, markdowns, discounts, returns, transfers between stores, and sales. The following formulas are used in inventory valuation methods.

- The cost complement of book inventory is total cost valuation divided by total retail valuation.
- Ending inventory at cost is computed by multiplying the adjusted ending book value at retail with the cost complement book inventory.
- The cost of goods sold equals total inventory valuation at cost minus ending inventory at cost.
- Gross margin equals sales minus the cost of goods sold.
- Net profit before taxes equals gross margin minus total operating expenses.

Retail Inventory Estimation Methods

Retailers can use either the retail method or the gross profit method to estimate a period ending inventory. These methods are used by management for internal merchandise planning and control purposes.

In using the retail method to estimate inventory, the retail prices of all merchandise acquired are accumulated. The inventory at retail is determined by deducting sales for the period from the retail price of the goods that were available for sale during the period. The inventory at retail is then converted to cost on the basis of the ratio of cost to selling (retail) price for the merchandise available for sale.

In using the gross profit method to estimate inventory, the estimated gross profit is deducted from the sales to determine the estimated cost of merchandise sold. This amount is then deducted from the cost of merchandise available for sale to determine the estimated ending inventory.

Retail Inventory Pricing Systems

First-in and first-out (FIFO) and last-in and first-out (LIFO) are two popular inventory pricing systems for a retailer. Most retailers prefer to use the LIFO system for planning purposes because it accurately reflects replacement costs.

The FIFO method reflects what happens in a retail store and best represents true merchandise cost. It assumes that the oldest merchandise is sold first.

Once a retailer has completed a physical inventory count, it must place a dollar value on that count. A major problem occurs when identical units of a particular product have been acquired at various prices. Both FIFO and LIFO yield different values for ending inventories and cost of goods sold.

The LIFO method is designed to cushion the impact of inflationary pressures by matching current costs against current revenues. Cost-of-goods sold is based on the costs of the most recently purchased inventory, whereas the older inventory is regarded as the unsold inventory. The LIFO method results during inflationary periods in the application of higher unit costs to the merchandise sold and a lower unit cost to the inventory unsold. In times of rapid inflation, most retailers use the LIFO method, resulting in lower profits on the income statement, but also lower income taxes.

The FIFO method assumes that the oldest merchandise is sold before the more recently purchased merchandise. Therefore, merchandise on the shelf will reflect the most current replacement price. During inflationary periods, the FIFO method allows "inventory profits" to be included as income.

Summary of LIFO and FIFO Methods

	LIFO	FIFO
Ending inventory value	Lower	Higher
Cost of goods sold	Higher	Lower
Gross margin	Lower	Higher
Net income	Lower	Higher
Taxes	Lower	Higher

In summary, LIFO yields a high cost of goods sold, lower inventory value, lower gross margin, lower net income, and lower income taxes. FIFO yields higher ending inventory values, lower cost of goods sold, higher gross margin, higher net income, and higher income taxes.

Merchandise Profitability Analysis

The word *profit* has many meanings and interpretations: gross profit, gross margin, net profit, net income, and operating profit. The most common way to define *profit* is the aggregate total of net profit after taxes or net income after taxes—the bottom of the income statement, often referred to as the "bottom line." Different managers focus on different profit levels based on their specific needs and objectives. For example, the CEO of a company focuses on net income after taxes, while the product manager in his marketing department focuses on gross margin for his product or product line.

The following formulas can be used in assessing the profitability of a store or retailer.

Annual Sales = Total Number of Transactions × Average Transaction Size

Gross Margin = Sales − Cost of Goods Sold

Gross Margin Amount = Gross Margin % × Sales

Gross Margin % = Gross Margin/Sales

Total Operating Costs = Total Variable Costs + Total Fixed Costs

Operating Profit = Gross Margin − Total Operating Costs

Net Income after Taxes = Operating Profit − Interest − Taxes

The closure rate is calculated as total number of transactions divided by the annual store traffic.

Retail Inventory Turns and Levels

Inventory turnover is the number of times per year, on average, that a retailer sells its inventory. Thus, an inventory turnover of twelve times indicates that, on average, the retailer turns over or sells its average inventory once a month. Likewise, an average inventory of $50,000 (retail) and annual sales of $300,000 means the retailer has turned over its inventory six times in one year or every two months.

The following formulas are used to compute inventory turnover ratios and inventory levels (average inventory).

Inventory Turnover Ratio = Annual Sales/Average Inventory at Retail, or

Inventory Turnover Ratio = Costs of Goods Sold/Average Inventory

Average Inventory = Cost of Goods Sold (COGS)/Inventory Turnover Ratio

Average Daily COGS = COGS/365 days

The number of day's sales in inventory is computed by dividing the inventory at the end of the year by the average daily COGS.

APPLICATION 14. RETAIL MANAGEMENT ANALYSIS

High-performance retailers are those who achieve financial excellence in terms of high gross margin percent, high inventory turnover ratio, and high net income after taxes. Retailers can be classified into four groups.

Low-margin/low-turnover retailers
Low-margin/high-turnover retailers
High-margin/low-turnover retailers
High-margin/high-turnover retailers

When a retailer achieves a high gross margin and high inventory turnover, the retailer can expect to achieve a high net income after taxes, assuming he or she is controlling operating costs, such as selling and administrative expenses.

Store Productivity and Performance

Profit is related to productivity in that productivity is a key determinant of profit. Major resources of a retailer include space, people, merchandise, and money. Productivity increase in each of these resources will yield greater productivity for the retailer as a whole. There are at least four ways to measure productivity of a retailer.

- Space productivity, which is defined as net sales divided by the total square feet of retail floor space.
- Labor productivity, which is defined as net sales divided by the number of full-time-equivalent employees.
- Merchandise productivity, which is defined as net sales divided by the average dollar investment in inventory. This is also called sales-to-stock ratio.
- Sales productivity, which is defined as net sales divided by the number of customers.

A retail store's productivity and performance can be measured, in part, with the following metrics: sales/square foot, sales/employee, sales/inventory dollars, and sales/customer. A decrease in any of the individual metrics can decrease the overall metric, return on assets (ROA). Notice that the common denominator in all the metrics is sales, which should be improved all the time.

Net Requirements Schedule

The net requirement schedule for a product indicates how many units should be released to purchasing. Net requirements can be calculated using the following formula.

Net Requirements = Estimated Demand + Ending Inventory − Beginning Inventory

Here, estimated demand is the same as gross requirements.

Economic Order Quantity and Costs

Economic order quantity (EOQ) is a type of fixed order quantity model that determines the amount of an item to be purchased at one time. The intent is to minimize the combined costs of acquiring and carrying inventory. EOQ can be used to set inventory policy. The basic EOQ model follows.

Total Stocking Cost (TSC) = $(Q/2) C + (D/Q) S$

where Q is average current order quantity, C is carrying cost per unit per year, D is annual demand in units, and S is ordering cost per order.

EOQ can also be calculated as the square root of $2DS/C$.

Fixed Order Period Model

The fixed order period model is a lot-sizing technique in materials requirements planning (MRP) or inventory management that will always cause planned or actual orders to be generated for a predetermined fixed quantity, or multiples thereof, if net requirements for the period exceed the fixed order quantity. The following formulas are used in the fixed order period model.

Fixed Order Period = T = Square Root of $2S/DC$

where D is annual demand, T is time interval for ordering, C is carrying cost (acquisition cost multiplied by annual carrying cost), and S is order cost.

Order Quantity = Upper Inventory Target − Current Inventory Level + EDDLT

where EDDLT is expected demand during lead time.

Total Stocking Cost (TSU) = $(DT/2) C + S/T$

ABC Inventory Classification System

The ABC inventory classification system helps companies manage their inventories more efficiently. The ABC classification is a group of inventory items arranged in decreasing order of annual dollar volume, which is price multiplied by projected inventory volume. This data is then split into class A, B, and C, as follows.

- Class A contains 10 to 20 percent of inventory items and represents 50 to 70 percent of dollar volume.
- Class B contains about 20 percent of inventory items and represents about 20 percent of dollar volume.
- Class C contains 60 to 70 percent of inventory items and represents 10 to 30 percent of dollar volume.

The ABC principle states that effort and money can be saved through applying looser controls to low-dollar-volume class items than will be applied to high-dollar-volume class items. This principle (also called the *80/20 rule* or *Pareto principle*) can be applied to many areas such as inventory, purchasing, sales, marketing, and production.

The following formula can be used in the ABC classification system.

Item Value = Item Cost × Item Demand or Usage

Retail Store Layout

Two important elements of store layout include store image and space productivity. Store image is the overall perception the consumer has of the store's environment. Space productivity represents how effectively the retailer utilizes its space and is usually measured by sales per square foot of selling space or gross margin dollars per square foot of selling space. When these two elements are maximized for a store, sales will be maximized as well.

Decision rules for better store layout include the following.

- Departments that have the most hourly customer traffic between them should be located next to each other.
- Departments that have the least hourly customer traffic between them should be located farthest from each other.

Service Management Analysis

This application is related to Operations Management (Module 200), and specifically to Sections 265 (Service Strategy), 270 (Service Capacity Management), and 275 (Waiting Time Management in Services).

Yield Management

Yield management is a revenue management concept in that it manages available capacity as effectively as possible to maximize revenues. It combines three techniques: (1) overbooking, (2) assigning capacity amounts to different market segments, and (3) differential pricing in different market segments. It is used extensively by industries such as airlines, hotels, vacation cruises and resorts, and rental car agencies.

The following formula can be used to establish the overbooking policy.

Number of Customers to Be Overbooked = $C_o /(C_s + C_o)$

where C_o is cost of overage and C_s is cost of stockouts.

Forecasting Retail Store Sales

The gravity model assumes that customers will spend more of their money in a store that requires less travel time from each area of living to each store and vice versa. The probability of customer traffic is higher for the nearest store.

Efficient Retail Stores

Data envelopment analysis (DEA) is a linear programming technique for measuring the relative efficiency of facilities. DEA is a practical measurement tool for businesses with many different facilities performing similar tasks when a single measure, such as profit or ROI, is not sufficient. The basic thought behind the DEA is that performance equals results obtained divided by resources used, or efficiency equals outputs divided by inputs.

DEA combines results obtained (outputs) and the resources used to create those results (inputs) into a single performance number that represents the efficiency of using resources to create results. For example, a retail store's management may want to study how many of its stores are efficient given the sales (inputs), profit (outputs), and customer outcome (satisfaction rates).

Profitable Sales Call

A retail company can decide whether certain potential customers should be the targets of a telephone solicitation. It needs to collect the following data on profits and loss.

- Average profit for a successful call
- Average loss for an unsuccessful call

From this data, the customer score and the appropriate cut-off point for a telephone call can be determined using the formula $Ln [P/(1 - P)]$.

Service Facility Layout

A service company is interested in determining new layout for its facilities to better serve its customers. The company can use a technique called *closeness rating* to determine where to locate its departments.

Closeness rating is used to reflect the desirability of placing one department near another. Ratings are 1 (necessary), 2 (very important), 3 (important), 4 (slightly important), 5 (unimportant), and 6 (undesirable). Usually, trial-and-error analysis is used in applying the closeness rating to develop good facility layouts. Several objectives should be considered when developing layouts, such as minimizing the sum of pairs of closeness ratings and minimizing the total distance between departments.

Decision rules for service facility include the following.

Departments that have a closeness rating of 1 are necessary, and therefore should be located next to each other.

Departments that have a closeness rating of 6 are undesirable, and therefore should not be located next to each other.

Site Location

Companies look for locations for their new offices, branches, or factories. Usually, they search for more locations before finalizing on one location. Management should define location attributes that are important to the business. Some of these attributes include office size, population, competition, and visibility. Then each attribute is assigned a weight factor. Each attribute is multiplied by its weight factor for each location, and the location with the highest weighted score is selected.

Another approach to site selection is the relative-aggregate-scores approach. Management collects data on various factors such as labor cost per hour, labor availability, government regulations, and transportation costs for each location. Each factor is assigned a weight between 0 and 1. This approach assigns weights to each factor before the decision is made. A weighted average number is obtained for each location, and the location with the highest score is selected.

Departmental Work Sequence

Identifying the proper sequence for a company's work departments requires careful planning. A technique called *load-distance analysis* can be used to determine the best layout. Management needs to collect information about distances between departments, departmental work sequence and volume, and how long each task stays in each department. The goal is to minimize the distance traveled from one department to the other considering the available workload.

Waiting Line Management

Models have been developed to help managers understand and make better decisions concerning the operation of waiting lines. A waiting line is also known as a *queue*, and the body of knowledge dealing with waiting lines is known as *queuing theory*.

Waiting line models consist of mathematical formulas and relationships that can be used to determine operating characteristics such as the probability that no units are in the system or the average number of units in the waiting line. These characteristics can become performance measures for a service company such as bank, university, or retail store.

The following formulas can be used in waiting line management.

Idle Time = 1 − (Utilization %)

The utilization is λ/μ. Utilization tells us the percentage of time the server is busy, where λ (lambda) is arrival rate (for example, the number of people per hour) and μ (mu) is service rate (for example, number of people serviced per hour). The average time between arrivals (for example, minutes per person) is 1 divided by λ. The average service time (for example, minutes per person) is 1 divided by μ.

To determine the length of the waiting line and how much time customers spend waiting, on average, the following equation can be used.

nl = Average Number in Line = $\lambda^2/\mu(\mu - \lambda)$
ns = Average Number in the System = $\lambda/(\mu - \lambda)$
tl = Average Time in Line = $\lambda/\mu(\mu - \lambda)$
ts = Average Time in the System = $1/(\mu - \lambda)$
Pn = Probability of *n* people in the system = $(1 - \lambda/\mu)(\lambda/\mu), n$

where λ (lambda) is arrival rate (for example, number of people per hour) and μ (mu) is service rate (for example, number of people serviced per hour).

Cost Analysis

This application is related to Accounting (Module 600), and specifically to Sections 630 (Cost Behavior, Control, and Decision Making), 640 (Product and Service Costs), and 660 (Decision Making and Accounting).

Characteristics of Costs

Different managers use different costs for different purposes, all for valid reasons. Important cost terms include *direct costs, indirect costs, sunk costs, book value, differential* or *incremental costs, opportunity costs,* and *controllable* or *uncontrollable costs.*

- Direct cost is traceable to a particular department, operation, or product (for example, the salary of a carpenter in a furniture plant).
- Indirect cost cannot be traced to a particular department, operation, or product (for example, the salary of general manager in a furniture plant).
- Sunk cost has been incurred in the past and cannot be altered by any current or future decision. Sunk cost is the result of past decision.
- Book value is the acquisition cost of an asset minus its accumulated depreciation. It is the remaining value of an asset according to the accounting books. For example, the book value of a machine is its original cost minus its accumulated depreciation. Book value is not relevant to current or future decision. It is a sunk cost because the decision was made in the past to acquire the machine. Nothing will change that now.
- Differential cost is the difference in costs between alternatives. It is also known as incremental cost. Incremental cost is the amount by which the cost of one action exceeds that of another. For example, incremental sales will require incremental costs, resulting in incremental profits.
- Opportunity cost is the cost of a foregone opportunity. It is the potential benefit given up when the choice of one action precludes selection of a different action. For example, plant space used by sales staff has an opportunity cost because plant management can use that space for something other than the sales office. Opportunity costs are real, and are not captured by the accounting system. The business manager should consider opportunity costs during the decision-making process.
- Controllable costs are those that can be influenced or changed by a particular manager or individual. Similarly, uncontrolled costs are those that a manager or an individual at a lower level cannot control or influence. Other managers at higher levels can control these costs.

Cost Structure and Production Volume

Cost structure refers to the amount of total fixed costs and total variable costs in a firm's total costs. Total fixed costs remain the same over the relevant range of activity, whether the activity is sales or production. Variable cost per unit will remain the same over the relevant activity range. Total variable costs are equal to variable costs per unit multiplied by the volume (sales or production).

Total Costs = Total Fixed Costs + Total Variable Costs

For any company, total fixed costs and variable costs per unit do not change within the relevant range. Fixed costs per unit are not meaningful because of their nonlinearity nature with volume. However, total costs do change within the relevant range of volume (sales or production). Once production jumps outside the relevant range, total fixed costs usually go up because additional overhead (fixed) costs are needed to support the additional activity.

Manufacturing Costs

Total manufacturing costs include materials (both direct and indirect), labor (both direct and indirect), and manufacturing overhead costs (factory burden). The interrelationship between cost elements in a manufacturing company is as follows.

Cost of Goods Sold = Beginning Inventory of Finished Goods + Costs of Goods Manufactured − Ending Inventory of Finished Goods

Sales − Cost of Goods Sold = Gross Margin

A lower cost of goods sold gives a higher gross margin and vice versa. The cost of goods manufactured is direct materials plus direct labor plus manufacturing overhead plus beginning work-in-process (WIP) inventory minus ending WIP.

Avoidable and Unavoidable Costs

Avoidable and unavoidable costs should be identified prior to deciding whether to keep or discontinue a department.

Avoidable costs are those that will no longer be incurred if a business unit or activity is eliminated. Unavoidable costs are those that will continue to be incurred if a business unit or activity is eliminated. Contribution margin analysis will be very useful in deciding which department to eliminate. Also, the opportunity cost of eliminating a department, store, or operation should be considered.

Cost Concepts and Cost Components

Various cost concepts and cost components exist as they relate to a manufacturing company. The goal is to match the cost concepts with the cost components. The following cost concepts should be considered.

- Prime costs consist of direct materials and direct labor with wages and fringe benefits.

    Prime Costs = Direct Material Costs + Direct Labor Costs

- Manufacturing overhead (factory burden or factory overhead) costs consist of depreciation on the factory building, indirect labor (including wages and fringe benefits), the production supervisor's salary and fringe benefits, and the overtime premium.

    Manufacturing Overhead Costs = Total Manufacturing Costs − Direct Labor Cost − Direct Material Cost

- Conversion costs include direct labor (including wages and fringe benefits), depreciation on the factory building, indirect labor (including wages and fringe benefits), the production supervisor's salary and fringe benefits, and the overtime premium.

    Conversion Costs = Direct Labor Cost + Factory Overhead Cost

- Product costs include direct materials, direct labor (including wages and fringe benefits), depreciation on the factory building, indirect labor (including wages and fringe benefits), the production supervisor's salary and fringe benefits, and the overtime premium.

    Product Costs = Direct Materials Cost + Direct Labor Cost + Factory Overhead Cost

- Period costs include advertising expenses, sales commissions, product promotion costs, rent for the sales office, and administrative salaries and fringe benefits. They do not include manufacturing costs.

    Period Costs = Selling Expenses + Administrative Expenses

A department supervisor in a food manufacturing plant can control the use of ingredients and utilities. A department supervisor in a food manufacturing plant cannot control depreciation on the factory building, the cost of property taxes, the cost of the plant manager's salary, and the wages of security staff.

APPLICATION 16. COST ANALYSIS

Sell-a-Product-As-Is-or-Process-It-Further Analysis

In process industries such as food, chemicals, or oil businesses, management is often faced with the decision about whether to sell a product at a stage of production or sell it later at a higher price after modification. Additional processing is required to make the product more valuable to customers (for example, selling cocoa powder as is or selling it as instant cocoa mix after modification).

Incremental revenues from additional processing should be compared with the incremental cost of additional processing. Incremental profit is incremental revenue minus incremental costs. If the incremental profit is positive, then additional processing should be undertaken. Otherwise, the product should be sold as is.

Special Orders

Management receives special order offers from major customers. The key issue here is to decide what price to charge the customer. The minimum price is variable cost per unit. Only variable costs are relevant in the short run, while all costs are relevant in the long run. The same variable costs are relevant to the special order because these are the additional costs that will be incurred. Fixed costs are assumed to be constant.

Management should consider the following factors before finalizing the special order decision: current inventory levels, current production capacity, customer relations, and accuracy of relevant costs. If inventory levels are high and if there is excess production capacity, it makes sense to accept the special order at a low price because both inventory and capacity will be put to good use. Some regular customers may not be happy if they find out the special price discount given to the local retailer. Because the entire decision is based on relevant costs, they must be accurate; otherwise special order costs will cut into profits.

Application 17

Corporate Performance Analysis

This application is related to Finance (Module 700) and Accounting (Module 600), and specifically to Sections 760 (Mergers, Acquisitions, and Business Valuations) and 650 (Operating Budgets and Performance Evaluation).

Economic-Value-Added and Return-on-Investment Analysis

The economic-value-added (EVA) is a better measure of corporate performance than return on investment (ROI), as the former adjusts for capital employed and incorporates business risk through the use of cost of capital. Although ROI is expressed as a percentage, it is not that significant when compared to EVA, which is expressed in absolute dollar amounts. Both ROI and EVA consider the net income. EVA is calculated as net income or operating net income minus (cost of capital $\times$ assets employed). ROI is calculated by dividing the net income with the assets employed or investment.

Market-Value-Added and Economic Profit Analysis

Market-value-added (MVA) is a better performance measure than economic profits because it is what investors use to assign value to a company's stock. Economic profit is similar in concept to accounting profit. Economic profit is invested capital $\times$ (ROIC $-$ WACC), where ROIC is return on invested capital and is computed as net income divided by the invested capital and WACC is weighted average cost of capital, which is the cost of money.

Economic Profit = Invested Capital $\times$ (ROIC $-$ WACC)

First, compute the book value per share to use the market-to-book (M/B) ratio in order to determine the market price per share. The book value per share is owner's equity divided by the total number of shares outstanding. The market price per share is book value per share multiplied by the M/B ratio. The market value of stock is market price per share multiplied by the total number of shares outstanding. The total market-value-added for a company is market value of stock plus the present value of debt minus capital invested since inception.

Economic-Value-Added and Market-Value-Added Analysis

EVA is operating profit minus a charge for the opportunity cost of capital invested. One of the reasons for a lower EVA compared to target could be that operating managers are not motivated. MVA is the difference between the market value of a company's debt and equity and the amount of capital invested since its inception. When actual MVA is higher than the target for successive years, investors show confidence in the overall performance of the company.

The MVA method measures the amount by which a company's stock market capitalization increases in a period. Market capitalization, which is the ultimate value of a company, is simply the number of shares outstanding multiplied by the market price per share. It is the value placed by investors. Market capitalization of a public company equals the number of shares outstanding multiplied by the market price per share.

An advantage of the EVA method is its integration of revenues and costs of short-term decisions into the long-term capital budgeting process. Disadvantages of the EVA method are that it focuses only on a single period and does not consider risks. MVA is an external measurement indicator, whereas EVA is an internal measurement for a company. In conclusion, MVA is better than EVA, and EVA is better than ROI.

Financial Management Analysis

This application is related to Accounting (Module 600) and Finance (Module 700), and specifically to Sections 620 (Analysis and Use of Financial Statements), 704 (Working Capital Policy), 720 (Financial Forecasting, Planning, and Control), and 725 (Cost of Capital, Capital Structure, and Dividend Policy).

Financial Condition

In order to asses the financial condition of a company, we need to collect not only the company's internal financial data (actual and target) for several years, but also the industry averages. The goal is to determine whether financial ratios are strong or weak, and, if weak, to find out the root causes of the problem. The overall financial condition of a company can be assessed by analyzing four areas of interest: liquidity, profitability, asset utilization, and market value measures.

Liquidity

The ability of a business to meet its financial obligations (debts) is called *liquidity* or *solvency*. Liquidity analysis focuses on the ability of a business to pay its current and noncurrent liabilities. It is normally assessed by examining balance sheet relationships, using the following major analyses.

Current position analysis can be divided into two areas: short-term and long-term. Short-term measures include current ratio (current assets divided by current liabilities), acid-test or quick ratio ([current assets minus inventory minus prepaid expenses] divided by current liabilities), cash ratio (cash divided by current liabilities), and working capital (current assets minus current liabilities) situation. Working capital is also called *net working capital*. Current ratio is a more reliable indicator of solvency than working capital or net working capital. A company with a higher acid-test ratio will have greater debt-paying ability.

Working capital and current ratios do not consider the makeup of current assets. The ability of each company to pay its debts is different. Some companies may have more inventories in their current assets. Some of these inventories must be sold and the receivable collected before current liabilities can be paid in full. Thus, inventories are not as liquid as cash. Inventories and prepaid expenses are subtracted from current assets in computing the acid-test ratio.

Long-term measures include financial leverage ratios such as total debt ratio ([total assets minus total equity] divided by total assets), times interest earned (EBIT divided by interest), and cash coverage ratios ([EBIT plus depreciation] divided by interest). Here, EBIT equals earnings before interest and taxes.

The ratio of fixed assets to long-term liabilities indicates the margin of safety available to noteholders and bondholders.

The ratio of liabilities to stockholders' equity indicates the margin of safety to creditors other than noteholders and bondholders.

Profitability

The ability of a business to earn profits depends on the effectiveness and efficiency of its operations as well as the resources available to it. Profitability analysis, therefore, focuses primarily on the relationship between operating results as reported in the income statement and resources available to the business as reported in the balance sheet. Major analyses include the following.

Profit Margin = Net Income After Taxes/Sales
Return on Assets (ROA) = Net Income After Taxes/Average Total Assets
Return on Equity (ROE) = Net Income After Taxes/Average Total Equity
Earning Power = Earnings Before Interest and Taxes (EBIT)/Total Assets

The following relationships hold true between ROA, ROE, and debt:

- When the ROA equals the cost of debt, ROE stays the same at different levels of debt.
- When the ROA is greater than the cost of debt, ROE increases at different levels of debt.
- When the ROA is less than the cost of debt, ROE decreases at different levels of debt.

Asset Utilization

The following turnover ratios tell us how efficiently or intensively a firm uses its assets to generate sales.

- Inventory turnover ratio (cost of goods sold divided by inventory) and number of days' sales in inventory (365 days divided by inventory turnover)
- Accounts receivable turnover ratio (sales divided by accounts receivable) and number of days' sales in receivables (365 days divided by receivables turnover)
- Total assets turnover is net sales divided by average total assets.

Market Value Measures

The following measures are useful to investors.

- The price-earnings (P/E) ratio is market price per share divided by earnings per share.
- The market-to-book (M/B) ratio is market value per share divided by book value per share.
- Earnings per share (EPS) is net income after taxes divided by the number of shares of stock outstanding. This is applicable when there is only one class of stock. A higher EPS does not always mean that stock price will increase.
- Earnings per share on common stock is net income after taxes minus preferred dividends divided by the number of shares of common stock outstanding.
- Dividends per share (DPS) on common stock is annual cash dividends paid divided by the number of shares of common stock outstanding. Stock dividends are not relevant.
- Dividend payout ratio is the amount of cash paid out divided by net income.

- Dividend yield on common stock is annual cash dividends per share on common stock divided by the market price per common stock on a specific date. Cash per share should not be listed because of its misleading nature. The dividends per share, dividend yield, and price-earnings (P/E) ratio of common stock are normally quoted on the daily listing of stock prices in the *Wall Street Journal* and other financial publications.

Dividends per Share and Earnings per Share

Dividends per share (DPS) can be reported with earnings per share (EPS) to indicate the relationship between dividends and earnings. Comparing these ratios indicates the extent to which a corporation is retaining its earnings for use in operations.

The DPS and the EPS are commonly used by investors in assessing alternative stock investments. The dividend yield is a profitability measure that shows the rate of return to common stockholders. The P/E ratio is an indicator of a company's earnings prospect.

Price-Earnings Ratio and Market-to-Book Ratio

A high or low price/earnings (P/E) ratio is not necessarily good or bad. A company's P/E ratio should be compared with industry norms rather than the previous year's performance. If the P/E ratio is significantly below the industry norm, one can conclude that this company is not performing as well as it should.

There is a relationship between book value per share, EPS, P/E ratio, and market-to-book (M/B) ratio. Book value per share is total assets divided by the number of common shares outstanding. If the M/B ratio were 2, then market price per share would be 2 times the book value per share. On the other hand, the book value per share can be multiplied by the M/B ratio to obtain the market price per share which, in turn, is divided by the EPS to result in the P/E ratio.

Acquisition-minded management always looks for companies with low price-earnings (P/E) ratios, hoping to improve stock price after acquisition. Stock may or may not increase after acquisition.

Working Capital Financing Policy

There are three short-term (working capital) financing polices: (1) the aggressive strategy, where a firm uses more short-term sources, its debt costs are low, profits are high, and solvency/liquidity is low; (2) the conservative strategy, where a firm uses more long-term sources, its debt costs are high, profits are low, and solvency/liquidity is high; and (3) the moderate strategy, where a firm operates in between the aggressive and conservative strategies.

Weighted Average Cost of Capital and Capital Structure

Cost of capital means determining the cost of money incurred in raising capital. The components of capital structure include debt, common stock, preferred stock, and retained earnings. Each component of the capital structure is weighted and each component's cost is calculated on both a before- and after-tax basis. Total cost is expressed as a percentage of total capital. Then, after-tax weighted average cost of capital (WACC) is computed. When we say that the cost of capital or WACC for a company is 10.5 percent, we mean that it costs 10.5 cents to raise every additional dollar. A lower WACC will mean a higher stock price and vice versa.

Company Recapitalization

A company that is changing its existing capital structure composition, that is, altering the make up of debt and equity is said to be recapitalizing or restructuring. Recapitalization is a financial issue for the company in that (1) it can issue some new bonds and use the proceeds to buy back some of its stock, thereby increasing its debt-equity ratio, or (2) it can issue new stock and use the money to pay off some debt, thereby reducing its debt-equity ratio. Assets of the company remain unchanged during the restructuring process.

APPLICATION 18. FINANCIAL MANAGEMENT ANALYSIS

Residual Dividend Policy

Dividends are paid out of net income and are mainly dictated by the dividend policy of the company (stable, variable, residual). To analyze a residual dividend policy, find the amount of retained earnings needed to fund the capital budget, determine the amount of net income available for dividends, and then compute the dividend payout ratio.

Lease Versus Purchase Analysis

The cost of lease should be compared with the after-tax cost of borrowing money and purchasing equipment.

A Comprehensive Financial Analysis

The following formulas will be useful when analyzing the overall financial condition of a company.
Return on Assets (ROA) = EBIT/Total Average Assets (Check: ROA = ROS × Asset Turnover)
Return on Sales (ROS) = EBIT/Net Sales
Asset Turnover = Net Sales/Total Average Assets
Financial Leverage = Total Average Assets/Total Average Common Stockholders' Equity
Return on Equity (ROE) = EBIT/Average Common Stockholders' Equity (Check: ROE = ROA × Financial Leverage)
Earnings per Share (EPS) = Net Income/Average Number of Common Shares Outstanding
Price/Earnings (P/E) Ratio = Market Price per Share/EPS
Market-to-Book (M/B) Ratio = Market Price per Share/Book Value per Share
Book Value per Share = Total Average Assets /Average Number of Common Shares Outstanding

Application 19

International Trade and Financing Analysis

This application is related to International Business (Module 1000), General Management and Organization (Module 100), and Information Technology (Module 800) and specifically to Sections 1070 (Economics and International Business), 1050 (International Payment), 1075 (International Banking), 170 (Economics and Management), and 850 (Systems Development and Acquisition).

Tariffs

The nominal tariff rate gives us a general idea of the level of protection afforded the home industry in a country. But it may not always truly indicate the actual, or effective, protection given.

Value Added = Price − Cost

The effective rate tariff rate is an indicator of the actual level of protection that a nominal tariff rate provides the domestic import-competing producers. It signifies the total increase in domestic productive activities (value added) that an existing tariff structure makes possible, compared to what would occur under free-trade conditions. The effective rate tells us how much more expensive domestic production can be relative to foreign production and still compete in the market.

The formula for the effective rate, e, is $(n - ab)/(1 - a)$, where e is the effective rate of protection, n is the nominal tariff rate on the final product, a is the ratio of the value of the imported input to the value of the final product, and b is the nominal tariff rate on the imported input.

Dumping Practices

Dumping is recognized as a form of international price discrimination. It occurs when foreign buyers are charged lower prices than domestic buyers for an identical product, after allowing for transportation costs and tariff duties. Selling in foreign markets at a price below the cost of production is also considered dumping.

Commodity Terms of Trade

The commodity terms of trade (also referred to as the *barter terms of trade*) is the most frequently used measure of the direction of trade gains for a country. It measures the relationship between the prices a nation gets for its exports and the prices it pays for its imports. The terms of trade, in short, is computed by dividing the export price index by the import price index, multiplying the result with 100 to express it in percentages.

International Balance of Payments

The measurement of all international economic transactions between the residents of a country and foreign residents is called the *balance of payments* (BOP). Many interested parties analyze the BOP in terms of three major accounts: the current account, the capital account, and the financial account.

The official reserve account is the total currency and metallic reserves held by official monetary authorities within a country. These reserves are normally composed of the major currencies used in international trade and financial transactions (for example, U.S. dollar, German mark, and Japanese yen) and gold. Note that the official reserve account should offset the total of current account, capital account, financial account, and net errors and omissions account. If the total of these four accounts is negative (deficit), the reserve account should be positive (surplus), and vice versa.

Incremental Analysis in Export Business

Companies in many countries, especially those less developed, can often sell their products at a higher price in more advanced countries. Company management in less-developed countries should consider price elasticities in foreign markets, greater economies of scale in their own production operations, foreign government restrictions, and market share in both domestic and foreign markets. Such management may want to develop various scenarios based on selling prices, variable costs, fixed costs, exporting costs, and transportation costs. For each scenario, contribution margin per unit should be calculated and additional earnings calculated from selling additional units. Incremental revenues and incremental costs should be calculated, and the final decision should be based on incremental profits, moving from one scenario to another.

Effective Financing Rates

We wish to determine the expected value of the effective financing rate of a foreign currency. To do this, we need percentage changes of currency values and their probability of occurrence. Then, we compute the effective financing rate for each value as (100 percent plus interest rate) multiplied by (100 percent minus the percentage change) minus 1. The result is multiplied by the probability of occurrence to get the expected value.

International Debt Financing Costs

Occasionally, U.S. multinational corporations (MNCs) raise money by issuing debt from foreign capital markets to finance their operations or to develop new products. Consider the foreign currency appreciation or depreciation variables when calculating the annual cost of debt financing.

Project Management Analysis

This application is related to General Management and Organization (Module 100), and specifically to Section 190 (Project Management).

Earned Value Management Method

Earned value management (EVM) is a reporting method to manage projects. The following formulas are used in an EVM report.

- The cost performance index (CPI) is earned value divided by actual cost = EV/AC. A CPI of more than or equal to 1 is good, while less than 1 is not so good.
- The schedule performance index (SPI) is earned value divided by planned value = EV/PV. A SPI of more than or equal to 1 is good, while less than 1 is not so good.
- The cost variance (CV) is earned value minus actual cost = EV − AC. A positive variance is good, while a negative variance is not so good.
- The schedule variance (SV) is earned value minus planned value = EV − PV. A positive variance is good, while a negative variance is not so good.
- The cost estimate at completion (EAC) is budget at completion (BAC) divided by cost performance index = BAC/CPI.
- The cost estimate to complete (ETC) a project is estimate at completion (EAC) minus actual cost (AC) = EAC − AC. The ETC is the remaining budget required to complete the project if work continues at the present performance rate.

Critical Path Method and Program Evaluation and Review Technique Method

Projects are scheduled and resources are committed and controlled with the use of the critical path method (CPM) and the program evaluation and review technique (PERT). Key concerns are when the project will be completed and at what cost. There are many possible paths to complete a project from beginning to end. But we are interested in only one path—that is, the critical path. The critical path is the one that takes the longest time to complete a project. We need to compute the total time required for all possible paths and select the one with the longest time as the critical path. Delaying any activity on the critical path will automatically delay the entire project.

Critical Paths and Slack Times

An activity on a critical path will have a slack time of zero. Slack is latest start (LS) minus early start (ES), or latest finish (LF) minus early finish (EF). Activities other than critical path activities will have a positive number.

Expected Values, Variance, Standard Deviation, and Probability

Sometimes a project may have three possible time estimates for each activity: optimistic, most likely, and pessimistic. We need to compute a single number for use in project planning and controlling. This is called the *expected duration*, which is computed as follows.

The expected duration for an activity is $t_e = (t_o + 4t_m + t_p)/6$

Variance is $= V_t = [(t_p - t_o)/6]**2$

Standard deviation is the square root of variance

**means raised to the power of 2.

We can also compute the probability of completing the project within a specified time frame using the following formula.

$Z = (T - D)/$Standard Deviation of Critical Path

Crashing a Project

Management may not accept the project manager's initial completion date for a project because of management's priorities and other commitments. In this case, management will ask the project manager to reduce the completion time of the project. This is called "crashing the project," which means reducing a project's completion time at a cost. Crash time is the shortest estimated length of time in which an activity can be completed. Crash cost is the estimated cost of completing an activity in the crash time.

Only activities on the critical path need to be crashed because they are the only ones that can make a difference in the project's completion time. In crashing a project's schedule, find the largest schedule reduction for the least incremental cost.

The following formulas can be used in computing the crash cost.

Crash cost for an activity is (crash cost minus normal cost)/(normal time minus crash time).

Total cost is normal cost plus crash cost. The normal cost is the summation of normal cost for all activities.

Economic Analysis

This application is related to General Management and Organization (Module 100), and specifically to Section 170 (Economics and Management).

Economic Cost Concepts

Business managers use the following economic concepts in a variety of business situations. A major use of these concepts is in deciding whether to accept a special order from a customer or to increase plant capacity.

Variable cost per unit is total variable costs divided by the quantity produced. This rate stays the same over the relevant range of production.

An additional unit of production incurs a cost equal to marginal cost. This can be verified by the difference in total costs divided by the differences in quantity of production. Marginal or incremental cost per unit is the same as the variable cost per unit because fixed costs are the same for the relevant range of production.

Average cost is simply total costs at a particular production quantity divided by that production quantity. The average cost per unit will be different at different quantities of production.

Regarding special orders, as long as the special order price per unit is more than the variable cost per unit, the special order should be accepted. This is because fixed costs stay the same when the company has excess production capacity. The cost structure changes when the company does not have excess capacity. Fixed costs will increase due to overtime, additional operating shifts, and additional overhead.

Application 22

Cash Flow Analysis

This application is related to Accounting (Module 600) and Finance (Module 700), and specifically to Sections 610 (Assets, Liabilities, and Owner's Equity) and 735 (Capital Budgeting).

Project Operating Cash Flows

Every project yields cash flows over a time period. We can compute operating cash flows as follows.

EBIT = Sales − Variable Costs − Fixed Costs − Depreciation
Operating Cash Flows = EBIT + Depreciation − Taxes
Net Income = EBIT − Taxes

Cash Flow From Operations

Cash flow from operations is obtained by subtracting taxes and incremental investment in inventory (working capital) and fixed assets from net operating profit.

Cash Flow From Operations = Net Operating Profit − Taxes − Incremental Investments

The total value of a project is the summation of the present value of current cash flows from operations and the present value of terminal cash flows.

Cash Flow Adequacy Ratio and Free Cash Flows

According to Jackson and Sawyers,[28] the cash flow adequacy ratio is computed as cash flow from operating activities minus interest paid minus taxed paid minus capital expenditures divided by the average amount of debt maturing over the next five years.

In general, if the cash flow adequacy ratio is less than 1, it indicates that cash flow is insufficient to repay average annual long-term debt over the next five years. If this ratio is above 1, it indicates sufficient cash flow to repay long-term debt obligation. This ratio should be compared to that of previous time periods as well as against industry averages.

Free cash flow is computed as cash flow from operating activities minus cash used to purchase fixed assets to maintain productive capacity used up in producing income during the period minus cash used for dividends. A company that has free cash flow is able to fund internal growth, retire debt, and enjoy financial flexibility. Lack of free cash flow can be an early indicator of liquidity problems.

Cash Flows From Operating, Financing, and Investing Activities

Cash flows come from three sources: operating, financing, and investing activities of a company. Operating activities include acquiring and selling products in the normal course of business. It includes income, cash receipts from cash sales, and interest. It also includes cash payments for payroll, insurance, interest, taxes, materials purchase, and rent.

Financing activities include cash flows from selling or repurchasing capital stock, long-term borrowing, and contributions from owners. It includes issuance of stocks and bonds, repurchase of the company's own stock, contribution from and withdrawal by owners, and payment of cash dividends.

Investing activities include the purchase and sale of property, plant, and equipment, the purchase and sale of investment securities, and making loans as investments. It includes sale of fixed assets, investment securities, and intangible assets, purchase of fixed assets, investment securities, and intangible assets.

Noncash activities do not involve cash. Rather, they involve issuance of stocks and bonds in exchange for assets, debt, and stocks. They also include stock dividends.

Fraud Analysis

This application is related to Corporate Control and Governance (Module 900), and specifically to Section 930 (Corporate Fraud).

Income Reconciliation Ratio

Timing and other elements create differences between a company's cash flows and its accrued-based net income. Over the life of a firm, however, these differences should even out so that the cash generated from operations is approximately equal to the net income that is reported. This condition should be tested by computing the income reconciliation ratio, as follows.

Income Reconciliation Ratio = (Net Income − Cash Flows From Operations)/Total Assets

Over a time period, this ratio should be around zero, with some positive years and some negative years. Progressive deterioration in this ratio, as measured by increasingly longer positive numbers, can signal trouble and hint that financial statement fraud is occurring, with reported net income increasing and cash flows from operations decreasing.

While the income reconciliation ratio does not provide information about the kind of fraud that may be occurring, it is an excellent warning sign to show (1) that financial statement fraud may be occurring and that net income is being manipulated; or (2) that even if fraud is not occurring, the company is having serious cash flow problems (that is, liquidity or solvency problems).

Fraud Losses and Indicators of Fraud

It is difficult to know exactly the amount of fraud losses because such information is not reported either internally or externally. Experts estimate this amount based on a number of subjective factors.

Companies need to generate additional sales to recover fraud-related losses. Two companies in the same industry will need different sales amounts due to differences in their gross margin percentages.

Reviewing the following indicators of fraud can reveal some clues as to the occurrence of fraud.

Current ratio

Acid-test ratio

Accounts payable/purchases ratio

Accounts payable/cost of goods sold ratio
Accounts payable/total liabilities ratio
Accounts payable/inventory ratio

For example, increases in the current ratio and acid-test ratio and decreases in the accounts payable/inventory ratio indicate the possibility of accounts payable fraud, that is, underreporting of accounts payable balances. Increase in the accounts payable/total liabilities ratio cannot be due to underreporting of accounts payable when the numerator is increasing.

Some "red flags" for fraud include the following.

- A large and sudden increase in sales is a possible red flag for revenue overstatement.
- When the cost of goods sold as a percentage of sales decreases considerably in two consecutive years, it is an alarming trend, and a possible red flag for cost of goods sold understatement.
- When the gross margin as a percentage of sales increases significantly in two consecutive years, this is an alarming trend, and a possible red flag for gross margin manipulation. In many cases, management bonus is based on gross margin performance.

Incorrect Reporting of Liabilities

The balance sheet reports two liabilities: accounts payable and notes payable. These liabilities arise from two transactions: purchasing and borrowing. When purchasing raw materials and merchandise, management may choose not to record purchases and understate accounts payable.

When borrowing money, management may choose not to record the liability and understate notes payable. Large changes in these two liabilities could be a symptom of understatement of liability.

Application 24

Quality Analysis

This application is related to Quality and Process Management (Module 400) and Operations Management (Module 200), and specifically to Sections 420 (Quality, Costs, and Profits), 440 (Statistics and Quality Control), and 255 (Purchasing Management).

Poor Quality Costs

Poor quality costs can be organized into four major categories: prevention, appraisal, internal failure, and external failure.

Prevention costs are investments made to keep nonconforming products from occurring and reaching the customer. These costs include specific costs such as quality planning, statistical process control costs and tools, information systems costs, quality education and training, general management costs, operator inspection costs, supplier ratings, supplier reviews, purchase-order technical data reviews, supplier certification, design reviews, pilot projects, prototype tests, vendor surveys, quality design, quality department review costs, customer surveys, product design, service design, process design, supplier reviews and ratings, field trials and tests, quality administration and quality system audits, design equipment, quality tools and equipment, design and engineering costs, and supplier quality surveys.

Six-sigma is a quality control approach that emphasizes a relentless pursuit of higher quality and lower costs. Six-sigma can achieve a competitive advantage. Investment in a six-sigma program should be considered a prevention effort.

Appraisal costs are those associated with efforts to ensure conformance to requirements, generally through measurements and analysis of data to detect nonconformances. Specific items in this category include test and inspection costs, instrument maintenance costs, process measurements and control costs, purchasing appraisal costs, qualification of supplier products, equipment calibration, receiving and shipping inspection costs of materials, tests, product quality audits, receiving inspections, test materials, setup inspections and special tests, laboratory support and supplies, measurement equipment and supplies, maintenance labor, external appraisal costs, evaluation of inventory and parts, review of test and inspection data, outside certification costs, product quality audits, service quality audits, operations inspections and tests, and source inspection costs.

Internal failure costs are incurred as a result of unsatisfactory quality found before the delivery of a product to the customer. Some examples in this category include scrap, rework, and waste costs, design, operations, and supplier corrective action costs, downgrading costs, process failures, repair, redesign, reinspection, retesting, sorting, operations failure costs, disposition costs for nonconforming materials, operations troubleshooting costs, product liability investigation support costs, cost of site visits to correct supplier quality problems, and uncontrolled labor and material costs.

External failure costs occur after poor-quality products reach the customer. Specifically, it includes costs due to customer complaints and returns, product recall costs and warranty claims costs, and product liability costs resulting from legal action and settlements, field service staff training costs, customer complaint investigation, design retrofit costs, loss of customer goodwill, and lost sales and profits.

Poor quality costs should be compared from period to period of a company with its targets as well as to that of the industry. A common measure is the percentage of quality costs to sales. The key question is whether a company is spending enough money on prevention efforts. When the company spends more money on preventing quality problems in the short run it will reduce both appraisal costs and failure costs in the long run.

Supplier Quality Evaluation

Three types of supplier performance measurement techniques are the categorical system, the weighted-point system, and the cost-based system. The categorical system is easy to implement and carries low implementation cost, but it is the least reliable due to its subjectivity. The weighted-point system is flexible and carries moderate implementation costs, but it tends to focus on unit price. The cost-based system is the most thorough and objective, but high costs and greater complexity may prohibit its use.

The cost-based system focuses on cost of nonconformance to specifications. An organization must calculate the additional costs that result whenever a supplier fails to perform as expected. Quality is one of the elements of performance. The supplier quality rating index (SQRI) with a base value of 1 is a total cost index calculated for each item or commodity provided by a supplier. The formula for SQRI follows.

SQRI = (Supplier Quality Costs + Total Purchase Costs)/Total Purchase Costs

Here, supplier quality costs are costs of nonconformance. The higher the SQRI, the greater the need for corrective action. The SQRI for a perfect supplier would be 1.0, as there are no supplier quality-related costs incurred.

Quality and Financial Statements

Quality affects financial statements in that good quality increases net income (through increased sales and decreased costs) whereas poor quality decreases net income (through decreased sales and increased costs). A common financial ratio is return on investment (ROI) or return on quality (ROQ), which can be calculated using the following formulas.

ROI is savings divided by investment or cost.

ROQ is (net present value of benefits or savings divided by net present value of cost or investment) − 1, and the result is multiplied by 100.

ROQ is better than ROI because it takes time value into account and discounts future cash flows to present value.

The following quality-related cost savings affect income statement accounts: savings in reduced direct labor costs, savings from reduced inspection costs, and savings from reduced raw materials costs.

The following quality-related cost savings affect balance sheet accounts: savings in decreased inventory, savings from decreased accounts receivables, and savings from decreased working capital.

Control Charts

A control chart is a statistical tool that distinguishes between natural (common) and unnatural (special) variations. The control chart method is used to measure variations in quality. It is a picture of a process over time. It shows whether a process is in a stable state and is used to improve process quality. There are three lines in the control chart: the central (average) line, the upper limit line, and the lower limit line. The following formulas can be used to measure the upper limit and lower limit lines.

Upper Limit = p-bar + (3) {Square Root of [p (100 − p)]/n}
Lower Limit = p-bar − (3) {Square Root of [p (100 − p)]/n}

where p-bar and p are percent defective and n is the number of sample observations.

Variable Control Charts

Two types of variable control charts exist: the X bar chart, which is used to record the variation in the average value of samples (process average) and the R chart, which measures range or dispersion (process spread, standard deviation, or variability). The following statements indicate the salient difference between the X bar and the R chart.

The X bar chart deals with the process average.

The R chart deals with the process spread.

Next, we will show the calculations for the X bar chart.

Upper Limit = X-Double Bar + A (R-Bar)
Lower Limit = X-Double Bar − A (R-Bar)

where X-double bar is process average, A is the control limit factor for the sample mean with a sample size of n, and the R-bar is range of data.

Next, we will show the calculations for the R chart.

Lower Limit = (Dl) (R-Bar)
Upper Limit = (D2) (R-Bar)

where D1 is the lower control limit factor for the sample range with a sample size of n, D2 is the upper control limit factor for the sample range with a sample size of n, and R-bar is the range of data.

System Reliability and Redundancy

Unreliable systems are poor quality systems. The reliability measure of a total system before backup involves multiplication of the reliabilities of each component.

The reliability of a product or system is increased with redundancy or backup. Redundant components add cost and complexity to a product, so we want to add such backups in the most cost-effective manner. If only one component can have a redundant unit, the greatest improvement in reliability can be achieved by assigning the redundant unit to the component with the lowest reliability. Sometimes we have to add redundancy to the most reliable component if cost differentials are not that large. The following formulas will be useful in improving a system's reliability.

Failure Rate for a Component = Number of Failures/Number Tested
Component Reliability = (1 − Failure Rate)

The mean time between failures (MTBF) for a component is calculated as follows.

MTBF = Unit-Hours of Operation/Number of Failures

Sensitivity and Scenario Analysis

This application is related to Finance (Module 700) and Accounting (Module 600), and specifically to Sections 735 (Capital Budgeting) and 630 (Cost Behavior, Control, and Decision Making).

Cash Flow Scenario Analysis

Sensitivity analysis is a technique that shows exactly how much output will change in response to a given change in input, other things held constant. Although sensitivity analysis probably is the most widely used risk analysis technique, it does have a limitation. It presents the output as a single value, instead of a range of values.

Scenario analysis eliminates the limitation of sensitivity analysis. It is a risk analysis technique that considers both the sensitivity of the output variable to changes in key variables and the likely range of variable values. Managers will develop a "bad" set of circumstances (for example, low unit sales, low sales price, high variable cost per unit, high fixed costs) and a "good" set (for example, high unit sales, high sales price, and low variable cost per unit, low fixed costs). These numbers are then compared to the expected, base case. The following statements express the interrelationships between the three scenarios.

The best-case scenario defines the upper bound.

The worst-case scenario defines the lower bound.

The base case is a most likely scenario, which is in between the best case and the worst case.

When a project involves cash flows spread over a period of time, the best approach is to develop the probability of each outcome (scenario) and compute the net present value (NPV). The following formulas can be used.

Expected NPV is the summation of NPVs multiplied by the probability of each outcome.

The coefficient of variation (CV) is standard deviation divided by expected NPV.

The CV measures the riskiness of a project. The greater the CV, the riskier a project is. A CV of 1.0 is normal. Choose the scenario with the lowest CV number.

Another approach to scenario analysis follows. Management is not sure about the sales volume, prices, and costs used in the base case, and wishes to use different scenarios of best case and worst case within, say, 5 percent of the base case. The best-case scenario adds 5 percent to the base case for unit sales and selling price, and subtracts 5 percent from the base case for all costs. The worst-case scenario subtracts 5 percent from the base case for unit sales and sales price, and adds 5 percent to the base case for all costs. The worst-case numbers are just opposite of the best-case. EBIT, cash flows, and NPVs must be computed for each case, as follows.

EBIT for any case = Total sales minus total variable costs minus total fixed costs minus depreciation

Cash flows for any case = EBIT plus depreciation expense minus taxes

NPV for any case = Present value of future cash flows minus initial investment or cost

Project Sensitivity Analysis

Sensitivity analysis can be applied to a single project. It is used when the project manager is uncertain about projected cash flows and is asking for various managers' input regarding probabilities of each cash flow outcome. The following is the suggested approach to handle this situation.

- Compute the expected value (EV) for each manager by multiplying the manager's probability with the cash flows project by that manager.
- Compute the total present value (PV) by combining the PV amount of cash flows and the PV of working capital recovery.
- Subtract the investment amount from the total PV to result in the net present value (NPV) for each manager.

Financial Sensitivity Analysis

Sales volumes and costs change very frequently for many corporations, and management wishes to know the impact of such changes on profits. Sensitivity analysis can help management in this area through break-even point (BEP) calculations as follows.

- A company will have a zero profit at BEP, that is, revenues are exactly equal to expenses (no profit or loss).
- The BEP in units is computed as fixed costs divided by unit contribution margin (CM), where CM is selling price per unit minus variable cost per unit.
- The BEP in dollars is computed as fixed costs divided by unit CM percentage or BEP in units multiplied by the selling price per unit.
- BEP with target net income is computed as (fixed costs + target net income)/unit contribution margin.
- Net income before tax is computed as net income after tax divided by the (1 − tax rate).

If fixed costs increase, then break-even point will increase and vice versa. The same thing holds true for variable costs. When both fixed costs and variable costs change simultaneously, the effect cannot be predicted precisely. If selling price is increased, then break-even point is decreased and vice versa.

Application 26

Divisional Performance Analysis

This application is related to Accounting (Module 600), and specifically to Section 650 (Operating Budgets and Performance Evaluation).

Return on Investment and Residual Income

Responsibility accounting is the process of measuring and reporting operating data by a responsibility center. Three common types of responsibility centers in a decentralized business are cost centers, profit centers, and investment centers. In a cost center, the business unit manager has the responsibility and authority for controlling the costs incurred. In a profit center, the business unit manager has the responsibility and authority to make decisions that affect both costs and revenues, and thus profits. In an investment center, the business unit manager has the responsibility and authority to make decisions that affect not only costs and revenues, but also the assets invested in the center. Investment centers are widely used in highly diversified companies organized by divisions.

Two methods are commonly used in measuring the performance of a divisional manager. These methods include return on investment (ROI) and residual income (RI). Both ROI and RI are calculated as follows.

ROI equals net operating income divided by average operating assets, where the latter is equal to the invested capital. When sales revenues are increased and operating expenses are decreased, the contribution margin will be increased. Decreasing the investment in operating assets will increase the ROI.

ROI = Profit Margin × Asset Turnover
Profit Margin (PM) = Net Operating Income/Sales Revenue
Asset Turnover (AT) = Sales Revenue/Average Operating Assets
RI = Net Operating Income − Minimum Required Return on Assets

where the latter is equal to imputed interest charge on the capital invested.

Residual income (RI) is measured in absolute dollars, not in percentages. Absolute dollars give clear size or magnitude of the amount, which is more appealing than percentages.

An advantage of ROI is that it shows the precise measure of return as a percentage, which can be compared to the target return percentage. A disadvantage of ROI is that it may lead divisional managers to reject new investments that could be profitable for the company as a whole, and to accept investments yielding returns above the division's target return percentage. The logic is that accepting individual projects with lower return could lower the average return for the entire division.

The major advantage of residual income as a performance measure is that it considers both the minimum acceptable rate of return and the total amount of the income from operations earned by each division. Residual income encourages division managers to maximize income from operations in excess of the minimum. This provides an incentive to accept any project that is expected to have a rate of return in excess of the minimum. Thus, the residual income number supports both divisional and overall company objectives the ROI does not.

The Balanced Scorecard System

The balanced scorecard system is a comprehensive management control system that balances traditional financial measures with operational measures relating to a company's critical success factors. The number of product or service warranty claims filed, the number of returned products, customer response time, and percentage of on-time deliveries are critical success factors for operations.

The balanced scorecard system started as a management control system is now becoming a strategic management system because of its importance to the overall progress of a company in terms of long-term value, vision, and strategy.

The balanced scorecard approach integrates financial and nonfinancial performance measures of a company. Costs and sales margins are financial measures, while items such as quality and customer service are nonfinancial measures.

Financial measures are lag indicators focusing on past actions and promoting short-term behavior. Companies also need lead indicators focusing on value creators or drivers, promoting long-term behavior, and equally emphasizing nonfinancial measures such as quality and service.

The four perspectives of the balanced scorecard include measures of quality, productivity, efficiency and timeliness, and marketing success. The balanced scorecard approach requires looking at performance from four different but related perspectives: financial, customer, internal business processes, and learning and growth. Financial perspectives include measures such as gross margin, net income, return on assets (ROA) return on investment (ROI), and return on equity (ROE). The customer perspective deals with taking care of the interests of customers, and acquiring and retaining more of them. Examples of customer-performance scorecard measures include new, dissatisfied, satisfied, or lost customers; target market awareness or preference; relative product or service quality; and on-time delivery. The scope of internal business process includes improving quality throughout the production process, increasing productivity, and increasing efficiency of resources and timeliness of information. The value chain of a company, which is a part of the internal business process, includes all activities from research and development (R&D) to post-sale customer service. Learning and growth perspectives deal with product improvement and innovation, information systems capabilities, efficient and effective use of employees, and overall company growth. Time to market a new product is part of the learning and growth measure.

Traditional measures are basically financial and are not adequate to fully assess the performance of companies. Traditional measures mainly deal with historical accounting data and cannot answer questions relating to customer satisfaction, quality improvement, productivity, efficient utilization of resources, and employee satisfaction.

Stakeholder-based performance scorecard measurements are more difficult to identify and implement than market-based, manufacturing-based, or human resource-based measurements. This is because of (1) the various constituents that are involved (stockholders, employees, unions, governments, investors and creditors, banks, distributors, wholesalers and retailers, and suppliers and vendors); (2) difficulty in reaching them on a day-to-day basis; (3) difficulty in communicating with them; (4) difficulty in coordinating them; and (5) difficulty in reaching a conclusion on issues due to divergent viewpoints and conflicting objectives.

An example of a market-based scorecard measure is the time to market a new product. Examples of manufacture-based scorecard measures include machine downtime, rework time, and plant waste. Examples of human resource-based scorecard measures include developing an employee skill inventory system, timely forecasting of workforce needs, increasing job efficiency of employees, and increasing core competencies of employees.

Organizational and General Management Analysis

This application is related to General Management and Organization (Module 100), and specifically to Sections 120 (Directing and Leading), 140 (Motivating and Communicating), 150 (Problem Solving and Decision Making), 175 (Organizational Behavior and Culture), 180 (Organizational Structure and Change Management), 110 (Planning and Organizing), and 160 (Business Policy and Ethics).

Leadership Styles

The five varieties of leader power include legitimate power, referent power, reward power, coercive power, and expert power.

Legitimate power is the power that stems from a formal management position in an organization and the authority granted to it. The command and control concept believes in job hierarchy and position power, which is the same as legitimate power. Referent power is the power that results from characteristics that command subordinates' identification with, respect and admiration for, and desire to emulate the leader. Reward power is the power that results from the authority to bestow rewards on other people. Coercive power is the power that stems from the authority to punish or recommend punishment. Expert power is the power that stems from special knowledge of or skill in the tasks performed by subordinates.

Blake and Mouton of the University of Texas have developed a two-dimensional leadership grid proposing five management styles. Each style is ranked on a scale of 1 to 9, one being low concern and 9 high concern. The two dimensions include concern for people and concern for production.

Team management style (9,9) often is considered the most effective style of leadership and is recommended for managers because organization members work together to accomplish a task. Country club management style (1,9) occurs when primary emphasis is given to people rather than to work outputs. Authority-compliance management style (9,1) occurs when efficiency in operations is the dominant orientation. Middle-of-the-road management style (5,5) reflects a moderate amount of concern for both people and production. Impoverished management style (1,1) denotes the absence of a management philosophy; managers exert little effort toward interpersonal relationships or work accomplishments.

Fiedler's contingency theory states that managers or leaders should match their style with the situation most favorable for their success. A leader's style is either relationship oriented or task oriented. Leadership style can be measured with a questionnaire known as the *least preferred coworker* (LPC) *scale*. If the leader describes the least preferred coworker using positive concepts, he or she is considered relationship oriented, that is, a leader who cares about and is sensitive to other people's feelings. Conversely, if the leader uses negative concepts to describe the least preferred coworker, he or she is considered task oriented, that is, a leader who sees other people in negative terms and places greater value on task activities than on people.

Communication

Organization-wide communications typically flow in three directions: downward, upward, and horizontally. These three directions make up the formal channels of communication, which is based on chain of command and task responsibility defined by the organization. In addition to formal channels, management can use informal channels, which means managers get out of their offices and mingle with employees.

Downward communication occurs when messages are sent from top management down to subordinates. Implementation of goals and strategies, performance feedback, job instructions, and procedures and practices are examples of downward communication.

Upward communication occurs when messages are transmitted from lower to higher levels in the organization's hierarchy. Suggestions for improvement, problems and exception reporting, grievances and disputes, financial and accounting information, and performance reports are examples of upward communication.

Horizontal communication is the lateral or diagonal exchange of messages among peers or coworkers. Intradepartmental problem solving, interdepartmental coordination, and change initiatives and improvements are examples of horizontal communication.

Presenting hard facts and figures is a verbal message. Nonverbal messages convey thoughts and feelings with greater force than most carefully selected words.

Effective listening and engaged listening are key characteristics of successful communication. Poor listeners are passive, laid back, tune out dry subjects, are easily distracted, tend to daydream, is minimally involved, tunes out if delivery is poor, has preconceptions, starts to argue, listens for facts, shows no energy output, fakes attention, and resists difficult materials used in presentations.

Good listeners ask questions, look for opportunities to learn, fight distractions, tolerate bad habits, know how to concentrate, show interest, judge content, listen to central themes, work hard, and maintain eye contact.

Decision Making

The decision-making process involves six basic steps: problem recognition, diagnosis of causes, development of alternatives, choice of an alternative, implementation of the alternative, and feedback and evaluation.

The Vroom-Jago model was designed to help managers gauge the amount of subordinate participation in decision making. The basic five leader participation styles include decide, consult individually, consult group, facilitate, and delegate.

The "decide" style is when the leader makes the decision alone. The "consult individually" style is manifested when the leader presents the problem to subordinates individually for their suggestions and then makes the decision. Using the "consult group" style, the leader presents the problem to subordinates as a group, collectively obtaining their ideas and suggestions. The leader who "facilitates" shares the problem with subordinates as a group and acts as a facilitator to help the group arrive at a decision. The leader who "delegates" assigns the problem to the group and has them make the decision within prescribed limits. Selecting a leadership participation style is not directly related to the decision-making process.

Three decision-making models exist: the classical model, the administrative model, and the political model. The classical model is good when problems and goals are clear, conditions are certain, individuals choose rational choices for maximizing outcomes, and full information is available about alternatives and their outcomes. The administrative model is good for handling vague problems and goals, or when conditions are uncertain, individuals choose satisfying choices for resolving problems using intuition, and limited information is available about alternatives and their outcomes. The political model is good when handling conflicting goals, when conditions are uncertain, when inconsistent viewpoints and ambiguous information are present, and bargaining and discussion are required among coalition members.

Corporate Culture

Each and every company operates between its external environment and internal environment. The organization's external environment can be conceptualized as having two layers: the general environment and the task environment. The general environment affects the organization indirectly. The task environment directly influences the organization's operations and performance.

The organization also has an internal environment, which includes the elements within the organization's boundaries. It is composed of current employees, management, and especially corporate culture, which defines employee behavior in the internal environment and how well the organization will adapt to the external environment. The internal culture must fit the needs of the external environment and company strategy. When this fit occurs, highly committed employees create a high-performance organization that is tough to beat. Stories about company officers are told to new employees to keep the organization's primary value and culture alive.

In considering what cultural values are important for the organization, managers consider the external environment as well as the company's strategy and goals. Studies have suggested that the right fit among culture, strategy, and environment is associated with four categories or types of culture. These four categories are based on two dimensions: (1) the extent to which the external environment requires flexibility or stability, and (2) the extent to which a company's strategic focus is internal or external. The four categories of cultures associated with these differences are adaptability, achievement, clan, and bureaucratic.

The adaptability culture has an external focus with flexibility in mind and emerges in an environment that requires fast response and high-risk decision making. Managers encourage values that support the company's ability to rapidly detect, interpret, and translate signals from the environment into new behavior responses. Employees have autonomy to make decisions and act freely to meet new needs; responsiveness to customers is highly valued. Managers also actively create change by encouraging and rewarding creativity, experimentation, and risk taking.

The achievement culture has an external focus with stability in mind. It is suited to organizations that are concerned with serving specific customers in the external environment, but without the intense need for flexibility and rapid change. This is a results-oriented culture that values competitiveness, aggressiveness, personal initiative, and willingness to work long and hard to achieve results. An emphasis on winning and achieving specific, ambitious goals is the glue that holds the organization together.

The clan culture has an internal focus and flexibility, and emphasizes the involvement and participation of employees to rapidly meet changing needs from the environment. This culture places high value on meeting the needs of employees, and the organization may be characterized by a caring, family-like atmosphere. Managers emphasize values such as cooperation, consideration for both employees and customers, and avoiding status differences.

The bureaucratic culture has an internal focus and a consistent orientation for a stable environment. Following the rules and being thrifty are valued, and the culture supports and rewards a methodical, rational, and orderly way of doing things. More and more companies are shifting away from a bureaucratic culture because of a need for greater flexibility.

Teamwork

Teams can increase organizational productivity as well as the productivity of individuals in the team due to the synergistic effect. Many team structures exist, which are described next.

A vertical team is a formal team composed of a manager and his or her subordinates in the formal chain of command. Sometimes called a *functional team* or a *command team,* the vertical team may, in some cases, include three or four levels of hierarchy within a functional department. The functional team is different from task forces and committees, which are cross-functional teams.

As part of the horizontal structure of an organization, task forces and committees offer several advantages. They allow organization members to exchange information; they help coordinate the organizational units that are represented; they develop new ideas and solutions for existing organizational problems; and they assist in developing new organizational practices and policies.

For a team to be successful, it must be structured so as to both maintain its members' social well-being and accomplish its task. In successful teams, the requirements for task performance and social satisfaction are met by the emergence of two types of roles: task specialist and socioemotional.

Task specialists initiate ideas, give opinions, seek information, summarize ideas, and energize the team into action. People who play the task specialist role spend time and energy helping the team reach its goal.

People who adopt a socioemotional role support team members' emotional needs and help strengthen the social entity. They display encouragement and harmonization, reduce tension, go along with the team (follow-approach), and compromise.

Some team members play a dual role. People with dual roles both contribute to the task and meet members' emotional needs. Such people often become team leaders. People in nonparticipatory roles contribute little to either the task or the social needs of team members. They are held in low esteem by the team.

Five stages of team development exist: forming, storming, norming, performing, and adjourning. Forming is characterized by orientation and acquaintance to the team. In storming, individual personalities and roles, and resulting conflicts, emerge. In norming, conflicts developed during the storming stage are resolved and team harmony and unity emerge. In performing, team members focus on problem solving and accomplishing the team's assigned task. Team members prepare for the team's disbandment in the adjourning stage.

Change Management

Organizational change is the adoption of a new idea or behavior by an organization. Forces for organizational change exist both in the external and internal environments. External forces to monitor include global competition, customers, competitors, and economic and political factors. Internal forces to monitor include plans, goals, company problems, and needs. Usually, performance gap is the driving force behind the change. Performance gap is the difference between existing and desired performance levels.

There are four roles in organizational change: inventor, champion, sponsor, and critic. Conceptual fluency and open mindedness, originality, a focused approach, and commitment are characteristics of a creative manager.

The following situations can create resistance to a new system: self-interest of resisting employees, lack of understanding of the new system, uncertainty or lack of information, and the pursuit of different goals by different departments.

Several techniques can be used to overcome resistance to a new system: education and communication, participation in designing the system, negotiation, coercion, and top management support.

Personality, Behavior, and Perception

The Big Five personality factors refer to an individual's extroversion, agreeableness, conscientiousness, emotional stability, and openness to experience. Extroversion is the degree to which a person is sociable, talkative, assertive, and comfortable with interpersonal relationships. Agreeableness is the degree to which a person is able to get along with others by being good-natured, cooperative, forgiving, understanding, and trusting. Conscientiousness is the degree to which a person is focused on a few goals, thus behaving in ways that are responsible, dependable, persistent, and achievement oriented. Emotional stability is the degree to which a person is calm, enthusiastic, and secure, rather than tense, nervous, depressed, moody, or insecure. Openness to experience is the degree to which a person has a broad range of interests and is imaginative, creative, artistically sensitive, and willing to consider new ideas.

An individual's personality influences a wide variety of work-related attitudes and behaviors. Among those that are of particular interest to managers are locus of control, authoritarianism, Machiavellianism, and problem-solving styles. The locus of control is the tendency to place the primary responsibility for one's success or failure either within oneself (internally) or on outside forces (externally). A high internal locus of control is a belief by individuals that their future is within their control and that external forces will have little influence. Authoritarianism is the belief that power and status differences should exist within the organization. Machiavellianism is the tendency to direct much of one's behavior toward the acquisition of power and the manipulation of other people for personal gain. Managers also need to understand that individuals differ in the way they go about gathering and evaluating information for problem solving and decision making.

Another aspect of understanding behavior is perception. Perception is the cognitive process people use to make sense out of the environment by selecting, organizing, and interpreting information. Perceptual distortions can occur in the workplace. These are perceptual errors in judgment that arise from inaccuracies in any part of the perceptual process. Examples include stereotyping, the halo effect, projection, and perceptual defense.

Stereotyping is placing an employee into a class category based on one or a few traits or characteristics. The halo effect is an overall impression of a person based on one characteristic, either favorable or unfavorable. Projection is the tendency to see one's own personal traits in other people. Perceptual defense is the tendency of perceivers to protect themselves by disregarding ideas, objects, or people that are threatening to them.

Planning

Management by objectives (MBO) is a method whereby managers and employees define goals for every department, project, and process, and use them to monitor subsequent performance. Four major activities in MBO include setting goals, developing action plans, reviewing progress, and appraising overall performance.

Goals should be established based on mutual interests, not dictated by supervisors. After objectives are established, action plans with timetables should be developed, and milestones should be defined.

There are several advantages (benefits) of the MBO program. Orientation toward goal achievement increases, performance can improve at all company levels, and employees are more motivated. Disadvantages of (problems with)

MBO include the following: constant changes in MBO can prevent the accomplishment of goal, an environment of poor employer-employee relations can reduce the MBO's effectiveness, strategic goals may be displaced by operational goals, and too much paperwork can sap MBO energy.

Motivation

Motivation is the art of arousal, direction, and persistence of behavior. Managers may make different assumptions about employees. This is stated in three theories: Theory X, Theory Y, and Theory Z. Theory X managers believe that the average human being has an inherent dislike of work and will avoid it if possible. Theory Y managers believe that an average human being learns, under proper conditions, not only to accept but to seek responsibility. Theory Z believes in teamwork and taking care of employees as family members.

Two-factor motivation theory states that employees are motivated or unmotivated for different reasons. These factors include motivators (satisfiers) and hygiene factors (dissatisfiers). Motivators include achievement, recognition, responsibility, work itself, and personal growth. Motivators influence the level of satisfaction. Hygiene factors include working conditions, pay and security, company policies, supervisors, and interpersonal relationships. Hygiene factors influence the level of dissatisfaction. It has been said that satisfied and happy employees are productive employees, whereas dissatisfied and unhappy employees are unproductive employees.

The most famous content theory states that humans are motivated by multiple needs and that these needs exist in a hierarchical order. The elements include physiological needs (basic needs at the lowest level), safety needs (freedom from threats), belongingness needs (friendship and love), esteem needs (self-image), and self-actualization needs (self-fulfillment at the highest level).

Physiological needs are met by pay or salary to employees. Safety needs are met by safe jobs, fringe benefits, and job security. Belongingness needs are met by good relationships with coworkers, participation in a work group, and a positive relationship with supervisors. Esteem needs are met by public recognition, increase in responsibility, high status, and credit for contribution to the organization. Self-actualization needs are met by providing employees with opportunities to grow, be creative, and acquire training for challenging assignments and advancement.

Process theories explain how workers select behavioral actions to meet their needs and determine whether their choices were successful. There are two basic process theories: equity theory and expectancy theory. Equity theory focuses on individuals' perceptions of how fairly they are treated relative to others. The most common methods for reducing perceived inequity include changing inputs, changing outcomes, distorting perceptions, or leaving the job. Expectancy theory proposes that motivation depends on individuals' expectations about their ability to perform tasks and receive desired rewards.

Managerial Ethics

Ethics deal with deciding and acting upon what is right or wrong in a particular situation. The following guidelines can assist a business manager in being ethical in a business setting.

Most ethical dilemmas involve a conflict between the needs of the part and those of the whole—the individual versus the organization or the organization versus society as a whole. Managers faced with tough ethical choices often benefit from a normative approach—one based on norms and values—to guide their decision making. Four normative approaches are the utilitarian approach, the individualism approach, the moral-rights approach, and the justice approach.

The utilitarian approach is based on the ethical concept that moral behaviors produce the greatest good for the greatest number. The individualism approach is based on the ethical concept that acts are moral when they promote the individual's best long-term interests, which ultimately leads to the greater good. The moral-rights approach is based on the ethical concept that moral decisions are those that best maintain the rights of those people affected by them. The justice approach is based on the ethical concept that moral decisions must be based on standards of equity, fairness, and impartiality.

Three types of justice are of concern to business managers. They are distributive, procedural, and compensatory justice. Distributive justice requires that different treatment of people not be based on arbitrary characteristics. Procedural justice emerges from the concept that rules should be clearly stated and consistently and impartially enforced. Compensatory justice requires that individuals should be compensated for the cost of their injuries by the party responsible and that individuals should not be held responsible for matters over which they have no control.

Organizational Structure, Design, and Development

New Perspectives in Management

Management is, by nature, complex and dynamic. Three recent trends that grew out of a humanistic perspective are systems theory, the contingency view, and total quality management (TQM). Systems theory describes organizations as open systems that are characterized by entropy, synergy, and subsystem interdependence. The contingency view states that the successful resolution of organizational problems is thought to depend on managers' identification of key variations in the situation at hand. TQM focuses on managing the total organization to deliver quality products or services to customers. Four significant elements of TQM are employee involvement, focus on the customer, benchmarking, and continuous improvement.

Organizational Structure and Design

There are four factors to consider in shaping organizational structure: (1) structure follows strategy, (2) structure reflects the environment, (3) structure fits technology, and (4) structure follows the workflow.

Structure follows strategy, ranging from pure functional structure to the new learning organization. Strategic goals in pure functional structure include cost leadership, efficiency, and stability. Strategic goals in the new learning organization include differentiation, innovation, and flexibility.

The relationship between the environment and organization structure can exist in four combinations: unstable/vertical, unstable/horizontal, stable/vertical, stable/horizontal. Both stable/vertical and unstable/horizontal are correct fits while the other two structures are incorrect fits. An uncertain (unstable) environment causes three things to happen within an organization: (1) increased differences occur among departments, (2) the organization needs increased coordination to keep departments working together, and (3) the organization must adapt to change.

Organization structure fits technology as it relates to a manufacturing situation, including small-batch and unit production, large-batch and mass production, and continuous process production. Small-batch and unit production is a type of technology that involves the production of goods in batches of one or a few products designed to customer specifications. Large-batch and mass production is a type of technology that is distinguished by standardized production runs, a large volume of products is produced, and all customers receiving the same product. Continuous process production is a type of technology involving mechanization of the entire workflow and nonstop production.

Structure follows the workflow including pooled, sequential, and reciprocal interdependence. Pooled interdependence means that each department is part of the organization and contributes to the common good, but each department is relatively independent because work does not flow between units. Sequential interdependence means that outputs of one department become inputs to another department in a serial fashion. Reciprocal interdependence means that the output of Operation A is the input to Operation B, and the output of Operation B is the input back again to Operation A.

Organizational Development

Organizational development (OD) is the application of behavioral science techniques to improve an organization's health and effectiveness through its ability to cope with environmental changes, improve internal relationships, and increase learning and problem-solving capabilities. The following are three types of current problems that OD can help managers address: mergers and acquisitions, organizational decline and revitalization, and conflict management.

OD activities include team building, survey feedback, and large-group intervention. OD steps include unfreezing (first stage), changing (second stage), and refreezing (third, stage). Unfreezing is the stage in which participants are made aware of problems in order to increase their willingness to change their behavior. Changing is intervention stage in which individuals experiment with new workplace behavior. A change agent is an OD specialist who contracts with an organization to facilitate change. Refreezing is the reinforcement stage in which individuals acquire a desired new skill or attitude and are rewarded for it by the organization.

Human Resource Management Analysis

This application is related to Human Resources Management (Module 500), and specifically to Sections 540 (Workforce Diversity Management), 530 (Staffing, Development, and Employment Practices), and 510 (Employee Performance and Retention Management).

Workforce Diversity Analysis—Internal Disparate Impact

Senior management at a company headquarters is concerned about whether certain business units are complying with laws covering protected-class employees. One such concern is internal disparate impact, which can result from inappropriate local employment practices at local business units. An internal disparate impact can exist when the selection rate for women is less than 4/5ths or 80 percent of the selection rate for men.

Workforce Diversity Analysis—External Disparate Impact

Senior management of a company headquarters is concerned about proper representation of protected-class members in the workforce. Here, the issue is whether protected-class employees working in the local business units are drawn from relevant local labor markets. An external disparate impact exists when a local business unit has fewer protected-class employees than the local labor market area.

Workforce Forecasting—Fill Rates

An employee transition matrix can be used to model the internal flow of human resources (fill rates) as well as in succession planning. The fill rate is a decision rule about the percentage of jobs that will be filled from internal sources or external sources. For example, a company's policy on fill rates may state that 20 percent of promotions into a specific job should come from one level below it. Succession planning is a process of identifying a longer-term plan for the orderly replacement of key employees. Replacement charts can be used in the succession planning.

Workforce Forecasting—Staffing Levels

Forecasting the internal supply of people for a given department or division for the upcoming planning year is not an easy task for the human resource management of a company. A staffing model, similar to the cash flow model in finance, can be used as follows: the department's internal supply of people for the next year equals the current staffing level plus projected inflows this year minus projected outflows this year.

Sources of inflows into the department include external hires, internal transfers, promotions into the department, and recalls/rehires. Sources of outflows from the department include promotions into other departments, voluntary turnover, terminations, demotions, retirements, deaths, and layoffs.

Employee Turnover Rates and Costs

Employee turnover rates and costs are a major concern to management of any company. The turnover rate is the number of employees leaving the organization during a month divided by the total number of employees at midmonth multiplied by 100.

Determining turnover costs can be relatively simple or complex, depending upon the nature of the efforts expended and data available. The following model is an example for job #154.

A. Find out the annual pay for Job #154, multiply it by the employee benefits percentage, and add them together. This is the total employee annual cost.
B. Determine how many employees voluntarily left this job in the past twelve months.
C. Find out how long it takes for one employee to become fully productive (in months) in this job.
D. Determine per person turnover cost as $(C/12) \times A \times 50\%$. Here, we are assuming that a new employee will be productive in half the time, that is, 50 percent productivity rate.
E. Determine the annual turnover cost for Job #154 as per person turnover cost multiplied by the number of employees voluntarily leaving the job in the past twelve months.

More detailed and sophisticated turnover costing models consider a number of factors such as hiring costs, training costs, productivity costs (with learning curve effect), separation costs, and so on.

Recruiting Yield Ratios

Management of a company is concerned about the effectiveness of employee recruiting efforts, which can give clue to turnover rates and costs. One means for evaluating recruiting efforts is to determine yield ratios. These ratios are comparisons of the number of applicants at one stage of the recruiting process to the number at the next stage.

Overall selection rate is the number of applicants hired divided by the total number of applicants, multiplied by 100.

Yield ratio for offers to hires is the number of applicants hired divided by the number of offers made, multiplied by 100.

Yield ratio for final interviews to offers is the number of offers made divided by the number of final interviews, multiplied by 100.

Yield ratio for initial contacts to final interviews is the number of final interviews divided by the total applicants, multiplied by 100.

Ways to increase recruiting effectiveness include (1) applicant tracking systems, to collect data on applicants and provide various analyses; (2) realistic job previews that provide job candidates honest and accurate details about the organization and the job; and (3) a responsive recruitment process in which applicants receive timely responses, get feedback on the process when promised, and are treated with consideration and respect.

Logistics Analysis

This application is related to Operations Management (Module 200) and Information Technology (Module 800), and specifically to Sections 260 (Logistical Management), 855 (Managing Information Technology Resources), and 880 (Information Technology Contingency Plans).

Costs and Outputs

The logistics system is the physical link connecting a company's customers, raw material suppliers, manufacturing plants, warehouses, and distribution channel members.

Management evaluates alternate logistics systems for cost reduction, efficiency gains, and competitive edge. To do this, it needs data on variable cost per unit and total fixed system for each logistics system. It also needs different output volumes to determine the most economical output level.

The approach is to calculate total costs of operating each logistics system. This includes total fixed costs and total variable costs for each system. The output level that is economical to each system is selected.

Cost of Lost Sales and Cost of Stockouts

Carrier transit time and reliability affect inventory and stockout costs (which take the form of lost sales). Shorter transit times result in lower inventories, while more dependability of carrier causes lower inventory levels or stockout costs. With a given level of lead time, a firm can minimize inventories and inventory carrying costs. But if transit time is not consistent, the firm must increase inventories above the level that a consistent transit time would require. This means a firm now must hold larger amounts of inventory as a safety factor against stockouts that could arise from inconsistent service.

Management should use the net profit per lost item to compute the cost of lost sale because that is the net result of all activities. The firm can save money if it stocks additional units and the cost of stockout is greater than the cost of carrying an additional item. Here, total cost per stockout is compared with the cost of an additional item.

Cost of Alternate Transportation Systems

Transportation modal choices include rail, water (barge), truck, air, and pipeline. Transportation cost analysis is oriented toward evaluating alternative modes since the rates, minimum weights, loading and unloading facilities, packaging, and blocking will vary from one mode to another. A trade-off exists between the service a carrier provides and facility operation costs. The cost of transportation alternatives can be calculated as follows.

Cost of Each Transportation Alternative = Total Fixed Costs + (Variable Cost/Unit × Number of Units Handled)

Inventory Levels at Distribution Centers

Many companies are searching for new ways to reduce levels of inventory without adversely affecting customer service. A popular approach now is to consolidate inventories into fewer stocking locations (distribution centers) in order to reduce aggregate inventories and their associated costs while maintaining or improving customer service levels.

The square root law (SRL) helps determine the extent to which inventories may be reduced through such a logistics strategy. Two principles undergird SRL: (1) the greater the number of stocking locations, the greater the amount of inventory needed to maintain customer service levels; and (2) as inventories are consolidated into fewer stocking locations, aggregate inventory levels will decrease. Assumptions made by the SRL include (1) inventory transfers between stocking locations are not a common practice; (2) lead times do not vary, and thus inventory centralization is not affected by inbound supply uncertainty; (3) customer service level, as measured by inventory availability, is constant regardless of the number of stocking locations; and (4) demand at each stocking location is normally distributed.

The following is the formula for the square root law.

$X_2 = (X_1)$ (square root of n_2/n_1)
X_2 is total inventory in future distribution centers
X_1 is total inventory in current distribution centers
n_2 is number of future distribution centers
n_1 is number of current distribution centers

Quick Response System

Quick response (QR) is a very effective approach to synchronizing product and information flows in a logistics network. It operates on a partnership basis between manufacturers, wholesalers, and retailers. The QR approach to a retailer or wholesaler is comparable to the just-in-time (JIT) approach for a manufacturer to reduce inventory investment by scheduling the delivery of parts or raw materials close to production lines. Critical success factors for the effective functioning of the QR system include low cycle times, high service levels, inventory turns (as high as possible), and fill rates (a target of 100 percent).

Management wishes to implement the quick response system in terms of greater accuracy of sales demand forecasts and improved in-stock percentages.

Efficient Consumer Response System

The efficient consumer response (ECR) system focuses on the efficiency of the total grocery supply chain system, rather than the efficiency of individual components. ECR represents an attempt to reengineer the logistics system across a company's product or business lines, enabled by information technology (IT). The goal of ECR is to maintain a continual product flow matched to consumption. Suppliers, distributors, and retailers work together as business allies to maximize consumer satisfaction and minimize costs. The role of IT here is to maintain a timely and accurate information flow, and to facilitate a paperless system between manufacturing, trading partners, and retailers with minimum degradation or interruption of computer services.

The ECR system involves a reversal of processes from the traditional approach to supply chain management. The ECR system approach is sell (retailer), move (distributor), make (manufacturer), and buy (consumer). The traditional approach is buy (consumer), make (manufacturer), move (distributor), and sell (retailer). Research finds that most retailers who are customer-oriented prefer increased inventory turns, better fill rates, and reduced cycle times from order to delivery.

International Distribution Selection

U.S. multinational corporations plan to open sales offices and distribution centers outside the United States to serve international markets. Critical selection factors must be identified and weights assigned to each factor in order to evaluate each location option.

The scoring system used can be a quantitative method, which should be supplemented by qualitative factors such as cultural impact, education levels, and attitude toward foreign companies. Economic factors, labor supply factors, and labor demand factors are examples of quantitative factors.

The approach is to multiply the weight of each factor with the weight (score) given to each location, and add them up. The location with the lowest score is the one to be selected.

Domestic Carrier Evaluation

Similar to reducing the number of suppliers providing raw materials, parts, and finished goods, companies are looking to reducing the number of transportation carriers. By reducing the number of carriers it uses, a shipping firm increases the freight volume and freight revenue that it gives to a carrier, thereby increasing its ability to have the carrier provide the rates and service levels the shipper needs.

Carrier evaluation criteria may include pick-up schedules, delivery schedules, transit time, claims handling, equipment condition, driver characteristics, billing errors, and financial stability.

When sales increase at an unexpected rate, it puts a lot of pressure or stress on the distribution system, thus decreasing its efficiency. Distribution capacity may need to be increased to accommodate unexpected sales growth.

The inventory carrying cost, the cost of inventory in transit, the cost of capital, the cost per order, and the cost of raw material are not relevant to carrier selection because they will be incurred regardless of the delivery service used. What is important is to find the differential operating cost of each alternative.

Distribution Resource Planning

Distribution resource (requirements) planning (DRP) technique is a powerful outbound logistics system to help determine the appropriate level of inventory and synchronize the flow and storage of finished goods destined for the marketplace. With the DRP system, companies can improve customer service (that is, decrease stockout situations), reduce the overall level of finished goods inventories, reduce transportation costs, and improve the efficiency of distribution center operations.

The following relationships are indicated in the DRP system. The planned order release is the quantity of material to be ordered in each time period. The planned order receipt is the amount of planned order considering lead time. The scheduled receipts (open orders) are quantities ordered and expected to be available. When a planned order receipt is canceled, a scheduled receipt is created in its place. Net requirements are gross requirements minus scheduled receipts minus available inventory.

DRP System Versus MRP System

The materials requirements planning (MRP) system takes output from the master production schedule and then "explodes" demand into gross and net requirements for raw materials and parts. Therefore, the MRP system is classified as a dependent demand system. The DRP system begins with customer demand, classified as independent demand, and works backward toward establishing a realistic and economically justifiable plan for ordering necessary inventory (finished goods). Using the best available forecasts of finished product demand, the DRP system develops a time-phased plan for distributing products from plants and warehouses to retailers or points where it is available to customers. Because DRP allocates available inventory to meet marketplace demands, it is a pull approach. On the other hand, the MRP system is a push system because it encourages purchase order and production order development taken from the master production schedule. DRP is more responsive than MRP to real marketplace needs in terms of product availability and receipt timing. DRP can adjust and readjust its ordering patterns to accommodate dynamic inventory needs, whereas MPR is subject to a single manufacturing facility or plant.

Application 30

New Product Development and Product Management Analysis

This application is related to Marketing Management (Module 300), and specifically to Sections 310 and 315 (New Product Development and Product Management).

New Product Opportunity Rating Analysis

Developing competitively advantaged products consistently over time is aided by having a strategy for what will be done and a process for how it will be accomplished. Firms with both a new product development strategy and a formal process for doing so demonstrate superior performance in terms of percentage of sales by new products, success rates, and meeting sales and profit objectives.

For example, 3M Company uses the opportunity rating method for its new development process. The product with the highest opportunity rating is moved to the next step of the product development process.

The formula for calculating opportunity rating in dollars is $(CS \times TS \times MS)/(LB + OC)$, where CS is five-year cumulative sales, TS is probability of technical success, MS is probability of marketing success, LB is laboratory costs (development costs), and OC is other costs (marketing costs).

The objective of 3M's team review process is to improve the product development process in a nonthreatening and nonpunitive environment. A punitive environment stifles creativity. Falling short of product development objectives provides an opportunity to improve the development process by learning from past mistakes. The most common reasons for missing a product's development objectives include poor internal planning, technical difficulties, and poor support from outside functions. Teams meeting or exceeding their objectives receive recognition and a small reward as a team, not as individuals on a team. Team reward is a critical factor in maintaining a team effort versus an individual effort.

New Products and Payback Period

As part of economical justification of a new product, some companies use payback technique to determine which product will be profitable quickly. Companies establish a payback cutoff point. Payback period is initial cost or investment divided by annual cash flows.

New Products and Equity Financing

Companies can raise additional funds needed to develop a new product requiring huge sums of money, as in the pharmaceutical industry. Usually, equity financing is used by selling stock to the general public. An underwriter is involved in selling the stock to the public.

Securities filing fees are added to the initial investment amount. Required total funds are computed after considering the underwriter's spread. From this, the total number of shares to be offered is computed at the stock price decided.

New Products and Profit Margin

Profit margin is the key ratio in product profitability analysis. Profit margin is net profit divided by net sales, with the result multiplied by 100 to express it as a percentage. Profit margin can be increased by increasing sales or decreasing costs.

Product Management–Product Line Profitability Analysis

Marketing management wants to determine which product lines are profitable and which can be discontinued. Management needs to compute net income from each product line.

Usually, production data and common fixed costs are not relevant. Only traceable fixed costs are relevant when computing net income for each product line. When evaluating the performance of each product line, only variable costs and traceable fixed costs are relevant because common fixed costs will be incurred at the corporate level regardless of individual product lines. Common fixed costs are nontraceable fixed costs to a product or market.

The following formulas can be used to determine net income.

Contribution Margin (CM) = Sales Revenue − Variable Costs
Net Income = CM − Traceable Fixed Costs

Product Management Concepts

Product line profitability analysis shows which product line is contributing to fixed costs and profits. With this information, management can decide which products or product lines should be kept, improved, reduced, expanded, or eliminated. This requires corrective action.

Product management interacts with cost accounting in deciding which cost system is better for each product or product line. An activity-based cost accounting system focuses on activities that can increase or decrease costs. Accurate and appropriate costs, in turn, will help in analyzing the true profitability picture of product lines or markets. Full-cost accounting suggests that all costs, whether traceable or not, should be considered when evaluating the profitability of products or markets.

Due to the variety of products and product lines available, the best organizational structure for the marketing department is the product-management structure. Product managers can focus on one or two products or product lines and make them grow in terms of investment, profit, and market share.

Sales Analysis

This application is related to Marketing Management (Module 300), and specifically to Section 390 (Sales Administration and Management).

Sales and Strategic Management

Sales management understands customer needs, competitive conditions, and product applications better than product costs. The latter costs are better understood by production and accounting management.

Sales Force Structure

Determining the average revenue per sales call should be the focus of a salesperson because everything depends on revenues generated. Costs support the revenue-generating process. Marketing expense-to-sales ratio will ensure that a company is not overspending to achieve its sales goals.

First, companies must define the specific objectives they expect their sales force to achieve. After setting objectives, strategy, structure, and size come into play.

A sales force structure can be territorial, product, market, or complex. If a firm has one product line selling to one end-using industry, it follows the territorial sales force structure. If a firm sells many products to many types of customers, it might follow a product or market sales force structure. A complex structure uses a combination of territorial, product, and market structures.

Personal selling is more effective in "closing" a sale. Sales staff have a better handle on costs incurred than revenues generated from a potential customer.

Cost of Sales Calls

When computing the average cost per sales call, overhead should be ignored since it is going to be incurred anyway, whether the salesperson makes three calls, ten calls, or no calls. Also, profit margin data are not relevant to cost of sales calls.

The break-even sales volume is the average cost per call $\times$ number of calls required to close a sale divided by the sales cost percentage.

Break-Even Point for Sales Effort

We need to compute the break-even point in dollars between two alternative methods of selling (sales agents versus company sales staff). We have to solve the two alternative methods by setting them as two equations and solve for unknown sales volume that makes these two alternatives equal.

Sales Variance Analysis

Variances between the actual sales volume in units and dollars to the planned sales volume in units and dollars as well as the variance between the actual price and the planned price are common. Marketing management wants to know which part caused what variance so that corrective action can be taken as well as for planning purposes. The following formulas are used in this situation.

> Price variance due to price decline is (plan price − actual price) × actual quantity sold.
>
> Volume variance due to volume decline is (plan volume − actual volume) × plan price.
>
> Sales performance variance is planned revenues minus actual revenues. This variance is due to price variance and volume variance.
>
> The marketing department needs to analyze reasons for sales variance in terms of both physical units and selling price.

Sales Forecasting

Sales management uses both quantitative and qualitative forecasting techniques to estimate future sales. Examples of quantitative techniques include simple moving average, weighted moving average, and exponential smoothing methods. The sales forecast can be done using the time series equation. Examples of qualitative techniques include intuition, heuristics, group consensus (the delphi method), scenario writing, expert judgment, and naive approaches. (Refer to Application 38, Quantitative and Qualitative Analysis, for details about these methods.)

Risk Analysis

This application is related to Finance (Module 700) and Corporate Control and Governance (Module 900), and specifically to Sections 755 (Financial Risk Management), 799 (International Issues), and 940 (Corporate Risk Management).

Investment Risks

Risk is uncertainty, which creates both problems and opportunities for businesses and individuals. Risk regarding the possibility of loss can be problematical. If a loss is certain to occur, it may be planned for in advance and treated as a definite, known expense. It is when there is uncertainty about the occurrence of loss that risk becomes a problem.

To evaluate risks in investment opportunities, we need expected returns from potential stock products, variance, and standard deviation. For example, an investment product is riskier because it has the highest standard deviation compared to other products. Similarly, a product is riskier because it has the highest coefficient of variation (CV) compared to other products. The CV shows the risk per unit of return, and it provides a more meaningful basis for comparison when the expected returns on alternative products are not the same.

The following approach is suggested to evaluate investment risk. First, compute the standard deviation for each product to measure its risk level. The standard deviation is the square root of variance. Compute the CV, which is standard deviation divided by the expected return or mean. Then select the product with the lowest CV number.

> Standard deviation is the square root of variance.
>
> The CV is calculated as standard deviation divided by the mean.

Risk-Related Concepts

Risks are of two types: systematic or unsystematic. Systematic risk cannot be eliminated. It is also called *nondiversifiable* or *market risk*. Market risks stem from external factors such as inflation that systematically affect most firms. Examples of market or nondiversifiable, or systematic, risk include war, inflation, recession, and high interest rates. Because most stocks tend to be affected negatively by these market conditions, systematic risk cannot be eliminated by portfolio diversification.

APPLICATION 32. RISK ANALYSIS

An element of riskiness in any individual stock can be eliminated through portfolio diversification. The part of a stock's risk that can be eliminated is called *diversifiable, firm-specific,* or *unsystematic risk.* Examples of firm-specific, diversifiable, or unsystematic risks include lawsuits, strikes, successful and unsuccessful marketing programs, the winning and losing of major contracts, and other events that are unique to a particular firm.

Objective Risks

Objective risk is probable variation of actual losses from expected losses divided by expected losses, with the result subtracted from 100 percent. For example, expected losses are equal to the number of employees multiplied by the chance of injury to employees.

Project Risks

Project managers often need contingency reserves to accommodate specific and known risks in a project. The project manager needs to develop an expected value of the project risks. Contingency reserves deal with known risks and use expected values. Project costs and impacts are not relevant here since they do not have probabilities associated with them. Risks have probabilities associated with them.

Business Risks and Financial Risks

Business risk is the risk inherent in the operation of a company, prior to the financing decision. It is the uncertainty inherent in future operating income and is caused by two major factors such as sales or revenue variability and operating leverage.

Financing risk is the risk added by the use of debt financing. Debt increases the variability of earnings before taxes, thus, along with business risk; it contributes to the uncertainty of net income and earnings per share. Business risk comes first followed by financial risk because it is the business operations that are the major purposes and the primary reasons for the existence of a company. Total risk of a corporation is business risk plus financial risk.

The following actions are unethical and create risk to a corporation. Off-the-books accounts hide business transactions such as leases, debt, and equity, from the balance sheet and income statements. Earnings management is manipulating the net income to fit management's goals. Creative accounting is stretching the accounting standards and rules to the convenience of a company management.

Financial engineering is a modeling technique to develop new financial products. When the technique is applied to currency real options, the result is the value of a project that contains embedded options. Financial engineering is a valid and legitimate approach to solve investment-related problems or issues.

Exchange Rate Exposure—Currency Derivatives

Currency derivatives include forward contracts, futures contracts, and currency options. All currency derivatives are subject to exchange rate risk because the value of currencies fluctuates over time. Exchange rate fluctuations make it difficult to estimate the dollars that foreign operations will produce. The exchange rate risk is the risk of losses due to fluctuations in the value of the dollars relative to the value of foreign currencies.

A forward contract specifies a standard volume of a particular currency to be exchanged on a particular date. Such a contract can be purchased by a firm to hedge accounts payables or sold by a firm to hedge accounts receivables.

Long-term forward contracts are available to cover positions of five years or longer. Currency swaps are available whereby an arrangement is made for two firms to swap currencies for a specified future time period at a specified exchange rate. Parallel loans can be used to exchange currencies and re-exchange the currencies at a specified future exchange rate and date.

Futures contracts on a particular currency can be purchased by corporations that have accounts payables in that currency and wish to hedge against the possible appreciation of that currency. Conversely, these contracts can be sold by corporations that have accounts receivables in that currency and wish to hedge against the possible depreciation of that currency.

Currency options are classified as call options or put options. Call options allow the right to purchase a specified currency at a specified exchange rate by a specified expiration date. Put options allow the right to sell a specified currency at a specified exchange rate by a specified expiration date.

Currency call options are commonly purchased by corporations that have accounts payables in a currency that is expected to appreciate. Currency put options are commonly purchased by corporations that have accounts receivables in a currency that is expected to depreciate.

Transaction Exposure—Hedging Foreign Transactions

Transaction exposure is the degree to which the value of future cash transactions can be affected by exchange rate fluctuations. Multinational corporations (MNCs) use the following techniques to hedge transaction exposure: (1) futures hedge, (2) forward hedge, (3) money market hedge, and (4) currency options hedge.

To hedge accounts payables, a futures or forward contract on the foreign currency can be purchased. Alternatively, a money market hedge strategy can be used; in this case, the MNC borrows its home currency and converts the proceeds into the foreign currency that will be needed in the future. Finally, call options on the foreign currency can be purchased.

To hedge accounts receivables, a futures or forward contract on the foreign currency can be sold. Alternatively, a money market hedge strategy can be used; in this case, the MNC borrows the foreign currency to be received and converts the funds into its home currency; the loan is to be repaid by the receivables. Finally, put options on the foreign currency can be purchased.

Futures contracts and forward contracts normally yield similar results. Forward contracts are more flexible because they are not standardized. The money market hedge yields results similar to those of the forward hedge if interest rate parity exists. The theory of interest rate parity focuses on the relationship between the interest rate differential and the forward rate premium (or discount) at a given point in time. The currency options hedge has an advantage over other hedging techniques in that it does not have to be exercised if the MNC would be better off unhedged. A premium must be paid to purchase currency options, however, so there is a cost for the flexibility they provide.

When the above hedging techniques are not available, there are methods of reducing transaction exposure, such as leading and lagging strategies, cross-hedging, and currency diversification.

Leading strategy is used when a company's subsidiary is expecting its currency to depreciate against an invoice currency on goods it imported. It may "lead" its payments, that is, make payments early. Lagging strategy is used when a company's subsidiary is expecting its currency to appreciate against an invoice currency on goods it imported. It may "lag" its payments, that is, make a late payment.

Cross-hedging is hedging an open position in one currency (first currency) with hedge on another currency (second currency) that is highly correlated with the first currency. This occurs when, for some reason, common hedging techniques cannot be applied to the first currency. A cross-hedge is not a perfect hedge, but can substantially reduce the exchange exposure.

Currency diversification is a process of using more than one currency as an investing or financing strategy. Exposure to a diversified currency portfolio typically results in less exchange rate risk than if all of the exposure were in a single foreign currency.

Examples of Hedging Foreign Transactions

The following are specific examples of hedging foreign transactions by a U.S.-based MNC.

- A forward purchase contract, a futures buy contract, and a call option purchase transaction will be impacted when a U.S. company purchases Japanese goods denominated in yen.
- A forward sell contract, a futures sell contract, and a put option purchase transaction will be impacted when a U.S. subsidiary in Australia remits funds to its parent.

- A forward sell contract, a futures sell contract, and a put option purchase transaction will be impacted when a U.S. company plans to sell goods to Japan, denominated in yen.
- A forward purchase contract, a futures buy contract, and a call option purchase transaction will be impacted when a U.S. company needs to pay off existing loans that are denominated in Canadian dollars.

International Cash Management

The first line of defense in managing foreign exchange exposure is to develop an information system that allows a company to track its current and expected daily cash flows in all currencies in which it does business. This allows the cash manager to net outflows in one currency against inflows of the same currency, reducing foreign exchange exposure to only the net difference.

Leading is the practice of accelerating collections or payments, and lagging is the practice of delaying collections or payments. Hedging is practiced externally by an exchange market or a bank, and it includes financial instruments such as futures, forwards, options, and swaps. Most firms implement internal strategies such as netting, re-invoicing, and leading and lagging practices prior to using hedging techniques. Re-invoicing is done by a company-owned subsidiary. The subsidiary buys goods from an exporting subsidiary in the subsidiary's currency and sells those goods to an importing subsidiary in its own currency. The re-invoicing center re-invoices only the net difference owed to each subsidiary. The center manages a firm's foreign currency exposure that results from the netting process.

Both the netting system and the re-invoicing system can be used to implement a leading and lagging cash flows management system that can be effective in managing the liquidity of an MNC by timing the cash inflows and outflows within a company's system. On the other hand, hedging is done outside the company through banks or external foreign exchange markets.

Economic Exposure and Translation Exposure

Economic exposure is the degree to which a firm's present value of future cash flows can be influenced by exchange rate fluctuations. Economic exposure can be managed by balancing the sensitivity of revenue and expenses with exchange rate fluctuations. To accomplish this, the firm must first recognize how its revenues and expenses are affected by exchange rate fluctuations. For some firms, revenue is more susceptible. These firms are most concerned that their home currency will appreciate against foreign currencies, since the unfavorable effects on revenue will more than offset favorable effects on expenses. Conversely, firms whose expenses are more sensitive to exchange rates than their revenues are most concerned that their home currency will depreciate against foreign currencies. When firms reduce their economic exposure, they reduce not only these unfavorable effects, but also the favorable effects if the home currency value moves in the opposite direction. This means an MNC should match its revenues and expenses in a foreign country's subsidiary.

Translation exposure is the degree to which a firm's consolidated financial statements are exposed to fluctuations in exchange rates. This exposure can be reduced by selling the forward foreign currency that is used to measure a subsidiary's income. If the foreign currency depreciates against the home currency, the adverse impact on the consolidated income statement can be offset by the gain on the forward sale in that currency. If the foreign currency appreciates over the time period of concern, there will be a loss on the forward sale that is offset by a favorable effect on the reported consolidated earnings.

Spot Rates and Forward Exchange Rates

Spot rates are the rates paid for delivery of currency "on the spot," while the forward exchange rate is the rate paid for delivery at some agreed-upon future date, usually 30, 90, or 180 days from the day the transaction is negotiated. The forward rate can be at either a premium or a discount to the spot rate.

Decision Analysis

This application is related to General Management and Organization (Module 100), and specifically to Section 195 (Quantitative Techniques and Management).

Payoff Analysis

Decision analysis can be used to determine optimal strategies in situations involving several alternatives and an uncertain or risk-filled pattern of future events. Payoff tables and decision trees are used in decision analysis.

A payoff is a measure of the consequence of a decision, such as profit, cost, utility, or time. Each combination of a decision alternative and a state of nature has an associated payoff. A payoff table is a tabular representation of the payoffs for a decision problem. Payoff tables deal with outcomes (choices) and states of nature along with their probabilities.

Some decision choices are inadmissible for further consideration because they are dominated by other choices, which are better in the payoff table. These decision choices will have a low expected payoff since they are inadmissible. The criterion for inadmissibility is that there is at least one value that is less than or equal to others.

Expected value is the weighted average of the payoffs for a chance node. It is calculated for each choice by multiplying the probability of each choice with the weight assigned to each state of nature. The expected value of perfect information (EVPI) is the absolute difference between expected value with perfect information about the states of nature (EVwPI) and expected value without perfect information about the states of nature (EVwoPI). That is, EVPI = EVwPI − EVwoPI.

In the profit payoff analysis, profit is the main consideration. In the cost payoff analysis, cost is the main consideration. Similarly, utility is the main consideration in the utility payoff analysis.

There are three approaches to decision-making: the optimistic approach, the conservative approach, and the minimax regret approach. The three approaches do not use probabilities.

- For a maximization problem, the optimistic approach leads to choosing the decision alternative corresponding to the largest payoff; for a minimization problem, it leads to choosing the decision alternative corresponding to the smallest payoff.
- For a maximization problem, the conservative approach leads to choosing the decision alternative that maximizes the minimum payoff; for a minimization problem, it leads to choosing the decision alternative that minimizes the maximum payoff.
- For each alternative, the maximum regret is computed, which leads to choosing the decision alternative that minimizes the maximum regret. Both maximization and minimization effects are combined in the minimax regret approach.

Utility takes into account the decision maker's attitude toward the profit, loss, and risk associated with a consequence. Differences in decision making are due to differences in attitude toward risk. The decision maker can be classified as risk taker, risk neutral, and risk avoider. The risk taker prefers decisions that, although risky, have a possibility for an extremely good (big) payoff. The risk neutral person chooses the decision alternative with the best expected monetary value that is identical to the alternative with the highest expected utility. The risk avoider ignores decisions that have the risk of an extremely bad (small) payoff.

Simulation of Stock Prices

Stock prices can be simulated prior to making an investment decision. In simulation, the sum of all probabilities must be equal to 1. We need to compute the cumulative probability that a specific random number is going to fall into the range (interval). A stock price is computed from this interval.

Simulation of Equipment Maintenance Times

A variety of routine maintenance checks are made on equipment, airplanes, trucks, buses, and other machines. Management wants to know the time it takes to carry out such maintenance checks. Simulation technique combined with random numbers can help in this situation.

$$\text{Time} = a + r(b - a)$$

where a is minimum time, b is maximum time, and r is random number between 0 and 1.

Capacity Planning—Decision Trees

Manufacturing management considers expansion of production capacity to meet growing demand for its new product line. Possible alternatives include building a new plant, expanding the old plant, or doing nothing (status quo).

To solve this problem, we need market situation (up, down, or stable) with its probabilities of happening and annual cash flows for each of these market situations. Decision trees and payoff tables are very useful in solving this type of problem. We need to compute the expected values for each alternative and select the alternative with the highest cash flows.

Tradeoff Analysis

In the tradeoff analysis, one variable is traded against another variable during the evaluation of alternatives. It is a decision-making process whereby one variable is decreased while the other variable is increased. It is a form of cost-benefit analysis in that cost is traded against benefit. It also equates to opportunity costs. Business managers will often encounter situations that involve tradeoffs and opportunity costs. Other examples of tradeoff situations include the following:

One variable	Another variable
Risk	Return
Time	Cost
Short-term performance	Long-term performance
Make	Buy
Insourcing	Outsourcing
Advertising expenditures	Improving product features
Lease	Purchase
Product/service features	Product/service costs
Project scope	Project time and cost

Application 34

Operating Budget Analysis

This application is related to Accounting (Module 600), and specifically to Section 650 (Operating Budgets and Performance Evaluation).

Determining Income, Retained Earnings, and Assets

The business manager needs to know how accountants measure income, retained earnings, and assets for his or her company. The first stop is to determine net income, followed by retained earnings, and finally the balance sheet for asset information.

Net Income = Revenues − Expenses

Retained Earnings This Period = Retained Earnings From Previous Period + Net Income for This Period − Dividends Paid This Period

Total assets (left-hand side of the balance sheet) are always equal to the total liabilities and stockholders' equity (right-hand side of the balance sheet).

Linking Operating Budgets for Consecutive Years

Net income from the income statement is linked to the retained earnings statement which, in turn, is linked to the balance sheet. Some specific relationships include the following.

- The net income for this year equals the change in retained earnings plus dividends paid.
- The book value of the plant and equipment that will be sold equals book value minus cash received equals the loss or gain on sale.
- The amount of new plant and equipment planned to be purchased this year equals the previous year's amount plus this year's addition minus the sale of plant and equipment.
- The amount of new patents planned to be purchased this year equals the previous year's amount plus this year's addition minus the amortization expense this year.

Missing Numbers in Cash Budget

Business managers need to know how cash receipts are forecasted each month, quarter, and year. Total cash receipts include receipts from cash sales and credit sales. Based on historical sales data, companies estimate how much of each month's sales are on account (that is, credit sales) and how much are cash sales. Based on past customer payment practices, for example, companies may estimate that 60 percent of credit sales is collected in the month of sale and 40 percent of credit sales collected in the following month.

Missing Numbers in Cash Forecasting

Both accounting and finance management work on the yearly budget along with other functional management. Management wants to know what the net cash inflow, beginning cash, and ending cash items represent so that financing arrangements can be made to handle cash deficits or investment opportunities for cash surpluses. The following formulas can be used to forecast cash needs.

Net Cash Inflow = Total Cash Receipts − Total Cash Disbursements

Ending Cash Balance = Net Cash Inflow + Beginning Cash Balance

Cash Surplus or Cash Deficit = Ending Cash Balance − Minimum (Target) Cash Balance Required

Retained Earnings Forecast

Retained earnings for a month are forecasted as follows.

First, find out earnings before interest and taxes (EBIT) as sales minus total operating costs.

Next, compute net income as EBIT minus interest and taxes.

Finally, subtract dividends paid from the net income.

Operating Budget Concepts

Operating budgets take one of two approaches: top-down and bottom-up. In top-down budgeting, the budget is imposed on lower-level managers by higher-level managers without the involvement of the lower-level managers. In bottom-up budgeting, lower-level managers submit their budget to the next-higher-level managers who, in turn, submit their budget to the next-higher-level managers, and so on.

An advantage of bottom-up budgeting is that lower-level managers are more involved in the process. It increases the ownership of the budget numbers by the managers involved and encourages positive behavior among employees.

Application 35

Cost-Volume-Profit Analysis

This application is related to Accounting (Module 600) and Finance (Module 700), and specifically to Sections 660 (Decision Making and Accounting) and 735 (Capital Budgeting).

Break-Even Point and Capital Budgeting Analysis

Costs behave in a certain way according to changes in sales and production volume. *Cost behavior* refers to the manner in which a cost changes as a related activity changes. Here, activity is referred to sales or production. To understand cost behavior, two factors must be considered: (1) the activity base (activity driver) that causes the cost to be incurred, and (2) the relevant range, which is a range of activity over which changes in cost are of interest to management.

Three types of break-even point (BEP) determination exist: operating (accounting) BEP, financial BEP, and cash BEP.

- Operating BEP = (total fixed costs + depreciation expense)/(selling price per unit − variable cost per unit). Net income is zero and operating cash flows are equal to depreciation expenses.
- Financial BEP = (total fixed costs + operating cash flows)/(selling price per unit − variable cost per unit). The financial BEP considers cash flows from the project. The project will have a zero net present value (NPV) when the present value of operating cash flows equals the initial investment. Because cash flow is the same every year, we can view it as an ordinary annuity. The operating cash flow = cash flow or investment/annuity or discount factor.
- Cash BEP = total fixed costs/(selling price per unit − variable cost per unit). A project that breaks even on an accounting basis has a net income of zero and a zero operating cash flow.

The three types of break-even points can be related to capital budgeting techniques such as net present value (NPV) and internal rate of return (IRR) as follows.

- NPV of a Project = Present Value of Cash Flows − Initial Investment. If NPV is zero or positive, the project should be accepted. If NPV is negative, the project should be rejected.
- Project's Operating Cash Flows = Project's Net Income + Depreciation Expense
- Project's Net Income = (Sales − Total Variable Costs − Total Fixed Costs − Depreciation Expense − Taxes)
- Present Value of Future Cash Flows = Future Cash Flows × Discount Factor

A project that breaks even on an operating basis has a payback exactly equal to its life, a negative NPV, and an IRR of zero. Discounted payback considers the time value of money, which is not considered by the operating break-even method.

A project that breaks even on a financial basis has a discounted payback equal to its life, a zero NPV, and an IRR equal to the required return (a positive number).

A project that breaks even on a cash basis never pays back (zero payback), has a negative NPV and is equal to the initial outlay, and has an IRR of negative 100 percent.

Contribution Margin and Operating Profit Analysis

Contribution margin (CM) per unit is selling price per unit minus variable cost per unit. The CM ratio is (sales-variable costs)/sales. The CM ratio indicates the percentage of each sales dollar available to cover fixed costs and to provide income from operations. Multiplying the CM ratio (for example, 30 percent) by the change in sales volume (for example, $60,000) indicates that income from operations will increase by $18,000.

$$\text{Additional Income From Operations} = \text{Additional Sales Volume in Dollars} \times \text{CM Ratio}$$

The unit contribution margin is most useful when the increase or decrease in sales volume is measured in sales units (quantities). If the unit contribution margin is say, $15, and if sales increase by 5,000 units, the operating income will increase by $75,000 ($15 × 5,000).

$$\text{Additional Income From Operations} = \text{Additional Sales Volume in Units} \times \text{CM per Unit}$$

Operating profit is another term for income from operations. It is computed as actual sales revenues minus variable costs minus fixed costs.

Break-Even Point, Margin of Safety, Operating Income, and Fixed Costs

Another financial relationship between actual sales and break-even point (BEP) sales is margin of safety. The margin of safety is actual sales minus BEP sales. The margin of safety expressed as a percentage of sales is margin of safety in dollars divided by actual sales. The following statements express the relationships between BEP, margin of safety, operating income, and fixed costs.

Break-Even Point = Actual Sales − Margin of Safety in Dollars
Margin of Safety in Dollars = Actual Sales × Margin of Safety %
Operating Income = Margin of Safety in Dollars × the CM Ratio

A company with high fixed costs will require a higher break-even point and vice versa.

Sales Mix, Break-Even Point, and Operating Income

The sales mix is the relative distribution of sales among the various products sold by a company. The sales volume necessary to break even or to earn a target profit for a company selling two or more products depends upon the sales mix. Operating income depends on how many products with a high contribution margin (CM) are sold compared to low CM products. Products with a high CM will contribute more toward recovering fixed costs faster and leaving the remainder as operating income.

Control Analysis

This application is related to General Management and Organization (Module 100) and Corporate Control and Governance (Module 900), and specifically to Sections 130 (Controlling and Motivating) and 901 (Corporate Control Strategies).

Control Concepts

Organizational Controls

Organizational controls are of three types: feedforward, concurrent, and feedback. Feedforward control (pre-action or input control) attempts to identify and prevent deviations before they occur. It is also called *preliminary* or *preventive* control. This type of control should be in place during the selection and hiring of new employees, the managing of enterprise risks, and in maintaining the quality of products and services.

Concurrent control assesses employee work activities, relies on performance standards, and includes rules and regulations for guiding employee tasks and behaviors. Control that monitors ongoing employee activities to ensure they are consistent with performance standards is called *concurrent control*. For example, direct supervision is an effective concurrent control.

Feedback control (post-action or output control) focuses on the organization's outputs, in particular, the quality of an end product or service. Well-designed feedback control systems include four key measures: establish standards of performance, measure actual performance, compare performance to standards, and take corrective action as necessary. Actual performance should be measured against standards before taking any action. In addition, the manager should discover the cause of any problem before taking action. Personal judgment and intuition are not substitutes for numerical indicators (such as sales or profits) or red flags.

Budgets and Controls

Organizational budget is a management control with strategic focus. Budgets and controls are interrelated. Top-down budgeting fits with the bureaucratic control. Bureaucratic control involves monitoring and influencing employee behavior through extensive use of rules, policies, and hierarchy of authority. Top-down budgeting means that the budgeted amounts for the coming year are imposed on middle- and lower-level managers by top managers.

Control Categories

Two categories of control are bureaucratic control and decentralized control. Bureaucratic control is implemented through the administrative system. It includes monitoring and influencing employee behavior through extensive use of rules, policies, a hierarchy of authority, reward systems, and written documentation (handbook).

Decentralized control relies on cultural values and norms, traditions, shared beliefs, and trust to foster compliance with organizational goals. Minimum standards, little direction, and trust are characteristics of decentralized control. Decentralized control is not weak control. It includes a management control system, technology, the quality control department, and total quality management (TQM). TQM is a management philosophy that emphasizes commitment to continuous improvement and that focuses on teamwork, customer satisfaction, and lowering costs. With TQM, employees are trained and empowered to think in terms of prevention—not detection or correction. Employees are empowered to control their own destiny and reach organizational goals.

There are four types of controls from an action perspective: preventive, directive, detective, and corrective. Detecting an exception in a business transaction or process is detective in nature, but reporting it is an example of corrective control. Preventive and directive controls neither detect nor correct an error, they simply stop or deter it, if possible.

Controls in the New Workplace

Controls in the new workplace include open-book management, economic value-added system, activity-based costing, market-value-added system, and the balanced scorecard system. Open-book management allows sharing of financial information and results with all employees in the organization. The economic value-added system is a new system used to measure corporate performance. The activity-based costing system identifies various activities needed to produce a product or service and determine the cost of those activities. Market-value-added system is total market value of a firm (equity plus debt) minus capital invested since its inception. The balanced scorecard is a system that considers and balances both financial (traditional) and operational (nonfinancial) measures relating to a company's critical success factors.

Risks and Controls

The purpose of a control mechanism is to ensure that the goals of a firm are being achieved. Controls should facilitate the achievement of an organization's objectives. Controls should not limit operational practices, processes, and people's actions. Control levers include belief systems, interactive control systems, boundary systems, and diagnostic control systems. Belief systems and interactive control systems create positive and inspirational forces. Boundary systems and diagnostic control systems create negative forces, such as rules and constraints.

Control involves the use of incentives and rewards to motivate employees in order to help them accomplish organizational goals and objectives. Controls should be seen as positive actions rather than negative actions (punishments).

There is a direct relationship between risk level and control level. That is, high-risk situations require stronger controls, low-risk situations require weaker controls, and medium-risk situations require moderate controls.

Customer Analysis

This application is related to Marketing Management (Module 300) and Quality and Process Management (Module 400), and specifically to Sections 385 (Services Marketing) and 425 (Quality Models and Awards).

Cost of Lost Customers

Companies lose a sale for a variety of reasons. Losing a sale has a minor impact, while losing a customer has a major impact on the selling company. From a company's viewpoint, a buyer (customer) waiting for a product is good, the seller (company) losing a sale is bad, and the seller losing a customer is to be circumvented.

To compute the cost of a lost sale, we need the percentage of repurchase, the average annual purchase amount per customer, and the number of lost customers. *Cost* here refers to loss of gross profit on the customer purchase. Fixed costs will remain the same whether a customer's sale is lost or not.

The cost of a lost sale is computed as follows.

Lost Sales Percent = 100% − Repurchase %
Estimated Lost Sales = Number of Lost Customers × Lost Sales % × Average Annual Purchase Amount per Customer
Lost Gross Profit = Estimated Lost Sales × Gross Profit

Value/Price Ratio and Value Offering Analysis

Value is the ratio between what the customer gets and what the customer gives. The customer gets benefits and assumes costs. Value equals benefits divided by costs. Value can also be defined as the combination of benefits received and costs paid by the customer.

The value/price ratio is simply value divided by price. The higher the value/price ratio, the better for the customer. The lower the value/price ratio, the worse for the customer.

The marketer can increase the value of the customer offering in many ways, including increasing benefits, decreasing costs, increasing benefits and decreasing costs, increasing benefits by more than the increase in costs, and decreasing benefits by less than the decrease in costs.

To a customer, value is changing all the time. Nowadays, the customer wants to buy a product or service with the important attributes of high conformance to quality, fast delivery, and high product reliability at the lowest price (manufacturing futures survey).[29]

Cost of Acquisition, Defection Rate, and Lifetime Value of a Customer

The cost of acquiring a new customer is the number of phone calls made by the sales person multiplied by cost per sales call. A company with a high customer turnover rate has a high rate of acquisition and a high rate of defection. Establishing high switching costs or barriers and delivering high customer service can strengthen the customer retention rate. Merely reducing the defection rate will not necessarily improve the retention rate.

The most effective method for reducing the customer defection rate is listening to the customer. This creates loyalty and customer satisfaction and turns defecting customers into retained customers. Relationship marketing can also create a strong customer loyalty base.

The formula used to find the customer's lifetime value is number of years to become a loyal customer × average revenue per customer × the profit margin.

Customer-Related Concepts

The major objective of the customer relationship management (CRM) program is to increase service to customers. A customer-centered company focuses more on customer developments in formulating its strategies. It pays close attention to market situations and reactions. Losing a current customer, whether large or small, is riskier than losing a potential customer.

Berry and Parasuraman[30] suggest that a company that wants to adopt a customer value-building approach should implement a Frequency Marketing Program, in which 20 percent of its customers account for 80 percent of its business. This is also called the *Pareto principle,* or the *20/80 rule.*

Terry Hill[31] coined the terms *order winners* and *order qualifiers.* An order-winner is a criterion that differentiates the products or services of one firm from another. It is an order-getting power. An order qualifier is a screening criterion that permits a firm's product or service to be considered as a possible candidate for purchase. It is important to remember that order-winning and order-qualifying criteria may change over time. What is order-winning today may become order-qualifying tomorrow. According to a survey conducted by Boston University (Manufacturing Futures Survey), low price is emerging as the order winner.

A Japanese professor, Kano, suggested three customer requirements in understanding customers' needs in the marketplace. Customers become dissatisfiers when the features or requirements that they are expecting in a product or service are not present. Customers become satisfiers when the features or requirements they want are being met, although those features are not expected. Customers become exciters or delighters when a product or service contains features that they are not expecting.

Application 38

Quantitative and Qualitative Analysis

This application is related to General Management and Organization (Module 100) and Operations Management (Module 200), and specifically to Sections 195 (Quantitative Techniques and Management), 220 (Product Demand Management and Forecasting), and 235 (Manufacturing Planning and Scheduling).

Quantitative Analysis—Basic Statistics

There are many aspects to basic statistics, including mean, median, mode, mean absolute deviation, variance, standard deviation, coefficient of variation, and mean squared error.

- Mean is the simple average of observed measurements.
- Median is the halfway point of the data, that is, half of the numbers are above it and half are below.
- Mode is the value that occurs most frequently.
- Mean absolute deviation (MAD) is a measure of dispersion in the data. This measure is the average of the absolute values of all the forecast errors. A smaller MAD is better.

- Variance, similar to MAD, measures the average distance from each number to the mean. We need to square each deviation and then take the average of all the squared deviations. Variance is difficult to interpret.
- Standard deviation is the square root of the variance. Assuming normal distribution, 68 percent of the data will be within one standard deviation of the mean, 95 percent of the data will be within two standard deviations of the mean, and 99 percent of the data will be within three standard deviations of the mean.
- The coefficient of variation tells us whether the dispersion is large or small relative to the average. It is computed by dividing the standard deviation by the mean. Smaller dispersion is good.
- Mean squared error (MSE) measures the average of the sum of the squared differences between the actual time series data and the forecasted data. A smaller MSE is preferred.

The choice between MAD and MSE is up to the individual making the decision. For the same set of data, the value of MSE is larger than that of MAD. Both MAD and MSE measure forecast errors.

Quantitative Analysis—Basic Probabilities

A probability is a numerical measure of the likelihood that an event or outcome will occur. Basic requirements of probability include that (1) for each experimental outcome, the value must be between 0 and 1, and (2) all individual probabilities must add up to one.

There are three methods to assign probabilities: the classical method, the relative frequency method, and the subjective method. The classical method assigns probabilities based on the assumption that experimental outcomes are equally likely. The relative frequency method assigns probabilities based on experimentation or historical data. The subjective method assigns probabilities based on judgment of the person assigning the probabilities. Business managers use the subjective method more frequently than the other methods.

Quantitative Analysis—Regression Analysis

Regression analysis is one example of a quantitative forecasting method. It is a causal forecasting method that can be used to develop forecasts when time series data are not available. Regression analysis is a statistical technique that can be used to develop a mathematical equation showing how variables are related. Two types of regression analysis are simple linear regression and multiple regression. In simple linear regression, there will be only two variables: one dependent variable and one independent variable. In multiple regression, there will be more than two variables: one dependent variable and more than one independent variable.

The following equation is an example of a simple linear regression model.

$$Y = mx + b$$

where Y is the dependent variable (sales), m is slope, X is the independent variable (disposable income), and b is the intercept.

A histogram or a bar diagram provides a frequency distribution of the measured data.

A scatter diagram is used to determine whether a relationship exists between the dependent variable (vertical, Y axis) and an independent variable (horizontal, X axis). With the regression equation, management can estimate future period sales by knowing the future period's disposable income.

MSE is an approach to measuring the accuracy of a forecasting model. The MSE is a quantity used in regression to estimate the unknown value of the variance of the error term.

Regression analysis deals with two statistical values: (1) value of the coefficient of determination and (2) value of correlation or correlation coefficient. The value of the coefficient of determination is always between 0 and 1. The higher this value, the better the regression line fits the data. For example, a coefficient of determination value of 0.97 means that 97 percent of the variations in sales can be explained by variations in disposal income. The value of correlation or correlation coefficient is always between -1 and $+1$. A correlation value near $+1$ or -1 indicates that there is a very strong linear relation between the sales and income variables. For example, a correlation coefficient value of 0.985 indicates a very strong linear relation between these two variables.

Quantitative Analysis—Sales Seasonality and Deseasonality

Sales for many businesses exhibit seasonality over time. Seasonal index is a measure of the seasonal effect on a time series. Time series is a set of observations measured at successive points in time or over successive periods of time. A seasonal index above 1 indicates a positive effect, a seasonal index of 1 indicates no seasonal effect, and a seasonal index less than 1 indicates a negative effect.

A deseasonalized times series is one that has had the effect of season removed. Deseasonalized sales are calculated by dividing original time series data by corresponding seasonal index values. The monthly or quarterly forecast is obtained by multiplying the trend forecast by seasonal index values.

Quantitative Analysis—Forecasting Methods

Management frequently estimates sales, costs, income, market share, interest rates, inflation, and manufacturing capacity utilization. There are six forecasting methods: simple moving average, weighted moving average, exponential smoothing, heuristics, conjoint analysis, and Markov analysis.

The simple moving average method smoothes time series data by averaging each successive group of data points. The weighted moving average method smoothes time series data by computing a weighted average of past time series data. The sum of the weights must equal 1. The exponential smoothing method uses a weighted average of past time series data to arrive at smoothed time series data that can be used as the forecasts. Smoothing constants are used in the exponential smoothing method. The smoothing constant is a parameter that provides the weight given to the most recent time series data. The exponential smoothing method is better than the moving average because it uses a weighted average of past time series data to arrive at smoothed time series data.

The heuristics method uses a set of rules of thumb that shorten the time or work required to find a reasonably good solution to a complex problem. One aspect of it is a naive approach based on intuition, where it assumes that this month's sales are equal to last month's sales. The heuristics method uses a trial-and-error approach.

Conjoint analysis is a statistical technique where customers' preferences for different attributes (such as product offers or advertisement impacts) are decomposed to determine the customer's inferred utility function and relative value for each attribute.

Markov analysis shows the probability of moving from a current state to any future state. Typical applications include determining the market share for a company, finding bad debts in accounts receivables, and identifying employee fill rates and succession planning moves.

Quantitative Analysis—Linear Programming, Transportation, Assignment, and Transshipment Problems

Linear programming is a mathematical model with a linear objective function, a set of linear constraints, and nonnegative decision variables. *Objective function* is the expression that defines the quantity to be maximized or minimized in a linear programming model. *Constraint* is an equation or inequality that rules out certain combinations of decision variables as feasible solutions. *Decision variable* is a controllable input for a linear programming model.

The transportation problem is a network flow problem that often involves minimizing the cost of shipping goods from a set of origins to a set of destinations; it can be formulated and solved as a linear program by including a variable for each arc and a constraint for each node.

The assignment problem is a network flow problem that often involves the assignment of agents to tasks; it can be formulated as a linear program and is a special case of the transportation problem.

The transshipment problem is an extension of the transportation problem to product distribution problems involving transfer points and possible shipments between any pair of nodes.

Quantitative Analysis—Quantitative Data Variables

Quantitative data variables are nominal, ordinal, interval, and ratio. In nominal variables, attributes have no inherent order. Ordinal, interval, and ratio variables have an order.

Qualitative Analysis

The tools and techniques used to analyze and interpret qualitative data include content analysis, factor analysis, cluster analysis, link analysis, canonical analysis, discriminant analysis, causal analysis, cost-benefit analysis, and conversation analysis. Conversation analysis is used to analyze spoken words, while all the other techniques listed here are used to analyze written words.

Content analysis is a set of procedures for transforming unstructured written material into a format for analysis. It is also used for making numerical comparisons among and within documents. It is a means of extracting insights from already existing data sources. Its potential applications include identifying goals, describing activities, and determining results.

Factor analysis is used in the exploration or confirmation of "interdependence" among variables. Factor analysis assumes that the observed variables are linear combinations of some underlying factors, which can be hypothetical or unobservable. Some of these factors can be common, while others can be unique.

Cluster analysis can be used to create a classification. It involves clustering elements that "go together" by using single or multiple dimensions. It involves coding and identifying patterns in data.

Link analysis connects relevant data segments with each other, forming categories, clusters, or networks of information.

Canonical analysis considers possible interrelationships among independent variables and dependent variables. Canonical analysis extends the basic relationship to an entire set of dependent variables. Canonical analysis depends on an understanding of factor analysis.

Discriminant analysis is an identification procedure. This technique can be applied to a wide variety of research and predictive problems, and interpretation and classification of data. It studies the differences between two or more groups and a set of discriminant variables.

Causal analysis and cost-benefit analysis are performed with both qualitative and quantitative data. Causal analysis is a method for analyzing possible causal associations among a set of variables. Causal association is a relationship between two variables in which a change in one brings about a change in the other. For example, causal analysis is used in marketing research to test cause-and-effect relationships. The common problem with cost-benefit analysis is understatement of cost and overstatement of benefits.

Conversation analysis is the study of talk-in-interaction with people (that is, analyzing spoken words). It studies the order and organization of discursive practices in terms of sayings, tellings, and doings of people.

Link Between Qualitative and Quantitative Data

Quantitative forecasting methods include time series methods and causal methods. The three time series methods are simple moving average, weighted moving average, and exponential smoothing. Of the three, the exponential smoothing method is the best because more weight is given to the most recent time series values.

The Delphi method, scenario writing, expert judgment, and the intuitive approach are examples of qualitative forecasting methods, which are good to use (1) when little or no historical data are available, and (2) when the historical pattern of the time series is not expected to continue into the future.

Qualitative data should be linked with quantitative data to (1) enable confirmation or corroboration of each other via triangulation; (2) elaborate or develop analysis, providing better, richer detail; and (3) initiate new lines of thinking through attention to surprises or paradoxes, "turning ideas around," and providing fresh insight.

Productivity Analysis

This application is related to Operations Management (Module 200), and specifically to Section 285 (Economics and Operations).

Productivity

Productivity has many meanings and definitions. A popular definition is outputs divided by inputs. Examples of outputs might be the number of units produced in a factory or the number of claims processed in an office. Corresponding inputs include the number of direct labor hours used in the factory or the number of administrative hours spent in the office. It has been said that motivated and happy workers are productive workers, whereas unmotivated and unhappy workers are unproductive workers.

Productivity is a key determinant of profits for many businesses, and is related to efficiency, not effectiveness. Effectiveness is accomplishing objectives; resources used are not considered, and results (outcomes) only are looked at. Efficiency is more closely related to economy in using resources. Productivity is the value added by an organization to its products or services. The higher the productivity of a nation, the higher the standards of living for people in that nation.

Efficiency refers to a single factor (labor) while productivity refers to multiple factors (for example, labor, capital, and material). Personal efficiency is more closely related to personal performance which is results obtained divided by resources used. For example, incentive pay (piece rate) systems were initiated to increase employees' efficiency.

The following is a clarification of the productivity and efficiency measures:

Productivity is outputs divided by inputs.

The numerator in the productivity equation, outputs, can be finished goods, dividends, bonds, or stocks.

The denominator in the productivity equation, inputs, can be all resources used such as labor, capital, material, and energy.

General efficiency is standard hours allowed divided by actual hours used.

Personal efficiency is results obtained divided by resources used.

Productivity, which is the amount of products or services produced with the given amount of resources used, can be increased by the following actions:

1. Increase the amount of production using the same or a smaller amount of resources.
2. Reduce the amount of resources used while maintaining the same amount of production or increasing the production.
3. Increase the amount of resources used less than the amount of production increased.
4. Decrease the amount of production more than the amount of resources used decreased.

Because productivity is a relative measure, it must be analyzed in several ways for the measure to be meaningful. A company can compare its productivity data with other similar companies; it can compare its productivity data with its industry average; it can compare its productivity data to a standard that it established; and it can compare its productivity data in one time period with that of the next.

Work measurement refers to the process of estimating the amount of worker time required to generate one unit of output. The scope of work measurement includes establishing labor standards, which are used in an incentive pay system. Three approaches are used to set labor standards: time study, work sampling, and predetermined time methods. Methods-time-measurement is an example of predetermined time methods.

Learning curve can improve a worker's productivity. Learning-curve concept states that, as workers learn their jobs, their output per day will increase up to a point, and then level off to a constant output rate. Learning-curve problems can be solved using arithmetic analysis, logarithmic analysis, and learning-curve tables.

One way to increase a company's productivity is to reduce the cycle time for a process. Cycle time is total time to complete a product or process. The scope of activities in a product or process can include transportation time, assembly time, wait time, and finishing time.

Competitive Analysis

This application is related to General Management and Organization (Module 100) and Marketing Management (Module 300), and specifically to Sections 101 (Corporate Strategies) and 301 (Marketing Strategies).

Benchmarking and Core Competencies

Benchmarking can be used in performing competitive analysis because it tells a company where it stands in relation to its competitors. A core competence is a business activity that an organization does particularly well in comparison to competitors.

Porter's Competitive Forces and Strategies

Porter's five competitive forces include (1) potential new entrants, (2) threat of substitute products, (3) bargaining power of buyers, (4) bargaining power of suppliers, and (5) rivalry among competitors. Porter's three competitive strategies include differentiation, cost leadership, and focus.

Differentiation is a type of competitive strategy with which the organization seeks to distinguish its products or services from competitors'. In cost leadership strategy, a company seeks efficient facilities, cuts costs, and employs tight controls to be more efficient than competitors. In focus strategy, a company emphasizes concentration on a specific regional market or buyer group.

Customer Value Analysis and Competition

Managers should conduct customer value analysis to reveal the company's strengths and weaknesses related to various competitors. The first step is to identify the major attributes customers value most.

After a company has conducted its customer value analysis, it can focus its attack strategies on one of the following classes of competitors: strong versus weak competitors, close versus distant competitors, and good versus bad competitors.

Kotler's Competitive Strategies

According to Philip Kotler,[32] an organization can look into the following defensive strategies against its competitors: contraction defense, position defense, and bypass attack. Contraction defense, or planned contraction, involves giving up weaker territories and reassigning resources to stronger territories. It is a move to consolidate competitive strength in the market and concentrate mass at pivotal positions. Planned contraction is also called *strategic withdrawal*.

Position defense is the basic defensive marketing strategy to build an impregnable fortification around one's own marketing territory. The bypass attack is the most indirect assault strategy. For example, technological leapfrogging (bypass attack) is practiced in high-tech industries.

Competitive Moves

According to the *Harvard Business Review* article titled "Global Gamesmanship" by Ian C. MacMillan and others,[33] the following competitive moves or strategies are available to a company. The article suggests the use of game theory, where the results of any moves a player makes stem in large part from the choices his opponent makes. Competitive moves are discussed next.

- The *onslaught* is a direct attack, where the goal is to take major market share in a target arena and force the competitor to retreat. Tactics employed include price cutting, heavy expenditures on marketing, and replacing existing product distribution patterns.
- A *feint* is designed to divert a defender's attention and resources from the instigator's target arena by launching an attack elsewhere (the focal arena).
- A *contest* is more subtle and narrowly focused than an onslaught and hence is less costly. Attacks are not easily matched by the competitor.
- In a *guerrilla campaign,* the defender has lower reactiveness in the undeserved segments than it does to the arena as a whole. The objective is to use these segments to drive a wedge into the target market, which can be exploited later.
- *Harvesting* is a competitive move in which both parties focus on extracting profit from an arena that neither finds attractive for future exploitation. Harvesting can also occur through cross-licensing agreements between two companies.
- *Gambit* often occurs when competitors are evenly matched in terms of market clout. A direct attack on the target arena is very costly. Like the feint, the gambit involves both a target arena and a focal arena.

Appendix

Mathematical Tables

Table A-1: *Present Value of $1 Due at the End of n Periods*

EQUATION:

$$PVIF_{i,n} = \frac{1}{(1+i)^n}$$

FINANCIAL CALCULATOR KEYS:

n → N
i → I
0 → PMT
1.0 → FV
PV → Table Value

Period	1%	2%	3%	4%	5%	6%	7%	8%	9%	10%
1	.9901	.9804	.9709	.9615	.9524	.9434	.9346	.9259	.9174	.9091
2	.9803	.9612	.9426	.9246	.9070	.8900	.8734	.8573	.8417	.8264
3	.9706	.9423	.9151	.8890	.8638	.8396	.8163	.7938	.7722	.7513
4	.9610	.9238	.8885	.8548	.8227	.7921	.7629	.7350	.7084	.6830
5	.9515	.9057	.8626	.8219	.7835	.7473	.7130	.6806	.6499	.6209
6	.9420	.8880	.8375	.7903	.7462	.7050	.6663	.6302	.5963	.5645
7	.9327	.8706	.8131	.7599	.7107	.6651	.6227	.5835	.5470	.5132
8	.9235	.8535	.7894	.7307	.6768	.6274	.5820	.5403	.5019	.4665
9	.9143	.8368	.7664	.7026	.6446	.5919	.5439	.5002	.4604	.4241
10	.9053	.8203	.7441	.6756	.6139	.5584	.5083	.4632	.4224	.3855
11	.8963	.8043	.7224	.6496	.5847	.5268	.4751	.4289	.3875	.3505
12	.8874	.7885	.7014	.6246	.5568	.4970	.4440	.3971	.3555	.3186
13	.8787	.7730	.6810	.6006	.5303	.4688	.4150	.3677	.3262	.2897
14	.8700	.7579	.6611	.5775	.5051	.4423	.3878	.3405	.2992	.2633
15	.8613	.7430	.6419	.5553	.4810	.4173	.3624	.3152	.2745	.2394
16	.8528	.7284	.6232	.5339	.4581	.3936	.3387	.2919	.2519	.2176
17	.8444	.7142	.6050	.5134	.4363	.3714	.3166	.2703	.2311	.1978
18	.8360	.7002	.5874	.4936	.4155	.3503	.2959	.2502	.2120	.1799
19	.8277	.6864	.5703	.4746	.3957	.3305	.2765	.2317	.1945	.1635
20	.8195	.6730	.5537	.4564	.3769	.3118	.2584	.2145	.1784	.1486
21	.8114	.6598	.5375	.4388	.3589	.2942	.2415	.1987	.1637	.1351
22	.8034	.6468	.5219	.4220	.3418	.2775	.2257	.1839	.1502	.1228
23	.7954	.6342	.5067	.4057	.3256	.2618	.2109	.1703	.1378	.1117
24	.7876	.6217	.4919	.3901	.3101	.2470	.1971	.1577	.1264	.1015
25	.7798	.6095	.4776	.3751	.2953	.2330	.1842	.1460	.1160	.0923
26	.7720	.5976	.4637	.3607	.2812	.2198	.1722	.1352	.1064	.0839
27	.7644	.5859	.4502	.3468	.2678	.2074	.1609	.1252	.0976	.0763
28	.7568	.5744	.4371	.3335	.2551	.1956	.1504	.1159	.0895	.0693
29	.7493	.5631	.4243	.3207	.2429	.1846	.1406	.1073	.0822	.0630
30	.7419	.5521	.4120	.3083	.2314	.1741	.1314	.0994	.0754	.0573
35	.7059	.5000	.3554	.2534	.1813	.1301	.0937	.0676	.0490	.0356
40	.6717	.4529	.3066	.2083	.1420	.0972	.0668	.0460	.0318	.0221
45	.6391	.4102	.2644	.1712	.1113	.0727	.0476	.0313	.0207	.0137
50	.6080	.3715	.2281	.1407	.0872	.0543	.0339	.0213	.0134	.0085
55	.5785	.3365	.1968	.1157	.0683	.0406	.0242	.0145	.0087	.0053

(continued)

Table A-1 *Continued*

Period	12%	14%	15%	16%	18%	20%	24%	28%	32%	36%
1	.8929	.8772	.8696	.8621	.8475	.8333	.8065	.7813	.7576	.7353
2	.7972	.7695	.7561	.7432	.7182	.6944	.6504	.6104	.5739	.5407
3	.7118	.6750	.6575	.6407	.6086	.5787	.5245	.4768	.4348	.3975
4	.6355	.5921	.5718	.5523	.5158	.4823	.4230	.3725	.3294	.2923
5	.5674	.5194	.4972	.4761	.4371	.4019	.3411	.2910	.2495	.2149
6	.5066	.4556	.4323	.4104	.3704	.3349	.2751	.2274	.1890	.1580
7	.4523	.3996	.3759	.3538	.3139	.2791	.2218	.1776	.1432	.1162
8	.4039	.3506	.3269	.3050	.2660	.2326	.1789	.1388	.1085	.0854
9	.3606	.3075	.2843	.2630	.2255	.1938	.1443	.1084	.0822	.0628
10	.3220	.2697	.2472	.2267	.1911	.1615	.1164	.0847	.0623	.0462
11	.2875	.2366	.2149	.1954	.1619	.1346	.0938	.0662	.0472	.0340
12	.2567	.2076	.1869	.1685	.1372	.1122	.0757	.0517	.0357	.0250
13	.2292	.1821	.1625	.1452	.1163	.0935	.0610	.0404	.0271	.0184
14	.2046	.1597	.1413	.1252	.0985	.0779	.0492	.0316	.0205	.0135
15	.1827	.1401	.1229	.1079	.0835	.0649	.0397	.0247	.0155	.0099
16	.1631	.1229	.1069	.0930	.0708	.0541	.0320	.0193	.0118	.0073
17	.1456	.1078	.0929	.0802	.0600	.0451	.0258	.0150	.0089	.0054
18	.1300	.0946	.0808	.0691	.0508	.0376	.0208	.0118	.0068	.0039
19	.1161	.0829	.0703	.0596	.0431	.0313	.0168	.0092	.0051	.0029
20	.1037	.0728	.0611	.0514	.0365	.0261	.0135	.0072	.0039	.0021
21	.0926	.0638	.0531	.0443	.0309	.0217	.0109	.0056	.0029	.0016
22	.0826	.0560	.0462	.0382	.0262	.0181	.0088	.0044	.0022	.0012
23	.0738	.0491	.0402	.0329	.0222	.0151	.0071	.0034	.0017	.0008
24	.0659	.0431	.0349	.0284	.0188	.0126	.0057	.0027	.0013	.0006
25	.0588	.0378	.0304	.0245	.0160	.0105	.0046	.0021	.0010	.0005
26	.0525	.0331	.0264	.0211	.0135	.0087	.0037	.0016	.0007	.0003
27	.0469	.0291	.0230	.0182	.0115	.0073	.0030	.0013	.0006	.0002
28	.0419	.0255	.0200	.0157	.0097	.0061	.0024	.0010	.0004	.0002
29	.0374	.0224	.0174	.0135	.0082	.0051	.0020	.0008	.0003	.0001
30	.0334	.0196	.0151	.0116	.0070	.0042	.0016	.0006	.0002	.0001
35	.0189	.0102	.0075	.0055	.0030	.0017	.0005	.0002	.0001	*
40	.0107	.0053	.0037	.0026	.0013	.0007	.0002	.0001	*	*
45	.0061	.0027	.0019	.0013	.0006	.0003	.0001	*	*	*
50	.0035	.0014	.0009	.0006	.0003	.0001	*	*	*	*
55	.0020	.0007	.0005	.0003	.0001	*	*	*	*	*

*The factor is zero to four decimal places.

Table A-2 *Present Value of an Annuity of $1 per Period for n Periods*

EQUATION:

$$PVIFA_{i,n} = \sum_{t=1}^{N} \frac{1}{(1+i)^n} = \frac{1 - \frac{1}{(1+i)^n}}{i} = \frac{1}{i} = \frac{1}{i(1+i)^n}$$

FINANCIAL CALCULATOR KEYS:

n	i	Table Value	1.0	0
N	I	PV	PMT	FV

Number of Periods	1%	2%	3%	4%	5%	6%	7%	8%	9%
1	0.9901	0.9804	0.9709	0.9615	0.9524	0.9434	0.9346	0.9259	0.9174
2	1.9704	1.9416	1.9135	1.8861	1.8594	1.8334	1.8080	1.7833	1.7591
3	2.9410	2.8839	2.8286	2.7751	2.7232	2.6730	2.6243	2.5771	2.5313
4	3.9020	3.8077	3.7171	3.6299	3.5460	3.4651	3.3872	3.3121	3.2397
5	4.8534	4.7135	4.5797	4.4518	4.3295	4.2124	4.1002	3.9927	3.8897
6	5.7955	5.6014	5.4172	5.2421	5.0757	4.9173	4.7665	4.6229	4.4859
7	6.7282	6.4720	6.2303	6.0021	5.7864	5.5824	5.3893	5.2064	5.0330
8	7.6517	7.3255	7.0197	6.7327	6.4632	6.2098	5.9713	5.7466	5.5348
9	8.5660	8.1622	7.7861	7.4353	7.1078	6.8017	6.5152	6.2469	5.9952
10	9.4713	8.9826	8.5302	8.1109	7.7217	7.3601	7.0236	6.7101	6.4177
11	10.3676	9.7868	9.2526	8.7605	8.3064	7.8869	7.4987	7.1390	6.8052
12	11.2551	10.5753	9.9540	9.3851	8.8633	8.3838	7.9427	7.5361	7.1607
13	12.1337	11.3484	10.6350	9.9856	9.3936	8.8527	8.3577	7.9038	7.4869
14	13.0037	12.1062	11.2961	10.5631	9.8986	9.2950	8.7455	8.2442	7.7862
15	13.8651	12.8493	11.9379	11.1184	10.3797	9.7122	9.1079	8.5595	8.0607
16	14.7179	13.5777	12.5611	11.6523	10.8378	10.1059	9.4466	8.8514	8.3126
17	15.5623	14.2919	13.1661	12.1657	11.2741	10.4773	9.7632	9.1216	8.5436
18	16.3983	14.9920	13.7535	12.6593	11.6896	10.8276	10.0591	9.3719	8.7556
19	17.2260	15.6785	14.3238	13.1339	12.0853	11.1581	10.3356	9.6036	8.9501
20	18.0456	16.3514	14.8775	13.5903	12.4622	11.4699	10.5940	9.8181	9.1285
21	18.8570	17.0112	15.4150	14.0292	12.8212	11.7641	10.8355	10.0168	9.2922
22	19.6604	17.6580	15.9369	14.4511	13.1630	12.0416	11.0612	10.2007	9.4424
23	20.4558	18.2922	16.4436	14.8568	13.4886	12.3034	11.2722	10.3711	9.5802
24	21.2434	18.9139	16.9355	15.2470	13.7986	12.5504	11.4693	10.5288	9.7066
25	22.0232	19.5235	17.4131	15.6221	14.0939	12.7834	11.6536	10.6748	9.8226
26	22.7952	20.1210	17.8768	15.9828	14.3752	13.0032	11.8258	10.8100	9.9290
27	23.5596	20.7069	18.3270	16.3296	14.6430	13.2105	11.9867	10.9352	10.0266
28	24.3164	21.2813	18.7641	16.6631	14.8981	13.4062	12.1371	11.0511	10.1161
29	25.0658	21.8444	19.1885	16.9837	15.1411	13.5907	12.2777	11.1584	10.1983
30	25.8077	22.3965	19.6004	17.2920	15.3725	13.7648	12.4090	11.2578	10.2737
35	29.4086	24.9986	21.4872	18.6646	16.3742	14.4982	12.9477	11.6546	10.5668
40	32.8347	27.3555	23.1148	19.7928	17.1591	15.0463	13.3317	11.9246	10.7574
45	36.0945	29.4902	24.5187	20.7200	17.7741	15.4558	13.6055	12.1084	10.8812
50	39.1961	31.4236	25.7298	21.4822	18.2559	15.7619	13.8007	12.2335	10.9617
55	42.1472	33.1748	26.7744	22.1086	18.6335	15.9905	13.9399	12.3186	11.0140

(continued)

MATHEMATICAL TABLES

Table A-2   *Continued*

Number of Periods	10%	12%	14%	15%	16%	18%	20%	24%	28%	32%
1	0.9091	0.8929	0.8772	0.8696	0.8621	0.8475	0.8333	0.8065	0.7813	0.7576
2	1.7355	1.6901	1.6467	1.6257	1.6052	1.5656	1.5278	1.4568	1.3916	1.3315
3	2.4869	2.4018	2.3216	2.2832	2.2459	2.1743	2.1065	1.9813	1.8684	1.7663
4	3.1699	3.0373	2.9137	2.8550	2.7982	2.6901	2.5887	2.4043	2.2410	2.0957
5	3.7908	3.6048	3.4331	3.3522	3.2743	3.1272	2.9906	2.7454	2.5320	2.3452
6	4.3553	4.1114	3.8887	3.7845	3.6847	3.4976	3.3255	3.0205	2.7594	2.5342
7	4.8684	4.5638	4.2883	4.1604	4.0386	3.8115	3.6046	3.2423	2.9370	2.6775
8	5.3349	4.9676	4.6389	4.4873	4.3436	4.0776	3.8372	3.4212	3.0758	2.7860
9	5.7590	5.3282	4.9464	4.7716	4.6065	4.3030	4.0310	3.5655	3.1842	2.8681
10	6.1446	5.6502	5.2161	5.0188	4.8332	4.4941	4.1925	3.6819	3.2689	2.9304
11	6.4951	5.9377	5.4527	5.2337	5.0286	4.6560	4.3271	3.7757	3.3351	2.9776
12	6.8137	6.1944	5.6603	5.4206	5.1971	4.7932	4.4392	3.8514	3.3868	3.0133
13	7.1034	6.4235	5.8424	5.5831	5.3423	4.9095	4.5327	3.9124	3.4272	3.0404
14	7.3667	6.6282	6.0021	5.7245	5.4675	5.0081	4.6106	3.9616	3.4587	3.0609
15	7.6061	6.8109	6.1422	5.8474	5.5755	5.0916	4.6755	4.0013	3.4834	3.0764
16	7.8237	6.9740	6.2651	5.9542	5.6685	5.1624	4.7296	4.0333	3.5026	3.0882
17	8.0216	7.1196	6.3729	6.0472	5.7487	5.2223	4.7746	4.0591	3.5177	3.0971
18	8.2014	7.2497	6.4674	6.1280	5.8178	5.2732	4.8122	4.0799	3.5294	3.1039
19	8.3649	7.3658	6.5504	6.1982	5.8775	5.3162	4.8435	4.0967	3.5386	3.1090
20	8.5136	7.4694	6.6231	6.2593	5.9288	5.3527	4.8696	4.1103	3.5458	3.1129
21	8.6487	7.5620	6.6870	6.3125	5.9731	5.3837	4.8913	4.1212	3.5514	3.1158
22	8.7715	7.6446	6.7429	6.3587	6.0113	5.4099	4.9094	4.1300	3.5558	3.1180
23	8.8832	7.7184	6.7921	6.3988	6.0442	5.4321	4.9245	4.1371	3.5592	3.1197
24	8.9847	7.7843	6.8351	6.4338	6.0726	5.4509	4.9371	4.1428	3.5619	3.1210
25	9.0770	7.8431	6.8729	6.4641	6.0971	5.4669	4.9476	4.1474	3.5640	3.1220
26	9.1609	7.8957	6.9061	6.4906	6.1182	5.4804	4.9563	4.1511	3.5656	3.1227
27	9.2372	7.9426	6.9352	6.5135	6.1364	5.4919	4.9636	4.1542	3.5669	3.1233
28	9.3066	7.9844	6.9607	6.5335	6.1520	5.5016	4.9697	4.1566	3.5679	3.1237
29	9.3696	8.0218	6.9830	6.5509	6.1656	5.5098	4.9747	4.1585	3.5687	3.1240
30	9.4269	8.0552	7.0027	6.5660	6.1772	5.5168	4.9789	4.1601	3.5693	3.1242
35	9.6442	8.1755	7.0700	6.6166	6.2153	5.5386	4.9915	4.1644	3.5708	3.1248
40	9.7791	8.2438	7.1050	6.6418	6.2335	5.5482	4.9966	4.1659	3.5712	3.1250
45	9.8628	8.2825	7.1232	6.6543	6.2421	5.5523	4.9986	4.1664	3.5714	3.1250
50	9.9148	8.3045	7.1327	6.6605	6.2463	5.5541	4.9995	4.1666	3.5714	3.1250
55	9.9471	8.3170	7.1376	6.6636	6.2482	5.5549	4.9998	4.1666	3.5714	3.1250

Table A-3 *Future Value of $1 at the End of n Periods*

EQUATION:

$FVIF_{i,n} = (1 + i)^n$

FINANCIAL CALCULATOR KEYS:

N	I	PV	PMT	FV
n	i	0	1.0	Table Value

Period	1%	2%	3%	4%	5%	6%	7%	8%	9%	10%
1	1.0100	1.0200	1.0300	1.0400	1.0500	1.0600	1.0700	1.0800	1.0900	1.1000
2	1.0201	1.0404	1.0609	1.0816	1.1025	1.1236	1.1449	1.1664	1.1881	1.2100
3	1.0303	1.0612	1.0927	1.1249	1.1576	1.1910	1.2250	1.2597	1.2950	1.3310
4	1.0406	1.0824	1.1255	1.1699	1.2155	1.2625	1.3108	1.3605	1.4116	1.4641
5	1.0510	1.1041	1.1593	1.2167	1.2763	1.3382	1.4026	1.4693	1.5386	1.6105
6	1.0615	1.1262	1.1941	1.2653	1.3401	1.4185	1.5007	1.5869	1.6771	1.7716
7	1.0721	1.1487	1.2299	1.3159	1.4071	1.5036	1.6058	1.7138	1.8280	1.9487
8	1.0829	1.1717	1.2668	1.3686	1.4775	1.5938	1.7182	1.8509	1.9926	2.1436
9	1.0937	1.1951	1.3048	1.4233	1.5513	1.6895	1.8385	1.9990	2.1719	2.3579
10	1.1046	1.2190	1.3439	1.4802	1.6289	1.7908	1.9672	2.1589	2.3674	2.5937
11	1.1157	1.2434	1.3842	1.5395	1.7103	1.8983	2.1049	2.3316	2.5804	2.8531
12	1.1268	1.2682	1.4258	1.6010	1.7959	2.0122	2.2522	2.5182	2.8127	3.1384
13	1.1381	1.2936	1.4685	1.6651	1.8856	2.1329	2.4098	2.7196	3.0658	3.4523
14	1.1495	1.3195	1.5126	1.7317	1.9799	2.2609	2.5785	2.9372	3.3417	3.7975
15	1.1610	1.3459	1.5580	1.8009	2.0789	2.3966	2.7590	3.1722	3.6425	4.1772
16	1.1726	1.3728	1.6047	1.8730	2.1829	2.5404	2.9522	3.4259	3.9703	4.5950
17	1.1843	1.4002	1.6528	1.9479	2.2920	2.6928	3.1588	3.7000	4.3276	5.0545
18	1.1961	1.4282	1.7024	2.0258	2.4066	2.8543	3.3799	3.9960	4.7171	5.5599
19	1.2081	1.4568	1.7535	2.1068	2.5270	3.0256	3.6165	4.3157	5.1417	6.1159
20	1.2202	1.4859	1.8061	2.1911	2.6533	3.2071	3.8697	4.6610	5.6044	6.7275
21	1.2324	1.5157	1.8603	2.2788	2.7860	3.3996	4.1406	5.0338	6.1088	7.4002
22	1.2447	1.5460	1.9161	2.3699	2.9253	3.6035	4.4304	5.4365	6.6586	8.1403
23	1.2572	1.5769	1.9736	2.4647	3.0715	3.8197	4.7405	5.8715	7.2579	8.9543
24	1.2697	1.6084	2.0328	2.5633	3.2251	4.0489	5.0724	6.3412	7.9111	9.8497
25	1.2824	1.6406	2.0938	2.6658	3.3864	4.2919	5.4274	6.8485	8.6231	10.835
26	1.2953	1.6734	2.1566	2.7725	3.5557	4.5494	5.8074	7.3964	9.3992	11.918
27	1.3082	1.7069	2.2213	2.8834	3.7335	4.8223	6.2139	7.9881	10.245	13.110
28	1.3213	1.7410	2.2879	2.9987	3.9201	5.1117	6.6488	8.6271	11.167	14.421
29	1.3345	1.7758	2.3566	3.1187	4.1161	5.4184	7.1143	9.3173	12.172	15.863
30	1.3478	1.8114	2.4273	3.2434	4.3219	5.7435	7.6123	10.063	13.268	17.449
40	1.4889	2.2080	3.2620	4.8010	7.0400	10.286	14.974	21.725	31.409	45.259
50	1.6446	2.6916	4.3839	7.1067	11.467	18.420	29.457	46.902	74.358	117.39
60	1.8167	3.2810	5.8916	10.520	18.679	32.988	57.946	101.26	176.03	304.48

(continued)

Table A-3 *Continued*

Period	12%	14%	15%	16%	18%	20%	24%	28%	32%	36%
1	1.1200	1.1400	1.1500	1.1600	1.1800	1.2000	1.2400	1.2800	1.3200	1.3600
2	1.2544	1.2996	1.3225	1.3456	1.3924	1.4400	1.5376	1.6384	1.7424	1.8496
3	1.4049	1.4815	1.5209	1.5609	1.6430	1.7280	1.9066	2.0972	2.3000	2.5155
4	1.5735	1.6890	1.7490	1.8106	1.9388	2.0736	2.3642	2.6844	3.0360	3.4210
5	1.7623	1.9254	2.0114	2.1003	2.2878	2.4883	2.9316	3.4360	4.0075	4.6526
6	1.9738	2.1950	2.3131	2.4364	2.6996	2.9860	3.6352	4.3980	5.2899	6.3275
7	2.2107	2.5023	2.6600	2.8262	3.1855	3.5832	4.5077	5.6295	6.9826	8.6054
8	2.4760	2.8526	3.0590	3.2784	3.7589	4.2998	5.5895	7.2058	9.2170	11.703
9	2.7731	3.2519	3.5179	3.8030	4.4355	5.1598	6.9310	9.2234	12.166	15.917
10	3.1058	3.7072	4.0456	4.4114	5.2338	6.1917	8.5944	11.806	16.060	21.647
11	3.4785	4.2262	4.6524	5.1173	6.1759	7.4301	10.657	15.112	21.199	29.439
12	3.8960	4.8179	5.3503	5.9360	7.2876	8.9161	13.215	19.343	27.983	40.037
13	4.3635	5.4924	6.1528	6.8858	8.5994	10.699	16.386	24.759	36.937	54.451
14	4.8871	6.2613	7.0757	7.9875	10.147	12.839	20.319	31.691	48.757	74.053
15	5.4736	7.1379	8.1371	9.2655	11.974	15.407	25.196	40.565	64.359	100.71
16	6.1304	8.1372	9.3576	10.748	14.129	18.488	31.243	51.923	84.954	136.97
17	6.8660	9.2765	10.761	12.468	16.672	22.186	38.741	66.461	112.14	186.28
18	7.6900	10.575	12.375	14.463	19.673	26.623	48.039	85.071	148.02	253.34
19	8.6128	12.056	14.232	16.777	23.214	31.948	59.568	108.89	195.39	344.54
20	9.6463	13.743	16.367	19.461	27.393	38.338	73.864	139.38	257.92	468.57
21	10.804	15.668	18.822	22.574	32.324	46.005	91.592	178.41	340.45	637.26
22	12.100	17.861	21.645	26.186	38.142	55.206	113.57	228.36	449.39	866.67
23	13.552	20.362	24.891	30.376	45.008	66.247	140.83	292.30	593.20	1178.7
24	15.179	23.212	28.625	35.236	53.109	79.497	174.63	374.14	783.02	1603.0
25	17.000	26.462	32.919	40.874	62.669	95.396	216.54	478.90	1033.6	2180.1
26	19.040	30.167	37.857	47.414	73.949	114.48	268.51	613.00	1364.3	2964.9
27	21.325	34.390	43.535	55.000	87.260	137.37	332.95	784.64	1800.9	4032.3
28	23.884	39.204	50.066	63.800	102.97	164.84	412.86	1004.3	2377.2	5483.9
29	26.750	44.693	57.575	74.009	121.50	197.81	511.95	1285.6	3137.9	7458.1
30	29.960	50.950	66.212	85.850	143.37	237.38	634.82	1645.5	4142.1	10143.
40	93.051	188.88	267.86	378.72	750.38	1469.8	5455.9	19427.	66521.	*
50	289.00	700.23	1083.7	1670.7	3927.4	9100.4	46890.	*	*	*
60	897.60	2595.9	4384.0	7370.2	20555.	56348.	*	*	*	*

*FVIF > 99,999.

Table A-4 *Future Value of an Annuity of $1 per Period for n Periods*

EQUATION:

$$PVIFA_{i,n} = \sum_{t=1}^{N}(1+i)^{n-t} = \frac{(1+i)^n - 1}{i}$$

FINANCIAL CALCULATOR KEYS:

n | i | 1.0 | 0 |
N | I | PV | PMT | FV
Table Value

Number of Periods	1%	2%	3%	4%	5%	6%	7%	8%	9%	10%
1	1.0000	1.0000	1.0000	1.0000	1.0000	1.0000	1.0000	1.0000	1.0000	1.0000
2	2.0100	2.0200	2.0300	2.0400	2.0500	2.0600	2.0700	2.0800	2.0900	2.1000
3	3.0301	3.0604	3.0909	3.1216	3.1525	3.1836	3.2149	3.2464	3.2781	3.3100
4	4.0604	4.1216	4.1836	4.2465	4.3101	4.3746	4.4399	4.5061	4.5731	4.6410
5	5.1010	5.2040	5.3091	5.4163	5.5256	5.6371	5.7507	5.8666	5.9847	6.1051
6	6.1520	6.3081	6.4684	6.6330	6.8019	6.9753	7.1533	7.3359	7.5233	7.7156
7	7.2135	7.4343	7.6625	7.8983	8.1420	8.3938	8.6540	8.9228	9.2004	9.4872
8	8.2857	8.5830	8.8923	9.2142	9.5491	9.8975	10.260	10.637	11.028	11.436
9	9.3685	9.7546	10.159	10.583	11.027	11.491	11.978	12.488	13.021	13.579
10	10.462	10.950	11.464	12.006	12.578	13.181	13.816	14.487	15.193	15.937
11	11.567	12.169	12.808	13.486	14.207	14.972	15.784	16.645	17.560	18.531
12	12.683	13.412	14.192	15.026	15.917	16.870	17.888	18.977	20.141	21.384
13	13.809	14.680	15.618	16.627	17.713	18.882	20.141	21.495	22.953	24.523
14	14.947	15.974	17.086	18.292	19.599	21.015	22.550	24.215	26.019	27.975
15	16.097	17.293	18.599	20.024	21.579	23.276	25.129	27.152	29.361	31.772
16	17.258	18.639	20.157	21.825	23.657	25.673	27.888	30.324	33.003	35.950
17	18.430	20.012	21.762	23.698	25.840	28.213	30.840	33.750	36.974	40.545
18	19.615	21.412	23.414	25.645	28.132	30.906	33.999	37.450	41.301	45.599
19	20.811	22.841	25.117	27.671	30.539	33.760	37.379	41.446	46.018	51.159
20	22.019	24.297	26.870	29.778	33.066	36.786	40.995	45.762	51.160	57.275
21	23.239	25.783	28.676	31.969	35.719	39.993	44.865	50.423	56.765	64.002
22	24.472	27.299	30.537	34.248	38.505	43.392	49.006	55.457	62.873	71.403
23	25.716	28.845	32.453	36.618	41.430	46.996	53.436	60.893	69.532	79.543
24	26.973	30.422	34.426	39.083	44.502	50.816	58.177	66.765	76.790	88.497
25	28.243	32.030	36.459	41.646	47.727	54.865	63.249	73.106	84.701	98.347
26	29.526	33.671	38.553	44.312	51.113	59.156	68.676	79.954	93.324	109.18
27	30.821	35.344	40.710	47.084	54.669	63.706	74.484	87.351	102.72	121.10
28	32.129	37.051	42.931	49.968	58.403	68.528	80.698	95.339	112.97	134.21
29	33.450	38.792	45.219	52.966	62.323	73.640	87.347	103.97	124.14	148.63
30	34.785	40.568	47.575	56.085	66.439	79.058	94.461	113.28	136.31	164.49
40	48.886	60.402	75.401	95.026	120.80	154.76	199.64	259.06	337.88	442.59
50	64.463	84.579	112.80	152.67	209.35	290.34	406.53	573.77	815.08	1163.9
60	81.670	114.05	163.05	237.99	353.58	533.13	813.52	1253.2	1944.8	3034.8

(continued)

MATHEMATICAL TABLES

Table A-4 Continued

Number of Periods	12%	14%	15%	16%	18%	20%	24%	28%	32%	36%
1	1.0000	1.0000	1.0000	1.0000	1.0000	1.0000	1.0000	1.0000	1.0000	1.0000
2	2.1200	2.1400	2.1500	2.1600	2.1800	2.2000	2.2400	2.2800	2.3200	2.3600
3	3.3744	3.4396	3.4725	3.5056	3.5724	3.6400	3.7776	3.9184	4.0624	4.2096
4	4.7793	4.9211	4.9934	5.0665	5.2154	5.3680	5.6842	6.0156	6.3624	6.7251
5	6.3528	6.6101	6.7424	6.8771	7.1542	7.4416	8.0484	8.6999	9.3983	10.146
6	8.1152	8.5355	8.7537	8.9775	9.4420	9.9299	10.980	12.136	13.406	14.799
7	10.089	10.730	11.067	11.414	12.142	12.916	14.615	16.534	18.696	21.126
8	12.300	13.233	13.727	14.240	15.327	16.499	19.123	22.163	25.678	29.732
9	14.776	16.085	16.786	17.519	19.086	20.799	24.712	29.369	34.895	41.435
10	17.549	19.337	20.304	21.321	23.521	25.959	31.643	38.593	47.062	57.352
11	20.655	23.045	24.349	25.733	28.755	32.150	40.238	50.398	63.122	78.998
12	24.133	27.271	29.002	30.850	34.931	39.581	50.895	65.510	84.320	108.44
13	28.029	32.089	34.352	36.786	42.219	48.497	64.110	84.853	112.30	148.47
14	32.393	37.581	40.505	43.672	50.818	59.196	80.496	109.61	149.24	202.93
15	37.280	43.842	47.580	51.660	60.965	72.035	100.82	141.30	198.00	276.98
16	42.753	50.980	55.717	60.925	72.939	87.442	126.01	181.87	262.36	377.69
17	48.884	59.118	65.075	71.673	87.068	105.93	157.25	233.79	347.31	514.66
18	55.750	68.394	75.836	84.141	103.74	128.12	195.99	300.25	459.45	700.94
19	63.440	78.969	88.212	98.603	123.41	154.74	244.03	385.32	607.47	954.28
20	72.052	91.025	102.44	115.38	146.63	186.69	303.60	494.21	802.86	1298.8
21	81.699	104.77	118.81	134.84	174.02	225.03	377.46	633.59	1060.8	1767.4
22	92.503	120.44	137.63	157.41	206.34	271.03	469.06	812.00	1401.2	2404.7
23	104.60	138.30	159.28	183.60	244.49	326.24	582.63	1040.4	1850.6	3271.3
24	118.16	158.66	184.17	213.98	289.49	392.48	723.46	1332.7	2443.8	4450.0
25	133.33	181.87	212.79	249.21	342.60	471.98	898.09	1706.8	3226.8	6053.0
26	150.33	208.33	245.71	290.09	405.27	567.38	1114.6	2185.7	4260.4	8233.1
27	169.37	238.50	283.57	337.50	479.22	681.85	1383.1	2798.7	5624.8	11198.0
28	190.70	272.89	327.10	392.50	566.48	819.22	1716.1	3583.3	7425.7	15230.3
29	214.58	312.09	377.17	456.30	669.45	984.07	2129.0	4587.7	9802.9	20714.2
30	241.33	356.79	434.75	530.31	790.95	1181.9	2640.9	5873.2	12941.	28172.3
40	767.09	1342.0	1779.1	2360.8	4163.2	7343.9	22729.	69377.	*	*
50	2400.0	4994.5	7217.7	10436.	21813.	45497.	*	*	*	*
60	7471.6	18535.	29220.	46058.	*	*	*	*	*	*

*FVIFA > 99,999.

Glossary*

Numbers

4/5ths Rule Rule stating that discrimination generally is considered to occur if the selection rate for a protected group is less than 80 percent (4/5ths) of the selection rate for the majority group or less than 80 percent of the group's representation in the relevant labor market.

8-K Monthly report to the SEC when significant events occur.

10-K Annual report filed by publicly traded companies to the SEC.

10-Q Quarterly report filed by publicly traded companies to the SEC.

40/30/30 rule A rule that identifies the sources of scrap, rework, and waste as 40 percent product design, 30 percent manufacturing processing, and 30 percent from suppliers.

360-degree feedback A process that uses multiple raters, including self-rating, to appraise employee performance and guide development.

401(k) plan An agreement in which a percentage of an employee's pay is withheld and invested in a tax-deferred account.

A

Abandoned product ranges The outcome of a firm narrowing its range of products to obtain economies of scale, which provides opportunities for other firms to enter the markets for the abandoned products.

ABC classification The classification of a group of items in decreasing order of annual dollar volume (price multiplied by projected volume) or other criteria. This array is then split into three classes, called A, B, and C. The A group usually represents 10 percent to 20 percent by number of items and 50 percent to 70 percent by projected dollar volume. The next grouping, B, usually represents about 20 percent of the items and about 20 percent of the dollar volume. The C class contains 60 percent to 70 percent of the items and represents about 10 percent to 30 percent of the dollar volume. The ABC principle states that effort and money can be saved through applying looser controls to the low-dollar-volume class items than will be applied to high-dollar-volume class items. The ABC principle is applicable to inventories, purchasing, sales, and so on. *Syn:* ABC analysis, distribution by value, Pareto analysis.

Ability test An assessment device that measures a person's capability to learn or acquire skills. Also referred to as an *aptitude test*.

Abnormal demand Demand in any period that is outside the limits established by management policy. This demand may come from a new customer or from existing customers whose own demand is increasing or decreasing. Care must be taken in evaluating the nature of the demand: Is it a volume change, is it a change in product mix, or is it related to the timing of the order?

Absolute advantage The ability to produce a good or service more cheaply than it can be produced elsewhere.

Absolute form of purchasing power parity Also called the "law of one price," this theory suggests that prices of two products of different countries should be equal when measured by a common currency.

Absorption costing A product costing approach that assigns all fixed and variable manufacturing costs to the units produced.

Accelerated depreciation method A depreciation method that provides for a high depreciation expense in the first year of use of an asset and a gradually declining expense thereafter.

Acceptable Quality Level (AQL) When a continuing series of lots is considered, a quality level that, for the purposes of sampling inspection, is the limit of a satisfactory process average.

Acceptance sampling Inspection of a sample from a lot to decide whether to accept or not accept that lot. There are two types: attributes sampling and variables sampling. In attributes sampling, the presence or absence of a characteristic is noted in each of the units inspected. In variables sampling, the numerical magnitude of a characteristic is measured and recorded for each inspected unit; this involves reference to a continuous scale of some kind.

Acceptance sampling plan A specific plan that indicates the sampling sizes and the associated acceptance or nonacceptance criteria to be used. In attributes sampling, for example, there are single, double, multiple, sequential, chain, and skip-lot sampling plans. In variables sampling, there are single, double, and sequential sampling plans.

Access control Hardware and software measures, such as user IDs and passwords, used to control access to information systems.

Account The form used to record additions and deductions for each individual asset, liability, owner's equity, revenue, and expense.

Account form The form of balance sheet with the assets section presented on the left-hand side and the liabilities and owner's equity sections presented on the right-hand side.

Account parameters and records Credit customer identifiers such as name, address, and the customer's bank transit routing number. These items are included in the customer's credit file.

Account receivable A claim against a customer for services rendered or goods sold on credit.

---

*Selected terms in Glossary from *APICS Dictionary,* 10th edition, © 2002 by APICS—The Educational Society for Resource Management, Alexandria, Virginia, USA. Reprinted with permission.

Glossary from the *Certified Quality Manager Handbook* by Duke Okes and Russell T. Westcott (eds), Second Edition. © 2001 by ASQ Quality Press, Milwaukee, Wisconsin, USA. Reprinted with permission.

Account reconciliation A disbursement-related service in which the bank develops a detailed report of checks paid as well as miscellaneous debits and stopped payments. In a full account reconciliation, the company also provides the bank with a record of checks drawn, and the bank informs the company of which checks remain outstanding.

Accountability The fact that the people with authority and responsibility are subject to reporting and justifying task outcomes to those above them in the chain of command.

Accounting The process of identifying, measuring, and communicating economic information to permit informed judgments and decisions by users of the information.

Accounting and Auditing Enforcement Release (AAER) Public document released by the SEC when a company commits financial statement fraud or other inappropriate activities.

Accounting anomalies Inaccuracies in source documents, journal entries, ledgers, or financial statements.

Accounting cycle 1: Procedures for analyzing, recording, classifying, summarizing, and reporting the transactions of a business. **2:** The sequence of basic accounting procedures during a fiscal period.

Accounting diversity The range of differences in national accounting practices.

Accounting equation The expression of the relationship between assets, liabilities, and owner's equity; it is most commonly stated as Assets = Liabilities + Owner's Equity.

Accounting exposures The transaction and translation risk exposures.

Accounting period concept An accounting principle that requires accounting reports be prepared at periodic intervals.

Accounting principles *See:* Accounting standards.

Accounting Principles Board (APB) Opinion No. 15 A standard issued by the Accounting Principles Board in the United States that outlines all the factors pertinent to the computation of earnings per common share.

Accounting profit A firm's net income as reported on its income statement.

Accounting standards The rules that govern the measuring and recording of economic activities and the reporting of accounting information to external users.

Accounting system 1: The methods and procedures used by a business to record and report financial data for use by management and external users. **2:** Policies and procedures for recording economic transactions in an organized manner.

Accounts payable 1: A liability that is generated by purchasing a good or service on credit. **2:** A financial obligation is created when good or services are purchased on credit.

Accounts receivable financing Indirect financing provided by an exporter for an importer by exporting goods and allowing for payment to be made at a later date.

Accounts receivable turnover 1: Computed by dividing days' sales outstanding into the number of days in the calculation period, which is usually 365. Indicates how many times per year the seller's investment in accounts receivable "turns over" into sales, which is an efficiency measure giving the same signal as days' sales outstanding. **2:** A measure used to determine a company's average collection period for receivables; computed by dividing net sales (or net credit sales) by average accounts receivable. **3:** Sales divided by average accounts receivable; a measure of the efficiency with which receivables are being collected.

Accounts receivable turnover ratio The rate at which a company collects its receivables; computed by dividing sales by average accounts receivable.

Accreditation Certification by a duly recognized body of the facilities, capability, objectivity, competence, and integrity of an agency, service, or operational group or individual to provide the specific service or operation needed. For example, the Registrar Accreditation Board (U.S.) accredits those organizations that register companies to the ISO 9000 series standards.

Accrual 1: A liability account that results from expenses incurred during the operating process that are not yet paid. **2:** Continually recurring short-term liabilities; liabilities such as wages and taxes that increase spontaneously with operations.

Accrued expenses Expenses that have been incurred but not paid. Sometimes called *accrued liabilities*.

Accrued liability Liabilities arising from end-of-period adjustments, not from specific transactions.

Accrued revenues Revenues that have been earned but not collected. Sometimes called *accrued assets*.

Acculturation The process of adjusting and adapting to a specific culture other than one's own.

Accumulated depreciation account The contra asset account used to accumulate the depreciation recognized to date on plant assets.

Accuracy A characteristic of measurement which addresses how close an observed value is to the true value. It answers the question, "Is it right?"

ACH credit Payment order transmitted through the automated clearing house system and originated by the payor. The routing bank (originating institution) in this case is the payor's disbursement bank.

ACH debit Payment order for payment through the automated clearing house system and originated by the payee, based on the prior authorization by the payor. This order is routed through the payee's bank (originating financial depository institution, or OFDI). Another name for an electronic depository transfer.

Acid-test ratio A ratio that measures the "instant" debt-paying ability of a company. Also known as *quick ratio*.

Acquisition The purchase of something, such as the purchase of one company by another company.

ACSI The American Customer Satisfaction Index, released for the first time in October 1994, is a new economic indicator, a cross-industry measure of the satisfaction of U.S. household customers with the quality of the goods and services available to them—both those goods and services produced within the United States and those provided as imports from foreign firms that have substantial market shares or dollar sales. The ACSI is cosponsored by the University of Michigan Business School and ASQ.

Act of state doctrine Rule that a court should not question the validity of actions taken by a foreign government in its own country.

Action plan The detail plan to implement the actions needed to achieve strategic goals and objectives (similar, but not as comprehensive as a project plan).

Active investment strategy An approach to investing which involves relatively more trading and active monitoring of the portfolio, and many times is motivated by a philosophy that the investor can "beat the market." Active strategy managers would rarely buy a security with the intention of holding it to maturity. For example, when an analyst forecasts a change in interest rates, trading strategies can be devised to enhance investment profits.

Active listening Paying attention solely to what others are saying (for example, rather than what you think of what they're saying or what you want to say back to them).

Active practice The performance of job-related tasks and duties by trainees during training.

ActiveX A Microsoft scripting language for small applications for specific tasks.

Activity A defined piece of work that consumes time; task.

Activity analysis The study of employee effort and other business records to determine the cost of activities.

Activity base The measure used to allocate factory overhead. Also known as *allocation base,* or *activity driver.*

Activity base usage The amount of activity base used by a particular product.

Activity-based costing (ABC) An accounting framework based on determining the cost of activities and allocating these costs to products, using activity rates. An approach to costing that focuses on activities as the fundamental cost objects. It uses the cost of these activities as the basis for assigning costs to other cost objects such as products, services, or customers. It provides more accurate allocation of indirect costs than traditional methods.

Activity-based management (ABM) 1: A discipline that focuses on the management of activities for improving the value received by the customer and the profit achieved by providing this value. **2:** Managing with an accounting system that allocates costs to products based on resources employed to produce the product.

Activity cost pools Cost accumulations that are associated with a given activity, such as machine usage, inspections, moving, and production setups.

Activity in the box (AIB) A form of network diagramming in which activities are represented by boxes.

Activity network diagram (AND) *See:* arrow diagram.

Activity on the arrow (AOA) A form of network diagramming in which activities are represented by arrows.

Activity rates The cost of an activity per unit of activity base, determined by dividing the activity cost pool by the activity base.

Activity ratios *See:* Efficiency ratios.

Actual cost The amount that has actually been expended.

Actual demand Actual demand is composed of customer orders (and often allocations of items, ingredients, or raw materials to production or distribution). Actual demand nets against or "consumes" the forecast, depending upon the rules chosen over a time horizon. For example, actual demand will totally replace forecast inside the sold-out customer order backlog horizon (often called the demand time fence), but will net against the forecast outside this horizon based on the chosen forecast consumption rule.

Actual (realized) rate of return, $\bar{k}_s$ The rate of return on a common stock actually received by stockholders. $\bar{k}_s$ may be greater than or less than $\hat{k}_s$ and/or k_s.

Actual volume Actual output expressed as a volume of capacity. It is used in the calculation of variances when compared with demonstrated capacity (practical capacity) or budgeted capacity.

Acute crisis stage The stage at which a crisis actually occurs.

Ad hoc groups Problem-specific teams or groups consisting of individuals who possess the relevant knowledge to address a particular organizational problem.

Ad hoc reports Unplanned, special reports designed to help solve specific problems. Also called *on-demand reports.*

Adaptability screening A selection procedure that usually involves interviewing both the candidate for an overseas assignment and his or her family members to determine how well they are likely to adapt to another culture.

Adaptable management A firm's management is able to adapt managerial techniques to the unique needs of specific countries.

Adaptation Refers to the stage in the expatriation process in which the expatriate must learn to cope with cultures, laws, political systems, legal processes, and other subtleties that are different from his or her own.

Adaptation problems Difficulties that arise for expatriates during the adaptation process. They are especially common when the physical and sociocultural environments are at odds with the expatriate's own value system and living habits.

Adaptive transformative innovations Modify and adjust existing modern technologies (for example, in farming, a modern, more efficient tractor replaces an older, less efficient model).

Additional funds needed (AFN) Funds that a firm must raise externally through borrowing or by selling new stock.

Additional paid-in capital Funds received in excess of par value when a firm issues new stock.

Add-on interest Interest that is calculated and then added to the amount borrowed to obtain the total dollar amount to be paid back in equal installments.

Adjourning The stage of team development in which members prepare for the team's disbandment.

Adjustable-rate preferred stock (ARPS) Preferred stock on which the dividend is reset quarterly.

Adjusted r^2 A measure for a statistical model's goodness of fit which compensates for the upward bias in goodness-of-fit resulting from the inclusion of additional predictor variables.

Adjusted trial balance The trial balance which is prepared after all the adjusting entries have been posted. Used to verify the equality of the total debit balances and total credit balances before preparing the financial statements.

Adjusting entries Entries required at the end of an accounting period to bring the ledger up to date.

Adjusting process The process of updating the accounts at the end of a period.

Administrative expenses (general expenses) Expenses incurred in the administration or general operations of a business.

Administrative model A decision-making model that describes how managers actually make decisions in situations characterized by nonprogrammed decisions, uncertainty, and ambiguity.

Administrative principles A subfield of the classical management perspective that focused on the total organization rather than the individual worker, delineating the management functions of planning, organizing, commanding, coordinating, and controlling.

ADSL (Asynchronous DSL) DSL Technology in which the downstream communication (to the subscriber) is several times greater than the upstream communication (from the subscriber). *See:* DSL.

Adult learning principles Key issues about how adults learn, which impact how education and training of adults should be designed.

Advance pricing agreement An agreement between a company and tax authorities that gives the company approval for using certain transfer pricing methods and the procedures for its application.

Advanced determination ruling (ADR) A transfer pricing guideline in the United States that allows a company to get approval for a parent-subsidiary specific product pricing.

Adverse selection Situation in which only higher-risk employees select and use certain benefits.

Advertising Nonpersonal communication that is paid for by an identified sponsor, and involves either mass communication via newspapers, magazines, radio, television, and other media (for example, billboards, bus stop signage) or direct-to-consumer communication via direct mail.

Advised line A standard lending service used abroad, which is very similar to credit lines in the United States. The advised line involves unsecured lending of up to one year maturity, available on short notice to the borrower.

Advising bank Corresponding bank in the beneficiary's country to which the issuing bank sends the letter of credit.

Affidavit Written statement or declaration given under oath.

Affiliate programs Advertisers pay for each person who enters their Web site via a link on the host site or pays for each sale generated.

Affinity diagram A management and planning tool used to organize ideas into natural groupings in a way that stimulates new, creative ideas. Also known as the "KJ" method.

Affirmative action 1: A policy requiring employers to take positive steps to guarantee equal employment opportunities for people within protected groups. **2:** Process in which employers identify problem areas, set goals, and take positive steps to enhance opportunities for protected-class members.

Affirmative Action Plan (AAP) Formal document that an employer compiles annually for submission to enforcement agencies.

After-tax cost of debt, k_{dT} The relevant cost of new debt, taking into account the tax deductibility of interest; used to calculate the WACC.

Agencies Securities issued by governmental agencies and several private financing institutions that have governmental backing.

Agency problem 1: A potential conflict of interest between (1) the principals (outside shareholders) and the agent (manager) or (2) stockholders and creditors (debtholders). **2:** May develop when the interests of the shareholders are not aligned with the interests of the manager.

Agent 1: A representative or intermediary for the firm that works to develop business and sales strategies and that develops contacts. **2:** Marketing intermediary who does not take title to the products but develops marketing strategy and establishes contacts abroad.

Agent of change Any person (such as an employee, a consultant, or a board member) whose work results in significant changes in the way workers perform their jobs. Often, systems analysts are agents of change because they drive companies to take fuller advantage of information technology.

Agents/brokers Independent middlemen who bring buyers and sellers together, provide market information to one or the other parties, but never take title to the merchandise. While most agents/brokers work for the seller, some do work for buyers.

Aggregate forecast An estimate of sales, often time phased, for a grouping of products or product families produced by a facility or firm. Stated in terms of units, dollars, or both, the aggregate forecast is used for sales and production planning (or for sales and operations planning) purposes.

Aggregate plan 1: *n:* A plan that includes budgeted levels of finished goods, inventory, production backlogs, and changes in the workforce to support the production strategy. Aggregated information (for example, product line, family) rather than product information is used, hence the name aggregate plan. **2: Aggregate planning** *v:* A process to develop tactical plans to support the organization's business plan. Aggregate planning usually includes the development, analysis, and maintenance of plans for total sales, total production, targeted inventory, and targeted customer backlog for families of products. The production plan is the result of the aggregate planning process. Two approaches to aggregate planning exist—production planning and sales and operations planning.

Aggressive approach A policy where all of the fixed assets of a firm are financed with long-term capital, but *some* of the firm's permanent current assets are financed with short-term nonspontaneous sources of funds.

Aggressive strategy A strategy that minimizes the amount of long-term financing used. This strategy generally results in a lower current ratio and higher but more volatile profitability during periods of normal yield curves.

Agile approach or agility *See:* lean approach

Agility The ability to successfully manufacture and market a broad range of low-cost, high-quality products and services with short lead times and varying volumes that provide enhanced value to customers through customization. Agility merges the four distinctive competencies of cost, quality, dependability, and flexibility.

Aging schedule A report showing how long accounts receivable have been outstanding; the report divides receivables into specified periods, which provides information about the proportion of receivables that is current and the proportion that is past due for given lengths of time. Shows a percent breakdown of present receivables, with the categories shown typically as follows: current, 0–30 days past due, 31–60 days past due, and over 90 days past due.

Aging the receivables The process of analyzing the accounts receivable and classifying them according to various age groupings, with the due date being the base point for determining age.

Airfreight Transport of goods by air; accounts for less than 1 percent of the total volume of international shipments, but more than 20 percent of value.

Airway bill Receipt for a shipment by air, which includes freight charges and title to the merchandise.

Algorithm A sequence of steps one takes to solve a problem. Often, these steps are expressed as mathematical formulas.

Alliances Firms with unique strengths that join to be more effective and efficient than their competitors. *See:* partnership/alliances.

All-in-rate Rate used in charging customers for accepting banker's acceptances, consisting of the discount interest rate plus the commission.

Allocated item In an MRP system, an item for which a picking order has been released to the stockroom but not yet sent from the stockroom.

Allocation mentality The tradition of acquiring resources based not on what is needed but on what is available.

Allowance for doubtful accounts A contra-asset (receivable) account representing the amount of receivables that are estimated to be uncollectible.

Allowance for uncollectible assets as a percentage of receivables Allowance for doubtful accounts divided by accounts receivable; a measure of the percentage of receivables estimated to be uncollectible.

Allowance method A method of accounting for uncollectible receivables, whereby advance provision for the uncollectibles is made.

Allowances for deferred income tax assets A contra account to the deferred income tax assets account.

Alpha risk *See:* producer's risk

Alternative evaluation Stage in the consumer decision process when consumers select one of the several alternatives (brands, dealers, and so on) available to them.

Ambiguity The goal to be achieved or the problem to be solved is unclear, alternatives are difficult to define, and information about outcomes is unavailable.

American-based leadership and motivation theories Traditionally, these theories advance the notion that participative leadership behavior is more effective than authoritative leadership behavior. Popular theories include McGregor's *Theory X and Theory Y Managers* and Likert's *System 4 Management*.

American depository receipts (ADRs) Certificates representing ownership in stocks of foreign companies, which are held in trust by a bank located in the country in which the stock is traded. ADRs are traded on stock exchanges in the United States.

American Institute of Certified Public Accountants (AICPA) An organization that issues the generally accepted auditing standards in the form of Statements on Auditing Standards in the United States.

American terms Quoting a currency rate as the U.S. dollar against a country's currency (for example, U.S. dollars/yen).

Amortization The periodic expense attributed to the decline in usefulness of an intangible asset.

Amortized loan A loan that is repaid in equal payments over its life.

Analog model While physical in form, an analog model does not have a physical appearance similar to the real object or situation it represents.

Analog signal A continuous signal, for example a human voice or the movement of the hands in an analog watch, that represents different degrees of mechanical or electrical power.

Analogy 1: A method for estimating market potential when data for the particular market do not exist. **2:** A technique used to generate new ideas by translating concepts from one application to another.

Analysis of means (ANOM) A statistical procedure for troubleshooting industrial processes and analyzing the results of experimental designs with factors at fixed levels. It provides a graphical display of data. Ellis R. Ott developed the procedure in 1967 because he observed that nonstatisticians had difficulty understanding analysis of variance. Analysis of means is easier for quality practitioners to use because it is an extension of the control chart. In 1973, Edward G. Schilling further extended the concept, enabling analysis of means to be used with nonnormal distributions and attributes data where the normal approximation to the binomial distribution does not apply. This is referred to as analysis of means for treatment effects.

Analysis of variance (ANOVA) A basic statistical technique for analyzing experimental data. It subdivides the total variation of a data set into meaningful component parts associated with specific sources of variation in order to test a hypothesis on the parameters of the model or to estimate variance components. There are three models: fixed, random, and mixed.

Analytical anomalies Relationships, procedures, or events that do not make sense.

Analytical thinking Breaking down a problem or situation into discrete parts to understand how each part contributes to the whole.

Anchor stores Dominant, large-scale stores that are expected to draw customers to a shopping center.

Andon board A visual device (usually lights) displaying status alerts that can easily be seen by those who should respond.

Angel financing Financing provided by a wealthy individual who believes in the idea for a start-up and provides personal funds and advice to help the business get started.

Annual compounding The arithmetic process of determining the final value of a cash flow or series of cash flows when interest is added once a year.

Annual percentage rate (APR) The rate reported to borrowers—it is the periodic rate times the number of periods in the year; thus, interest compounding is not considered. The periodic rate × the number of periods per year.

Annual report A report issued annually by a corporation to its stockholders. It contains basic financial statements, as well as management's opinion of the past year's operations, and the firm's future prospects.

Annuity A series of payments of an equal amount at fixed intervals for a specified number of periods.

Annuity due An annuity whose payments occur at the beginning of each period.

ANOVA *See:* analysis of variance.

ANSI American National Standards Institute.

Antecedent The *if* component of an *if-then* rule knowledge representation.

Anticipation This transfer rule initiates a cash transfer before the related deposit is made.

Antidumping Laws that many countries use to impose tariffs on foreign imports. They are designed to help domestic industries that are injured by unfair competition from abroad due to imported products being sold at less than fair market value.

Antidumping laws Laws designed to help domestic industries that are injured by unfair competition from abroad due to imports being sold at less than fair value.

Antiplanning Belief that any attempt to lay out specific and "rational" plans is either foolish or dangerous and downright evil. Correct approach is to live in existing systems, react in terms of one's own experience, and not try to change them by means of some grandiose scheme or mathematical model.

Antitrust laws Laws that prohibit monopolies, restraint of trade, and conspiracies to inhibit competition. Apply to unfair methods of competition that have a direct, substantial, and reasonably foreseeable effect on the domestic, import, or export commerce of the United States.

Antivirus software Software designed to detect and intercept computer viruses.

AOQ Average outgoing quality.

AOQL Average outgoing quality limit.

Appellate Court Review court to which participants in lower court cases can have their cases reviewed or retried if they are unhappy with the outcome.

Applet A small software application, usually written in Java or another programming language for the Web.

Applicant pool All persons who are actually evaluated for selection.

Applicant population A subset of the labor force population that is available for selection using a particular recruiting approach.

Application A computer program that addresses a general or specific business or scientific need. General applications include electronic spreadsheets and word processors. Specific applications are written especially for a business unit to accommodate special activities.

Application controls Programmed procedures in application software and related manual procedures, designed to help ensure the completeness and accuracy of information processing. Examples include computerized edit checks of input data, and numerical sequence checks and manual procedures to follow up on items listed in exception reports.

Application/Data independence A situation in which an application can be developed to manipulate data without regard to the physical organization of the data in the files. This is achieved in the database approach to data management.

Application form A device for collecting information about an applicant's education, previous job experience, and other background characteristics.

Application generator A software tool that expedites the application development process. Often, the term is synonymous with fourth generation language. Modern application generators include graphical user interfaces.

Application service provider (ASP) A firm that rents the use of software applications through an Internet link.

Application-specific software A collective term for all computer programs that are designed specifically to address certain business problems, such as a program specifically written to deal with a company's market research effort.

Appraisal costs Costs to detect, measure, evaluate, and audit products and processes to ensure that they conform to customer requirements and performance standards.

Appreciation Increase in the value of a currency.

Appropriation The amount of a corporation's retained earnings that has been restricted and therefore is not available for distribution to shareholders as dividends.

AQL Acceptable quality level.

Arbitrage 1: An activity done to take advantage of rate discrepancies by buying the currency in the low-cost markets and selling in the high-cost markets. **2:** Action to capitalize on a discrepancy in quoted prices; in many cases, there is no investment of funds tied up for any length of time.

Arbitration The procedure for settling a dispute in which an objective third party hears both sides and makes a decision; a procedure for resolving conflict in the international business arena through the use of intermediaries such as representatives of chambers of commerce, trade associations, or third-country institutions.

Area expertise A knowledge of the basic systems in a particular region or market.

Area structure An organizational structure in which geographic divisions are responsible for all manufacturing and marketing in their respective areas.

Area studies Training programs that provide factual preparation prior to an overseas assignment.

Arithmetic logic unit (ALU) The electronic circuitry in the central processing unit of a computer responsible for arithmetic and logic operations.

Arm's-length price A price that unrelated parties would have reached.

Arraignment Court hearing where charges against the defendant are read. At the arraignment, the defendants may plead guilty, not guilty, or nolo contendere.

Arrow diagram A management and planning tool used to develop the best possible schedule and appropriate controls to accomplish the schedule; the critical path method (CPM) and the program evaluation review technique (PERT) make use of arrow diagrams.

Artificial intelligence The study and creation of computer programs that mimic human behavior. This discipline combines the interests of computer science, cognitive science, linguistics, and management information systems. The main subfields of AI are: robotics, artificial vision, natural language processors, and expert systems.

Artificial vision A subfield of artificial intelligence devoted to the development of hardware and software that can mimic human vision.

AS-9100 A standard for the aeronautics industry embracing the ISO 9001 standard.

ASCII (pronounced: AS-kee) American Standard Code for Information Interchange, a computer encoding scheme whereby each group of 8 bits (a byte) uniquely represents a character.

Asian dollar market Market in Asia in which banks collect deposits and make loans denominated in U.S. dollars.

Asia-Pacific Economic Cooperation (APEC) An organization committed to the trade and investment concept of open regionalism. Its twenty-member countries include Australia, Brunei, Canada, Chile, China (including Hong Kong), Indonesia, Japan, Korea, Malaysia, Mexico, New Zealand, Papua New Guinea, Peru, Philippines, Russia, Singapore, Chinese Taipei, Thailand, the United States, and Vietnam.

Ask price Price at which a trader of foreign exchange (typically a bank) is willing to sell a particular currency.

ASP *See:* Application Service Provider.

ASQ American Society for Quality, a society of individual and organizational members dedicated to the ongoing development, advancement, and promotion of quality concepts, principles, and technologies.

Assembler A compiler for an assembly language.

Assemble-to-order A production environment where a good or service can be assembled after receipt of a customer's order. The key components (bulk, semifinished, intermediate, subassembly, fabricated, purchased, packing, and so on) used in the assembly or finishing process are planned and usually stocked in anticipation of a customer order. Receipt of an order initiates assembly of the customized product. This strategy is useful where a large number of end products (based on the selection of options and accessories) can be assembled from common components. *Syn:* finish-to-order. *See:* make-to-order, make-to-stock.

Assembly languages Second-generation programming languages that assemble several bytes into groups of characters that are human-readable, to expedite programming tasks.

Assessment An estimate or determination of the significance, importance, or value of something.

Assessment center A technique for selecting individuals with high managerial potential based on their performance on a series of simulated managerial tasks.

Asset-and-liability approach The recognition of deferred tax liabilities or deferred tax assets for the income tax that will be levied or recovered on temporary timing differences between the taxable income amount and the pretax financial income amount.

Asset-based lending A form of collateralized lending which has a claim on an asset or group of assets, ordinarily receivables or inventory, which could be easily sold if the borrower defaults on the loan.

Asset-based loans A source of financing obtained from a bank or commercial finance company secured by accounts receivable or inventory.

Asset fraud Financial statement fraud in which assets are recorded at higher amounts than they should be.

Asset management ratios A set of ratios that measures how effectively a firm is managing its assets.

Asset misappropriations Theft that is committed by stealing receipts, stealing assets on hand, or by committing some type of disbursement fraud.

Asset securitization Has become prevalent in the United States because of the need for banks to increase their capital-to-assets ratio.

Asset swap A swap created to hedge cash flows related to assets or investments.

Asset turnover Total sales divided by average total assets; a measure of the amount of sales revenue generated with each dollar of assets.

Assets Physical items (tangible) or rights (intangible) that have value and that are owned by the business entity.

Assignable cause *See:* special causes.

Assignment of proceeds Arrangement which allows the original beneficiary of a letter of credit to pledge or assign proceeds to an end supplier.

Associated firms *See:* Representative firms.

Association of Certified Fraud Examiners (ACFE) An international organization, based in Austin, Texas, dedicated to fighting fraud and white-collar crime.

Association of Southeast Asian Nations (ASEAN) The most important trading bloc in Southeast Asia. The member countries include Brunei, Cambodia, Indonesia, Laos, Malaysia, Myanmar, the Philippines, Singapore, Thailand, and Vietnam. The member countries established a free-trade area.

Asymmetric information The situation in which managers have different (better) information about their firm's prospects than do outside investors.

Asymmetric key encryption Encryption technology in which a message is encrypted with one key and decrypted with another.

Asynchronous communications Data communications whereby the communications devices must synchronize the transmission and reception after the transmission of each byte. Each byte is accompanied by synchronization bits, such as start and stop bits.

Atomic transaction A transaction whose entry is not complete until all entries into the appropriate files have been successfully completed. A data entry control.

Attitude 1: A cognitive and affective evaluation that predisposes a person to act in a certain way. **2:** Learned predispositions to respond to an object or class of objects in a consistently favorable or unfavorable way.

Attitude survey One that focuses on employees' feelings and beliefs about their jobs and the organization.

Attribute data Go/no-go information. The control charts based on attribute data include fraction defective chart, number of affected units chart, count chart, count per-unit chart, quality score chart, and demerit chart.

Attributions Judgments about what caused a person's behavior—either characteristics of the person or of the situation.

Auction preferred stock (APS) Preferred stock on which the dividend is reset every forty-nine days through an auction bidding process.

Audit A planned, independent, and documented assessment to determine whether agreed-upon requirements are being met.

Audit command language (ACL) Popular commercial data-mining software; helps investigators detect fraud.

Audit committee Responsible for assessing the adequacy of internal control systems and the integrity of financial statements.

Audit program The organizational structure, commitment, and documented methods used to plan and perform audits.

Audit team The group of individuals conducting an audit under the direction of a team leader, relevant to a particular product, process, service, contract, or project.

Audit trail 1: Documents and records that can be used to trace transactions. **2:** Names, dates, and other references in computer files that can help an auditor track down the person who used an IS for a transaction, legal or illegal.

Auditee The individual or organization being audited.

Auditor An individual or organization carrying out an audit.

Auditor's report A report that communicates the results of the external audit, and the format of the report is necessarily mandated by the nature of the audit. Because there are no worldwide uniform accounting and auditing standards, there is no worldwide uniform format of an auditor's report.

Autarky Self-sufficiency: a country that is not participating in international trade.

Authentication The process of ensuring that the person who sends a message to or receives a message from another party is indeed that person.

Authoritarianism The belief that power and status differences *should* exist within the organization.

Authoritative decision making Refers to a style of decision making in which the leader simply makes a decision and instructs followers what to do without consulting or involving them in the decision-making process.

Authority The formal and legitimate right of a manager to make decisions, issue orders, and allocate resources to achieve organizationally desired outcomes.

Autocratic leader A leader who tends to centralize authority and rely on legitimate, reward, and coercive power to manage subordinates.

Autocratic management 1: Autocratic managers are concerned with developing an efficient workplace and have little concern for people (theory X assumptions about people). They typically make decisions without input from subordinates, relying on their positional power. **2:** Management conducted by a few key people who do not accept advice or participation from other employees.

Automated clearing house (ACH) A quick and relatively inexpensive means of electronically processing large numbers of routine transactions. This system is comprised of a loosely tied network of associations spread across the country. The electronic equivalent of the paper check clearing system.

Automated storage/retrieval system (AS/RS) A high-density rack inventory storage system with vehicles automatically loading and unloading the racks.

Autonomation 1: Automated shutdown of a line, process, or machine upon detection of an abnormality or defect. **2:** (Jidoka) Use of specially equipped automated machines capable of detecting a defect in a single part, stopping the process, and signaling for assistance.

Autonomy The extent of individual freedom and discretion in the work and its scheduling.

Autoregressive model A time series model that uses a regression relationship based on historical time series values to predict the future time series values.

Availability The ability of a product to be in a state to perform its designated function under stated conditions at a given time. Availability can be expressed by the ratio:

$$\frac{uptime}{uptime + downtime}$$

Availability analysis An analysis that identifies the number of protected-class members available to work in the appropriate labor markets in given jobs.

Availability float The delay from the time a check is deposited and the time when funds are available to be spent. This time lag may not always coincide with the amount of time it takes the check to actually clear, but generally the two are closely linked. Delays in collecting checks caused by delays in the check clearing process after the check has been deposited.

Availability schedule Listing of how long after deposit checks will become "good funds" for spending by the depositor. Prior to recording available funds, the bank will credit the depositor's ledger balance, but the portion of the total deposit available as "good funds" ready to be spent varies according to the bank's schedule.

Available-for-sale security A debt or equity security that is not classified as either a held-to-maturity or a trading security.

Available inventory The on-hand inventory balance minus allocations, reservations, backorders, and (usually) quantities held for quality problems. Often called beginning available balance. *Syn:* beginning available balance, net inventory.

Available-to-promise (ATP) The uncommitted portion of a company's inventory and planned production maintained in the master schedule to support customer-order promising. The ATP quantity is the uncommitted inventory balance in the first period and is normally calculated for each period in which an MPS receipt is scheduled. In the first period, ATP includes on-hand inventory less customer orders that are due and overdue. Three methods of calculation are used: discrete ATP, cumulative ATP with lookahead, and cumulative ATP without lookahead. *See:* discrete available-to-promise, cumulative available-to-promise.

Average *See:* mean

Average chart A control chart in which the subgroup average, $\overline{X}$, is used to evaluate the stability of the process level.

Average collection period How long the typical customer is taking to pay its bills. Alternately, how long, on average, the seller is taking to collect its receivables. It is computed by dividing accounts receivable by daily sales. Also known as *days sales outstanding*.

Average cost method 1: The method of inventory costing that is based on the assumption that costs should be charged against revenue in accordance with the weighted average unit costs of the items sold. **2:** An accounting principle by which the value of inventory is estimated as the average cost of the items in inventory.

Average inventory One-half the average lot size plus the safety stock, when demand and lot sizes are expected to be relatively uniform over time. The average can be calculated as an average of several inventory observations taken over several historical time periods; for example, 12-month ending inventories may be averaged. When demand and lot sizes are not uniform, the stock level versus time can be graphed to determine the average.

Average outgoing quality (AOQ) The expected average quality level of outgoing product for a given value of incoming product quality.

Average outgoing quality limit (AOQL) The maximum average outgoing quality over all possible levels of incoming quality for a given acceptance sampling plan and disposal specification.

Average rate of return A method of evaluating capital investment proposals that focuses on the expected profitability of the investment.

Average tax rate Taxes paid divided by taxable income.

Avoidance The pricing of invoices in the seller's currency.

B

B2B marketplace An electronic marketplace set up by an intermediary where buyers and sellers meet.

Back scheduling A technique for calculating operation start dates and due dates. The schedule is computed starting with the due date for the order and working backward to determine the required start date and/or due dates for each operation. *Syn:* backward scheduling. *Ant:* forward scheduling.

Back value date The date that cleared checks are assigned and may cause funds to be drawn from an account before the check actually arrives at the drawee bank.

Backbone The network of copper lines, optical fibers, and radio satellites that supports the Internet.

Backflush A method of inventory bookkeeping where the book (computer) inventory of components is automatically reduced by the computer after completion of activity on the component's upper-level parent item based on what should have been used as specified on the bill of material and allocation records. This approach has the disadvantage of a built-in differential between the book record and what is physically in stock. *Syn:* explode-to-deduct, post-deduct inventory transaction processing.

Backflush costing The application of costs based on the output of a process. Backflush costing is usually associated with repetitive manufacturing environments.

Backtranslation The retranslation of text to the original language by a different person than the one who made the first translation. Useful to find translation errors.

Backup Periodic duplication of data in order to guard against loss.

Backward chaining (backward reasoning) The processes in which an expert system searches the conditions that would bring about the achievement of a specified goal. For example, an ES uses backward chaining to determine how long to invest how much money in which stocks to achieve a specified yield.

Backward innovation The development of a drastically simplified version of a product.

Bad debt expense An expense representing receivables and/or revenues that are presumed not to be collectible.

Badwill What international corporations create when they exploit foreign markets without sharing benefits with locals.

Balance fractions, inventory The percent of an inventory purchase order that remains as inventory over succeeding months.

Balance fractions, payables The dollar amount remaining to be paid in succeeding months as a percent of the original accounts payable balance.

Balance of payments 1: Statement of inflow and outflow payments for a particular country. **2:** A statement of all transactions between one country and the rest of the world during a given period; a record of flows of goods, services, and investments across borders.

Balance of payments deficit When a country's cumulative imports exceed its cumulative exports.

Balance of payments surplus When a country's cumulative exports exceed its cumulative imports.

Balance of the account The amount of difference between the debits and the credits that have been entered into an account.

Balance of trade Difference between the value of merchandise exports and merchandise imports.

Balance on goods and services Balance of trade, plus the net amount of payments of interest and dividends to foreign investors and from investment, as well as receipts and payments resulting from international tourism and other transactions.

Balance reporting services Means by which the treasurer may inquire by phone or PC hook-up about the balance positions in many different accounts and about transactions affecting the accounts.

Balance sheet 1: A financial statement that shows the firm's financial position with respect to assets and liabilities at a specific point in time. **2:** A financial statement listing the assets, liabilities, and owner's equity of a business entity as of a specific date.

Balance-sheet approach Compensation package that equalizes cost differences between international assignments and those in the home country.

Balance sheet recognition Information presented within the balance sheet.

Balanced scorecard 1: Translates an organization's mission and strategy into a comprehensive set of performance measures to provide a basis for strategic measurement and management, utilizing four balanced views: financial, customers, internal business processes, and learning and growth. **2:** A comprehensive management control system that balances traditional financial measures with measures of customer service, internal business processes, and the organization's capacity for learning and growth. **3:** A set of financial and nonfinancial measures that reflect multiple performance dimensions of a business.

Balanced tenancy Occurs where the stores complement each other in merchandise offerings.

Balancing operations In repetitive Just-in-Time production, matching actual output cycle times of all operations to the demand or use for parts as required by final assembly and, eventually, as required by the market.

Balassa-Samuelson Theory A theory that states inflation is difficult to get rid of in a fast-growing economy.

Bandwidth The capacity of the communications channel; the number of signal streams the channel can support. A greater bandwidth also supports a greater bit rate, that is, transmission speed.

Bank deposit notes Short-term debt securities issued by banks, which range from nine months to thirty years in maturity, and have an active secondary market.

Bank draft A financial withdrawal document drawn against a bank.

Banker's acceptance (BA) A corporate time draft drawn on the buyer, whose bank agrees to pay ("accepts") the amount if the buyer does not. Related to this, a short-term acceptance facility allows the selling firm to initiate drafts (called bills of exchange) against the buyer's bank instead of against the buyer, which can be discounted at the bank. A time draft drawn against a deposit in a commercial bank but with payment at maturity guaranteed by the bank.

Bank for International Settlements (BIS) Institution that facilitates cooperation among countries involved in international transactions and provides assistance to countries experiencing international payment problems.

Bank Holding Company Act of 1956 Prohibited further acquisitions by bank holding companies unless specifically allowed by state law in the state of the proposed acquisition.

Bank Letter of Credit Policy Policy that enables banks to confirm letters of credit by foreign banks supporting the purchase of U.S. exports.

Bank notes Technically not deposits, these bank debt obligations thereby avoid FDIC insurance premiums which also forfeits deposit insurance coverage.

Bank reconciliation The analysis that details the items responsible for the difference between the cash balance reported in the bank statement and the balance of the cash account in the ledger.

Bank relationship policy Document that establishes the company's objectives, compensations, and review process for the banks with which it has a relationship.

Bank selection process Involves assembling a system of banks to serve all of a company's cash management and related needs.

Banking Act, 1991 Prohibited the FDIC from voluntarily covering a bank's uninsured depositors except when the Department of Treasury, the Federal Reserve Board, the FDIC, and the President all agree that the financial system would be endangered by the bank's closure.

Bankruptcy A legal process that either allows a debtor to work out an orderly plan to settle debts or to liquidate a debtor's assets and distribute them to creditors.

Bankruptcy Code Title 11 of the U.S. Code—the federal statute that governs the bankruptcy process.

Bankruptcy Courts Federal courts that hear only bankruptcy cases.

Banner ad Animated GIF graphic placed on a host site and hyperlinked to the URL of the advertiser.

Banners Advertisements that appear on a Web page.

Bar chart *See:* Gantt chart.

Bar code A series of wide and narrow lines that represents data. Usually printed on product tags for ease of data entry and the recording of shipment and sales by a specific machine used to read the code.

Barriers Elements that inhibit the implementation and maintenance of various business programs and strategies.

Barriers to entrants Any and all of the measures that a business can take to prevent potential competitors from entering the market.

Barter Exchange of goods between two parties without the use of any currency as a medium of exchange.

Base case An analysis in which all of the input variables are set at their most likely values.

Base-case scenario Determining the output given the most likely values for the probabilistic inputs of a model.

Base demand The percentage of a company's demand that derives from continuing contracts and/or existing customers. Because this demand is well known and recurring, it becomes the basis of management's plans. *Syn:* baseload demand.

Base inventory level The inventory level made up of aggregate lot-size inventory plus the aggregate safety stock inventory. It does not take into account the anticipation inventory that will result from the production plan. The base inventory level should be known before the production plan is made. *Syn:* basic stock.

Base pay The basic compensation an employee receives, usually as a wage or salary.

Base salary Salary not including special payments such as allowances paid during overseas assignments.

Base stock system A method of inventory control that includes as special cases most of the systems in practice. In this system, when an order is received for any item, it is used as a picking ticket, and duplicate copies, called replenishment orders, are sent back to all stages of production to initiate replenishment of stocks. Positive or negative orders, called base stock orders, are also used from time to time to adjust the level of the base stock of each item. In actual practice, replenishment orders are usually accumulated when they are issued and are released at regular intervals.

Baseband link A communications channel that allows only a very low bit rate in telecommunications, such as unconditioned telephone twisted pair cables.

Basel Accord Agreement among country representatives in 1988 to establish standardized risk-based capital requirements for banks across countries.

Baseline plan The original plan, or roadmap, laying out the way in which the project scope will be accomplished on time and within budget.

Batch processing 1: A mode of transaction processing in which all the transactions of the same type for a given period of time are collected, and then entered into a computer system together and processed. **2:** Running large batches of a single product through the process at one time, resulting in queues awaiting next steps in the process.

Bathtub curve Also called "life-history curve." A graphic demonstration of the relationship of life of a product versus the probable failure rate. Includes three portions: early or infant failure (break-in), a stable rate during normal use, and wearout.

Baud After J. M. Emile Baudot, a French scientist; the number of signals per second that a communications channel can support.

Bayes theorem A probability expression that enables the use of sample information to revise prior probabilities.

BCG matrix A concept developed by the Boston Consulting Group (BCG) that evaluates SBUs with respect to the dimensions of business growth rate and market share.

Bearer bond A bond owned officially by whoever is holding it.

Behavior modeling Copying someone else's behavior.

Behavior modification The set of techniques by which reinforcement theory is used to modify human behavior.

Behavioral interview Interview in which applicants give specific examples of how they have performed a certain task or handled a problem in the past.

Behavioral rating approach Assesses an employee's behaviors instead of other characteristics.

Behavioral sciences approach A subfield of the humanistic management perspective that applies social science in an organizational context, drawing from economics, psychology, sociology, and other disciplines.

Behaviorally anchored rating scale (BARS) A rating technique that relates an employee's performance to specific job-related incidents.

Benchmark job Job found in many organizations and performed by several individuals who have similar duties that are relatively stable and require similar KSAs.

Benchmarking 1: An improvement process in which a company measures its performance against that of best-in-class companies (or others who are good performers), determines how those companies achieved their performance levels, and uses the information to improve its own performance. The areas that can be benchmarked include strategies, operations, processes, and procedures. **2:** Comparing specific measures of performance against data on those measures in other "best practice" organizations. **3:** The measurement of time intervals and other important characteristics of hardware and software, usually when testing them before a decision to purchase or reject. **4:** An ongoing, systematic approach by which a public affairs unit measures and compares itself with higher performing and world-class units in order to generate knowledge and action about public affairs roles, practices, processes, products, services, and strategic issues that will lead to improvement in performance. Originated in the Total Quality Management (TQM) movement.

Benefit Indirect compensation given to an employee or group of employees as a part of organizational membership.

Benefit concept Encapsulation of the benefits of a product in the customer's mind.

Benefit-cost analysis Collection of the dollar value of benefits derived from an initiative and the associated costs incurred and computing the ratio of benefits to cost.

Benefits needs analysis A comprehensive look at all aspects of benefits.

Best and final offer (BAFO) A final price for a project, submitted by a contractor at the request of a customer who is considering proposals from several contractors for the same project.

Best-case scenario An analysis in which all of the input variables are set at their best reasonably forecasted values.

Best efforts arrangement Agreement for the sale of securities in which the investment bank handling the transaction gives no guarantee that the securities will be sold.

Best practices Refer to approaches that produce exceptional results.

Beta coefficient, β A measure of the extent to which the returns on a given stock move with the stock market.

Beta (market) risk That part of a project's risk that cannot be eliminated by diversification; it is measured by the project's beta coefficient.

Beta probability distribution A distribution that is frequently used to calculate the expected duration and variance for an activity based on the activity's optimistic, most likely, and pessimistic time estimates.

Beta risk *See:* consumer's risk.

Beta site An organization that agrees to use a new application for a specific period and report errors and unsatisfactory features to the developer in return for free use and support.

Betterment An expenditure that increases operating efficiency or capacity for the remaining useful life of a plant asset.

Bias A characteristic of measurement that refers to a systematic difference.

Biased expectations hypothesis A theory of the term structure of interest rates in which market expectations are modified by some degree of liquidity preference.

Biculturalism The sociocultural skills and attitudes used by racial minorities to move back and forth between the dominant culture and their own ethnic or racial culture.

Bid/ask spread Difference between the price at which a bank is willing to buy a currency and the price at which it will sell that currency.

Bid/no-bid decision An evaluation by a contractor of whether to go ahead with the preparation of a proposal in response to a customer's request for proposal.

Bid price Price that a trader of foreign exchange (typically a bank) is willing to pay for a particular currency.

Bid-rigging scheme Collusive fraud wherein an employee helps a vendor illegally obtain a contract that was supposed to involve competitive bidding.

Big Five Public accounting firms that have the capability to perform external audits in different parts of the world. The Big Five accounting firms include Andersen, KPMG Peat Marwick, Deloitte Touche Tohmatsu, Ernst & Young, and PricewaterhouseCoopers.

Big Five personality factors Dimensions that describe an individual's extroversion, agreeableness, conscientiousness, emotional stability, and openness to experience.

Big Q, little q A term used to contrast the difference between managing for quality in all business processes and products (big Q) and managing for quality in a limited capacity, traditionally in only factory products and processes (little q).

Bilan Social (social report) A required report in France. It contains mainly employee-related information covering topics such as pay structure, hiring policies, health and safety conditions, training, and industrial relations.

Bilateral advance pricing agreement When the multinational company receives the approval of proposed transfer pricing approaches from tax authorities of two countries.

Bilateral and multilateral netting systems Are centralized bookkeeping entries made to eliminate ("net out") offsetting amounts owed by divisions or subsidiaries within a company.

Bilateral negotiations Negotiations carried out between two nations focusing only on their interests.

Bilateral netting system Netting method used for transactions between two units.

Bill of batches A method of tracking the specific multilevel batch composition of a manufactured item. The bill of batches provides the necessary where-used and where-from relationships required for lot traceability.

Bill of exchange (draft) Promise drawn by one party (usually an exporter) to pay a specified amount to another party at a specified future date, or upon presentation of the draft.

Bill of labor A structured listing of all labor requirements for the fabrication, assembly, and testing of a parent item. *See:* bill of resources, capacity bill procedure, routing.

Bill of lading 1: Document serving as a receipt for shipment and a summary of freight charges and conveying title to the merchandise. **2:** A contract between an exporter and a carrier indicating that the carrier has accepted responsibility for the goods and will provide transportation in return for payment.

Bill of lading (uniform) A carrier's contract and receipt for goods the carrier agrees to transport from one place to another and to deliver to a designated person. In case of loss, damage, or delay, the bill of lading is the basis for filing freight claims.

Bill of material (BOM) 1: A listing of all the subassemblies, intermediates, parts, and raw materials that go into a parent assembly showing the quantity of each required to make an assembly. It is used in conjunction with the master production schedule to determine the items for which purchase requisitions and production orders must be released. A variety of display formats exist for bills of material, including the single-level bill of material, indented bill of material, modular (planning) bill of material, transient bill of material, matrix bill of material, and costed bill of material. **2:** A list of all the materials needed to make one production run of a product, by a contract manufacturer, of piece parts/components for its customers. The bill of material may also be called the formula, recipe, or ingredients list in certain process industries. **3:** A list showing an explosion of the materials that go into the production of an item. Used in planning the purchase of raw materials.

Bill-of-material explosion The process of determining component identities, quantities per assembly, and other parent/component relationship data for a parent item. Explosion may be single level, indented, or summarized.

Bill of resources A listing of the required capacity and key resources needed to manufacture one unit of a selected item or family. Rough-cut capacity planning uses these bills to calculate the approximate capacity requirements of the master production schedule. Resource planning may use a form of this bill. *Syn:* bill of capacity. *See:* bill of labor, capacity planning using overall factors, product load profile, resource profile, rough-cut capacity planning, routing.

Bill presentation Sending a bill (especially for telephone use, electricity, and similar services) via e-mail; usually with an option to pay online by credit card or bank transfer.

Billing scheme Submission of a false or altered invoice that causes an employer to willingly issue a check.

Binary number system A number system in which 2 is the base (rather than 10, which is the normal base human beings use in everyday counting). Used in computers.

Biometric A unique, measurable characteristic or trait of a human being used for automatically authenticating a person's identity. Biometrics include digitized fingerprints, retinal pictures, and voice. Used with special hardware to uniquely identify a person who tries to access a facility or an IS, instead of a password.

Bit Binary digit; either a zero or a one. The smallest unit of information used in computing.

Bit map The arrangement of bits representing an image for display on a computer monitor or a paper printout.

Bits per second (bps) The measurement of the capacity (or transmission rate) of a communications channel.

Black hole The situation that arises when an international marketer has a low-competence subsidiary—or none at all—in a highly strategic market.

Blackouts and brownouts Periods of power loss or a significant fall in power. Such events may cause computers to stop working, or even damage them. Computers can be protected against these events by using proper equipment, such as UPS (uninterruptible power supply) systems.

Bleeding edge The situation in which a business fails because it tries to be on the technological leading edge.

Blemish An imperfection that is severe enough to be noticed but should not cause any real impairment with respect to intended normal or reasonably foreseeable use. *See:* defect, imperfection, and nonconformity.

Block diagram A diagram that shows the operation, interrelationships, and interdependencies of components in a system. Boxes, or blocks (hence the name) represent the components; connecting lines between the blocks represent interfaces. There are two types of block diagrams: a functional block diagram, which shows a system's subsystems and lower-level products, their interrelationships, and interfaces with other systems; and a reliability block diagram, which is similar to the functional block diagram except that it is modified to emphasize those aspects influencing reliability.

Blocked operation An upstream work center that is not permitted to produce because of a full queue at a downstream work center or because no kanban authorizes production.

Blue sky laws State laws that prevent the sale of securities that have little or no asset backing.

Board of Governors The main Federal Reserve System's policy-making body, which is comprised of seven members. Governors are appointed by the President and confirmed by the U.S. Senate. The Board of Governors supervises the district Federal Reserve banks, limiting to some extent the powers and privileges of their stockholders.

Body language Includes eye contact, physical distance and touching, hand movements, pointing, and facial expressions.

Bona fide occupational qualification (BFOQ) Characteristic providing a legitimate reason why an employer can exclude persons on otherwise illegal bases of consideration.

Bond A form of interest-bearing note employed by corporations to borrow on a long-term basis.

Bond anticipation notes Short-term debt instrument which provides working capital financing for states and localities as they await anticipated revenues from upcoming bond issuance.

Bond indenture The contract between a corporation issuing bonds and the bondholders.

Bonus A one-time payment that does not become part of the employee's base pay.

Book value The amount at which an asset or liability is reported on the balance sheet. Also called *basis* or *carrying value*.

Book value of the asset The difference between the balance of a fixed asset account and its related accumulated depreciation account.

Book value per share The accounting value of a share of common stock; equal to common equity (common stock plus additional paid-in capital plus retained earnings) divided by the number of shares outstanding.

Boot The cash balance owed the seller when an old asset is traded for a new asset.

Bottleneck A facility, function, department, or resource whose capacity is less than the demand placed upon it. For example, a bottleneck machine or work center exists where jobs are processed at a slower rate than they are demanded.

Bottom-up budgeting A budgeting process in which lower-level managers budget their departments' resource needs and pass them up to top management for approval.

Bottom-up planning An approach to planning based on satisfying the needs of individual business units. Reactive in nature.

Bottom-up replanning In MRP, the process of using pegging data to solve material availability or other problems. This process is accomplished by the planner (not the computer system), who evaluates the effects of possible solutions. Potential solutions include compressing lead time, cutting order quantity, substituting material, and changing the master schedule.

Boundary-spanning roles Roles assumed by people and/or departments that link and coordinate the organization with key elements in the external environment.

Boundaryless organization An organization without the internal or external boundaries limiting the traditional structures. Also known as a *network organization,* a *modular corporation,* or a *virtual corporation.*

Bounded rationality The concept that people have the time and cognitive ability to process only a limited amount of information on which to base decisions.

Box-Jenkins model A type of time-series forecasting technique. Named after two pioneers in the field of time series modeling, this approach lets the data specify the best model.

Boycott An organized effort to refrain from conducting business with a particular seller of goods or services; used in the international arena for political or economic reasons.

BPR (business process reengineering) *See:* reengineering.

Brain drain A migration of professional people from one country to another, usually for the purpose of improving their incomes or living conditions.

Brainstorming A problem-solving tool that teams use to generate as many ideas as possible related to a particular subject. Team members begin by offering all their ideas; the ideas are not discussed or reviewed until after the brainstorming session.

Branch Lines showing the alternatives from decision nodes and the outcomes from chance nodes.

Brand equity Marketplace value of a brand based on reputation and goodwill.

Brands Name, representative symbol or design, or any other feature that identifies one firm's product as distinct from another firm's. Trademark is the legal term for a brand. Brands may be associated with one product, a family of products, or with all of the products sold by a firm.

Breadth Refers to the number and size of parties that are potential buyers of the instruments in a market.

Break-even point 1: Literally, "to have zero profit." It is that point at which total cost and total revenue are equal. **2:** The level of business operations at which revenues and expired costs are equal.

Break point (BP) The dollar value of new capital that can be raised before an increase in the firm's weighted average cost of capital occurs.

Breakthrough A method of solving chronic problems that results from the effective execution of a strategy designed to reach the next level of quality. Such change often requires a paradigm shift within the organization.

Bretton Woods Agreement 1: An agreement signed by the major trading countries following World War II which returned the world economy to a type of gold standard. The U.S. dollar was pegged to the dollar at $35 per ounce. Currencies of all other countries were then fixed in price to the dollar and the countries agreed to maintain the established exchange rate within 1 percent. **2:** An agreement reached in 1944 among finance ministers of 45 Western nations to establish a system of fixed exchange rates.

Bribery 1: The offering, giving, receiving, or soliciting anything of value to influence an official act. **2:** The use of payments or favors to obtain some right or benefit to which the briber has no legal right; a criminal offense in the United States but a way of life in many countries.

Bridge A device connecting two communications networks that use similar hardware.

Broadband link A communications channel that supports high-speed communication.

Broadbanding Practice of using fewer pay grades having broader ranges than in traditional compensation systems.

Brokers Middlemen which do not inventory the securities they arrange transactions for.

Browsers Special software designed to search the Web for specific sites and retrieve information in the form of text, pictures, sound, and animation.

Browsing Using a special application called a Web browser to move from one Web site to another.

Bucketed system An MRP, DRP, or other time-phased system in which all time-phased data are accumulated into time periods, or buckets. If the period of accumulation is one week, then the system is said to have weekly buckets.

Bucketless system An MRP, DRP, or other time-phased system in which all time-phased data are processed, stored, and usually displayed using dated records rather than defined time periods, or buckets.

Budget An outline of a business's future plans, stated in financial terms. A budget is used to plan and control operational departments and divisions.

Budget performance report A report comparing actual results with budget figures.

Buffer 1: A quantity of materials awaiting further processing. It can refer to raw materials, semifinished stores or hold points, or a work backlog that is purposely maintained behind a work center. *Syn:* bank. **2:** In the theory of constraints, buffers can be time or material and support throughput and/or due date performance. Buffers can be maintained at the constraint, convergent points (with a constraint part), divergent points, and shipping points.

Buffer management In the theory of constraints, a process in which all expediting in a shop is driven by what is scheduled to be in the buffers (constraint, shipping, and assembly buffers). By expediting this material into the buffers, the system helps avoid idleness at the constraint and missed customer due dates. In addition, the causes of items missing from the buffer are identified, and the frequency of occurrence is used to prioritize improvement activities.

Buffer stock Stock of a commodity kept on hand to prevent a shortage in times of unexpectedly great demand; under international commodity and price agreements, the stock controlled by an elected or appointed manager for the purpose of managing the price of the commodity.

Bug An error in a computer program. Despite a famous story about a real insect that interrupted the work of a 1940s computer, the word "bug" had been used for "error" a long time before the advent of computers, and has nothing to do with that event.

Build cycle The time period between a major setup and a cleanup. It recognizes cyclical scheduling of similar products with minor changes from one product/model to another.

Bulk service Ocean shipping provided on contract either for individual voyages or for prolonged periods of time.

Bullwhip effect An extreme change in the supply position upstream in a supply chain generated by a small change in demand downstream in the supply chain. Inventory can quickly move from being backordered to being excess. This is caused by the serial nature of communicating orders up the chain with the inherent transportation delays of moving product down the chain. The bullwhip effect can be eliminated by synchronizing the supply chain.

Bureaucratic control The use of rules, policies, hierarchy of authority, reward systems, and other formal devices to influence employee behavior and assess performance.

Bureaucratic organizations A subfield of the classical management perspective that emphasized management on an impersonal, rational basis through such elements as clearly defined authority and responsibility, formal record-keeping, and separation of management and ownership.

Bus The set of wires or soldered conductors in the computer through which the different components (such as the CPU and RAM) communicate. It also refers to a data communications topology whereby communicating devices are connected to a single, open-ended medium.

Business An organization in which basic resources (inputs), such as materials and labor, are assembled and processed to provide goods or services (outputs) to customers.

Business continuity plan Organizational plan that prepares for disruption in information systems, detailing what should be done and by whom, if critical information systems fail or become untrustworthy; also called *business recovery plan* and *disaster recovery plan.*

Business entity concept The concept that accounting applies to individual economic units and that each unit is separate from the persons who supply its assets.

Business ethics Concerned with good and bad or right and wrong behavior and practices that take place within a business context.

Business ethics gap Compared with other capitalistic societies, the approach to ethics is more individualistic, legalistic, and universalistic in the United States.

Business ethics visibility gap The people of the United States read and hear far more about business misconduct than people in other countries.

Business incubator An innovation that provides shared office space, management support services, and management advice to entrepreneurs.

Business-level strategy The level of strategy concerned with the question "How do we compete?" Pertains to each business unit or product line within the organization.

GLOSSARY

Business market All organizations that buy goods and services for use in the production of other goods and services or for resale.

Business model The manner in which businesses generate income.

Business necessity A practice necessary for safe and efficient organizational operations.

Business partnering The creation of cooperative business alliances between constituencies within an organization or between an organization and its customers or suppliers. Partnering occurs through a pooling of resources in a trusting atmosphere focused on continuous, mutual improvement. *See:* customer–supplier partnership.

Business plan A document specifying the business details prepared by an entrepreneur in preparation for opening a new business.

Business planning The general idea or explicit statement of where an organization wishes to be at some time in the future.

Business processes Processes that focus on what the organization does as a business and how it goes about doing it. A business has functional processes (generating output within a single department) and cross-functional processes (generating output across several functions or departments).

Business Recovery Plan (BRP) *See:* Business Continuity Plan.

Business report A report that covers many of the matters typically found in the Management Discussion and Analysis part of companies' annual reports in North America.

Business risk The possibility that a company will not be able to meet ongoing operating expenditures. The risk associated with projections of a firm's future returns on assets (ROA) or returns on equity (ROE) if the firm uses no debt.

Business stakeholder A person or entity that has an interest in the economic performance of the business.

Business transaction The occurrence of an economic event or a condition that must be recorded in the accounting records.

Bustarella Italian term for bribery/payoffs.

Bustout A planned bankruptcy.

Buy-and-hold strategy An approach to investing that involves holding until maturity securities purchased. Quite often, this is part of a "maturity matching" approach to investing that prescribes investing in a security that will mature at the end of the investment horizon.

Buy-back A refinement of simple barter with one party supplying technology or equipment that enables the other party to produce goods, which are then used to pay for the technology or equipment that was supplied.

Buy hedge A hedge created by purchasing a futures contract.

Buyers Consumers who actually purchase the product.

Buying center Those individuals who participate in the purchasing decision and who share the goals and risks arising from the decision.

Buzzword A new or existing word that takes on a very specific meaning when used in a particular context. Buzzwords are usually used to impress someone with new jargon or to promote a product, service, or idea.

Bylaws A set of rules drawn up by the founders of the corporation that indicate how the company is to be governed; includes procedures for electing directors, whether the common stock has a preemptive right, and how to change the bylaws when necessary.

Byte A standard group of bits. In ASCII, a byte comprises 7 bits. In ASCII-8 and EBCDIC, a byte comprises 8 bits.

C

C chart Count chart. *See:* attribute data.

Cache From French, pronounced "cash." A part of RAM devoted to the most frequently used instructions and data of a program for faster retrieval.

CAD A production technology in which computers perform new-product design.

Calibration The comparison of a measurement instrument or system of unverified accuracy to a measurement instrument or system of a known accuracy to detect any variation from the true value.

Call *See:* currency call option.

Call option A contract that allows the owner to purchase the underlying asset at a specific price over a specific span of time. An option to buy, or "call," a share of stock at a certain price within a specified period.

Call option on real assets Project that contains an option of pursuing an additional venture.

Call premium The amount in excess of par value that a company must pay when it calls a security.

Call provision A provision in a bond contract that gives the issuer the right to redeem ("recall") the bonds under specified terms prior to the normal maturity date.

Callback A telecommunications security measure whereby the communications device at the destination end disconnects and calls the user back at the user-provided telephone number, to ensure the authenticity of the caller.

CAM A production technology in which computers help guide and control the manufacturing system.

Canonical analysis Considers possible interrelationships among independent variables and dependent variables.

Can-order point An ordering system used when multiple items are ordered from one vendor. The can-order point is a point higher than the original order point. When any one of the items triggers an order by reaching the must-order point, all items below their can-order point are also ordered. The can-order point is set by considering the additional holding cost that would be incurred should the item be ordered early.

Capability ratio (Cp) Is equal to the specification tolerance width divided by the process capability.

Capable-to-promise (CTP) The process of committing orders against available capacity as well as inventory. This process may involve multiple manufacturing or distribution sites. Capable-to-promise is used to determine when a new or unscheduled customer order can be delivered. Capable-to-promise employs a finite-scheduling model of the manufacturing system to determine when an item can be delivered. It includes any constraints that might restrict the production, such as availability of resources, lead times for raw materials or purchased parts, and requirements for lower-level components or subassemblies. The resulting delivery date takes into consideration production capacity, the current manufacturing environment, and future order commitments. The objective is to reduce the time spent by production planners in expediting orders and adjusting plans because of inaccurate delivery-date promises.

Capacity 1: The capability of a system to perform its expected function. **2:** The capability of a worker, machine, work center, plant, or organization to produce output per time period. Capacity required represents the system capability needed to make a given product mix (assuming technology, product specification, and so on). As a planning function, both capacity available and capacity required can be measured in the short term (capacity requirements plan), intermediate term (rough-cut capacity plan), and long term (resource requirements plan). Capacity control is the execution through the I/O control report of the short-term plan. Capacity can be classified as budgeted, dedicated, demonstrated, productive, protective, rated, safety, standing, or theoretical. *See:* capacity available, capacity required. **3:** Required mental ability to enter into a contract.

Capacity control The process of measuring production output and comparing it with the capacity requirements plan, determining if the variance exceeds preestablished limits, and taking corrective action to get back on plan if the limits are exceeded.

Capacity management The function of establishing, measuring, monitoring, and adjusting limits or levels of capacity in order to execute all manufacturing schedules; that is, the production plan, master production schedule, material requirements plan, and dispatch list. Capacity management is executed at four levels: resource requirements planning, rough-cut capacity planning, capacity requirements planning, and input/output control.

Capacity planning The process of determining the amount of capacity required to produce in the future. This process may be performed at an aggregate or product-line level (resource requirements planning), at the master-scheduling level (rough-cut capacity planning), and at the material requirements planning level (capacity requirements planning). *See:* capacity requirements planning, resource planning, rough-cut capacity planning.

Capacity requirements planning (CRP) The function of establishing, measuring, and adjusting limits or levels of capacity. The term capacity requirements planning in this context refers to the process of determining in detail the amount of labor and machine resources required to accomplish the tasks of production. Open shop orders and planned orders in the MRP system are input to CRP, which through the use of parts routings and time standards translates these orders into hours of work by work center by time period. Even though rough-cut capacity planning may indicate that sufficient capacity exists to execute the MPS, CRP may show that capacity is insufficient during specific time periods. *See:* capacity planning.

Capacity strategy One of the strategic choices that a firm must make as part of its manufacturing strategy. There are three commonly recognized capacity strategies: lead, lag, and tracking. A lead capacity strategy adds capacity in anticipation of increasing demand. A lag strategy does not add capacity until the firm is operating at or beyond full capacity. A tracking strategy adds capacity in small amounts to attempt to respond to changing demand in the marketplace.

Capital account 1: Account reflecting changes in country ownership of long-term and short-term financial assets. **2:** An account in the BOP statement that records transactions involving borrowing, lending, and investing across borders. It is also called financial account.

Capital asset pricing model (CAPM) A model used to determine the required return on an asset, which is based on the proposition that any asset's return should be equal to the risk-free rate of return plus a risk premium that reflects the asset's nondiversifiable risk.

Capital budget 1: The financial evaluation of a proposed investment to determine whether the expected returns are sufficient to justify the investment expenses. **2:** A budget that plans and reports investments in major assets to be depreciated over several years.

Capital budgeting 1: The process of identifying, evaluating, and planning long-term investment decisions. **2:** The process of planning and evaluating expenditures on assets whose cash flows are expected to extend beyond one year.

Capital component One of the types of capital used by firms to raise money.

Capital expenditures Costs that add to the usefulness of assets for more than one accounting period.

Capital expenditures budget The budget summarizing future plans for acquiring fixed assets.

Capital flight The flow of private funds abroad because investors believe that the return on investment or the safety of capital is not sufficiently ensured in their own countries.

Capital gain (loss) The profit (loss) from the sale of a capital asset for more (less) than its purchase price.

Capital gains yield The change in price (capital gain) during a given year divided by the price at the beginning of the year.

Capital investment analysis The process by which management plans, evaluates, and controls long-term capital investments involving property, plant, and equipment.

Capital lease A lease treated as a purchase of property by the lessee. Leases that treat the leased assets as purchased assets in the accounts.

Capital markets The financial markets for stocks and long-term debt (generally longer than one year).

Capital rationing 1: The process by which management allocates available investment funds among competing capital investment proposals. **2:** A situation in which a constraint is placed on the total size of the firm's capital investment.

Capital stock The portion of a corporation's owner's equity contributed by investors (owners) in exchange for shares of stock.

Capital structure The combination of debt and equity used to finance a firm.

Capital structure ratios *See:* Coverage ratios.

Capitalization Recording expenditures as assets rather than as expenses. (For example, start-up costs that are "capitalized" are recorded as assets and amortized.)

Captive finance companies A financing subsidiary of a corporation that facilitates arranging financing for customers of the firm's products.

Captive finance subsidiary Separate entity within a company that provides financing for parent company or its customers, and which is thought to provide a marketing advantage or debt capacity advantage.

Captive insurer A type of insurer that is generally formed and owned by potential insureds to meet their own distinctive needs.

Career The series of work-related positions a person occupies throughout life.

Caribbean Basin Initiative (CBI) Extended trade preferences to Caribbean countries and granted them special access to the markets of the United States.

Carriage and insurance paid to (CIP) The price quoted by an exporter for shipments not involving waterway transport, including insurance.

Carriage paid to (CPT) The price quoted by an exporter for shipments not involving waterway transport, not including insurance.

Carryforwards Tax losses that are applied in a future year to offset income in the future year.

Carrying amount The amount at which a long-term investment or a long-term liability is reported on the balance sheet.

Cartel 1: Organization of firms in an industry where the central organization makes certain management decisions and functions (often regarding pricing, outputs, sales, advertising, and distribution) that would otherwise be performed within the individual firms. **2:** Groups of private businesses that agree to set prices, share markets, and control production. An association of producers of a particular good, consisting either of private firms or of nations, formed for the purpose of suppressing the market forces affecting prices.

Cascading training Training implemented in an organization from the top down, where each level acts as trainers to those below.

CASE (Computer-Aided Software Engineering) Software tools that expedite systems development. The tools provide a 4GL or application generator for fast code writing, facilities for flowcharting or data-flow diagramming, data-dictionary facility, word-processing capability, and other features required to develop and document the new software. Modern CASE is often called I-CASE (integrated CASE).

Case study A prepared scenario (story) which when studied and discussed serves to illuminate the learning points of a course of study.

Cash Coins, currency (paper money), checks, money orders, and money on deposit that is available for unrestricted withdrawal from banks or other financial institutions.

Cash and securities mix decision The proportional breakdown of cash and securities held by a company as part of its current asset holdings.

Cash application Crediting the account upon payment for a credit sale, this process frees up that amount of the credit limit for additional orders from this customer.

Cash basis A basis of accounting in which revenue is recognized in the period cash is received, and expenses are recognized in the period cash is paid.

Cash budget 1: One of the most important elements of the budgeted balance sheet. It presents the expected receipts (inflows) and payments (outflows) of cash for a period of time. **2:** A budget that estimates and reports cash flows on a daily or weekly basis to ensure that the company has sufficient cash to meet its obligations. **3:** Forecast showing cash receipts and disbursements on a monthly basis for a minimum horizon of one year, typically assembled before the beginning of a new fiscal year.

Cash collection system A management-designed system that converts checks to cash and considers mail float, processing float, and availability float.

Cash concentration The process of moving dollar balances from deposit banks to concentration banks.

Cash conversion cycle The length of time from the payment for the purchase of raw materials to manufacture a product until the collection of accounts receivable associated with the sale of the product.

Cash conversion period A liquidity measure that takes a going-concern approach. It measures the difference in time from when cash is received from credit customers and when cash is paid to suppliers. The length of time from when cash is paid out for purchases and when cash is received from collections on credit sales.

Cash cycle The time that elapses from the purchase of raw materials until cash is received from the sale of the final product.

Cash discount The percentage amount that can be subtracted from the invoice if the customer pays within a stated period of time.

Cash dividend A cash distribution of earnings by a corporation to its shareholders.

Cash equivalents Highly liquid investments that are usually reported on the balance sheet with cash.

Cash flow The actual cash, as opposed to accounting net income, that a firm receives or pays during some specified period.

Cash flow cycle The way in which actual net cash, as opposed to accounting net income, flows into or out of the firm during some specified period.

Cash flow from operations One of the most direct measures of liquidity found by subtracting operating cash disbursements from operating cash receipts.

Cash flow timeline An important tool used in time value of money analysis; it is a graphical representation used to show the timing of cash flows.

Cash flows from financing activities The section of the statement of cash flows that reports cash flows from transactions affecting the equity and debt of the entity.

Cash flows from investing activities The section of the statement of cash flows that reports cash flows from transactions affecting investments in noncurrent assets.

Cash flows from operating activities The section of the statement of cash flows that reports the cash transactions affecting the determination of net income.

Cash inflows The cash benefits arising from sources of cash increases.

Cash items Deposited checks given immediate, provisional credit by the bank.

Cash letter The accompanying listing of checks that are bundled by the deposit bank for routing through the check clearing process.

Cash management Optimization of cash flows and investment of excess cash.

Cash management systems Information systems that help reduce the interest and fees that organizations have to pay when borrowing money, and increase the yield that organizations can receive on unused funds.

Cash outflows Cash being disbursed.

Cash payback period The expected period of time that will elapse between the date of a capital expenditure and the complete recovery in cash (or equivalent) of the amount invested.

Cash pooling Used by multinational firms to centralize individual units' cash flows, resulting in less spending or foregone interest unnecessary cash balances.

Cash short and over account An account which has recorded errors in cash sales or errors in making change causing the amount of actual cash on hand to differ from the beginning amount of cash plus the cash sales for the day.

Catchball A term used to describe the interactive process of developing and deploying policies and plans with hoshin planning.

Category killers A name that comes from a marketing strategy in which a company carries such a large amount of merchandise in a single category at such good prices that they make it impossible for customers to walk out without purchasing what they needed, thus "killing" the competition.

Category management Process of managing and planning all SKUs within a product category as a distinct business.

Cathode-ray tube A display (for a computer or television set) that uses an electronic gun to draw and paint on the screen by bombarding pixels on the internal side of the screen.

Causal analysis A method for analyzing the possible causal associations among a set of variables.

Causal distributions A set of outcomes characterized by situations where a predictor variable has changed from what was expected, causing the forecast variable to deviate from what was expected.

Causal forecasting methods Forecasting methods that relate a time series to other variables that are believed to explain or cause its behavior.

Causal techniques Forecasting methods linking the forecast values of an effect variable to one or more hypothesized causes.

Cause-and-effect diagram A tool for analyzing process variables. It is also referred to as the Ishikawa diagram, because Kaoru Ishikawa developed it and the fishbone diagram, because the complete diagram resembles a fish skeleton. The diagram illustrates the main causes and sub-causes leading to an effect (symptom). The cause-and-effect diagram is one of the seven tools of quality.

Cause-related marketing Form of corporate philanthropy that links a company's contributions (usually monetary) to a predesignated worthy cause with the purchasing behavior of consumers.

CBT Computer-based training is training delivered via computer software.

CD-ROM (Compact Disc Read-Only Memory) A compact disc whose data were recorded by the manufacturer and cannot be changed.

Cell A layout of workstations and/or various machines for different operations (usually in a U-shape) in which multi-tasking operators proceed, with a part, from machine to machine, to perform a series of sequential steps to produce a whole product or major subassembly.

Cellular layout A facility's layout in which machines dedicated to sequences of production are grouped into cells in accordance with group-technology principles.

Cellular manufacturing A manufacturing process that produces families of parts within a single line or cell of machines controlled by operators who work only within the line or cell.

Center of excellence The location of product development outside the home country because of an advantage of skills.

Central exchange rate Exchange rate established between two European currencies through the European Monetary System arrangement; the exchange rate between the two currencies is allowed to move within bands around that central exchange rate.

Central IS organization Organizational structure that includes a corporate information systems team to whom all units turn with their information systems needs.

Central plan The economic plan for the nation devised by the government of a socialist state; often a five-year plan that stipulated the quantities of industrial goods to be produced.

Central planning department A group of planning specialists who develop plans for the organization as a whole and its major divisions and departments and typically report to the president or CEO.

Central Processing Unit (CPU) The circuitry of a computer microprocessor that fetches instructions and data from the primary memory and executes the instructions. The CPU is the most important electronic unit of the computer.

Central tendency The propensity of data collected on a process to concentrate around a value situated somewhere midway between the lowest and highest value.

Central tendency error Rating all employees in a narrow range in the middle of the rating scale.

Centralization The concentrating of control and strategic decision making at headquarters. Most of the important decisions relative to local matters are made by headquarters management rather than by managers in the local subsidiary.

Centralized architecture Information systems architecture in which all applications and data are stored in a single mainframe.

Centralized cash flow management Policy that consolidates cash management decisions for all MNC units, usually at the parent's location.

Centralized disbursing An organizational structure that disburses corporate cash from a central area, allowing the corporate headquarters' staff to check each disbursement and possibly initiate each payment as well.

Centralized internal audit model In this type of organization, there is only one central internal audit organization that is located at the headquarters of the parent company. The internal auditors travel to various parts of the world where operations are located to perform internal audits, and to perform other functions such as quality control, audit research, liaison with external auditors, training, and technical support.

Centralized multinational organizations Organizations that retain to a great extent the authority to make decisions at parent company headquarters.

Centralized network A team communication structure in which team members communicate through a single individual to solve problems or make decisions.

Centralized processing system A cash collection system where corporate headquarters receives all customer remittances.

Centralized transfer initiation The timing and amount of the transfer is centered either at the concentration bank or corporate headquarters.

Certainty All the information the decision maker needs is fully available.

Certificate of deposit (CD) An interest-bearing account that evidences (certifies) that a certain amount of money has been deposited at the bank for a prespecified period of time, and that will be redeemed with interest at the end of that time (maturity).

Certified internal auditor (CIA) A certification program sponsored by the Institute of Internal Auditors consisting of an examination and a mandatory two years of practical experience in internal auditing before certification.

Certified public accountant (CPA) The professional designation for public accountants and independent (external) auditors in the United States and some other countries.

Chain of command An unbroken line of authority that links all individuals in the organization and specifies who reports to whom.

Chain of custody Maintaining detailed records about documents from the time they are received in the investigation process until the trial is completed. Helps to substantiate that documents have not been altered or manipulated since coming into the investigator's hands.

Chaku-chaku (Japanese) Meaning "load-load" in a cell layout where a part is taken from one machine and loaded into the next.

Champion 1: An individual who has accountability and responsibility for many processes or who is involved in making strategic-level decisions for the organization. The champion ensures ongoing dedication of project resources and monitors strategic alignment (also referred to as a *sponsor*). **2:** An executive with much clout who supports a project and endeavors to muster support from top management. A champion is important for the success of a project, such as developing a new information system.

Chance event An uncertain future event affecting the consequence, or payoff, associated with a decision.

Chance nodes Nodes indicating points where an uncertain event will occur.

Change agent 1: A person or institution that facilitates change in a firm or in a host country. **2:** An organizational development specialist who contracts with an organization to facilitate change. **3:** The person who takes the lead in transforming a company into a quality organization by providing guidance during the planning phase, facilitating implementation, and supporting those who pioneer the changes.

Changeover Changing a machine or process from one type of product or service to another.

Changing An intervention stage of organizational development in which individuals experiment with new workplace behavior.

Channel (link, path) The guiding or nonguiding environment in which communications signals are transmitted.

Channel design The length and width of the distribution channel.

Channel intensity The number of intermediaries at each level of the marketing channel.

Channel length Number of levels in a marketing channel.

Channel richness The amount of information that can be transmitted during a communication episode.

Channel strategy Broad set of principles by which a firm seeks to achieve its distribution objectives to satisfy its customers.

Channel structure All of the businesses and institutions (including producers or manufacturers and final customers) who are involved in performing the functions of buying, selling, or transferring title.

Chapter 7 bankruptcy Complete liquidation or "shutting down of a business" and distribution of any proceeds to creditors.

Chapter 11 bankruptcy Bankruptcy that allows the bankrupt entity time to reorganize its operational and financial affairs, settle its debts, and continue to operate in a reorganized fashion.

Character The smallest piece of data in the data hierarchy.

Characteristic A property that helps to identify or to differentiate between entities and that can be described or measured to determine conformance or nonconformance to requirements.

Chargeback A method used to manage the expenses involved in rendering information system services. The greater part of the expense is charged to the budget of the business unit that ordered it.

Charismatic leader A leader who has the ability to motivate subordinates to transcend their expected performance.

Charter A documented statement officially initiating the formation of a committee, team, project, or other effort in which a clearly stated purpose and approval is conferred.

Chart of accounts The system of accounts that make up the ledger for a business.

Chase production method A production planning method that maintains a stable inventory level while varying production to meet demand. Companies may combine chase and level production schedule methods. *Syn:* chase strategy.

Check processing float Delays in collecting cash caused by delays between the time a check is received and when it is deposited in the banking system.

Check sheet A simple data-recording device. The check sheet is custom-designed for the particular use, allowing ease in interpreting the results. The check sheet is one of the seven tools of quality. Check sheets are often confused with data sheets and checklists. *See:* checklist.

Check tampering Scheme in which dishonest employees (1) prepare fraudulent checks for their own benefit or (2) intercept checks intended for a third party and convert the checks for their own benefit.

Check truncation Involves expediting clearing by scanning the data on the check's MICR line, and then processing only that data back to the payee's bank.

Checklist 1: A tool used to ensure that all important steps or actions in an operation have been taken. Checklists contain items that are important or relevant to an issue or situation. Checklists are often confused with check sheets and data sheets. *See:* check sheet. **2:** Performance appraisal tool that uses a list of statements or words that are checked by raters.

Chief Executive Officer (CEO) The top leader in an organization, to whom a small group of executives reports.

Chief learning officer Responsible for developing on a worldwide scale the organization's human talent and for using the human knowledge present in the organization. *See:* CKO.

Children The data records linked to a parent record.

Chip A flat piece of silicon in which electronic circuitry is integrated.

CHIPS Short for Clearing House Interbank Payment System, the institution which was established in 1970 to handle interbank transactions needed to settle international transactions. CHIPS is a private association of banks that operates through the New York Clearinghouse Association.

Chronic crisis stage The lingering period of a crisis; may involve investigations, audits, or in-depth news stories.

Chronic problem A long-standing adverse situation that can be remedied by changing the status quo. For example, actions such as revising an unrealistic manufacturing process or addressing customer defections can change the status quo and remedy the situation.

CIO (Chief Information Officer) The highest-ranking IS officer in the organization, usually a vice president, who oversees the planning, development, and implementation of IS and serves as leader to all IS professionals in the organization.

Ciphertext A coded message designed to authenticate users and maintain secrecy.

Circuit switching A communication process in which a dedicated channel (circuit) is established for the duration of a transmission; the sending node signals the receiving node; the receiver acknowledges the signal and then receives the entire message.

Circular cultures Belief that since individuals can see what has happened in the past, their past is ahead of them, and since they cannot see into the future, their future is behind them.

CISG United Nations Convention on Contracts for the International Sales of Goods governs all contracts for international sales of goods between parties located in different nations that have ratified the CISG.

Civil law Body of law that provides remedies for violation of private rights deals with rights and duties between individuals.

CKO (Chief Knowledge Officer) A relatively new position in some large organizations. The CKO is responsible for garnering knowledge and making it available for future operations in which employees can learn from previous experience. The CKO works closely with the CIO, who is in charge of the technical means for garnering the necessary information. In some firms, the position is called chief learning officer.

Classic system A national tax system that subjects income to taxes when income is received by the taxable entity.

Classical model A decision-making model based on the assumption that managers should make logical decisions that will be in the organization's best economic interests.

Classical perspective A management perspective that emerged during the nineteenth and early twentieth centuries that emphasized a rational, scientific approach to the study of management and sought to make organizations efficient operating machines.

Classified stock Common stock that is given a special designation, such as Class A, Class B, and so forth, to meet special needs of the company.

Cleansing phase The stage at which database builders modify data into a form that allows insertion into the data warehouse.

Clearing agent Often a Federal Reserve bank, branch or RCPC, an entity that uses the information printed at the bottom of the check to process the check.

Clearing bank(s) When checks are deposited, the bank(s) used for processing those checks into the clearing system. Sometimes called *deposit bank(s)*.

Clearing float Sometimes called "availability float," the delay in availability incurred after deposit. The length of this component of float is linked to the bank's availability schedule in connection with the location of the payor's bank.

Clearing house A central location where representatives of area banks meet, and each bank settles its balances with one institution (the clearing house) instead of with each bank individually.

Click through Term that describes the act of clicking on an advertising banner located at a host site and being transported electronically to the advertiser's site.

Clientele effect The tendency of a firm to attract the type of investor who likes its dividend policy.

Client/server An information system arrangement in which one large computer holds large databases that are tapped by the users of smaller local microcomputers, but much discretion and the creation of the applications that manipulate the data are in the hands of the users. The larger computer is the server, while the local computers are the clients.

Clock rate The rate of repetitive machine cycles that a computer can perform. Also called *frequency*.

Closed-loop MRP A system built around material requirements planning that includes the additional planning processes of production planning (sales and operations planning), master production scheduling, and capacity requirements planning. Once this planning phase is complete and the plans have been accepted as realistic and attainable, the execution processes come into play. These processes include the manufacturing control processes of input-output (capacity) measurement, detailed scheduling and dispatching, as well as anticipated delay reports from both the plant and suppliers, supplier scheduling, and so on. The term closed loop implies not only that each of these processes is included in the overall system, but also that feedback is provided by the execution processes so that the planning can be kept valid at all times.

Closed system 1: A system that stands alone, with no connection to another system. **2:** A system that does not interact with the external environment.

Closely held corporation A corporation that is owned by a few individuals who are typically associated with the firm's management.

Closing entries Entries necessary to eliminate the balances of temporary accounts in preparation for the following accounting period.

Cluster analysis 1: Geographical grouping and labeling of individuals based on their buying behavior, demographics, and lifestyles. **2:** Used to create a classification by using single or multiple dimensions.

Clusters Geographic concentrations of interconnected companies and institutions in a particular field.

Coaching A continuous improvement technique by which people receive one-to-one learning through demonstration and practice and that is characterized by immediate feedback and correction.

Coalition An informal alliance among managers who support a specific goal.

Coaxial cable A transmission medium consisting of thick copper wire insulated and shielded by a special sheath of meshed wires to prevent electromagnetic interference. Supports high-speed telecommunication.

Code law Law based on a comprehensive set of written statutes.

Code of ethics A formal statement of the organization's values regarding ethics and social issues.

Codetermination A management approach in which employees are represented on supervisory boards to facilitate communication and collaboration between management and labor.

Coding Categorizing customers based on how profitable their past business has been.

Coefficient of determination Measure of the percentage variation in the dependent variable that can be explained by the independent variables when using regression analysis.

Coefficient of variation (CV) Standardized measure of the risk per unit of return; calculated as the standard deviation divided by the expected return.

Coercive power Power that stems from the authority to punish or recommend punishment.

Cofinancing agreements Arrangement in which the World Bank participates along with other agencies or lenders in providing funds to developing countries.

Cognitive ability tests Tests that measure an individual's thinking, memory, reasoning, and verbal and mathematical abilities.

Cognitive dissonance A condition in which two attitudes or a behavior and an attitude conflict.

Coin and currency services Procedures provided by banks that include receiving of bulk cash deposits sent by armed courier, sorting of deposit items, same day verification of the total deposit if received by the bank's cutoff time, and supply of coins and currency for the company's cash payment needs.

Cold calling Contacting prospective customers without a prior appointment.

Cold turkey conversion A swift switch from an old information system to the new; also called *cut-over conversion.*

Collaborative problem-solving strategy Firms emphasize long-term relationships with a variety of external constituencies and broad problem-solving perspectives on the resolution of social issues affecting their businesses and industries.

Collected balance Sometimes called the *available balance,* this amount represents how much of a deposit balance is immediately spendable. It may be somewhat less than the ledger balance because of availability delays applied to the checks by the bank.

Collection bank The bank of deposit that encodes the dollar amount of the check in magnetic ink on the bottom right side of the check and then routes the check through the clearing process.

Collection float The sum of the delays in collecting cash from customers caused by mail, process, and availability delays.

Collection policy The procedures followed by a firm to collect its accounts receivables.

Collection procedures Detailed statements regarding when and how the company will carry out collection of past due accounts. These policies specify how long the company will wait past the due date to initiate collection efforts, the method(s) of contact with delinquent customers and whether and at what point accounts will be referred to an outside collection agency.

Collective In stage six of the social interaction paradigm, leaders look for opportunities that benefit the group as a whole.

Collectivism 1: A preference for a tightly knit social framework in which individuals look after one another and organizations protect their members' interests. **2:** The belief that interests of the organization should have top priority.

Collusion Fraud perpetrated by two or more employees or others, each of whose job responsibilities is necessary to complete the fraud.

Comarketing agreement Two or more companies who share the risks and rewards of long-term marketing programs.

Comment cards Printed cards or slips of paper used to solicit and collect comments from users of a service or product.

Commercial data-mining software Commercial software packages that use query techniques to detect patterns and anomalies in data that may suggest fraud.

Commercial enterprises Sector of the business market represented by manufacturers, construction companies, service firms, transportation companies, professional groups, and resellers that purchase goods and services.

Commercial/industrial market Refers to business market customers who are described by variables such as location, SIC code, buyer industry, technological sophistication, purchasing process, size, ownership, and financial strength.

Commercial invoice A bill for transported goods that describes the merchandise and its total cost and lists the addresses of the shipper and seller and delivery and payment terms.

Commercial letter of credit A guarantee of payment by an importer, made by its bank, that becomes binding when the shipping and other documents related to the goods sold are presented to the bank.

Commercial paper An unsecured IOU issued mainly by financial companies such as banks, their parent holding companies, and consumer or commercial finance companies. A short-term promissory note issued by a corporation for a fixed maturity generally in the 30 day range but can be as much as 270 days. Unsecured, short-term promissory notes issued by large, financially sound firms to raise funds.

Commercial Service A department of the U.S. Department of Commerce that gathers information and assists business executives in business abroad.

Commission Compensation computed as a percentage of sales in units or dollars.

Commitment An important reciprocal relationship in which the employee is committed to the organization and its goals and is matched by the employer's commitment to the employee's welfare.

Commitment fee A fee charged on the *unused* balance of a revolving credit agreement to compensate the bank for guaranteeing that the funds will be available when needed by the borrower; the fee normally is about 1/4 percent of the unused balance.

Committed cost The funds that are unavailable to be spent elsewhere because they will be needed at some later time to pay for an item, such as material, that has been ordered; commitment; encumbered cost.

Committed facility Lending arrangement in which the bank charges a fee to compensate it for agreeing to lend upon request for a period of five to seven years.

Committed line A line of credit where the firm pays a commitment fee that obligates the bank to provide funding for the credit line with a formal written agreement.

Committee A long-lasting, sometimes permanent team in the organization structure created to deal with tasks that recur regularly.

Committee of Sponsoring Organizations (COSO) Organization made up of representatives from major accounting firms that focus on internal controls and financial statement fraud.

Committee on Foreign Investments in the United States (CFIUS) A federal committee, chaired by the U.S. Treasury, with the responsibility to review major foreign investments to determine whether national security or related concerns are at stake.

Commodity analysis Researching the requirements for a commodity purchase. Some of the elements of a thorough commodity analysis include the buyer's/supplier's needs and objectives, importance of the item cost/quality/delivery/packaging requirements, manufacturing process, cost structure and pricing trends, substitutions, major suppliers and customers, and other relevant information that can facilitate a sound sourcing decision.

Commodity price agreement An agreement involving both buyers and sellers to manage the price of a particular commodity, but often only when the price moves outside a predetermined range.

Common agricultural policy (CAP) An integrated system of subsidies and rebates applied to agricultural interests in the European Union.

Common causes Are factors internal to a process.

Common causes of variation Causes that are inherent in any process all the time. A process that has only common causes of variation is said to be stable or predictable or in-control. Also called "chance causes."

Common equity The sum of the firm's common stock, paid-in capital, and retained earnings, which equals the common stockholders' total investment in the firm stated at book value.

Common Gateway Interface (CGI) Special software used in Internet servers that allows the capture of data from a form displayed on a page and the storage of the data in a database.

Common law Law based on tradition and depending less on written statutes and codes than on precedent and custom—used in the United States.

Common market A group of countries that agree to remove all barriers to trade among members, to establish a common trade policy with respect to nonmembers, and also to allow mobility for factors of production—labor, capital, and technology.

Common-size financial statements 1: Financial statements that have been converted to percentages. **2:** A financial statement in which all items are expressed only in relative terms.

Common stock The basic ownership class of corporate stock.

Common stockholders' equity (net worth) The capital supplied by common stockholders—capital stock, paid-in capital, retained earnings, and, occasionally, certain reserves.

Communication The process by which information is exchanged and understood by two or more people, usually with the intent to motivate or influence behavior.

Communication services Services that are provided in the areas of videotext, home banking, and home shopping, among others.

Communications channel Any medium that supports the transmission and reception of data and information. May be a guided channel, such as wires, or an unguided channel, such as the atmosphere or space. Also called *communications link* and *communications path*.

Communications protocol The set of rules that govern data communications. When more than two parties participate in the communication, it is also called *network protocol*.

Compact disc (CD) A plastic disk in which pits and flat areas represent bits. A laser beam "reads" the data. Also called "optical disc" and "laser disc." CDs have a storage capacity 100–150 times that of regular magnetic disks. Used as the predominant medium for storing musical works and archival data.

Company/brand sites Web sites that provide information about a company, such as history, mission, financial statements, and so on.

Company processing center An administrative office or area within the corporation that processes payments received from customers.

Company-wide quality control (CWQC) Similar to Total Quality Management.

Compa-ratio Current pay level divided by the midpoint of the pay range.

Comparative advantage 1: Results when a strategic advantage is held relative to the competition. **2:** Theory suggesting that specialization by countries can increase worldwide production. **3:** The ability to produce a good or service more cheaply, relative to other goods and services, than is possible in other countries.

Comparative ratio analysis An analysis based on a comparison of a firm's ratios with those of other firms in the same industry.

Compensable factor Identifies a job value commonly present throughout a group of jobs.

Compensating balance (CB) A minimum checking account balance that a firm must maintain with a bank to borrow funds—generally 10 to 20 percent of the amount of loans outstanding.

Compensation 1: Monetary payments (wages, salaries) and nonmonetary goods/commodities (benefits, vacations) used to reward employees. **2:** Arrangement in which the delivery of goods to a party is compensated for by buying back a certain amount of the product from that same party.

Compensation committee 1: Has the responsibility of evaluating executive performance and recommending terms and conditions of employment. **2:** A subgroup of the board of directors composed of directors who are not officers of the firm.

Compensatory Financing Facility (CFF) Facility that attempts to reduce the impact of export instability on country economies.

Compensatory justice The concept that individuals should be compensated for the cost of their injuries by the party responsible and also that individuals should not be held responsible for matters over which they have no control.

Compensatory time off Hours given in lieu of payment for extra time worked.

Competence Refers to a person's ability to learn and perform a particular activity. Competence generally consists of skill, knowledge, experience, and attitude components.

Competencies Basic characteristics that can be linked to enhanced performance by individuals or teams.

Competency-based training A training methodology which focuses on building mastery of a redetermined segment or module before moving on to the next.

Competitive advantage 1: A position in which one dominates a market; also called *strategic advantage*. **2:** The ability to produce a good or service more cheaply than other countries due to favorable factor conditions and demand conditions, strong related and supporting industries, and favorable firm strategy, structure, and rivalry conditions.

Competitive analysis The gathering of intelligence relative to competitors in order to identify opportunities or potential threats to current and future strategy.

Competitive assessment A research process that consists of matching markets to corporate strengths and providing an analysis of the best potential for specific offerings.

Competitive bids Offers to buy securities at a given price or yield. In the Treasury auctions, these are mainly entered by financial institutions, including dealers.

Competitive environment This environment is affected by bribery and the existence of cartels.

Competitive Equality Banking Act of 1987 Allows existing nonbank banks to continue to operate, but prohibits the establishment of new nonbank banks.

Competitively advantaged product Product that solves a set of customer problems better than any competitor's product. This product is made possible due to this firm's unique technical, manufacturing, managerial, or marketing capabilities, which are not easily copied by others.

Compiler A program whose purpose is to translate code written in a high-level programming language into the equivalent code in machine language for execution by the computer.

Complaint 1: Request filed by a plaintiff to request civil proceedings against someone—usually to seek damages. **2:** Indication of employee dissatisfaction.

Complementary marketing Contractual arrangement where participating parties carry out different but complementary activities.

Complete enumeration A lockbox model that analyzes all possible lockbox sites to determine the optimal combination that maximizes shareholder wealth.

Compliance An affirmative indication or judgment that the supplier of a product or service has met the requirements of the relevant specifications, contract, or regulation; also the state of meeting the requirements.

Compliance strategy Is focused on obedience to the law as its driving force.

Components of internal control The internal control components are the control environment, risk assessment, control activities, information and communication, and monitoring.

Composite key In a data file, a combination of two fields that can serve as a unique key to locate specific records.

Composition of trade The ratio of primary commodities to manufactured goods in a country's trade.

Compounded interest Interest earned on interest.

Compounding The process of determining the value of a cash flow or series of cash flows some time in the future when compound interest is applied.

Comprehensive income All changes in stockholders' equity during a period, except those resulting from dividends and stockholders' investments.

Comprehensive payables Is the outsourcing of part or all of the accounts payable and/or disbursement functions.

Compressed workweek One in which a full week's work is accomplished in fewer than five days.

Compression (data compression) The restorage or communication of data, using special software techniques, so that the new file takes up significantly less space on the storage medium, or takes less time to communicate over a channel.

Computer-aided design (CAD) Special software used by engineers and designers that facilitates engineering and design work.

Computer controls 1: Controls performed by a computer, that is, controls programmed into computer software (contrast with manual controls). **2:** Controls over computer processing of information, consisting of general controls and application controls (both programmed and manual).

Computer virus (virus) Destructive software that propagates and is activated by unwary users; a virus usually damages applications and data files or disrupts communications.

Computerized numeric control (CNC) Control by computers that take data and create instructions that tell robots how to manufacture and assemble parts and products.

Concealment investigative methods Investigating a fraud by focusing on the cover-up efforts, such as the manipulation of source documents.

Concentration account Deposit account into which funds are pooled at the endpoint(s) of a company's collection system.

Concentration bank A bank that receives balance transfers from several deposit or gathering banks.

Concentration banking A technique used to move funds from many bank accounts to a more central cash pool in order to more effectively manage cash.

Concentration services Closely linked to collection services, these services mobilize and pool collected cash in order to increase interest income and reduce interest expense.

Concentration strategy Market development strategy that involves focusing on a smaller number of markets.

Concept Written description or visual depiction of a new product idea. A concept includes the product's primary features and benefits.

Conceptual skill The cognitive ability to see the organization as a whole and the relationship among its parts.

Conclusion The *then* component of an *if-then* rule in knowledge representation.

Concurrent control Control that consists of monitoring ongoing activities to ensure their consistency with standards.

Concurrent engineering A process in which an organization designs a product or service using input and evaluations from business units and functions early in the process, anticipating problems, and balancing the needs of all parties. The emphasis is on upstream prevention versus downstream correction.

Concurrent validity Measured when an employer tests current employees and correlates the scores with their performance ratings.

Conditional probabilities The probability of one event given the known outcome of a (possibly) related event.

Confiscation Governmental taking of foreign-owned property without payment (or for a highly inadequate payment) or for a nonpublic purpose.

Conflict Antagonistic interaction in which one party attempts to thwart the intentions or goals of another.

Conflict in marketing channels Occurs when one channel member believes that another channel member is impeding the attainment of its goals.

Conflict resolution A process for resolving disagreements in a manner acceptable to all parties.

Conformance An affirmative indication or judgment that a product or service has met the requirements of a relevant specification, contract, or regulation.

Confucianism A system of practical ethics based on a set of pragmatic rules for daily life derived from experience.

Congeneric merger A merger of firms in the same general industry, but for which no customer or supplier relationship exists.

Conglomerate merger A merger of companies in totally different industries.

Conquest marketing Strategy for constantly seeking new customers by offering discounts and markdowns and developing promotions that encourage new business.

Consensus 1: Finding a proposal acceptable enough that all team members can support the decision and no member opposes it. **2:** Employed in choice and implementation tactics within collectivist cultures to maintain harmony and unity.

Consequence The result obtained when a decision alternative is chosen and a chance event occurs. A measure of the consequence is often called a payoff.

Conservative approach 1: An approach to choosing a decision alternative without using probabilities. For a maximization problem, it leads to choosing the decision alternative that maximizes the minimum payoff; for a minimization problem, it leads to choosing the decision alternative that minimizes the maximum payoff. **2:** A policy where all of the fixed assets, all of the permanent current assets, and some of the temporary current assets of a firm are financed with long-term capital.

Conservative strategy A strategy that uses a majority of long-term sources to fulfill its financing needs. This strategy results in a higher current ratio but a lower level but more stable level of profitability during periods of normal yield curves.

Consideration A type of leader behavior that describes the extent to which a leader is sensitive to subordinates, respects their ideas and feelings, and establishes mutual trust.

Consigned stocks Inventories, generally of finished goods, that are in the possession of customers, dealers, agents, and so on, but remain the property of the manufacturer by agreement with those in possession. *Syn:* consignment inventory.

Consignment An arrangement whereby a retailer obtains an inventory item without obligation. If not sold, the inventory can be returned.

Consistency principle A requirement that accounting methods be used consistently from one period to the next unless conditions have changed that make it appropriate to switch to another method to provide more useful information.

Consistent norms Values that are more culturally specific, but that are consistent with hypernorms and other legitimate norms.

Consol A perpetual bond issued by the British government to consolidate past debts; in general, any perpetual bond.

Consolidated financial statements Financial statements resulting from combining parent and subsidiary company statements. The statements prepared by the parent company that essentially portray the financial position and results of operations of the parent and its subsidiaries as though they were one economic unit.

Consolidation The creation of a new corporation by the transfer of assets and liabilities from two or more existing corporations.

Constancy of purpose Occurs when goals and objectives are properly aligned to the organizational vision and mission.

Constant dollar accounting *See:* Constant monetary unit restatement.

Constant growth model Also called the Gordon Model, it is used to find the value of a stock that is expected to experience constant growth.

Constant monetary unit restatement A general term for restating historical cost basis financial statements for changes in general purchasing power of the monetary unit.

Constant payout ratio Payment of a constant *percentage* of earnings as dividends each year.

Constraint 1: Restriction or limitation imposed on a problem **2:** A constraint may range from the intangible (for example, beliefs, culture) to the tangible (for example, posted rule prohibiting smoking, buildup of work-in-process awaiting the availability of a machine or operator).

Constraint management Pertains to identifying a constraint and working to remove or diminish the constraint, while dealing with resistance to change.

Construct A formally proposed concept representing relationships between empirically verifiable events and based on observed facts.

Construct validity Validity showing a relationship between an abstract characteristic and job performance.

Consultative Decision-making approach in which a person talks to others and considers their input before making a decision.

Consultative selling Process of helping customers reach their strategic goals by using the products and expertise of the sales organization.

Consulting services Services that are provided in the areas of management expertise on such issues as transportation and logistics.

Consumer behavior Process by which individuals or groups select, use, or dispose of goods, services, ideas, or experiences to satisfy needs and wants.

Consumer decision making Process that typically involves whether to purchase, what to purchase, when to purchase, from whom to purchase, and how to pay for a purchase.

Consumer market customers End users of a product or service.

Consumer profiling The collection of information about individual shoppers in order to know and serve consumers better.

Consumer's risk For a sampling plan, refers to the probability of acceptance of a lot, the quality of which has a designated numerical value representing a level that is seldom desirable. Usually the designated value will be the lot tolerance percent defective (LTPD). Also called beta risk or type 2 error.

Consumption satiation Occurs when the more units of a product that are consumed in a short period of time, the less the added value of consuming another unit of the same product and the greater the variety-seeking behavior.

Container ships Ships designed to carry standardized containers, which greatly facilitate loading and unloading as well as intermodal transfers.

Content analysis A set of procedures for transforming unstructured written material into a format for analysis.

Content theories A group of theories that emphasize the needs that motivate people.

Content validity Validity measured by use of a logical, nonstatistical method to identify the KSAs and other characteristics necessary to perform a job.

Contingency An amount a contractor may include in a proposal to cover unexpected costs that may arise during a project; management reserve.

Contingency approach A model of leadership that describes the relationship between leadership styles and specific organizational situations.

Contingency decision making A style of decision making committed to recognizing the uniqueness of different situations and therefore using different approaches when confronting varying situations, cultures, and so on.

Contingency graph Graph showing the net profit to a speculator in currency options under various exchange rate scenarios.

Contingency plans Plans that define company responses to specific situations, such as emergencies, setbacks, or unexpected conditions.

Contingency view An extension of the humanistic perspective in which the successful resolution of organizational problems is thought to depend on managers' identification of key variables in the situation at hand.

Contingent liability A possible liability. If the likelihood of payment is "probable," the contingent liability must be reported as a liability on the financial statements; if likelihood of payment is reasonably possible, it must be disclosed in the footnotes to the financial statements; if likelihood of payment is remote, no mention of the possible liability needs to be made.

Contingent workers People who work for an organization, but not on a permanent or full-time basis, including temporary placements, contracted professionals, or leased employees.

Continuous budgeting A method of budgeting that provides for maintaining a twelve-month projection into the future.

Continuous compounding A situation in which interest is added continuously rather than at discrete points in time.

Continuous improvement A management philosophy embraced by companies who constantly improve the quality and productivity of their operations in order to survive. A wide range of approaches to continuous improvement exist, including total quality management (TQM), and statistical process control (SPC).

Continuous probability distribution 1: A graph or formula representing the probability of a particular numeric value of continuous (variable) data, based on a particular type of process that produces the data. **2:** The number of possible outcomes is unlimited or infinite.

Continuous process improvement Includes the actions taken throughout an organization to increase the effectiveness and efficiency of activities and processes in order to provide added benefits to the customer and organization. It is considered a subset of total quality management and operates according to the premise that organizations can always make improvements. Continuous improvement can also be equated with reducing process variation.

Continuous reinforcement schedule A schedule in which every occurrence of the desired behavior is reinforced.

Continuously compounding When compounding is done every moment.

Contra accounts Accounts that are offset against other accounts.

Contra asset An account that affects an asset account, such as the allowance for uncollectible accounts receivable or accumulated depreciation.

Contract 1: An agreement between two or more parties that can be legally enforced. A contractual relationship between two or more commercial entities allows the shifting of risk between the entities in order to obtain the stated purpose of the contract. **2:** An agreement between a contractor, who agrees to provide a product or service (deliverables), and a customer, who agrees to pay the contractor a certain amount of money in return.

Contract enforcement Usually, a contract entered into by firms from different nations stipulates whose law is applied in the event of default. However, some countries' legal systems mandate that the laws of the nation where the contract was signed shall be applied. Other legal systems mandate that the laws of the country where the contract was executed shall be applied.

Contract manufacturing Using another firm for the manufacture of goods so that the marketer may concentrate on the research and development as well as marketing aspects of the operation.

Contract rate The interest rate specified on a bond; sometimes called the *coupon rate of interest*.

Contract review Systematic activities carried out by an organization before agreeing to a contract to ensure that requirements for quality are adequately defined, free from ambiguity, documented, and can be realized by the supplier.

Contracting cost motive Theoretical motive for trade credit extension in which the buyers' sales contracting costs are reduced in that they can inspect the quantity and quality of the goods prior to payment due to the delayed payment offered.

Contractual alliances Many enterprises enter foreign markets via non–equity-based joint ventures, often referred to as contractual alliances or strategic alliances.

Contractual hedging A multinational firm's use of contracts to minimize its transaction exposure.

Contrast error Tendency to rate people relative to others rather than against performance standards.

Contribution margin Sales less variable costs and variable selling and administrative expenses.

Contribution margin analysis The systematic examination of the differences between planned and actual contribution margins.

Contribution margin ratio The percentage of each sales dollar that is available to cover the fixed costs and provide an operating income.

Contributor A national subsidiary with a distinctive competence, such as product development.

Contributory plan Pension plan in which the money for pension benefits is paid in by both employees and employers.

Control 1: A policy or procedure that is part of internal control. **2:** Refers to restrictions on what a foreign investor may own or control in another country.

Control activities or procedures Specific error-checking routines performed by company personnel.

Control chart Basic tool that consists of a chart with upper and lower control limits on which values of some statistical measure for a series of samples or subgroups are plotted. It frequently shows a central line to help detect a trend of plotted values toward either control limit. It is used to monitor and analyze variation from a process to see whether the process is in statistical control.

Control environment The actions, policies, and procedures that reflect the overall attitudes of top management, the directors, and the owners about control and its importance to the entity.

Control limits Trigger points that signal a purchase or sale of securities, and are part of the decision-making apparatus in the Miller-Orr cash management model.

Control plan Document that may include the characteristics for quality of a product or service, measurements, and methods of control.

Control sample That part of a sample group that is left unchanged and receives no special treatment, and serves as a basis of comparison to allow analysis of the results of an experiment.

Control system A system that compares the actual performance (results) with planned performance (goals) so that management may take appropriate action as necessary.

Control unit The circuitry in the CPU that fetches instructions and data from the primary memory, decodes the instructions, passes them to the ALU for execution, and stores the results in the primary memory.

Controllable costs Cost that can be influenced (increased, decreased, or eliminated) by someone such as a manager or factory worker.

Controllable expenses Costs that can be influenced by the decisions of a manager.

Controllable input The decision alternatives or inputs to a simulation model that can be specified by the decision maker.

Controllable variance The difference between the actual amount of variable factory overhead cost incurred and the amount of variable factory overhead budgeted for the standard product.

Controls Constraints applied to a system to ensure proper use and security standards.

Controlled disbursement accounts (CDA) Checking accounts in which funds are not deposited until checks are presented for payment, usually on a daily basis.

Controller The chief management accountant of a business.

Controlling account The account in the general ledger that summarizes the balances of the accounts in a subsidiary ledger.

Convenience quota sample Sample of consumers that is not randomly sampled from a population (for example, users of the product) but is obtained through approaching people in a mall to participate. Quotas are placed on how many men and women should be interviewed (for example, 200 of each) or some other demographic categorization such as age, education, or income.

Convenience translation Translation of currency using the year-end exchange rates.

Conversation analysis A study of talk-in-interaction with people (that is, analyzing spoken words).

Conversational principles Those principles governing verbal and nonverbal communication applicable in all aspects of cross-cultural communication.

Conversion The process of abandoning an old information system and implementing a new one.

Conversion costs The combination of direct labor and factory overhead costs.

Conversion ratio, CR The number of shares of common stock that can be obtained by converting a convertible bond or a share of convertible preferred stock.

Conversion value The equivalent amount of another currency at a given exchange rate.

Convertible bond A bond that is exchangeable, at the option of the holder, for common stock of the issuing firm.

Convertible security A security, usually a bond or preferred stock, that is exchangeable at the option of the holder for the common stock of the issuing firm.

Cookie A small file that a Web site places on a visitor's hard disk so that the Web site can remember something about the visitor later, such as an ID number or user name.

Coordinated decentralization The providing of overall corporate strategy by headquarters while granting subsidiaries the freedom to implement it within established ranges.

Coordinated intervention A currency value management method whereby the central banks of the major nations simultaneously intervene in the currency markets, hoping to change a currency's value.

Coordination The quality of collaboration across departments.

Coordination costs The time and energy needed to coordinate the activities of a team to enable it to perform its task.

Co-payment Employee's payment of a portion of the cost of both insurance premiums and medical care.

Copromotion agreement A product that is promoted jointly by two companies under the same brand name and marketing plan. Generally the manufacturing company handles receivables, inventory, and so on and pays a commission to the copromotor. Compensation is almost always based on the product sales level.

Copyright The exclusive right to publish and sell a literary, artistic, or musical composition.

Core benefit proposition (CBP) Primary benefit or purpose for which a customer buys a product. The CBP may reside in the physical good or service performance, or it may come from augmented dimensions of the product.

Core competence 1: A business activity that an organization does particularly well in comparison to competitors. **2:** A unique capability that creates high value and that differentiates the organization from its competition.

Core processes Will have a major impact on the strategic goals of an organization.

Corporate agency services Security-related services, some of which are related to short-term borrowing and investing, offered by financial institutions to publicly held corporations.

Corporate charter A document filed with the secretary of the state in which the firm is incorporated that provides information about the company, including its name, address, directors, and amount of capital stock.

Corporate citizenship Includes corporate social responsiveness and corporate social performance.

Corporate culture 1: (While the word "corporate" typically appears, the culture referred to may be that of any type of organization, large or small) relates to the collective beliefs, values, attitudes, manners, customs, behaviors, and artifacts unique to an organization. **2:** Refers to an organization's practice, such as its symbols, heroes, and rituals, and its values, such as its employees' perception of good/evil, beautiful/ugly, normal/abnormal, and rational/irrational. The practice aspects differ from corporation to corporation within a national culture, and the value aspects vary from country to country.

Corporate governance The method by which a firm is being governed, directed, administered, or controlled and to the goals for which it is being governed. Corporate governance is concerned with the relative roles, rights, and accountability of such stakeholder groups as owners, boards of directors, managers, employees, and others who assert to be stakeholders.

Corporate income tax A tax applied to all residual earnings, regardless of what is retained or what is distributed as dividends.

Corporate-level strategy The level of strategy concerned with the question "What business are we in?" Pertains to the organization as a whole and the combination of business units and product lines that make it up.

Corporate public affairs and public affairs management The management processes that focus on the formalization and institutionalization of corporate public policy. The public affairs function is a logical and increasingly prevalent component of the overall strategic management process.

Corporate public policy A firm's posture, stance, strategy, or position regarding the public, social, and ethical aspects of stakeholders and corporate functioning.

Corporate social performance model Includes social responsibility categories, philosophy (or mode) of social responsiveness, and social (or stakeholder) issues involved.

Corporate social responsibility An objective to respond appropriately everywhere possible to societal expectations and environmental needs.

Corporate social responsiveness The action-oriented variant of corporate social responsibility.

Corporate sponsorships Involve investments in events or causes for the purpose of achieving various corporate objectives, such as increasing sales volume, enhancing a company's reputation or a brand's image, and increasing brand awareness.

Corporate university An in-house training and education facility that offers broad-based learning opportunities for employees.

Corporate (within-firm) risk Risk that does not take into consideration the effects of stockholders' diversification; it is measured by a project's effect on the firm's earnings variability.

Corporation 1: A legal entity created by a state, separate and distinct from its owners and managers, having unlimited life, easy transferability of ownership, and limited liability. **2:** An artificial entity created by the state and existing apart from its owners. **3:** A separate legal entity that is organized in accordance with state or federal statutes and in which ownership is divided into shares of stock.

Corrective action Action taken to eliminate the root cause(s) and symptom(s) of an existing deviation or nonconformity to prevent recurrence.

Corrective control An action or procedure that will ensure the correction of an error or omission.

Correlation Refers to the measure of the relationship between two sets of numbers or variables.

Correlation coefficient 1: Describes the magnitude and direction of the relationship between two variables. **2:** Index number giving the relationship between a predictor and a criterion variable.

Correlation coefficient, r A measure of the degree of relationship between two variables.

Correspondent banks Banks located in different countries and unrelated by ownership that have a reciprocal agreement to provide services to each other's customers.

Correspondent firms *See:* Representative firms.

Corruption Dishonesty that involves the following schemes: (1) bribery, (2) conflicts of interest, (3) economic extortion, and (4) illegal gratuities.

Cost 1: The amount the customer has agreed to pay for acceptable project deliverables. **2:** A disbursement of cash (or a commitment to pay cash in the future) for the purpose of generating revenues.

Cost accounting system A system used to accumulate manufacturing costs for financial reporting and decision-making purposes.

Cost allocation The process of assigning indirect cost to a cost object, such as a job.

Cost and freight (CFR) Seller quotes a price for the goods, including the cost of transportation to the named port of debarkation. Cost and choice of insurance are left to the buyer.

Cost-based transfer pricing The price one segment of a company charges another segment of the same company for the transfer of a good or a service based on some type of cost. Examples include variable manufacturing costs, full manufacturing (absorption) costs, and full product costs.

Cost-benefit analysis An evaluation of the costs incurred by a system or project and the benefits gained by the system or the project.

Cost behavior The manner in which a cost changes in relation to its activity base (driver).

Cost center A responsibility center in which a manager is accountable for costs only. A decentralized unit in which the department or division manager has responsibility for the control of costs incurred and the authority to make decisions that affect these costs.

Cost concept The basis for entering the exchange price, or cost, into the accounting records.

Cost distortion Inaccurate product costs that are the result of applying a cost allocation method that is inappropriate for the situation.

Cost driver Any factor that causes a change in the cost of an activity.

Cost driver analysis In activity-based cost accounting, the examination of the impact of cost drivers. The results of this analysis are useful in the continuous improvement of cost, quality, and delivery times.

Cost estimate Estimate of total cost of an activity based on the types and quantities of resources required for that activity.

Cost, insurance, and freight (CIF) Seller quotes a price including insurance, all transportation, and miscellaneous charges to the point of debarkation from the vessel or aircraft.

Cost leadership 1: A pricing tactic where a company offers an identical product or service at a lower cost than the competition. **2:** A type of competitive strategy with which the organization aggressively seeks efficient facilities, cuts costs, and employs tight cost controls to be more efficient than competitors.

Costly trade credit Credit taken in excess of "free" trade credit, whose cost is equal to the discount lost.

Cost method A method of accounting for an investment in common stock, by which the investor recognizes as income its share of cash dividends of the investee.

Cost object Any customer, product, service, project, or other work unit for which a separate cost measurement is desired.

Cost of communication The cost of communicating electronically or by telephone with other locations. These costs have been drastically reduced through the use of fiber-optic cables.

Cost of goods sold The cost of goods sold to customers; calculated by subtracting ending inventory from the sum of beginning inventory plus purchases.

Cost of goods sold budget A budget in which the desired ending inventory and the estimated beginning inventory data are combined with data from direct materials budget, direct labor budget, and factory overhead cost budget.

Cost of living allowance (COLA) An allowance paid during assignment overseas to enable the employee to maintain the same standard of living as at home.

Cost of merchandise sold The cost of merchandise purchased by a merchandise business and sold.

Cost of new common equity, k^e The cost of external equity; based on the cost of retained earnings, but increased for flotation costs.

Cost of poor quality (COPQ) Costs associated with providing poor-quality products or services.

Cost of preferred stock, k_{ps} The rate of return investors require on the firm's preferred stock. k_{ps} is calculated as the preferred dividend, D_{ps}, divided by the net issuing price, NP.

Cost of production report A report prepared periodically by a processing department, summarizing 1) the units for which the department is accountable and the disposition of those units and 2) the costs incurred by the department and the allocation of those costs between completed and incomplete production.

Cost of quality (COQ) Costs incurred in assuring quality of a product or service. There are four categories of poor quality costs: internal failure costs (costs associated with defects found before delivery of the product or service); external failure costs (costs associated with defects found during or after product or service delivery); appraisal costs (costs incurred to determine the degree of conformance to quality requirements); and prevention costs (costs incurred to keep failure and appraisal costs to a minimum).

Cost of quality report A report summarizing the costs, percent of total, and percent of sales by appraisal, prevention, internal failure, and external failure cost of quality categories.

Cost of retained earnings, k_s The rate of return required by stockholders on a firm's existing common stock.

Cost of risk The sum of 1) outlays to reduce risks, 2) the opportunity cost of activities forgone due to risk considerations, 3) expenses of strategies to finance potential losses, and 4) the cost of reimbursed losses.

Cost per equivalent unit The rate used to allocate costs between completed and partially completed production in a process costing system.

Cost per thousand Calculated by dividing the cost of an ad placed in a particular ad vehicle (for example, certain magazine) by the number of people (expressed in thousands) who are exposed to that vehicle.

Cost performance index (CPI) A measure of the cost efficiency with which the project is being performed; the cumulative earned value divided by the cumulative actual cost.

Cost price approach An approach to transfer pricing that uses cost as the basis for setting the transfer price.

Cost-plus method A pricing policy in which there is a full allocation of foreign and domestic costs to the product.

Cost-reimbursement contract A contract in which a customer agrees to pay a contractor for all actual costs incurred during a project, plus some agreed-upon profit.

Cost variance (CV) 1: An indicator of cost performance; the cumulative earned value minus the cumulative actual cost. **2:** The difference between actual cost and the flexible budget at actual volumes.

Cost-volume-profit analysis The systematic examination of the relationships among selling prices, volume of sales and production, costs, expenses, and profits.

Cost-volume-profit chart A chart used to assist management in understanding the relationships among costs, expenses, sales, and operating profit or loss.

Count chart Control chart for evaluating the stability of a process in terms of the count of events of a given classification occurring in a sample.

Counterpurchase 1: A refinement of simple barter that unlinks the timing of the two transactions. **2:** Exchange of goods between two parties under two distinct contracts expressed in monetary terms.

Countertrade 1: A buyer of a product pays the seller with another product of the equivalent monetary value. **2:** Sale of goods to one country which is linked to the purchase or exchange of goods from that same country.

Count-per-unit chart Control chart for evaluating the stability of a process in terms of the average count of events of a given classification per unit occurring in a sample.

Country-related cultural factors framework Identifies certain national cultural dimensions and their impact on decision-making behavior.

Country risk Characteristics of the host country, including political and financial conditions, that can affect the MNC's cash flows. The possibility of loss of assets due to political, economic, or regulatory instability in a nation in which business is being conducted.

Coupon-equivalent yield Interest return figure calculated based on a 365-day year instead of 360 days. For a discount security maturing within one year, it is also adjusted to account for the fact that the price paid is less than the face value, which increases the true yield.

Coupon interest rate The stated annual rate of interest paid on a bond.

Coupon payment The specified number of dollars of interest paid each period, generally each six months, on a bond.

Coupon security One which pays interest periodically prior to maturity.

Coups d'état A forced change in a country's government, often resulting in attacks of foreign firms and policy changes by the new government.

Coverage ratios Ratios that measure the degree of protection for long-term creditors and investors.

Covered interest arbitrage Investment in a foreign money market security with a simultaneous forward sale of the currency denominating that security.

Covert operations Placing an agent in an undercover role in order to observe the suspect.

Cp Widely used process capability index. It is expressed as:

$$\frac{\text{upper spec limit} - \text{lower spec limit}}{6\sigma}$$

Cpk a widely used process capability index. It is expressed as:

(ratio with smallest answer)
$$\frac{\text{upper specification limit} - \overline{X}}{3\sigma}$$

or

$$\frac{\overline{X} - \text{lower specification limit}}{3\sigma}$$

CQI Continuous quality improvement.

Crash cost The estimated cost of completing an activity in the shortest possible time (the crash time).

Crash time The shortest estimated length of time in which an activity can be completed.

Crawford Slip Method Method of gathering and presenting anonymous data from a group.

Creativity The generation of novel ideas that may meet perceived needs or offer opportunities for the organization.

Credence attributes Cannot be evaluated confidently even immediately after consumption.

Credit The right side of an account; the amount entered on the right side of an account; to enter an amount on the right side of an account.

Credit administration The establishment of credit policy and planning, organizing, directing, and controlling all aspects of the credit function.

Credit decision process Sequence beginning with the marketing contact with potential customers and ending with the credit extension decision. Includes credit investigation, customer information contacts, written document preparation, credit file establishment, and financial analysis.

Credit extension The decision to sell on credit to a customer.

Credit-granting decision Determination of whether and how much credit to give customers, a process which involves four distinct steps: development of credit standards, getting necessary information about customers, application of credit standards, and setting credit limits.

Credit interchange bureaus Departments of local credit associations that provide information on the credit history of local businesses and individuals.

Credit limit Where credit is extended, the maximum dollar amount that cumulative credit purchases can reach for a given customer. Also known as the credit line.

Credit memorandum The form issued by a seller to inform a buyer that a credit has been posted to the buyer's account receivable.

Credit period The length of time for which credit is granted; after that time, the credit account is considered delinquent.

Credit policy A set of decisions that includes a firm's credit standards, credit terms, methods used to collect credit accounts, and credit monitoring procedures.

Credit reporting agencies Sources of business credit information, such as Dun & Bradstreet.

Credit scoring models Evaluation approach that weights variables depending on their helpfulness in discriminating between "good" and "bad" applicants, based on past payment histories. These models are developed with the assistance of computerized statistical techniques such as multiple discriminant analysis.

Credit standards Standards that indicate the minimum financial strength a customer must have to be granted credit.

Credit terms Specification of when invoiced amounts are due and whether a cash discount can be taken for earlier payment.

Creditor A person or entity owed money by a debtor.

Criminal law Branch of law that deals with offenses of a public nature or against society.

Crisis A major, unpredictable event that has potentially negative results. The event and its aftermath may significantly damage an organization and its employees, products, services, financial condition, and reputation.

Crisis resolution stage The final stage of a crisis and the goal of all crisis management efforts.

Criteria A set of standards against which an internal control system can be measured in determining its effectiveness.

Criteria for successful segmentation Includes target markets that are heterogeneous, measurable, substantial, actionable, and accessible.

Criterion Standard, rule, or test upon which a judgment or decision can be based.

Criterion-related validity Validity measured by a procedure that uses a test as the predictor of how well an individual will perform on the job.

Critical commodities list A U.S. Department of Commerce file containing information about products that are either particularly sensitive to national security or controlled for other purposes.

Critical incident Event that has greater than normal significance, often used as a learning or feedback opportunity.

Critical path 1: The sequence of tasks that takes the longest time and determines a project's completion date. **2:** In a network diagram, any path of activities with zero or negative total slack. *See:* Most critical path.

Critical path method (CPM) 1: Activity-oriented project management technique that uses arrow-diagramming techniques to demonstrate both the time and cost required to complete a project. It provides one time estimate—normal time. **2:** A network planning technique.

Critical ratio A dispatching rule that calculates a priority index number by dividing the time to due date remaining by the expected elapsed time to finish the job. For example,

$$\text{critical ratio} = \frac{\text{time remaining}}{\text{work remaining}} = \frac{30}{40} = .75$$

A ratio less than 1.0 indicates the job is behind schedule, a ratio greater than 1.0 indicates the job is ahead of schedule, and a ratio of 1.0 indicates the job is on schedule.

Critical success factors Processes and their results that are critical to the success of business units. One approach to defining requirements for information systems is the outlining of CSFs by managers.

Cross-border factoring Factoring by a network of factors across borders. The exporter's factor can contact correspondent factors in other countries to handle the collections of accounts receivable.

Cross-cultural communication Effective communication across nations/cultures can only take place when the sender encodes the message using language, idioms, norms and values, and so on, that are familiar to the receiver or when the receiver is familiar with the language, idioms, and so on, used by the sender. Also, the sender and receiver must be aware of both his or her own and the other's environmental, cultural, sociocultural, and psychocultural contexts.

Cross-cultural message adjustment The process of adjusting and adapting incoming signifiers to the existing repository of signs, and of adapting and adjusting the repository of signifieds to create new signs.

Cross-cultural research Conducted by researchers from one culture to ascertain how people in one or more other cultures behave—usually to identify the similarities and differences existing among the cultures.

Cross-cultural social responsibility A firm's actions must take into account not only the well-being of stockholders, but also the well-being of the community, the employees, and the customers.

Cross-currency swap An agreement by two parties to exchange their liabilities or assets in different currencies.

Cross exchange rate Exchange rate between currency A and currency B, given the values of currencies A and B with respect to a third currency.

Cross-functional team A group of employees from various functional departments that meet as a team to resolve mutual problems.

Cross hedge A hedge that uses a futures contract that has a different underlying instrument from the cash market instrument being hedged.

Cross-hedging Hedging an open position in one currency with a hedge on another currency that is highly correlated with the first currency. This occurs when for some reason the common hedging techniques cannot be applied to the first currency. A cross-hedge is not a perfect hedge, but can substantially reduce the exposure.

Cross-marketing activities A reciprocal arrangement whereby each partner provides the other access to its markets for a product.

Cross rates Exchange rate quotations which do not include the U.S. dollar as one of the two currencies quoted.

Crossover rate The discount rate at which the NPV profiles of two projects cross and, thus, at which the projects' NPVs are equal.

Cross-sectional analysis Analysis of relationships among a cross-section of firms, countries, or some other variable at a given point in time.

Cross-subsidization The use of resources accumulated in one part of the world to fight a competitive battle in another.

Cultural assimilator A program in which trainees for overseas assignments must respond to scenarios of specific situations in a particular country.

Cultural barriers Business behavior in one culture does not transfer well to another culture due to cultural differences. For example, Americans' "spirit of competitiveness" culture does not transfer well to "spirit of cooperation" cultures, such as Japan.

Cultural briefing Predeparture education and orientation of the expatriate and his or her family about the foreign country. The briefing includes the country's cultural traditions, history, government, economy, living conditions, and so on.

Cultural contexts *See:* Cross-cultural communication.

Cultural convergence Increasing similarity among cultures accelerated by technological advances.

Cultural differences The many ways in which people from different countries vary in their tastes, gestures, treatment of others, attitudes, and opinions.

Cultural environment To develop an effective international business strategy, the critical aspects of culture must be identified.

Cultural fluency A strong command of not only the language of a foreign country, but also its culture. This is required for effective cross-cultural communication.

Cultural imperialism Criticism by some that the United States is forcing its products and culture on other cultures through technological advances and the globalization of business.

Cultural leader A manager who uses signals and symbols to influence corporate culture.

Cultural relativism The belief that no culture's ethics are any better than any other's.

Cultural risk The risk of business blunders, poor customer relations, and wasted negotiations that results when firms fail to understand and adapt to the differences between their own and host countries' cultures.

Cultural-toughness dimension Through a battery of tests, an assessor determines if an applicant for an expatriate assignment has the ability to adapt to the "toughness" of a specific culture.

Cultural universals Manifestations of the total way of life of any group of people.

Culture 1: Comprises an entire set of social norms and responses that condition people's behavior; it is acquired and inculcated, a set of rules and behavior patterns that an individual learns but does not inherit at birth. **2:** System of values, beliefs, and behaviors inherent in an organization or society. *See:* corporate culture.

Culture-free A theory proposing that managerial behavior is affected by specific situations in all cultures.

Culture/people change A change in employees' values, norms, attitudes, beliefs, and behavior.

Culture gap The difference between an organization's desired cultural norms and values and actual norms and values.

Culture shock The more pronounced reactions to the psychological disorientation that most people feel when they move for an extended period of time into a markedly different culture. What expatriates experience after the novelty of living in a new culture wears out.

Culture shock phase The third phase in the expatriation process usually begins two months into the disillusionment phase. After two months of day-to-day confusion, the expatriate faces culture shock and wishes to go back to his or her old, familiar environment.

Culture-specific A theory proposing that managerial behavior is affected by a nation's culture.

Cumulative actual cost (CAC) The amount that has actually been expended to accomplish all the work performed up to a specific point in time.

Cumulative available-to-promise (ATP) A calculation based on the available-to-promise (ATP) figure in the master schedule. Two methods of computing the cumulative available-to-promise are used, with and without lookahead calculation. The cumulative with lookahead ATP equals the ATP from the previous period plus the MPS of the period minus the backlog of the period minus the sum of the differences between the backlogs and MPSs of all future periods until, but not to include, the period where point production exceeds the backlogs. The cumulative without lookahead procedure equals the ATP in the previous period plus the MPS, minus the backlog in the period being considered. *See:* available-to-promise.

Cumulative budgeted cost (CBC) The amount budgeted to accomplish all the work scheduled to be performed up to a specific point in time.

Cumulative dividends A protective feature on preferred stock that requires preferred dividends previously not paid to be paid before any common dividends can be paid.

Cumulative earned value (CEV) The value of the work actually performed up to a specific point in time; total budgeted cost multiplied by the percent of the work estimated to be complete.

Cumulative lead time The longest planned length of time to accomplish the activity in question. For any item planned through MRP, it is found by reviewing the lead time for each bill of material path below the item; whichever path adds up to the greatest number defines cumulative lead time. *Syn:* aggregate lead time, combined lead time, composite lead time, critical path lead time, stacked lead time. *See:* planning time fence.

Cumulative manufacturing lead time The cumulative planned lead time when all purchased items are assumed to be in stock. *Syn:* composite manufacturing lead time.

Cumulative MRP The planning of parts and subassemblies by exploding a master schedule, as in MRP, except that the master-scheduled items and therefore the exploded requirements are time phased in cumulative form. Usually these cumulative figures cover a planning year.

Cumulative preferred stock Preferred stock that is entitled to current and past dividends before dividends may be paid on common stock.

Cumulative receipts A cumulative number, or running total, as a count of parts received in a series or sequence of shipments. The cumulative receipts provide a number that can be compared with the cumulative figures from a plan developed by cumulative MRP.

Cumulative sum control chart Control chart on which the plotted value is the cumulative sum of deviations of successive samples from a target value. The ordinate of each plotted point represents the algebraic sum of the previous ordinate and the most recent deviations from the target.

Cumulative transaction adjustment (CTA) A balance sheet account created to maintain a balanced translation for the purchase of a subsidiary; the CTA has no effect on the firm until the subsidiary is either sold or liquidated.

Cumulative trauma disorders (CTDs) Muscle and skeletal injuries that occur when workers repetitively use the same muscles to perform tasks.

Currency Board System for maintaining the value of the local currency with respect to some other specified currency.

Currency call option Contract that grants the right to purchase a specific currency at a specific price (exchange rate) within a specific period of time.

Currency cocktail bond Bond denominated in a mixture (or cocktail) of currencies.

Currency diversification Process of using more than one currency as an investing or financing strategy. Exposure to a diversified currency portfolio typically results in less exchange rate risk than if all of the exposure was in a single foreign currency.

Currency exchange rate 1: The rates at which currency in another country can be exchanged for U.S. dollars. **2:** Countries' currency exchange rates fluctuate. Fluctuations can be dirty or clean. Dirty fluctuations result when a government adjusts the exchange rate up or down. Clean fluctuations are the result of supply and demand.

Currency flows The movement of currency from nation to nation, which in turn determine exchange rates.

Currency futures contract Contract specifying a standard volume of a particular currency to be exchanged on a specific settlement date.

Currency options contract A contract giving one of the parties the right to decide in the future whether an exchange will actually take place at a certain price.

Currency put option Contract granting the right to sell a particular currency at a specified price (exchange rate) within a specified period of time.

Currency swap 1: Agreement to exchange one currency for another at a specified exchange rate and date. Banks commonly serve as intermediaries between two parties who wish to engage in a currency swap. **2:** An agreement by which a firm exchanges or swaps its debt service payments in one currency for debt service payments in a different currency. The equivalent of the interest rate swap, only the currency of denomination of the debt is different.

Current account An account in the BOP statement that records the results of transactions involving merchandise, services, and unilateral transfers between countries.

Current assets Cash or other assets that are expected to be converted to cash or sold or used up, usually within a year or less, through the normal operations of a business.

Current cost accounting *See:* Current value accounting.

Current exchange rate The exchange rate on the balance sheet date.

Current liabilities Liabilities that will be due within a short time (usually one year or less) and that are to be paid out of current assets.

Current liquidity index A cash coverage ratio found by adding beginning of period balance of cash assets and the cash flow from operations during the period and then dividing this sum by the sum of beginning of period notes payable and current maturing debt.

Current maturity The length of time remaining until a security matures. When first issued a five-year Treasury note has an original maturity of five years; one year later it has a current maturity of four years.

Current-noncurrent method A translation method in which balance sheet items classified as "current" are translated at the current exchange rate on the balance sheet date, and items classified as "noncurrent" are translated at appropriate historical rates.

Current purchasing power accounting *See:* Constant monetary unit restatement.

Current rate method A translation method that translates all assets and all liabilities at the current exchange rate—the rate on the balance sheet date. Paid-in capital accounts are translated at the applicable historical rates, dividends at the exchange rate on the date of declaration and on the income statement, and all revenue and expense items at the weighted average exchange rate for the period.

Current ratio Measure of the liquidity of a business; equal to current assets divided by current liabilities. It indicates the extent to which current liabilities are covered by assets expected to be converted into cash in the near future.

Current reality tree Technique used in applying Goldratt's Theory of Constraints.

Current transfer A current account on the Balance of Payments statement that records gifts from the residents of one country to the residents of another.

Current value accounting Valuation systems designed to show the effects of changes in prices of individual items on financial statements.

Current yield The annual interest payment on a bond divided by its current market value.

Currently attainable standards Standards that represent levels of operation that can be attained with reasonable effort.

Custody account Specialized account in which financial institution holds securities, automatically reinvests interest and other investment-related cash receipts, transfers funds per corporate instructions, monitors issuers actions such as calls and refundings, and provides a monthly statement on all account transactions.

Custom-designed software Software designed to meet the specific needs of a particular organization or department; also called *tailored software*.

Customer 1: The entity that provides the funds necessary to accomplish a project. A customer may be a person, an organization, or a group of people or organizations. **2:** Recipient of a product or service provided by a supplier. *See:* external customer and internal customer.

Customer-centric companies Companies that set explicit targets for retaining customers and make extraordinary efforts to exceed their customer loyalty goals.

Customer council Group usually composed of representatives from an organization's largest customers who meet to discuss common issues.

Customer delight Result achieved when customer requirements are exceeded in ways the customer finds valuable.

Customer fraud Customers not paying for goods purchased, getting something for nothing, or deceiving organizations into giving them something they should not have.

Customer involvement The active participation of customers; a characteristic of services in that customers often are actively involved in the provision of services they consume.

Customer loyalty/retention Result of an organization's plans, processes, practices, and efforts designed to deliver their services or products in ways which create retained and committed customers.

Customer-oriented The salesperson seeks to elicit customer needs/problems and then takes the necessary steps to meet those needs or solve the problem in a manner that is in the best interest of the customer.

Customer prototypes Detailed pictures and descriptions of individuals or firms in the target market for a product. Creating these descriptions helps firms envision how products and the marketing mix might best be combined to maximize profits.

Customer relationship management (CRM) 1: The process of identifying, attracting, differentiating, and retaining customers; relies on systematized processes to profile key segments so that marketing and retention strategies can be customized for these customers. **2:** Refers to an organization's knowledge of their customers' unique requirements and expectations, and using the information to develop a closer and more profitable link to business processes and strategies.

Customer relationship management (CRM) systems Systems that help companies track customers' interaction with the firm and allow employees to call up information on past transactions.

Customer requirements Specifications for a project and/or attributes of a deliverable specified by a customer in a request for proposal. Requirements may include size, quantity, color, speed, and other physical or operational parameters that a contractor's proposed solution must satisfy.

Customer retention Focusing a firm's marketing efforts toward the existing customer base.

Customer satisfaction Short-term, transaction-specific measure of whether customer perceptions meet or exceed customer expectations. Result of delivering a product or service that meets customer requirements, needs, and expectations. An important measure of quality.

Customer segmentation Process of differentiating customers based on one or more dimensions for the purpose of developing a marketing strategy to address specific segments.

Customer service 1: A total corporate effort aimed at customer satisfaction; customer service levels in terms of responsiveness that inventory policies permit for a given situation. **2:** Activities of dealing with customer questions; also sometimes the department that takes customer orders or provides post-delivery services. **3:** The function within an organization responsible for taking orders from customers and ensuring that the finished goods or services are delivered at the right time and in the right condition and quantity, and are billed correctly. This function may be located in the marketing, logistics, or operations part of an organization.

Customer structure An organizational structure in which divisions are formed on the basis of customer groups.

Customer–supplier partnership Long-term relationship between a buyer and supplier characterized by teamwork and mutual confidence. The supplier is considered an extension of the buyer's organization. The partnership is based on several commitments. The buyer provides long-term contracts and uses fewer suppliers. The supplier implements quality assurance processes so that incoming inspection can be minimized. The supplier also helps the buyer reduce costs and improve product and process designs.

Customer value Market-perceived quality adjusted for the relative price of a product.

Customization Products are modified to fit the needs of specific markets.

Customized application A computer program designed especially for an organization, to satisfy particular business needs.

Customs union Collaboration among trading countries in which members dismantle barriers to trade in goods and services and also establish a common trade policy with respect to nonmembers.

Cutoff time Deposit deadline for receiving a given day's stated availability.

Cybermall A virtual shopping mall on the Web.

Cybernetic system A system that enables corporations to monitor and coordinate the activities of its subsidiaries around the globe.

Cycle counting An inventory accuracy audit technique where inventory is counted on a cyclic schedule rather than once a year. A cycle inventory count is usually taken on a regular, defined basis (often more frequently for high-value or fast-moving items and less frequently for low-value or slow-moving items). Most effective cycle counting systems require the counting of a certain number of items every workday with each item counted at a prescribed frequency. The key purpose of cycle counting is to identify items in error, thus triggering research, identification, and elimination of the cause of the errors.

Cycle stock One of the two main conceptual components of any item inventory, the cycle stock is the most active component, that is, that which depletes gradually as customer orders are received and is replenished cyclically when supplier orders are received. The other conceptual component of the item inventory is the safety stock, which is a cushion of protection against uncertainty in the demand or in the replenishment lead time. *Syn:* cycle inventory.

Cycle time 1: In industrial engineering, the time between completion of two discrete units of production. For example, the cycle time of motors assembled at a rate of 120 per hour would be 30 seconds. **2:** In materials management, it refers to the length of time from when material enters a production facility until it exits. *Syn:* throughput time.

Cycle time reduction To reduce the time that it takes, from start to finish, to complete a particular process.

Cyclical component The component of the time series model that results in periodic above-trend and below-trend behavior of the time series lasting more than one year.

D

Daily NPV Is the difference between the present value of a project's daily inflows and the present value of its daily outflows.

Daily transfer rule The simplest and most common transfer rule that initiates a daily transfer from the deposit bank to the concentration bank in the amount of the daily deposit.

DASD (Direct Access Storage Device) An external storage medium that allows direct storage and retrieval of records from stored files. Example: magnetic disks and optical discs.

Data 1: Facts about people, other subjects, and events. May be manipulated and processed to produce information. **2:** Raw, unsummarized, and unanalyzed facts and figures. **3:** Facts presented in descriptive, numeric, or graphic form.

Data communication The transmission and reception of digitized data in the computer, between the computer and its peripheral devices, and between computers. Data communication over a distance is called *telecommunication*.

Data definition language The part of the database management system that allows the builder of a database to define the characteristics of fields and records, and the relationships among records.

Data dictionary The part of the database that contains information about the different sets of records and fields.

Data entry control Software controls whose purpose is to minimize errors in data entry, such as rejecting a Social Security number with more or fewer than nine digits.

Data flow diagram A convention of four symbols used to describe external entities, data stores, processes, and direction of data flow in an information system.

Data management module In a decision support system, a database or data warehouse that allows a decision maker to conduct the intelligence phase of decision making.

Data manipulation language The part of a database management system that allows the user to enter commands to retrieve, update, and manipulate data in a database.

Data mining Using a special application that scours large databases for relationships among business events, such as items typically purchased together on a certain day of the week, or machinery failures that occur along with a specific use mode of a machine. Instead of the user querying the databases, the application dynamically looks for such relationships.

Data privacy Electronic information security that restricts secondary use of data according to laws and preferences of the subjects.

Data processing The operation of changing and manipulating data.

Data range The amount of data from which information is extracted, in terms of the number of organizational units supplying data or the length of time the data cover.

Data redundancy The existence of the same data in more than one place in a computer system. Although some data redundancy is unavoidable, efforts should be made to minimize it.

Data store Any form of data at rest, such as a filing cabinet or a database.

Data theft Theft of data or personal information through such means as sniffing, spoofing, and customer impersonation.

Data warehouse 1: A huge collection of data that supports management decision making. **2:** The use of a huge database that combines all of a company's data and allows users to access the data directly, create reports, and obtain answers to what-if questions.

Database 1: Set of interrelated, centrally controlled data files that are stored with as little redundancy as possible. A database consolidates many records previously stored in separate files into a common pool of data and serves a variety of users and data processing applications. **2:** A collection of shared, interrelated records, usually in more than one file. An approach to data management that facilitates data entry, update, and manipulation.

Database administrator (DBA) The individual in charge of organizational databases.

Database approach An approach to maintaining data that contains a mechanism for tagging, retrieving, and manipulating data.

Database marketing Collecting and electronically storing (in a database) information about present, past, and prospective customers.

Database model The general logical structure in which records are stored within a database.

Daylight overdrafts Bookkeeping negative account balances which occur when a bank's Federal Reserve account book balance is negative during the day or it sends more funds via Fedwire than it receives, prior to final end-of-day settlements. Many of the overdrafts occur because of international funds transfers of government securities transactions.

Days of cost of goods sold invested in inventory An inventory activity measure which indicates the average number of days it takes to sell inventory.

Days inventory held The average number of days a firm holds inventory found by dividing average daily cost of goods sold into the balance sheet inventory account.

Days payables outstanding The average number of days the firm takes to pay for its purchases found by dividing average daily purchases into the balance sheet accounts payable balance.

Days purchases outstanding The average number of days a firm takes to pay its payables.

Days sales outstanding (DSO) Measure of how long a company is taking to collect receivables. Also known as average collection period. It is computed by taking the latest period's accounts receivables and dividing it by daily credit sales. Daily credit sales, in turn, are computed by taking the period's sales and dividing by the number of days in the period—365 when computing DSO over a yearly period. The average number of days credit customers take to pay for their purchases found by dividing average daily sales into the accounts receivable balance.

DBA (Database administrator) The IS professional in charge of building and maintaining the organization's databases.

DBMS (Database Management System) A computer program that allows the user to construct a database, populate it with data, and manipulate the data.

Dealers Market participants which typically "take a position" in the security instrument(s) they trade, meaning they hold an inventory of securities.

Debenture A long-term bond that is not secured by a mortgage on specific property.

Debit 1: The left side of an account. **2:** The amount entered on the left side of an account. **3:** To enter an amount on the left side of an account.

Debit cards Similar to credit cards except the transaction amount is immediately (or within two business days) charged against the user's checking account balance. These cards allow consumers to pay grocery and other bills through an electronic charge to their bank accounts.

Debit memorandum The form issued by a buyer to inform a seller that a debit has been posted to the seller's account payable.

Debt capital Capital that is financed by borrowing.

Debt financing Borrowing money that has to be repaid at a later date in order to start a business.

Debt ratio The ratio of total debt to total assets. It is a measure of the percentage of funds provided by creditors.

Debtor A person or entity declaring bankruptcy.

Debt-to-equity ratio The number of dollars of borrowed funds for every dollar invested by owners; computed as total liabilities divided by total equity.

Debugging The process of finding and correcting errors in software programs.

Decentralization 1: The separation of a business into more manageable operating units. **2:** Managers at the subsidiary are given the autonomy to make most of the important decisions relative to local matters.

Decentralized control The use of organization culture, group norms, and a focus on goals, rather than rules and procedures, to foster compliance with organizational goals.

Decentralized disbursing Corporate arrangement which allows payments to be made by divisional offices or individual stores, usually from accounts held at nearby banks.

Decentralized internal audit model In this type of organization, the internal auditors are on locations throughout the world, wherever international operations are located. Each international operation has its own internal audit organization.

Decentralized multinational organizations Organizations that give managements of the subsidiaries considerable independence of action.

Decentralized network A team communication structure in which team members freely communicate with one another and arrive at decisions together.

Decentralized planning Managers work with planning experts to develop their own goals and plans.

Decentralized processing system A collection system that has the company's various field offices or stores receive payments from the company's customers.

Decentralized transfer initiation The cash transfer decision initiated by the field office manager.

Decision A choice that must be made from between two or more alternatives.

Decision making The process of defining the problem, identifying the alternatives, determining the criteria, evaluating the alternatives, and choosing an alternative.

Decision matrix Matrix used by teams to evaluate problems or possible solutions. For example, after a matrix is drawn to evaluate possible solutions, the team lists them in the far-left vertical column. Next, the team selects criteria to rate the possible solutions, writing them across the top row. Then, each possible solution is rated on a scale of 1 to 5 for each criterion and the rating recorded in the corresponding grid. Finally, the ratings of all the criteria for each possible solution are added to determine its total score. The total score is then used to help decide which solution deserves the most attention.

Decision nodes Nodes indicating points where a decision is made.

Decision strategy A strategy involving a sequence of decisions and chance outcomes to provide the optimal solution to a decision problem.

Decision style Differences among people with respect to how they perceive problems and make decisions.

Decision support system (DSS) 1: An interactive, computer-based system that uses decision models and specialized databases to support an organization's decision makers. **2:** Information systems that aid managers in making decisions based on built-in models. DSSs comprise three modules: data management, model management, and dialog management.

Decision tree A graphical representation of the decision problem that shows the sequential nature of the decision-making process.

Decision variable Another term for controllable input.

Declining-balance depreciation method A method of depreciation that provides declining periodic depreciation expense over the estimated life of an asset.

Decode To translate the symbols used in a message for the purpose of interpreting its meaning.

Decomposition method Analysis of collection experience which involves segregating the period-to-period changes in receivables into three effects: the collection effect, the sales effect, and the interaction effect.

Decoupling inventory An amount of inventory kept between entities in a manufacturing or distribution network to create independence between processes or entities. The objective of decoupling inventory is to disconnect the rate of use from the rate of supply of the item. *See:* buffer.

Dedicated capacity A work center that is designated to produce a single item or a limited number of similar items. Equipment that is dedicated may be special equipment or may be grouped general-purpose equipment committed to a composite part.

Deductive fraud detection Determining the types of frauds that can occur and then using query techniques and other methods to determine if those frauds may actually exist.

Deemed exports Addresses people rather than products where knowledge transfer could lead to a breach of export restrictions.

Default risk The possibility that the issuer will not meet contractual obligations to pay interest or repay principal or will violate a covenant in a debt agreement.

Default risk premium (DRP) The difference between the interest rate on a U.S. Treasury bond and a corporate bond of equal maturity and marketability.

Defect A product's or service's nonfulfillment of an intended requirement or reasonable expectation for use, including safety considerations. They are often classified, such as:

- Class 1, Critical, leads directly to severe injury or catastrophic economic loss
- Class 2, Serious, leads directly to significant injury or significant economic loss
- Class 3, Major, is related to major problems with respect to intended normal or reasonably foreseeable use
- Class 4, Minor, is related to minor problems with respect to intended normal or reasonably foreseeable use. *See:* blemish, imperfection, and nonconformity.

GLOSSARY

Defensive merger A merger designed to make a company less vulnerable to a takeover.

Deferred asset Expenditure that has been capitalized to be expensed in the future.

Deferred expenses Items that are initially recorded as assets but are expected to become expenses over time or through the normal operations of the business. Sometimes called prepaid expenses.

Deferred income tax asset The future tax benefits from earnings that have already been taxed but have not been reported in the income statement yet.

Deferred income tax liability The future tax liability that results from current or past periods' earnings that have already been reported in the financial statements but have not been taxed yet.

Deferred revenues Items that are initially recorded as liabilities but are expected to become revenues over time or through the normal operations of the business. Sometimes called unearned revenues.

Deficiency A perceived, potential, or real internal control shortcoming, or an opportunity to strengthen the internal control system to provide a greater likelihood that the entity's objectives will be achieved.

Defined-benefit plan One in which an employee is promised a pension amount based on age and service.

Defined-contribution plan One in which the employer makes an annual payment to an employee's pension account.

Degree of financial leverage (DFL) The percentage change in earnings available to common stockholders associated with a given percentage change in earnings before interest and taxes.

Degree of individualism Extent to which individual interests prevail over group interests.

Degree of operating leverage (DOL) The percentage change in operating income (EBIT) associated with a given percentage change in sales.

Degree of total leverage (DTL) The percentage change in EPS that results from a given percentage change in sales; DTL shows the effects of both operating leverage and financial leverage.

Delay tactics Another form of leverage. A pause, or delay, by one party during a negotiation may make the other party overly anxious, causing them to make concessions. A delay tactic also allows a negotiator time to rest, recuperate, assess progress, obtain other information, and reformulate strategy.

Delegation The process managers use to transfer authority and responsibility to positions below them in the hierarchy.

Deliverables The tangible items or products that the customer expects the contractor to provide during performance of the project.

Delivery duty paid (DDP) Seller delivers the goods, with import duties paid, including inland transportation from import point to the buyer's premises.

Delivery duty unpaid (DDU) Only the destination customs duty and taxes are paid by the consignee.

Delphi method A qualitative forecasting method that obtains forecasts through group consensus.

Delphi studies A research tool using a group of participants with expertise in the area of concern to state and rank major future developments.

Delphi technique Collection of independent opinions without group discussion by the assessors who provide the opinions; used for various types of assessments (such as country risk assessment).

Demand A need for a particular product or component. The demand could come from any number of sources, for example, customer order or forecast, an interplant requirement, or a request from a branch warehouse for a service part or for manufacturing another product. At the finished goods level, demand data are usually different from sales data because demand does not necessarily result in sales (that is, if there is no stock, there will be no sale). There are generally up to four components of demand: cyclical component, random component, seasonal component, and trend component.

Demand deposit account (DDA) Noninterest bearing checking accounts. This account is the foundation for all other cash management services the bank might offer to the corporate client.

Demand flow An inventory system similar to the just-in-time system, but more encompassing.

Demand management 1: The function of recognizing all demands for goods and services to support the market place. It involves prioritizing demand when supply is lacking. Proper demand management facilitates the planning and use of resources for profitable business results. **2:** In marketing, the process of planning, executing, controlling, and monitoring the design, pricing, promotion, and distribution of products and services to bring about transactions that meet organizational and individual needs. *Syn:* marketing management.

Demand pull The triggering of material movement to a work center only when that work center is ready to begin the next job. It in effect eliminates the queue from in front of a work center, but it can cause a queue at the end of a previous work center.

Demand schedules Provide a systematic look at the relationship between price and quantity sold.

Demand-side market failure Cumulative effect of the marketing practice of many thousands of advertising campaigns that has a residual negative impact on the values of buyers and the demand for various products (for example, voting).

Demerit chart A control chart for evaluating a process in terms of a demerit (or quality score), such as, a weighted sum of counts of various classified nonconformities.

Deming Cycle *See:* plan-do-check-act cycle.

Deming Prize Award given annually to organizations that, according to the award guidelines, have successfully applied company-wide quality control based on statistical quality control and will keep up with it in the future. Although the award is named in honor of W. Edwards Deming, its criteria are not specifically related to Deming's teachings. There are three separate divisions for the award: the Deming Application Prize, the Deming Prize for Individuals, and the Deming Prize for Overseas Companies. The award process is overseen by the Deming Prize Committee of the Union of Japanese Scientists and Engineers in Tokyo.

Democratic leader A leader who delegates authority to others, encourages participation, and relies on expert and referent power to manage subordinates.

Demodulation The transformation of an analog signal (from a phone line) into a digital signal (so a computer can understand it).

Demographics Variables among buyers in the consumer market, which include geographic location, age, sex, marital status, family size, social class, education, nationality, occupation, and income.

Demonstrated capacity Proven capacity calculated from actual performance data, usually expressed as the average number of items produced multiplied by the standard hours per item.

Denial of service (DoS) The inability of legitimate visitors to log on to a Web site when too many malicious requests are launched by an attacker.

Denomination Refers to a security's dollar amount or face value.

Density Weight-to-volume ratio; often used to determine shipping rates.

Departmentalization The basis on which individuals are grouped into departments and departments into total organizations.

Dependability Degree to which a product is operable and capable of performing its required function at any randomly chosen time during its specified operating time, provided that the product is available at the start of that period. (Non-operation-related influences are not included.) Dependability can be expressed by the ratio:

$$\frac{\text{time available}}{\text{time available} + \text{time required}}$$

Dependent demand Demand that is directly related to or derived from the bill of material structure for other items or end products. Such demands are therefore calculated and need not and should not be forecast. A given inventory item may have both dependent and independent demand at any given time. For example, a part may simultaneously be the component of an assembly and sold as a service part. *See:* independent demand.

Dependent demand inventory Inventory in which item demand is related to the demand for other inventory items.

Dependent variable Term used in regression analysis to represent the variable that is dependent on one or more other variables.

Depletion The cost of metal ores and other minerals removed from the earth.

Deployment (to spread around) Used in strategic planning to describe the process of cascading plans throughout an organization.

Deposit reconciliation One type of account reconciliation, this service minimizes the number of depository accounts a company must have while offering the added advantage of convenience.

Deposit reporting service Information on account balances offered by a bank or third-party vendor, which enables the treasury staff to know when and where the company's operations have deposited money into bank accounts.

Deposition Sworn testimony taken before a trial begins. At depositions, the opposing side's attorneys ask questions of witnesses.

Depository Institution Deregulation and Monetary Control Act of 1980 Landmark legislation which enabled savings and loans, mutual savings banks, and credit unions to operate more like commercial banks. Also established reserve requirement ranges for various deposit accounts.

Depository transfer checks (DTC) Nonnegotiable, unsigned checks used by firms to move funds from one account to another. They are often used to move (concentrate) monies collected in many different locations into a pooled account in a "concentration bank," where the money can be invested as a single large amount.

Depreciation 1: Decrease in the value of a currency. **2:** In a general sense, the decrease in usefulness of plant assets other than land. In accounting, refers to the systematic allocation of a fixed asset's cost to expense.

Depreciation expense The portion of the cost of a fixed asset that is recorded as an expense each year of its useful life.

Depth A characteristic of a market in which a very large dollar amount of securities can be easily absorbed without large changes in the market price.

Deregulation Removal of government regulation.

Derivative A contract whose market value fluctuates in direct proportion to fluctuations in the market value of a commodity or a financial instrument or a foreign currency.

Derived demand Demand for component products that arises from the demand for final design products. For example, the demand for steel is derived from the demand for automobiles.

Descriptive An approach that describes how managers actually make decisions rather than how they should.

Descriptive ethics Concerned with describing, characterizing, and studying the morality of a people, a culture, or a society.

Deseasonalized time series A time series that has had the effect of season removed by dividing each original time series observation by the corresponding seasonal index.

Design engineering The discipline consisting of process engineering and product engineering.

Design for manufacturability Simplification of parts, products, and processes to improve quality and reduce manufacturing costs.

Design for manufacture and assembly A product development approach that involves the manufacturing function in the initial stages of product design to ensure ease of manufacturing and assembly. *See:* early manufacturing involvement.

Design for quality A product design approach that uses quality measures to capture the extent to which the design meets the needs of the target market (customer attributes), as well as its actual performance, aesthetics, and cost. *See:* total quality engineering.

Design of experiments (DOE) Branch of applied statistics dealing with planning, conducting, analyzing, and interpreting controlled tests to evaluate the factors that control the value of a parameter or group of parameters.

Design review Documented, comprehensive, and systematic examination of a design to evaluate its capability to fulfill the requirements for quality.

Designing in quality vs. inspecting in quality *See:* prevention vs. detection.

Desired quality Additional features and benefits a customer discovers when using a product or service which lead to increased customer satisfaction. If missing, a customer may become dissatisfied.

Desktop publishing Using word processing programs and high-quality printers to prepare books and pamphlets for publication.

Detachable warrant A warrant that can be detached from a bond and traded independently of it.

Detective control A control designed to discover an unintended event or undesirable result that has been detected.

Deterministic model 1: Data input for deterministic models are single point estimates. **2:** A model in which all uncontrollable inputs are known and cannot vary.

Development Efforts to improve employees' ability to handle a variety of assignments.

Deviation Nonconformance or departure of a characteristic from specified product, process, or system requirements.

Devil's advocate A decision-making technique in which an individual is assigned the role of challenging the assumptions and assertions made by the group to prevent premature consensus.

DFD (Data Flow Diagram) A graphical method to communicate the data flow in a business unit. Usually serves as a blueprint for a new information system in the development process. The DFD uses four symbols, for entity, process, data store, and data flow.

Diagnosis The step in the decision-making process in which managers analyze underlying causal factors associated with the decision situation.

Diagnostic journey and remedial journey A two-phase investigation used by teams to solve chronic quality problems. In the first phase, the diagnostic journey, the team moves from the symptom of a problem to its cause. In the second phase, the remedial journey, the team moves from the cause to a remedy.

Dialog module The part of a decision-support system, or any other system, that allows the user to interact with it.

Dialogue A group communication process aimed at creating a culture based on collaboration, fluidity, trust, and commitment to shared goals.

Differential analysis The area of accounting concerned with the effect of alternative courses of action on revenues and costs.

Differential cost The amount of increase or decrease in cost expected from a particular course of action as compared with an alternative.

Differential piece-rate system A system in which employees are paid one piece-rate wage for units produced up to a standard output and a higher piece-rate wage for units produced over the standard.

Differential revenue The amount of increase or decrease in revenue expected from a particular course of action as compared with an alternative.

Differentiation 1: A type of competitive strategy with which the organization seeks to distinguish its products or services from competitors. **2:** Takes advantage of the company's real or perceived uniqueness on elements such as design or after-sales service. **3:** Process of creating and sustaining a strong, consistent, and unique image about one product in comparison to others.

Diffusion of innovation The process by which innovation is communicated through certain channels over time among members of a social system.

Digital certificates Computer files that serve as the equivalent of ID cards.

Digital signal An expression of discrete, noncontinuous signals produced by electrical or electromagnetic bursts of different power levels. Only a digital signal can represent bits, and therefore be processed by a computer.

Digital signature An encrypted digest of the text that is sent along with a message, that authenticates the identity of the sender and guarantees that no one has altered the sent document.

Digital signatures and certificates A signature sent over the Internet.

Digital subscriber line (DSL) Technology that relieves individual subscribers of the need for the conversion of digital signals into analog signals between the telephone exchange and the subscriber jack. DSL lines are linked to the Internet on a permanent basis and support bit rates significantly greater than a normal telephone line between the subscriber's jack and the telephone exchange. The service is not offered everywhere.

Digital technology Technology characterized by use of the Internet and other digital processes to conduct or support business operations.

Dimensions of quality Different ways in which quality may be viewed, for example, meaning of quality, characteristics of quality, drivers of quality, and so on.

Direct access The manner in which a record is retrieved from a storage device, without the need to seek it sequentially. The record's address is calculated from the value in its logical key field.

Direct deposit Service in which the employer's bank automatically deposits employees' wages and salaries. The bank sorts out the on-us checks for employees having checking accounts at that bank, and credits their accounts. Employees banking elsewhere are paid through the local clearing house or ACH-initiated transactions. Direct deposit of payroll is easily the most popular electronic payment application.

Direct export sales Seller contracts directly with the buyer in the other country.

Direct exporting The firm produces at home and creates a division to export to foreign markets.

Direct-financing lease A lease where the lessor provides financing only, and assumes financial risks but does not assume inventory risk.

Direct foreign investment (DFI) Investment in real assets (such as land, buildings, or even existing plants) in foreign countries.

Direct format One possible format allowed for presenting the Statement of Cash Flows that computes cash inflows and cash outflows directly, showing the major components of operating cash receipts and operating cash disbursements.

Direct hedge A hedge using a futures contract that is of the same type as the cash market instrument being hedged.

Direct intervention The process governments used in the 1970s if they wished to alter the current value of their currency. It was done by simply buying or selling their own currency in the market using their reserves of other major currencies.

Direct investing 1: An entry strategy in which the organization is involved in managing its production facilities in a foreign country. **2:** Established operations in a country.

Direct investment account An account in the BOP statement that records investments with an expected maturity of more than one year and an investor's ownership position of at least 10 percent.

Direct involvement Participation by a firm in international business in which the firm works with foreign customers or markets to establish a relationship.

Direct labor cost Wages of factory workers who are directly involved in converting materials into a finished product.

Direct labor rate variance The cost associated with the difference between the standard rate and the actual rate paid for direct labor used in producing a commodity.

Direct labor time variance The cost associated with the difference between the standard hours and the actual hours of direct labor spent producing a commodity.

Direct loan program Program in which Ex-Im Bank offers fixed-rate loans directly to the foreign buyer to purchase U.S. capital equipment and services.

Direct materials cost The cost of materials that are an integral part of the finished product.

Direct materials price variance The cost associated with the difference between the standard price and the actual price of direct materials used in producing a commodity.

Direct materials quantity variance The cost associated with the difference between the standard quantity and the actual quantity of direct materials used in producing a commodity.

Direct method A method of reporting the cash flows from operating activities as the net income from operations adjusted for all deferrals of past cash receipts and payments and all accruals of expected future cash receipts and payments.

Direct presenting Situation in which checks are sent to the drawee bank or its local clearinghouse via courier. Direct presenting is mainly used for large checks.

Direct quotation 1: A foreign exchange quotation that specifies the amount of home country currency needed to purchase one unit of foreign currency. **2:** Exchange rate quotations representing the value measured by number of dollars per unit.

Direct taxes Taxes applied directly to income.

Direct write-off method A method of accounting for uncollectible receivables, whereby an expense is recognized only when specific accounts are judged to be uncollectible.

Directive An order to take a certain action.

Disabled person Someone who has a physical or mental impairment that substantially limits life activities, who has a record of such an impairment, or who is regarded as having such an impairment.

Disassembly bill of material In remanufacturing, a bill of material used as a guide for the inspection in the teardown and inspection process. On the basis of inspection, this bill is modified to a bill of repair defining the actual repair materials and work required. *Syn:* teardown bill of material.

Disaster recovery plan *See:* Business Continuity Plan.

Disbursement float The delay between the time when the company writes the check and the time when its bank charges the checking account for the amount of the check.

Disbursement fraud Having an organization pay for something it shouldn't pay for or pay too much for something it purchases.

Disbursement policy Whether an informal strategy or a formal written document, specifies which payment mechanism to utilize for a given disbursement, when to pay a given invoice, and the setup of guidelines regarding the disbursement system (including which bank(s) might be involved).

Disbursement system A company's payment methods, disbursement banks, and disbursing locations.

Disbursements and receipts method (scheduling) The net cash flow is determined by estimating the cash disbursements and the cash receipts expected to be generated each period.

Disbursing bank Bank used to pay from.

Disclosure Financial statements.

Disclosure fraud The issuance of fraudulent or misleading statements or press releases without financial statement line-item effect or the lack of appropriate disclosures that should have been, but were not, made by management.

Discontinued operations The operations of a business segment that has been disposed of.

Discount 1: The interest deducted from the maturity value of a note. The excess of the face amount of bonds over their issue price. The excess of par value of stock over its sales price. **2:** As related to forward rates, represents the percentage amount by which the forward rate is less than the spot rate.

Discount basis When the selling price of a financial instrument is less than its face value or value at maturity.

Discount bond A bond that sells below its par value; occurs whenever the going rate of interest rises above the coupon rate.

Discount interest loan A loan in which the interest, which is calculated on the amount borrowed, is paid at the beginning of the loan period; interest is paid in advance.

Discount rate 1: In a capital project evaluation it is the opportunity cost of the use of funds, which is used to determine the present value of cash flows. **2:** The rate used in computing the interest to be deducted from the maturity value of a note.

Discount rate (Fed) The rate charged depository institutions when they borrow reserves from the Fed in order to meet their reserve requirements or meet unusual loan demand.

Discount security One which does not pay regular interest payments, but compensates the investor for implied interest by returning at maturity a principal amount greater than the purchase price.

Discount yield The difference between the maturity cash flow and the purchase price on a discount (noninterest bearing) security, expressed as a percentage of the purchase price.

Discounted cash flow (DCF) techniques Methods of evaluating investment proposals that employ time value of money concepts; two of these are the net present value and the internal rate of return.

Discounted payback The length of time it takes for a project's *discounted* cash flows to repay the cost of the investment.

Discounting The process of finding the present value of a cash flow or a series of cash flows; the reverse of compounding.

Discovery Legal process by which each party's attorneys try to find all information about the other side's case before a trial begins.

Discovery sampling Sampling used in fraud detection that assumes a zero expected error rate. The methodology allows an auditor to determine confidence levels and make inferences from the sample to the population.

Discrepancies between production and consumption Differences in quantity, assortment, time, and place that must be overcome to make goods available to final customers.

Discrete available-to-promise (ATP) calculation based on the available-to-promise figure in the master schedule. For the first period, the ATP is the sum of the beginning inventory plus the MPS quantity minus backlog for all periods until the item is master scheduled again. For all other periods, if a quantity has been scheduled for that time period then the ATP is this quantity minus all customer commitments for this and other periods until another quantity is scheduled in the MPS. For those periods where the quantity scheduled is zero, the ATP is zero (even if deliveries have been promised). The promised customer commitments are accumulated and shown in the period where the item was most recently scheduled. *Syn:* incremental available-to-promise. *See:* available-to-promise.

Discrete-event simulation model A simulation model that describes how a system evolves over time by using events that occur at discrete points in time.

Discrete probability distribution The measured process variable takes on a finite or limited number of values; no other possible values exist.

Discriminant analysis An identification procedure to interpret and classify data.

Discrimination The hiring or promoting of applicants based on criteria that are not job relevant.

Discriminatory regulations Regulations that impose larger operating costs on foreign service providers than on local competitors, that provide subsidies to local firms only, or that deny competitive opportunities to foreign suppliers.

Dishonored note receivable A note that the maker fails to pay on its due date.

Disillusionment phase Beginning two months into the expatriation process, the novelty of the new culture wears out, and day-to-day inconveniences caused by different practices in the local culture along with the inability to communicate effectively create disillusionment for the expatriate.

Disparate impact Occurs when substantial underrepresentation of protected-class members results from employment decisions that work to their disadvantage.

Disparate treatment Situation that exists when protected-class members are treated differently from others.

Displacement Act of moving employment opportunities from the country of origin to host countries.

Disposition Activities that involve the management of excess or waste packaging and materials. In the past, organizations frequently used landfills for disposition. Today, more organizations are increasingly exploring alternative environmentally friendly forms of disposition, including recycling, reuse, remanufacturing, and other similar options. This approach is sometimes referred to as reverse logistics.

Disposition of nonconformity Action taken to deal with an existing nonconformity; action may include: correction (repair), rework, regrade, scrap, obtain a concession, or amendment of a requirement.

Dissatisfiers Those features or functions which the customer or employee has come to expect and which, if they were no longer present, would result in dissatisfaction.

Distance learning Learning where student(s) and instructor(s) are not co-located, often carried out through electronic means.

Distributed Denial of Service (DDoS) Multiple log-in requests from many computers to the same Web site, so that the Web site is jammed with requests and cannot accept inquiries of legitimate visitors.

Distributed earnings The proportion of a firm's net income after taxes which is paid out or distributed to the stockholders of the firm.

Distribution 1: Amount of potential variation in outputs of a process; it is usually described in terms of its shape, average, and standard deviation. **2:** Moving finished products to customers; also called *order fulfillment*.

Distribution method A regression-based cash forecasting approach which spreads, or "distributes," a monthly total across the weeks or days within that month. This method has also been used to model payroll-related cash disbursements by relating cash outflows to how many business days have elapsed since payroll checks have been issued.

Distribution requirements planning (DRP) 1: The function of determining the need to replenish inventory at branch warehouses. A time-phased order point approach is used where the planned orders at the branch warehouse level are "exploded" via MRP logic to become gross requirements on the supplying source. In the case of multilevel distribution networks, this explosion process can continue down through the various levels of regional warehouses (master warehouse, factory warehouse, and so on.) and become input to the master production schedule. Demand on the supplying sources is recognized as dependent, and standard MRP logic applies. **2:** More generally, replenishment inventory calculations, which may be based on other planning approaches such as period order quantities or "replace exactly what was used," rather than being limited to the time-phased order point approach.

Distributive justice 1: Focuses on the specific outcome of a firm's recovery efforts. **2:** The concept that different treatment of people should not be based on arbitrary characteristics. In the case of substantive differences, people should be treated differently in proportion to the differences among them. **3:** Perceived fairness in the distribution of outcomes.

Distributor Marketing intermediary that purchases products from the domestic firm and assumes the trading risk.

Distributorship MNE sells to a foreign distributor who takes title to the merchandise.

Diversification 1: A market expansion policy characterized by growth in a relatively large number of markets or market segments. **2:** Process of spreading risk through a firm's involvement in various businesses or through the location of its operations in different geographic areas.

Diversification strategy Market development strategy that involves expansion to a relatively large number of markets.

Diversity The differences among people.

Diversity awareness training Special training designed to make people aware of their own prejudices and stereotypes.

Diverting Occurs when a manufacturer restricts an off-invoice allowance to a limited geographical area, resulting in some wholesalers and retailers buying abnormally large quantities at the deal price and then transshipping the excess quantities to other geographical areas.

Dividend capture strategy Corporate investment strategy involving buying a common or preferred stock shortly before it pays its dividend, or buying a preferred stock having an adjustable dividend payment. Because intercorporate dividends have been largely excludable for income tax purposes (presently there is a 70 percent exclusion), corporate investors buy stocks with high dividend yields, hold them at least forty-nine days (until the record date for payment), and then sell.

Dividend irrelevance theory The theory that a firm's dividend policy has no effect on either its value or its cost of capital.

Dividend policy decision The decision as to how much of current earnings to pay out as dividends rather than to retain for reinvestment in the firm.

Dividend relevance theory The value of a firm is affected by its dividend policy—the optimal dividend policy is the one that maximizes the firm's value.

Dividend reinvestment plan (DRIP) A plan that enables a stockholder to automatically reinvest dividends received back into the stock of the paying firm.

Dividend roll An investment approach that involves buying stocks with high dividend yields, holding them at least forty-nine days to collect the dividend, and then selling the stocks.

Dividend yield 1: The expected dividend divided by the current price of a share of stock. **2:** The rate of return to stockholders in terms of cash dividend distributions.

Dividends Distributions made to stockholders from the firm's earnings, whether those earnings were generated in the current period or in previous periods.

Dividends per share The cash dividends per common shares commonly used by investors in assessing alternative stock investments, computed by dividing dividends by the number of shares of stock outstanding.

Division A decentralized organizational unit that is structured around a common function, product, customer, or geographical territory. Divisions can be cost, profit, or investment centers.

Division of labor The premise of modern industrial production where each stage in the production of a good is performed by one individual separately, rather than one individual being responsible for the entire production of the good.

Divisional structure An organization structure in which departments are grouped based on similar organizational outputs.

DMAIC Methodology used in the six-sigma approach: define, measure, analyze, improve, control.

Document examiner Specialized investigator who applies forensic chemistry, microscopy, photography, and other scientific methods to determine whether documents or other evidence are genuine, forged, counterfeit, or fraudulent.

Documentary collections Trade transactions handled on a draft basis.

Documentary evidence Evidence gathered from paper, documents, computer records, and other written, printed, or electronic sources.

Documents against acceptance Situation in which the buyer's bank does not release shipping documents to the buyer until the buyer has accepted (signed) the draft.

Documents against payment Shipping documents that are released to the buyer once the buyer has paid for the draft.

Documents and records Documentation of all transactions in order to create an audit trail.

Dodge–Romig sampling plans Plans for acceptance sampling developed by Harold F. Dodge and Harry G. Romig. Four sets of tables were published in 1940: single-sampling lot tolerance tables, double-sampling lot tolerance tables, single-sampling average outgoing quality limit tables, and double-sampling average outgoing quality limit tables.

Dollar-day float A measure of delay that considers both the dollar amount and the time lag.

Domain name The name assigned to an Internet server.

Domestic enterprises Companies that derive all of their revenues from their home market.

Domestic environment Home country factors, including the political, competitive, economic, and legal and governmental climates, affect the enterprise.

Domestication Government demand for partial transfer of ownership and management responsibility from a foreign company to local entities, with or without compensation.

Dominant Securities which provide a higher expected return for a given amount of risk than other securities.

Doomsday ratio The ratio of cash and cash equivalents to current liabilities.

Dot-matrix printer A printer on which the print head consists of a matrix of little pins; thus, each printed character is made up of tiny dots.

Double counting This can either occur when a bank counts the same balances as compensation for a loan and as compensation for cash management services, or if the company has written a depository check for which it has been granted availability at the concentration bank, but has not had its checking account debited.

Double-entry accounting A system for recording transactions, based on recording increases and decreases in accounts so that debits always equal credits.

Double-entry bookkeeping Accounting methodology where each transaction gives rise to both a debit and a credit of the same currency amount. It is used in the construction of the Balance of Payments.

Double taxation The situation in which an expatriate is taxed by both the home-country and host-country governments. In some cases the firm will pay for the over-taxation.

Downloading The copying of data or applications from a computer to your computer, for example from a mainframe computer to a notebook computer. The term has come to mean the copying from another computer to your own computer, regardless of computer size.

Downsizing Planned reduction in workforce due to economics, competition, merger, sale, restructuring, or reengineering.

Downstream Used as a relative reference within a firm or supply chain to indicate moving in the direction of the end customer.

Downward communication Messages sent from top management down to subordinates.

Draft A written order to make payment to a third party, where the entity ordered to pay the draft is usually a bank. Any party holding a credit balance for the person writing the draft may have a draft drawn on it.

Draft (bill of exchange) Unconditional promise drawn by one party (usually the exporter) instructing the buyer to pay the face amount of the draft upon presentation.

Draw An amount advanced from and repaid to future commissions earned by the employee.

Drawee bank The bank on which a check or draft was written ("drawn").

Drill down The process of finding the most relevant information for executive decision making within a database or data warehouse.

Driver The software that enables an operating system to control a device, such as an optical disc drive or joystick.

Drivers of quality Include customers, products/services, employee satisfaction, total organizational focus.

Driving variable A key variable in most financial planning models to which most relationships are tied. Sales is generally such a variable in many financial planning models.

Drum-buffer-rope In the theory of constraints, the generalized process used to manage resources to maximize throughput. The drum is the rate or pace of production set by the system's constraint. The buffers establish the protection against uncertainty so that the system can maximize throughput. The rope is a communication process from the constraint to the gating operation that checks or limits material released into the system to support the constraint. *See:* finite scheduling, synchronized production.

Dual balance The same dollar balance that is temporarily on deposit at two different banks.

Dual pricing Price-setting strategy in which the export price may be based on marginal cost pricing, resulting in a lower export price than domestic price; may open the company to dumping charges.

Dual role A role in which the individual both contributes to the team's task and supports members' emotional needs.

Dual translation Using an interpreter in a country to translate a sender's message into a foreign language and then using an interpreter in the foreign country to translate the message back into the sender's language.

Dual use items Goods and services that are useful for both military and civilian purposes.

Due date The date, specified in a request for proposal, by which a customer expects potential contractors to submit proposals.

Dummy activity A special type of activity, used in the activity-on-the-arrow form of network diagramming, that consumes no time. A dummy activity is represented by a dashed arrow.

Dummy or shell company Fictitious entity created for the sole purpose of committing fraud; usually involves an employee making fraudulent payments to the dummy company.

Dummy variables Variables included in the regression equation when modeling seasonal or monthly effects. The number included is one less than the number of seasons. Each dummy variable that is included as an independent variable takes on a value of 1 only when the season it represents is the season for which the forecast is being made, and 0 at all other times.

Dumping 1: Selling products overseas at unfairly low prices (a practice perceived to result from subsidies provided to the firm by its government). **2:** The practice by an MNC of selling a product in a foreign market at a price lower than the price for which it sells the product in its own market and/or below production cost with the intent to eliminate its competition.

DuPont chart A chart designed to show the relationships among return on investment, asset turnover, the profit margin, and leverage.

DuPont equation A formula that gives the rate of return on assets by multiplying the profit margin by the total assets turnover.

Duration A tool for evaluating the interest rate risk of interest-bearing notes and bonds. It is defined as the weighted average time until the investor receives an investment's discounted cash flows.

Duration estimate The estimated total time an activity will take from start to finish, including associated waiting time; time estimate.

Duty A larger work segment composed of several tasks that are performed by an individual.

DVD (Digital Video Disc) A collective term for several types of high-capacity storage optical discs, used for data storage and motion pictures.

Dynamic hedging Strategy of hedging in those periods when existing currency positions are expected to be adversely affected, and remaining unhedged in other periods when currency positions are expected to be favorably affected.

Dynamic IP number The IP number assigned to a computer that is connected to the Internet intermittently for the duration of the computer's connection.

Dynamic risks Uncertainties, either pure or speculative, that are produced because of societal changes.

Dynamic simulation model A simulation model used in situations where the state of the system affects how the system changes or evolves over time.

E

Earliest finish time (EF) The earliest time by which a particular activity can be completed; the activity's earliest start time plus the activity's estimated duration.

Earliest start time (ES) The earliest time at which a particular activity can begin; the project's estimated start time plus the estimated duration of preceding activities.

Early manufacturing involvement The process of involving manufacturing personnel early in the product design activity and drawing on their expertise, insights, and knowledge to generate better designs in less time and to generate designs that are easier to manufacture. Early involvement of manufacturing, field service, suppliers, customers, and so on means drawing on their expertise, knowledge, and insight to improve the design. Benefits include increased functionality, increased quality, ease of manufacture and assembly, ease of testing, better testing procedures, ease of service, decreased cost, and improved aesthetics. *See:* design for manufacture and assembly, participative design/engineering.

Early supplier involvement (ESI) The process of involving suppliers early in the product design activity and drawing on their expertise, insights, and knowledge to generate better designs in less time and designs that are easier to manufacture with high quality. *See:* participative design/engineering.

Earned value (EV) The value of the work actually performed.

Earnings credit rate (ECR) A rate that banks credit collected balances with as compensation for leaving the balances in the account.

Earnings flexibility *See:* Income smoothing.

Earnings per share (EPS) Net income divided by the number of shares of common stock outstanding. A measure of profitability.

Earnings per share (EPS) on common stock The profitability ratio of net income available to common shareholders to the number of common shares outstanding.

EBCDIC (Extended Binary Coded Decimal Interchange Code) A binary computer encoding scheme devised by IBM. Consists of 8 bits per byte, each byte uniquely representing a character.

E-Business 1: The use of information technology and electronic communication networks to exchange business information and conduct transactions in electronic, paperless form. **2:** Work an organization does using electronic linkages; any business that takes place by digital processes over a computer network rather than in a physical space.

E-commerce 1: Business activity that is electronically executed between parties, such as between two businesses or between a business and a consumer. **2:** The ability to offer goods and services over the Web.

Economic and monetary union (EMU) The ideal among European leaders that economic integration should move beyond the four freedoms; specifically, it entails (1) closer coordination of economic policies to promote exchange rate stability and convergence of inflation rates and growth rates, (2) creation of a European central bank, and (3) replacement of national monetary authorities by the European Central Bank and adoption of the euro as the European currency.

Economic environment The way in which people of a society manage their material wealth and the results of their management.

Economic exposure Refers to the possibility that the long-term net present value of a firm's expected cash flows will change due to unexpected changes in exchange rates.

Economic extortion scheme Involves an employee demanding payment from a vendor in order to make or influence a decision in that vendor's favor.

Economic feasibility study An evaluation of whether the benefits outweigh the costs of a proposed information system over the life of the system.

Economic forces Forces that affect the availability, production, and distribution of a society's resources among competing users.

Economic infrastructure The transportation, energy, and communication systems in a country.

Economic Order Quantity (EOQ) 1: The optimal quantity of a specific raw material that allows a business to minimize overstocking and save cost without risking understocking and missing production deadlines. **2:** A type of fixed order quantity model that determines the amount of an item to be purchased or manufactured at one time. The intent is to minimize the combined costs of acquiring and carrying inventory. The basic formula is

$$\text{Quantity} = \sqrt{\frac{2(d)(c)}{(i)(u)}}$$

where d = annual demand, c = average cost of order preparation, i = annual inventory carrying cost percentage, and u = unit cost. *Syn:* economic lot size, minimum cost order quantity.

Economic risk The uncertainty surrounding key elements of the investment process.

Economic security Perception of a business activity as having an effect on a country's financial resources, often used to restrict competition from firms outside the country.

Economic union A union among trading countries that has the characteristics of a common market and also harmonizes monetary policies, taxation, and government spending and uses a common currency.

Economic value added (EVA) 1: A firm's net operating profit after the cost of capital is deducted. **2:** A control system that measures performance in terms of after-tax profits minus the cost of capital invested in tangible assets.

Economies of scale 1: Achievement of lower average cost per unit by means of increased production. **2:** Production economies made possible by the output of larger quantities.

Economies of scale and economies of scope Obtained by spreading the costs of distribution over a large quantity of products (scale) or over a wide variety of products (scope).

ECU The outgrowth of the European Monetary System is a new currency, referred to as the ECU, which represents a basket of currencies of the members of the EEC.

Education Process undertaken to learn required additional knowledge. *See:* training.

Education allowance Reimbursement by company for dependent educational expenses incurred while a parent is assigned overseas.

EEC The European Economic Community.

Effective annual rate (EAR) The annual rate earned or paid considering interest compounding during the year (that is, the annual rate that equates to a given periodic rate compounded for m periods during the year).

Effective interest rate The rate of interest that is equal to or greater than the stated interest rate because of out-of-pocket expenses and usable funds that are less than the face value of the loan.

Effective interest rate method One method of amortizing a bond discount. Also known as the interest method.

Effective internal control This reflects a state or condition of internal control. While internal control is a process, its effectiveness is a state or condition of the process at a point in time.

Effective rate of interest The market rate of interest when bonds are issued.

Effective tax rate Actual total tax burden after including all applicable tax liabilities and credits.

Effective yield Yield or return to an MNC on a short-term investment after adjustment for the change in exchange rates over the period of concern.

Effectiveness 1: The degree to which the organization achieves a stated goal. **2:** The measure of how well a job is performed.

Efficiency A measurement (usually expressed as a percentage) of the actual output to the standard output expected. Efficiency measures how well something is performing relative to existing standards; in contrast, productivity measures output relative to a specific input, for example, tons/labor hour. Efficiency is the ratio of 1) actual units produced to the standard rate of production expected in a time period or 2) standard hours produced to actual hours worked (taking longer means less efficiency) or 3) actual dollar volume of output to a standard dollar volume in a time period. Illustrations of these calculations follow. 1) There is a standard of 100 pieces per hour and 780 units are produced in one eight-hour shift; the efficiency is 780/800 converted to a percentage, or 97.5 percent. 2) The work is measured in hours and took 8.21 hours to produce eight standard hours; the efficiency is 8/8.21 converted to a percentage or 97.5 percent. 3) The work is measured in dollars and produces $780 with a standard of $800; the efficiency is $780/$800 converted to a percentage, or 97.5 percent.

Efficiency ratios Ratios that measure how effectively the enterprise is using the assets employed.

Efficient markets Where prices change freely and instantly in response to supply and demand and are not significantly affected by poor information or tax code barriers.

Efficient markets hypothesis (EMH) The hypothesis that securities are typically in equilibrium—that they are fairly priced in the sense that the price reflects all publicly available information on each security.

Eighth Directive, The The EU Eighth Directive deals with auditing of financial statements of companies in EU countries, and specifies that they be consistent with EU law. It also sets qualifications for auditors and the firms conducting audits, including education and experience requirements. In addition, the Directive deals with ethical matters such as independence, and includes sanctions for cases in which audits are not conducted as prescribed by statute. *See:* Fourth Directive, Seventh Directive.

Eighty-twenty (80–20) rule Term referring to the Pareto principle, which suggests that most effects come from relatively few causes; that is, 80 percent of the effects come from 20 percent of the possible causes.

Elasticity of demand Relationship between changes in price and quantity sold.

e-learning The use of the Internet or an organizational intranet to conduct training on-line.

Electronic agent A computer program that searches Internet sites and other resources in a telecommunications network to respond to a request made by its user.

Electronic brochures Digital versions of a company's brochures.

Electronic business data interchange (EBDI) The electronic movement of information such as invoices between corporate trading partners.

Electronic check presentment Is an arrangement in which the image of the MICR line of a check is presented to the paying back, instead of presenting the physical check, shortening clearance float.

Electronic commerce Information systems that allow transactions between parties in a supply chain to be automatically completed via electronic data interchange (EDI), electronic funds transfer (EFT), bar codes, and a variety of other electronic mediums. The "paper" transactions of the past are becoming increasingly obsolete. At the same time, the proliferation of new telecommunications and computer technology has also made instantaneous communications a reality. Such information systems—like Wal-Mart's satellite network—can link together suppliers, manufacturers, distributors, retail outlets, and ultimately, customers, regardless of location.

Electronic corporate trade payment An arrangement between two corporations (a buyer and a seller) and the banks of the two parties so that payment is effected without a paper check being issued.

Electronic data interchange (EDI) 1: A network that links the computer systems of buyers and sellers to allow the transmission of structured data primarily for ordering, distribution, and payables and receivables. **2:** Computer-to-computer exchange of invoices, orders, and other business documents; a computer-to-computer communications protocol that allows basic information on purchases and invoices to be transferred.

Electronic depository transfer (EDT) Payment process in which a local or regional account is debited electronically and the amount sent through an automated clearing house to the concentration bank account. Also known as an ACH debit, is an electronic equivalent to the paper DTC. The electronic transaction provides quicker availability in the concentration account for the company.

Electronic funds transfer (EFT) A payment system that uses computerized information rather than paper (money, checks, and so on.) to effect a cash transaction between trading partners.

Electronic intermediary Profit model based on commissions received by bringing buyers and sellers together.

Electronic lockbox Collection system offered by banks for companies to receive payments, via wire transfers or ACH, from customers.

Electronic superhighway The Internet. Often called *the information superhighway.*

Electronic surveillance Using video, e-mail, wiretapping, and so on to watch fraud suspects.

Elements of fraud The theft act, concealment, and conversion that are present in every fraud.

Elements of internal control The control environment, risk assessment, control activities, information and communication, and monitoring.

E-mail (electronic mail) The exchange of messages between computers either in the same building or over great distances.

E-marketing The set of activities that bring customers and companies together using electronic means such as the Internet.

Embargo A governmental action, usually prohibiting trade entirely, for a decidedly adversarial or political rather than economic purpose.

Embezzlement Theft or fraudulent appropriation of money through deception; often used interchangeably with the term fraud.

Emotions 1: Even though behavior in business and negotiations is mainly intuitive, it should never be judgmental. To be able to listen to other negotiators, one should exclude his or her subjective opinions, preconceptions, or emotional filters. It is important to prevent emotions from controlling negotiations. **2:** Strong, relatively uncontrolled feelings that affect our behavior.

Employee assistance program One program that provides counseling and other help to employees having emotional, physical, or other personal problems.

Employee embezzlement Employees deceiving their employers by taking company assets.

Employee fraud The intentional act of deceiving an employer for personal gain.

Employee involvement Practice within an organization whereby employees regularly participate in making decisions on how their work areas operate, including making suggestions for improvement, planning, objectives setting, and monitoring performance.

Employee network groups Groups based on social identity, such as gender or race, and organized by employees to focus on concerns of employees from that group.

Employee stock ownership plan (ESOP) A plan whereby employees gain stock ownership in the organization for which they work.

Employee's earnings record A detailed record of each employee's earnings.

Employment test 1: Any employment procedure used as the basis for making an employment-related decision. **2:** A written or computerbased test designed to measure a particular attribute such as intelligence or aptitude.

Empowerment Condition whereby employees have the authority to make decisions and take action in their work areas, within stated bounds, without prior approval. For example, an operator can stop a production process upon detecting a problem, or a customer service representative can send out a replacement product if a customer calls with a problem.

Encapsulated development Situation in which an individual learns new methods and ideas in a development course and returns to a work unit that is still bound by old attitudes and methods.

Encode To select symbols with which to compose a message.

Encoding scheme A convention of representing characters with another, small, set of characters or special marks. Morse code, EBCDIC, and ASCII are encoding schemes.

Encryption The conversion of plaintext to an unreadable stream of characters, especially to prevent a party that intercepts telecommunicated messages from reading them. Special encryption software is used by the sending party to encrypt messages, and by the receiving party to decipher them.

End users External customers who purchase products/services for their own use.

Engineering change order A document that initiates a change in the specification of a product or process.

Engineering services Services that are provided in the areas of construction, design, and engineering.

Engineer-to-order Products whose customer specifications require unique engineering design, significant customization, or new purchased materials. Each customer order results in a unique set of part numbers, bills of material, and routings. *Syn:* design-to-order.

Enterprise Application Systems Information systems that fulfill a number of functions together, such as inventory planning, purchasing, payment, and billing.

Enterprise-level strategy The overarching strategy level that poses the basic questions, "What is the role of the organization in society?" and "What do we stand for?"

Enterprise resource planning (ERP) 1: An information system that supports different activities for different departments, assisting executives with planning and running different functions. **2:** Systems that unite a company's major business functions—order processing, product design, purchasing, inventory, and so on; a networked information system that collects, processes, and provides information about an organization's entire enterprise, from identification of customer needs and receipt of orders to distribution of products and receipt of payments. **3:** Accounting-oriented information systems used for identifying and planning the enterprise-wide resources needed to take, make, ship, and account for customer orders.

Enterprise resources planning (ERP) system 1: An ERP system differs from the typical MRP II system in technical requirements such as graphical user interface, relational database, use of fourth-generation language, and computer-assisted software engineering tools in development, client/server architecture, and open-system portability. **2:** More generally, a method for the effective planning and control of all resources needed to take, make, ship, and account for customer orders in a manufacturing, distribution, or service company.

Enterprise risk management Approach for managing both pure and speculative risks together. Another name for *integrated risk-management*.

Entity Any object about which an organization chooses to collect data.

Entity relationship diagram One of several conventions for graphical rendition of the data elements involved in business processes and the logical relationships among the elements.

Entrepreneur Someone who recognizes a viable idea for a business product or service and carries it out.

Entrepreneurship The process of initiating a business venture, organizing the necessary resources, and assuming the associated risks and rewards.

Entropy The tendency for a system to run down and die.

Environmental analysis/scanning Relates to monitoring factors from both inside and outside the organization that may impact the long-term viability of the organization.

Environmental contexts *See:* Cross-cultural communication.

Environmental monitoring stage Focuses on the tracking of specific trends and events with an eye toward confirming or disconfirming trends or patterns.

Environmental protection Actions taken by governments to protect the environment and resources of a country.

Environmental scanning 1: Obtaining ongoing data about a country. **2:** Process of studying the environment of the organization to pinpoint opportunities and threats. **3:** Identifies important trends in the microand macroenvironments, then considers the potential impact of these changes on a firm's existing marketing strategy.

Environmental scanning stage Focuses on identification of precursors or indicators of potential environmental changes and issues.

Environment-specific An accounting system designed to provide information for making decisions in a given environment. Five major environmental influences on accounting consist of the economic system, political system, legal system, educational system, and religion.

E → P expectancy Expectancy that putting effort into a given task will lead to high performance.

EPA Environmental Protection Agency.

EPS indifference point The level of sales at which EPS will be the same whether the firm uses debt or common stock financing.

Equal employment opportunity (EEO) Individuals should have equal treatment in all employment-related actions.

Equilibrium The condition under which the expected return on a security is just equal to its required return, $\hat{k} = k$, and the price is stable.

Equilibrium exchange rate Exchange rate at which demand for a currency is equal to the supply of the currency for sale.

Equity 1: A situation that exists when the ratio of one person's outcomes to inputs equals that of another. **2:** The perceived fairness of what the person does compared with what the person receives.

Equity capital Capital that is financed by shares (stocks).

Equity financing Financing that consists of funds that are invested in exchange for ownership in the company.

Equity method A method of accounting for investments in common stock, by which the investment account is adjusted for the investor's share of periodic net income and dividends of the investee. A method in which income of a subsidiary is recognized by the parent company according to ownership percentage. The investment in the subsidiary account balance is adjusted accordingly.

Equity multiplier Assets divided by equity.

Equity reserves A general term to describe many different types of reserves that serve different purposes.

Equity security A security that represents ownership in a business, such as stock in a corporation.

Equity theory 1: A process theory that focuses on individuals' perceptions of how fairly they are treated relative to others. **2:** Theory that states that job motivation depends upon how equitable the individual believes the rewards or punishment to be.

Equivalent annual annuity (EAA) method A method that calculates the annual payments a project would provide if it were an annuity. When comparing projects of unequal lives, the one with the higher equivalent annual annuity should be chosen.

Equivalent units of production The number of units that could have been completed within a given accounting period with respect to direct materials and conversion costs. Equivalent units are used to allocate departmental costs incurred during the period between completed units and in-process units at the end of the period.

ERG theory A modification of the needs hierarchy theory that proposes three categories of needs: existence, relatedness, and growth.

Ergonomics 1: The study and design of the work environment to address physiological and physical demands on individuals. **2:** The science of designing and modifying machines to better suit people's health and comfort.

Error distribution The shape or pattern of the array of forecast errors.

Escalating commitment Continuing to invest time and resources into a failing decision.

Essential job functions Fundamental duties of a job.

Estimated start time The time or date when a project is expected to begin.

Ethernet The design, introduced and named by Xerox, for the contention data communications protocol.

Ethical What members of a given society generally accept as being "right."

Ethical dilemma A situation that arises when all alternative choices or behaviors have been deemed undesirable because of potentially negative ethical consequence, making it difficult to distinguish right from wrong.

Ethical impact statement An attempt to assess the underlying moral justifications for corporate actions and the consequent results of those actions.

Ethical relativism Picking and choosing which source of norms to use based on what will justify current actions or maximize freedom.

Ethical responsibilities Those activities and practices that are expected or prohibited by societal members even though they are not codified into law.

Ethical values Moral values that enable a decision maker to determine an appropriate course of behavior; these values should be based on what is "right," which may go beyond what is "legal."

Ethical vigilance Paying constant attention to whether one's actions are "right" or "wrong," and if ethically "wrong," asking why one is behaving in that manner.

Ethics 1: Code of conduct that is based on moral principles, and which tries to balance what is fair for individuals with what is right for society. **2:** The code of moral principles and values that govern the behaviors of a person or group with respect to what is right or wrong. **3:** The discipline that deals with what is good and bad and with moral duty and obligation.

Ethnocentric Tending to regard one's own culture as superior; tending to be home-market oriented.

Ethnocentric staffing outlook The belief that key positions in foreign subsidiaries should be staffed by citizens from the parent company's home country.

Ethnocentric strategy Companies produce unique goods and services that they offer primarily to their domestic market, and when they export, they do not modify the product or service for foreign consumption.

Ethnocentrism A cultural attitude marked by the tendency to regard one's own culture as superior to others; the belief that one's own group or subculture is inherently superior to other groups or cultures.

Ethnorelativism The belief that groups and subcultures are inherently equal.

Euro A single currency proposed for use by the European Union that will eventually replace all the individual currencies of the participating member states.

Euro cp Similar in concept to domestic commercial paper except issued in the Euromarket which has fewer restrictions, is unrated, and generally has a longer maturity averaging from sixty to ninety days.

Eurobanks Commercial banks that participate as financial intermediaries in the Eurocurrency market.

Eurobond A bond that is denominated in a currency other than the currency of the country in which the bond is sold.

Euro-clear Telecommunications network that informs all traders about outstanding issues of Eurobonds for sale.

Euro-commercial paper Debt securities issued by MNCs for short-term financing.

Eurocredit loans Loans of one year or longer extended by Eurobanks.

Eurocredit market Collection of banks that accept deposits and provide loans in large denominations and in a variety of currencies. The banks that comprise this market are the same banks that comprise the Eurocurrency market; the difference is that the Eurocredit loans are longer term than so-called Eurocurrency loans.

Eurocurrency A bank deposit in a currency other than the currency of the country where the bank is located; not confined to banks in Europe.

Eurocurrency market Collection of banks that accept deposits and provide loans in large denominations and in a variety of currencies.

Eurodebt Debt sold in a country other than the one in whose currency the debt is denominated.

Eurodollar Term used to describe United States dollar deposits placed in banks located in Europe.

Eurodollar CDs Dollar-denominated deposits held in banks or bank branches outside the U.S. or in International Banking Facilities (IBFs, which can offer Eurodollar deposits only to non-U.S. residents) located within the United States.

Eurodollars United States dollars deposited in banks outside the United States; not confined to banks in Europe.

Euromarkets Money and capital markets in which transactions are denominated in a currency other than that of the place of the transaction; not confined to Europe.

Euronotes Unsecured debt securities issued by MNCs for short-term financing.

European Article Numbering (EAN) system European version of the Universal Product Code located on a product's package that provides information read by optical scanners.

European Central Bank (ECB) Central bank created to conduct the monetary policy for the countries participating in the single European currency, the euro.

European Confederation of Institutes of Internal Auditing This organization, comprised of seventeen internal audit organizations representing eighteen European nations plus Israel, helps in the development of internal auditing standards.

European Currency Unit (ECU) Unit of account representing a weighted average of exchange rates of member countries within the European Monetary System.

European Monetary System (EMS) An organization formed in 1979 by eight EC members committed to maintaining the values of their currencies within 2 1/4 percent of each other's.

European terms Quoting a currency rate as a country's currency against the U.S. dollar (for example, yen/U.S. dollars).

European Union (EU) The January 1, 1994, organization created by the twelve member countries of the European Community (now fifteen members). A single trading block currently linking fifteen European nations into a single market in order to eliminate tariff and custom restrictions. The fifteen nations include Austria, Belgium, Denmark, Finland, France, Germany, Great Britain, Greece, Ireland, Italy, Luxembourg, Netherlands, Portugal, Spain, and Sweden.

European Union directives Rules issued by the European Union. These are binding on member countries.

Evaluated receipt settlement An electronic payment process in which receipt of shipment (not receipt of invoice) triggers payment by the purchasing company.

Evaluation criteria The standards, specified in a request for proposal, that a customer will use to evaluate proposals from competing contractors.

Evaluative criteria Specifications that organizational buyers use to compare alternative goods and services.

Event 1: An instantaneous occurrence that changes the state of the system in a simulation model. **2:** Starting or ending point for a task or group of tasks. **3 (*pl*):** Interconnecting points that link activities in the activity-on-the-arrow form of network diagramming. An event is represented by a circle.

Event risk Includes any security feature or possible event that subjects the investor to a disruption to or reduction in the expected yield.

Event-related marketing (ERM) Form of brand promotion that ties a brand to a meaningful cultural, social, athletic, or other type of high-interest public activity.

Every day low pricing (EDLP) Pricing strategy in which a firm charges the same low price every day.

Evidence square A categorization of fraud investigative procedures that includes testimonial evidence, documentary evidence, physical evidence, and personal observation.

Evidential matter The underlying data and all corroborating information available about a fraud.

EVOP Process of adjusting variables in a process in small increments in a search for a more optimum point on the response surface.

Exception reports Periodic or ad hoc reports that flag facts or numbers that deviate from preset standards.

Excess capacity A situation where the output capabilities at a nonconstraint resource exceed the amount of productive and protective capacity required to achieve a given level of throughput at the constraint.

Excess inventory Any inventory in the system that exceeds the minimum amount necessary to achieve the desired throughput rate at the constraint or that exceeds the minimum amount necessary to achieve the desired due date performance. Total inventory = productive inventory + protective inventory + excess inventory.

Exchange controls Controls on the movement of capital in and out of a country, sometimes imposed when the country faces a shortage of foreign currency.

Exchange principle Maintains that when an exchange benefits both trading partners, the exchange adds value. This principle is derived from the raw material scarcity, labor specialization, and consumption satiation principles.

Exchange rate The amount of one currency needed to obtain one unit of another currency.

Exchange Rate Mechanism (ERM) The acceptance of responsibility by a European Monetary System member to actively maintain its own currency within agreed-upon limits versus other member currencies established by the European Monetary System.

Exchange rate risk The uncertainty associated with the price at which the currency from one country can be converted into the currency of another country. The risk that a firm faces when buying or selling in one or more currencies different from its domestic currency.

Excited quality Additional benefit a customer receives when a product or service goes beyond basic expectations. Excited quality "wows" the customer and distinguishes the provider from the competition. If missing, the customer will still be satisfied.

Exclusive distribution Only one intermediary is used at a particular level in the marketing channel.

Ex-dividend date The date on which the right to the next dividend no longer accompanies a stock; it usually is two working days prior to the holder-of-record date.

Execution error A program error in which a certain operation cannot be carried out, such as division by zero.

Executive education Education (and training) provided to top management.

Executive information system (EIS) 1: A management information system designed to facilitate strategic decision making at the highest levels of management by providing executives with easy access to timely and relevant information. **2:** An information system that extracts high-level organization-wide information from large amounts of data stored in the business' databases. Typically, an EIS presents information graphically as charts and diagrams, allowing for a quick grasp of patterns and trends. Also called *executive support system*.

Executive stock option A type of incentive plan that allows managers to purchase stock at some future time at a given price.

Exempt employees Employees to whom employers are not required to pay overtime under the Fair Labor Standards Act.

Exercise price (strike price) Price (exchange rate) at which the owner of a currency call option is allowed to buy a specified currency; or the price (exchange rate) at which the owner of a currency put option is allowed to sell a specified currency.

Exit interview An interview in which individuals are asked to identify reasons for leaving the organization.

Exit measurement *See:* Output price measurement.

Expansion decisions Whether to purchase capital projects and add them to existing assets to *increase* existing operations.

Expansion project A project that is intended to increase sales.

Expatriate 1: An employee, working in an operation, who is not a citizen of the country in which the operation is located, but is a citizen of the country of the headquarters organization. **2:** Employees who live and work in a country other than their own.

Expatriation Preparing and sending global employees to their foreign assignments.

Expatriation program Takes place while the expatriate is working in the foreign operations; certain delivery and communications programs are required.

Expectancy theory A process theory that proposes that motivation depends on individuals' expectations about their ability to perform tasks and receive desired rewards.

Expectations theory The theory that the shape of the yield curve depends on investors' expectations about future inflation rates.

Expected duration (t_e) Also called the mean or average duration. The expected duration for an activity, calculated from the activity's optimistic, most likely, and pessimistic time estimates, as follows:

$$t_e = \frac{t_o + 4(t_m) + t_p}{6}$$

Expected quality Also known as *basic quality*, the minimum benefit a customer expects to receive from a product or service.

Expected rate of return, $\hat{k}_s$ The rate of return on a common stock that an individual stockholder expects to receive; equal to the expected dividend yield plus the expected capital gains yield.

Expected return on a portfolio, $\hat{k}_p$ The weighted average expected return on the stocks held in the portfolio.

Expected utility (EU) The weighted average of the utilities associated with a decision alternative. The weights are the state-of-nature probabilities.

Expected value (EV) For a chance node, it is the weighted average of the payoffs. The weights are the state-of-nature probabilities.

Expected value approach An approach to choosing a decision alternative that is based on the expected value of each decision alternative. The recommended decision alternative is the one that provides the best expected value.

Expected value of perfect information (EVPI) The expected value of information that would tell the decision maker exactly which state of nature is going to occur (that is, perfect information).

Expected value of sample information (EVSI) The difference between the expected value of an optimal strategy based on sample information and the "best" expected value without any sample information.

Expedited check processing Speedier check clearing provided by the clearing bank if the depositor is willing to perform extra tasks or pay the bank the extra charge involved.

Expedited Funds Availability Act of 1987 Required that shorter availability schedules be put in place to reduce arbitrarily long holds on deposited checks.

Expense budget A budget that outlines the anticipated and actual expenses for each responsibility center.

Expense liability reserves An equity reserve used to achieve income smoothing or to show a steady growth in income from year to year.

Expense scheme Scheme in which perpetrators produce false documents to claim false expenses.

Expenses Assets used up or services consumed in the process of generating revenues.

Experience attributes Can be evaluated only during and after consumption.

Experiential knowledge Knowledge acquired through involvement (as opposed to information, which is obtained through communication, research, and education).

Experimental design Formal plan that details the specifics for conducting an experiment, such as which responses, factors, levels, blocks, treatments, and tools are to be used.

Experimentation A research tool to determine the effects of a variable on an operation.

Expert power Power that stems from special knowledge of or skill in the tasks performed by subordinates.

Expert System (ES) A computer program that mimics the decision process of a human expert in providing a solution to a problem. Current expert systems deal with problems and diagnostics in narrow domains. An ES consists of a knowledge base, an inference engine, and a dialog management module.

Expert system shell An expert system without a knowledge base. A tool that eases the building of an expert system by prompting the designer for facts and relationships among the facts that are built into the shell as a knowledge base.

Expert witness Trial witness who can offer opinions about a matter, based on unique experience, education, or training.

Expertise The skill and knowledge, primarily gained from experience, whose input into a process results in performance that is far above the norm.

Explicit knowledge Represented by the captured and recorded tools of the day, for example, procedures, processes, standards, and other like documents.

Exponential distribution Continuous distribution where data are more likely to occur below the average than above it. Typically used to describe the break-in portion of the "bathtub" curve.

Exponential smoothing 1: A forecasting technique that uses a weighted average of past time series values to arrive at smoothed time series values that can be used as forecasts. **2:** Statistical forecasting technique similar to a moving average, but overcoming the slowness of adaptation to changing patterns inherent in the moving average by allowing a greater weighting for more recent data.

Export complaint systems Allow customers to contact the original supplier of a product in order to inquire about products, make suggestions, or present complaints.

Export-control system A system designed to deny or at least delay the acquisition of strategically important goods to adversaries; in the United States, based on the Export Administration Act and the Munitions Control Act.

Export-Import Bank (Ex-Im Bank) Bank that attempts to strengthen the competitiveness of U.S. industries involved in foreign trade.

Export license A license obtainable from the U.S. Department of Commerce Bureau of Export Administration, which is responsible for administering the Export Administration Act.

Export management companies (EMCs) Domestic firms that specialize in performing international business services as commissioned representatives or as distributors.

Export trading company (ETC) The result of 1982 legislation to improve the export performance of small and medium-sized firms, the export trading company allows businesses to band together to export or offer export services. Additionally, the law permits bank participation in trading companies and relaxes antitrust provisions.

Exporting An entry strategy in which the organization maintains its production facilities within its home country and transfers its products for sale in foreign markets.

Expropriation Government takeover of a company's operations frequently at a level lower than the value of the assets.

Extended enterprise An organizing principle that views multiple tiers of suppliers and multiple tiers of customers as part of the integrated supply chain.

Extensible Markup Language (XML) A programming language that tags data elements in order to indicate what the data mean.

External collaboration *See:* External cooperation.

External cooperation To be more effective and efficient, a firm focuses on what it can do best, and forms an alliance with other firms to obtain the additional organizational capabilities needed to be more effective and efficient than their competitors.

External customer Person or organization who receives a product, a service, or information but is not part of the organization supplying it. *See:* internal customer.

External data Data that are collected from a wide array of sources outside the organization, including mass communications media, specialized newsletters, government agencies, and the Web.

External economies of scale Lower production costs resulting from the free mobility of factors of production in a common market.

External failure costs Costs associated with defects found during or after delivery of the product or service.

External locus of control The belief by individuals that their future is not within their control but rather is influenced by external forces.

External review A company's management becoming familiar with the domestic, international, and foreign factors that affect its business activities.

Externalities The effect accepting a project will have on the cash flows in other parts (areas) of the firm.

Extortion An official in a foreign country in a position of power seeking payment from an individual or corporation for an action to which the individual or corporation may be lawfully entitled.

Extra dividend A supplemental dividend paid in years when the firm does well, and excess funds are available for distribution.

Extraction phase The stage of data warehouse building in which the builders create the files from transactional databases and save them on the server that will hold the data warehouse.

Extranet A company communications system that gives access to suppliers, partners, and others outside the company; an external communications system that uses the Internet and is shared by two or more organizations.

Extraordinary items Events or transactions that are unusual and infrequent.

Extraordinary repair An expenditure that increases the useful life of an asset beyond the original estimate.

Extraterritoriality An exemption from rules and regulations of one country that may challenge the national sovereignty of another. The application of one country's rules and regulations abroad.

Extrinsic forecast A forecast based on a correlated leading indicator, such as estimating furniture sales based on housing starts. Extrinsic forecasts tend to be more useful for large aggregations, such as total company sales, than for individual product sales. *Ant:* intrinsic forecast method.

Extrinsic reward A reward given by another person.

Ex-works (EXW) Price quotes that apply only at the point of origin; the seller agrees to place the goods at the disposal of the buyer at the specified place on a date or within a fixed period.

F

Face value Investors holding an investment to maturity will receive this amount back from the issuer. Also called the *investment's principal.* The amount of the loan, or the amount borrowed; also called the principal amount of the loan.

Facilitating payments Payments made to influence an official to take an action that the official must take anyway.

Facilitator Individual who is responsible for creating favorable conditions that will enable a team to reach its purpose or achieve its goals by bringing together the necessary tools, information, and resources to get the job done.

Factor Firm specializing in collection on accounts receivable; exporters sometimes sell their accounts receivable to a factor at a discount.

Factor analysis 1: Used in the exploratory or confirmatory of "interdependence" among the variables. **2:** Statistical technique that examines the relationships between a single dependent variable and multiple independent variables. For example, it is used to determine which questions on a questionnaire are related to a specific question such as "Would you buy this product again?"

Factor intensities The proportion of capital input to labor input used in the production of a good.

Factor mobility The ability to freely move factors of production across borders, as among common market countries.

Factor proportions theory Systematic explanation of the source of comparative advantage.

Factoring Purchase of receivables of an exporter by a factor without recourse to the exporter. The outright sale of receivables.

Factors of production All inputs into the production process, including capital, labor, land, materials, machines, buildings, and technology, that are necessary for bringing the good to the market.

Factory overhead cost All of the costs of operating the factory except for direct materials and direct labor.

Factual cultural knowledge Knowledge obtainable from specific country studies published by governments, private companies, and universities and also available in the form of background information from facilitating agencies such as banks, advertising agencies, and transportation companies.

Failsafe work methods Methods of performing operations so that actions that are incorrect cannot be completed. For example, a part without holes in the proper place cannot be removed from a jig, or a computer system will reject invalid numbers or require double entry of transaction quantities outside the normal range. Called poka-yoke by the Japanese. *Syn:* failsafe techniques, mistake-proofing, poka-yoke.

Failure mode analysis (FMA) Procedure to determine which malfunction symptoms appear immediately before or after a failure of a critical parameter in a system. After all the possible causes are listed for each symptom, the product is designed to eliminate the problems.

Failure mode effects analysis (FMEA) Procedure in which each potential failure mode in every subitem of an item is analyzed to determine its effect on other subitems and on the required function of the item.

Failure mode effects and criticality analysis (FMECA) Procedure that is performed after a failure mode effects analysis to classify each potential failure effect according to its severity and probability of occurrence.

Falsified identity (customer impersonation) Pretending to be someone you're not—a major problem in e-business transactions.

FASB Statement 95 The accounting standard that created the Statement of Cash Flows.

Fatalism A view that individuals cannot control their destiny, that God has predetermined the course of their life.

Fault tree analysis A logical approach to identify the probabilities and frequencies of events in a system that are most critical to uninterrupted and safe operation. This analysis may include failure mode effects analysis (determining the result of component failure interactions toward system safety) and techniques for human error prediction.

Fault-tolerant computer system A computer system that has extra hardware, software, and power lines that guarantee that the system will continue running even when a mishap occurs.

Feasibility studies A series of studies conducted to determine if a proposed information system can be built, and whether or not it will benefit the business; the series includes technical, economic, and operational feasibility studies.

Feasible solution A decision alternative or solution that satisfies all constraints.

Features The way that benefits are delivered to customers. Features provide the solution to customer problems.

Fed float Part of the clearing float for a mailed check, it arises because the Fed may grant availability to the clearing bank before it presents the check (and debits the account of) the payee's bank. Fed float has been greatly reduced since 1980, because the 1980 Monetary Control Act mandated that the Fed eliminate or charge for Fed float.

Fed funds rate The rate charged on reserve borrowings, mostly overnight, transacted between banks.

Federal Advisory Council Is a group of prominent commercial bankers which gives input into Fed decision making.

Federal Courts Courts established by the federal government to enforce federal laws and statutes.

Federal Deposit Insurance Corp. Improvement Act of 1991 Requires the FDIC to give acquiring banks the choice of whether to bid for all of a failed bank's deposits or just the insured deposits, signaling a reduction in coverage for uninsured deposits.

Federal Open Market Committee (FOMC) The seven members of the Board of Governors are also members of this group, which makes most of the monetary policy for the United States in its eight regularly scheduled meetings per year. The FOMC effects changes in the money supply by buying and selling Treasury securities (open market operations), which affects the reserve position of banks, and ultimately the money supply.

Federal Reserve Act (1913) Established the Federal Reserve System to oversee and regulate the national money and credit system.

Federal Reserve member banks *See:* member banks.

Federal Reserve System (Fed) The nation's central bank, this organization oversees the national money and credit system by acting as lender of last resort, lending money to banks through the "discount window," and facilitating the payments mechanism, and is one of several national bodies that supervises and regulates banks.

Fedwire A linked network of the twelve Fed district banks which transfers funds for banks (and by extension their customers) by debiting or crediting the banks' reserve accounts. It is a major part of the Federal Reserve System's payment system involvement.

Feedback 1: Return of information in interpersonal communication; it may be based on fact or feeling and helps the party who is receiving the information judge how well he/she is being understood by the other party. More generally, information about a process that is used to make decisions about its performance and to adjust the process when necessary. **2:** The amount of information received about how well or how poorly one has performed.

Feedback control Control that focuses on the organization's outputs; also called *postaction* or *output control.*

Feedback loops Open-loop and closed-loop feedback.

Feedforward control Control that focuses on human, material, and financial resources flowing into the organization; also called *preliminary* or *preventive quality control.*

Femininity 1: A cultural preference for cooperation, group decision making, and quality of life. **2:** The quality of life, nurturing, and relationships.

FICA tax Federal Insurance Contributions Act tax used to finance federal programs for old-age and disability benefits (Social Security) and health insurance for the aged (Medicare).

Field A data element in a record, describing one aspect of an entity or event.

Field experience Experience acquired in actual rather than laboratory settings; training that exposes a corporate manager to a different cultural environment for a limited amount of time.

Field selling Involves calling on prospective customers in either their business or home locations.

Field warehouse agreement Inventories pledged as collateral and physically segregated from other inventory generally on the borrower's premises.

FIFO Method of valuation of inventories for accounting purposes, meaning First-In-First-Out. The principle rests on the assumption that costs should be charged against revenue in the order in which they occur.

File A collection of records of the same type, for different entities or events.

File transfer protocol (ftp) Software that allows the transfer of files over communications lines.

Filters Relative to human to human communication, those perceptions (based on culture, language, demographics, experience, and so on.) that affect how a message is transmitted by the sender and how a message is interpreted by the receiver.

Final assembly schedule (FAS) A schedule of end items to finish the product for specific customers' orders in a make-to-order or assemble-to-order environment. It is also referred to as the finishing schedule because it may involve operations other than just the final assembly; also, it may not involve assembly, but simply final mixing, cutting, packaging, and so on. The FAS is prepared after receipt of a customer order as constrained by the availability of material and capacity, and it schedules the operations required to complete the product from the level where it is stocked (or master scheduled) to the end-item level.

Finance lease *See:* Capital lease.

Financial accounting A component of an organization's internal accounting system that provides information primarily for users outside the organization. The branch of accounting that is concerned with the recording of transactions using generally accepted accounting principles (GAAP) for a business or other economic unit and with a periodic preparation of various statements from such records.

Financial Accounting Standards Board (FASB) The main body responsible for promulgating accounting standards in the United States.

Financial Accounting Standards Board (FASB) Statement 95 Provides a set of guidelines to help classify cash receipts and disbursement according to type of activity.

Financial break-even analysis Determining the operating income (EBIT) the firm needs to just cover all of its fixed financing costs and produce earnings per share equal to zero.

Financial break-even point The level of EBIT at which EPS equals zero.

Financial control The phase in which financial plans are implemented; control deals with the feedback and adjustment process required to ensure adherence to plans and modification of plans because of unforeseen changes.

Financial EDI (FEDI) The exchange of electronic business information such as lockbox information reports, daily balance reports, and monthly account analysis reports between a firm and its bank. In the context of payments, financial EDI refers to electronic data interchange combined with payment instructions. This allows customers to include invoice data and payment instructions in the same payment order.

Financial engineering A unique model is developed for a specific real currency option. Used when the results of a decision tree analysis are not adequate and cannot find a standard option that corresponds to the real option.

Financial flexibility The ability of the firm to augment its future cash flows to cover any unforeseen needs or to take advantage of any unforeseen opportunities.

Financial incentives Monetary offers intended to motivate; special funding designed to attract foreign direct investors that may take the form of land or building, loans, or loan guarantees.

Financial infrastructure Facilitating financial agencies in a country; for example, banks.

Financial Institution Buyer Credit Policy Policy that provides insurance coverage for loans by banks to foreign buyers of exports.

Financial Institutions Reform, Recovery and Enforcement Act (1989) Allowed bank holding companies to buy healthy savings and loan associations.

Financial intermediaries Specialized financial firms that facilitate the transfer of funds from savers to borrowers.

Financial lease A lease that does not provide for maintenance services, is not cancelable, and is fully amortized over its life. Also called a *capital lease.*

Financial leverage The extent to which fixed-income securities (debt and preferred stock) are used in a firm's capital structure. The use of debt financing.

Financial markets "Mechanisms" by which borrowers and lenders get together.

Financial motive One of the theoretical motives for trade credit extension, applies where the seller has a lower cost of capital than the buyer and is able to pass along some of the difference.

Financial planning The projection of sales, income, and assets based on alternative production and marketing strategies, as well as the determination of the resources needed to achieve these projections.

Financial ratio analysis An evaluation of financial performance and financial position between two or more firms.

Financial reporting disclosures The information presented in financial statements. Such disclosures may be either within the statements or in the accompanying notes.

Financial restructuring Situation in which the company changes its product lines or its relative use of assets with heavy fixed operating costs altering the company's business risk.

Financial risk 1: The portion of stockholders' risk, over and above basic business risk, resulting from the manner in which the firm is financed. The possibility that a company will not be able to cover financing related expenditures such as lease payments, interest, principal repayment, and referred stock dividends. **2:** Risk involving credit, foreign exchange, commodity trading, and interest rate; may involve chance for gain as well as loss.

Financial Services Modernization Act of 1999 Also known as the Gramm-Leach-Bliley Act, this law repealed the 1933 Glass-Steagall Act's prohibition on bank-investment company affiliations.

Financial shenanigans Actions or omissions intended to hide or distort the real financial performance or financial condition of a business entity.

Financial statement analysis The conversion of the data in financial statements into useful information.

Financial statement fraud Intentional misstatement of financial statements by omitting critical facts or disclosures, misstating amounts, or misapplying GAAP.

Financial statements Financial reports such as the balance sheet, income statement, and statement of cash flows that summarize the profitability and cash flows of an entity for a specific period and the financial position of the entity as of a specific date.

Financing activities Defined as cash flows resulting from proceeds of issuance of securities, retirement of debt, and payments of dividends or other distributions to shareholders.

Financing cash flows The cash flows arising from the firm's funding activities.

Financing feedbacks The effects on the income statement and balance sheet of actions taken to finance forecasted increases in assets.

Finding Conclusion of importance based on observation(s).

Finished-goods inventory 1: Inventory consisting of items that have passed through the complete production process but have yet to be sold. **2:** The cost of finished products on hand that have not been sold.

Finished goods ledger The subsidiary ledger that contains the individual accounts for each kind of commodity or product produced.

Finite forward scheduling An equipment scheduling technique that builds a schedule by proceeding sequentially from the initial period to the final period while observing capacity limits. A Gantt chart may be used with this technique. *See:* finite scheduling.

Finite loading Assigning no more work to a work center than the work center can be expected to execute in a given time period. The specific term usually refers to a computer technique that involves calculating shop priority revisions in order to level load operation by operation.

Finite scheduling A scheduling methodology where work is loaded into work centers such that no work center capacity requirement exceeds the capacity available for that work center. *See:* drum-buffer-rope, finite forward scheduling.

Firewall Hardware and software designed to control access by Internet surfers to an information system, and access to Internet sites by organizational users.

Firm planned order (FPO) A planned order that can be frozen in quantity and time. The computer is not allowed to change it automatically; this is the responsibility of the planner in charge of the item that is being planned. This technique can aid planners working with MRP systems to respond to material and capacity problems by firming up selected planned orders. In addition, firm planned orders are the normal method of stating the master production schedule. *See:* planning time fence.

Firm-specific, or diversifiable, risk That part of a security's risk associated with random outcomes generated by events, or behaviors, specific to the firm; it can be eliminated by proper diversification.

First differencing A means of correcting a data series for autocorrelation, which is accomplished by subtracting the previous value for the dependent variable from the current value, and then using the differences as the dependent variable (in lieu of the original values of the dependent variable).

First generation languages (1GL) Machine languages.

First-in, first-out (FIFO) method A method of inventory costing based on the assumption that the costs of merchandise sold should be charged against revenue in the order in which the costs were incurred.

First-line manager A manager who is at the first or second management level and is directly responsible for the production of goods and services.

Fiscal incentives Incentives used to attract foreign direct investment that provide specific tax measures to attract the investor.

Fiscal year The annual accounting period adopted by a business.

Fishbone diagram *See:* cause-and-effect diagram.

Fisher effect Theory that nominal interest rates are composed of a real interest rate and anticipated inflation.

Fitness for use Term used to indicate that a product or service fits the customer's defined purpose for that product or service.

Five (5)-Ss Five practices for maintaining a clean and efficient workplace (Japanese). These include sort, set in order, shine, standardize, and sustain.

Five C's of credit Traditional means of evaluating a corporate credit applicant by investigating character, collateral, capacity, conditions, and capital. Character is thought to be the single most important aspect in this approach.

Five focusing steps In the theory of constraints, a process to continuously improve organizational profit by evaluating the production system and market mix to determine how to make the most profit using the system constraint. The steps consist of 1) identifying the constraint to the system, 2) deciding how to exploit the constraint to the system, 3) subordinating all nonconstraints to the constraint, 4) elevating the constraint to the system, 5) returning to step 1 if the constraint is broken in any previous step, while not allowing inertia to set in.

Five stages of national economic development A theory proposing that nations advance from an agricultural economy to an advanced industrial economy in five stages.

Five whys Persistent questioning technique to probe deeper to surface the root cause of a problem.

Fixed assets 1: Physical resources that are owned and used by a business and are permanent or have a long life. **2:** Property, plant, and equipment assets of an organization; also called *long-term* and *noncurrent assets.*

Fixed assets turnover ratio The ratio of sales to net fixed assets.

Fixed charge coverage ratio This ratio expands the TIE ratio to include the firm's annual long-term lease payments and sinking fund payments.

Fixed costs The portion of the total costs that do not depend on the volume; these costs remains the same no matter how much is produced.

Fixed exchange rate The government of a country officially declares that its currency is convertible into a fixed amount of some other currency.

Fixed exchange rate system Monetary system in which exchange rates are either held constant or allowed to fluctuate only within very narrow boundaries.

Fixed-for-floating rate swap In this type of swap, Party A, with floating rate debt, agrees to pay Party B, who has fixed rate debt, a fixed-rate interest payment based on the notional dollar amount stated in the agreement, in exchange for receipt of a floating-rate interest payment.

Fixed-interval review system A hybrid inventory system in which the inventory analyst reviews the inventory position at fixed time periods. If the inventory level is found to be above a preset reorder point, no action is taken. If the inventory level is at or below the reorder point, the analyst orders a variable quantity equal to $M - x$ where M is a maximum stock level and x is the current quantity on hand and on order (if any). This hybrid system does not reorder every review interval. It therefore differs from the fixed-interval order system, which automatically places an order whenever inventory is reviewed.

Fixed order quantity A lot-sizing technique in MRP or inventory management that will always cause planned or actual orders to be generated for a predetermined fixed quantity, or multiples thereof, if net requirements for the period exceed the fixed order quantity.

Fixed point surveillance Watching a fraud suspect from a fixed point, such as a restaurant, office, or other set location.

Fixed-position layout A facility's layout in which the product remains in one location and the required tasks and equipment are brought to it.

Fixed-price contract A contract in which a customer and a contractor agree on a price that will not change no matter how much the project actually costs the contractor.

Fixed rate currency Currency with a fixed rate of exchange within narrow limits against a major currency, such as the U.S. dollar or the British pound.

Fixed reorder cycle inventory model A form of independent demand management model in which an order is placed every n time units. The order quantity is variable and essentially replaces the items consumed during the current time period. Let M be the maximum inventory desired at any time, and let x be the quantity on hand at the time the order is placed. Then, in the simplest model, the order quantity will be $M - x$. The quantity M must be large enough to cover the maximum expected demand during the lead time plus a review interval. The order quantity model becomes more complicated whenever the replenishment lead time exceeds the review interval, because outstanding orders then have to be factored into the equation. These reorder systems are sometimes called fixed-interval order systems, order level systems, or periodic review systems. *Syn:* fixed-interval order system, fixed-order quantity system, order level system, periodic review system, time-based order system. *See:* fixed reorder quantity inventory model, hybrid inventory system, independent demand item management models, optional replenishment model.

Fixed reorder quantity inventory model A form of independent demand item management model in which an order for a fixed quantity, Q, is placed whenever stock on hand plus on order reaches a predetermined reorder level, R. The fixed order quantity Q may be determined by the economic order quantity, by a fixed order quantity (such as a carton or a truckload), or by another model yielding a fixed result. The reorder point, R, may be deterministic or stochastic, and in either instance is large enough to cover the maximum expected demand during the replenishment lead time. Fixed reorder quantity models assume the existence of some form of a perpetual inventory record or some form of physical tracking, for example, a two-bin system that is able to determine when the reorder point is reached. These reorder systems are sometimes called fixed order quantity systems, lot-size systems, or order point-order quantity systems. *Syn:* fixed order quantity system, lot size system, order point-order quantity system, quantity-based order system. *See:* fixed reorder cycle inventory model, hybrid inventory system, independent demand item management models, optional replenishment model, order point, order point system, statistical inventory control, time-phased order point.

Flash memory A memory chip that can be rewritten and hold its content without electric power.

Flat structure A management structure characterized by an overall broad span of control and relatively few hierarchical levels.

Flat yield curve Horizontally shaped graph of the yields to maturity of securities with various maturities, implying a "no change" forecast of future interest rates.

Flexible benefits plan One that allows employees to select the benefits they prefer from groups of benefits established by the employer.

Flexible budget A budget that adjusts for varying rates of activity.

Flexible capacity The ability to operate manufacturing equipment at different production rates by varying staffing levels and operating hours or starting and stopping at will.

Flexible manufacturing system (FMS) A group of numerically controlled machine tools interconnected by a central control system. The various machining cells are interconnected via loading and unloading stations by an automated transport system. Operational flexibility is enhanced by the ability to execute all manufacturing tasks on numerous product designs in small quantities and with faster delivery.

Flexible spending account Account that allows employees to contribute pretax dollars to buy additional benefits.

Flexible staffing Use of recruiting sources and workers who are not traditional employees.

Flextime A modification of work scheduling that allows workers to determine their own starting and ending times within a broad range of available hours.

Float The delay between the time a payment is initiated and the time when the payment is debited to the payor (disbursement float) or credited to the payee (collection float). Within ethical limits companies try to maximize it on payments or minimize it on collections, and float continues to be an important fact of life that must be coped with. The difference between the balance shown in a firm's (or individual's) checkbook and the balance on the bank's records. *See:* total slack.

Floating exchange rate Under this system, the government possesses no responsibility to declare that its currency is convertible into a fixed amount of some other currency; this diminishes the role of official reserves.

Floating lien A financing arrangement where a borrower's inventory in general is pledged as collateral for a loan.

Floating rate bond A bond whose interest rate fluctuates with shifts in the general level of interest rates.

Floating rate currency Currency whose exchange rate is determined by market forces.

Floating rate notes (FRNs) 1: Provision of some Eurobonds, in which the coupon rate is adjusted over time according to prevailing market rates. **2:** Type of loan in which the interest rate is reset either daily, weekly, monthly, quarterly, or semi-annually.

Floor planning The common name used for trust receipt loans made to automobile dealerships.

Flotation costs The costs associated with issuing new stocks or bonds.

Flow of capital International Monetary Fund facilitates the expansion and balanced growth of international trade, assists in eliminating foreign exchange restrictions, and smoothes the international balance of payments.

Flow of labor Controlled through passport, visa, and immigration regulations.

Flow of trade Controlled by trade barriers on imports and exports.

Flowchart 1: A graphical method used to describe an information system, including hardware pieces and logical processes. Over thirty symbols represent various types of operations, processes, input and output devices, and communication. **2:** Graphical representation of the steps in a process. Flowcharts are drawn to better understand processes. The flowchart is one of the seven tools of quality. **3:** Movement of products, negotiation, ownership, information, and promotion through each participant in the marketing channel.

FOB (free on board) destination Terms of agreement between buyer and seller whereby ownership passes when merchandise is received by the buyer and the seller pays the transportation costs.

FOB (free on board) shipping point Terms of agreement between buyer and seller whereby ownership passes when merchandise is delivered to the freight carrier and the buyer pays the transportation costs.

Focus A type of competitive strategy that emphasizes concentration on a specific regional market or buyer group.

Focus group Qualitative discussion group consisting of eight to ten participants, invited from a segment of the customer base to discuss an existing or planned product or service, lead by a facilitator working from predetermined questions (focus groups may also be used to gather information in a context other than customers).

Focused factory A plant established to focus the entire manufacturing system on a limited, concise, manageable set of products, technologies, volumes, and markets precisely defined by the company's competitive strategy, technology, and economics. *See:* cellular manufacturing.

Footnote disclosure Information contained in a note accompanying the financial statements.

Footnotes Information that accompanies a company's financial statements and that provides interpretive guidance to the financial statements or includes related information that must be disclosed.

Forced distribution Performance appraisal method in which ratings of employees' performance are distributed along a bell-shaped curve.

Force-field analysis Technique for analyzing the forces that aid or hinder an organization in reaching an objective.

Forecast A projection or prediction of future values of a time series.

Forecast bias Tendency for a forecasting model to systematically over- or under-predict the variable of interest. It can often be detected on a graph of forecast errors over time or across values of an important predictor variable.

Forecast horizon How far ahead the cash balance is being projected.

Forecast interval The units the horizon is segmented into, such as months in a year-ahead forecast.

Forecasted cost at completion (FCAC) The projected total cost of all the work required to complete a project.

Forecasting 1: An important activity that provides operations and supply chain managers with the numbers needed to make both long-term capacity decisions and short-term planning decisions. For example: What will the total demand for a new product be over the next five years? How many customers will we serve next week? **2:** Use of information from the past and present to identify expected future conditions.

Foreign agents A local agent in the host country is used to provide limited involvement for an MNE.

Foreign availability The ability of a firm's products to be obtained in markets outside the firm's home country.

Foreign bond Bonds that are issued by a country's borrowers in other countries, subject to the same restrictions as bonds issued by domestic borrowers.

Foreign Corrupt Practices Act (FCPA), The An established U.S. code of conduct making it illegal for U.S. businesses to bribe foreign government officials, political parties, and political candidates, even if it is an acceptable practice in the foreign country; requires appropriate accounting controls for full disclosure of firms' foreign transactions.

Foreign currency transactions Transactions denominated in a currency other than the reporting currency of the entity.

Foreign currency translation A conversion of amounts in accounts of international subsidiaries (recorded in a foreign currency) to the currency used for consolidated financial statements.

Foreign debt A debt instrument sold by a foreign borrower but denominated in the currency of the country in which it is sold.

Foreign direct investment 1: International entry strategy that is achieved through the acquisition of foreign firms. **2:** The establishment or expansion of operations of a firm in a foreign country. Like all investments, it assumes a transfer of capital.

Foreign environment Refers to factors in a country that affect international business, including the country's cultural, legal, political, competitive, economic, and technological systems.

Foreign exchange market Market composed primarily of banks, serving firms and consumers who wish to buy or sell various currencies.

Foreign exchange rate The price of one currency stated in relation to the price of another currency.

Foreign exchange risk The possibility that exchange rates will move adversely, causing results of foreign business activities to have a reduced value when converted into the company's home currency.

Foreign exchange risk management The management of the risk of loss from currency exchange rate movements on transactions, translation, or remeasurement involving foreign currency.

Foreign investment Many countries' laws dictate that foreign investments in their nation must be in the form of a joint venture with local partners and that the local partners must be majority owners.

Foreign investment risk matrix (FIRM) Graph that displays financial and political risk by intervals, so that each country can be positioned according to its risk ratings.

Foreign key In a relational database: a field in a file that is a primary key in another file. Foreign keys allow association of data between the two files.

Foreign market opportunity analysis Broad-based research to obtain information about the general variables of a target market outside a firm's home country.

Foreign policy The area of public policy concerned with relationships with other countries.

Foreign service premium A financial incentive to accept an assignment overseas, usually paid as a percentage of the base salary.

Foreign subsidiary An international firm's operating unit established in foreign countries. It typically has its own management structure.

Foreign tax credit Credit applied to home-country tax payments due for taxes paid abroad.

Foreign trade zones Special areas where foreign goods may be held or processed without incurring duties and taxes.

Forfaiting Method of financing international trade of capital goods.

Form utility Achieved by the conversion of raw and component materials into finished products that are desired by the marketplace.

Formal communication Officially sanctioned data within an organization, which includes publications, memoranda, training materials/events, public relations information, and company meetings.

Formal communication channel A communication channel that flows within the chain of command or task responsibility defined by the organization.

Formal team A team created by the organization as part of the formal organization structure.

Formalization 1: Represents decision making through bureaucratic mechanisms such as formal systems, established rules, and prescribed procedures. **2:** The written documentation used to direct and control employees.

Fortress Europe Suspicion raised by trading partners of Western Europe, claiming that the integration of the European Union may result in increased restrictions on trade and investment by outsiders.

Forward buying (bridge buying) Retailers purchase enough product during a manufacturer's off-invoice allowance period to carry the retailers over until the manufacturer's next regularly scheduled deal.

Forward chaining (forward reasoning) The process in which an expert system looks for an outcome under the constraints of given conditions. Example: A medical ES accepts the conditions (age, temperature, and so on) of a patient and provides a diagnosis of the patient's disease.

Forward contract Agreement between a commercial bank and a client about an exchange of two currencies to be made at a future point in time at a specified exchange rate.

Forward discount Percentage by which the forward rate is less than the spot rate; typically quoted on an annualized basis.

Forward exchange contract An agreement to buy (or sell) a foreign currency in the future at a fixed rate called a forward rate.

Forward premium Percentage by which the forward rate exceeds the spot rate; typically quoted on an annualized basis.

Forward pricing Setting the price of a product based on its anticipated demand before it has been introduced to the market.

Forward rate(s) 1: The fixed future rate used in a forward exchange contract. **2:** Contracts that provide for two parties to exchange currencies on a future date at an agreed-upon exchange rate. **3:** Prices or yields which the market collectively forecasts today for future periods. In foreign exchange markets, forward rates refer to exchange rates between currencies which is contracted to exist at a future value date.

Forward scheduling A scheduling technique where the scheduler proceeds from a known start date and computes the completion date for an order, usually proceeding from the first operation to the last. Dates generated by this technique are generally the earliest start dates for operations. *Syn:* forward pass. *Ant:* back scheduling.

Forward value date The date that good funds will be credited to the account (similar to availability schedules in the United States).

Founders' shares Stock owned by the firm's founders who have sole voting rights; this type of stock generally has restricted dividends for a specified number of years.

Fourteen (14) points Both W. Edwards Deming and Philip B. Crosby have advocated fourteen management practices to help organizations increase their quality and productivity.

Fourth Directive, The The EU Fourth Directive contains comprehensive accounting rules relevant to corporate accounting. It covers financial statements, their contents, methods of presentation, valuation methods, and disclosure of information. *See:* Eighth Directive, Seventh Directive.

Fourth-generation languages (4GLs) High-level programming languages that allow the programmer to concentrate on what the program should do, rather than on how it should do it. 4GLs contain many preprogrammed functions to expedite code writing. Sometimes called *application generators.*

Fraction defective chart (p chart) Attribute control chart used to track the proportion of defective units.

Franchise holding/loading Includes manufacturers' efforts to hold on to their franchise of current users by rewarding them for continuing to purchase the promoted brand, or to load them so they have no need to switch to another brand.

Franchising 1: A form of licensing in which an organization provides its foreign franchisees with a complete assortment of materials and services; an arrangement by which the owner of a product or service allows others to purchase the right to distribute the product or service with help from the owner. **2:** A form of licensing that allows a distributor or retailer exclusive rights to sell a product or service in a specified area. **3:** Agreement by which a firm provides a specialized sales or service strategy, support assistance, and possibly an initial investment in the franchise in exchange for periodic fees. **4:** Form of licensing that grants a wholesaler or a retailer exclusive rights to sell a product or a service in a specified area.

Fraud A generic term that embraces all the multifarious means which human ingenuity can devise, which are resorted to by one individual, to get an advantage over another by false representations. No definite and invariable rule can be laid down as a general proposition in defining fraud, as it includes surprise, trickery, cunning and unfair ways by which another is cheated. The only boundaries defining it are those which limit human knavery.

Free alongside ship (FAS) Exporter quotes a price for the goods, including charges for delivery of the goods alongside a vessel at a port. Seller handles cost of unloading and wharfage; loading, ocean transportation, and insurance are left to the buyer.

Free carrier (FCA) Applies only at a designated inland shipping point. Seller is responsible for loading goods into the means of transportation; buyer is responsible for all subsequent expenses.

Free cash flow The amount of operating cash flow remaining after replacing current productive capacity and maintaining current dividends.

Free cash flow hypothesis All else equal, firms that pay dividends from cash flows that cannot be reinvested in positive net present value projects, which are termed *free cash flows,* have higher values than firms that retain free cash flows.

Free market economic system An economic concept used to denote the economic system of a country unimpeded by government restrictions, and ideally subject to the laws of supply and demand of the market.

Free on board (FOB) Applies only to vessel shipments. Seller quotes a price covering all expenses up to and including delivery of goods on an overseas vessel provided by or for the buyer.

Free on board (FOB) pricing Leaves the cost and responsibility of transportation to the customer.

Free rider A person who benefits from team membership but does not make a proportionate contribution to the team's work.

Free slack (FS) The amount of time that a particular activity can be delayed without delaying the earliest start time of its immediately succeeding activities; the relative difference between the amounts of total slack for activities entering into that same activity. It's always a positive value.

Free trade area An area in which all barriers to trade among member countries are removed, although sometimes only for certain goods or services.

Free Trade Area of the Americas (FTAA) A hemispheric trade zone covering all of the Americas. Organizers hope for it to be operational by 2005.

"Free" trade credit Credit received during the discount period.

Freely floating exchange rate system Monetary system in which exchange rates are allowed to move due to market forces without intervention by country governments.

Freight forwarders Specialists in handling international transportation by contracting with carriers on behalf of shippers.

Fringe benefits A variety of employee benefits that may take many forms, including vacations, pension plans, and health, life, and disability insurance.

Frustration-regression principle The idea that failure to meet a high-order need may cause a regression to an already satisfied lower-order need.

Fulfillment Picking, packing, and shipping after a customer places an order online.

Full compensation An arrangement in which the delivery of goods to one party is fully compensated for by buying back more than 100 percent of the value that was originally sold.

Full disclosure One of the responsibilities of a public corporation to its shareholders and potential shareholders.

Full reconciliation Service which provides detailed checks outstanding information along with the checks paid data from company-supplied check issue detail.

Full-duplex Telecommunications whereby a party can transmit and receive data at the same time while the other party also transmits and receives.

Full-service merchant wholesalers Provide a wide range of services for retailers and business purchasers.

Functional currency The currency of the primary environment in which the international subsidiary operates.

Functional manager A manager who is responsible for a department that performs a single functional task and has employees with similar training and skills.

Functional organization Organization organized by discrete functions, for example, marketing/sales, engineering, production, finance, human resources.

Functional organization structure An organizational structure in which groups are made up of individuals who perform the same function, such as engineering or manufacturing, or have the same expertise or skills, such as electronics engineering or testing.

Functional structure An organization structure in which positions are grouped into departments based on similar skills, expertise, and resource use.

Functional-level strategy Addresses the question, "How should a firm integrate its various subfunctional activities and how should these activities be related to changes taking place in the various functional areas?" Pertains to all of the organization's major departments.

Fundamental attribution error The tendency to underestimate the influence of external factors on another's behavior and to overestimate the influence on internal factors.

Fundamental forecasting Forecasting based on fundamental relationships between economic variables and exchange rates.

Funded debt Long-term debt; "funding" means replacing short-term debt with securities of longer maturity.

Funnel experiment Experiment that demonstrates the effects of tampering. Marbles are dropped through a funnel in an attempt to hit a flat-surfaced target below. The experiment shows that adjusting a stable process to compensate for an undesirable result or an extraordinarily good result will produce output that is worse than if the process had been left alone.

Future reality tree Technique used in the application of Goldratt's Theory of Constraints.

Future value (FV) The amount to which a cash flow or series of cash flows will grow over a given period of time when compounded at a given interest rate.

Future value interest factor for an annuity (FVIFA$_{i,n}$) The future value interest factor for an annuity of n periods compounded at i percent.

Future value interest factor for *i* and *n* (FVIF$_{i,n}$) The future value of $1 left on deposit for n periods at a rate of i percent per period—the multiple by which an initial investment grows because of the interest earned.

Futures contract A standardized contract that obligates the buyer (issuer) to purchase (sell) a specified amount of the item represented by the contract at a set price at the expiration of the contract.

Futures option An option contract that gives the buyer (issuer) the right to purchase (sell) the futures contract underlying the options contract.

Futures rates An exchange rate at which currencies can be traded at a future date. Futures differ from forwards in that the futures contract is standardized and traded on a national exchange.

Fuzzy logic A rule-based method used in artificial intelligence to solve problems with imprecise conditions. The method uses membership functions to characterize a situation.

FVA$_n$ The future value of an ordinary annuity over n periods.

FVIFA(DUE)$_{i,n}$ The future value interest factor for an annuity due—FVIFA(DUE)$_{i,n}$ = FVIFA$_{i,n}$ × (1 + i).

G

Gainsharing Type of program that rewards individuals financially on the basis of organizational performance.

Game theory General framework to help decision making when a firm payoff depends on actions taken by other firms.

Gantt chart Type of bar chart used in process/project planning and control to display planned work and finished work in relation to time. Also called a *milestone chart*.

Gap analysis Technique that compares a company's existing state to its desired state (as expressed by its long-term plans) to help determine what needs to be done to remove or minimize the gap.

Garnishment A court action in which a portion of an employee's wages is set aside to pay a debt owed a creditor.

Garn-St. Germain Depository Institutions Act (1982) Enacted alterations allowing: (1) depository institutions to pay interest on money market deposit accounts in order to compete with money market mutual funds and (2) savings and loans associations to lend to businesses.

Gatekeeping Role of an individual (often a facilitator) in a group meeting in helping ensure effective interpersonal interactions (for example, someone's ideas are not ignored due to the team moving on to the next topic too quickly).

Gateway A device that connects two communications networks, each consisting of different hardware devices, for example an IBM- and a Macintosh-based network.

Gauge repeatability and reproducibility (GR&R) Evaluation of a gauging instrument's accuracy by determining whether the measurements taken with it are repeatable (that is, there is close agreement among a number of consecutive measurements of the output for the same value of the input under the same operating conditions) and reproducible (that is, there is close agreement among repeated measurements of the output for the same value of input made under the same operating conditions over a period of time).

Gearing adjustment A gearing adjustment equals the average borrowing divided by average operating assets multiplied by total current value adjustments for cost of goods sold, depreciation, and so on. It shows the benefit (or disadvantage) to shareholders from debt financing during a period of changing prices. The amount of gearing adjustment is added (deducted) to current cost income.

General adaptation syndrome (GAS) The physiological response to a stressor, beginning with an alarm response, continuing to resistance, and sometimes ending in exhaustion if the stressor continues beyond the person's ability to cope.

General Agreement on Tariffs and Trade (GATT), now called World Trade Organization (WTO) A 124-nation organization that provides the conditions under which a nation can impose trade barriers such as tariffs. The new World Trade Organization was created to settle trade disputes.

General Agreement on Trade in Services (GATS) A legally enforceable pact among GATT participants that covers trade and investments in the services sector.

General controls Policies and procedures that help ensure the continued, proper operation of computer information systems. They include controls over data center operations, system software acquisition and maintenance, access security, and application system development and maintenance. General controls support the functioning of programmed application controls. Other terms sometimes used to describe general controls are general computer controls and information technology controls.

General ledger The primary ledger, when used in conjunction with subsidiary ledgers, that contains all of the balance sheet and income statement accounts.

General manager A manager who is responsible for several departments that perform different functions.

General obligation The banking for the interest principal payments of these securities is simply future general revenues and the issuer's capacity to raise taxes.

General price index An index used to estimate the amount of inflation or deflation in an economy.

General price-level accounting *See:* constant monetary unit restatement.

General purpose application software Programs that serve varied purposes, such as developing decision-making tools or creating documents; examples include spreadsheets and word processors.

General reserve An equity reserve that normally serves the same purpose as an appropriation of retained earnings, that is, it temporarily restricts the maximum amount that can be declared for dividends.

Generally accepted accounting principles (GAAP) Accounting principles in the United States that are recognized by a standard-setting body or by authoritative support for the preparation of financial statements.

Generally accepted manufacturing practices (GAMP) A group of practices and principles, independent of any one set of techniques, that defines how a manufacturing company should be managed. Included are such elements as the need for data accuracy, frequent communication between marketing and manufacturing, top management control of the production planning process (sales and operations planning process), systems capable of validly translating high-level plans into detailed schedules, and so on. Today GAMP includes such paradigms as Just-in-Time, theory of constraints, total quality management, business process reengineering, and supply chain management.

Genetic algorithms Sets of algorithms used in artificial intelligence to solve complex problems for which the number of models for a solution is huge. The algorithms are either eliminated or combined with other algorithms to eventually produce the one that can solve the problem optimally. Called *genetic algorithms* because the method mimics the evolution of species over millions of years through changes in their genetic codes.

Geocentric staffing outlook Holds that nationality should not make any difference in the assignment of key positions anywhere (local subsidiary, regional headquarters, or central headquarters); that competence should be the prime criterion for selecting managerial staff.

Geodemographic information Allows identification of customer segments based on geographical location and demographic information.

Geographic Information Systems (GIS) Information systems that exhibit information visually on a computer monitor with local, regional, national, or international maps, so that the information can easily be related to locations or routes on the map. GISs are used, for example, in the planning of transportation and product distribution, or the examination of government resources distributed over an area.

Geographic organization Organization structured by geography, territory, region, and so on.

Geometric dimensioning and tolerancing (GDT) Method to minimize production costs by considering the functions or relationships of part features in order to define dimensions and tolerances.

Giro acceptance Foreign payment method in which computer-processable stub card is signed by the customer, who then takes it to the post office. The bill mailed to the customer has a stub attached to it that includes the seller's bank and account number.

GIRO systems A collection system for consumer payments that is commonplace in Europe. Sellers send customers an invoice with a payment stub encoded with the seller's bank account number. The customer signs the stub and then takes it to a GIRO processor. The processor delivers the stubs to the nearest GIRO bank which then debits the customer's account and credits the seller's account.

Glasnost The Soviet policy of encouraging the free exchange of ideas and discussion of problems, pluralistic participation in decision making, and increased availability of information.

Glass ceiling 1: Discriminatory practices that have prevented women and other protected-class members from advancing to executive-level jobs. **2:** Invisible barrier that separates women and minorities from top management positions.

Global Worldwide interdependencies of financial markets, technology, and living standards.

Global account management Global customers of a company may be provided with special services including a single point of contact for domestic and international operations and consistent worldwide service.

Global capital markets Capital markets in a global economy that attract investors and investees from throughout the world.

Global corporate culture Corporate core values that cut across all of a firm's subsidiaries located around the globe.

Global corporations International businesses that view the world as their marketplace.

Global manager An international executive with the ability to manage enterprises in diverse cultures.

Global mind-set In today's global environment, even for employees who may not go abroad, it is necessary to constantly sensitize everyone to the notion that the company is in a global business.

Global organization One having corporate units in a number of countries integrated to operate worldwide.

Global outsourcing Engaging in the international division of labor so as to obtain the cheapest sources of labor and supplies regardless of country; also called *global sourcing*.

Global reporting initiative An international, multistakeholder effort to create a common framework for voluntary reporting of the economic, environmental, and social impact of organization-level activity.

Global strategy A corporation using this strategy uses all of its resources against its competition in a very integrated fashion—all of its foreign subsidiaries and divisions are highly interdependent in both operations and strategy.

Global team A work team made up of members of different nationalities whose activities span multiple countries; may operate as a virtual team or meet face to face.

Global village A term used to refer to our world in the age of information and telecommunications because people are highly accessible to each other.

Globalization 1: Refers to the global economic integration of many formerly national economies into one global economy. **2:** The notion that in the future more and more companies will have to conduct their business activities in a highly interconnected world, thus presenting their managements with the challenge of re-engineering their systems to cope with this new environment. Awareness, understanding, and response to global developments as they affect a company. **3:** The standardization of product design and advertising strategies throughout the world.

Globalization approach Approach to international marketing in which differences are incorporated into a regional or global strategy that will allow for differences in implementation.

Glocalization 1: A term coined to describe the networked global organization approach to an organizational structure. **2:** The planning and designing of global Web sites so that they also cater to local needs and preferences.

Go/no-go State of a unit or product. Two parameters are possible: go conforms to specifications, and no-go does not conform to specifications.

Goal 1: A desired future state that the organization attempts to realize. **2:** Statement of general intent, aim, or desire; it is the point toward which management directs its efforts and resources; goals are often nonquantitative.

Goal conflict Occurs when an employee's self-interest differs from business objectives.

Going concern concept The accounting concept that an economic entity will continue in operation for the foreseeable future.

Going public The act of selling stock to the public at large by a closely held corporation or its principal stockholders.

Gold standard 1: A standard for international currencies in which currency values were stated in terms of gold. **2:** Era in which each currency was convertible into gold at a specified rate, allowing the exchange rate between two currencies to be determined by their relative convertibility rates per ounce of gold.

Golden parachute A contract in which a corporation agrees to make payments to key officers in control of the corporation.

Goods Objects, devices, or things.

Goods trade An account of the BOP statement that records funds used for merchandise imports and funds obtained from merchandise exports.

Goodwill 1: The amount paid by the buyer of a business for above-normal profits. An intangible asset of a business due to such favorable factors as location, product superiority, reputation, and managerial skill. **2:** What international corporations create when they share with locals the benefits derived from the markets they exploit.

Government policies Extreme social and economic conditions may sometimes force a political party into radical policy changes. Generally, however, governments change their policies gradually; they implement new policies to attract the foreign investments needed by the nation to attain its economic development objectives.

Government regulation Interference in the marketplace by governments.

Government warrant Essentially a payable-through-draft issued by a government agency.

Governmental units Comprise the sector of the business market represented by federal, state, and local governmental units that purchase goods and services.

Grade Planned or recognized difference in requirements for quality.

Gramm-Leach Bliley Act Passed in 1999, this law prohibits the use of false pretenses to access the personal information of others. It does allow banks and other financial institutions to share or sell customer information, unless customers proactively "opt out" and asks that their information not be shared.

Grand jury Body of four to twenty-three individuals who deliberate in secret to decide whether there is sufficient evidence to charge someone in a preliminary hearing.

Grand strategy The general plan of major action by which an organization intends to achieve its long-term goals.

Grapevine Informal communication channels over which information flows within an organization, usually without a known origin of the information and without any confirmation of its accuracy or completeness (sometimes referred to as the *rumor mill*).

Graphic rating scale A scale that allows the rater to mark an employee's performance on a continuum.

Graphical evaluation and review technique (GERT) A type of network planning technique.

Graphical user interface (GUI) Icons, frames, scroll bars, and other graphical means that make software easy and intuitive to learn and use.

Gray market A market entered in a way not intended by the manufacturer of the goods.

Gray marketing Marketing of authentic, legally trademarked goods through unauthorized channels.

Grease payments Minor, facilitating payments to officials for the primary purpose getting them to do whatever they are supposed to do anyway.

Green-circled employee An incumbent who is paid below the range set for the job.

Greenfield venture The most risky type of direct investment, whereby a company builds a subsidiary from scratch in a foreign country.

Greenmail A situation in which a firm, trying to avoid a takeover, buys back stock at a price above the existing market price from the person(s) trying to gain control of the firm.

Gross margin Net sales minus the cost of goods sold.

Gross margin percentage Shows how much gross margin a retailer makes as a percentage of sales.

Gross pay The total earnings of an employee for a payroll period.

Gross profit The excess of net sales over the cost of merchandise sold.

Gross profit margin Gross profit margin divided by net sales; a measure of markup.

Gross profit method A means of estimating inventory based on the relationship of gross profit to sales.

Gross rating points (GRPs) Accumulation of rating points including all vehicles in a media purchase over the span of a particular campaign.

Gross requirement The total of independent and dependent demand for a component before the netting of on-hand inventory and scheduled receipts.

Group decision support system A set of personal computers and one large screen with special software that facilitates brainstorming, the examination of ideas, voting, and reaching a decision by a group of decision makers.

Group technology (GT) An engineering and manufacturing philosophy that identifies the physical similarity of parts (common routing) and establishes their effective production. It provides for rapid retrieval of existing designs and facilitates a cellular layout.

Groupware Any of several types of software that enable users of computers in remote locations to work together on the same project. The users can create and change documents and graphic designs on the same monitor.

Growth rate, g The expected rate of change in dividends per share.

H

Hacker A person who accesses a computer system without permission.

Half-duplex Telecommunications whereby the receiving party must wait until the transmitting party finishes, before transmitting to the party. A party cannot receive while transmitting or transmit while receiving.

Halo effect An overall impression of a person or situation based on one characteristic, either favorable or unfavorable; a type of rating error that occurs when an employee receives the same rating on all dimensions regardless of his or her performance on individual ones.

Hand-held computers Computers that are small enough to fit in the palm of a person's hand. Also called *palm computers* or *personal digital assistants (PDAs)*.

Handling costs Costs to a firm associated with the act of transferring inventory to customers.

Hands-on consumer research Conducted by direct observation by managers of the way current customers use specific products and brands. The opposite is arm's-length research, which is undertaken by external suppliers.

Hard controls Based on objective evidence, hard controls are formal and tangible, and easier to measure and evaluate. An example is budget.

Hard currencies Money that is readily acceptable as payment in international business transactions—usually the currencies of industrially advanced countries (for example, dollars and pounds).

Hard disk A stack of several rigid aluminum platters usually installed in the same box that holds the CPU and other computer components; may be portable.

Hard sell Trying every means to get the prospective customer to buy, regardless of whether it is in the prospect's best interest.

Hard skills Include technical skills such as functional skills, problem-solving skills, and decision-making skills. In a way hard skills are acquired.

Hardship allowance An allowance paid during an assignment to an overseas area that requires major adaptation.

Harmonization Keeping the differences among national accounting standards to a minimum. Alternative accounting rules or practices may exist in different countries as long as they are "in harmony" with one another and can be reconciled.

Hawthorne studies A series of experiments on worker productivity begun in 1924 at the Hawthorne plant of Western Electric Company in Illinois; attributed employees' increased output to managers' better treatment of them during the study.

Health A general state of physical, mental, and emotional well-being.

Health maintenance organization (HMO) Managed care plan that provides services for a fixed period on a pre-paid basis.

Health promotion A supportive approach to facilitate and encourage employees to enhance healthy actions and lifestyles.

Hedge inventory A form of inventory buildup to buffer against some event that may not happen. Hedge inventory planning involves speculation related to potential labor strikes, price increases, unsettled governments, and events that could severely impair a company's strategic initiatives. Risk and consequences are unusually high, and top management approval is often required.

Hedge To counterbalance a present sale or purchase with a sale or purchase for future delivery as a way to minimize loss due to price fluctuations; to make counterbalancing sales or purchases in the international market as protection against adverse movements in the exchange rate.

Hedger A person who has a cash position or an anticipated cash position that he or she is trying to protect from adverse interest rate movements.

Hedging 1: A transfer of risk from one party to another; similar to speculation and may be used to handle risks not subject to insurance, such as price fluctuations. **2:** Measures taken to protect against risks associated with foreign exchange fluctuations.

Held-to-maturity securities Investments in bonds or other debt securities that management intends to hold to their maturity.

Help desk The group of small teams who specialize in troubleshooting problems in different areas of an information system—hardware, software, communications, and so forth.

Heterogeneity Distinguishing characteristic of services that reflects the variation in consistency from one service transaction to the next.

Heuristics Rules that cannot be formulated as a result of ordinary, proven knowledge but only through experience.

Hierarchical database A database model that generally follows an upside-down tree structure, in which each record can have only one parent record.

Hierarchy of needs theory A content theory that proposes that people are motivated by five categories of needs—physiological, safety, belongingness, esteem, and self-actualization—that exist in a hierarchical order.

Hierarchy structure Organization that is organized around functional departments/product lines or around customers/customer segments and is characterized by top-down management. Also referred to as a *bureaucratic model* or *pyramid structure*.

High-context culture A culture in which behavioral and environmental nuances are an important means of conveying information. In the course of business, participants establish social trust first, value personal relations and goodwill, make agreements on the basis of general trust, and like to conduct slow and ritualistic business negotiations.

High dollar group sort A special expediting of large dollar amounts through the clearing system, with the Fed granting the depositing bank immediate credit if it deposits the check early in the morning.

High liquidity strategy Current asset allocation strategy which prescribes a high proportion of assets to be held in cash and securities in order to reduce the chance of running out of cash.

High-low method A technique that uses the highest and lowest total costs as a basis for estimating the variable cost per unit and the fixed cost component of a mixed cost.

High performance work Defined by the MBNQA criteria as work approaches systematically directed toward achieving ever higher levels of overall performance, including quality and productivity.

High power distance culture A state in which a person at a higher position in the organizational hierarchy makes the decision and the employees at the lower levels simply follow the instructions.

Higher trial courts State courts that try felony (larger crimes) and civil cases above a predetermined amount.

Histogram Graphic summary of variation in a set of data. The pictorial nature of the histogram lets people see patterns that are difficult to see in a simple table of numbers. The histogram is one of the seven tools of quality.

Historical cost convention A method of accounting using data in terms of the units of currency in which a transaction originally took place.

Historical yield spread analysis Study of risk-related and maturity-related interest rate differences, motivated by a desire to detect profitable trading strategies.

Hold point Point, defined in an appropriate document, beyond which an activity must not proceed without the approval of a designated organization or authority.

Holder-of-record date (date of record) The date the company opens the ownership books to determine who will receive the dividend; the stockholders of record on this date receive the dividend.

Holding costs The costs associated with the storage of inventory.

Holistic planning Organizational planning that focuses on the big picture, including objectives and goals; also called *top-down planning*.

Home page The opening page of a Web site.

Horizontal analysis Financial analysis that compares an item in a current statement with the same item in prior statements.

Horizontal communication The lateral or diagonal exchange of messages among peers or coworkers.

Horizontal dependency The relationship between the components at the same level in the bill of material, in which all must be available at the same time and in sufficient quantity to manufacture the parent assembly. *See:* vertical dependency.

Horizontal information interchange The sharing of information by organizations in a horizontal market.

Horizontal market A market in which all players buy or sell the same type of product, making them competitors.

Horizontal merger A combination of two firms that produce the same type of good or service.

Horizontal promotions Instead of slowly climbing the organizational ladder, workers and managers make lateral movements, acquiring expertise in different functions such as marketing or manufacturing.

Horizontal structure Organization that is organized along a process or value-added chain, eliminating hierarchy and functional boundaries (also referred to as a *systems structure*).

Horizontal team A formal team composed of employees from about the same hierarchical level but from different areas of expertise.

Hoshin kanri, hoshin planning Japanese-based strategic planning/policy deployment process which involves consensus at all levels as plans are cascaded throughout the organization, resulting in actionable plans and continual monitoring and measurement.

Host-country national An employee working for a firm in an operation who is a citizen of the country where the operation is located, but where the headquarters for the firm are in another country.

Hostile environment Sexual harassment where an individual's work performance or psychological well-being is unreasonably affected by intimidating or offensive working conditions.

Hostile takeover The acquisition of a company over the opposition of its management.

House of Quality Diagram (named for its house-shaped appearance) that clarifies the relationship between customer needs and product features. It helps correlate market or customer requirements and analysis of competitive products with higher level technical and product characteristics and makes it possible to bring several factors into a single figure. Also known as *Quality Function Deployment* (QFD).

Household decision making Occurs when significant decisions are made by individuals jointly with other members of their household, and for joint use by the members of the household.

Housing allowance An allowance paid during assignment overseas to provide living quarters.

HR audit A formal research effort that evaluates the current state of HR management in an organization.

HR research The analysis of data from HR records to determine the effectiveness of past and present HR practices.

HR strategies Means used to anticipate and manage the supply of and demand for human resources.

Human capital The economic value of the knowledge, experience, skills, and capabilities of employees.

Human relations movement A movement in management thinking and practice that emphasized satisfaction of employees' basic needs as the key to increased worker productivity.

Human relations theory Theory focusing on the importance of human factors in motivating employees.

Human resource information system (HRIS) An integrated computer system designed to provide data and information used in HR planning and decision making.

Human resource management (HRM) 1: Activities undertaken to attract, develop, and maintain an effective workforce within an organization. **2:** The design of formal systems in an organization to ensure effective and efficient use of human talent to accomplish organizational goals.

Human resource (HR) planning Process of analyzing and identifying the need for and availability of human resources so that the organization can meet its objectives.

Human resources perspective A management perspective that suggests jobs should be designed to meet higher-level needs by allowing workers to use their full potential.

Human skill The ability to work with and through other people and to work effectively as a group member.

Hybrid production method A production planning method that combines the aspects of both the chase and level production planning methods. *Syn:* hybrid strategy. *See:* chase production method, level production method, production planning method.

Hygiene factors 1: Factors that involve the presence or absence of job dissatisfiers, including working conditions, pay, company policies, and interpersonal relationships. **2:** Term used by Frederick Herzberg to label "dissatisfiers." *See:* dissatisfiers.

Hypergeometric distribution Discrete distribution defining the probability of r occurrences in n trials of an event, when there are a total of d occurrences in a population of N.

Hypermedia Perhaps the Web's most essential ingredient, this feature enables a computer user to access additional information by clicking on selected text or graphics displayed on-screen.

Hypernorms Transcultural values, including fundamental human rights.

Hypertext Computer-generated text that allows the reader to click designated words (typically colored or boldfaced) to open a linked file that elaborates on the topic, or to invoke images or sound associated with the topic.

Hypertext Markup Language (HTML) A programming language for Web pages and Web browsers.

Hypertext Transfer Protocol (HTTP) Software that allows browsers to log on to Web sites.

I

Iconic model A physical replica, or representation, of a real object.

Idea champion A person who sees the need for and champions productive change within the organization.

Idea incubator An in-house program that provides a safe harbor where ideas from employees throughout the organization can be developed without interference from company bureaucracy or politics.

Idle capacity The unused capacity of a selling segment that is not needed for producing products or services to meet demand from the external market.

If-then **rules** A method of knowledge representation that holds the facts in the form of if-then statements; also called *production rules*.

Illegal gratuities Similar to bribery, except that there is no intent to influence a particular business decision, but rather to reward someone for making a favorable decision.

Illegitimate norms Norms that are incompatible with hypernorms (for example, exposing employees to unacceptable levels of carcinogens).

Image reinforcement Careful selection of the right premium object, or appropriate sweepstakes prize, to reinforce a brand's desired image.

Imaging The transformation of text and graphical documents into digitized files. The document can be electronically retrieved and printed to reconstruct a copy of the original. Imaging has saved much space and expense in paper-intensive business areas.

Immoral management A posture that is devoid of ethical principles or precepts and that implies a positive and active opposition to what is ethical.

Impact printer A printer that reproduces an image on a page using mechanical impact.

Imperfect market 1: A market where factors of production are somewhat immobile. **2:** The condition where, due to the costs to transfer labor and other resources used for production, firms may attempt to use foreign factors of production when they are less costly than local factors.

Imperfect market theory A firm engages in international trade to gain access to factors of production.

Imperfection Quality characteristic's departure from its intended level or state without any association to conformance to specification requirements or to the usability of a product or service. *See also:* blemish, defect, and nonconformity.

Implementation 1: The step in the decision-making process that involves using managerial, administrative, and persuasive abilities to translate the chosen alternative into action. **2:** The phase of implementing a new information system that includes training and conversion. Also called *delivery*.

Implementor A type of leader who takes a newly initiated vision and systematically puts into operation the desired changes. The typical subsidiary role, which involves implementing strategy that originates with headquarters.

Implosion The process of determining the where-used relationship for a given component. Implosion can be single-level (showing only the parents on the next higher level) or multilevel (showing the ultimate top-level parent). *See:* where-used list. *Ant:* explosion.

Import/export letters of credit Trade-related letters of credit.

Import substitution A policy for economic growth adopted by many developing countries that involves the systematic encouragement of domestic production of goods formerly imported.

Importing and exporting Selling and buying goods and services with organizations in other countries.

Improper accumulation Retention of earnings by a business for the purpose of enabling stockholders to avoid personal income taxes.

Incentives Bonuses or rewards (sweepstakes, coupons, premiums, display allowances, and so on.) for purchasing one brand rather than another.

Income bond A bond that pays interest to the holder only if the interest is earned by the firm.

Income elasticity of demand A means of describing change in demand in relative response to a change in income.

Income from operations (operating income) The excess of gross profit over total operating expenses.

Income leveling *See:* Income smoothing.

Income smoothing Use of reserves to transfer income between periods.

Income statement 1: A financial statement that summarizes the firm's financial performance for a given time interval; sometimes called a profit-and-loss statement. **2:** A summary of the revenues and expenses of a business entity for a specific period of time. **3:** A statement summarizing the firm's revenues and expenses over an accounting period, generally a quarter or a year. **4:** Financial statement that reports the amount of net income earned by a company during a specified period.

Income summary The account used in the closing process for transferring the revenue and expense account balances to the retained earnings account at the end of the period.

In-control process Process in which the statistical measure being evaluated is in a state of statistical control; that is, the variations among the observed sampling results can be attributed to a constant system of chance/common causes. *See:* out-of-control process.

Incoterms International Commerce Terms. Widely accepted terms used in quoting export prices.

Incremental cash flow The change in a firm's net cash flow attributable to an investment project.

Incremental operating cash flows The changes in day-to-day cash flows that result from the purchase of a capital project and continue until the firm disposes of the asset.

Indented bill of material A form of multilevel bill of material. It exhibits the highest level parents closest to the left margin, and all the components going into these parents are shown indented toward the right. All subsequent levels of components are indented farther to the right. If a component is used in more than one parent within a given product structure, it will appear more than once, under every subassembly in which it is used.

Indented where-used A listing of every parent item, and the respective quantities required, as well as each of their respective parent items, continuing until the ultimate end item or level-0 item is referenced. Each of these parent items calls for a given component item in a bill-of-material file. The component item is shown closest to the left margin of the listing, with each parent indented to the right, and each of their respective parents indented even further to the right.

Indenture A formal agreement (contract) between the issuer of a bond and the bondholders.

Independent checks Procedures for verifying and monitoring other controls.

Independent contractors Workers who perform specific services on a contract basis.

Independent demand The demand for an item that is unrelated to the demand for other items. Demand for finished goods, parts required for destructive testing, and service parts requirements are examples of independent demand. *See:* dependent demand.

Independent demand item management models Models for the management of items whose demand is not strongly influenced by other items managed by the same company. These models can be characterized as follows: 1) stochastic or deterministic, depending on the variability of demand and other factors; 2) fixed quantity, fixed cycle, or hybrid (optional replenishment). *See:* fixed reorder cycle inventory model, fixed reorder quantity inventory model, optional replenishment model.

Independent projects Projects whose cash flows are not affected by decisions made about other projects.

Independent variable Term used in regression analysis to represent the variable that is expected to influence another (so-called "dependent") variable.

Index fund A managed portfolio assembled to mirror a particular financial market composite.

Indexed (purchasing power) bond A bond that has interest payments based on an inflation index to protect the holder from inflation.

Indexed file A data file that contains an index, a directory-like table that indicates where each record physically resides on the storage medium by the value of its key field. The records are usually organized sequentially, so that retrieval can be carried out either sequentially, without using the index, or through the index. To retrieve a record, a lookup is performed to find the record's location.

Indexed sequential organization A method of file organization that allows direct access to specific records in a sequential file by using an index of key fields.

Indirect costs *See:* Overhead.

Indirect exporting The firm manufactures at home and employs a middle person to export its product(s) to foreign markets.

Indirect format One possible format allowed for presenting the Statement of Cash Flows that begins with net profit and then presents adjustments for items that do not results in current-period cash transactions including depreciation and changes in the various working capital accounts.

Indirect investment Buying equity or debt securities originating from a country as investments.

Indirect involvement Participation by a firm in international business through an intermediary, in which the firm does not deal with foreign customers or firms.

Indirect method A method of reporting the cash flows from operating activities as the net income from operations adjusted for all deferrals of past cash receipts and payments and all accruals of expected future cash receipts and payments.

Indirect quotation 1: Foreign exchange quotation that specifies the units of foreign currency that could be purchased with one unit of the home currency. **2:** Exchange rate quotations representing the value measured by number of units per dollar.

Indirect taxes Taxes applied to nonincome items, such as value-added taxes, excise taxes, tariffs, and so on.

Individual/adversarial external affairs strategy Executives deny the legitimacy of social claims on their businesses and minimize the significance of challenges they receive from external critics.

Individual-centered career planning Career planning that focuses on individuals' careers rather than on organizational needs.

Individual development Process that may include education and training, but also includes many additional interventions and experiences to enable an individual to grow and mature both intellectually as well as emotionally.

Individual retirement account (IRA) A special account in which an employee can set aside funds that will not be taxed until the employee retires.

Individualism 1: A preference for a loosely knit social framework in which individuals are expected to take care of themselves. **2:** Dimension of culture that refers to the extent to which people in a country prefer to act as individuals instead of members of groups. **3:** The trait in which the employee attaches higher importance to personal and family interests than to the organization. **4:** Refers to the degree to which people in a society look after primarily their own interests or belong to and depend on "in-groups."

Individualism approach The ethical concept that acts are moral when they promote the individual's best long-term interests, which ultimately leads to the greater good.

Inductive fraud detection Proactively searching for fraud by identifying anomalies or unusual or unexpected patterns and/or relationships, without determining in advance the kinds of fraud for which you are looking.

Inefficient targeting Results when advertising and distribution reach too broad an audience, most of whom are not interested in the product.

Infeasible solution A decision alternative or solution that violates one or more constraints.

Inference engine The part of an expert system that links facts and relationships in the knowledge base to reach a solution to a problem.

Inflation A period when prices in general are rising and the purchasing power of money is declining.

Inflation accounting Accounting to cope with changing price levels.

Inflation premium (IP) A premium for expected inflation that investors add to the real risk-free rate of return.

Inflow A receipt of cash from an investment, an employer, or other sources.

Influence diagram A graphical device that shows the relationship among decisions, chance events, and consequences for a decision problem.

Influence peddling Providing monetary or nonmonetary benefits to a person in a position of authority in exchange for an action by that person that benefits the company—normally an action that would not have been taken without the monetary or nonmonetary benefit.

Informal communication Unofficial communication that takes place in an organization as people talk freely and easily; examples include impromptu meetings and personal conversations (verbal or e-mail).

Informal communication channel A communication channel that exists outside formally authorized channels without regard for the organization's hierarchy of authority.

Informal integration Allowing a foreign subsidiary to adopt the corporation's global vision, core values, and cultural principles in its own way. That is, the corporation's central management does not formally force these on the foreign subsidiaries; rather it listens to people at the local level and communicates with them.

Informal training Training that occurs through interactions and feedback among employees.

Information 1: Data transferred into an ordered format that makes it usable and allows one to draw conclusions. **2:** The product of processing data so that they can be used in a context by human beings.

Information-based services The provision of these services involves collecting, manipulating, interpreting, and transmitting data to create value. Examples include such services as accounting, banking, consulting, education, insurance, legal services, and news.

Information center The unit within an organization that provides coordination, control, and support for all aspects of the organization's information systems and its users.

Information content (signaling) hypothesis The theory that investors regard dividend changes as signals of management's earnings forecasts.

Information map The description of data and information flow within an organization set out in a visual chart or map.

Information overload A situation in which people have too much information from which to choose for their problem solving and decision making.

Information reporting system A system that organizes information in the form of prespecified reports that managers use in day-to-day decision making.

Information search Stage in the consumer decision process when consumers collect information on only a select subset of brands.

Information sites Web sites that generate revenue through advertising or the subscription rates that are charged to members.

Information system (IS) 1: A computer-based set of hardware, software, and telecommunications components, supported by people and procedures, to process data and turn them into useful information. **2:** Technology-based systems used to support operations, aid day-to-day decision making, and support strategic analysis (other names often used include: management information system, decision system, information technology (IT), data processing). **3:** Can provide the decision maker with basic data for most ongoing decisions.

Information systems auditor The information systems professional whose job is to find erroneous or fraudulent transactions and investigate them; auditing.

Information Technology (IT) 1: Refers to all technologies that collectively facilitate construction and maintenance of information systems. **2:** The hardware, software, telecommunications, database management, and other technologies used to store, process, and distribute information.

Infrastructure A country's physical facilities that support economic activities.

Infrastructure shortages Problems in a country's underlying physical structure, such as transportation, utilities, and so on.

Inherent limitations The limitations that apply to all internal control systems. The limitations relate to the limits of human judgment, resource constraints and the need to consider the cost of controls in relation to expected benefits, the reality that breakdowns can occur, and the possibility of management override and collusion.

Inherent risks A business's susceptibility to fraud, assuming that appropriate controls are not in place.

Inhwa Influences South Korean business behavior; stresses harmony; links people who are unequal in rank, prestige, and power; and stresses loyalty to hierarchical rankings and superiors' concern for the well-being of subordinates.

Initial investment Expenses necessary to implement a capital budgeting proposal must be determined. This may include set-up costs, physical asset acquisition or disposition costs, permanent increases in the company's investment in cash, receivables, and inventories, and other cash outflows incurred at the time the project is initiated.

Initial investment outlay Includes the incremental cash flows associated with a project that will occur only at the start of a project's life, $\hat{C}F_0$.

Initial phase The first phase in the expatriation process. When the expatriate transfers to the foreign assignment, the newness of the culture creates a great deal of excitement for him or her.

Initial pleading Complaint filed by a plaintiff to request legal proceedings against someone.

Initial public offering (IPO) market The market consisting of stocks of companies that have just gone public.

Initiating structure A type of leader behavior that describes the extent to which a leader is task oriented and directs subordinates' work activities toward goal achievement.

Ink-jet printer Inexpensive type of printer that sprays ink to create the printed text or pictures of a computer-generated document.

Innovator A type of leader who identifies new ideas and visions and "sells" them to the institution.

Input Raw data entered into a computer for processing.

Input device A tool, such as a keyboard or voice recognition system, used to enter data into an information system.

Input-output analysis A method for estimating market activities and potential that measures the factor inflows into production and the resultant outflow of products.

Input price measurement A current value is assigned to an item on the basis of its replacement cost.

In-sample validation Involves gauging forecast errors by using the data set on which the model is fitted. This gives an upward bias to forecast accuracy.

Inseparability Distinguishing characteristic of services that reflects the interconnection among the service provider, the customer receiving the service, and other customers sharing the service experience.

Inside directors Persons with some sort of ties to the firm.

Insider trading The practice of obtaining critical information inside a company and then using that information for one's own personal financial gain.

Insiders Officers, directors, major stockholders, or others who might have inside, or privileged, information on a company's operations.

Insourcing Assigning an IS service function to the organization's own IS unit. The term was invented to emphasize a decision not to outsource.

Inspection Measuring, examining, testing, and gauging one or more characteristics of a product or service and comparing the results with specified requirements to determine whether conformity is achieved for each characteristic.

Instant messaging 1: Technology that provides a way to send quick notes from PC to PC over the Internet so two people who are online at the same time can communicate instantly. **2:** The capability for several online computer users to share messages in real time; also called *chatting online*.

Institute of Internal Auditors (IIA) The most influential international organization in the development of internal auditing standards. It was established in 1941.

Institutional customers Comprise the sector of the business market represented by health care organizations, colleges and universities, libraries, foundations, art galleries, and clinics that purchase goods and services.

Instrument A class of similar investments. Examples are agency notes, commercial paper, Treasury bills, certificates of deposit (CDs), banker's acceptances, and repurchase agreements.

Insurance services Services that are provided in underwriting, risk evaluation, and operations.

Intangibility The inability to be seen, tasted, or touched in a conventional sense; the characteristic of services that most strongly differentiates them from products.

Intangible assets 1. Long-lived assets that are useful in the operations of a business, are not held for sale, and are without physical qualities. **2:** Assets that have no tangible existence (for example, goodwill).

Integrated circuits Electronic semiconductors within computers that integrate a large number of circuits into one silicon chip.

Integrated disability management programs A benefit that combines disability insurance programs and efforts to reduce workers' compensation claims.

Integrated international operation A foreign operation whose economic activities have a direct impact on the reporting (parent) entity.

Integrated marketing communications (IMC) System of management and integration of marketing communication elements—advertising, publicity, sales promotion, sponsorship marketing, and point-of-purchase communications—with the result that all elements adhere to the same message.

Integrated risk management Approach for managing both pure and speculative risks together; another name for *enterprise risk management.*

Integrated system A national tax system that attempts to eliminate double taxation by taxing corporate income differently depending on whether it is distributed to shareholders.

Integrity The quality or state of being of sound moral principle; uprightness, honesty, and sincerity; the desire to do the right thing and to profess and live up to a set of values and expectations.

Integrity strategy Is driven by ethical values that provide a common frame of reference and that serve to unify different functions, lines of business, and employee groups.

Intellectual property rights 1: Legal rights resulting from industrial, scientific, literary, or artistic activity. **2:** Protection provided by patents, copyrights, and trademarks.

Intelligence (1) The ability to learn, think, and deduce; (2) The first phase in the decision-making process: gathering relevant data.

Intelligent agent A sophisticated program that can be instructed to perform services for human beings, especially on the Internet.

Intensive distribution Occurs when all possible intermediaries at a particular level of the channel are used.

Intentional amoral management Does not factor ethical considerations into decisions, actions, and behaviors because of the belief that business activity resides outside the sphere to which moral judgments apply.

Interactional justice Human interaction during service recovery efforts.

Interactive leadership A leadership style characterized by values such as inclusion, collaboration, relationship building, and caring.

interactive multimedia Term encompassing technology that allows the presentation of facts and images with interaction by the viewer.

Interbank interest rates The interest rate charged by banks to banks in the major international financial centers.

Interbank market Market that facilitates the exchange of currencies between banks.

Interdependence The extent to which departments depend on each other for resources or materials to accomplish their tasks.

Interdistrict Transportation System Redesign of the Federal Reserve's routing modes and techniques to shorten delays and minimize system-wide float.

Interest-bearing When the interest paid is based on a quoted rate based on the face value of the financial instrument.

Interest Equalization Tax (IET) Tax imposed by the U.S. government in 1963 to discourage U.S. investors from investing in foreign securities.

Interest rate cap A financial contract which limits the rise in a selected interest rate.

Interest rate collar A financial contract which restricts the movement of a selected interest rate within a narrow band referred to as a collar. It is essentially a combination of an interest rate floor and cap.

Interest rate floor A financial contract which limits the decline in a selected interest rate.

Interest rate parity 1: Holds that investors should expect to earn the same return on their money in all countries after adjusting for risk. **2:** Theory specifying that the forward premium (or discount) is equal to the interest rate differential between the two currencies of concern.

Interest rate parity (IRP) line Diagonal line depicting all points on a four-quadrant graph that represent a state of interest rate parity.

Interest rate parity theory Theory suggesting that the forward rate differs from the spot rate by an amount that reflects the interest differential between two currencies.

Interest rate price risk The risk of changes in bond prices to which investors are exposed due to changing interest rates.

Interest rate reinvestment risk The risk that income from a bond portfolio will vary because cash flows have to be reinvested at current market rates.

Interest rate risk The possibility that interest rates will increase, causing the prices of existing fixed-income securities to drop.

Interest rate swap 1: Agreement to swap interest payments, whereby interest payments based on a fixed interest rate are exchanged for interest payments based on a floating interest rate. **2:** A firm uses its credit standing to borrow capital at low fixed rates and exchange its interest payments with a slightly lower credit-rated borrower who has debt service payments at floating rates.

Interface The connection of two systems to establish interaction.

Intermediate customers Distributors, dealers, or brokers who make products and services available to the end user by repairing, repackaging, reselling, or creating finished goods from components or subassemblies.

Intermodal movements The transfer of freight from one mode or type of transportation to another.

Internal audit 1: Audit conducted within an organization by members of the organization to measure its strengths or weaknesses against its own procedures and/or external standards—a "first-party audit." **2:** An objective evaluation of operations and control systems of an organization to determine whether its policies and procedures are being followed, and also whether its resources are safeguarded and used efficiently to achieve organizational objectives.

Internal bank A multinational firm's financial management tool that actually acts as a bank to coordinate finances among its units.

Internal capability analysis Detailed view of the internal workings of the organization (for example, determine how well the capabilities of the organization match to strategic needs).

Internal collaboration *See:* Internal cooperation.

Internal control A process effected by an entity's board of directors, management, and other personnel that is designed to provide reasonable assurance regarding the achievement of objectives such as 1) effectiveness and efficiency of operations, 2) reliability of financial reporting, and 3) compliance with applicable laws and regulations.

Internal control structure Specific policies and procedures designed to provide management with reasonable assurance that the goals and objectives it believes important to the entity will be met.

Internal control weakness Weakness in the control environment, accounting system, or the control activities or procedures.

Internal cooperation The organization develops an internal environment where there is downward, upward, and horizontal communication, as well as a focal point to coordinate the communication, for the purpose of making effective and efficient decisions.

Internal customer Recipient, person, or department of another person's or department's output (product, service, or information) within an organization. *See:* external customer.

Internal data Data that are collected within the organization, usually by transaction processing systems but also through employee and customer surveys.

Internal economies of scale Lower production costs resulting from greater production for an enlarged market.

Internal failure costs The costs associated with defects that are discovered by the organization before the product or service is delivered to the consumer.

Internal locus of control The belief by individuals that their future is within their control and that external forces will have little influence.

Internal memory The memory circuitry inside the computer, communicating directly with the CPU. Consists of RAM and ROM.

Internal rate of return (IRR) The discount rate that forces the PV of a project's expected cash flows to equal its initial cost. IRR is similar to the YTM on a bond.

Internal rate of return method A method of analysis of proposed capital investments that focuses on using present value concepts to compute the rate of return from the net cash flows expected from the investment.

Internal review A company's management becoming familiar with the firm's ability to implement a strategy aimed at coping with external demands.

Internalization Occurs when a firm establishes its own multinational operation, keeping information that is at the core of its competitiveness within the firm.

International *See:* Global.

International accounting Accounting for international transactions, comparisons of accounting principles in different countries, harmonization of diverse accounting standards worldwide, and accounting information for the management and control of global operations.

International Accounting Standard (IAS) An accounted rule developed by the International Accounting Standards Committee in order to harmonize accounting standards worldwide.

International Bank for Reconstruction and Development (IBRD) Bank established in 1944 to enhance economic development by providing loans to countries. Also referred to as the World Bank.

International bond Bond issued in domestic capital markets by foreign borrowers (foreign bonds) or issued in the Eurocurrency markets in currency different from that of the home currency of the borrower (Eurobonds).

International competitiveness The ability of a firm, an industry, or a country to compete in the international marketplace at a stable or rising standard of living.

International contracts Involve additional issues beyond those in domestic contracts, such as differences in language, legal systems, and currency.

International corporation International business that produces products in its home country and exports to other countries.

International Court of Justice Judicial branch of the United Nations having voluntary jurisdiction over nations.

International debt load Total accumulated negative net investment of a nation.

International Development Association (IDA) Association established to stimulate country development; it was especially suited for less prosperous nations, since it provided loans at low interest rates.

International division A unit established to supervise a firm's exports, foreign distribution agreements, foreign sales forces, foreign sales branches, and foreign subsidiaries.

International environment Refers to groupings of nations (such as the European Union), worldwide bodies (such as the World Bank), and organizations of nations by industry (such as the Organization of Petroleum Exporting Countries).

International Federation of Accountants (IFAC) An organization engaged in efforts to harmonize auditing standards worldwide.

International Financial Corporation (IFC) Firm established to promote private enterprise within countries; it can provide loans to and purchase stock of corporations.

International Fisher Effect (IFE) line Diagonal line on a graph that reflects points at which the interest rate differential between two countries is equal to the percentage change in the exchange rate between their two respective currencies.

International human resource management function Consists of interplay among three dimensions: the broad function, country categories, and types of employees.

International intermediaries Marketing institutions that facilitate the movement of goods and services between the originator and customer.

International labor relations The management of an MNC interacting with organized labor units in each country.

International law Includes law that deals with the conduct and relations of nation-states and international organizations as well as some of their relations with persons; such law is enforceable by the courts of a nation that has adopted the international law as domestic law.

International management The management of business operations conducted in more than one country.

International marketing Process of planning and conducting transactions across national borders to create exchanges that satisfy the objectives of individuals and organizations.

International Monetary Fund (IMF) A specialized agency of the United Nations established in 1944. An international financial institution for dealing with Balance of Payment problems; the first international monetary authority with at least some degree of power over national authorities.

International mutual funds Mutual funds containing securities of foreign firms.

International Organization of Securities Commission (IOSCO) A private organization of securities market regulators that promotes the integration of securities markets worldwide.

International Organization for Standardization (ISO) Nongovernmental organization that promotes the development of standardization to facilitate the international exchange of goods and services.

International organizational structures The firm's organizational structure is its "skeleton"; it provides support and ties together disparate functions.

International pricing A managerial decision about what to charge for goods produced in one nation and sold in another.

International product life cycle (IPLC) A theory that many products that are exported to foreign countries are eventually produced abroad, and that foreign producers subsequently obtain a competitive edge over the original producers, forcing them to either create a new product or go out of business.

International relocation and orientation The making of arrangements for predeparture training, immigration and travel details, and finalizing compensation details between the expatriate and the home country.

International Standards on Auditing (ISA) A comprehensive set of auditing standards issued by the International Federation of Accountants. Audits conducted in accordance with these standards can be relied on by securities regulatory authorities for multinational reporting purposes.

International Trade Organization (ITO) A forwardlooking approach to international trade and investment embodied in the 1948 Havana Charter; due to disagreements among sponsoring nations, its provisions were never ratified.

International treaties Agreements between or among independent nations, such as the General Agreement on Tariffs and Trade (GATT), now called the World Trade Organization.

Internationalization A process by which firms increase their awareness of the influence of international activities on their future and establish and conduct transactions with firms from other countries.

Internet 1: A global collection of computer networks linked together for the exchange of data and information. **2:** Worldwide network of interconnected computer networks originally built by the U.S. government. **3:** An international network of networks providing millions of people with access to rich information resources.

Internet domain The part of an Internet address, such as .com, .edu, or .gov, that is shared by many users and indicates the particular community of their owners.

Internet hosts Provide high-speed connections to the Web.

internet Protocol (IP) number A unique number assigned to a server or another device that is connected to the Internet, for identification purposes consists of 32 bits.

Internet Relay Chat (IRC) Internet software that allows remote users to correspond in real time.

Internet servers The computers that are linked directly to the Internet backbone and carry the files accessed over the Internet.

Internet Service Provider (ISP) An individual or organization that provides Internet connection, and sometimes other related services, to subscribers.

Interorganizational context Channel management that extends beyond a firm's own organization into independent businesses.

Interorganizational information systems Systems that are shared by two or more organizations to transfer data electronically.

Interpreter A programming language translator that translates the source code, one statement at a time, and executes it. If the instruction is erroneous, the interpreter produces an appropriate error message.

Interpretive knowledge An acquired ability to understand and appreciate the nuances of foreign cultural traits and patterns.

Interrelationship digraph Management and planning tool that displays the relationship between factors in a complex situation. It identifies meaningful categories from a mass of ideas and is useful when relationships are difficult to determine.

Interrogatory A series of written questions that specifically identify information needed from the opposing party.

Interstate Banking and Branching Efficiency Act (1994) Permitted interstate bank acquisitions, mergers, and branching.

Interval scale Intervals of measure that stay constant along the scale. For example, the interval between the measures of 1 and 3 on the scale is the same as the interval between 5 and 7.

Intervention 1: Action taken by a leader or a facilitator to support the effective functioning of a team or work group. **2:** An action taken by the central bank of a country to influence the exchange rate of its currency in the market.

Intervention intensity Strength of the intervention by the intervening person; intensity is affected by words, voice inflection, and nonverbal behaviors.

Interviews A face-to-face research tool to obtain in-depth information.

In-the-money option When it is beneficial financially for the option holder to exercise the option.

Intracompany trade International trade between subsidiaries that are under the same ownership.

Intra-industry trade The simultaneous export and import of the same good by a country. It is of interest due to the traditional theory that a country will either export or import a good, but not do both at the same time.

Intranet 1: An internal communication system that uses the technology and standards of the Internet but is accessible only to people within the organization. **2:** A process that integrates a company's information assets into a single accessible system using Internet-based technologies such as e-mail, news groups, and the World Wide Web.

Intransit lead time The time between the date of shipment (at the shipping point) and the date of receipt (at the receiver's dock). Orders normally specify the date by which goods should be at the dock. Consequently, this date should be offset by intransit lead time for establishing a ship date for the supplier.

Intrinsic forecast method A forecast based on internal factors, such as an average of past sales. Ant: extrinsic forecast.

Intrinsic reward The satisfaction received in the process of performing an action.

Intrinsic value, $\hat{P}_0$ The value of an asset that in the mind of a particular investor is justified by the facts; $\hat{P}_0$ may be different from the asset's current market price, its book value, or both.

Intuition The immediate comprehension of a decision situation based on past experience but without conscious thought.

Inventory 1: The goods that the organization keeps on hand for use in the production process up to the point of selling the final products to customers. **2:** Materials used in producing a final product. Raw materials inventory includes items purchased from suppliers to directly support production requirements. Work in process inventory is the total inventory that exists within and among all processing centers located throughout the operations system. Finished goods inventory includes completed items or products that are available for shipment or future customer orders. Maintenance, repair, and operating (MRO) inventory includes all the items used to support operations but which are not directly in the finished product. Pipeline or in-transit inventory includes items on their way to customers or located throughout a firm's distribution channels.

Inventory carrying costs The expense of maintaining inventories.

Inventory control systems An information system employed to help control inventory.

Inventory financing A very important component of the total financial plan of most corporations because inventory makes up a significant portion of total working capital.

Inventory management Activities involved in ensuring that the right materials and goods are in the right place at the right time at the lowest cost possible. Inventory management (also called materials management in some organizations) may involve automated and/or manual systems for tracking inventory, as well the physical facilities for storing the materials.

Inventory ordering system Inventory models for the replenishment of inventory. Independent demand inventory ordering models include but are not limited to fixed reorder cycle, fixed reorder quantity, optional replenishment, and hybrid models. Dependent demand inventory ordering models include material requirements planning, kanban, and drum-buffer-rope.

Inventory shrinkage Loss of inventory due to shoplifting, employee theft, or errors in recording or counting inventory.

Inventory turnover 1: The number of times that an inventory cycles, or "turns over" during the year. A frequently used method to compute inventory turnover is to divide the average inventory level into the annual cost of sales. For example, an average inventory of $3 million divided into an annual cost of sales of $21 million means that inventory turned over seven times. Syn: inventory turns, inventory velocity, turnover. **2:** A ratio that measures the relationship between the volume of goods (merchandise) sold and the amount of inventory carried during the period.

Inventory turnover ratio 1: Measure of the efficiency with which inventory is managed; computed by dividing cost of goods sold by average inventory for a period. **2:** A measure of inventory usage that is found by dividing cost of goods sold by either the year-end inventory balance or by the average inventory balance.

Inverted "abnormal" yield curve Downward-sloping graph of yields to maturity of securities with different maturities. Given the possibility to engage in arbitrage (simultaneously buy and sell otherwise identical securities having different maturities), this slope implies that the market collectively anticipates future shorter-term interest rates to decline.

Investing activities On the statement of cash flows items that are defined as receipts of cash from loans, sale of property, and cash disbursed for loans to other business entities and payments for property, plant, and equipment.

Investment banker An organization that underwrites and distributes new issues of securities; helps businesses and other entities obtain needed financing.

Investment center A responsibility center where the manager is responsible for costs, revenues, profits, and investment in assets. A decentralized unit in which the manager has the responsibility and authority to make decisions that affect not only costs and revenues but also the plant assets available to the center.

Investment grade bonds Bonds rated A or triple-B; many banks and other institutional investors are permitted by law to hold only investment-grade or better bonds.

Investment income The proportion of net income that is paid back to a parent company.

Investment opportunity schedule (IOS) A graph of the firm's investment opportunities ranked in order of the projects' internal rates of return.

Investment policy Defines the company's posture toward risk and return and specifies how that posture is to be implemented.

Investment scams The selling of fraudulent and worthless investments to unsuspecting investors.

Investment turnover A component of the rate of return on investment, computed as the ratio of sales to invested assets.

Investments The balance sheet caption used to report long-term investments in stocks or bonds not intended as a source of cash in the normal operations of the business.

Invigilation Imposing strict temporary controls on an activity so that, during the observation period, fraud is virtually impossible. Involves keeping detailed records before, during, and after the invigilation period and comparing suspicious activity during the three periods to obtain evidence about whether fraud is occurring.

Invoice The bill provided by the seller (who refers to it as a sales invoice) to a buyer (who refers to it as a purchase invoice) for items purchased.

Involvement Degree of personal relevance of a product to a consumer.

IRR (internal rate of return) Discount rate that causes net present value to equal zero.

Irregular component The component of the time series model that reflects the random variation of the actual time series values beyond what can be explained by the trend, cyclical, and seasonal components.

Irrevocable letter of credit Letter of credit issued by a bank that cannot be cancelled or amended without the beneficiary's approval.

Ishikawa diagram *See:* cause-and-effect diagram.

IS architecture The manner in which an organization's IS assets are deployed and connected.

IS infrastructure The IS resources that an organization owns, including hardware, software, and telecommunications devices and lines.

IS planning Planning for the deployment and for the resources needed to develop and maintain information systems.

IS subsidiaries Independent corporations that offer services not only to the parent company but also to other companies.

ISDN (Integrated Services Digital Network) A set of hardware and software standards that support the transmission of text, images, and sounds through the same communications channel. ISDN will result in the combination of the telephone, fax, computer, and television into one device.

ISO "equal" (Greek). A prefix for a series of standards published by the International Organization for Standardization.

ISO 9000 A set of international standards for quality management, setting uniform guidelines for processes to ensure that products conform to customer requirements. Requires each enterprise to define and document its own quality process and provide evidence of their implementation. ISO stands for International Organization for Standardization.

ISO 9000 series standards Set of individual but related international standards and guidelines on quality management and quality assurance developed to help companies effectively document the quality system elements to be implemented to maintain an efficient quality system. The standards, initially published in 1987, revised in 1994 and 2000, are not specific to any particular industry, product, or service. The standards were developed by the International Organization for Standardization, a specialized international agency for standardization composed of the national standards bodies of nearly 100 countries.

ISO 14000-series Set of standards and guidelines relevant to developing and sustaining an environmental management system.

Issues management and crisis management Two major ways by which business has responded to critical situations.

Issuing bank Bank that issues a letter of credit.

J

J-curve effect Effect of a weaker dollar on the U.S. trade balance, in which the trade balance initially deteriorates; it only improves once U.S. and non-U.S. importers respond to the change in purchasing power that is caused by the weaker dollar.

Jamaica Agreement As a result of the inflation and balance of payment problems after World War II, causing many countries great difficulty in maintaining their appropriate exchange rate, the major trading nations signed the Jamaica Agreement in 1976 to demonetize gold and create a system of floating exchange rates.

Java Object-oriented programming language that allows Web browsers to download applets that can run on any computer with any operating system.

Jidoka Japanese method of autonomous control involving the adding of intelligent features to machines to start or stop operations as control parameters are reached, and to signal operators when necessary.

Job Grouping of tasks, duties, and responsibilities that constitutes the total work assignment for employees.

Job aid Any device, document, or other media which can be provided a worker to aid in correctly performing their tasks (for example, laminated setup instruction card hanging on machine, photos of product at different stages of assembly, metric conversion table).

Job analysis Systematic way to gather and analyze information about the content, context, and the human requirements of jobs.

Job anxiety Tension caused by the pressures of the job.

Job characteristics model A model of job design that comprises core job dimensions, critical psychological states, and employee growth-need strength.

Job cost sheet An account in the work in process subsidiary ledger in which the costs charged to a particular job order are recorded.

Job criteria Important elements in a given job.

Job description Narrative explanation of the work, responsibilities, and basic requirements of the job.

Job design 1: The application of motivational theories to the structure of work for improving productivity and satisfaction. **2:** Organizing tasks, duties, and responsibilities into a productive unit of work.

Job enlargement A job design that combines a series of tasks into one new, broader job to give employees variety and challenge.

Job enrichment 1: A job design that incorporates achievement, recognition, and other high-level motivators into the work. **2:** Increasing the depth of a job by adding the responsibility for planning, organizing, controlling, and evaluating the job.

Job evaluation The process of determining the value of jobs within an organization through an examination of job content.

Job order cost system A type of cost accounting system that provides for a separate record of the cost of each particular quantity of product that passes through the factory.

Job posting A system in which the employer provides notices of job openings and employees respond to apply.

Job rotation A job design that systematically moves employees from one job to another to provide them with variety and stimulation.

Job satisfaction A positive emotional state resulting from evaluating one's job experience.

Job simplification A job design whose purpose is to improve task efficiency by reducing the number of tasks a single person must do.

Job specifications The knowledge, skills, and abilities (KSAs) an individual needs to perform a job satisfactorily.

Join The joining of data from multiple tables.

Joint Application Development (JAD) A method of systems development that facilitates analysis and design by involving representatives of the prospective users in all of the phases and by using prototyping wherever possible.

Joint occurrence Occurrence of a phenomenon affecting the business environment in several locations simultaneously.

Joint planning meetings Meeting involving representatives of a key customer and the sales and service team for that account to determine how better to meet the customer's requirements and expectations.

Joint probabilities The probabilities of both sample information and a particular state of nature occurring simultaneously.

Joint Research and Development Act A 1984 act that allows both domestic and foreign firms to participate in joint basic-research efforts without fear of U.S. antitrust action.

Joint ventures 1: Two or more firms that band together to establish operations in foreign markets in order to capitalize on each other's resources and reduce risk. They share profits, liabilities, and duties. **2:** Result from the participation of two or more companies in an enterprise in which each party contributes assets, owns the new entity to some degree, and shares risk.

Journal The initial record in which the effects of a transaction on accounts are recorded.

Journal entry The form of recording a transaction in a journal.

Journalizing The process of recording a transaction in a journal.

Judgmental approach Relies heavily on intuition to adjust what is known about upcoming cash flows to arrive at the cash forecast.

Junk bond A high-risk, high-yield bond used to finance mergers, leveraged buyouts, and troubled companies.

Juran's Trilogy *See:* quality trilogy.

Jurisdiction The limit or territory over which an organization has authority.

JUSE Union of Japanese Scientists and Engineers.

Justice approach The ethical concept that moral decisions must be based in standards of equity, fairness, and impartiality.

Just-in-Time (JIT) A philosophy of manufacturing based on planned elimination of all waste and on continuous improvement of productivity. It encompasses the successful execution of all manufacturing activities required to produce a final product, from design engineering to delivery, and includes all stages of conversion from raw material onward. The primary elements of Just-in-Time are to have only the required inventory when needed; to improve quality to zero defects; to reduce lead times by reducing setup times, queue lengths, and lot sizes; to incrementally revise the operations themselves; and to accomplish these activities at minimum cost. In the broad sense, it applies to all forms of manufacturing—job shop, process, and repetitive—and to many service industries as well. *Syn:* short-cycle manufacturing, stockless production, zero inventories.

Just-in-time (JIT) inventory Materials scheduled to arrive precisely when they are needed on a production line.

Just-in-time inventory system An inventory system designed to reduce the levels of inventory kept at the manufacturing site increasing quality in the production process and by shifting the inventory burden to the supplier.

Just-in-time manufacturing 1: A business philosophy that focuses on eliminating time, cost, and poor quality within manufacturing processes. **2:** Optimal material requirement planning system for a manufacturing process in which there is little or no manufacturing material inventory on hand at the manufacturing site and little or no incoming inspection.

Just-in-time processing A processing approach that focuses on eliminating time, cost, and poor quality within manufacturing and nonmanufacturing processes.

Just-in-time training Providing job training coincidental with, or immediately prior to its need for the job.

K

Kaikaku (Japanese) Breakthrough improvement in eliminating waste.

Kaizen Japanese term that means gradual unending improvement by doing little things better and setting and achieving increasingly higher standards. The term was made famous by Masaaki Imai in his book *Kaizen: The Key to Japan's Competitive Success*. *See:* continuous process improvement.

Kaizen blitz/event Intense, short time-frame, team approach to employ the concepts and techniques of continuous improvement (for example, to reduce cycle time, increase throughput).

Kanban 1: A method of just-in-time production that uses standard containers or lot sizes with a single card attached to each. It is a pull system in which work centers signal with a card that they wish to withdraw parts from feeding operations or suppliers. The Japanese word kanban, loosely translated, means card, billboard, or sign. The term is often used synonymously for the specific scheduling system developed and used by the Toyota Corporation in Japan. *See:* move card, production card, synchronized production. **2:** System inspired by Tauchi Ohno's (Toyota) visit to a U.S. supermarket. The system signals the need to replenish stock or materials or to produce more of an item. Also called a "pull" approach.

Kano model Representation of the three levels of customer satisfaction defined as dissatisfaction, neutrality, and delight.

Keiretsu A form of cooperative relationship among companies in Japan where the companies largely remain legally and economically independent, even though they work closely in various ways such as sole sourcing and financial backing. A member of a keiretsu generally owns a limited amount of stock in other member companies. A keiretsu generally forms around a bank and a trading company but "distribution" (supply chain) keiretsus exist linking companies from raw material suppliers to retailers.

Keogh plan A type of individualized pension plan for self-employed individuals.

Key A field in a database table whose values identify records either for display or for processing. Typical keys are part number (in an inventory file) and Social Security number (in a human resources file).

Key buying influentials Individuals in the buying organization who have the power to influence the buying decision.

Kickback fraud Fraud perpetrated by an employee and the employee's vendor or customer. Usually involves the employee buying goods or services from the vendor at an overstated price or giving the customer a lower-than-normal price, and in return the vendor or customer pays the employee a "kickback."

Kiting Fraud that conceals cash shortages by 1) transferring funds from one bank to another and 2) recording the receipt on or before the balance sheet date and the disbursement after the balance sheet date.

KJ method *See:* affinity diagram.

Knowledge base The collection of facts and the relationships among them that mimic the decision-making process in an expert's mind and constitute a major component of an expert system.

Knowledge engineer A programmer whose expertise is the extraction of knowledge from a domain expert and the transformation of the knowledge into code, that is, into the knowledge base of an expert system. Knowledge engineers construct expert systems.

Knowledge management 1: The efforts to systematically find, organize, and make available a company's intellectual capital and to foster a culture of continuous learning and knowledge sharing; the process of systematically gathering knowledge, making it widely available throughout the organization, and fostering a culture of learning. **2:** Transforming data into information, the acquisition or creation of knowledge, as well as the processes and technology employed in identifying, categorizing, storing, retrieving, disseminating, and using information and knowledge for the purposes of improving decisions and plans.

Knowledge management portal A single point of access for employees to multiple sources of information that provides personalized access on the corporate intranet.

Knowledge worker Any worker who produces information. The term roughly overlaps with "professional."

L

Labeling Teaching and training.

Labor force population All individuals who are available for selection if all possible recruitment strategies are used.

Labor laws Laws in many countries provide extensive security for workers and make it extremely expensive to terminate an employee.

Labor markets The external supply pool from which organizations attract employees.

Labor productivity A measure of the relationship between workers' hours and the actual output produced.

Labor specialization Occurs when labor and management undertake specific activities and processes, the repetition and focus increase the effectiveness, efficiency, and learning of labor and management.

Laddering A method of showing the logical precedential relationship of a set of activities that is repeated several times consecutively.

Lagged regression analysis A quick and relatively inexpensive way of determining a company's collection experience by determining a mathematical equation relating cash collections to the sales that gave rise to them.

Lagging Strategy used by a firm to stall payments, normally in response to exchange rate projections. The practice of delaying collections or payments.

Lags Paying a debt late to take advantage of exchange rates.

Lambda A liquidity measure from a function of the likelihood that a firm will exhaust its liquid reserve. The measure's numerator is the sum of the firm's initial liquid reserve and total anticipated net cash flow during the analysis horizon and denominator is the standard deviation of the net cash flow during the analysis horizon.

LAN (Local Area Network) A computer network confined to a building or a group of adjacent buildings, as opposed to a wide area network.

Land bridge Transfer of ocean freight on land among various modes of transportation.

Language translator Fluent in both languages being used in a cross-cultural communication, translators help eliminate the verbal and nonverbal communication barriers.

Lapping Fraud that involves stealing one customer's payment and then crediting that customer's account when a subsequent customer pays.

Larceny Intentionally taking an employer's cash or other assets without the consent and against the will of the employer, after it has been recorded in the company's accounting system.

Large power distance culture The culture where a person at a higher position in the organizational hierarchy makes the decisions, and the employees at the lower levels simply follow the instructions.

Large-group intervention An approach that brings together participants from all parts of the organization (and may include key outside stakeholders as well) to discuss problems or opportunities and plan for major change.

Laser printer A nonimpact printer that uses laser beams to produce high-quality printouts.

Last-in, first-out (LIFO) method A method of inventory costing based on the assumption that the most recent merchandise costs incurred should be charged against revenue.

Latest finish time (LF) The latest time by which a particular activity must be completed in order for the entire project to be finished by its required completion time.

Latest start time (LS) The latest time by which a particular activity must be started in order for the entire project to be finished by its required completion time; the activity's latest finish time minus the activity's estimated duration.

Law of effect The assumption that positively reinforced behavior tends to be repeated and unreinforced or negatively reinforced behavior tends to be inhibited.

Law of one price The theory that the relative prices of any single good between countries, expressed in each country's currency, is representative of the proper or appropriate exchange rate value.

Lead, or managing, underwriter The member of an underwriting syndicate that actually *manages* the distribution and sale of a new security offering.

Lead time The elapsed time between starting a unit of product into the beginning of a process and its completion.

Leader Individual, recognized by others, as the person to lead an effort. One cannot be a "leader" without one or more "followers." The term is often used interchangeably with "manager" (*see*: manager). A "leader" may or may not hold an officially designated management-type position.

Leadership Essential part of a quality improvement effort. Organization leaders must establish a vision, communicate that vision to those in the organization, and provide the tools, knowledge, and motivation necessary to accomplish the vision.

Leadership grid A two-dimensional leadership theory that measures a leader's concern for people and concern for production.

Leading 1: The management function that involves the use of influence to motivate employees to achieve the organization's goals. **2:** Strategy used by a firm to accelerate payments, normally in response to exchange rate expectations. The practice of accelerating collections or payments.

Leads Paying a debt early to take advantage of exchange rates.

Leaky bucket theory Traditionally associated with conquest marketing where new customers replace disloyal customers at the same rate; hence, the firm never grows.

Lean approach/lean thinking ("lean" and "agile" may be used interchangeably) Focus on reducing cycle time and waste using a number of different techniques and tools, for example, value stream mapping, and identifying and eliminating "monuments" and non-value-added steps.

Lean manufacturing Applying the lean approach to improving manufacturing operations.

Lean production A philosophy of production that emphasizes the minimization of the amount of all the resources (including time) used in the various activities of the enterprise. It involves identifying and eliminating non-value-adding activities in design, production, supply chain management, and dealing with the customers. Lean producers employ teams of multiskilled workers at all levels of the organization and use highly flexible, increasingly automated machines to produce volumes of products in potentially enormous variety. It contains a set of principles and practices to reduce cost through the relentless removal of waste and through the simplification of all manufacturing and support processes. *Syn:* lean, lean manufacturing.

Learner-controlled instruction (also called *self-directed learning*) The learner working without an instructor, at their own pace, building mastery of a task (computer-based training is a form of LCI).

Learning 1: Change in the content of long-term memory. As consumers, we learn to adapt better to our environment. **2:** A change in behavior or performance as the result of experience.

Learning curve 1: A curve reflecting the rate of improvement in time per piece as more units of an item are made. A planning technique, the learning curve is particularly useful in project-oriented industries in which new products are frequently phased in. The basis for the learning curve calculation is that workers will be able to produce the product more quickly after they get used to making it. *Syn:* experience curve, manufacturing progress curve. **2:** Time it takes to achieve mastery of a task or body of knowledge.

Learning objectives (also called *terminal objectives*) The objectives to be met upon completion of a course of study or the learning of a skill.

Learning organization 1: An organization in which everyone is engaged in identifying and solving problems, enabling the organization to continuously experiment, improve, and increase its capability. **2:** Organization that has as a policy to continue to learn and improve its products, services, processes and outcomes; "an organization that is continually expanding its capacity to create its future" (Senge). **3:** The concept of an organization that accumulates knowledge through the experiences of its employees. Information systems facilitate learning by organizations.

Lease A contract between a lessor and a lessee that gives the lessee the right to use specific property owned by the lessor, for a given time period, in exchange for cash or other consideration—typically a commitment to make future cash payments.

Leaves The lowest-level records in a hierarchical database.

Ledger The group of accounts used by a business.

Ledger balance Reflects all credits and debits posted to an account as of a certain time, but this balance may not be entirely spendable.

Legacy system An old information system still in use. Usually, the term is used when contrasting such a system with a new information system, or a new type of information system.

Legal environment Includes rules of competition, packaging laws, patents, trademarks, copyright laws and practices, labor laws, and contract enforcement.

Legitimate power Power that stems from a formal management position in an organization and the authority granted to it.

Legitimation Dynamic process by which a business seeks to perpetuate its acceptance.

Leontief Paradox Wassily Leontief's studies of U.S. trade indicated that the United States was a labor-abundant country, exporting labor-intensive products. This was a paradox because of the general belief that the United States was a capital-abundant country which should be exporting capital-intensive products.

Less-developed country (LDC) 1: An emerging or developing nation. **2:** A country with a less diversified economy, a lower than average gross national product, and a lower than average per capita income.

Lessee The party that uses, rather than the one who owns, the leased property.

Lessor The owner of the leased property.

Letter of credit (L/C) A promise by a bank to make payment to a party upon presentation of a draft provided that the party complies with certain documentary requirements. This guarantees the investor of principal repayment, and the use of backup bank financing allows the bank's credit rating to be substituted for the issuer's.

Level of detail The degree to which the information generated is specific.

Level of equality Extent to which less powerful members accept that power is distributed unequally.

Level of service A measure (usually expressed as a percentage) of satisfying demand through inventory or by the current production schedule in time to satisfy the customers' requested delivery dates and quantities. In a make-to-stock environment, level of service is sometimes calculated as the percentage of orders picked complete from stock upon receipt of the customer order, the percentage of line items picked complete, or the percentage of total dollar demand picked complete. In make-to-order and design-to-order environments, level of service is the percentage of times the customer-requested or acknowledged date was met by shipping complete product quantities. *Syn:* measure of service, service level.

Level production method A production planning method that maintains a stable production rate while varying inventory levels to meet demand. *Syn:* level strategy, production leveling. *See:* level schedule.

Level schedule 1: In traditional management, a production schedule or master production schedule that generates material and labor requirements that are as evenly spread over time as possible. Finished goods inventories buffer the production system against seasonal demand. *See:* level production method. **2:** In JIT, a level schedule (usually constructed monthly) in which each day's customer demand is scheduled to be built on the day it will be shipped. A level schedule is the output of the load-leveling process. *Syn:* JIT master schedule, level production schedule. *See:* load leveling.

Leverage 1: Generally refers to the power you have in a negotiation. In negotiations, the more leverage (options) you have, the more concessions your opponent will have to make. **2:** The tendency of the rate earned on stockholders' equity to vary from the rate earned on total assets because the amount earned on assets acquired through the use of funds provided by creditors varies from the interest paid to these creditors.

Leverage ratios *See:* Coverage ratios.

Leveraged buyout (LBO) A transaction in which a firm's publicly owned stock is bought up in a mostly debt-financed tender offer, and a privately owned, highly leveraged firm results.

Liabilities Debts owed to outsiders (creditors).

Liability frauds Financial statement fraud in which liabilities (amounts owed to others) are understated.

Liability swap A swap created to hedge cash flows related to liabilities.

LIBOR The London InterBank Offer Rate. The rate of interest charged by top-quality international banks on loans to similar quality banks in London. This interest rate is often used in both domestic and international markets as the rate of interest on loans and other financial agreements.

Licensing 1: Arrangement in which a local firm in the host country produces goods in accordance with another firm's (the licensing firm's) specifications; as the goods are sold, the local firm can retain part of the earnings. **2:** MNE sells a foreign company the right to use technology or information. A firm gives a license to another firm to produce or package its product.

Licensing agreement Arrangement in which one firm permits another to use its intellectual property in exchange for compensation, typically a royalty.

Licensing program Proprietary information, such as patent rights or expertise, that is licensed by the owner (licenser) to another party (licensee). Compensation paid to the licenser usually includes license issuance fees, milestone payments, and/or royalties.

Lien Claim on property for the satisfaction of just debt.

Life cycle Product life cycle is the total time frame from product concept to the end of its intended use; a project life cycle is typically divided into five stages: concept, planning, design, implementation, evaluation and close-out.

LIFO Method of valuation of inventories for accounting purposes, meaning Last-In-First-Out. The principle rests on the practice of recording inventory by "layer" of the cost at which it was incurred.

Limited-service merchant wholesalers Perform only a few services for manufacturers or other customers, or they perform all of them on a more restricted basis than do full-service wholesalers.

Limiting operation The operation with the least capacity in a series of operations with no alternative routings. The capacity of the total system can be no greater than the limiting operation, and as long as this limiting condition exists, the total system can be effectively scheduled by scheduling the limiting operation and providing this operation with proper buffers.

Line 1: A specific physical space for the manufacture of a product that in a flow shop layout is represented by a straight line. In actuality, this may be a series of pieces of equipment connected by piping or conveyor systems. **2:** A type of manufacturing process used to produce a narrow range of standard items with identical or highly similar designs. Production volumes are high, production and material handling equipment is specialized, and all products typically pass through the same sequence of operations.

Line authority A form of authority in which individuals in management positions have the formal power to direct and control immediate subordinates.

Line balancing 1: The balancing of the assignment of the tasks to workstations in a manner that minimizes the number of workstations and minimizes the total amount of idle time at all stations for a given output level. In balancing these tasks, the specified time requirement per unit of product for each task and its sequential relationship with the other tasks must be considered. **2:** A technique for determining the product mix that can be run down an assembly line to provide a fairly consistent flow of work through that assembly line at the planned line rate.

Line efficiency A measure of actual work content versus cycle time of the limiting operation in a production line. Line efficiency (percentage) is equal to the sum of all station task times divided by the longest task time multiplied by the number of stations. In an assembly line layout, the line efficiency is 100 percent minus the balance delay percentage.

Line extensions New products that are developed as variations of existing products.

Line loading The loading of a production line by multiplying the total pieces by the rate per piece for each item to come up with a finished schedule for the line.

Line of credit An arrangement in which a bank agrees to lend up to a specified maximum amount of funds during a designated period. Short-term lending arrangement which allows the company to borrow up to a prearranged dollar amount during the one-year term.

Linear cultures View the past as being behind them and the future in front of them; they view change as good and attempt to take advantage of business opportunities that they foresee.

Linear regression Mathematical application of the concept of a scatter diagram where the correlation is actually a cause-and-effect relationship.

Linear responsibility matrix Matrix providing a three-dimensional view of project tasks, responsible person, and level of relationship.

Liner service Ocean shipping characterized by regularly scheduled passage on established routes.

Lingua franca The language habitually used among people of diverse speech to facilitate communication.

Link analysis Connects relevant data segments with each other, forming categories, clusters, or networks of information.

Liquid asset An asset that can be easily converted into cash without significant loss of its original value.

Liquid crystal display (LCD) A flat-panel computer monitor in which a conductive-film-covered screen is filled with a liquid crystal whose molecules can align in different planes when charged with certain electrical voltage, which either blocks light or allows it to pass through the liquid. The combination of light and dark produces images of characters and pictures.

Liquidity The ability to sell an asset quickly, at or very close to the present market price. For a company the ability of the firm to pay its bills on time.

Liquidity preference hypothesis Theoretical explanation for the term structure of interest rates that hypothesizes that higher yields will be necessary to induce investors to tie their funds up for long time periods (in other words, to be illiquid) in light of the increasing interest rate risk. Preference for liquidity is thought to characterize enough investors that the yield curve (in the absence of expectations or other influences on other than the shortest-term securities) should slope upward from left to right. The longer the maturity, the larger the liquidity premium must be to attract investors.

Liquidity preference theory The theory that, all else equal, lenders prefer to make short-term loans rather than long-term loans; hence, they will lend short-term funds at lower rates than long-term funds.

Liquidity premium (LP) A premium added to the rate on a security if the security cannot be converted to cash on short notice and at close to the original cost.

Liquidity ratios Ratios that show the relationship of a firm's cash and other current assets to its current liabilities.

Liquidity risk The inability to sell quickly at or very near the current market price, which is tied to the marketability of a security.

Listening The skill of receiving messages to accurately grasp facts and feelings to interpret the genuine meaning.

Listening post data Customer data and information gathered from designated "listening posts."

Little's law Relates three performance measures of a business process: average flow rate (R, throughput), average flow time (T), and average inventory (I). $I = R \times T$

Load The amount of planned work scheduled for and actual work released to a facility, work center, or operation for a specific span of time. Usually expressed in terms of standard hours of work or, when items consume similar resources at the same rate, units of production. *Syn:* workload.

Load balancing The transfer of visitor inquiries from a busy server to a less busy server.

Load leveling Spreading orders out in time or rescheduling operations so that the amount of work or similar considerations make it more economical to purchase or produce in larger lots than are needed for immediate purposes.

Loan participation After a bank or syndicate of banks arranges a large loan, part or all of the loan may be sold off to corporate or other institutional investors, as well as to other banks.

Lobbyist Typically, a well-connected person or firm that is hired by a business to influence the decision making of policymakers and legislators.

Local content Regulations to gain control over foreign investment by ensuring that a large share of the product is locally produced or a larger share of the profit is retained in the country.

Location decision A decision concerning the number of facilities to establish and where they should be situated.

Locational arbitrage Action to capitalize on a discrepancy in quoted exchange rates between banks.

Lock out/tag out regulations Requirements that locks and tags be used to make equipment inoperative for repair or adjustment.

Lockbox A special post office box where customers are instructed to mail their remittances.

Lockbox arrangement A technique used to reduce float by having payments sent to post office boxes located near the customers.

Lockbox collection system A cash collection system that intercepts customer remittances close to the sending location and deposits the checks in the banking system prior to the company receiving notification.

Lockbox consortium A system composed of several independent banks operating under a contractual agreement to provide lockbox services for each other's customers.

Lockbox optimization model A set of variables, relationships, and rules that determine the optimal number of lockboxes, their locations, and the customer allocations to the selected lockbox sites.

Lockbox services A collection service offered by banks, with the emphasis being to reduce collection float. Banks receiving one million or more pieces of mail per year can have a unique zip code set up for them, saving one or more sorts by post office personnel.

Lockbox study A study usually conducted by a bank consulting group to help a corporation decide the structure of its collection system.

Locus of control The tendency to place the primary responsibility for one's success or failure either within oneself (internally) or on outside forces (externally).

Log-linear regression An approach to estimating a variable's growth rate, which takes into account all of the variable's observed values.

Logic bomb A destructive computer program that is inactive until it is triggered by an event taking place in the computer, such as the deletion of a certain record from a file. When the event is the occurrence of a particular time, the logic bomb is referred to as a *time bomb*.

Logic error A program error that occurs when the logic of the program does not achieve its goals.

Logical design A translation of user requirements into detailed functions of a proposed information system.

Logistical service standards Kinds of quantifiable distribution services performed by a logistical system to meet the needs of customers.

Logistics Also called physical distribution, logistics focuses on the physical movement and storage of goods and materials. Managers in this area must evaluate various transportation options, develop and manage networks of warehouses when needed, and manage the physical flow of materials into and out of the organization, what are often called inbound and out-bound logistics. In some cases, logistics managers help decide on the appropriate type of packaging for the product. Logistics must also work closely with marketing to determine the appropriate channels (for example, wholesalers, retailers, mail order) by which to market the firm's products and services.

Logistics (or physical distribution) Planning, implementing, and controlling of the physical flows of materials and final products from points of origin to points of use to meet customers' needs at a profit.

Logistics platform Vital to a firm's competitive position, it is determined by a location's ease and convenience of market reach under favorable cost circumstances.

London Interbank Offer Rate (LIBOR) The short-term interest rate at which banks offer Eurodollar loans to each other.

Longitudinal analysis A method of estimating market demand by factoring in the time lag of demand patterns.

Long-term forward contracts Contracts that state any exchange rate at which a specified amount of a specified currency can be exchanged at a future date (more than one year from today). Also called long forwards.

Long-term goals Goals that an organization hopes to achieve in the future, usually in three to five years. They are commonly referred to as strategic goals.

Long-term liabilities Liabilities that are not due for a long time (usually more than one year).

Long-term orientation 1: A greater concern for the future and high value on thrift and perseverance. **2:** Dimension of culture that refers to values people hold that emphasize the future, as opposed to short-term values focusing on the present and the past. **3:** The adaptation of traditions to meet current needs.

Loss control Actions taken to reduce the frequency and/or severity of losses (risk reduction or mitigation).

Loss exposure A potential loss that may be associated with a specific type of risk.

Loss exposure checklist A risk identification tool used by businesses and individuals that lists many different potential losses. The user can determine which of the potential losses is relevant.

Loss from operations The excess of operating expenses over gross profit.

Lot Defined quantity of product accumulated under conditions that are considered uniform for sampling purposes.

Lot tolerance percent defective (LTPD) *See:* consumer's risk.

Lottery A hypothetical investment alternative with a probability p of obtaining the best payoff and a probability of $(1-p)$ of obtaining the worst payoff.

Louvre Accord 1987 agreement between countries to attempt to stabilize the value of the U.S. dollar.

Low-context culture A culture in which communication is used to exchange facts and information.

Low liquidity strategy Aggressive current asset allocation strategy which entails driving the company's investment in cash and securities to a minimum.

Low power distance culture A state in which employees perceive few power differences and follow a superior's instructions only when either they agree or feel threatened.

Lower control limit (LCL) Control limit for points below the central line in a control chart.

Lower-of-cost-or-market (LCM) method A method of valuing inventory that reports the inventory at the lower of its cost or current market value (replacement cost).

Lower trial courts State courts that try misdemeanors (small crimes) and pretrial issues.

Lubrication bribes A payment made to an official to facilitate, expedite, and speed up routine government approvals or other actions to which the firm would be legally entitled. They are also called *grease payments*.

Lump-sum increase (LSI) A one-time payment of all or part of a yearly pay increase.

Lumpy assets Assets that cannot be acquired in small increments; instead, they must be obtained in large, discrete amounts.

M

Maastricht Treaty The agreement signed in December 1991 in Maastricht, the Netherlands, in which European Community members agreed to a specific timetable and set of necessary conditions to create a single currency for the EU countries.

Machiavellianism The tendency to direct much of one's behavior toward the acquisition of power and the manipulation of others for personal gain.

Machine center A production area consisting of one or more machines (and, if appropriate for capacity planning, the necessary support personnel) that can be considered as one unit for capacity requirements planning and detailed scheduling.

Machine cycle The four steps that the CPU follows repeatedly: fetch an instruction, decode the instruction, execute the instruction, and store the result.

Machine language Binary programming language that is specific to a computer. A computer can execute a program only after the program's source code is translated to object code expressed in the computer's machine language.

Machine loading The accumulation by workstation, machine, or machine group of the hours generated from the scheduling of operations for released orders by time period. Machine loading differs from capacity requirements planning in that it does not use the planned orders from MRP but operates solely from released orders. It may be of limited value because of its limited visibility of resources.

Machine productivity A partial productivity measure. The rate of output of a machine per unit of time compared with an established standard or rate of output. Machine productivity can be expressed as output per unit of time or output per machine hour.

Machine utilization A measure of how intensively a machine is being used. Machine utilization compares the actual machine time (setup and run time) to available time.

MacOS The family of Macintosh operating systems.

Macro processes Broad, far-ranging processes that often cross functional boundaries.

Macroassessment Overall risk assessment of a country without considering the MNC's business.

Macroeconomic level Level at which trading relationships affect individual markets.

Magnetic disk A disk, or set of disks sharing a spindle, coated with an easily magnetized substance to record data in the form of tiny magnetic fields.

Magnetic-ink character recognition (MICR) A technology that allows a special electronic device to read data printed with special magnetic ink. The data are later processed by a computer. MICR is widely used in banking. The bank code, account number, and the amount of a check are printed on the bottom of checks.

Magnetic Ink Character Recognition (MICR) line The clearing agent, often a Federal Reserve bank, branch, or RCPC, uses the information printed at the bottom of the check to process the check. This information can be read by scanning machines and indicates several items about the drawee bank.

Magnetic tape Coated polyester tape used to store computer data; similar to tape recorder or VCR tape.

Mail float The time that elapses from the point when the check is written until it is received by the payee. It may range from a day for local checks immediately mailed out to ten days for a check sent to New York from Rome, Italy.

Mainframe A computer larger than a midrange computer, but smaller than a supercomputer.

Maintainability The probability that a given maintenance action for an item under given usage conditions can be performed within a stated time interval when the maintenance is performed under stated conditions using stated procedures and resources. Maintainability has two categories: serviceability, the ease of conducting scheduled inspections and servicing, and repairability, the ease of restoring service after a failure.

Maintenance Ironing out bugs that went undetected in the final testing of a program and modifying a program to meet new business needs.

Maintenance margin The level that the margin account returns to after a margin call.

Make-to-order A production environment where a good or service can be made after receipt of a customer's order. The final product is usually a combination of standard items and items custom-designed to meet the special needs of the customer. Where options or accessories are stocked before customer orders arrive, the term assemble-to-order is frequently used. *See:* assemble-to-order, make-to-stock.

Make-to-stock A production environment where products can be and usually are finished before receipt of a customer order. Customer orders are typically filled from existing stocks, and production orders are used to replenish those stocks. *See:* assemble-to-order, make-to-order.

Malcolm Baldrige National Quality Award (MBNQA) An award established by Congress in 1987 to raise awareness of quality management and to recognize U.S. companies that have implemented successful quality management systems. A *Criteria for Performance Excellence* is published each year. Three awards may be given annually in each of five categories: manufacturing businesses, service businesses, small businesses, education institutions, and healthcare organizations. The award is named after the late Secretary of Commerce Malcolm Baldrige, a proponent of quality management. The U.S. Commerce Department's National Institute of Standards and Technology (NIST) manages the award, and ASQ administers it. The major emphasis in determining success is achieving results.

Managed care Approaches that monitor and reduce medical costs using restrictions and market system alternatives.

Managed earnings *See:* Income smoothing.

Managed float Exchange rate system in which currencies have no explicit boundaries, but central banks may intervene to influence exchange rate movements.

Management The attainment of organizational goals in an effective and efficient manner through planning, organizing, leading, and controlling organizational resources.

Management accounting A component of an organization's internal accounting system that provides financial and nonfinancial information used by managers and others within the organization for use in planning, controlling, and decision making.

Management by exception (MBE) An approach for reducing the amount of information that managers must consume that allows managers to review only exceptions from expected results that are of a certain size or type.

Management by fact Business philosophy that decisions should be based on data.

Management by objectives (MBO) 1: A method of management whereby managers and employees define goals for every department, project, and person and use them to monitor subsequent performance. **2:** Specifies the performance goals that an individual and her or his manager agree to try to attain within an appropriate length of time.

Management by policy Organizational infrastructure that ensures that the right things are done at the right time.

Management by walking around (MBWA) A manager's planned, but usually unannounced, walk-through of their organization to gather information from employees and make observations; may be viewed in a positive light by virtue of giving employees opportunity to interact with top management; has the potential of being viewed negatively if punitive action is taken as a result of information gathered.

Management by wandering around (MBWA) A communication technique in which managers interact directly with workers to exchange information.

Management contract An international business alternative in which the firm sells its expertise in running a company while avoiding the risk or benefit of ownership.

Management controls Controls performed by one or more managers at any level in an organization.

Management Discussion and Analysis (MDA) A required disclosure in the annual report filed with the Securities and Exchange Commission; it provides critical information in interpreting financial statements.

Management fraud Deception perpetrated by an organization's top management through the manipulation of financial statement amounts or disclosures.

Management information system (MIS) A computer-based system that provides information and support for effective managerial decision making.

Management intervention Management's actions to overrule prescribed policies or procedures for legitimate purposes; management intervention is usually necessary to deal with nonrecurring and nonstandard transactions or events that otherwise might be handled inappropriately by the system.

Management override Management's overruling of prescribed policies or procedures for illegitimate purposes with the intent of personal gain or an enhanced presentation of an entity's financial condition or compliance status.

Management process The series of actions taken by management to run an entity. An internal control system is a part of and integrated with the management process.

Management reserve *See:* Contingency.

Management review Formal evaluation by top management of the status and adequacy of the quality system in relation to the quality policy and objectives.

Management science perspective A management perspective that emerged after World War II and applied mathematics, statistics, and other quantitative techniques to managerial problems.

Management styles Predominant personal styles used by managers; styles may be based on prevalent management theories or assumptions about people.

Management training Training and/or education provided to any management or professional level person from front-line supervision up to, but not including executives.

Manager Individual who manages and is responsible for resources (people, material, money, time). A person officially designated with a management-type position title. A "manager" is granted authority from above, whereas a "leader's" role is derived by virtue of having followers. However, the terms "manager" and "leader" are often used interchangeably.

Managerial accounting The branch of accounting that uses both historical and estimated data in providing information that management uses in conducting daily operations, in planning future operations, and in developing overall business strategies.

Managerial commitment Desire and drive on the part of management to act on an idea and support it in the long run.

Managerial grid Management theory developed by Robert Blake and Jane Mouton, that maintains that a manager's management style is based on his or her mind-set toward people; it focuses on attitudes rather than behavior. The theory uses a grid to measure concern with production and concern with people.

Managing about a target rule Rather than make daily transfers, this transfer rule makes only one transfer for several days of deposits and the amount transferred takes into consideration a desired target balance that is to be left at the deposit bank.

Mandated benefits Benefits that employers in the United States must provide to employees by law.

Manufacturability A measure of the design of a product or process in terms of its ability to be produced easily, consistently, and with high quality.

Manufacturer's agents Independent middlemen who handle a manufacturer's marketing functions by selling part or all of a manufacturer's product line in an assigned geographic area.

Manufacturer's sales branches Sales outlets owned by the manufacturer.

Manufacturing businesses A type of business that changes basic inputs into products that are sold to individual customers.

Manufacturing cells A grouping of production processes where employees are cross-trained to perform more than one function.

Manufacturing cycle efficiency The ratio of value-added time to manufacturing lead time or cycle time. Manufacturing cycle time can be improved by the reduction of manufacturing lead time by eliminating non-value-added activities such as inspecting, moving, and queuing.

Manufacturing environment The framework in which manufacturing strategy is developed and implemented. Elements of the manufacturing environment include external environmental forces, corporate strategy, business unit strategy, other functional strategies (marketing, engineering, finance, and so on), product selection, product/process design, product/process technology, and management competencies. Often refers to whether a company, plant, product, or service is make-to-stock, make-to-order, or assemble-to-order. *Syn:* production environment.

Manufacturing execution system An information system that helps pinpoint bottlenecks in production lines.

Manufacturing lead time The total time required to manufacture an item, exclusive of lower level purchasing lead time. For make-to-order products, it is the length of time between the release of an order to the production process and shipment to the final customer. For make-to-stock products, it is the length of time between the release of an order to the production process and receipt into finished goods inventory. Included here are order preparation time, queue time, setup time, run time, move time, inspection time, and putaway time. *Syn:* manufacturing cycle, production cycle, production lead time.

Manufacturing margin The variable cost of goods sold deducted from sales.

Manufacturing organization An organization that produces physical goods.

Manufacturing process The series of operations performed upon material to convert it from the raw material or a semifinished state to a state of further completion. Manufacturing processes can be arranged in a process layout, product layout, cellular layout, or fixed-position layout. Manufacturing processes can be planned to support make-to-stock, make-to-order, assemble-to-order, and so on, based on the strategic use and placement of inventories. *See:* production process, transformation process.

Manufacturing Resource Planning (MRP II) 1: The combination of MRP with other manufacturing-related activities to plan the entire manufacturing process, not just inventory. **2:** A method for the effective planning of all resources of a manufacturing company. Ideally, it addresses operational planning in units, financial planning in dollars, and has a simulation capability to answer what-if questions. It is made up of a variety of processes, each linked together: business planning, production planning (sales and operations planning), master production scheduling, material requirements planning, capacity requirements planning, and the execution support systems for capacity and material. Output from these systems is integrated with financial reports such as the business plan, purchase commitment report, shipping budget, and inventory projections in dollars. Manufacturing resource planning is a direct outgrowth and extension of closed-loop MRP.

Manufacturing strategy A collective pattern of decisions that acts upon the formulation and deployment of manufacturing resources. To be most effective, the manufacturing strategy should act in support of the overall strategic direction of the business and provide for competitive advantages (edges).

Manufacturing volume strategy An element of manufacturing strategy that includes a series of assumptions and predictions about long-term market, technology, and competitive behavior in the following areas: 1) the predicted growth and variability of demand, 2) the costs of building and operating different sized plants, 3) the rate and direction of technological improvement, 4) the likely behavior of competitors, and 5) the anticipated impact of international competitors, markets, and sources of supply. It is the sequence of specific volume decisions over time that determines an organization's long-term manufacturing volume strategy.

Maquiladoras Mexican border plants that make goods and parts or process food for export back to the United States. They benefit from lower labor costs.

Margin A small percentage of the contract price that is put up rather than paying the full price of the contract.

Margin call A call from a broker asking for more money to support a stock purchase loan.

Margin requirement Deposit placed on a contract (such as a currency futures contract) to cover the fluctuations in the value of that contract; this minimizes the risk of the contract to the counterparty.

Margin of safety The difference between current sales revenue and the sales at the break-even point.

Marginal cost The rate of change of the total cost with respect to volume.

Marginal cost method This method considers the direct costs of producing and selling goods for export as the floor beneath which prices cannot be set.

Marginal cost of capital (MCC) The cost of obtaining another dollar of new capital; the weighted average cost of the last dollar of new capital raised.

Marginal costs Change in a firm's total costs-per-unit change in its output level.

Marginal functions Duties that are part of a job but are incidental or ancillary to the purpose and nature of a job.

Marginal revenue Change in a firm's total revenue-per-unit change in its sales level.

Marginal tax rate The tax applicable to the last unit of income.

Marked-to-market When changes in the market price of the futures contract impact the margin account on a daily basis.

Market audit A method of estimating market size by adding together local production and imports, with exports subtracted from the total.

Market-based forecasting Use of a market-determined exchange rate (such as the spot rate or forward rate) to forecast the spot rate in the future.

Market-based transfer pricing The price one segment of a company charges another segment of the same company for the transfer of a good or a service based on its current market price.

Market/book (M/B) ratio The ratio of a stock's market price to its book value.

Market-differentiated pricing Price-setting strategy based on demand rather than cost.

Market entry strategy An organizational strategy for entering a foreign market.

Market line The line on a graph showing the relationship between job value, as determined by job evaluation points and pay survey rates.

Market microstructure Consists of the participants and mechanics involved in making transactions.

Market, or nondiversifiable, risk That part of a security's risk that *cannot* be eliminated by diversification because it is associated with economic, or market, factors that systematically affect most firms.

Market-perceived quality The customer's opinion of your products or services as compared to those of your competitors.

Market potential Level of sales that might be available to all marketers in an industry in a given market.

Market price approach An approach to transfer pricing that uses the price at which the product or service transferred could be sold to outside buyers as the transfer price.

Market price, P_0 The price at which a stock sells in the market.

Market risk premium, RP_M The additional return over the risk-free rate needed to compensate investors for assuming an average amount of risk.

Market (price) skimming Strategy of pricing the new product at a relatively high level and then gradually reducing it over time.

Market segment 1: Overlapping ranges of trade targets with common ground and levels of sophistication. **2:** A portion of business that can be assigned to a manager for profit responsibility. **3:** Those segments of the market or submarkets that seek similar benefits from product usage, and that shop and buy in similar ways that are different from other market segments and submarkets; consist of groups of consumers who are alike based on some characteristic(s).

Market segmentation hypothesis A theoretical explanation of the term structure of interest rates which contends that instead of being close substitutes, securities with short, medium, and long maturities are seen by investors (fund suppliers) and issuers (funds demanders) as quite different. Thus interest rates for securities with different maturities are set by diverse supply and demand conditions.

Market segmentation theory The theory that each borrower and lender has a preferred maturity and that the slope of the yield curve depends on the supply of and demand for funds in the long-term market relative to the short-term market.

Market transparency Availability of full disclosure and information about key market factors such as supply, demand, quality, service, and prices.

Market value-added (MVA) system A control system that measures the stock market's estimate of the value of a company's past and expected capital investment projects.

Market value ratios A set of ratios that relate the firm's stock price to its earnings and book value per share.

Marketable securities 1: Securities that can be sold on short notice without loss of principal or original investment. **2:** Stocks, bonds, and other noncash assets; sometimes called *short-term investments*.

Marketing Process of planning and executing the conception, pricing, promotion, and distribution of ideas, goods, and services to create exchanges that satisfy individual and organizational goals.

Marketing channel Network of organizations that creates time, place, and possession utilities.

Marketing channel management Analysis, planning, organizing, and controlling of a firm's marketing channels.

Marketing channel power Capacity of one channel member to influence the behavior of another channel member.

Marketing concept How organizational goals are achieved by identifying the needs and wants of customers and delivering products that satisfy customers more effectively than competitors could.

Marketing environment Involves the micro- and macroenvironmental influences, including the company's own objectives and resources, the sociocultural environment, the competitive environment, the economic environment, the technological environment, and the political and legal environment.

Marketing infrastructure Facilitating marketing agencies in a country; for example, market research firms, channel members.

Marketing mix Composed of product, price, place (distribution), and promotion decisions and programs that the company decides to pursue in implementing its marketing strategy.

Marketing myopia Too narrowly defining one's business.

Marketing strategy Using vision and planning to create and deploy a company's assets and capabilities most profitably.

Marking the evidence Placing unique identification tags or descriptions on documents when they are received, so that they can be identified during the investigation and trial process.

Markup An amount that is added to a "cost" amount to determine product price.

Markup laws Require a specified markup above cost in particular industries.

Masculinity 1: A cultural preference for achievement, heroism, assertiveness, work centrality, and material success. **2:** The relative importance of the qualities associated with men, such as assertiveness and materialism. **3:** Refers to the degree to which people in a society stress material success and assertiveness and assign different roles to males and females.

Masculinity/femininity Dimension of cultures that refers to the degree to which "masculine" values prevail over "feminine" values.

Maslow's hierarchy of needs Classification scheme of needs satisfaction where higher level needs are dormant until lower level needs are satisfied.

Mass customization The creation of a high-volume product with large variety so that a customer may specify his or her exact model out of a large volume of possible end items while manufacturing cost is low because of the large volume. An example is a personal computer order in which the customer may specify processor speed, memory size, hard disk size and speed, removable storage device characteristics, and many other options when PCs are assembled on one line and at low cost.

Massed practice The performance of all of the practice at once.

Master budget The comprehensive budget plan encompassing all the individual budgets related to sales, cost of goods sold, operating expenses, capital expenditures, and cash.

Master note Open-ended commercial paper, which allow the investor to add or withdraw monies on a daily basis, up to a specified maximum amount.

Master of destiny A view that individuals can substantially influence their future, that they control their destiny, and through hard work they can make things happen.

Master operating budget A plan for achieving the corporate goals for a period of time (normally one year).

Master planning A group of business processes that includes the following activities: demand management (which includes forecasting and order servicing); production and resource planning; and master scheduling (which includes the master schedule and the rough-cut capacity plan).

Master planning of resources A grouping of business processes that includes the following activities: demand management, which includes the forecasting of sales, the planning of distribution, and the servicing of customer orders; sales and operations planning, which includes sales planning, production planning, inventory planning, backlog planning, and resource planning; master scheduling, which includes the preparation of the master production schedule and the rough-cut capacity plan.

Master Production Schedule (MPS) 1: The component of an MRP II system that specifies production capacity to meet customer demands and maintain inventories. **2:** The master production schedule is a line on the master schedule grid that reflects the anticipated build schedule for those items assigned to the master scheduler. The master scheduler maintains this schedule, and in turn, it becomes a set of planning numbers that drives material requirements planning. It represents what the company plans to produce expressed in specific configurations, quantities, and dates. The master production schedule is not a sales item forecast that represents a statement of demand. The master production schedule must take into account the forecast, the production plan, and other important considerations such as backlog, availability of material, availability of capacity, and management policies and goals. *Syn:* master schedule.

Matching concept The concept that expenses incurred in generating revenue should be matched against the revenue in determining the net income or net loss for the period.

Matching model An employee selection approach in which the organization and the applicant attempt to match each other's needs, interests, and values.

Material achievement Extent to which the dominant values in society are success, money, and things.

Material possessions Individuals in some cultures equate success with material wealth. However, individuals in many cultures place relatively little importance on material possessions and view the flaunting of wealth as disrespectful.

Material requirements planning (MRP) 1: An inventory planning system that focuses on the amount and timing of finished goods demanded and translates this into the derived demand for raw materials and subassemblies at various stages of production. **2:** A set of techniques that uses bill of material data, inventory data, and the master production schedule to calculate requirements for materials. It makes recommendations to release replenishment orders for material. Further, because it is time-phased, it makes recommendations to reschedule open orders when due dates and need dates are not in phase. Time-phased MRP begins with the items listed on the MPS and determines 1) the quantity of all components and materials required to fabricate those items and 2) the date that the components and material are required. Time-phased MRP is accomplished by exploding the bill of material, adjusting for inventory quantities on hand or on order, and offsetting the net requirements by the appropriate lead times. **3:** A dependent demand inventory planning and control system that schedules the precise amount of all materials required to support the production of desired end products.

Materiality concept A concept of accounting that accounts for items that are deemed significant for a given size of operations. This concept, requiring use of professional judgment, describes information that must be included or disclosed to prevent financial statements from misleading their users.

Materials inventory The cost of materials that have not yet entered into the manufacturing process.

Materials ledger The subsidiary ledger that contains the individual accounts for each type of material.

Materials management 1: An approach to management that seeks to organize and coordinate the activities responsible for managing the inbound flow of materials and information from suppliers through to the point of finished goods. The various functions that often fall under the materials umbrella include *material planning and control, materials and procurement research, purchasing, incoming traffic, receiving, incoming quality control, stores, materials movement,* and *scrap* and *surplus disposal.* **2:** The timely movement of raw materials, parts, and supplies into and through the firm.

Materials Requirement Planning (MRP) Inventory control that includes a calculation of future need.

Materials requisitions The form or electronic transmission used by a manufacturing department to authorize materials issuances from the storeroom.

Materials review board (MRB) Quality control committee or team, usually employed in manufacturing or other materials-processing installations, that has the responsibility and authority to deal with items or materials that do not conform to fitness-for-use specifications. An equivalent, error review board, is sometimes used in software development.

Mathematical model Mathematical symbols and expressions used to represent a real situation.

Matrix approach An organization structure that utilizes functional and divisional chains of command simultaneously in the same part of the organization.

Matrix chart/diagram Management and planning tool that shows the relationships among various groups of data; it yields information about the relationships and the importance of task/method elements of the subjects.

Matrix organization An organization in which managers report to both a divisional executive and a functional executive. For instance, the marketing manager of the Manufacturing Division reports both to the division's president and to the corporate vice president of marketing.

Matrix organization structure A hybrid of the functional and project organizational structures, in which resources from appropriate functional components of a company are temporarily assigned to particular projects.

Matrix structure 1: Describes an organization that is organized into a combination of functional and product departments; it brings together teams of people to work on projects and is driven by product scope. **2:** An organizational structure that uses functional and divisional structures simultaneously. This structure is strongly decentralized: it allows local subsidiaries to develop products that fit into local markets. And yet at its core, it is very centralized; it allows companies to coordinate activities across the globe and capitalize on synergies and economies of scale.

Maturity curve Curve that depicts the relationship between experience and pay rates.

Maturity date A specified date on which the par value of a bond must be repaid.

Maturity extension swap Situation where a security is sold and replaced or exchanged with another security which will increase the yield or dollar return, while affecting credit risk minimally. The swap is executed when the manager wishes to ride the yield curve, but to make the investment he must liquidate another security.

Maturity matching, or "self-liquidating," approach A financing policy that matches asset and liability maturities. This would be considered a moderate current asset financing policy.

Maturity risk premium (MRP) A premium that reflects interest rate risk; bonds with longer maturities have greater interest rate risk.

Maturity value The amount due (face value plus interest) at the maturity or due date of a note.

Maximization of shareholder value The ultimate goal of the management of a multinational firm is to increase the value of the shareholder's investment as much as possible.

MBO In this approach, the manager and subordinate meet, and together set objectives for the subordinate.

McFadden Act (1927) Limited branch banking by national banks to the same areas in which state-chartered banks in that state were permitted to branch, effectively prohibiting interstate branching.

M-commerce Mobile commerce, spawned by advances in technology for mobile communications devices.

Mean Measure of central tendency and is the arithmetic average of all measurements in a data set.

Mean absolute deviation (MAD) A measure of forecast accuracy. The average of the absolute values of the forecast errors.

Mean absolute error (MAE) Measure of forecast error calculated by adding up the absolute values of the difference between forecasted and actual values, and then dividing by the number of forecasts.

Mean square error Weights large errors more than small ones, and thus favors forecasting models that rarely if ever miss by a large amount.

Mean squared error (MSE) An approach to measuring the accuracy of a forecasting model. This measure is the average of the sum of the squared differences between the actual time series values and the forecasted values.

Mean time between failures (MTBF) Average time interval between failures for repairable product for a defined unit of measure (for example, operating hours, cycles, or miles).

Means (in the hoshin planning usage) The step of identifying the ways by which multi-year objectives will be met, leading to the development of action plans.

Measurement 1: Reference standard or sample used for the comparison of properties. **2:** Recording economic transactions in the accounting system.

Mechanistic organization Roles and objectives are clearly and rigidly outlined for employees—managers and subordinates are allowed little or no discretion. Historically, large organizations have tended to adopt the mechanistic form.

Media strategy 1: Strategy applied to the selection of media vehicles and the development of a media schedule. **2:** Four sets of interrelated activities: 1) selecting the target audience, 2) specifying media objectives, 3) selecting media categories and vehicles, and 4) buying media.

Median Middle number or center value of a set of data when all the data are arranged in an increasing sequence.

Mediation Process by which a third party assists negotiators in reaching a settlement.

Mediators In some situations within cultures, it is not wise to send messages directly to the receiver(s); it is wise to use a mediator. The encoder sends the message to a mediator (a third party), who in turn conveys it to the receiver(s).

Medium Anything through which data are transmitted; may be guided or unguided.

Medium-Term Guarantee Program Program conducted by Ex-Im Bank in which commercial lenders are encouraged to finance the sale of U.S. capital equipment and services to approved foreign buyers; Ex-Im Bank guarantees the loan's principal and interest on these loans.

Member banks Commercial banks which belong to the Federal Reserve System. Being a member of the Federal Reserve System has historically been a requirement of all national banks, and many state-chartered banks joined voluntarily. Subsequent to the 1980 Monetary Control Act membership has been much less important, in that all depository institutions must adhere to reserve requirements and can now borrow from the Fed.

Mentor A higher-ranking, senior organizational member who is committed to providing upward mobility and support to a protégé's professional career.

Mentoring A relationship in which experienced managers aid individuals in the earlier stages of their careers.

Mercantilism Political and economic policy in the seventeenth and early eighteenth centuries aimed at increasing a nation's wealth and power by encouraging the export of goods in return for gold.

Merchandise inventory Merchandise on hand and available for sale to customers.

Merchandising businesses A type of business that purchases products from other businesses and sells them to customers.

Merchant wholesalers Independent firms that purchase a product from a manufacturer and resell it to other manufacturers, wholesalers, or retailers, but not to the final consumer.

Merger The combining of two corporations by the acquisition of the properties of one corporation by another, with the dissolution of one of the corporations.

Message The tangible formulation of an idea to be sent to a receiver.

Methods analysis That part of methods engineering normally involving an examination and analysis of an operation or a work cycle broken down into its constituent parts to improve the operation, eliminate unnecessary steps, and/or establish and record in detail a proposed method of performance.

Metric A standard of measurement.

Metrology Science and practice of measurements.

Micro managing Managing every little detail (for example, approving requisition for paper clips).

Micro processes Narrow processes made up of detailed steps and activities that could be accomplished by a single person.

Microassessment The risk assessment of a country as related to the MNC's type of business.

Microcomputer The smallest type of computer; includes desktop, laptop, and hand-held computers. The term is used less and less. Trade journals now use the terms *PC* and *PDA*.

Microeconomic level Level of business concerns that affect an individual firm or industry.

Micromarkets Very small market segments, such as zip code areas or even neighborhoods.

Microprocessor An electronic chip that contains the circuitry of either a CPU or a processor with a dedicated and limited purpose, for example a communications processor.

Middle manager A manager who works at the middle levels of the organization and is responsible for major departments.

Midrange computer A computer larger than a microcomputer but smaller than a mainframe.

Migration The move from old hardware or software to new hardware or software.

Milestone Point in time when a critical event is to occur; a symbol placed on a milestone chart to locate the point when a critical event is to occur.

Milestone chart Another name for a *Gantt chart*.

MIL-STD Military standard.

Mind mapping Technique for creating a visual representation of a multitude of issues or concerns by forming a map of the interrelated ideas.

Minimax regret approach An approach to choosing a decision alternative without using probabilities. For each alternative, the maximum regret is computed, which leads to choosing the decision alternative that minimizes the maximum regret.

Mininationals Newer companies with sales between $200 million and $1 billion that are able to serve the world from a handful of manufacturing bases.

Minority interest The portion of a subsidiary corporation's stock that is not owned by the parent corporation.

Minority participation Participation by a group having less than the number of votes necessary for control.

MIPS Millions of instructions per second.

Mirror An Internet server that holds the same software and data as another server, which may be located thousands of miles away.

Miscellaneous fraud Deception that doesn't fall into any of the other five categories of fraud.

Mission The organization's reason for existence.

Mission-critical applications Applications without which a business cannot conduct its operations.

Mission-critical hardware or software Hardware or software without which the business cannot operate and survive.

Mission statement A broadly stated definition of the organization's basic business scope and operations that distinguishes it from similar types of organizations.

Mixed aid credits Credits at rates composed partially of commercial interest rates and partially of highly subsidized developmental aid interest rates.

Mixed approach When applied to forecasting, involves the use of both quantitative and judgmental approaches.

Mixed cost A cost with both variable and fixed characteristics, sometimes called a semivariable or semifixed cost.

Mixed forecasting Development of forecasts based on a mixture of forecasting techniques.

Mixed instruments Specialized investment instruments which offer tailoring to the specific desires of the investor.

Mixed-model production Making several different parts or products in varying lot sizes so that a factory produces close to the same mix of products that will be sold that day. The mixed-model schedule governs the making and the delivery of component parts, including those provided by outside suppliers. The goal is to build every model every day, according to daily demand.

Mixed structure An organizational structure that combines two or more organizational dimensions; for example, products, areas, or functions.

Mobile observation Another term for *tailing*.

Mode Value that occurs most frequently in a data set.

Model A representation of a real object or situation.

Model audit The monitoring of an existing model to ensure its continued validity.

Model estimation Includes the selection of an appropriate forecasting technique and model calibration.

Model management module A collection of models that a decision-support system draws on to assist in decision making.

Modeling 1: The process of establishing a relationship between a set of independent variables in order to produce an estimate of a dependent variable. **2:** Setting an example.

Modem (modulator/demodulator) A communications device that transforms digital signals to analog telephone signals, and vice versa, for data communications over voice telephone lines. Almost all of the commercial modems currently offered on the market also serve as fax devices, and are, therefore, called fax/modems. ("Fax" comes from the Latin words *fac simile,* "make alike" or "copy.")

Moderate current asset investment policy A policy that is between the relaxed and restrictive policies.

Moderate liquidity strategy An approach to liquidity management which implies an intermediate concentration of current assets in the form of cash and securities, with corresponding intermediate levels of risk. This strategy falls between and should be contrasted with conservative and aggressive liquidity strategies.

Moderate strategy In short-term financing, a strategy that is a blend of the aggressive and conservative financing strategies.

Modified accrual technique Sometimes called the "accrual addback technique" or "adjusted net income technique," this cash forecasting approach begins with accounting reports or the operating budget and then adjusts these number to reflect the timing of cash flows related to these transactions.

Modified buy-and-hold strategy An approach to investing in which the investor plans to hold the security to maturity, but will selectively sell securities on which capital gains might be realized. This strategy might be utilized when the investor wishes to take advantage of anticipated favorable interest rate movements.

Modified IRR (MIRR) The discount rate at which the present value of a project's cost is equal to the present value of its terminal value, in which the terminal value is found as the sum of the future values of the cash inflows, compounded at the firm's required rate of return (cost of capital).

Modified rebuy Purchase where the buyers have experience in satisfying the need but feel the situation warrants reevaluation of a limited set of alternatives before making a decision.

Modular approach A manufacturing company uses outside suppliers to provide the large components of the product, which are then assembled into a final product by a few workers.

Modular bill of material A type of planning bill that is arranged in product modules or options. It is often used in companies where the product has many optional features, for example, assemble-to-order companies such as automobile manufacturers. *See:* pseudo bill of material.

Modulation The modification of a digital signal (from a computer) into an analog signal (for a phone line to transmit).

Moment-of-truth A *MOT* is described by Jan Carlzon, former CEO of Scandinavian Air Services, in the 1980s as: "Any episode where a customer comes into contact with any aspect of your company, no matter how distant, and by this contact, has an opportunity to form an opinion about your company."

Monetary barriers Sometimes employed by governments to restrict trade, reduce competition, or encourage certain imports. Monetary barriers occur when governments sell foreign currencies needed to pay for undesired imports at a higher rate than the one charged for currencies needed to pay for desired imports.

Monetary items All assets and liabilities expressed in fixed amounts of currency.

Monetary-nonmonetary method A translation method that restates monetary items on the balance sheet at the current exchange rate on the balance sheet date and nonmonetary items at their historical exchange rates.

Money market A financial market in which funds are borrowed or loaned for short periods (generally one year or less).

Money market deposit accounts Savings accounts offered by depository institutions which pay interest. These were introduced to give depository institutions an account to compete with money market mutual funds.

Money market hedge Use of international money markets to match future cash inflows and outflows in a given currency.

Money market mutual fund A mutual fund that invests in short-term, low-risk securities and allows investors to write checks against their accounts.

Monoculture A culture that accepts only one way of doing things and one set of values and beliefs.

Monte Carlo simulation A risk analysis technique in which probable future events are simulated on a computer, generating a probability distribution that indicates the most likely outcomes.

Monument The point in a process which necessitates a product must wait in a queue before processing further; a barrier to continuous flow.

Moods Emotions that are less intense and transitory.

Moral free space Norms that are inconsistent with at least some legitimate norms existing in other economic cultures.

Moral management Conforms to the highest standards of ethical behavior or professional standards of conduct; strives to be ethical in terms of its focus on high ethical norms and professional standards of conduct, motives, goals, orientation toward the law, and general operating strategy.

Moral-rights approach The ethical concept that moral decisions are those that maintain the rights of those people affected by them.

Mortgage Long-term loan secured by property, such as a home mortgage.

Mortgage bond A bond backed by fixed assets. First mortgage bonds are senior in priority to claims of second mortgage bonds.

Most critical path In a network diagram, the most time-consuming (longest) path of activities; the path of activities that has the lowest value—either least positive or most negative—for total slack.

GLOSSARY

Most-Favored Nation (MFN) A term describing a GATT/WTO clause that calls for member countries to grant other member countries the same most favorable treatment they accord any country concerning imports and exports.

Most likely time estimate (t_m) The time in which an activity can most frequently be completed under normal conditions.

Motion Response to a complaint or pleading by the defendant. Sometimes "motion" refers to any request made to the judge for a ruling in a case by either party.

Motion for dismissal Request to the judge to dismiss a claim because there is no genuine issue of a material fact.

Motivating channel members Action taken by a manufacturer or franchiser to get channel members to implement its channel strategies.

Motivation 1: The arousal, direction, and persistence of behavior. **2:** The desire within a person causing that person to act. **3:** State of drive or arousal that moves us toward a goal-object.

Motivational research Research method directed at discovering the conscious or subconscious reasons that motivate a person's behavior.

Motivators Factors that influence job satisfaction based on fulfillment of high-level needs such as achievement, recognition, responsibility, and opportunity for growth.

Moving average 1: Statistical forecasting technique which evens out temporary ups and downs by taking the mean of the most recent observations. **2:** A method of forecasting or smoothing a time series by averaging each successive group of data points.

Moving surveillance Another term for tailing; involves following suspects wherever they go (within limits) and observing or recording their activities.

Muda (Japanese) Activity that consumes resources but creates no value; seven categories are correction, processing, inventory, waiting, over-production, internal transport, and motion.

Multiattribute evaluation Simpler than QFD, this process rank orders and weights customer requirements relative to the competition. In addition it estimates the cost of each requirement in order to prioritize improvement actions.

Multibuyer policy Policy administered by Ex-Im Bank that provides credit risk insurance on export sales to many different buyers.

Multicollinearity Presence of moderate or high correlation between predictor variables in a regression equation. This condition is a violation of one of the assumptions of ordinary least squares regression modeling, the most common form of regression analysis.

Multicriteria decision problem A problem that involves more than one criterion; the objective is to find the "best" solution, taking into account all the criteria.

Multicultural centers Some countries, such as the United States, are multicultural centers. These countries' residents came from many parts of the world and maintain much of their former country's culture.

Multicultural team Team whose members represent diverse views and come from varied cultures.

Multidimensional development The ninth stage in the social interaction paradigm is characterized by "stepping aside," that is, leaving an important position and distributing political and economic power across private and public sectors.

Multidomestic approach Approach to international marketing in which local conditions are adapted to in each and every target market.

Multidomestic strategy 1: The modification of product design and advertising strategies to suit the specific needs of individual countries. **2:** A business strategy where each individual country organization is operated as a profit center.

Multilateral Investment Guarantee Agency (MIGA) Agency established by the World Bank that offers various forms of political risk insurance to corporations.

Multilateral negotiations Trade negotiations among more than two parties; the intricate relationships among trading countries.

Multilateral netting system Complex interchange for netting between a parent and several subsidiaries.

Multilevel bill of material A display of all the components directly or indirectly used in a parent, together with the quantity required of each component. If a component is a subassembly, blend, intermediate, and so on, all its components and all their components also will be exhibited, down to purchased parts and raw materials.

Multilevel master schedule A master scheduling technique that allows any level in an end item's bill of material to be master scheduled. To accomplish this, MPS items must receive requirements from independent and dependent demand sources. *See:* two-level master schedule.

Multilevel where-used A display for a component listing all the parents in which that component is directly used and the next higher level parents into which each of those parents is used, until ultimately all top-level (level 0) parents are listed.

Multimedia Computer-based technology that provides information comprising text, images, motion pictures, and sound from the same source.

Multinational corporation (MNC) 1: An organization that receives more than 25 percent of its total sales revenues from operations outside the parent company's home country; also called global corporation or transnational corporation. **2:** Company that has production operations in at least one country in addition to its domestic base. **3:** A company that considers the globe as a single marketplace. **4:** Companies that invest in countries around the globe. International businesses that establish subsidiaries in foreign markets.

Multinational enterprise (MNE) 1: Any business that engages in transactions involving the movement of goods, information, money, people, or services across national borders. **2:** An organization with operating units located in foreign countries. *See:* Multinational corporation.

Multinational restructuring Restructuring of the composition of an MNC's assets or liabilities.

Multiple-drawee checks Negotiable payment order having more than one bank listed on the face of the check, with one of the banks being a bank located near the disbursing location, for which the check is an "on us" item.

Multiple IRRs The situation in which a project has two or more IRRs.

Multiple processing centers Processing centers established around the country to pick up lockbox mail and do the processing while the processed checks are deposited in accounts at correspondent banks in the company's name. Cash is then concentrated in the company's account at the lockbox bank's headquarters.

Multiple production department factory overhead rate method A method that allocates factory overhead to products by using factory overhead rates for each production department.

Multiple regression Statistical model incorporating two or more predictor variables to explain the movement in the variable of interest. The form of a multiple regression model having two predictor variables is generally of the form: $Y = a + b_1 X_1 + b_2 X_2$.

Multiple-step income statement An income statement with several sections, subsections, and subtotals.

Multiplexer A device that allows a single channel to communicate data from multiple sources simultaneously.

Multiplicative time series model A model that assumes that the separate components of the time series can be multiplied together to identify the actual time series value. When the four components of trend, cyclical, seasonal, and irregular are assumed present, we obtain $Y^t \times T^t \times C^t \times S^t \times I^t$. When cyclical effects are not modeled, we obtain $Y^t = T^t \times S^t \times I^t$.

Multiprocessing The mode in which a computer uses more than one processing unit simultaneously to process data.

Multiprogramming The capacity to allow several people to use the same computer simultaneously via different terminals.

Multitasking The ability of a computer to run more than one program seemingly at the same time; it enables the notion of windows in which different programs are represented.

Multivariate control chart Control chart for evaluating the stability of a process in terms of the levels of two or more variables or characteristics.

Multivariate models Description of the relationship between three or more variables, typically with one of the variables being explained as the influence of two or more predictor variables.

Multivoting Decision-making tool that enables a group to sort through a long list of ideas to identify priorities.

Municipal obligations Securities issued by governmental authorities, governments, or government-authorized entities at other than the federal level. These securities, sometimes called "munis," pay interest that is not taxable for federal income tax purposes and usually not taxable for state income tax purposes in the state in which the issuer is located. Examples of issuers would be states, counties, localities, and school districts.

Mutually exclusive projects A set of projects in which the acceptance of one project means the others cannot be accepted.

Mystery shopper Person who pretends to be a regular shopper in order to get an unencumbered view of how a company's service process works.

N

n sample size The number of units in a sample.

NACHA The National Automated Clearing House Association. NACHA has been involved in developing five format options that allow the movement of funds electronically, each with varying amounts of data.

Name-your-price auction An online auction in which participants post the prices they are willing to pay for certain goods or services and sellers are given the opportunity to meet the terms; also called a *reverse auction*.

Narrow band A small-capacity communications channel.

National Crime Information Center (NCIC) The major criminal database maintained by the FBI. This database contains information on stolen vehicles, securities, boats, missing persons, and other information helpful in fraud investigations.

National-culture scheme Proposes that HSRs are affected by national cultural dimensions.

National security The ability of a nation to protect its internal values from external threats.

National sovereignty The supreme right of nations to determine national policies; freedom from external control.

Nationalization Occurs when a government takes over private property—reasonable compensation is usually paid by the government.

Native application A computer program originally written for the specific type of computer that is running it. As opposed to a native application, a cross-system application is one that was originally written for one type of machine, but then adapted for a newer computer. Usually, a cross-system application exhibits slow or poor performance.

Natural business year A year that ends when a business's activities have reached the lowest point in its annual operating cycle.

Natural hedging The structuring of a firm's operations so that cash flows by currency, inflows against outflows, are matched.

Natural Language Processors (NLPs) Programs that are designed to take human language input and translate it into a standard set of statements that a computer can execute.

Natural team Work group having responsibility for a particular process.

NDE Nondestructive evaluation. *See:* nondestructive testing and evaluation.

Nearby contract The futures contract with a maturity date that occurs nearest to, but after, the date of the cash market transaction that is to be hedged.

Need to achieve A human quality linked to entrepreneurship in which people are motivated to excel and pick situations in which success is likely.

Needs Unsatisfactory conditions of the consumer that prompt him or her to an action that will make the condition better.

Negative exposure A condition that exists when a foreign subsidiary has more current liabilities than current assets.

Negotiable bill of lading Contract that grants title of merchandise to the holder, which allows banks to use the merchandise as collateral.

Negotiable certificate of deposit Bank deposits that come in $100,000 and larger denominations. Negotiability means the security can be legally sold and exchanged between investors, circumventing the early withdrawal penalty charged by the issuing bank. Only the first $100,000 is insured by the Federal Deposit Insurance Corporation, however.

Negotiated price approach An approach to transfer pricing that allows managers of decentralized units to agree (negotiate) among themselves as to the transfer price.

Negotiated transfer pricing A system that requires managers of selling and buying divisions to negotiate a mutually acceptable transfer price.

Negotiation A process of formal communication, either face to face or electronic, where two or more people come together to seek mutual agreement about an issue or issues.

Nemawashi A Japanese term borrowed from gardening. In business terms, it means many private or semiprivate meetings in which true opinions are shared before a major decision-making meeting takes place.

Nepotism 1: Practice of allowing relatives to work for the same employer. **2:** Relatives of those in power tend to easily obtain business licenses, lucrative government contracts, real estate deals, and so on.

Net change MRP An approach in which the material requirements plan is continually retained in the computer. Whenever a change is needed in requirements, open order inventory status, or bill of material, a partial explosion and netting is made for only those parts affected by the change. *See:* requirements alteration. *Ant:* regeneration MRP.

Net errors and omissions account Makes sure the balance of payments (BOP) actually balances.

Net float The difference between disbursement float and collections float; the difference between the balance shown in the checkbook and the balance shown on the bank's books.

Net income An overall measure of the performance of a company; equal to revenues minus expenses for the period.

Net liquid balance Cash and marketable securities less notes payable and current maturities of long-term debt.

Net loss The amount by which expenses exceed revenues.

Net operating loss carrybacks Practice of applying losses to offset earnings in previous years.

Net operating loss carryforwards Practice of applying losses to offset earnings in future years.

Net pay Gross pay less payroll deductions; the amount the employer is obligated to pay the employee.

Net present value (NPV) 1: A measure of the present dollar equivalent of all cash inflows and outflows flowing from a capital investment proposal. To compute net present value each cash inflow and outflow must be converted to its dollar value at a standard point in time. Calculation of NPV involves discounting all cash flows to the beginning of the cash flow timeline, then subtracting the present value of the outflows from the present value of the inflows. **2:** The sum of the present values of all cash inflows and outflows from an investment project discounted at the cost of capital.

Net present value (NPV) method A method of evaluating capital investment proposals by finding the present value of future net cash flows, discounted at the rate of return required by the firm.

Net present value (NPV) profile A curve showing the relationship between a project's NPV and various discount rates (required rates of return).

Net profit margin on sales This ratio measures net income per dollar of sales; it is calculated by dividing net income by sales.

Net realizable value The valuation of an asset at an amount equal to the estimated selling price less any direct cost of disposal.

Net requirements In MRP, the net requirements for a part or an assembly are derived as a result of applying gross requirements and allocations against inventory on hand, scheduled receipts, and safety stock. Net requirements, lot-sized and offset for lead time, become planned orders.

Net transaction exposure Consideration of inflows and outflows in a given currency to determine the exposure after offsetting inflows against outflows.

Net working capital Current assets minus current liabilities—the amount of current assets financed by long-term liabilities.

Net worth method Analytical method that estimates a suspect's unexplained income. Liabilities are subtracted from assets to give net worth, then the previous year's net worth is subtracted to find the increase in net worth. Living expenses are then added to the change in net worth to determine a person's total income, and finally known income is subtracted from total income to determine the unknown income.

Netting 1: Combining of future cash receipts and payments to determine the net amount to be owed by one subsidiary to another. **2:** Cash flow coordination between a corporation's global units so that only one smaller cash transfer must be made.

Network 1: A combination of a communications device and a computer, or several computers, or two or more computers and terminals, so that the various devices can send and receive text or audiovisual information. **2:** A system in which everyone is linked and interconnected and where there is a free exchange of ideas and data.

Network diagram A graphic display of the activities to be performed to achieve the overall project work scope, showing their sequence and interdependencies.

Network model A type of database that has the ability to store a record only once in the entire database, while creating links that establish relationships with several records of another type of entity.

Network protocol The set of rules that governs a network of communications devices.

Network structure An organization structure that disaggregates major functions to separate companies that are brokered by a small headquarters organization.

Networks Similar to the contractual alliance arrangement, a corporation subcontracts its manufacturing functions to other companies.

Neural net An artificial intelligence computer program that emulates the way in which the human brain operates, especially its ability to learn.

Neutralizer A situational variable that counteracts a leadership style and prevents the leader from displaying certain behaviors.

New economy High productivity and low inflation.

Newsgroup A group of people who share questions, opinions, and information about a specific subject at a specific site.

New-task buying situation Purchase situation that results in an extensive search for information and a lengthy decision process.

New-venture fund A fund providing resources from which individuals and groups can draw to develop new ideas, products, or businesses.

New-venture team A unit separate from the mainstream of the organization that is responsible for developing and initiating innovations.

Next operation as customer Concept that the organization is comprised of service/product providers and service/product receivers or "internal customers."

Niche marketing Process of targeting a relatively small market segment with a specific, specialized marketing mix.

Node An intersection or junction point of an influence diagram or a decision tree.

Nolo contendere Plea by a defendant that does not contest the charges but does not admit guilt.

Nominal group technique Technique similar to brainstorming, used by teams to generate ideas on a particular subject. Team members are asked to silently come up with as many ideas as possible, writing them down. Each member is then asked to share one idea, which is recorded. After all the ideas are recorded, they are discussed and prioritized by the group.

Nominal interest rate The stated interest rate for an investment or borrowing opportunity, ignoring the effect of the frequency of compounding. In order to compare various investments, the nominal rate is usually converted to an effective annual rate.

Nominal (quoted) risk-free rate, k_{RF} The rate of interest on a security that is free of all risk; k_{RF} is proxied by the T-bill rate or the T-bond rate. k_{RF} includes an inflation premium.

Nominating committee Has the responsibility of ensuring that competent, objective board members are selected; usually composed of outside directors.

Nonbank banks Make loans or accept deposits, but not both.

Noncallable A feature of a security which stipulates that the investor need not worry about a forced buyback of the security if interest rates fall subsequent to issuance. The absence of a call feature allows the issuer to pay a slightly lower interest rate due to the lower risk to the investor.

Noncompetitive bid Bids that are entered directly through a tender offer to the nearest Federal Reserve district bank, or through a broker or commercial bank. Investors willing to accept the average yield of all accepted competitive bids enter a noncompetitive bid.

Nonconformity Nonfulfillment of a specified requirement. *See:* blemish, defect, and imperfection.

Nonconstant growth The part of the life cycle of a firm in which growth either is much faster or much slower than that of the economy as a whole.

Noncontributory plan Pension plan in which all the funds for pension benefits are provided by the employer.

Noncontrollable costs Costs that cannot be influenced (increased, decreased, or eliminated) by someone such as a manager or factory worker.

Nondeliverable Forward Contracts (NDFs) Like a forward contract, represents an agreement regarding a position in a specified currency, a specified exchange rate, and a specified future settlement date, but does not result in delivery of currencies. Instead, a payment is made by one party in the agreement to the other party based on the exchange rate at the future date.

Nondestructive testing and evaluation (NDT) Testing and evaluation methods that do not damage or destroy the product being tested.

Nondirective interview Interview that uses questions that are developed from the answers to previous questions.

Nonexempt employees Employees who must be paid overtime under the Fair Labor Standards Act.

Nonfinancial incentives Nonmonetary offers intended to motivate; special offers designed to attract foreign direct investors that may take the form of guaranteed government purchases, special protection from competition, or improved infrastructure facilities.

Nonfinancial measure A performance measure that has not been stated in dollar terms.

Nonimpact printer A printer that creates an image on a page without pressing any mechanism against the paper; includes laser, ink-jet, electrostatic, and electrothermal printers.

Nonmonetary item An item that does not represent a claim to, or for, a specified number of monetary units.

Nonparticipating preferred stock Preferred stock with a limited dividend preference.

Nonparticipator role A role in which the individual contributes little to either the task or members' socioemotional needs.

Nonprogrammed decision A decision made in response to a situation that is unique, is poorly defined and largely unstructured, and has important consequences for the organization.

Nonprogrammed decision making Entails analyzing current data and information, which was obtained through a systematic investigation of the current environment, for the purpose of identifying and solving a problem.

Nonrecourse or without recourse When a factor buys receivables and the selling firm is not ultimately responsible for final payment.

Nonresponse or participation bias Created by underrepresentation and overrepresentation in a sample of different groups. For example, most studies have an overrepresentation of consumers who are interested in the product and a nonresponse underrepresentation of consumers not interested in the product.

Nonroutine reports Reports prepared for the purpose of providing information to managers to assist them in formulating policies, preparing strategic plans, and preparing tactical (operational) plans.

Nonsampling risk Risk that a sample will be examined and the characteristics of the sample will be misinterpreted.

Nonsterilized Intervention Intervention in the foreign exchange market without adjusting for the change in money supply.

Nontariff barriers Include quotas, bans, safety standards, and subsidies. Sometimes employed by governments to restrict trade or reduce competition. Nontariff barriers occur when governments impose restrictive and costly administrative and legal requirements on imports.

Nonvalue-added Tasks or activities that can be eliminated with no deterioration in product or service functionality, performance, or quality in the eyes of the customer.

Nonvalue-added activities The cost of activities that are perceived as unnecessary from the customer's perspective and are thus candidates for elimination.

Nonvalue-added lead time The time that units wait in inventories, move unnecessarily, and wait during machine breakdowns.

Nonverbal communication A communication transmitted through actions and behaviors rather than through words.

Nonvolatile memory Storage media that keep data and programs unchanged because they do not need electric power to maintain the stored material. Examples: ROM chips and magnetic disks.

Norm A standard of conduct that is shared by team members and guides their behavior.

Normal cost The estimated cost of completing an activity under normal conditions, according to the plan.

Normal (constant) growth Growth that is expected to continue into the foreseeable future at about the same rate as that of the economy as a whole; g is a constant.

Normal distribution Bell-shaped distribution for continuous data where most of the data are concentrated around the average, and it is equally likely that an observation will occur above or below the average.

Normal probability distribution A bell-shaped distribution of values that is symmetrical around its mean value.

Normal profits/rates of return Those profits and rates of return that are close to the average for all firms and are just sufficient to attract capital.

Normal time The estimated length of time required to perform an activity under normal conditions, according to the plan.

Normal yield curve Upward-sloping graph of yields to maturity for securities with various maturities, with longer-term maturities yielding more than shorter-term maturities.

Normative An approach that defines how a decision maker should make decisions and provides guidelines for reaching an ideal outcome for the organization.

Normative ethics Concerned with supplying and justifying a coherent moral system of thinking and judging.

Normative integration The headquarters-foreign subsidiary control relationship relies neither on direct headquarters involvement nor on impersonal rules but on the socialization of managers into a set of shared goals, values, and beliefs that then shape their perspectives and behavior.

Norming The stage of team development in which conflicts developed during the storming stage are resolved and team harmony and unity emerge.

Norms Behavioral expectations, mutually agreed-upon rules of conduct, protocols to be followed, social practice.

North American Free Trade Agreement (NAFTA) A trade agreement among Canada, Mexico, and the United States with the objective of creating a single market with no trade barriers.

Notebook computer A computer as small as a book, yet with computing power similar to that of a desktop microcomputer.

Notes receivable A written promise to pay by the maker, representing an amount to be received by the payee.

Not-invented-here syndrome A defensive, territorial attitude that, if held by managers, can frustrate effective implementation of global strategies.

Notional amount The agreed upon face amount of the swap contract which exchange rates or interest rates are to be applied to calculate the cash flows which are to be swapped.

NPV (net present value) Discounted cash flow technique for finding the present value of each future year's cash flow.

Number of affected units chart (np chart) Control chart for evaluating the stability of a process in terms of the total number of units in a sample in which frequency of an event of a given classification occurs.

Number of days in receivables 365 (number of days in a year) divided by accounts receivable turnover; a measure of how long it takes to collect receivables.

Number of days of payables outstanding (DPO) A payables activity measure found by dividing the payables balance by average daily purchases (alternatively, average daily cost of goods sold can be used in the denominator).

Number of days' sales in inventory A measure of the length of time it takes to acquire, sell, and replace the inventory.

Number of days' sales in receivables An estimate of the length of time the accounts receivable have been outstanding.

Number of times the interest charges are earned A ratio that measures the risk that interest payments to debtholders will continue to be made if earnings decrease.

O

Object code Program code in machine language, immediately processable by the computer.

Object linking and embedding (OLE) The linking of different applications to the same software so that it can be addressed and used by any of these applications. The object may be text, graphic, or audiovisual material.

Object-oriented programming (OOP) A programming method that combines data and the procedures that process the data into a single unit called an "object," which can be invoked from different programs.

Objective 1: The expected result or product of a project, usually defined in terms of scope, schedule, and cost. **2:** Quantitative statement of future expectations and an indication of when the expectations should be achieved; it flows from goals and clarifies what people must accomplish.

Objective evidence Verifiable qualitative or quantitative observations, information, records, or statements of fact pertaining to the quality of an item or service or to the existence and implementation of a quality system element.

Objective function A mathematical expression that describes the problem's objective.

Objective risk The probable variation of actual from expected experience.

Objectivity concept Requires that the accounting records and reports be based upon objective evidence.

Observation 1: Item of objective evidence found during an audit. **2:** A research tool where the subjects' activity and behavior are observed.

Obsolescence costs Costs to a firm associated with holding inventory that is not selling due to a loss in demand for the product.

OC (operating characteristic) curve For a sampling plan, the OC curve indicates the probability of accepting a lot based on the sample size to be taken and the fraction defective in the batch.

Ocean bill of lading Receipt for a shipment by boat, which includes freight charges and title to the merchandise.

Ocean shipping The forwarding of freight by ocean carrier.

Off-balance-sheet financing Financing in which the assets and liabilities involved do not appear on the firm's balance sheet.

Off-invoice allowance Deals offered periodically to the trade that allow wholesalers and retailers to simply deduct a fixed amount, say 15 percent, from the full price at the time the order is placed.

Off-the-job training Training that takes place away from the actual work site.

Off-target The output of a process deviates from the established target.

Offering price The price at which common stock is sold to the public.

Office automation systems Systems that combine modern hardware and software to handle the tasks of publishing and distributing information.

Official reserves account An account in the BOP statement that shows 1) the change in the amount of funds immediately available to a country for making international payments and 2) the borrowing and lending that has taken place between the monetary authorities of different countries either directly or through the International Monetary Fund.

Offshore banking The use of banks or bank branches located in low-tax countries, often Caribbean islands, to raise and hold capital for multinational operations.

OLAP (online analytical processing) A type of application that operates on data stored in databases and data warehouses to produce summary tables with multiple combinations of dimensions. An OLAP server is connected to the database or data warehouse server at one end, and to the user's computer at the other.

Omitted variables Independent variables which should have been included in a regression model, and that could have helped the analyst predict the variable of interest. If important, omission may give rise to a violation of ordinary least squares assumption, a condition known as serial correlation.

Omnibus surveys Survey research service offered by a number of large marketing research companies where several companies' research studies and sets of questions are included in a single questionnaire sent to representative panels of households.

One-stop logistics Allows shippers to buy all the transportation modes and functional services from a single carrier.

One-to-one marketing Concept of knowing customers' unique requirements and expectations and marketing to these. *See:* customer relationship management.

One-transaction approach An approach used to translate foreign currency where the transaction is not considered to be completed until the final settlement. Any transaction gain or loss will be reflected on the settlement date in an adjustment to the value of the resource acquired.

Ongoing validation Involves continually checking a model's forecast accuracy by monitoring each period's forecast error and comparing it to past forecast errors.

On-the-job training (OJT) A type of training in which an experienced employee "adopts" a new employee to teach him or her how to perform job duties.

On-us When the payee deposits the check in the bank on which it is drawn.

Online processing Using a computer while in current interaction with the CPU, so that the data are processed as they are entered, as opposed to batch processing.

Open account (or open book account) Once approved for credit, a customer can make repeated purchases as long as the total amount owed at any one time is less than some predetermined ceiling.

Open account transaction Sale in which the exporter ships the merchandise and expects the buyer to remit payment according to agreed-upon terms.

Open-book management Approach to managing that exposes employees to the organization's financial information, provides instruction in business literacy, and enables employees to better understand their role and contribution and its impact on the organization.

Open communication Sharing all types of information throughout the company, across functional and hierarchical levels.

Open criticism A style of Chinese management in which the practice of public scolding (*ma ren*) is used frequently. Represents the Chinese view that the practice of quiet, subtle criticism is sneaky and therefore all communication, including criticism, should take place in the open.

Open-ended questions Allow respondents to determine the direction of the answer without being led by the question. They also prevent "yes" or "no" answers.

Open regionalism The use of declarations instead of treaties to combine an informal regional trading strategy with a commitment to global openness.

Open source software Software whose source code can be accessed by the general public.

Open system A system that interfaces and interacts with other systems.

Open Systems Interconnection (OSI) The dominant standard that works as a general model for wide area network protocols.

Operating activities Those cash flows that are not classified as either investing or financing activities. Generally operating cash flows are related to cash collected from sales and cash disbursed to supplies, workers, management, and taxes.

Operating break-even analysis An analytical technique for studying the relationship between sales revenues, operating costs, and profits.

Operating break-even point Represents the level of production and sales at which operating income is zero; it is the point at which revenues from sales just equal total operating costs.

Operating cash flows Those cash flows that arise from normal operations; the difference between cash collections and cash expenses.

Operating characteristic curve *See:* OC curve.

Operating cycle The process of funds flowing from inventory to receivables to payables.

Operating expenses Costs a retailer incurs in running a business, other than the cost of merchandise.

Operating lease A lease where the lessor retains most of the risks and rewards of ownership; commonly referred to as rentals. Leases that do not meet the criteria for capital leases and thus are accounted for as operating expenses. Also called a *service lease*.

Operating leverage 1: A measure of the relative mix of a business's variable costs and fixed costs, computed as contribution margin divided by operating income. **2:** The existence of fixed operating costs, such that a change in sales will produce a larger change in operating income (EBIT).

Operating motive Theoretical motive for trade credit extension in which the seller responds to variable and uncertain demand by altering its trade credit availability.

Operating performance ratio Net income divided by total sales; a measure of the percentage of revenues that become profits.

Operating or service lease A lease that transfers most but not all benefits and costs inherent in the ownership of the property to the lessee. Payments do not fully cover the cost of purchasing the asset or incurring the liability.

Operating risk The danger of interference by governments or other groups in one's corporate operations abroad.

Operating system System software that supports the running of applications developed to utilize its features and controls peripheral equipment.

Operation start date The date when an operation should be started so that its order due date can be met. It can be calculated based on scheduled quantities and lead times or on the work remaining and the time remaining to complete the job.

Operational feasibility study An evaluation made to determine whether a new information system will be used as intended.

Operational goals Specific, measurable results expected from departments, work groups, and individuals within the organization.

Operational managers Individuals who are in charge of small groups of workers.

Operational plans Plans developed at the organization's lower levels that specify action steps toward achieving operational goals and that support tactical planning activities.

Operational restructuring When a company changes its product lines or use of assets with heavy fixed operating costs and alters the company's business risk.

Operations 1: The collection of people, technology, and systems within a company that has primary responsibility for providing the organization's products or services. **2:** Used with "objectives" or "controls" and having to do with the effectiveness and efficiency of an entity's operations, including performance and profitability goals, and safeguarding resources.

Operations information system A computer-based information system that supports a company's day-to-day operations.

Operations management The design, implementation, and improvement of a firm's operations. All organizations have an operations function. But not all organizations manage their operations. A firm must constantly ask itself, "How can we use our operations to create the greatest value for our customers and to meet our business strategy?"

Operations scheduling The actual assignment of starting or completion dates to operations or groups of operations to show when these operations must be done if the manufacturing order is to be completed on time. These dates are used in the dispatching function. *Syn:* detailed scheduling, order scheduling, shop scheduling.

Operations sequence The sequential steps for an item to follow in its flow through the plant. For instance, operation 1: cut bar stock; operation 2: grind bar stock; operation 3: shape; operation 4: polish; operation 5: inspect and send to stock. This information is normally maintained in the routing file.

Operations sequencing A technique for short-term planning of actual jobs to be run in each work center based upon capacity (that is, existing workforce and machine availability) and priorities. The result is a set of projected completion times for the operations and simulated queue levels for facilities.

Operations strategy The recognition of the importance of operations to the firm's success and the involvement of operations managers in the organization's strategic planning.

Opportunity 1: A situation in which managers see potential organizational accomplishments that exceed current goals. **2:** A potential increase in revenue, reduction of costs, or gain in competitive advantage that can be achieved using an information system.

Opportunity cost 1: The return on the best alternative use of an asset; the highest return that will not be earned if funds are invested in a particular project. **2:** Cost incurred by a firm as the result of foreclosure of other sources of profit; for example, for the licenser in a licensing agreement, the cost of forgoing alternatives such as exports or direct investment.

Opportunity cost rate The rate of return on the best available alternative investment of equal risk.

Opportunity costs per unit The contribution margin per unit sacrificed by the selling segment due to the internal transfer of one unit of the good or service, rather than selling it in the external market.

Opportunity loss, or regret The amount of loss (lower profit or higher cost) from not making the best decision for each state of nature.

Optical character recognition (OCR) A way of capturing data from source documents, in which scanning devices read characters and transform them into digital data processable by the computer.

Optical disc A disc on which data are recorded by treating the disc surface so it reflects light in different ways; also called a *compact disc* (CD).

Optical fiber A thin fiberglass filament used as a medium for transmitting bursts of light that represent bits. The most advanced physical communications channel, now in use for data, voice, and image telecommunication.

Optical tape A storage device that uses the same principles as a compact disc.

Optimal dividend policy The dividend policy that strikes a balance between current dividends and future growth and maximizes the firm's stock price.

Optimal solution The specific decision variable value or values that provide the "best" output for the model.

Optimistic approach An approach to choosing a decision alternative without using probabilities. For a maximization problem, it leads to choosing the decision alternative corresponding to the largest payoff; for a minimization problem, it leads to choosing the decision alternative corresponding to the smallest payoff.

Optimistic time estimate (t^o) The time in which an activity can be completed if everything goes perfectly well and there are no complications.

Optimization Achieving planned process results that meet the needs of the customer and supplier alike and minimize their combined costs.

Opting-out right Right of customers to give written notice to financial institutions that prohibits the institution from sharing or selling customer's personal information.

Option A contract that gives the option holder the right to buy or sell an asset at some predetermined price within a specified period of time.

Option overplanning Typically, scheduling extra quantities of a master schedule option greater than the expected sales for that option to protect against unanticipated demand. This schedule quantity may only be planned in the period where new customer orders are currently being accepted, typically just after the demand time fence. This technique is usually used on the second level of a two-level master scheduling approach to create a situation where more of the individual options are available than of the overall family. The historical average of demand for an item is quantified in a planning bill of material. Option overplanning is accomplished by increasing this percentage to allow for demands greater than forecast. *See:* demand time fence, hedge, planning bills of material.

Order control Control of manufacturing activities by individual manufacturing, job, or shop orders, released by planning personnel and authorizing production personnel to complete a given batch or lot size of a particular manufactured item. Information needed to complete the order (components required, work centers and operations required, tooling required, and so on.) may be printed on paper or tickets, often called shop orders or work orders, which are distributed to production personnel. This use of order control sometimes implies an environment where all the components for a given order are picked and issued from a stocking location, all at one time, and then moved as a kit to manufacturing before any activity begins. It is most frequently seen in job shop manufacturing.

Order cycle time The total time that passes between the placement of an order and the receipt of the merchandise.

Order getter Salesperson who seeks to actively provide information to prospects, persuade prospective customers, and close sales.

Order handling Disposition of orders that are within credit limits and handling of orders which violate limits.

Order losers Capabilities of an organization in which poor performance can cause loss of business. Failure to meet customer expectations with delivery of the product is an order loser. *See:* order qualifiers, order winners.

Order management The planning, directing, monitoring, and controlling of the processes related to customer orders, manufacturing orders, and purchase orders. Regarding customer orders, order management includes order promising, order entry, order pick, pack and ship, billing, and reconciliation of the customer account. Regarding manufacturing orders, order management includes order release, routing manufacture, monitoring, and receipt into stores or finished goods inventories. Regarding purchasing orders, order management includes order placement, monitoring, receiving, acceptance, and payment of supplier.

Order point A set inventory level where, if the total stock on hand plus on order falls to or below that point, action is taken to replenish the stock. The order point is normally calculated as forecasted usage during the replenishment lead time plus safety stock. *Syn:* reorder point, statistical order point, trigger level. *See:* fixed reorder quantity inventory model.

Order point system The inventory method that places an order for a lot whenever the quantity on hand is reduced to a predetermined level known as the order point. *Syn:* statistical order point system. *See:* fixed reorder quantity inventory model, hybrid system.

Order promising The process of making a delivery commitment, that is, answering the question, When can you ship? For make-to-order products, this usually involves a check of uncommitted material and availability of capacity, often as represented by the master schedule available-to-promise. *Syn:* customer order promising, order dating. *See:* available-to-promise, order service.

Order qualifiers Those competitive characteristics that a firm must exhibit to be a viable competitor in the marketplace. For example, a firm may seek to compete on characteristics other than price, but in order to "qualify" to compete, its costs and the related price must be within a certain range to be considered by its customers. *Syn:* qualifiers. *See:* order losers, order winners.

Order taker Salesperson who only processes the purchase that the customer has already selected.

Order winners Those competitive characteristics that cause a firm's customers to choose that firm's goods and services over those of its competitors. Order winners can be considered to be competitive advantages for the firm. Order winners usually focus on one (rarely more than two) of the following strategic initiatives: price/cost, quality, delivery speed, delivery reliability, product design, flexibility, aftermarket service, and image. *See:* order losers, order qualifiers.

Ordering costs Costs associated with the inventory ordering process.

Ordinary (deferred) annuity An annuity whose payments occur at the end of each period.

Organic organization Allows employees considerable discretion in defining their roles and the organization's objectives. Historically, small organizations have tended to adopt the organic form.

Organization A social entity that is goal directed and deliberately structured.

Organization-centered career planning Career planning that focuses on jobs and on identifying career paths that provide for the logical progression of people between jobs in an organization.

Organization chart The visual representation of an organization's structure.

Organization development (OD) Organization-wide (usually) planned effort, managed from the top, to increase organization effectiveness and health through interventions in the organization's processes, using behavioral science knowledge.

Organization for Economic Cooperation and Development (OECD) An organization that promotes worldwide economic development in general, and economic growth and stability of its member countries in particular. Its work focuses primarily on providing financial accounting and reporting guidelines to multinational corporations for disclosures to host countries.

Organization structure The framework in which the organization defines how tasks are divided, resources are deployed, and departments are coordinated.

Organizational behavior An interdisciplinary field dedicated to the study of how individuals and groups tend to act in organizations.

Organizational change The adoption of a new idea or behavior by an organization.

Organizational citizenship Work behavior that goes beyond job requirements and contributes as needed to the organization's success.

Organizational commitment 1: Loyalty to and heavy involvement in one's organization. **2:** The degree to which employees believe in and accept organizational goals and desire to remain with the organization.

Organizational control The systematic process through which managers regulate organizational activities to make them consistent with expectations established in plans, targets, and standards of performance.

Organizational culture 1: The pattern of basic assumptions that a given group has invented, discovered, or developed in learning to cope with its problems of external adaptation and internal integration; having worked well enough to be considered valid, the pattern may therefore be taught to new members as the correct way to perceive, think, and feel in relation to those problems. **2:** An umbrella term referring to the general tone of a corporate environment.

Organizational development (OD) The application of behavioral science techniques to improve an organization's health and effectiveness through its ability to cope with environmental changes, improve internal relationships, and increase problem-solving capabilities.

Organizational socialization Process by which an individual adapts to and comes to appreciate the values, norms, and required behavior patterns of an organization.

Organized security exchange A formal organization, having a tangible physical location, that facilitates trading in designated ("listed") securities. The two major national security exchanges in the United States are the New York Stock Exchange (NYSE) and the American Stock Exchange (AMEX).

Organizing The management function concerned with assigning tasks, grouping tasks into departments, and allocating resources to departments; the deployment of organizational resources to achieve strategic goals.

Orientation The planned introduction of new employees to their jobs, co-workers, and the organization.

Orientation program A program that familiarizes new workers with their roles; the preparation of employees for assignment overseas.

Original maturity Length of time until principal is repaid, measured at the time the security is first sold.

Originating ACH The automated clearing house contacted by the bank initiating the transaction. The originating ACH must then transmit the payment order to the receiving institution's ACH (termed the receiving ACH).

Originating depository financial institution (ODFI) Bank that is contacted by the payment initiator.

Other expense An expense that cannot be traced directly to operations.

Other income Revenue from sources other than the primary operating activity of a business.

Out-of-control process Process in which the statistical measure being evaluated is not in a state of statistical control (that is, the variations among the observed sampling results cannot all be attributed to a constant system of chance causes); special or assignable causes exist. See: in-control process.

Out-of-the-money option When it is *not* beneficial financially for the option holder to exercise the option—a loss would be incurred if the option is exercised.

Out of pocket expenses Financing expenses that include interest and bank commitment fees.

Out-of-sample validation Using a new data set to assess a forecasting model's forecast accuracy.

Out of spec Term used to indicate that a unit does not meet a given specification.

Outflow A payment, or disbursement, of cash for expenses, investments, and so on.

Outpartnering The process of involving the supplier in a close partnership with the firm and its operations management system. Outpartnering is characterized by close working relationships between buyers and suppliers, high levels of trust, mutual respect, and emphasis on joint problem solving and cooperation. With outpartnering, the supplier is viewed not as an alternative source of goods and services (as observed under outsourcing) but rather as a source of knowledge, expertise, and complementary core competencies. Outpartnering is typically found during the early stages of the product life cycle when dealing with products that are viewed as critical to the strategic survival of the firm. See: customer-supplier partner, supplier partner.

Output The result of processing data by the computer; usually, information.

Output device A device, usually a monitor or printer, that delivers information from a computer to a person.

Output price measurement The current value of an item equals its net realizable value.

Outside directors Persons who are independent of the firm and its top managers.

Outsourcing 1: Using another firm for the manufacture of needed components or products or delivery of a service. **2:** Buying the services of an information service firm that undertakes some or all of the organization's IS operations. **3:** Strategy to relieve an organization of processes and tasks in order to reduce costs, improve quality, reduce cycle time (for example, by parallel processing), reduce the need for specialized skills, and increase efficiency.

Outstanding stock The stock that is in the hands of stockholders.

Overapplied factory overhead The amount of factory overhead applied in excess of the actual factory overhead costs incurred for production during a period.

Overcentralization Expatriates are unable to establish and maintain an effective relationship with local associates because their authority is constrained by headquarters management overcentralizing decision making.

Overdraft credit lines Whether uncommitted or committed, have the added feature of being automatically drawn down whenever the company writes a check for which it does not have the sufficient funds to cover when it clears. Used extensively in foreign countries.

Overdraft facility A banking service that allows a firm to overdraw its account. The overdraft is then charged interest as if it were a loan.

Overhead A percentage of the direct costs of a particular project, added to a contractor's proposal to cover costs of doing business, such as insurance, depreciation, general management, and human resources; indirect costs.

Overhead cost A general expense carried by all departments that is considered essential to running a company.

Overhedging Hedging an amount in a currency larger than the actual transaction amount.

Over-the-counter (OTC) market A large collection of brokers and dealers, connected electronically by telephones and computers, that provides for trading in securities not listed on the organized exchanges.

Owner's equity The owner's right to the assets of the business after the total liabilities are deducted.

Ownership risk The risk inherent in maintaining ownership of property abroad. The exposure of foreign owned assets to governmental intervention.

P

P chart Fraction defective chart. Also called a *proportion chart*.

Pacifier-oriented leader The type of leader needed in an organization that has achieved a certain level of stability and in which daily operations are running smoothly.

Packaged software General purpose applications that come ready to install from a magnetic disk, CD, or file downloaded from a vendor's Web site.

Packet Several bytes that make up a part of a telecommunicated message.

Packet switching A telecommunications method whereby messages are broken into groups of fixed amounts of bytes, and each group (packet) is transmitted through the shortest route available. The packets are assembled at the destination into the original message.

Paid-only reconciliation Bank-provided demand deposit report which indicates all paid checks by check number, with check number, dollar amount, and date paid.

Paid time-off plan Plan that combines all sick leave, vacation time, and holidays into a total number of hours or days that employees can take off with pay.

Palm computer A computer that is small enough to be held in a person's palm; also called a *hand-held computer* or *personal digital assistant* (PDA).

Panel interview Interview in which several interviewers interview the candidate at the same time.

Panels Groups of customers recruited by an organization to provide ad hoc feedback on performance or product development ideas.

Panels of households Groups of households (for example, 5,000) recruited by market research firms and rewarded for participating in market research surveys. The firm creates a panel by carefully selecting the composition of the group so that it is representative of the general population in terms of demographics such as geographical location, income, education, and age of the heads of households.

Par The monetary amount printed on a stock certificate.

Par value The nominal or face value of a stock or bond.

Parallel bonds Bonds placed in different countries and denominated in the respective currencies of the countries where they are placed.

Parallel conversion Using an old information system along with a new system for a predetermined period of time before relying only on the new one.

Parallel loan Loan involving an exchange of currencies between two parties, with a promise to reexchange the currencies at a specified exchange rate and future date.

Parallel processing The capacity for several CPUs in one computer to process different data at the same time.

Parallel structure Describes an organizational module in which groups, such as quality circles or a quality council, exist in the organization in addition to and simultaneously with the line organization (also referred to as collateral structure).

Parallel transmission Transmission of more than one bit at a time; usually the transmission of one byte at a time via parallel channels. Such transmission can take place only inside the computer or between the computer and its physically close peripheral equipment, such as a printer.

Parameter design (Taguchi) Use of design of experiments for identifying the major contributors to variation.

Parameters 1: The categories that are considered when following a sequence of steps in problem solving. **2:** Numerical values that appear in the mathematical relationships of a model. Parameters are considered known and remain constant over all trials of a simulation.

Parent 1: The company acquiring the stock of a subsidiary. **2:** In a hierarchical database, the data record to which several records of a lower level are linked.

Parent company The company owning a majority of the voting stock of another corporation.

Parent/subsidiary relationship A combination of companies where control of other companies, known as subsidiaries, is achieved by a company, known as the parent, through acquisition of voting stock.

Pareto chart Basic tool used to graphically rank causes from most significant to least significant. It utilizes a vertical bar graph in which the bar height reflects the frequency or impact of causes.

Parity check A method to reduce errors in data communication both inside the computer and among remote communications devices. An extra bit is added to each transmitted byte to ascertain that the number of 1s is odd (in an odd parity check) or even (if an even parity check).

Partial compensation An arrangement in which the delivery of goods to one party is partially compensated for by buying back a certain amount of product from the same party.

Partial productivity The ratio of total outputs to the inputs from a single major input category.

Partial reinforcement schedule A schedule in which only some occurrences of the desired behavior are reinforced.

Participation Involving employees in the decision-making process.

Participative decision making Refers to making decisions after consulting others. This style of decision making is perceived negatively in many cultures and causes the decision maker to lose credibility in the eyes of subordinates.

Participative design/engineering A concept that refers to the participation of all the functional areas of the firm in the product design activity. Suppliers and customers are often also included. The intent is to enhance the design with the inputs of all the key stakeholders. Such a process should ensure that the final design meets all the needs of the stakeholders and should ensure a product that can be quickly brought to the marketplace while maximizing quality and minimizing costs. *Syn:* co-design, concurrent design, concurrent engineering, neural network, parallel engineering, simultaneous design/engineering, simultaneous engineering, team design/engineering. *See:* early manufacturing involvement.

Participative management Management style that expects everyone in the organization to take ownership and responsibility for their conduct and responsibilities and that allows input into decisions.

Participatory design approach The design of the information system where all users must be actively involved.

Partnership An unincorporated business owned by two or more individuals.

Partnership/alliance Strategy leading to a relationship with suppliers or customers aimed at reducing costs of ownership, maintenance of minimum stocks, just-in-time deliveries, joint participation in design, exchange of information on materials and technologies, new production methods, quality improvement strategies, and the exploitation of market synergy.

Passive investment strategy Involves a minimal amount of oversight and very few transactions once the portfolio has been selected.

Passwords Secret codes or names that allow users to access networks and other computer systems.

Patent Cooperations Treaty (PCT) An agreement that outlines procedures for filing one international patent application rather than individual national applications.

Patents Exclusive rights to produce and sell goods with one or more unique features.

Path-goal theory A contingency approach to leadership specifying that the leader's responsibility is to increase subordinates' motivation by clarifying the behaviors necessary for task accomplishment and rewards.

Pax Americana An American peace between 1945 through 1990 that led to increased international business transactions.

Pay compression Situation in which pay differences among individuals with different levels of experience and performance in the organization becomes small.

Pay equity Similarity in pay for all jobs requiring comparable levels of knowledge, skill, and ability, even if actual duties and market rates differ significantly.

Pay-for-performance Incentive pay that ties at least part of compensation to employee effort and performance.

Pay grade A grouping of individual jobs having approximately the same job worth.

Pay survey A collection of data on compensation rates for workers performing similar jobs in other organizations.

Payable through draft (PTD) Gives the payor twenty-four hours to decide whether to honor or refuse payment after it has been presented to the payor's bank. They are used for claim reimbursement by insurance companies, which use the twenty-four hour period to verify the signature and endorsements.

Payables turnover ratio Found by dividing purchases over a given time period by the year-end or average payables balance. Indicates the firm's payment behavior.

Payback period Number of years it will take the results of a project or capital investment to recover the investment from net cash flows.

Payback period (PBP) method A capital budgeting method that measures the time it will take to recoup, in the form of net cash inflows, the net dollars invested in a project.

Payers Consumers who actually pay for the product.

Paying agent The bank performing this function makes interest and dividend payments to bondholders and shareholders, respectively, and repays the bond principal at maturity.

Payment (PMT) This term designates constant cash flows.

Payment date The date on which a firm actually mails dividend checks.

Payoff A measure of the consequence of a decision such as profit, cost, or time. Each combination of a decision alternative and a state of nature has an associated payoff (consequence).

Payoff table A tabular representation of the payoffs for a decision problem.

Payoffs Illegal payments made abroad by MNCs to foreign government officials and politicians in the course of conducting business.

Payroll The total amount paid to employees for a certain period.

Payroll fraud scheme Using the payroll function to commit fraud, such as creating ghost employees or overpaying wages.

Payroll register A multicolumn form used to assemble and summarize payroll data at the end of each payroll period.

PDSA cycle Plan-do-study-act cycle (a variation of PDCA developed by Deming).

Peer-to-peer (P2P) file sharing File sharing that allows PCs to communicate directly with one another over the Internet, bypassing central databases, servers, control points, and Web pages.

Peer-to-peer LAN A local area network (LAN) in which no central device controls communications.

Pegged exchange rate Exchange rate whose value is pegged to another currency's value or to a unit of account.

Pegging In MRP and MPS, the capability to identify for a given item the sources of its gross requirements and/or allocations. Pegging can be thought of as active where-used information.

Penetration strategy Requires that the firm enter the market at a relatively low price in an attempt to obtain market share and expand demand for its product.

Pension Postretirement cash benefits paid to former employees.

Pension liabilities The accumulating obligations of employers to fund the retirement or pension plans of employees.

Pension plans Retirement benefits established and funded by employers and employees.

People-processing services In these services, customers become part of the production process. Such services include passenger transportation, health care, food services, and lodging services.

Perceived opportunity A situation where people believe they have a favorable or promising combination of circumstances to commit fraud and not be detected.

Perceived pressure A situation where people perceive they have a need to commit fraud; a constraining influence on the will or mind, as a moral force.

Percent complete An estimate in percentage form of the proportion of the work involved in a particular work package that has been completed.

Percent of sales Forecasting model in which an expense or balance sheet amount is expressed as some fraction of sales.

Perception The cognitive process people use to make sense out of the environment by selecting, organizing, and interpreting information.

Perceptual defense The tendency of perceivers to protect themselves by disregarding ideas, objects, or people that are threatening to them.

Perceptual distortions Errors in perceptual judgment that arise from inaccuracies in any part of the perceptual process.

Perceptual mapping Commonly used, multidimensional scaling method of graphically depicting a product's performance on selected attributes or the "position" of a product against its competitors on selected product traits.

Perceptual selectivity The process by which individuals screen and select the various stimuli that vie for their attention.

Perfect forecast line A 45-degree line on a graph that matches the forecast of an exchange rate with the actual exchange rate.

Performance 1: The organization's ability to attain its goals by using resources in an efficient and effective manner. **2:** What an employee does or does not do.

Performance appraisal The process of evaluating how well employees perform their jobs when compared to a set of standards, and then communicating that information to employees.

Performance-based pay Pay related to and directly derived from performance.

Performance consulting A process in which a trainer and the organizational client work together to boost workplace performance in support of business goals.

Performance gap A disparity between existing and desired performance levels.

Performance management system 1: System that supports and contributes to the creation of high-performance work and work systems by translating behavioral principles into procedures. **2:** Processes used to identify, encourage, measure, evaluate, improve, and reward employee performance.

Performance plan Performance management tool that describes desired performance and provides a way to assess the performance objectively.

Performance report A routine report that compares actual performance against budgetary goals.

Performance shares A type of incentive plan in which managers are awarded shares of stock on the basis of the firm's performance over given intervals with respect to earnings per share or other measures.

Performance standards Expected levels of performance.

Performance test Assessment device that requires candidates to complete an actual work task in a controlled situation.

Performing The stage of team development in which members focus on problem solving and accomplishing the team's assigned task.

Period costs Those costs that are used up in generating revenue during the current period and that are not involved in the manufacturing process These costs are recognized as expenses on the current period's income statement.

Period order quantity A lot-sizing technique under which the lot size is equal to the net requirements for a given number of periods, for example, weeks into the future. The number of periods to order is variable, each order size equalizing the holding costs and the ordering costs for the interval.

Periodic inventory system A system of inventory accounting in which only the revenue from sales is recorded each time a sale is made. The cost of merchandise on hand at the end of a period is determined by a detailed listing (physical inventory) of the merchandise on hand.

Periodic rate The rate charged by a lender or paid by a borrower each interest period (for example, monthly, quarterly, annually, and so on).

Periodic replenishment A method of aggregating requirements to place deliveries of varying quantities at evenly spaced time intervals, rather than variably spaced deliveries of equal quantities.

Peripheral equipment The additional equipment, such as a printer and keyboard, connected to a computer.

Perishability Distinguishing characteristic of services in that they cannot be saved, their unused capacity cannot be reserved, and they cannot be inventoried.

Permanent current assets Current assets' balances that do not change due to seasonal or economic conditions; these balances exist even at the trough of a firm's business cycle. The minimum amount of funds that are invested in current assets over the firm's operating cycle.

Permanent differences Differences that are caused by certain types of revenues that are exempted from taxation and certain types of expenses that are not deductible for tax purposes.

Permanent teams A group of participants from several functions who are permanently assigned to solve ongoing problems of common interest.

Permissive issues Collective bargaining issues that are not mandatory but relate to certain jobs.

Perpetrator A person who has committed a fraud.

Perpetual inventory system A system of inventory accounting in which both the revenue from sales and the cost of merchandise sold are recorded each time a sale is made, so that the records continually disclose the amount of the inventory on hand.

Perpetuity A cash flow stream of equal dollar amounts that will last indefinitely into the future.

Perquisites (perks) Special benefits—usually noncash items—for executives.

Person-job fit 1: Matching the KSAs of people with the characteristics of jobs. **2:** The extent to which a person's ability and personality match the requirements of a job.

Person-organization fit The congruence between individuals and organizational factors.

Personal decision-support system A decision-support system that is built for the individual knowledge worker to use in his or her daily work.

Personal digital assistant (PDA) A small handheld computer. Many PDAs require the use of a special stylus to enter handwritten information that is recognized by the computer.

Personal observation evidence Evidence that is sensed (seen, heard, felt, and so on) by investigators.

Personal selling Person-to-person communication in which a seller informs and educates prospective customers and attempts to influence their purchase choices; direct oral communication designed to explain how an individual's or firm's goods, services, or ideas fit the needs of one or more prospective customers.

Personality The set of characteristics that underlie a relatively stable pattern of behavior in response to ideas, objects, or people in the environment.

Personality test Assessment device that measures a person's interaction skills and patterns of behavior.

Personnel competencies The ability of a firm's personnel to implement its strategy to internationalize its operations.

PERT chart A chart showing events, the activities required to reach the events, and the interdependencies among activities. The events are usually completion milestones.

Pessimistic time estimate (t_p) The time in which an activity can be completed under adverse conditions, such as in the presence of unusual or unforeseen complications.

Petrodollars Deposits of dollars by countries which receive dollar revenues due to the sale of petroleum to other countries; the term commonly refers to OPEC deposits of dollars in the Eurocurrency market.

Petty cash fund A special cash fund used to pay relatively small amounts.

Phantom bill of material A bill-of-material coding and structuring technique used primarily for transient (nonstocked) subassemblies. For the transient item, lead time is set to zero and the order quantity to lot-for-lot. A phantom bill of material represents an item that is physically built, but rarely stocked, before being used in the next step or level of manufacturing. This permits MRP logic to drive requirements straight through the phantom item to its components, but the MRP system usually retains its ability to net against any occasional inventories of the item. This technique also facilitates the use of common bills of material for engineering and manufacturing. *Syn:* blowthrough, transient bill of material. *See:* pseudo bill of material.

Phased conversion Implementing a new information system one module at a time.

Phased retirement Approach in which employees reduce their workloads and pay.

Philanthropic responsibilities Responsibilities viewed as such because they reflect current expectations of business by the public.

Philanthropy Contributions to charity and other worthy causes.

Physical ability tests Tests that measure individual abilities such as strength, endurance, and muscular movement.

Physical design The process of information system design that includes specifying the necessary software and hardware needed to support it.

Physical distribution The movement of finished products from suppliers to customers.

Physical distribution management An approach to management that seeks to organize and coordinate the activities responsible for managing the outbound flow of materials and information from finished goods operations through to end customers. The various functions that often fall under the physical distribution umbrella include distribution planning and control, forecasting, outbound transportation, material handling, inventory planning and control, and warehousing.

Physical evidence Evidence of a tangible nature—includes fingerprints, tire marks, weapons, stolen property, identification numbers or marks on stolen objects, and so on—that can be used in an investigation to provide information about a fraud or other crime.

Physical inventory The detailed listing of merchandise on hand.

Physical safeguards Vaults, fences, locks, and so on that protect assets from theft.

Piggyback Situation in which a bank is permitted to add a check or checks it is clearing and an accompanying listing to whatever checks the local Fed district bank is sending to the distant Fed office. This way the clearing bank can miss the local Fed's cutoff time but still meet the distant Fed's cutoff.

Piloting A trial conversion in which a new information system is introduced in one business unit before introducing it in others.

Pipeline stock Inventory in the transportation network and the distribution system, including the flow through intermediate stocking points. The flow time through the pipeline has a major effect on the amount of inventory required in the pipeline. Time factors involve order transmission, order processing, scheduling, shipping, transportation, receiving, stocking, review time, and so on. *Syn:* pipeline inventory. *See:* distribution system, transportation inventory.

Pipelining A technique in which one part of a CPU can do its job while others do theirs, allowing faster processing.

Pixel (picture element) A phosphor dot on the inside of a cathode-ray tube monitor. In a color monitor a triad of red, green, and blue dots is used. When the pixels are bombarded by electrons shot from the tube's electron gun, they emit light, thereby creating an image on the screen. The larger the number of pixels on the screen, the better the resolution.

Place/entry strategy Managers of business enterprises must determine how their products or services will reach the consumer. Distribution methods generally require variations from country to country as well as within each country.

Placement Fitting a person to the right job.

Plaintext An original message, before encryption.

Plan A blueprint specifying the resource allocations, schedules, and other actions necessary for attaining goals.

Plan-do-check-act cycle (PDCA) Four-step process for quality improvement. In the first step (plan), a plan to effect improvement is developed. In the second step (do), the plan is carried out, preferably on a small scale. In the third step (check), the effects of the plan are observed. In the last step (act), the results are studied to determine what was learned and what can be predicted. The plan-do-check-act cycle is sometimes referred to as the Shewhart cycle because Walter A. Shewhart discussed the concept in his book *Statistical Method from the Viewpoint of Quality Control* and as the Deming cycle because W. Edwards Deming introduced the concept in Japan. The Japanese subsequently called it the *Deming cycle*.

Planned issue receipt A transaction that updates the on-hand balance and the related allocation or open order.

Planned obsolescence Design of a product with features that the company knows will soon be superseded, thus making the model obsolete.

Planned order A suggested order quantity, release date, and due date created by the planning system's logic when it encounters net requirements in processing MRP. In some cases, it can also be created by a master scheduling module. Planned orders are created by the computer, exist only within the computer, and may be changed or deleted by the computer during subsequent processing if conditions change. Planned orders at one level will be exploded into gross requirements for components at the next level. Planned orders, along with released orders, serve as input to capacity requirements planning to show the total capacity requirements by work center in future time periods. *See:* planning time fence.

Planned order receipt The quantity planned to be received at a future date as a result of a planned order release. Planned order receipts differ from scheduled receipts in that they have not been released. *Syn:* planned receipt.

Planned order release A row on an MRP table that is derived from planned order receipts by taking the planned receipt quantity and offsetting to the left by the appropriate lead time. *See:* order release.

Planning The management function concerned with defining goals for future organizational performance and deciding on the tasks and resource use needed to attain them; the act of determining the organization's goals and the means for achieving them. The systematic arrangement of tasks to accomplish an objective; determining what needs to be done, who will do it, how long it will take, and how much it will cost.

Planning bill of material An artificial grouping of items or events in bill-of-material format used to facilitate master scheduling and material planning. It may include the historical average of demand expressed as a percentage of total demand for all options within a feature or for a specific end item within a product family and is used as the quantity per in the planning bill of material. *Syn:* planning bill.

Planning task force A group of managers and employees who develop a strategic plan.

Planning time fence A point in time denoted in the planning horizon of the master scheduling process that marks a boundary inside of which changes to the schedule may adversely affect component schedules, capacity plans, customer deliveries, and cost. Outside the planning time fence, customer orders may be booked and changes to the master schedule can be made within the constraints of the production plan. Changes inside the planning time fence must be made manually by the master scheduler. *Syn:* planning fence. *See:* cumulative lead time, demand time fence, firm planned order, planned order, planning horizon, time fence.

Platform Either the standard hardware or the standard operating system that the organization uses. The term has been used differently in different contexts by IS professionals and trade journals.

Plaza Accord Agreement among country representatives in 1985 to implement a coordinated program to weaken the dollar.

Plaza Agreement An accord reached in 1985 by the Group of Five that held that the major nations should join in a coordinated effort to bring down the value of the U.S. dollar.

Pledging receivables A lender makes a loan protected by a lien placed on a certain portion of the firm's receivables. Using accounts receivable as collateral for a loan.

Plug-and-play The ability of an operating system to recognize a new attachment and its function without a user's intervention.

Pluralism The organization accommodates several subcultures, including employees who would otherwise feel isolated and ignored.

PM theory of leadership A Japanese leadership theory; the P stands for showing a concern for subordinates and leadership that is oriented toward forming and reaching group goals; the M stands for leadership that is oriented toward preserving group stability.

P→O expectancy Expectancy that successful performance of a task will lead to the desired outcome.

Point-counterpoint A decision-making technique in which people are assigned to express competing points of view.

Point estimate Single value used to estimate a population parameter. Point estimates are commonly referred to as the points at which the interval estimates are centered; these estimates give information about how much uncertainty is associated with the estimate.

Point of presence (POP) A telephone number that a user can dial to log on to a server even if the server is many miles away, to save the user long-distance call charges.

Point-of-purchase communications Signage—displays, posters, signs, shelf cards, and a variety of other visual materials—designed to influence buying decisions at the point of sale.

Point to point protocol (PPP) A protocol for communication between two computers (as opposed to a network).

Poison pill 1: An action taken by management to make a firm unattractive to potential buyers and thus to avoid a hostile takeover. **2:** A shareholder rights plan aimed at discouraging or preventing a hostile takeover.

Poisson distribution Distribution used for discrete data, applicable when there are many opportunities for occurrence of an event but a low probability (less than 0.10) on each trial.

Poka-yoke Term that means to mistake-proof a process by building safeguards into the system that avoid or immediately find errors. It comes from poka, which means "error," and yokeru, which means "to avoid."

Policy Management's dictate of what should be done to effect control. A policy serves as the basis for procedures for its implementation.

Political environment A nation's political system, government policies, attitude toward the product, and management of scarce foreign exchange.

Political forces The influence of political and legal institutions on people and organizations.

Political instability Events such as riots, revolutions, or government upheavals that affect the operations of an international company.

Political risk 1: The risk of loss by an international corporation of assets, earning power, or managerial control as a result of political actions by the host country. **2:** Political actions taken by the host government or the public that affect the MNC's cash flows. The risk of expropriation (seizure) of a foreign subsidiary's assets by the host country or of unanticipated restrictions on cash flows to the parent company.

Political systems The types of political system—one-party, two-party, or multiparty—affects the level of stability and consistency in governmental policies as it relates to business.

Political union A group of countries that have common foreign policy and security policy and that share judicial cooperation.

Polling A protocol in which a communications processor conducts a continuous roll-call of the nodes.

Polycentric staffing outlook The belief that key positions in foreign subsidiaries should be staffed by host-country nationals (locals).

Polygamous loyalty Reflects the notion that customer loyalty tends to be divided among a number of providing firms.

PONC Price of nonconformance: the cost of not doing things right the first time.

Pooling A banking service offered by many banking systems outside the United States which allows a firm's excess balances spread across its bank branches to offset corporate deficit balances in other branches of the same bank.

Pooling-of-interests method An accounting method used for a business combination where the acquired entity's assets and equities are combined at book value. No goodwill is created in a pooling of interests. A method of accounting for an affiliation of two corporations resulting from an exchange of voting stock of one corporation for substantially all the voting stock of the other corporation.

Population Group of people, objects, observations, or measurements about which one wishes to draw conclusions.

Population increase The effect of changes in countries' populations on economic matters.

Population stabilization An attempt to control rapid increases in population and ensure that economic development exceeds population growth.

Port A socket on a computer to which external devices, such as printers, keyboards, and scanners, can be connected.

Portability A pension plan feature that allows employees to move their pension benefits from one employer to another.

Portal A site that offers a search engine and general information such as weather, news, and stock market quotations; Yahoo! is one example.

Portfolio analysis Process of comparing the value of proposed projects or acquisitions relative to the financial impacts on current projects as well as the potential impact on resources of the proposed project or acquisitions.

Portfolio approach A method used to manage economic exposure of a company by offsetting negative exposure in one country with positive exposure in another.

Portfolio investment account An account in the BOP statement that records investments in assets with an original maturity of more than one year and where an investor's ownership position is less than 10 percent.

Portfolio models Tools that have been proposed for use in market and competitive analysis. They typically involve two measures—internal strength and external attractiveness.

Portfolio risk The risk associated with an investment when it is held in combination with other assets, not by itself.

Portfolio strategy A type of corporate-level strategy that pertains to the organization's mix of SBUs and product lines that fit together in such a way as to provide the corporation with synergy and competitive advantage.

Ports Harbor towns or cities where ships may take on or discharge cargo; the lack of ports and port services is the greatest constraint in ocean shipping.

Positioning Image that customers have about a product, especially in relation to the product's competitors.

Positive adjustment phase Beginning at about month four of the expatriation phase, the expatriate begins to adapt, and by about month six of the assignment, the expatriate feels more positive about the foreign environment; in this phase, he or she will attain neither the "high" of the first phase nor the "low" of the second or third phases.

Positive exposure A condition that exists when a foreign subsidiary has more current assets than current liabilities.

Positive float The time period between receipt of the goods or services and the date on which cash payment is made.

Positive pay A company sends its daily check issue file to its disbursing bank. Before the bank honors incoming checks, it refers to the issue file to see if the payee and check amounts match up.

Possession-processing services Services of this nature involve tangible actions to tangible objects to enhance their value to customers. The customer may not be present. These services include transporting freight and installing and maintaining equipment.

Postal inspectors Inspectors or investigators hired by the U.S. Postal Service to handle major fraud cases that are perpetrated through the U.S. mail system.

Post-audit A comparison of the actual and expected results for a given capital project.

Post-closing trial balance A trial balance prepared after all of the temporary accounts have been closed.

Posterior (revised) probabilities The probabilities of the states of nature after revising the prior probabilities based on sample information.

Posting The process of transferring debits and credits from a journal to the accounts.

Postpurchase behavior Last stage in the consumer decision process, when the consumer experiences an intense need to confirm the wisdom of that decision.

Post-retirement benefits Rights to benefits that employees earn during their term of employment for themselves and their dependents after they retire.

Power The potential ability to influence others' behavior.

Power distance 1: The degree to which people accept inequality in power among institutions, organizations, and people. **2:** Dimension of culture that refers to the inequality among the people of a nation. **3:** Refers to the degree to which people in a society accept centralized power and depend on superiors for structure and direction.

Ppk Potential process capability used in the validation stage of a new product launch (uses the same formula as Cpk, but a higher value is expected due to the smaller time span of the samples).

PPM Parts per million.

Practices Cultural foundations of organizational behavior, including symbols, heroes, rituals, and values.

Preauthorized debit system A system that allows a customer's bank to periodically transfer funds from its account to a selling firm's bank account for the payment of bills.

Preauthorized debits Arrangement in which a customer agrees to allow his bank to automatically charge his checking account balance to make a fixed or variable payment each month.

Preauthorized draft Payment order initiated by the payee, who has been authorized to draw against the payor's account. Banks sometimes collect mortgage payments this way, and most automobile dealerships now make payments to Ford, GM, and Chrysler by these drafts.

Preauthorized payment The seller and buyer agree to a payment date and the seller initiates a request to the buyer's bank for payment of the predetermined amount.

Precautionary balances A cash balance held in reserve for unforeseen fluctuations in cash flows.

Precautionary motive Additional inventory held as a cushion for an unexpected increase in demand.

Precedence diagramming method (PDM) A type of network planning technique.

Precedential relationship The order in which activities must be finished before other activities can start.

Precision Characteristic of measurement that addresses the consistency or repeatability of a measurement system when the identical item is measured a number of times.

Pre-control Control process, with simple rules, based on tolerances. It is effective for any process where a worker can measure a quality characteristic (dimension, color, strength, and so on.) and can adjust the process to change that characteristic, and where there is either continuous output or discrete output totaling three or more pieces.

Predatory pricing Practice where one firm attempts to drive out rivals (usually smaller ones) by pricing at such a low level that the rival cannot make money.

Predecessor event The event at the beginning of an activity (tail of the arrow) in the activity-on-the-arrow form of network diagramming; start event.

Predetermined factory overhead rate The rate used to apply factory overhead costs to the goods manufactured. It is determined by dividing the budgeted overhead cost by the estimated activity usage at the beginning of the fiscal period.

Predication Circumstances that, taken as a whole, would lead a reasonable, prudent professional to believe that a fraud has occurred, is occurring, or will occur.

Predictive validity Measured when test results of applicants are compared with subsequent job performance.

Preemptive right A provision in the corporate charter or bylaws that gives common stockholders the right to purchase on a *pro rata* basis new issues of common stock (or convertible securities).

Pre-expatriation program Once the expatriate has been selected for the foreign assignment, but before leaving the home country, he or she is involved in certain training to prepare for what will be encountered in the foreign country.

Preferential policies Government policies that favor certain (usually domestic) firms; for example, the use of national carriers for the transport of government freight even when more economical alternatives exist.

Preferred provider organization (PPO) A health-care provider that contracts with an employer group to provide health-care services to employees at a competitive rate.

Preferred stock A class of stock with preferential rights over common stock.

Preliminary hearing Pretrial hearing to determine whether there is "probable cause" to charge the defendant with a crime.

Preloss activities Loss control methods implemented before any losses occur. All measures with a frequency-reduction focus, as well as some based on severity reduction, are of this type.

Premium As related to forward rates, represents the percentage amount by which the forward rate exceeds the spot rate. As related to currency options, represents the price of a currency option.

Premium bond A bond that sells above its par value; occurs whenever the going rate of interest falls below the coupon rate.

Prepaid expenses Purchased commodities or services that have not been used up at the end of an accounting period.

Prepayment Method which exporter uses to receive payment before shipping goods.

Prerequisite tree Technique used in the application of Goldratt's Theory of Constraints.

Present value (PV) The value today of a future cash flow or series of cash flows.

Present value concept A concept in which cash to be received (or paid) in the future is worth less than the same amount of money held today.

Present value index An index computed by dividing the total present value of the net cash flow to be received from a proposed capital investment by the amount to be invested.

Present value interest factor for an annuity ($PVIFA_{i,n}$) The present value interest factor for an annuity of n periods discounted at i percent.

Present value interest factor for i and n ($PVIF_{i,n}$) The present value of $1 due n periods in the future discounted at i percent per period.

Present value of an annuity The sum of the present values of a series of equal cash flows to be received at fixed intervals.

Presentation principles Those principles governing verbal and nonverbal communication that are applicable when making a presentation to a foreign audience.

Presentment Step seven in the check clearing process, when the check is returned to the drawee bank for payment.

Pretest Undertaken before the major study to test the validity and reliability of measures and other components of the study's research methodology.

Prevention costs 1: Costs incurred to prevent defects from occurring during the design and delivery of products or services. **2:** Costs incurred to keep internal and external failure costs and appraisal costs to a minimum.

Prevention vs. detection Term used to contrast two types of quality activities. Prevention refers to those activities designed to prevent nonconformances in products and services. Detection refers to those activities designed to detect nonconformances already in products and services. Another term used to describe this distinction is "designing in quality vs. inspecting in quality."

Preventive action Action taken to eliminate the causes of a potential nonconformity, defect, or other undesirable situation in order to prevent occurrence.

Preventive control A control designed to avoid an unintended event or result.

Price Some unit of value given up by one party in return for something from another party.

Price controls Government regulation of the prices of goods and services; control of the prices of imported goods or services as a result of domestic political pressures.

Price/cost analysis The ongoing evaluation of price and cost trends. Price analysis is the process of comparing supplier prices against external price benchmarks, without direct knowledge of the supplier's actual costs. Cost analysis is the process of analyzing each individual cost element that together add up to the final price.

Price discrimination A seller offers a lower price to some buyers than to other buyers.

Price/earnings (P/E) ratio The ratio of the price per share to earnings per share; it shows the dollar amount investors will pay for $1 of current earnings; computed by dividing the market price per share of common stock at a specific date by the company's earnings per share on common stock.

Price-elastic Sensitive to price changes.

Price escalation The establishing of export prices far in excess of domestic prices—often due to a long distribution channel and frequent markups.

Price factor The effect of a difference in unit sales price or unit cost on the number of units sold.

Price-fixing Conspiracy to fix competitive prices.

Price promotions Short-term price reductions designed to create an incentive for consumers to buy now rather than later and/or stock up on the specially priced product.

Price strategy Some firms are influenced by the view that pricing is an active tool by which to accomplish their marketing objectives, while some are influenced by the belief that price is a static element in business decisions.

Pricing market Also called the original issue market, is centered in money centers such as New York City, London, Frankfurt, Singapore, and Hong Kong. Investors can access this "over-the-counter" market from anywhere, as the market consists of phone and computer hook-ups among all participating dealers and brokers.

Pricing motive Theoretical motive for trade credit extension in which sellers unable to change prices, perhaps due to market conditions or regulation, alter trade credit instead in order to charge varying amounts to buyers.

Primacy effect Information received first gets the most weight.

Primary Process that refers to the basic steps or activities that will produce the output without the "nice-to-haves."

Primary audience In the communication process, those who receive a message directly.

Primary data Data obtained directly for a specific research purpose through interviews, focus groups, surveys, observation, or experimentation.

Primary key In a file, a field that holds values that are unique to each record. Only a primary key can be used to uniquely identify and retrieve a record.

Primary market The market in which firms issue new securities to raise corporate capital.

Primary memory (primary storage, main memory, main storage) The built-in memory chips in the computer, made of transistors. The majority of the memory is of the RAM type, and the rest is of the ROM type.

Primary research Research method in which data are gathered firsthand for the specific project being conducted.

Prime rate A published rate of interest charged by banks to short-term borrowers (usually large, financially secure corporations) with the best credit; rates on short-term loans generally are "pegged" to the prime rate.

Principal The original amount invested or borrowed.

Principal amount, face value, maturity value, par value The amount of money the firm borrows and promises to repay at some future date, often at maturity.

Prior-period adjustments Corrections of material errors related to a prior period or periods, excluded from the determination of net income.

Prior probabilities The probabilities of the states of nature prior to obtaining sample information.

Priorities matrix Tool used to choose between several options that have many useful benefits, but where not all of them are of equal value.

Privacy The ability to control information about ourselves. In a larger sense, "the right to be left alone." Information technology has made invasion of privacy a major issue in our society, due to its ability to collect, maintain, store, and manipulate huge amounts of personal information.

Private Branch Exchange (PBX) A computer-based digital switching device that simultaneously handles communications of internal voice telephones, computers, and the external telephone network.

Private placement 1: Security issuance transaction in which a large institution such as a retirement fund or insurance company buys the entire issue. **2:** The sale of debt securities to private or institutional investors without going through a public issuance like that of a bond issue or equity issue.

Private Securities Litigation Reform Act of 1995 Law that made it more difficult for companies to bring class-action lawsuits to federal court.

Privatization A policy of shifting government operations to privately owned enterprises to cut budget costs and ensure more efficient services.

Pro forma balance sheet approach Method of generating a cash forecast which involves determination of the amount of cash and marketable securities by computing the difference between projected assets (excluding cash and marketable securities) and the sum of projected liabilities and owner's equity.

Proactive marketing public relations (proactive MPR) Offensively rather than defensively oriented, and opportunity-seeking rather than problem-solving. The major role of proactive MPR is in the area of product introductions or product revisions.

Probabilistic input Input to a simulation model that is subject to uncertainty. A probabilistic input is described by a probability distribution.

Probability Likelihood of occurrence.

Probability distribution Mathematical formula that relates the values of characteristics to their probability of occurrence in a population.

Probability-impact matrix Assesses the probability of occurrence of an issue on one dimension and its impact on the company on the other dimension.

Problem 1: A situation in which organizational accomplishments have failed to meet established goals. **2:** Any undesirable situation.

Problem recognition Consumer's realization that he or she needs to buy something to get back to a normal state of comfort.

Problem solving Rational process for identifying, describing, analyzing, and resolving situations in which something has gone wrong without explanation.

Problem-solving team Typically five to twelve hourly employees from the same department who meet to discuss ways of improving quality, efficiency, and the work environment.

Procedural justice 1: The concept that rules should be clearly stated and consistently and impartially enforced. **2:** Examines the process a customer is required to travel in order to arrive at a final outcome. **3:** Perceived fairness of the process used to make decisions about employees.

Procedure Document that answers the questions: What has to be done? Where is it to be done? When is it to be done? Who is to do it? Why do it? (contrasted with a work instruction which answers: How is it to be done? With what materials and tools is it to be done?); in the absence of a work instruction, the instructions may be embedded in the procedure.

Proceeds The net amount available from discounting a note.

Process 1: Activity or group of activities that takes an input, adds value to it, and provides an output to an internal or external customer; a planned and repetitive sequence of steps by which a defined product or service is delivered. **2:** Any manipulation of data, usually with the goal of producing information. *See:* Management process.

Process capability Statistical measure of the inherent process variability for a given characteristic (*See:* Cp, Cpk, and Ppk).

Process capability index Value of the tolerance specified for the characteristic divided by the process capability. There are several types of process capability indexes, including the widely used Cp and Cpk.

Process control system A computer system that monitors and controls ongoing physical processes, such as temperature or pressure changes.

Process cost system A type of cost accounting system that accumulates costs for each of the various departments or processes within a manufacturing facility.

Process decision program chart (PDPC) Management and planning tool that identifies all events that can go wrong and the appropriate countermeasures for these events. It graphically represents all sequences that lead to a desirable effect.

Process improvement Act of changing a process to reduce variability and cycle time and make the process more effective, efficient, and productive.

Process improvement team (PIT) Natural work group or cross-functional team whose responsibility is to achieve needed improvements in existing processes. The life span of the team is based on the completion of the team purpose and specific goals.

Process layout A facilities layout in which machines that perform the same function are grouped together in one location.

Process management Collection of practices used to implement and improve process effectiveness; it focuses on holding the gains achieved through process improvement and assuring process integrity.

Process manufacturers Manufacturers that use machines to process a continuous flow of raw materials through various stages of completion into a finished state.

Process mapping Flowcharting of a work process in detail, including key measurements.

Process organization Form of departmentalization where each department specializes in one phase of the process.

Process-oriented layout Organizing work in a plant or administrative function around processes (tasks).

Process owner Manager or leader who is responsible for ensuring that the total process is effective and efficient.

Process quality audit Analysis of elements of a process and appraisal of completeness, correctness of conditions, and probable effectiveness.

Process structure A variation of the functional structure in which departments are formed on the basis of production processes.

Process theories A group of theories that explain how employees select behaviors with which to meet their needs and determine whether their choices were successful.

Process village Machines grouped by type of operation (contrast with a cell layout).

Processing float The amount of time that transpires from the point of receipt of the check at a post office box or company mail room and the time when the check is deposited at the bank is termed processing float.

Procurement Purchasing supplies, services, and raw materials for use in the production process.

Procurement costs Costs to a firm associated with the process of receiving customers' orders.

Prodromal crisis stage Warning or symptom stage of a crisis.

Producer's risk for a sampling plan The probability of not accepting a lot, the quality of which has a designated numerical value representing a level that is generally desirable. Usually the designated value will be the acceptable quality level (also called alpha risk and type 1 error).

Product cost concept A concept used in applying the cost-plus approach to product pricing in which only the costs of manufacturing the product, termed the product cost, are included in the cost amount to which the markup is added.

Product costing Determining the cost of a product.

Product costs The three components of manufacturing cost: direct materials, direct labor, and factory overhead costs.

Product cycle theory 1: Theory suggesting that a firm initially establish itself locally and expand into foreign markets in response to foreign demand for its product; over time, the MNC will grow in foreign markets; after some point, its foreign business may decline unless it can differentiate its product from competitors. **2:** A theory that views products as passing through four stages: introduction, growth, maturity, decline; during which the location of production moves from industrialized to lower-cost developing nations.

Product development process Clearly defined set of tasks and steps that describes the normal means by which product development proceeds. The process outlines the order and sequence of the tasks and indicates who is responsible for each.

Product differentiation The effort to build unique differences or improvements into products.

Product division structure Each of the enterprise's product divisions is responsible for the sale and profits of its product.

Product layout A facilities layout in which machines and tasks are arranged according to the sequence of steps in the production of a single product.

Product life cycle Cycle of stages that a product goes through from birth to death: introduction, growth, maturity, and decline.

Product line Set of products a firm targets to one general market. These products are likely to share some common features and technology characteristics or be complementary products. They also are likely to share several elements of the marketing mix, such as distribution channels.

Product load profile A listing of the required capacity and key resources needed to manufacture one unit of a selected item or family. The resource requirements are further defined by a lead-time offset to predict the impact of the product on the load of the key resources by specific time period. The product load profile can be used for rough-cut capacity planning to calculate the approximate capacity requirements of the master production schedule. *See:* bill of resources, resource profile, rough-cut capacity planning.

Product mix Full set of a firm's products across all markets served.

Product organization Departmentalization where each department focuses on a specific product type or family.

Product-oriented layout Organizing work in a plant or administrative function around products; sometimes referred to as product cells.

Product orientation Tendency to see customers' needs in terms of a product they want to buy, not in terms of the services, value, or benefits the product will produce.

Product positioning Refers to how customers perceive a product's position in the marketplace relative to the competition.

Product quality audit Quantitative assessment of conformance to required product characteristics.

Product/service liability Obligation of a company to make restitution for loss related to personal injury, property damage, or other harm caused by its product or service.

Product/service strategy Managers are typically concerned with what the product or service should look like and what it should be able to do. In foreign markets, they must determine whether their product or service can be sold in standard form or be customized to fit differing foreign market needs.

Product structure The sequence of operations that components follow during their manufacture into a product. A typical product structure would show raw material converted into fabricated components, components put together to make subassemblies, subassemblies going into assemblies, and so on.

Product tree A graphical (or tree) representation of the bill of material such as is shown below:

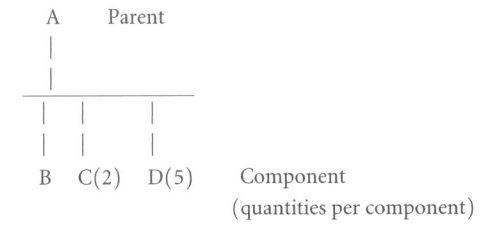

```
A     Parent
|
|
| | |
| | |
B C(2) D(5)   Component
              (quantities per component)
```

Production bottleneck A condition that occurs when product demand exceeds production capacity The bottleneck resource is a portion of the production process that is operating at 100 percent of capacity and is unable to meet product demand.

Production budget A budget of estimated production.

Production capability 1: The highest sustainable output rate that could be achieved for a given product mix, raw materials, worker effort, plant, and equipment. **2:** The collection of personnel, equipment, material, and process segment capabilities. **3:** The total of the current committed, available, and unattainable capability of the production facility. The capability includes the capacity of the resource.

Production forecast A projected level of customer demand for a feature (option, accessory, and so on.) of a make-to-order or an assemble-to-order product. Used in two-level master scheduling, it is calculated by netting customer backlog against an overall family or product line master production schedule and then factoring this product's available-to-promise by the option percentage in a planning bill of material. *See:* assemble-to-order, planning bill of material, two-level master production schedule.

Production management 1: The planning, scheduling, execution, and control of the process of converting inputs into finished goods. **2:** A field of study that focuses on the effective planning, scheduling, use, and control of a manufacturing organization through the study of concepts from design engineering, industrial engineering, management information systems, quality management, inventory management, accounting, and other functions as they affect the transformation process.

Production opportunities The returns available within an economy from investment in productive (cash-generating) assets.

Production plan The agreed-upon plan that comes from the production planning (sales and operations planning) process, specifically the overall level of manufacturing output planned to be produced, usually stated as a monthly rate for each product family (group of products, items, options, features, and so on). Various units of measurement can be used to express the plan: units, tonnage, standard hours, number of workers, and so on. The production plan is management's authorization for the master scheduler to convert it into a more detailed plan, that is, the master production schedule.

Production planning A process to develop tactical plans based on setting the overall level of manufacturing output (production plan) and other activities to best satisfy the current planned levels of sales (sales plan or forecasts), while meeting general business objectives of profitability, productivity, competitive customer lead times, and so on, as expressed in the overall business plan. The sales and production capabilities are compared, and a business strategy that includes a sales plan, a production plan, budgets, pro-forma financial statements, and supporting plans for materials and workforce requirements, and so on, is developed. One of its primary purposes is to establish production rates that will achieve management's objective of satisfying customer demand by maintaining, raising, or lowering inventories or backlogs, while usually attempting to keep the workforce relatively stable. Because this plan affects many company functions, it is normally prepared with information from marketing and coordinated with the functions of manufacturing, sales, engineering, finance, materials, and so on. *See:* aggregate planning.

Production planning and control strategies An element of manufacturing strategy that includes the design and development of manufacturing planning and control systems in relation to the following considerations: 1) market-related criteria—the required level of delivery speed and reliability in a given market segment, 2) process requirement criteria—consistency between process type (job shop, repetitive, continuous, and so on.) and the production planning and control system, 3) organization control levels—systems capable of providing long-term planning and short-term control capabilities for strategic and operational considerations by management. Production planning and control strategies help firms develop systems that enable them to exploit market opportunities while satisfying manufacturing process requirements.

Production possibilities frontier A theoretical method of representing the total productive capabilities of a nation used in the formulation of classical and modern trade theory.

Production rules A method of knowledge representation that holds the facts in the form of *if-then* statements; also called if-then *rules*.

Production scheduling The systems and activities involved with coordinating materials, manpower, and machines to produce a given amount of finished product or service and meet customer requirements.

Productivity 1: An overall measure of the ability to produce a good or a service. It is the actual output of production compared to the actual input of resources. Productivity is a relative measure across time or against common entities (labor, capital, and so on). In the production literature, attempts have been made to define total productivity where the effects of labor and capital are combined and divided into the output. One example is a ratio that is calculated by adding the dollar value of labor, capital equipment, energy, and material, and so on, and dividing it into the dollar value of output in a given time period. This is one measure of total factor productivity. *See:* efficiency, labor productivity, machine productivity, utilization. **2:** In economics, the ratio of output in terms of dollars of sales to an input such as direct labor in terms of the total wages. This is called single factor productivity or partial factor productivity.

Products Set of features, functions, and benefits that customers purchase. Products may consist primarily of tangible (physical) attributes or intangibles, such as those associated with services, or some combination of tangible and intangible.

Professional development plan Individual development tool for an employee. Working together, the employee and his/her supervisor create a plan that matches the individual's career needs and aspirations with organizational demands.

Profit center A responsibility center where the manager is responsible for both revenues and costs. A decentralized unit in which the manager has the responsibility and the authority to make decisions that affect both costs and revenues (and thus profits).

Profit margin Measure of the profit generated from each dollar of revenue; calculated by dividing net income by revenue. Also known as return on sales, profit margin percentage, profit margin ratio, or operating performance ratio.

Profit maximization The maximization of the firm's net income.

Profit repatriation limitations Restrictions set up by host governments in terms of a company's ability to pay dividends from its operations back to its home base.

Profit sharing A system to distribute a portion of the profits of the organization to employees.

Profit-volume chart A chart used to assist management in understanding the relationship between profit and volume.

Profitability The ability of a firm to earn income.

Profitability ratios 1: Ratios that measure the degree of success or failure of an enterprise or division for a given period of time. **2:** A group of ratios showing the effect of liquidity, asset management, and debt management on operating results.

Profound knowledge, system of As defined by W. Edwards Deming, states that learning cannot be based on experience only; it requires comparisons of results to a prediction, plan, or an expression of theory. Predicting why something happens is essential to understand results and to continually improve. The four components of the system of profound knowledge are: appreciation for a system, knowledge of variation, theory of knowledge, and understanding of psychology.

Program A set of instructions to a computer.

Program evaluation and review technique (PERT) Event-oriented project management planning and measurement technique that utilizes an arrow diagram or road map to identify all major project events and demonstrates the amount of time (critical path) needed to complete a project. It provides three time estimates: optimistic, most likely, and pessimistic.

Programmable problem A problem that can be solved by a computer program.

Programmed decision A decision made in response to a situation that has occurred often enough to enable decision rules to be developed and applied in the future.

Programmed decision making Making decisions based on precedent, custom, policies and procedures, and on training and development.

Programming The process of writing software.

Programming languages Sets of syntax for abbreviated forms of instructions that special programs can translate into machine language so a computer can understand the instructions.

Project 1 (*n*) An endeavor to accomplish a specific objective through a unique set of interrelated tasks and the effective utilization of resources. **2** (*v*): The selection of certain columns from a table.

Project control Regularly gathering data on actual project performance, comparing actual performance to planned performance, and taking corrective measures if actual performance is behind planned performance.

Project life cycle 1: The four phases through which a project moves: identification of a need, problem, or opportunity; development of a proposed solution; implementation of the proposed solution; and termination of the project. **2:** Five sequential phases of project management: concept, planning, design, implementation, and evaluation.

Project Finance Loan Program Program that allows banks, Ex-Im Bank, or a combination of both to extend long-term financing for capital equipment and related services for major projects.

Project management The set of activities that is performed to ensure the timely and successful completion of a project within the budget. Project management includes planning activities, hiring and managing personnel, budgeting, conducting meetings, and tracking technical and financial performance. Project management software applications facilitate these activities.

Project manager A manager responsible for a temporary work project that involves the participation of other people from various functions and levels of the organization; a person responsible for coordinating the activities of several departments on a full-time basis for the completion of a specific project.

Project manufacturing A type of manufacturing process used for large, often unique, items or structures that require a custom design capability (engineer-to-order). This type of process is highly flexible and can cope with a broad range of product designs and design changes. Product manufacturing usually uses a fixed-position type layout. *See:* batch (fourth definition), continuous production, job shop (second definition), process manufacturing, project, repetitive manufacturing.

Project organization structure An organization structure in which each project has its own project manager and project team and all the resources needed to accomplish an individual project are assigned full time to the project.

Project plan All the documents that comprise the details of why the project is to be initiated, what the project is to accomplish, when and where it is to be implemented, who will have responsibility, how the implementation will be carried out, how much it will cost, what resources are required, and how the project's progress and results will be measured.

Project required rate of return, k_{proj} The risk-adjusted required rate of return for an individual project.

Project scope All the work that must be done to accomplish the project's objective to the customer's satisfaction; scope of the project; work scope.

Project selection Evaluating various needs or opportunities and then deciding which of these should move forward as a project to be implemented.

Project strategy (protocol) Statement of the attributes the project is expected to have, the market at which it is targeted, and the purpose behind commercializing the product.

Projected (pro forma) balance sheet method A method of forecasting financial requirements based on forecasted financial statements.

Projection The tendency to see one's own personal traits in other people.

Promissory note A document specifying the terms and conditions of a loan, including the amount, interest rate, and repayment schedule.

Promotion strategy Problems related to international promotion strategy include the legal aspects of the country, tax considerations, language complexities, cultural diversity, media limitations, credibility of advertising, and degree of illiteracy.

Promotional message The content of an advertisement or a publicity release.

Proposal A document, usually prepared by a contractor, that outlines an approach to meeting a need or solving a problem for a potential customer.

Proposal for appropriation of retained earnings A report prepared for approval at the stockholders' meeting for dividend payments and bonus payments to members of the board of directors and statutory auditors.

Proprietorship An unincorporated business owned by one individual.

Prospectus A document describing a new security issue and the issuing company.

Protected class Individuals within a group identified for protection under equal employment laws and regulations.

Protection of intellectual property The owner of an intellectual property right must comply with each country's requirements to obtain from that country whatever protection is available.

Protectionistic legislation A trade policy that restricts trade to or from one country to another country.

Protocol A standard set of rules that governs telecommunication between two communications devices or in a network.

Prototype Product concept in physical form. A prototype may be a full working model that has been produced by hand or a nonworking physical representation of the final product. It is used to gather customer reaction to the physical form (aesthetics and ergonomics) or to initial operating capability. It is also used in internal performance tests to ensure that performance goals have been met.

Prototyping An approach to the development of information systems in which several analysis steps are skipped, to accelerate the development process. A "quick and dirty" model is developed and continually improved until the prospective users are satisfied.

Prox Payment due on a specific day in the following month.

Proxy A document giving one person the authority to act for another, typically the power to vote shares of common stock.

Proxy fight An attempt by a person or group of people to gain control of a firm by getting its stockholders to grant that person or group the authority to vote their shares in order to elect a new management team.

Proxy information Data used as a substitute for more desirable data that are unobtainable.

Proxy process The method by which shareholders elect boards of directors.

Prudence concept The concept that provision be made for all known liabilities and losses whether the amount is known with certainty or not.

Psychocultural contexts *See:* Cross-cultural communication.

Psychographic customer characteristics Variables among buyers in the consumer market that address lifestyle issues and include consumer interests, activities, and opinions.

Psychographics Characteristics of individuals that describe them in terms of their psychological and behavioral makeup.

Psychological contract The unwritten expectations employees and employers have about the nature of their work relationships.

Psychomotor tests Tests that measure dexterity, hand-eye coordination, arm-hand steadiness, and other factors.

Psychopath A person with a personality disorder, especially one manifested in aggressively antisocial behavior.

Public issues committee (public policy committee) A firm's mechanism for responding to public or social issues.

Public relations (PR)/Public affairs (PA) Principal distinctions are that, whereas PR deals with government as one of many publics, PA professionals are experts on government, and that whereas PR has many communication responsibilities, PA deals with issues management and serves as a corporate conscience.

Publicity Like advertising, is nonpersonal communication to a mass audience, but unlike advertising, publicity is not directly paid for by the company that enjoys the publicity.

Public-key encryption Encryption technology in which a public key is used to encrypt and a private key is used to decrypt.

Publicly-owned corporation A corporation that is owned by a relatively large number of individuals who are not actively involved in its management.

Pull manufacturing A just-in-time method wherein customer orders trigger the release of finished goods, which trigger production, which trigger release of materials from suppliers.

Pull strategy Heavy emphasis on consumer-oriented advertising to encourage consumer demand for a new brand and thereby obtain retail distribution. The brand is "pulled" through the channel system in the sense that there is a backward tug from the consumer to the retailer.

Pull system 1: In production, the production of items only as demanded for use or to replace those taken for use. *See:* pull signal. **2:** In material control, the withdrawal of inventory as demanded by the using operations. Material is not issued until a signal comes from the user. **3:** In distribution, a system for replenishing field warehouse inventories where replenishment decisions are made at the field warehouse itself, not at the central warehouse or plant. *See:* kanban

Punitive tariff A tax on an imported good or service intended to punish a trading partner.

Purchase Stage in the consumer decision process when transaction terms are arranged, title of ownership is transferred, the product is paid for, and the consumer takes possession of the product from the seller.

Purchase method An accounting method used for a business combination where the acquired entity's assets and equities are combined at fair market value. Goodwill is created to the extent that cost exceeds the fair market value of the identifiable assets of the unit acquired. The accounting method employed when a parent company acquires a controlling share of the voting stock of a subsidiary other than by the exchange of voting common stock.

Purchase order with payment voucher attached A draft coupled with a purchase order, which eliminates the need for a supplier to issue an invoice and for a customer to process the invoice and issue a check.

Purchase terms Terms of credit offered by suppliers.

Purchases discounts An available discount taken by a buyer for early payment of an invoice.

Purchases returns and allowances Reductions in purchases resulting from merchandise being returned to the seller or from the seller's reduction in the original purchase price.

Purchasing (or procurement) A functional activity carried out in just about every organization, most often referring to the day-to-day tactical management of material flows and information. It begins with the determination of needs and specifications for internal customers, matching market and commodity information to customer needs, developing a purchase order (a paper or electronic form that specifies that type and quantity of material or service required), tracking and follow-up on the order, and issuing a payment to the supplier.

Purchasing cards Are credit cards used by businesses to make small dollar purchases of maintenance, repair, and operating supplies. Use of purchasing, or procurement, cards greatly reduces the number of purchase orders and invoices processed and payments made.

Purchasing power gain A gain that arises from holding monetary items during times when the general purchasing power of the monetary unit changes.

Purchasing power loss A loss that arises from holding monetary items during times when the general purchasing power of the monetary unit changes.

Purchasing Power Parity (PPP) line Diagonal line on a graph that reflects points at which the inflation differential between two countries is equal to the percentage change in the exchange rate between the two respective currencies.

Purchasing Power Parity (PPP) theory Theory suggesting that exchange rates will adjust over time to reflect the differential in inflation rates in the two countries; in this way, the purchasing power of consumers when purchasing domestic goods will be the same as that when they purchase foreign goods.

Purchasing power risk The possibility that an investment's proceeds will not be worth as much as anticipated due to general price level increases in the economy. Anticipated inflation is built into the risk-free interest rate, but investors are still vulnerable to losses in purchasing power from unanticipated inflation and will require a higher yield when price levels are volatile.

Pure play method An approach used for estimating the beta of a project in which a firm identifies companies whose only business is the product in question, determines the beta for each firm, and then averages the betas to find an approximation of its own project's beta.

Pure risk Uncertainty as to whether a loss will occur.

Push manufacturing Materials are released into production and work in process is released into finished goods in anticipation of future sales.

Push strategy Aggressive trade allowances and personal selling efforts to obtain distribution for a new brand through wholesalers and retailers. The brand is "pushed" through the channel system in the sense that there is a forward thrust from the manufacturer to the trade.

Push system 1: In production, the production of items at times required by a given schedule planned in advance. **2:** In material control, the issuing of material according to a given schedule or issuing material to a job order at its start time. **3:** In distribution, a system for replenishing field warehouse inventories where replenishment decision making is centralized, usually at the manufacturing site or central supply facility.

Put *See:* currency put option.

Putable bond A bond that can be redeemed at the bondholder's option.

Put option A contract that allows the owners to sell the underlying asset at a specific price over a specific span of time. The option to sell a specified number of shares of stock at a prespecified price during a particular period.

Put option on real assets Project that contains an option of divesting part or all of the project.

PVA$_n$ The present value of an ordinary annuity with n payments.

PVIFA(DUE)$_{i,n}$ The present value interest factor for an annuity due—PVIFA(DUE)$_{i,n}$ = PVIFA$_{i,n}$ × (1 + i).

Pyramid forecasting A forecasting technique that enables management to review and adjust forecasts made at an aggregate level and to keep lower level forecasts in balance. The procedure begins with the roll up (aggregation) of item forecasts into forecasts by product group. The management team establishes a (new) forecast for the product group. The value is then forced down (disaggregation) to individual item forecasts so that they are consistent with the aggregate plan. The approach combines the stability of aggregate forecasts and the application of management judgment with the need to forecast many end items within the constraints of an aggregate forecast or sales plan.

Pyramid model A management structure in which the CEO is at the top, a small group of senior managers are one level down, a larger number of middle managers are the next level down, and so forth.

Q

Qualified sales leads Potential customers who have a need for the salesperson's product, and are able to buy; that is, they have the financial means to purchase the product and the authority to make the buying decision.

Qualitative information Data that have been analyzed to provide a better understanding, description, or prediction of given situations, behavioral patterns, or underlying dimensions.

Quality 1: Refers to products/services that meet or exceed consumers' expectations at the lowest cost possible. **2:** Subjective term for which each person has his or her own definition. In technical usage, quality can have two meanings: 1) the characteristics of a product or service that bear on its ability to satisfy stated or implied needs and 2) a product or service free of deficiencies.

Quality adviser Person (facilitator) who helps team members work together in quality processes and is a consultant to the team. The adviser is concerned about the process and how decisions are made rather than about which decisions are made.

Quality assessment Process of identifying business practices, attitudes, and activities that are enhancing or inhibiting the achievement of quality improvement in an organization.

Quality assurance/quality control (QA/QC) Two terms that have many interpretations because of the multiple definitions for the words *assurance* and *control*. For example, *assurance* can mean the act of giving confidence, the state of being certain, or the act of making certain; *control* can mean an evaluation to indicate needed corrective responses, the act of guiding, or the state of a process in which the variability is attributable to a constant system of chance causes. One definition of quality assurance is: all the planned and systematic activities implemented within the quality system that can be demonstrated to provide confidence that a product or service will fulfill requirements for quality. One definition for quality control is: the operational techniques and activities used to fulfill requirements for quality. Often, however, *quality assurance* and *quality control* are used interchangeably, referring to the actions performed to ensure the quality of a product, service, or process.

Quality audit Systematic, independent examination and review to determine whether quality activities and related results comply with planned arrangements and whether these arrangements are implemented effectively and are suitable to achieve the objectives.

Quality characteristics Unique characteristics of products and of services by which customers evaluate their perception of quality.

Quality circle Small group of employees who monitor productivity and quality and suggest solutions to problems.

Quality cost reports System of collecting quality costs that uses a spreadsheet to list the elements of quality costs against a spread of the departments, areas, or projects in which the costs occur and summarizes the data to enable trend analysis and decision making. The reports help organizations review prevention costs, appraisal costs, and internal and external failure costs.

Quality costs *See:* cost of quality. Same as *poor quality cost*.

Quality council (sometimes called "quality steering committee") Group driving the quality improvement effort and usually having oversight responsibility for the implementation and maintenance of the quality management system; operates in parallel with the normal operation of the business.

Quality culture Employee opinions, beliefs, traditions, and practices concerning quality.

Quality engineering Analysis of a manufacturing system at all stages to maximize the quality of the process itself and the products it produces.

Quality function Entire collection of activities through which an organization achieves fitness for use, no matter where these activities are performed.

Quality function deployment (QFD) Structured method in which customer requirements are translated into appropriate technical requirements for each stage of product development and production. The QFD process is often referred to as listening to the voice of the customer. *See:* house of quality.

Quality improvement Actions taken throughout the organization to increase the effectiveness and efficiency of activities and processes in order to provide added benefits to both the organization and its customers.

Quality level agreement (QLA) Internal service/product providers assist their internal customers in clearly delineating the level of service/product required in quantitatively measurable terms. A QLA may contain specifications for accuracy, timeliness, quality/usability, product life, service availability, responsiveness to needs, and so on.

Quality loop Conceptual model of interacting activities that influence quality at the various stages ranging from the identification of needs to the assessment of whether those needs are satisfied.

Quality loss function Parabolic approximation of the quality loss that occurs when a quality characteristic deviates from its target value. The quality loss function is expressed in monetary units: The cost of deviating from the target increases as a quadratic function the farther the quality characteristic moves from the target. The formula used to compute the quality loss function depends on the type of quality characteristic being used. The quality loss function was first introduced in this form by Genichi Taguchi.

Quality management All activities of the overall management function that determine the quality policy, objectives, and responsibilities, and implement them by means such as quality planning, quality control, quality assurance, and quality improvement within the quality system.

Quality manual Document stating the quality policy and describing the quality system of an organization.

Quality metrics Numerical measurements that give an organization the ability to set goals and evaluate actual performance versus plan.

Quality of life The standard of living combined with environmental factors, it determines the level of well-being of individuals.

Quality of work life Various corporate efforts in the areas of personal and professional development undertaken with the objectives of increasing employee satisfaction and increasing productivity.

Quality plan Document setting out the specific quality practices, resources, and sequence of activities relevant to a particular product, project, or contract.

Quality planning Activity of establishing quality objectives and quality requirements.

Quality policy Top management's formally stated intentions and direction for the organization pertaining to quality.

Quality principles Rules or concepts that an organization believes in collectively. The principles are formulated by senior management with input from others and are communicated and understood at every level of the organization.

Quality score chart (Q chart) Control chart for evaluating the stability of a process in terms of a quality score. The quality score is the weighted sum of the count of events of various classifications in which each classification is assigned a weight.

Quality system Organizational structure, procedures, processes, and resources needed to implement quality management.

Quality system audit Documented activity performed to verify, by examination and evaluation of objective evidence, that applicable elements of the quality system are suitable and have been developed, documented, and effectively implemented in accordance with specified requirements.

Quality trilogy Three-pronged approach to managing for quality. The three legs are quality planning (developing the products and processes required to meet customer needs), quality control (meeting product and process goals), and quality improvement (achieving unprecedented levels of performance). Attributed to Joseph M. Juran.

Quantitative approach Any forecasting technique which involves the use of a numerical model to forecast; the technique is usually implemented on a computer.

Quantity discounts A reduction in the cost per order based on the quantity ordered.

Quantity factor The effect of a difference in the number of units sold, assuming no change in unit sales price or unit cost.

Query An instruction to a database management system to retrieve records that meet certain conditions.

Questionnaires *See:* surveys.

Queue processing Processing in batches (contrast with continuous flow processing).

Queue time Wait time of product awaiting next step in process.

Quick (acid-test) ratio This ratio is calculated by deducting inventories from current assets and dividing the remainder by current liabilities. The quick ratio is a variation of the current ratio.

Quick assets The sum of cash, receivables, and marketable securities.

Quick ratio A financial ratio that measures the ability to pay current liabilities within a short period of time.

Quid pro quo Sexual harassment in which employment outcomes are linked to the individual's granting sexual favors.

Quincunx Tool that creates frequency distributions. Beads tumble over numerous horizontal rows of pins, which force the beads to the right or left. After a random journey, the beads are dropped into vertical slots. After many beads are dropped, a frequency distribution results. In the classroom, quincunxes are often used to simulate a manufacturing process. The quincunx was invented by English scientist Francis Galton in the 1890s.

Quotas Legal restrictions on the import quantity of particular goods, imposed by governments as barriers to trade.

R

Radar chart Visual method to show in graphic form the size of gaps among a number of both current organization performance areas and ideal performance areas; resulting chart resembles a radar screen.

RAID (Redundant Array of Independent Disks) A set of magnetic disk packs maintained for backup purposes. Sometimes RAIDs are used for storing large databases.

Random Access Memory (RAM) The major part of a computer's internal memory. RAM is volatile; that is, software is held in it temporarily and disappears when the machine is unplugged or turned off, or it may disappear when operations are interrupted or new software is installed or activated. RAM is made of microchips containing transistors. Many computers have free sockets that allow the expansion of RAM.

Random number generator Used to select a stated quantity of random numbers from a table of random numbers, the resulting selection is then used to pull specific items or records corresponding to the selected numbers to comprise a "random sample."

Random sample Set of items that have been drawn from a population in such a way that each time an item was selected, every item in the population had an equal opportunity to appear in the sample.

Random sampling Sampling method in which every element in the population has an equal chance of being included.

Range chart (R chart) Control chart in which the subgroup range, R, is used to evaluate the stability of the variability within a process.

Range Measure of dispersion; highest value minus lowest value.

Range reconciliation Provides subtotals of all checks within a range of check serial numbers. This is especially useful for identifying disbursements from the same account but from several locations.

Ranking Listing of all employees from highest to lowest in performance.

Rapid Application Development (RAD) Methods using I-CASE tools and 4GLs to quickly prototype an information system. Often, software is reused in RAD.

Rapid prototyping Using software and special output devices to create prototypes to test design in three dimensions.

Rate earned on common stockholders' equity A measure of profitability computed by dividing net income, reduced by preferred dividend requirements, by common stockholders' equity.

Rate earned on stockholders' equity A measure of profitability computed by dividing net income by total stockholders' equity.

Rate earned on total assets A measure of the profitability of assets, computed as net income plus interest expense divided by total average assets.

Rate of return on investment (ROI) A measure of managerial efficiency in the use of investments in assets, computed as income from operations divided by invested assets.

Rate-based scheduling A method for scheduling and producing based on a periodic rate, for example, daily, weekly, or monthly. This method has traditionally been applied to high-volume and process industries. The concept has recently been applied within job shops using cellular layouts and mixed-model level schedules where the production rate is matched to the selling rate.

Rated capacity The expected output capability of a resource or system. Capacity is traditionally calculated from such data as planned hours, efficiency, and utilization. The rated capacity is equal to hours available $\times$ efficiency $\times$ utilization. *Syn:* calculated capacity, effective capacity, nominal capacity, standing capacity.

Rater bias Error that occurs when a rater's values or prejudices distort the rating.

Ratio analysis Process of relating isolated business numbers, such as sales, margins, expenses, debt, and profits, to make them meaningful.

Ratio of fixed assets to long-term liabilities A financial ratio that provides a measure indicating the margin of safety to creditors.

Ratio of liabilities to stockholders' equity The relationship between the total claims of the creditors and owners.

Ratio of net sales to assets A profitability measure that shows how effectively a firm utilizes its assets.

Ratio scale Scale that measures length, weight, or income.

Rational subgroup Subgroup which is expected to be as free as possible from assignable causes (usually consecutive items).

Rationalization Self-satisfying but incorrect reasons for one's behavior.

Raw and in process inventory The capitalized cost of direct materials purchases, labor, and overhead charged to the production cell.

Raw material scarcity Occurs when valuable raw material resources are geographically concentrated in some locations and not in others, resulting in resource scarcity in some locations.

Raw materials inventory Inventory consisting of the basic inputs to the organization's production process.

Reach percentage The percentage of Web users who have visited a site in the past month, or the ratio of visitors to the total Web population.

Reactive MPR Form of defensively oriented public relations that deals with developments (such as product defects or flaws) having negative consequences for the organization. Reactive MPR attempts to repair a company's reputation, prevent market erosion, and regain lost sales.

Read-Only Memory (ROM) The minor part of a computer's internal memory. ROM is loaded by the manufacturer with software that cannot be changed. Usually, ROM holds very basic system software, but sometimes also applications. Like RAM, ROM consists of microchips containing transistors.

Real accounts Balance sheet accounts.

Real cost of hedging The additional cost of hedging when compared to not hedging (a negative real cost would imply that hedging was more favorable than not hedging).

Real interest rate Nominal (or quoted) interest rate minus the inflation rate.

Real options Implicit options on real assets.

Real risk-free rate of interest, k^* The rate of interest that would exist on default-free U.S. Treasury securities if no inflation were expected.

Realistic job preview (RJP) A recruiting approach that gives applicants all pertinent and realistic information about the job and the organization.

Realized gains Gains that are actually incurred.

Realized losses Losses that are actually incurred.

Realized rate of return, $\bar{k}$ The return that is actually earned. The actual return $(\bar{k})$ is usually different from the expected return $(\hat{k})$.

Reasonable accommodation A modification or adjustment to a job or work environment for a qualified individual with a disability.

Reasonable assurance The concept that internal control, no matter how well designed and operated, cannot guarantee that an entity's objectives will be met. This is because of inherent limitations in all internal control systems.

Receipts and disbursements method A commonly used cash forecasting approach which involves determining upcoming sources of cash inflows and outflows, then laying these out on a schedule to see the aggregate effect.

Receivables All money claims against other entities, including people, business firms, and other organizations.

Receivables control Procedures and methods for following up credit extensions, including monitoring and corrective actions.

Receivables monitoring The process of evaluating the credit policy to determine if a shift in the customers' payment patterns occurs.

Receiving depository financial institution (RDFI) ACH payee's bank in an ACH credit transaction.

Receiving report The form or electronic transmission used by the receiving personnel to indicate that materials have been received and inspected.

Recency effect Error in which the rater gives greater weight to recent events when appraising an individual's performance.

Record 1: A set of standard field types. All the fields of a record contain data about a certain entity or event. **2:** Document or electronic medium which furnishes objective evidence of activities performed or results achieved.

Recourse The lender can seek payment from the borrowing firm when receivables' accounts used to secure a loan are uncollectible. When a factor buys receivables with recourse, the selling firm is ultimately responsible for payment if the customer defaults.

Recruiting 1: The activities or practices that define the desired characteristics of applicants for specific jobs. **2:** The process of generating a pool of qualified applicants for organizational jobs.

Recursive least squares (RLS) In the context of receivables monitoring, a regression model which allows the estimated receivables collection fractions (the regression coefficients) to change over time.

Red bead experiment Experiment developed by W. Edwards Deming to illustrate that it is impossible to put employees in rank order of performance for the coming year based on their performance during the past year because performance differences must be attributed to the system, not to employees. Four thousand red and white beads, 20 percent red, in a jar and six people are needed for the experiment. The participants' goal is to produce white beads because the customer will not accept red beads. One person begins by stirring the beads and then, blindfolded, selects a sample of 50 beads. That person hands the jar to the next person, who repeats the process, and so on. When everyone has his or her sample, the number of red beads for each is counted. The limits of variation between employees that can be attributed to the system are calculated. Everyone will fall within the calculated limits of variation that could arise from the system. The calculations will show that there is no evidence one person will be a better performer than another in the future. The experiment shows that it would be a waste of management's time to try to find out why, say, John produced four red beads and Jane produced fifteen; instead, management should improve the system, making it possible for everyone to produce more white beads.

Red-circled employee An incumbent who is paid above the range set for the job.

Red-lining Practice of identifying and avoiding unprofitable types of neighborhoods or people.

Reengineering (also: business process engineering) Completely redesigning or restructuring a whole organization, an organizational component, or a complete process. It's a "start all over again from the beginning" approach, sometimes called a "breakthrough." In terms of improvement approaches, reengineering is contrasted with incremental improvement (*kaizen*).

Reference groups Groups such as the family, coworkers, and professional and trade associations that provide the values and attitudes that influence and shape behavior, including consumer behavior.

Referent power Power that results from characteristics that command subordinates' identification with, respect and admiration for, and desire to emulate the leader.

Referrals Usually obtained by the salesperson asking current customers if they know of someone else, or another company, who might need the salesperson's product.

Refreezing The reinforcement stage of organizational development in which individuals acquire a desired new skill or attitude and are rewarded for it by the organization.

Refunding Retiring an existing bond issue with the proceeds of a newly issued bond.

Regiocentric staffing outlook The belief that key positions at the regional headquarters should be staffed by individuals from one of the region's countries.

Regional audit staff internal audit model In this type of organization, the regional staff is responsible for performing audits in all of the operations in the region. This model has recently been gaining popularity among many multinationals.

Regional Check Processing Centers (RCPCs) Eleven Fed offices set up to help clear checks. Together the twelve district banks plus the twenty-five regional branches and eleven RCPCs gives the Fed a network of forty-eight offices to clear checks.

Regional structure An international corporate structure wherein regional heads are made responsible for specific territories, usually consisting of multiple countries, such as Europe, East Asia, and South America.

Regional trade communities International organizations, conferences, and treaties focusing on business and trade regulations; the EU (European Union) is the most prominent of these.

Register A fast memory location in the CPU, made of special semiconductors and circuitry.

Register disbursement scheme Scheme that involves false refunds or false voids.

Registrar Bank which keeps records of the number of shares of stock authorized, issued, and redeemed, and ensures that the number of share issued does not exceed those authorized.

Registration statement A statement of facts filed with the SEC about a company that plans to issue securities.

Registration to standards Process in which an accredited, independent third-party organization conducts an on-site audit of a company's operations against the requirements of the standard to which the company wants to be registered. Upon successful completion of the audit, the company receives a certificate indicating that it has met the standard requirements.

Regression analysis Study used to understand the relationship between two or more variables. Regression analysis makes it possible to predict one variable from knowledge about another. The relationship can be determined and expressed as a mathematical equation.

Regression coefficient Term measured by regression analysis to estimate the sensitivity of the dependent variable to a particular independent variable.

Regular reports Reports that assist managers in planning activities and controlling operations.

Regulation CC Effective September 1990, this ruling stipulates that from the day of deposit local checks must be given availability within two business days, and nonlocal checks within five days.

Regulation Q A Federal Reserve regulation that restricts banks from paying interest on demand deposit accounts.

Reinforcement Process of providing positive consequences when an individual is applying the correct knowledge and skills to the job. It has been described as "catching people doing things right and recognizing their behavior." Caution: less than desired behavior can also be reinforced unintentionally.

Reinforcement theory A motivation theory based on the relationship between a given behavior and its consequences.

Reinvestment rate assumption The assumption that cash flows from a project can be reinvested 1) at the cost of capital, if using the NPV method, or 2) at the internal rate of return, if using the IRR method.

Reinvestment rate risk The possibility that the investor will have to invest cash proceeds at a lower interest rate for the remainder of a predetermined investment horizon.

Reinvoicing The policy of buying goods from one unit and selling them to a second unit and reinvoicing the sale to the next unit, to take advantage of favorable exchange rates.

Reinvoicing center Facility that centralizes payments and charges subsidiaries fees for its function; this can effectively shift profits to subsidiaries where tax rates are low.

Relational database A database in which the records are organized in individual tables (called "relations"). In order for data from different tables to be related, tables must contain foreign keys, which are primary keys in other tables in the database. The ease of building and maintaining a relational database has made it more popular than the hierarchical and network models.

Relational operation An operation that creates a temporary table that is a subset of the original table or tables in a relational database.

Relationship approach One view of the corporation's link to its banks, in which the corporation chooses its bank services primarily based on preexisting business dealings. Loyalty to prior arrangements is considered to be more important than price when selecting banks for cash management or lending services. Usually implies that credit and cash management services will both be handled by the same bank or network of banks.

Relationship selling Requires the development of a trusting partnership in which the salesperson seeks to provide long-term customer satisfaction by listening, gathering information, educating, and adding value for the customer.

Relative form of purchasing power parity Theory stating that the rate of change in the prices of products should be somewhat similar when measured in a common currency, as long as transportation costs and trade barriers are unchanged.

Relaxed current asset investment policy A policy under which relatively large amounts of cash and marketable securities and inventories are carried and under which sales are stimulated by a liberal credit policy that results in a high level of receivables.

Relevant cash flows The specific cash flows that should be considered in a capital budgeting decision.

Relevant range The range of activity over which changes in cost are of interest to management.

Relevant risk The risk of a security that cannot be diversified away, or its market risk. This reflects a security's contribution to the risk of a portfolio.

Reliability 1: Dependability; the predictability of the outcome of an action. For example, the reliability of arrival time for ocean freight or airfreight. **2:** In measurement system analysis, refers to the ability of an instrument to produce the same results over repeated administration—to measure consistently. In reliability engineering it is the probability of a product performing its intended function under stated conditions for a given period of time. *See:* mean time between failures.

Religion Different societies develop different religious systems, which are major causes of cultural differences in many societies. Religious systems provide motivation and meaning beyond the material aspects of life.

Remanufacturing 1: An industrial process in which worn-out products are restored to like-new condition. In contrast, a repaired product normally retains its identity, and only those parts that have failed or are badly worn are replaced or serviced. **2:** The manufacturing environment where worn-out products are restored to like-new condition.

Remedy 1: Judgments asked for in civil cases (what it would take to right a private wrong). **2:** Something that eliminates or counteracts a problem cause; a solution.

Remittance advice A document that usually accompanies payment, indicating customer, account number, date, and invoice(s) being paid.

Rental A type of lease in which the lessor retains not only legal title, but most of the risks and rewards of ownership.

Reorder point The inventory level at which an order should be placed.

Repair Action taken on a nonconforming product so that it will fulfill the intended usage requirements although it may not conform to the originally specified requirements.

Repatriation Planning, training, and reassignment of global employees to their home countries.

Repatriation of earnings The process of sending cash flows from a foreign subsidiary back to the parent company.

Repatriation program Programs that assist the returning expatriate in readjusting to the home country's environment. Attempts to alleviate the effects of reverse culture shock.

Repeatability and reproducibility (R & R) Measurement validation process to determine how much variation exists in the measurement system (including the variation in product, the gage used to measure, and the individuals using the gage).

Repeater A device that strengthens signals and then sends them on their next leg toward their next destination.

Repetitive manufacturing The repeated production of the same discrete products or families of products. Repetitive methodology minimizes setups, inventory, and manufacturing lead times by using production lines, assembly lines, or cells. Work orders are no longer necessary; production scheduling and control are based on production rates. Products may be standard or assembled from modules. Repetitive is not a function of speed or volume. *Syn:* repetitive process, repetitive production.

Replacement chain (common life) approach A method of comparing projects of unequal lives that assumes each project can be replicated as many times as necessary to reach a common life span; the NPVs over this life span are then compared, and the project with the higher common life NPV is chosen.

Replacement cost The total cost to acquire another item that would perform the functions identical to those performed by an existing item.

Replacement decisions Whether to purchase capital assets to take the place of existing assets to maintain or improve existing operations.

Replication A process in which a full copy of an entire database is stored at all the sites that need access to it.

Report form The form of balance sheet with the liabilities and owner's equity sections presented below the assets section.

Reportable condition An internal control deficiency related to financial reporting; it is a significant deficiency in the design or operation of the internal control system that could adversely affect the entity's ability to record, process, summarize, and report financial data consistent with the assertions of management in the financial statements.

Reporting period The time interval at which actual project performance will be compared to planned performance.

Representative firms Locally owned accounting firms that have agreements with a Big Five or some other accounting firm. The agreement covers areas such as standards of performance and standards of conduct.

Representative office An office of an international bank established in a foreign country to serve the bank's customers in the area in an advisory capacity; does not take deposits or make loans.

Repurchase agreement (RP) 1: The sale of a portfolio of securities with a prearranged buyback one or several days later. A repurchase agreement, or "repo" as it is often called, involves the bank "selling" the investor a portfolio of securities, then agreeing to buy the securities back (repurchase) at an agreed-upon future date. **2:** Agreement to buy back something previously sold.

Request for admission Request that the opposing party admit designated facts relevant to litigation.

Request for information (RFI) A request to vendors for general, somewhat informal, information about their products.

Request for proposal (RFP) A document specifying all the system requirements and soliciting a proposal from vendors who might want to bid on a project or service.

Required completion time The time or date by which a project must be completed.

Required rate of return, k_s The minimum rate of return on a stock that stockholders consider acceptable.

Required rate of return, or hurdle rate The discount rate (cost of funds) that the IRR must exceed for a project to be considered acceptable.

Requirements explosion The process of calculating the demand for the components of a parent item by multiplying the parent item requirements by the component usage quantity specified in the bill of material. *Syn:* explosion.

Research and development costs The direct and indirect outlays for exploring potential new products and developing new products.

Research collaboration Two or more companies that participate in a defined research program and benefit from the results. Research costs can be funded entirely by one of the parties, shared equally by the parties, or shared according to some other agreed-upon proportion.

Reserve borrowing capacity The ability to borrow money at a reasonable cost when good investment opportunities arise; firms often use less debt than specified by the MM optimal capital structure to ensure that they can obtain debt capital later if they need to.

Resident staff and central reviewers internal audit model In this type of organization, the resident internal auditors located on site perform the audit work. Their work is periodically reviewed by the traveling members of the parent company's central internal audit staff.

Resident staff and regional and central reviewers internal auditing model In this type of organization, the resident staff conducts the internal audits. Regional reviewers, responsible for certain geographical areas, oversee their work to ensure compliance with the parent company policies. The central staff from headquarters makes periodic reviews to ensure reporting uniformity throughout all the regions.

Resident staff and regional reviewers internal audit model In this type of organization, the work of the resident internal auditors is reviewed by the regional reviewers to ensure uniformity. Independent review from regional staff also enhances the degree of reliability of the reports.

Residual dividend policy A policy in which the dividend paid is set equal to the actual earnings minus the amount of retained earnings necessary to finance the firm's optimal capital budget.

Residual income (RI) RI expresses performance in the form of a profit amount that is left after the cost of invested capital has been subtracted. The excess of income from operations over a "minimum" amount of desired income from operations.

Residual value 1: The estimated recoverable cost of a depreciable asset as of the time of its removal from service. **2:** The value of leased property at the end of the lease term.

Resiliency Condition of a market in which new orders enter when a temporary imbalance of buy or sell orders push the price away from its equilibrium level.

Resistance to change Unwillingness to change beliefs, habits, and ways of doing things.

Resolution The degree to which the image on a computer monitor is sharp. Higher resolution means a sharper image. Resolution depends on the number of pixels on the screen and the dot pitch.

Resource leveling A method for developing a schedule that attempts to minimize the fluctuations in requirements for resources without extending the project schedule beyond the required completion time; resource smoothing. *Syn:* leveling.

Resource-limited scheduling The scheduling of activities so that predetermined resource availability pools are not exceeded. Activities are started as soon as resources are available (with respect to logical constraints), as required by the activity. When not enough of a resource exists to do all tasks on a given day, a priority decision is made. Project finish may be delayed, if necessary, to alter schedules constrained by resource usage.

Resource requirements matrix Tool to relate the resources required to the project tasks requiring them (used to indicate types of individuals needed, material needed, subcontractors, and so on).

Respect-oriented leadership Prevalent in China, Japan, Korea, Singapore, and Turkey; characterized by avoiding confrontation, displaying patience, listening to others, and avoiding losing face.

Responsibility Obligation to perform certain tasks and duties.

Responsibility accounting The process of measuring and reporting operating data by areas of responsibility.

Responsibility center An organizational unit for which a manager is assigned responsibility for the unit's performance.

Responsibility matrix A table that lists the individuals or organizational units responsible for accomplishing each work item in a work breakdown structure.

Restricted current asset investment policy A policy under which holdings of cash and marketable securities, inventories, and receivables are minimized.

Restrictive covenant A provision in a debt contract that constrains the actions of the borrower.

Restructuring Reevaluation of a company's assets because of impairment of value or for other reasons. Restructured companies usually have lower amounts of assets and look quite different than before the restructuring.

Retail inventory method A means of estimating inventory based on the relationship of the cost and the retail price of merchandise.

Retail life cycle Description of competitive development in retailing that assumes that retail institutions pass through an identifiable cycle that includes four distinct stages: 1) introduction, 2) growth, 3) maturity, and 4) decline.

Retail lockbox Is set up for a business receiving a large volume of relatively small dollar checks. Processing costs must be considered here along with collection float, and optically scannable invoices are read by machine to minimize human processing.

Retail lockbox system A lockbox system structured to handle a large volume of standardized invoice materials where the remittance checks have a relatively low average dollar face value.

Retail market An exchange situation where the buyers and/or sellers are primarily small entities, especially individuals.

Retail mix Retailer's combination of merchandise, prices, advertising, location, customer services, selling, and store layout and design that is used to attract customers.

Retailing The final activity and steps needed to place merchandise made elsewhere into the hands of the consumer or to provide services to the consumer.

Retained earnings Net income retained in a corporation.

Retained earnings statement A summary of the changes in the earnings retained in the corporation for a specific period of time.

Retained earnings The balance sheet account that indicates the total amount of earnings the firm has not paid out as dividends throughout its history; these earnings have been reinvested in the firm.

Retaliation Punitive actions taken by employers against individuals who exercise their legal rights.

Return items Checks that bounce, leading to their return to the bank of first deposit through each bank involved in the forward presentment.

Return on assets (ROA) ROA equals net income divided by total assets.

Return on common equity (ROE) The ratio of net income to common equity; it measures the rate of return on common stockholders' investment.

Return on equity (ROE) Net profit after taxes, divided by last year's tangible stockholders' equity, and then multiplied by 100 to provide a percentage (also referred to as return on net worth).

Return on investment (ROI) 1: Calculation showing the value of expenditures for HR activities. **2:** ROI incorporates the investment base and profits to assess performance. **3:** Umbrella term for a variety of ratios measuring an organization's business performance and calculated by dividing some measure of return by a measure of investment and then multiplying by 100 to provide a percentage. In its most basic form, ROI indicates what remains from all money taken in after all expenses are paid.

Return on net assets (RONA) Measurement of the earning power of the firm's investment in assets, calculated by dividing net profit after taxes by last year's tangible total assets and then multiplying by 100 to provide a percentage.

Return on quality Measurement of the expected revenue against the expected costs associated with quality efforts.

Return on total assets The ratio of net income to total assets; it provides an idea of the overall return on investment earned by the firm.

Revaluation reserve An equity reserve used to value fixed assets at an appraised value or a replacement value. This is done by upward adjustment of the asset and correspondingly recording an equal amount in a revaluation reserve.

Revenue 1: Increases in a company's resources from the sale of goods or services. **2:** The gross increase in owner's equity as a result of business and professional activities that earn income.

Revenue anticipation notes Short-term debt instruments that provide working capital financing for states and localities as they await anticipated revenues from other sources of revenue.

Revenue budget A budget that identifies the forecasted and actual revenues of the organization.

Revenue center A responsibility center in which a manager is accountable for revenues only.

Revenue expenditures Expenditures that benefit only the current period.

Revenue recognition Determining that revenues have been earned and are collectible and thus should be reported on the income statement.

Revenue recognition concept The principle by which revenues are recognized in the period in which they are earned.

Revenue securities Issues which tie cash flows to pledged revenue from the facility(ies) being financed: rental revenue from a convention center, or tolls from a bridge or toll road.

Reverse auction An online auction in which participants post the price they want to pay for a good or service, and retailers compete to make the sale; also called a name-your-price auction.

Reverse culture shock What expatriates experience upon returning home after a long assignment in a foreign country.

Reverse discrimination When a person is denied an opportunity because of preferences given to protected-class individuals who may be less qualified.

Reverse distribution A system responding to environmental concerns that ensures a firm can retrieve a product from the market for subsequent use, recycling, or disposal.

Reverse engineering Learning to reproduce technology by taking it apart to determine how it works and then copying it.

Reverse positive pay The disbursing bank sends the check presentment file to the company to see if all the items should be honored.

Reverse repo The other side of a repurchase agreement. In this case a firm needing a temporary source of cash for a few days can negotiate with its bank to temporarily sell securities with an agreement to repurchase them at the end of the specified period.

Revocable letter of credit Letter of credit issued by a bank that can be cancelled at any time without prior notification to the beneficiary.

Revolving (guaranteed) line of credit A formal, committed line of credit extended by a bank or other lending institution.

Revolving credit agreement Allows the borrower to continually borrow and repay amounts up to an agreed-upon limit. The agreement is annually renewable at a variable interest rate during an interim period of anywhere from one to five years.

Reward power Power that results from the authority to bestow rewards on other people.

Rework Action taken on a nonconforming product so that it will fulfill the specified requirements (may also pertain to a service).

Riding the yield curve Investing strategy that involves buying securities with maturities longer than the investment horizon, fully intending to liquidate the position early.

Right the first time Term used to convey the concept that it is beneficial and more cost effective to take the necessary steps up front to ensure a product or service meets its requirements than to provide a product or service that will need rework or not meet customers' needs. In other words, an organization should engage in defect prevention rather than defect detection.

Rightsizing *See:* Downsizing.

Right-to-sue letter A letter issued by the EEOC that notifies a complainant that he or she has ninety days in which to file a personal suit in federal court.

Ring A communications network topology in which each computer (or other communications device) is connected to two other computers.

Ringi A group-oriented participative decision-making technique used in many Japanese organizations.

RISC (Reduced Instruction Set Computer) A computer whose CPU includes only the most commonly used functions. A reduced instruction set makes the computer significantly faster than the same computer with a full instruction set in its CPU.

Risk 1: A decision has clear-cut goals, and good information is available, but the future outcomes associated with each alternative are subject to chance. **2:** Uncertainty as to economic loss. **3:** In a financial market context, the chance that a financial asset will not earn the return promised.

Risk-adjusted discount rate Higher (lower) interest rate used in present value calculations when the project is of greater (lesser) risk than the average capital budgeting project invested in by the company.

Risk-adjusted return on capital (RAROC) Assesses how much capital would be required by the organization's various activities (such as products, projects, loans, and so on) to keep the probability of bankruptcy below a specified probability level.

Risk analysis The process of predicting the outcome of a decision in the face of uncertainty. The study of the possible payoffs and probabilities associated with a decision alternative or a decision strategy.

Risk arbitrage The opportunistic buying and selling of companies that appear on the verge of being taken over by other firms.

Risk assessment The identification, analysis, and management of risk, such as the risk associated with the possibility of fraud.

Risk assessment/management Process of determining what risks are present in a situation (for example, project plan) and what actions might be taken to eliminate or mediate them.

Risk aversion Risk-averse investors require higher rates of return to invest in higher-risk securities.

Risk avoidance A conscious decision not to expose oneself or one's firm to a particular risk of loss.

Risk avoider A decision-maker who tends to avoid decisions that have the risk of an extremely bad (low) payoff.

Risk classes An approach to risk adjusting potential capital projects by developing discount rates based on anticipated variability in the projects' cash flows. Proposals with longer time horizons, permanent effects on the firm's cash flows, or those with a short time horizon that might result in a very large range or standard deviation of outcomes would be assigned a higher discount rate.

Risk exposure Possible terrorism in a foreign country, especially in countries where some groups hold hostile feelings toward "capitalists," or where there is a high possibility of the expatriate being kidnapped for ransom.

Risk-free rate Determined primarily by investors' collective time preferences, the rate of inflation expected over the maturity period, and demand-side influences such as economic productivity.

Risk management 1: The identification of threats and the design of an approach to their containment. **2:** The process used to systematically manage pure risk exposures.

Risk-management policy A plan, procedure, or rule of action followed for the purpose of securing consistent action over a period of time.

Risk-management process 1) Identify risks, 2) evaluate risks as to frequency and severity, 3) select risk-management techniques, and 4) implement and review decisions.

Risk-management information system (RMIS) A computer software program that assists in tracking and statistical analysis of past losses.

Risk manager An individual charged with minimizing the adverse impact of losses on the achievement of a company's goals.

Risk mapping (risk profiling) Method of risk identification and assessment by arranging all risks in a matrix reflecting frequency, severity, and existing insurance coverage.

Risk neutral A decision-maker who is indifferent to risk where an alternative with the best expected monetary value is identical to an alternative with the highest expected utility.

Risk premium, RP The portion of the expected return that can be attributed to the additional risk of an investment; it is the difference between the expected rate of return on a given risky asset and that on a less risky asset.

Risk profile The probability distribution of the possible payoffs associated with a decision alternative or decision strategy.

Risk propensity The willingness to undertake risk with the opportunity of gaining an increased payoff.

Risk reduction A decrease in the total amount of uncertainty present in a particular situation.

Risk retention Handling risk by bearing the results of risk, rather than employing other methods of handling it, such as transfer or avoidance.

Risk spread The added yield necessary to compensate for risk factors other than maturity differences, such as default risk and liquidity risk.

Risk structure of interest rate Set of interest rate differences between various securities which arise due to any factor other than a different maturity. The main risk factors giving rise to this structure are default risk, reinvestment rate risk, and purchasing power risk.

Risk taker A decision maker that tends to prefer decisions that, although risky, have a possibility for an extremely good (high) payoff.

Risk transfer A risk-management technique whereby one party (transferor) pays another (transferee) to assume a risk that the transferor desires to escape.

Robotics The science and specialty of developing machines that can mimic human movement. Robots are highly automated machines controlled by computers.

Robustness Condition of a product or process design that remains relatively stable with a minimum of variation even though factors that influence operations or usage, such as environment and wear, are constantly changing.

ROI *See:* return on investment.

Role A set of expectations for one's behavior.

Role ambiguity 1: Uncertainty about what behaviors are expected of a person in a particular role. **2:** Anxiety caused by inadequate information about job responsibilities and performance-related goals.

Role conflict 1: Incompatible demands of different roles. **2:** Anxiety caused by conflicting job demands.

Role-playing Training technique whereby participants spontaneously perform in an assigned scenario.

Roll-on-roll-off (RORO) Transportation vessels built to accommodate trucks, which can drive on in one port and drive off at their destinations.

Root cause analysis Quality tool used to distinguish the source of defects or problems. It is a structured approach that focuses on the decisive or original cause of a problem or condition.

Root mean square error Has become increasingly popular in business and economic applications. It simply involves taking the square root of the mean square error (MSE).

Rough-cut capacity planning (RCCP) The process of converting the master production schedule into requirements for key resources, often including labor, machinery, warehouse space, suppliers' capabilities, and, in some cases, money. Comparison to available or demonstrated capacity is usually done for each key resource. This comparison assists the master scheduler in establishing a feasible master production schedule. Three approaches to performing RCCP are the bill of labor (resources, capacity) approach, the capacity planning using overall factors approach, and the resource profile approach. *See:* bill of resources, capacity planning, capacity planning using overall factors, product load profile, resource profile.

Routine reporting Reports that enable managers to plan activities and control operations.

Routing Process of directing incoming calls to customer service representatives in which more profitable customers are more likely to receive faster and better customer service.

Royalty Compensation paid by one firm to another under licensing and franchising agreements.

Rules of Professional Conduct A section in the American Institute of Certified Public Accountants' Code of Professional Conduct that contains rules that govern the performance of professional services and identify both acceptable and unacceptable behavior.

Run Consecutive points on one side of the centerline.

Run chart Line graph showing data collected during a run or an uninterrupted sequence of events. A trend is indicated when the series of collected data points head up or down.

S

S corporation A small corporation which, under Subchapter S of the Internal Revenue Code, elects to be taxed as a proprietorship or a partnership yet retains limited liability and other benefits of the corporate form of organization.

Safety Condition in which the physical well-being of people is protected.

Safety capacity The planned amount by which the available capacity exceeds current productive capacity. This capacity provides protection from planned activities, such as resource contention, and preventive maintenance and unplanned activities, such as resource breakdown, poor quality, rework, or lateness. Safety capacity plus productive capacity plus excess capacity is equal to 100 percent of capacity.

Safety lead time An element of time added to normal lead time to protect against fluctuations in lead time so that an order can be completed before its real need date. When used, the MRP system, in offsetting for lead time, will plan both order release and order completion for earlier dates than it would otherwise. *Syn:* protection time, safety time.

Safety stock 1: In general, a quantity of stock planned to be in inventory to protect against fluctuations in demand or supply. **2:** In the context of master production scheduling, the additional inventory and capacity planned as protection against forecast errors and short-term changes in the backlog. Overplanning can be used to create safety stock. *Syn:* buffer stock, reserve stock.

Salaries Consistent payments made each period regardless of number of hours worked.

Sale and leaseback An operation whereby a firm sells land, buildings, or equipment and simultaneously leases the property back for a specified period under specific terms.

Sales agents Dealers sometimes function as brokers in their role as for banks and other issuers of short-term securities. For a commission the agent will locate buyers for the institution's securities, again without risk because the agent does not have to buy and resell the securities.

Sales budget One of the major elements of the income statement budget that indicates the quantity of estimated sales and the expected unit selling price.

Sales call anxiety Fear of negative evaluation and rejection by customers.

Sales discounts An available discount granted by a seller for early payment of an invoice; a contra account to Sales.

Sales force automation Equipping traveling salespeople with notebook computers, PDAs, telecommunications devices, and other devices that allow them to communicate with the home office, retrieve and store information from and to other computers remotely, and fax information.

Sales forecast A forecast of a firm's unit and dollar sales for some future period; generally based on recent sales trends plus forecasts of the economic prospects for the nation, region, industry, and so forth.

Sales leveling Strategy of establishing a long-term relationship with customers to lead to contracts for fixed amounts and scheduled deliveries in order to smooth the flow and eliminate surges.

Sales mix The relative distribution of sales among the various products available for sale.

Sales potential Share of the market potential that a particular marketer may hope to gain over the long term.

Sales promotion All marketing activities that attempt to stimulate quick buyer action or, in other words, attempt to promote immediate sales of a product (thereby yielding the name *sales promotion*).

Sales return percentage (ratio) Sales returns divided by total sales; a measure of the percentage of sales being returned by customers.

Sales returns (sales returns and allowances) 1: Sold merchandise that is returned by customers and/or damaged, or other sold merchandise for which credit is given. **2:** Reductions in sales resulting from merchandise being returned by customers or from the seller's reduction in the original sales price; a contra account to Sales.

Sales-type lease In the United States, a type of capital lease where a dealer's or manufacturer's profit or loss is a basic part of the transaction for the lessor.

Same-day settlement Presentment of a check to the paying bank by 8:00 A.M. local time, with payment of the check required by Fedwire by the close of business day. This Fed initiative was enacted to reduce arbitrary holds or fees used by disbursing banks to slow check clearing.

Sample Finite number of items of a similar type taken from a population for the purpose of examination to determine whether all members of the population would conform to quality requirements or specifications.

Sample information New information obtained through research or experimentation that enables an updating or revision of the state-of-nature probabilities.

Sample size Number of units in a sample chosen from the population.

Sample standard deviation chart (*s* chart) Control chart in which the subgroup standard deviation, *s*, is used to evaluate the stability of the variability within a process.

Sampling risk Risk that a sample is not representative of the population.

Sanction A governmental action, usually consisting of a specific coercive trade measure, that distorts the free flow of trade for an adversarial or political purpose rather than an economic one.

Satisficing To choose the first solution alternative that satisfies minimal decision criteria regardless of whether better solutions are presumed to exist.

Scalability The ability to adapt applications as business needs grow.

Scale of market entities Displays a range of products along a continuum based on their tangibility.

Scanner A device that scans pictures and text and transforms them into digitized files.

Scanning system A system that enables corporations to monitor the activities taking place in markets around the globe for the purpose of responding to changing market needs.

Scatter diagram Graphical technique to analyze the relationship between two variables. Two sets of data are plotted on a graph, with the *y*-axis being used for the variable to be predicted and the *x*-axis being used for the variable to make the prediction. The graph will show possible relationships (although two variables might appear to be related, they might not be: Those who know most about the variables must make that evaluation). The scatter diagram is one of the seven tools of quality.

Scenario analysis A risk analysis technique in which "bad" and "good" sets of financial circumstances are compared with a most likely, or base case, situation.

Scenario building The identification of crucial variables and determining their effects on different cases or approaches.

Scenario planning Strategic planning process that generates multiple stories about possible future conditions, allowing an organization to look at the potential impact on them and different ways they could respond.

Scenario writing A qualitative forecasting method that consists of developing a conceptual scenario of the future based on a well-defined set of assumptions.

Schedule A timetable for a project plan.

Schedule of reinforcement The frequency with which and intervals over which reinforcement occurs.

Schema The structure of a database, detailing the names and types of fields in each set of records, and the relationships among sets of records.

Scientific management A subfield of the classical management perspective that emphasized scientifically determined changes in management practices as the solution to improving labor productivity.

Scrambled merchandising Handling of merchandise lines based solely on the profitability criterion and without regard to the consistency of the product or merchandise mix.

Scrap factor A factor that expresses the quantity of a particular component that is expected to be scrapped upon receipt from a vendor, completion of production, or while that component is being built into a given assembly. It is usually expressed as a decimal value. For a given operation or process, the scrap factor plus the yield factor is equal to one. If the scrap factor is 30 percent (or .3) then the yield is 70 percent (or .7). In manufacturing planning and control systems, the scrap factor is usually related to a specific item in the item master, but may be related to a specific component in the product structure. For example, if 50 units of a product are required by a customer and a scrap factor of 30 percent (a yield of 70 percent) is expected then 72 units (computed as 50 units divided by .7) should be started in the manufacturing process. *Syn:* scrap rate. *See:* yield, yield factor.

Sea bridge The transfer of freight among various modes of transportation at sea.

Search The process of learning about current developments inside or outside the organization that can be used to meet a perceived need for change.

Search attributes Physical properties that customers can evaluate prior to their purchase decision.

Search warrant Order issued by a judge that gives the investigator consent to search a suspect's personal information, such as bank records, tax returns, or their premises.

Seasonal component The component of the time series model that shows a periodic pattern over one year or less.

Seasonal dating Allows customers to purchase inventory before the peak buying season and defer payment until after the peak season.

Seasonal index A measure of the seasonal effect on a time series. A seasonal index above 1 indicates a positive effect, a seasonal index of 1 indicates no seasonal effect, and a seasonal index less than 1 indicates a negative effect.

Second generation languages (2GL) Assembly languages.

Secondary audience In the communication process, those who do not receive a message directly, but who will hear about the message, need to participate in the decision-making, or are affected by the message.

Secondary data Data originally collected to serve another purpose than the one in which the researcher is currently interested.

Secondary market The market in which "used" stocks are traded after they have been issued by corporations.

Secondary research Research method using data already gathered by others and reported in books, articles in professional journals, or other sources.

Secondary statement approach A complete set of financial statements including accompanying notes prepared according to the accounting standards of another country. Independent auditors express an opinion on secondary statements using the auditing standards of that country.

Secured loan A loan backed by collateral; for short-term loans, the collateral often is inventory, receivables, or both.

Securities and Exchange Commission (SEC) The U.S. government agency that regulates the issuance and trading of stocks and bonds.

Securities regulation Foreign issuers who issue securities, or whose securities are sold in the secondary market in the United States, must register them unless an exemption is available; the antifraud provisions apply where there is either *conduct* or *effects* in the United States relating to a violation of the federal securities laws.

Securitization Involves issuing debt securities collateralized by a pool of selected financial assets such a mortgages, auto loans or credit card receivables.

Security 1: A specific investment offered by a given issuer. **2:** Protection of employees and organizational facilities.

Security audit A comprehensive review of organizational security.

Security market line (SML) The line that shows the relationship between risk as measured by beta and the required rate of return for individual securities.

Security measures Systems or application programs that provide such services as tracking account numbers and passwords, and controlling access to files and programs.

Segregation of duties Division of tasks into two parts, so one person does not have complete control of the task.

Select In a relational database, the selection of records that meet certain conditions.

Selection Process of choosing individuals who have needed qualifications to fill jobs in an organization.

Selection criterion 1: Characteristic that a person must have to do a job successfully. **2:** Factor that a firm uses to choose which intermediaries will become members of its marketing channel.

Selection rate The percentage hired from a given group of candidates.

Selective distribution A carefully chosen group of intermediaries is used at a particular level in the marketing channel.

Selective listening One hears what he or she is predispositioned to hear.

Selective restatements Partial restatements of companies' reports used to help resolve the problems created by diversity in accounting standards throughout the world.

Self-concept A person's self-image.

Self-directed learning *See:* learner-controlled instruction.

Self-directed team A team consisting of five to twenty multiskilled workers who rotate jobs to produce an entire product or service, often supervised by an elected member.

Self-efficacy A person's belief that he/she can successfully learn the training program content.

Self-inspection Process by which employees inspect their own work according to specified rules.

Self-managed team Team that requires little supervision and manages itself and the day-to-day work it does; self-directed teams are responsible for whole work processes with each individual performing multiple tasks.

Self-management Independent decision making; a high degree of worker involvement in corporate decision making.

Self-reference criterion (SRC) The unconscious reference to one's own cultural values.

Self-serving bias The tendency to overestimate the contribution of internal factors to one's successes and the contribution of external factors to one's failures.

Self-sustaining international operation A foreign operation whose activities generally have no direct impact on the reporting entity's operations.

Sell hedge A hedge created by selling a futures contract.

Selling expenses Expenses incurred directly in the sale of merchandise.

Selling forward A market transaction in which the seller promises to sell currency at a certain future date at a pre-specified price.

Selling group A group (network) of brokerage firms formed for the purpose of distributing a new issue of securities.

Selling sites Web sites that provide products for purchase over the Internet.

Semantic nets A method of representing knowledge whereby facts are linked by relationships. The links create a "net."

Semantics The meaning of words and the way they are used.

Semiannual compounding The arithmetic process of determining the final value of a cash flow or series of cash flows when interest is added twice a year.

Semistrong-form efficient Description of foreign exchange markets, implying that all relevant public information is already reflected in prevailing spot exchange rates.

Semistructured problem An unstructured problem with which the decision maker may have had some experience. Requires expertise to resolve.

Seniority Time spent in the organization or on a particular job.

Sensitivity analysis 1: The study of how changes in the probability assessments for the states of nature and/or changes in the payoffs affect the recommended decision alternative. **2:** Using a model to determine the extent to which a change in a factor affects an outcome. The analysis is done by repeating *if-then* calculations. **3:** Means of incorporating risk in financial outcomes which involves varying key inputs, one at a time, and observing the effect on the decision variable(s). For example, the analyst might vary the sales level, and observe the effect on the company's cash forecast.

Sensitivity training Training in human relations that focuses on personal and interpersonal interactions; training that focuses on enhancing an expatriate's flexibility in situations quite different from those at home.

Sequential access A file organization for sequential record entry and retrieval. The records are organized as a list that follows a logical order, such as ascending order of ID numbers, or descending order of part numbers. To retrieve a record, the application must start the search at the first record and retrieve every record, sequentially, until the desired record is encountered.

Sequential oral interpreters Used by clients involved in cross-language business negotiations and social functions. Unlike simultaneous oral interpreters, they translate both language and culture.

Serial correlation The existence of correlated errors in a regression model of a time series of data points.

Serial port An outlet that accepts a cord for serial transmission.

Serial transmission Transmission of streams of bits one after another. This is the only kind of transmission possible in telecommunications.

Serious health condition A health condition requiring in-patient, hospital, hospice, or residential medical care or continuing physician care.

Servant leader A leader who works to fulfill subordinates' needs and goals as well as to achieve the organization's larger mission.

Server A computer connected to several less powerful computers that can utilize its databases and applications.

Service blueprint A service analysis method that allows service designers to identify processes involved in the service delivery system, isolate potential failure points in the system, establish time frames for the service delivery, and set standards for each step that can be quantified for measurement.

Service capacity The maximum level at which a service provider is able to provide services to customers.

Service consistency Uniform quality of service.

Service department charges The costs of services provided by an internal service department and transferred to a responsibility center.

Service gap The gap between customers' expectations of service and their perception of the service actually delivered, which is a function of the knowledge gap, the standards gap, the delivery gap, and the communications gap.

Service heterogeneity The difference from one delivery of a product to another delivery of the same product as a result of the inability to control the production and quality of the process.

Service level agreement (SLA) A document that lists all the types of services expected of an outsourcing vendor as well as the metrics that will be used to measure the degree to which the vendor has met the level of promised services. Usually, the client makes the list.

Service organization An organization that produces non-physical outputs that require customer involvement and cannot be stored in inventory.

Service quality Attitude formed by a long-term, overall evaluation of performance.

Service recovery A firm's reaction to a complaint that results in customer satisfaction and goodwill.

Service sites Web sites that provide a customer service interface for a company.

Service technology Technology characterized by intangible outputs and direct contact between employees and customers.

Serviceability 1: Design characteristic that facilitates the easy and efficient performance of service activities. Service activities include those activities required to keep equipment in operating condition, such as lubrication, fueling, oiling, and cleaning. **2:** A measurement of the degree to which servicing of an item will be accomplished within a given time under specified conditions. *See:* maintainability. **3:** The competitive advantage gained when an organization focuses on aspects such as the speed and courtesy in which customer complaints and questions are answered, following up with customers after the sale to ensure satisfaction, and offering on-site service for product repairs.

Services Deeds, efforts, or performances.

Services businesses A business providing services rather than products to customers.

Services trade The international exchange of personal or professional services, such as financial and banking services, construction, and tourism.

Servicescapes Use of physical evidence to design service environments.

Settlement Negotiated pretrial agreement between the parties to resolve a legal dispute.

Settlement date The date when payment of funds is made on the maturity of a foreign exchange contract.

Settlement range A phase of strategic planning in which a negotiation range (all possible settlements that a negotiator would be willing to take) must be established. During this phase, the LAR (least acceptable result) and MSP (most supportable position) must be identified.

Setup Changing the characteristics of a machine to produce a different product.

Setup time Time taken to change over a process to run a different product or service.

Seven basic tools of quality Help organizations understand their processes in order to improve them. The tools are the cause-and-effect diagram, check sheet, control chart, flowchart, histogram, Pareto chart, and scatter diagram. *See:* individual entries.

Seven management tools of quality Tools used primarily for planning and managing are activity network diagram (AND) or arrow diagram, affinity diagram (KJ method), interrelationship digraph, matrix diagram, priorities matrix, process decision program chart (PDPC), and tree diagram.

Seventh Directive, The The EU Seventh Directive addresses consolidated financial statement issues. *See:* Eighth Directive, Fourth Directive.

Severance pay A security benefit voluntarily offered by employers to employees who lose their jobs.

Sexual harassment Actions that are sexually directed, are unwanted, and subject the worker to adverse employment conditions or create a hostile work environment.

Shamrock team One composed of a core of members, resource experts who join the team as appropriate, and part-time/temporary members as needed.

Shape Pattern or outline formed by the relative position of a large number of individual values obtained from a process.

Shareholder value maximization Presumed goal of publicly held companies, in which decisions are made which will lead to the greatest anticipated increase in the value of the financial claims on the company. In practice, the company's stock price is utilized as a measure of the value of all financial claims.

Sharing Making key customer information accessible to all parts of the organization and in some cases selling that information to other firms.

Shelf registration Securities are registered with the SEC for sale at a later date; the securities are held "on the shelf" until the sale.

Sherman Antitrust Act Prohibits any contract, combination, or conspiracy that restrains trade. It was passed by Congress in 1890 in an effort to prevent companies from controlling (monopolizing) an industry.

Shewhart cycle *See:* plan-do-check-act cycle.

Shingo's seven wastes Shigeo Shingo, a pioneer in the Japanese Just-in-Time philosophy, identified seven barriers to improving manufacturing. They are the waste of overproduction, waste of waiting, waste of transportation, waste of stocks, waste of motion, waste of making defects, and waste of the processing itself.

Shipper's order A negotiable bill of lading that can be bought, sold, or traded while the subject goods are still in transit and that is used for letter of credit transactions.

Ship-to-stock program Arrangement with a qualified supplier whereby the supplier ships material directly to the buyer without the buyer's incoming inspection; often a result of evaluating and approving the supplier for certification.

Shop floor control A system for using data from the shop floor to maintain and communicate status information on shop orders (manufacturing orders) and on work centers. The major subfunctions of shop floor control are 1) assigning priority of each shop order; 2) maintaining work-in-process quantity information; 3) conveying shop order status information to the office; 4) providing actual output data for capacity control purposes; 5) providing quantity by location by shop order for work-in-process inventory and accounting purposes; and 6) providing measurement of efficiency, utilization, and productivity of the workforce and machines. Shop floor control can use order control or flow control to monitor material movement through the facility. *Syn:* production activity control.

Short-term credit Any liability originally scheduled for repayment within one year.

Short-term orientation A concern with the past and present and a high value on meeting social obligations.

Short-term orientation Values that respect tradition, personal stability, quick results from the efforts made, and concern with appearances.

Shrinkage Reduction of merchandise through theft, loss, and damage.

Sight draft A formal, written agreement whereby an importer (drawee) contracts to pay a certain amount on demand ("at sight") to the exporter. The bank is not extending credit, but simply helping in the payment process by receiving the draft and presenting it to the drawee. Sight drafts often must have documentation attached to verify that conditions for payment (receipt, or "sight" of goods) have been met.

Sigma Greek letter that stands for the standard deviation of a process.

Sign A signal that is recognized, structured into a category, and assigned meaning.

Signal 1: An action taken by a firm's management that provides clues to investors about how management views the firm's prospects. **2:** Transmitted by a sender to a receiver; the receiver must decode and try to understand the signal.

Signal-to-noise ratio (S/N ratio) Mathematical equation that indicates the magnitude of an experimental effect above the effect of experimental error due to chance fluctuations.

Signified The meaning attached to the signifier.

Signifier The sound or shape of the signal that is sensorially perceived without meaning yet attached to it.

Silo (as in *functional silo*) Organization where cross-functional collaboration and cooperation is minimal and where the functional "silos" tend to work toward their own goals to the detriment of the organization as a whole.

Simple (quoted) interest rate The contracted, or quoted, interest rate that is used to compute the interest paid per period.

Simple interest Arrangement in which interest is only added to the account at maturity. Because no compounding occurs, the nominal interest rate is also the annual effective rate.

Simple interest approximation formula Simple interest formula to approximate the present value effect of a financial decision. The simplicity of this approach makes its use desirable where the effect of ignoring cash flow compounding would not have a significant effect on the valuation of those flows.

Simple interest loan Both the amount borrowed and the interest charged on that amount are paid at the maturity of the loan; there are no payments made before maturity.

Simple, or quoted, rate, i_{SIMPLE} The rate quoted by borrowers and lenders that is used to determine the rate earned per compounding period (periodic rate).

Simple regression A statistical model in which the equation used to predict the value of the variable of interest (dependent variable) involves just one predictor (independent) variable.

Simplex Transmission from a device that can only transmit, to devices that can only receive. Example: radio and television broadcasts.

Simulation Technique for assessing the degree of uncertainty. Probability distributions are developed for the input variables; simulation uses this information to generate possible outcomes.

Simulation experiment The generation of a sample of values for the probabilistic inputs of a simulation model and computing the resulting values of the model outputs.

Simultaneous oral interpreters Used by speakers in formal situations such as conferences, where the audience and the speaker communicate using different languages.

Single European Act Act intended to remove numerous barriers imposed on trade and capital flows between European countries.

Single plantwide factory overhead rate method A method that allocates all factory overhead to products by using a single factory overhead rate.

Single-buyer policy Policy administered by Ex-Im Bank which allows the exporter to selectively insure certain transactions.

Single-criterion decision problem A problem in which the objective is to find the "best" solution with respect to just one criterion.

Single-minute exchange of dies (SMED) Goal to be achieved in reducing the setup time required for a changeover to a new process; the methodologies employed in devising and implementing ways to reduce setup.

Single-piece flow Method whereby the product proceeds through the process one piece at a time, rather than in large batches, eliminating queues and costly waste.

Single-source systems Measurement of the effectiveness of advertising (whether it leads to increased sales activity). They are unique in that all the relevant data is collected by a single source, processed, and then made available in a readily usable format to retailers and manufacturers.

Single-step income statement An income statement in which the total of all expenses is deducted in one step from the total of all revenues.

Single-use plans Plans that are developed to achieve a set of goals that are unlikely to be repeated in the future.

Sinking fund 1: A required annual payment designed to amortize a bond or preferred stock issue. **2:** Assets set aside in a special fund to be used for a specific purpose.

SIPOC Macro-level analysis of the suppliers, inputs, processes, outputs, and customers.

Situation analysis Analysis of the strengths, weaknesses, opportunities, and threats (SWOT) that affect organizational performance.

Situational ethics Societal condition where "right" and "wrong" are determined by the specific situation, rather than by universal moral principles.

Situational interview A structured interview composed of questions about how applicants might handle specific job situations.

Situational leadership Leadership theory that maintains that leadership style should change based on the person and the situation, with the leader displaying varying degrees of directive and supportive behavior.

Situational scheme Proposes that certain situational factors influence the HSR in all countries.

Situational theory A contingency approach to leadership that links the leader's behavioral style with the task readiness of subordinates.

Six-sigma quality 1: Term used generally to indicate that a process is well controlled, that is, process limits 63 sigma from the centerline in a control chart, and requirements/tolerance limits 66 sigma from the centerline. The term was initiated by Motorola. **2:** 3.4 defects per million units processed.

Six-sigma approach Quality philosophy; a collection of techniques and tools for use in reducing variation; a program of improvement.

Skill variety The extent to which the work requires several different activities for successful completion.

Skimming Removal of cash from a victim organization prior to its entry in an accounting system.

Skip-level meeting Evaluation technique which occurs when a member of senior management meets with persons two or more organizational levels below, without the intervening management present, to allow open expression about the effectiveness of the organization.

SKU Stock keeping unit and refers to a distinct merchandise item in the retailer's merchandise assortment.

Skunkworks A separate small, informal, highly autonomous, and often secretive group that focuses on breakthrough ideas for the business.

Slack time Time an activity can be delayed without delaying the entire project; it is determined by calculating the difference between the latest allowable date and the earliest expected date. *See:* project evaluation and review technique.

Slide The erroneous movement of all digits in a number, one or more spaces to the right or the left, such as writing $542 as $5,420.

Small business policy Policy providing enhanced coverage to new exporters and small businesses.

Small power distance culture A culture where employees perceive few power differences and follow a superior's instructions only when they either agree or feel threatened.

Smithsonian Agreement Conference between nations in 1971 that resulted in a devaluation of the dollar against major currencies and a widening of boundaries (2 percent in either direction) around the newly established exchange rates.

Smoot-Hawley Act A 1930 act that raised import duties to the highest rates ever imposed by the United States; designed to promote domestic production, it resulted in the downfall of the world trading system.

Smoothing *See:* Resource leveling.

Smoothing constant A parameter of the exponential smoothing model that provides the weight given to the most recent time series value in the calculation of the forecast.

Snail mail Regular mail handled by the Postal Service (as opposed to e-mail).

Snake Arrangement established in 1972, whereby European currencies were tied to each other within specified limits.

Social altruism An individual's major concern is the functioning of society. He or she acts to generate vital long-term benefits for others without the want or need to acquire rewards for him or herself.

Social audit A systematic attempt to identify, measure, monitor, and evaluate an organization's performance with respect to its social efforts, goals, and programs.

Social awareness Understanding human/societal needs outside one's own individual-based ends furnishes a base for interorganizational cooperative behavior and for molding effective strategies to merge human endeavors to solve difficult problems.

Social contribution Refers to the mixture of striving to fulfill other people's needs while simultaneously pursuing one's own growth and social power.

Social facilitation The tendency for the presence of others to influence an individual's motivation and performance.

Social forces The aspects of a culture that guide and influence relationships among people—their values, needs, and standards of behavior.

Social infrastructure The housing, health, educational, and other social systems in a country.

Social interaction paradigm Used to explain the inherent cooperative culture behind the economic success of the Pacific Rim economies; extends the hierarchy of needs beyond the self-actualization model.

Social responsibility 1: The notion that corporations have an obligation to constituent groups in society other than stockholders and beyond that prescribed by law or union contract. **2:** Collection of marketing philosophies, policies, procedures, and actions intended primarily to enhance society's welfare.

Social stratification The division of a particular population into classes.

Socially conscious (or ethical investing) movement A comprehensive investing approach complete with social and environmental screens, shareholder activism, and community investment.

Socially acceptable and unacceptable Standards or practices determined by each individual culture such that what is acceptable in one culture might be unacceptable in another.

Sociocultural contexts *See:* Cross-cultural communication.

Socioemotional role A role in which the individual provides support for team members' emotional needs and social unity.

Soft controls Based on subjective evidence, soft controls are informal and intangible, and difficult to measure and evaluate. An example is ethical behavior.

Soft currencies Refers to money that is not readily acceptable in international business transactions—usually the currencies of industrially less-advanced countries and of communist countries.

Soft skills Include interpersonal skills, motivation, leadership, and communication skills. Also known as people skills. In a way soft skills are innate.

Software Sets of instructions that control the operations of a computer.

Software piracy The phenomenon of copying software illegally.

Sogoshosha Trading companies of Japan, including firms such as Sumitomo, Mitsubishi, and Mitsui.

SOHO (Small Office/Home Office) The fastest growing type of business, thanks to the availability of inexpensive microcomputers and fax/modems. Also called TOHO (Tiny Office/Home Office).

Sole proprietorship An unincorporated business owned by an individual for profit.

Solvency The ability of a business to pay its debts. A firm is solvent when the dollar level of its assets exceed the dollar level of its liabilities.

Solvency ratios *See:* Liquidity ratios.

Source code An application's code written in the original high-level programming language.

Southeast Asian management The basis of an opposing theory to Theory X and Y known as Theory T and T+, representing two styles and attitudes found to be prevalent in Southeast Asian countries.

Sovereign immunity Foreign country's freedom from a host country's laws.

Spaced practice Several practice sessions spaced over a period of hours or days.

Spaghetti chart Before improvement chart of existing steps in a process and the many back and forth interrelationships (can resemble a bowl of spaghetti); used to see the redundancies and other wasted movements of people and material.

Span of control How many subordinates a manager can effectively and efficiently manage.

Span of management The number of employees reporting to a supervisor; also called *span of control.*

Special causes Causes of variation that arise because of special circumstances. They are not an inherent part of a process. Special causes are also referred to as assignable causes. *See:* common causes.

Special Drawing Rights (SDRs) Reserves established by the International Monetary Fund; they are used only for intergovernment transactions; the SDR also serves as a unit of account (determined by the values of five major currencies) that is used to denominate some internationally traded goods and services, as well as some foreign bank deposits and loans.

Special economic zones Areas created by a country to attract foreign investors, in which there are no tariffs, substantial tax incentives, and low prices for land and labor.

Special reports Reports that help managers formulate policies, prepare strategic plans, and prepare operational plans.

Specialization or division of labor Each participant in the marketing channel focuses on performing those activities at which it is most efficient.

Special-purpose team Organizational team formed to address specific problems, improve work processes, and enhance product and service quality.

Specie Gold and silver.

Specific price index An index that shows the price changes for a specific good or service over time.

Specification Engineering requirement, used for judging the acceptability of a particular product/service based on product characteristics, such as appearance, performance, and size. In statistical analysis, specifications refer to the document that prescribes the requirements with which the product or service has to perform.

Speculative balance A cash balance that is held to enable the firm to take advantage of any bargain purchases that might arise.

Speculative motive Additional inventory held to take advantage of unique business opportunities such as future shortages.

Speculative risk The uncertainty of an event that could produce either a profit or a loss, such as a business venture or a gambling transaction.

Speculator A person who has no operating cash flow position to protect and is trying to profit solely from interest rate movements.

Speech recognition The process of translating human speech into computer-readable data and instructions.

Speech synthesizing Technology that allows machines to create sounds emulating a human voice.

Sponsorship marketing Practice of promoting the interests of a company and its brands by associating the company with a specific event (for example, a golf tournament) or a charitable cause (for example, the Leukemia Society).

Spontaneous financing Those financing sources such as accounts payables and accruals that are generated as a part of the operations of the firm.

Spontaneously generated funds Funds that are obtained from routine business transactions.

Spoofing 1: Changing the information in an e-mail header or an IP address used to hide identities. **2:** Deception for the purpose of gaining access to a Web site, or deception of users to make them think they are logged on to a certain Web site when they are actually logged on to another.

Sporadic problem Sudden adverse change in the status quo that can be remedied by restoring the status quo. For example, actions such as changing a worn part or proper handling of an irate customer's complaint can restore the status quo.

Spot market Market in which exchange transactions occur for immediate exchange.

Spot rates 1: Contracts that provide for two parties to exchange currencies with delivery in two business days. **2:** Existing prices or interest rates in today's markets. In foreign exchange, the spot rate is an exchange rate quote based on immediate delivery of the currency being traded.

Spurious correlation Chance association between two variables, which the analyst should watch for because it might account for a high coefficient of determination.

SQL (Structured Query Language) A data manipulation language for relational database management systems that has become a de facto business standard.

Square root law States that total safety stock inventories in a future number of facilities can be approximated by multiplying the total amount of inventory at existing facilities by the square root of the number of future facilities divided by the number of existing facilities. Used to consolidate inventories at multiple distribution centers.

Stable distribution Pattern of outcomes which characterizes a variable with a well-defined, consistent trend or seasonal component.

Stable, predictable dividends Payment of a specific dollar dividend each year, or periodically increasing the dividend at a constant rate—the annual dollar dividend is relatively predictable by investors.

Staff authority A form of authority granted to staff specialists in their areas of expertise.

Stage of subsidiary development Traditionally, MNCs have staffed foreign subsidiaries with expatriates in the early stages of establishing operations in the foreign country. In the later stages, at least at the lower levels, host-country nationals are employed.

Stage-Gate process Common new product development process that divides the repeatable portion of product development into a time-sequenced series of stages, each of which is separated by a management decision gate. In each stage, a team completes a set of tasks that span the functions involved in product development. At the end of each stage, management reviews the results obtained and, based on the team's ability to meet the objectives in that stage, provides the resources to continue to the next stage ("go"), requests additional work ("recycle"), or stops the project ("kill").

Stages of creativity One model gives the following stages: generate, percolate, illuminate, and verify.

Stages of team growth Four development stages through which groups typically progress: forming, storming, norming, and performing. Knowledge of the stages help team members accept the normal problems that occur on the path from forming a group to becoming a team.

Stakeholder 1: People, departments, and organizations that have an investment or interest in the success or actions taken by the organization. **2:** The users of financial reports.

Stakeholder audit A systematic attempt to identify and measure an organization's stakeholders' issues and measure and evaluate their opinions with respect to its effective resolution.

Stakeholder environment Composed of trends, events, issues, expectations, and forecasts that may have a bearing on the strategic management process and the development of corporate public policy.

Stakeholders Individuals or entities that have an interest in the well-being of a firm—stockholders, creditors, employees, customers, suppliers, and so on.

Stand-alone risk The risk an asset would have if it were a firm's only asset; it is measured by the variability of the asset's expected returns.

Standard Statement, specification, or quantity of material against which measured outputs from a process may be judged as acceptable or unacceptable.

Standard check processing When the deposit bank verifies the depositor's cash letter—which lists the checks and their amounts—and then encodes the dollar amount on the MICR line and sends the checks to a correspondent bank or the nearest Federal Reserve facility to be cleared back to the disbursing bank on which the check was written.

Standard cost A detailed estimate of what a product should cost.

Standard cost systems Accounting systems that use standards for each element of manufacturing cost entering into the finished product.

Standard deviation σ **1.** A measure of the dispersion, or spread, of a distribution from its expected value; the square root of the variance. **2:** Calculated measure of variability that shows how much the data are spread around the mean. **3:** A measure of the tightness, or variability, of a set of outcomes.

Standard of living The level of material affluence of a group or nation, measured as a composite of quantities and qualities of goods.

Standard worldwide pricing Price-setting strategy based on average unit costs of fixed, variable, and export-related costs.

Standardization 1: The process of designing and altering products, parts, processes, and procedures to establish and use standard specifications for them and their components. **2:** Reduction of the total numbers of parts and materials used and products, models, or grades produced. **3:** The function of bringing a raw ingredient into standard (acceptable) range per the specification before introduction to the main process. **4:** Products sold unchanged or only slightly changed in all markets. **5:** Full comparability of accounting information.

Standardized approach Approach to international marketing in which products are marketed with little or no modification.

Standby letter of credit Document used to guarantee invoice payments to a supplier; it promises to pay the beneficiary if the buyer fails to pay.

Standing plans Ongoing plans used to provide guidance for tasks performed repeatedly within the organization.

Star A network topology in which many computers are linked to a single computer through which all messages must be passed.

Stated value A value approved by the board of directors of a corporation for no-par stock. Similar to par value.

Statement of cash flows Financial statement that reports an entity's cash inflows (receipts) and outflows (payments) during an accounting period.

Statement of Financial Accounting Standards No. 52 A U.S. foreign currency standard issued by the Financial Accounting Standards Board acknowledging that the functional currency of an entity is the currency of the primary environment in which the entity operates.

Statement of retained earnings A statement reporting the change in the firm's retained earnings as a result of the income generated and retained during the year. The balance sheet figure for retained earnings is the sum of the earnings retained for each year the firm has been in business.

Statement of stockholders' equity A summary of the changes in the stockholders' equity of a corporation that have occurred during a specific period of time.

Statement of work (SOW) Description of the actual work to be accomplished. It is derived from the work breakdown structure and, when combined with the project specifications, becomes the basis for the contractual agreement on the project (also referred to as scope of work).

Statements on Auditing Standards (SAS) Standards issued by the American Institute of Certified Public Accountants in the United States concerning generally accepted auditing standards.

State-owned enterprise A corporate form that has emerged in non-Communist countries, primarily for reasons of national security and economic security.

States of nature The possible outcomes for chance events that affect the payoff associated with a decision alternative.

Static budget A budget that does not adjust to changes in activity levels.

Static IP number An Internet Protocol number permanently associated with a device.

Static simulation model A simulation model used in situations where the state of the system at one point in time does not affect the state of the system at future points in time. Each trial of the simulation is independent.

Static surveillance Another term for fixed-point surveillance.

Stationary surveillance Locating a scene to be observed, anticipating the actions that are most likely to occur at the scene, and keeping detailed notes on tape or film on all activities involving the suspect.

Statistical analysis The use of statistics and number patterns to discover relationships in certain data, such as Benford's law.

Statistical confidence The level of accuracy expected of an analysis of data. Most frequently it is expressed as either a "95 percent level of significance," or "5 percent confidence level." Also called *statistical significance*.

Statistical decomposition A complex forecasting technique which uses the past observations of a variable to forecast future values. Sometimes called Census X-11 decomposition (after the computer software developed by the Census Bureau), this approach is especially useful for forecasting variables which have trend, seasonal, and cyclical variations.

Statistical process control (SPC) Application of statistical techniques to control a process.

Statistical quality control (SQC) Application of statistical techniques to control quality. Often the term "statistical process control" is used interchangeably with "statistical quality control" although statistical quality control includes acceptance sampling as well as statistical process control.

Statistical thinking Philosophy of learning and action based on fundamental principles:

- all work occurs in a system of interconnected processes
- understanding and reducing variation are vital to improvement
- variation exists in all processes

Statute A law or regulation; a law enacted by the legislative branch of a government.

Statutory (legal) reserve An equity reserve required by several countries to provide additional protection to creditors.

Statutory merger One company acquires the net assets of another company or companies.

Steering committee A group of representatives from a variety of key business units that establishes priorities for systems development and implementation of communications networks, prioritizes requests for new systems, and commits funds to projects.

Stepped-up exercise price An exercise price that is specified to be higher if a warrant is exercised after a designated date.

Stereotypes Generalizations about a particular culture and its members. Normally simple or brief, these are statements that characterize an entire group, culture, or its members. For example, "Americans are efficiency-oriented" or "The French are rude to non–French-speaking visitors."

Stereotyping Placing an employee into a class category based on one or a few traits or characteristics.

Sterilized intervention Intervention by the Federal Reserve in the foreign exchange market, with simultaneous intervention in the Treasury securities markets to offset any effects on the dollar money supply; thus, the intervention in the foreign exchange market is achieved without affecting the existing dollar money supply.

Stochastic model A model in which at least one uncontrollable input is uncertain and subject to variation; stochastic models are also referred to as probabilistic models.

Stock Shares of ownership of a corporation.

Stock dividend A dividend paid in the form of additional shares of stock rather than cash.

Stock option A plan that gives an individual the right to buy stock in a company, usually at a fixed price for a period of time.

Stock split 1: A reduction in the par or stated value of a share of common stock and the issuance of a proportionate number of additional shares. **2:** An action taken by a firm to increase the number of shares outstanding, such as doubling the number of shares outstanding by giving each stockholder two new shares for each one formerly held.

Stockholder wealth maximization The appropriate goal for management decisions; considers the risk and timing associated with expected earnings per share in order to maximize the price of the firm's common stock.

Stockholders The owners of a corporation.

Stone model Optimization process similar to Miller-Orr but allows the cash manager's knowledge of imminent cash flows to permit him to selectively override model directives.

Storage The operation of storing data and information in an information system.

Storage costs Costs to a firm associated with the act of storing inventory.

Storage service provider (SSP) A firm that rents storage space for software through an Internet link.

Storming The stage of team development in which individual personalities and roles, and resulting conflicts, emerge.

Storyboarding Technique that visually displays thoughts and ideas and groups them into categories, making all aspects of a process visible at once. Often used to communicate to others the activities performed by a team as they improved a process.

Straddle Combination of a put option and a call option.

Straight bill of lading A nonnegotiable bill of lading usually used in prepaid transactions in which the transported

GLOSSARY

goods involved are delivered to a specific individual or company.

Straight piece-rate system A pay system in which wages are determined by multiplying the number of units produced by the piece rate for one unit.

Straight rebuy Routine reordering from the same supplier of a product that has been purchased in the past.

Straight-line depreciation method A method of depreciation that provides for equal periodic depreciation expense over the estimated life of an asset.

Strategic activities Refers to activities that support the "long-term" objectives of an organization. Examples include strategic planning, strategic sourcing, and so on.

Strategic advantage A position in which one dominates a market; also called competitive advantage.

Strategic alliance 1: A firm's collaboration with companies in other countries to share rights and responsibilities as well as revenues and expenses as defined in a written agreement. Some common types of strategic alliances include research collaboration, a licensing program, and a copromotion deal. **2:** Two or more companies band together to attain efficiency. *See:* joint venture.

Strategic business unit (SBU) A division of the organization that has a unique business mission, product line, competitors, and markets relative to other SBUs in the same corporation.

Strategic fit review Process by which senior managers assess the future of each project to a particular organization in terms of its ability to advance the mission and goals of that organization.

Strategic goals Broad statements of where the organization wants to be in the future; pertain to the organization as a whole rather than to specific divisions or departments.

Strategic human resource management Organizational use of employees to gain or keep a competitive advantage against competitors.

Strategic information system Any information system that gives its owner a competitive advantage.

Strategic leader A highly competent firm located in a strategically critical market.

Strategic management The set of decisions and actions used to formulate and implement strategies that will provide a competitively superior fit between the organization and its environment so as to achieve organizational goals.

Strategic managers Individuals who make decisions that affect an entire organization, or large parts of it, and leave an impact in the long run.

Strategic marketing concept Company's mission to identify, generate, and sustain competitive advantage through superior positioning and vision.

Strategic objectives Guided by the enterprise's mission or purpose, they associate the enterprise with its external environment and provide management with a basis for comparing performance with that of its competitors, in relation to environmental demands.

Strategic plan A plan that integrates an organization's major goals, policies, and action sequences into a cohesive whole.

Strategic planning Process to set an organization's long range goals and identify the actions needed to reach the goals.

Strategic plans The action steps by which an organization intends to attain its strategic goals.

Strategic sourcing A cross-functional process that involves members of the firm other than those who work in the purchasing department. A strategic sourcing team may include members from engineering, quality, design, manufacturing, marketing, accounting, strategic planning and other departments. The focus of strategic sourcing management involves integrating supplier capabilities into organizational processes to achieve a competitive advantage through cost reduction, technology development, quality improvement, cycle time, and delivery capabilities to meet customer requirements.

Strategy The plan of action that prescribes resource allocation and other activities for dealing with the environment and helping the organization attain its goals.

Strategy formulation The stage of strategic management that involves the planning and decision making that lead to the establishment of the organization's goals and of a specific strategic plan.

Strategy implementation The stage of strategic management that involves the use of managerial and organizational tools to direct resources toward achieving strategic outcomes.

Stratified random sampling Technique to segment (stratify) a population prior to drawing a random sample from each strata, the purpose being to increase precision when members of different strata would, if not stratified, cause an unrealistic distortion.

Stress A physiological and emotional response to stimuli that place physical or psychological demands on an individual.

Stress interview Interview designed to create anxiety and put pressure on an applicant to see how the person responds.

Stretch goals Force an organization to think in a radically different way for major and incremental improvements.

Stretching accounts payable The practice of deliberately paying accounts payable late.

Strike price *See:* Exercise price.

Striking (exercise) price The price that must be paid (buying or selling) for a share of common stock when an option is exercised.

Strong-form efficient Description of foreign exchange markets, implying that all relevant public information and private information is already reflected in prevailing spot exchange rates.

Structural Adjustment Loan Facility (SAL) Facility established in 1980 by the World Bank to enhance a country's long-term economic growth through financing projects.

Structural causes Are factors both internal and external to a process.

Structural variation Variation caused by regular, systematic changes in output, such as seasonal patterns and long-term trends.

Structured data Numbers and facts that can be conveniently stored and retrieved in an orderly manner for operations and decision making.

Structured interview Interview that uses a set of standardized questions asked of all job applicants.

Structured problem A problem for whose solution there is a known set of steps to follow. Also called a *programmable problem*.

Structured Query Language (SQL) The data definition and manipulation language of choice for many developers of relational database management systems.

Stylus A penlike marking device used to enter commands and data on a computer screen.

Subjective risk The risk based on the mental state of an individual who experiences uncertainty or doubt as to the outcome of a given event.

Suboptimization Need for each business function to consider overall organizational objectives, resulting in higher efficiency and effectiveness of the entire system, although performance of a function may be suboptimal.

Subordinated debenture A bond having a claim on assets only after the senior debt has been paid off in the event of liquidation.

Subscription Fee paid by users to be granted access to certain online information or services.

Subsidiary 1: A subunit of a business entity established in a foreign country for the purpose of serving that market or other markets, including the business entity's home-country market. **2:** The company whose voting stock is acquired by a parent company to exercise control over it.

Subsidiary company The corporation that is controlled by a parent company.

Subsidiary ledger A ledger containing individual accounts with a common characteristic.

Substance abuse The use of illicit substances or the misuse of controlled substances, alcohol, or other drugs.

Substitute A situational variable that makes a leadership style redundant or unnecessary.

Subsystem 1: A component of a larger system. **2:** Parts of a system that depend on one another for their functioning.

Succession planning Process of identifying a longer-term plan for the orderly replacement of key employees.

Successor event The event at the end of an activity (head of the arrow) in the activity-on-the-arrow form of network diagramming; finish event.

Suggestion selling Occurs when the salesperson points out available complementary items in line with the selected item(s), in order to encourage an additional purchase.

Sugging Illegal survey conducted under the guise of research but with the intent of selling.

Suite A group of general software applications that are often used in the same environment. The strengths of the different applications can be used to build a single powerful document. Current suites are usually a combination of a spreadsheet, a word processor, and a database management system.

Sum-of-the-years-digits depreciation method A method of depreciation that provides for declining periodic depreciation expense over the estimated life of an asset.

Sunk cost 1: A cash outlay that already has been incurred and that cannot be recovered regardless of whether the project is accepted or rejected. **2:** A cost that is not affected by subsequent decisions.

Supercomputer The most powerful class of computers, used by large organizations, research institutions, and universities for complex scientific computations and the manipulation of very large databases.

Super-NOW accounts While banks continue to set higher minimum balance requirements for NOW accounts, in 1986 regulators removed interest rate distinctions between the accounts by eliminating the maximum NOW rate of 5 1/4 percent.

Superordinate goal A goal that cannot be reached by a single party.

Supplier Any provider whose goods and services may be used at any stage in the production, design, delivery, and use of another company's products and services. Suppliers include businesses, such as distributors, dealers, warranty repair services, transportation contractors, and franchises, and service suppliers, such as healthcare, training, and education. Internal suppliers provide materials or services to internal customers.

Supplier audits Reviews that are planned and carried out to verify the adequacy and effectiveness of a supplier's quality program, drive improvement, and increase value.

Supplier certification Process of evaluating the performance of a supplier with the intent of authorizing the supplier to self-certify shipments if such authorization is justified.

Supplier credit Credit provided by the supplier to itself to fund its operations.

Supplier development The process providing on-site help, training, or other improvement measures to suppliers.

Supplier evaluation and selection The process of determining if a given supplier is capable of meeting a purchasing organization's needs. This is typically carried out by an on-site visit to the supplier's facility.

Supplier identification The process of searching multiple sources (Internet, catalogs, interviews, trade shows, and so on) to find potential suppliers to meet a need.

Supplier integration The process of involving suppliers in new product development and ongoing production processes.

Supplier management The ongoing coordination of all suppliers being used. This is a broad term that often includes supplier identification, evaluation, performance measurement, and development.

Supplier network A group of organizations that provide inputs, either directly or indirectly, to the focal firm.

Supplier partnering A just-in-time method that views suppliers as a valuable contributor to the overall success of the business.

Supplier performance measurement The ongoing process of tracking cost, quality, delivery, and service performance of suppliers, as well as updating a database of all supplier's performance over time.

Supplier quality assurance Confidence that a supplier's product or service will fulfill its customers' needs. This confidence is achieved by creating a relationship between the customer and supplier that ensures the product will be fit for use with minimal corrective action and inspection. According to J. M. Juran, there are nine primary activities needed: 1) define product and program quality requirements, 2) evaluate alternative suppliers, 3) select suppliers, 4) conduct joint quality planning, 5) cooperate with the supplier during the execution of the contract, 6) obtain proof of conformance to requirements, 7) certify qualified suppliers, 8) conduct quality improvement programs as required, and 9) create and use supplier quality ratings.

Supplier selection strategy and criteria Selection of new suppliers is based on the type and uniqueness of the product or service to be purchased, and the total cost. Suppliers of commodity-type items and basic supplies may be selected from directories and catalogs. For more sophisticated products and services stringent evaluation criteria may be established.

Supply chain 1: The activities associated with the flow and transformation of goods from the raw materials stage (extraction), through to the end user, as well as the associated information flows. Material and information flows both up and down the supply chain. The supply chain includes systems management, manufacturing and assembly, sourcing and procurement, production scheduling, order processing, inventory management, warehousing, and customer service. **2:** Series of processes and/or organizations that are involved in producing and delivering a product to the final user.

Supply chain management (SCM) 1: The coordination of purchasing, manufacturing, shipping, and billing operations, often supported by an enterprise resource planning system. **2:** The integration of the activities in the supply chain through improved supply chain relationships, information systems, and other means to achieve a sustainable competitive advantage. The supply chain includes the management of information systems, sourcing and procurement, production scheduling, order processing, inventory management, warehousing, customer service, and aftermarket disposition of packaging and materials. **3:** Results where a series of value-adding activities connect a company's supply side with its demand side. **4:** Technique for linking a manufacturer's operations with those of all of its strategic suppliers and its key intermediaries and customers to enhance efficiency and effectiveness; managing logistical systems to achieve close cooperation and comprehensive interorganizational management so as to integrate the logistical operations of different firms in the marketing channel.

Supply side market failure Results when the individual activities of a supplier inadvertently lead to destructive effects on the overall supply.

Support processes Will provide infrastructure for core processes.

Support systems Starting with top-management commitment and visible involvement, support systems are a cascading series of interrelated practices or actions aimed at building and sustaining support for continuous quality improvement. Such practices/actions may include: mission statement, transformation of company culture, policies, employment practices, compensation, recognition and rewards, employee involvement, rules and procedures, quality-level agreements, training, empowerment, methods and tools for improving quality, tracking-measuring-evaluating-reporting systems, and so on.

Support The maintenance and provision for user help on an information system.

Surfers Computer users who have dial-up or faster access to the Internet and who visit Web sites.

Surveillance 1: Continual monitoring of a process. **2:** Investigation technique that relies on the senses, especially hearing and seeing.

Surveillance audit Regular audits conducted by registrars to confirm that a company registered to the ISO 9001 standard still complies; usually conducted on a six-month or one-year basis.

Survey Examination for some specific purpose; to inspect or consider carefully; to review in detail (survey implies the inclusion of matters not covered by agreed-upon criteria). Also, a structured series of questions designed to elicit a predetermined range of responses covering a preselected area of interest. May be administered orally by a survey-taker, by paper and pencil, or by computer. Responses are tabulated and analyzed to surface significant areas for change.

Survey feedback A type of OD intervention in which questionnaires on organizational climate and other factors are distributed among employees and the results reported back to them by a change agent.

Sustainable competitive advantage Competitive edge that cannot be easily or quickly copied by competitors in the short run.

Sustainable growth The rate of sales growth that is compatible with a firm's established financial policies including asset turnover, net profit margin, dividend payout, and debt to equity ratio and assumes that new equity is derived only through retained earnings, not new common stock.

Swap Exchange of securities between two parties, often with the assistance of an intermediary known as a swap dealer. In its simplest form, a company engaging in a swap exchanges a fixed interest rate obligation for one that has a variable, or floating interest rate.

Swap strategies *See for example:* maturity extension swap and yield spread swap.

Sweatshops Businesses characterized by child labor, low pay, poor working conditions, worker abuse, and health and safety violations.

Sweep accounts Special accounts whereby excess funds are automatically or at the cash manager's request transferred ("swept") from the demand deposit account into an interest-bearing overnight investment.

SWIFT The Society of Worldwide Interbank Financial Telecommunications, is a communication network for relaying payment instructions for international transactions. It boasts roughly 1,500 member banks in 68 counties, and almost 3,000 banks are connected to the network.

Switching costs Expenses that are incurred when a customer stops buying a product or service from one business and starts buying it from another.

Switching techniques Data communications mechanisms that allow messages to be routed through a variety of paths; if one is busy, another can be used.

SWOT analysis Assessment of an organization's key strengths, weaknesses, opportunities, and threats. It considers factors such as the organization's industry, the competitive position, functional areas, and management.

Symmetric encryption Encryption technology in which both the sender and recipient of a message use the same key for encryption and decryption.

Symmetric information The situation in which investors and managers have identical information about the firm's prospects.

Symptom Indication of a problem or opportunity.

Synchronized cash flows A situation in which cash inflows coincide with cash outflows, thereby permitting a firm to hold low transactions balances.

Synchronized production A manufacturing management philosophy that includes a consistent set of principles, procedures, and techniques where every action is evaluated in terms of the global goal of the system. Both kanban, which is a part of the JIT philosophy, and drum-buffer-rope, which is a part of the theory of constraints philosophy, represent synchronized production control approaches. *Syn:* synchronous manufacturing. *See:* drum-buffer-rope, kanban, synchronous scheduling.

Syndicate Sometimes a group of investment banks works together on the marketing and shares the risk involved with bringing a new issue to market, which may or may not be acceptable at the predetermined price. This grouping is called a syndicate.

Syndicated Eurocredit loans Loans provided by a group (or syndicate) of banks in the Eurocredit market.

Synergy From Greek "to work together." The attainment of output, when two factors work together, that is greater or better than the sum of their products when they work separately.

Syntax error A program error that is equivalent to a typo in regular written language.

Synthetic composite An artificial security which is devised to mirror the portfolio's average coupon interest rate, maturity, and risk rating.

System 1: A set of interrelated parts that function as a whole to achieve a common purpose. **2:** Network of connecting processes that work together to accomplish the aim of the system.

System clock Special circuitry within the computer control unit that synchronizes all tasks.

System of authorizations A system of limits on who can and cannot perform certain functions.

System of profound knowledge (SoPK) *See: profound knowledge.*

System requirements The functions that an information system is expected to fulfill and the features through which it will perform its tasks.

System software Software that executes routine tasks. System software includes operating systems, language translators, and communications software. Also called *support software*.

Systematic risk The degree of sensitivity of the company's stock returns to market-wide returns.

Systems analysis The early steps in the systems development process, to define the requirements of the proposed system and determine its feasibility.

Systems approach to management Management theory that views the organization as a unified, purposeful combination of interrelated parts; managers must look at the organization as a whole and understand that activity in one part of the organization affects all parts of the organization. Also known as *systems thinking*.

Systems concept A concept of logistics based on the notion that materials-flow activities are so complex that they can be considered only in the context of their interaction.

Systems concept of logistics Viewing all components of a logistical system together and understanding the relationships among them.

Systems design The evaluation of alternative solutions to a business problem and the specification of hardware, software, and communications technology for the selection solution.

Systems development led by users (SDLU) An approach to systems development that reflects the view that users, not information systems professionals, are responsible for their information systems.

Systems development life cycle (SDLC) The oldest method of developing an information system, consisting of several phases of analysis and design, which must be followed sequentially.

Systems integration Interfacing several information systems.

Systems integrator An individual or an organization that specializes in integrating several different hardware items and software applications for business operations. Often, the system integrator integrates one new information system into the existing information resources of the business.

Systems theory An extension of the humanistic perspective that describes organizations as open systems that are characterized by entropy, synergy, and subsystem interdependence.

Systems thinking The approach of thinking of an organization in terms of its suborganizations or systems; a framework for problem solving and decision making.

T

T account A form of account resembling the letter T, showing debits on the left and credits on the right.

T test Method for testing hypotheses about the population mean; the t statistic measures the deviation between the sample and population means, in terms of the number of standard errors.

Tablet computer A full-power personal computer in the form of a thick writing tablet.

Tacit knowledge 1: Knowledge that is implied by or inferred from actions or statements. **2:** Unarticulated heuristics and assumptions used by any individual or organization.

Tactical activities The short-term activities associated with the day-to-day management. Over time, tactical activities serve to eventually support the organization's long-term strategic goals.

Tactical goals Goals that define the outcomes that major divisions and departments must achieve in order for the organization to reach its overall goals.

Tactical managers Individuals who receive general directions and goals from their superiors and, within those guidelines, make decisions for their subordinates; also called middle managers.

Tactical objectives Guided by the enterprise's strategic objectives, they identify the key result areas in which specific performance is essential for the success of the enterprise, and aim to attain internal efficiency.

Tactical plans Short-term plans, usually of one- to two-year duration, that describe actions the organization will take to meet its strategic business plan.

Tactics Strategies and processes that help an organization meet its objectives.

Taguchi loss function Product characteristics deviate from the normal aim and losses increase according to a parabolic function; by merely attempting to produce a product within specifications doesn't prevent loss (loss is that inflicted on society after shipment of a product).

Taguchi methods The American Supplier Institute's trade-marked term for the quality engineering methodology developed by Genichi Taguchi. In this engineering approach to quality control, Taguchi calls for off-line quality control, on-line quality control, and a system of experimental design to improve quality and reduce costs.

Tailing Secretly following a fraud suspect in an attempt to gain additional information; another name for moving surveillance.

Takeover An action whereby a person or group succeeds in ousting a firm's management and taking control of the company.

Takt time Available production time divided by the rate of customer demand. Operating to takt time sets the production pace to customer demand.

Tall structure A management structure characterized by an overall narrow span of management and a relatively large number of hierarchical levels.

Tally sheet Another term for *checksheet*.

Tampering Action taken to compensate for variation within the control limits of a stable system. Tampering increases rather than decreases variation, as evidenced in the funnel experiment.

Target (optimal) capital structure The combination (percentages) of debt, preferred stock, and common equity that will maximize the price of the firm's stock.

Target (minimum) cash balance The minimum cash balance a firm desires to maintain in order to conduct business.

Target cost concept A concept used to design and manufacture a product at a cost that will deliver a target profit for a given market-determined price.

Target costing A costing method that sets cost targets for new products based on market price.

Target marketing Promoting products and services to the people who are most likely to purchase them.

Target markets Market segments whose needs and demands a company seeks to serve and satisfy.

Target zones Implicit boundaries established by central banks on exchange rates.

Targeting Offering the firm's most profitable customers special deals and incentives.

Tariff Tax imposed by a government on imported goods.

Tariffs Duties or taxes on imported goods and services, instituted by governments as a means to raise revenue and as barriers to trade.

Tariffs and quotas Often employed by governments to restrict trade or reduce competition. Tariffs are a form of tax imposed on incoming goods, and quotas specify the number of foreign units that can be imported.

Task A distinct, identifiable work activity composed of motions.

Task force A temporary team or committee formed to solve a specific short-term problem involving several departments.

Task identity The extent to which the job includes a "whole" identifiable unit of work that is carried out from start to finish and that results in a visible outcome.

Task significance The impact the job has on other people.

Task specialist role A role in which the individual devotes personal time and energy to helping the team accomplish its task.

Tax-advantaged instruments Those on which part or all of the income is exempted from taxation, or where the tax is deferred.

Tax anticipation notes Short-term debt instruments which provide working capital financing for states and localities as they await anticipated revenues from tax collections.

Tax courts Federal courts that hear only tax cases.

Tax credit The reduction of a tax liability by an amount equal to the amount of the tax credit.

Tax equalization Reimbursement by the company when an employee in an overseas assignment pays taxes at a higher rate than if he or she were at home.

Tax equalization plan Compensation plan used to protect expatriates from negative tax consequences.

Tax-exempt commercial paper States and localities also issue some of these items. The risks are very similar to those of anticipation notes.

Tax holiday The period of time during which a foreign investor is exempted from taxes.

Tax loss carryback and carryover Losses that can be carried backward or forward in time to offset taxable income in a given year.

Tax policy A means by which countries may control foreign investors.

Taxable-equivalent yield The yield of a tax-exempt security on an after-tax basis, which facilitates comparison with the yield of taxable securities. The taxable-equivalent yield is the nominal (stated) yield divided by (1 − corporation's marginal tax rate).

Taxable income 1: Gross income minus exemptions and allowable deductions as set forth in the tax code. **2:** The base on which the amount of income tax is determined.

Taxable instruments Security types that are not given preferential tax treatment, including commercial paper, domestic and Eurodollar certificates of deposit, banker's acceptances, repurchase agreements, and money market mutual funds invested in these instruments.

TCP/IP (Transmission Control Protocol/Internet Protocol) A packet-switching protocol that is actually a set of related protocols that can guarantee packets are delivered in the correct order and can handle differences in transmission and reception rates.

Teaching services Services that are provided in the areas of training and motivating as well as in teaching of operational, managerial, and theoretical issues.

Team 1: Set of two or more people who are equally accountable for the accomplishment of a purpose and specific performance goals; it is also defined as a small number of people with complimentary skills who are committed to a common purpose. **2:** Many organizations manage themselves through empowered self-managed teams.

Team-based structure 1: Describes an organizational structure in which team members are organized around performing a specific function of the business, such as handling customer complaints or assembling an engine. **2:** Structure in which the entire organization is made up of teams that coordinate their work and work directly with customers to accomplish the organization's goals.

Team building 1: A process that enhances the cohesiveness of a department or group by helping members learn how to organize their work and assume responsibility for it. **2:** A type of OD intervention that enhances the cohesiveness of departments by helping members learn to function as a team.

Team building/development Process of transforming a group of people into a team and developing the team to achieve its purpose.

Team cohesiveness The extent to which team members are attracted to the team and motivated to remain in it.

Team culture *See:* culture, as it pertains to teams.

Team dynamics Interactions which occur among team members under different conditions.

Team facilitation Deals with both the role of the facilitator on the team and the techniques and tools for facilitating the team.

Team interview Interview in which applicants are interviewed by the team members with whom they will work.

Team performance evaluation, rewards, and recognition Special metrics are needed to evaluate the work of a team (to avoid focus on any individual on the team) and as a basis for rewards and recognition for team achievements.

Team structure Type of organization based on teams.

Technical core The heart of the organization's production of its product or service.

Technical feasibility study An evaluation of whether the components of a proposed information system exist or can be developed with available tools.

Technical forecasting Development of forecasts using historical prices or trends.

Technical skill The understanding of and proficiency in the performance of specific tasks.

Technology The knowledge, tools, techniques, and activities used to transform the organization's inputs into outputs.

Technology transfer The transfer of systematic knowledge for the manufacture of a product, the application of a process, or the rendering of a service.

Telecommunications Communications over a long distance, as opposed to communication within a computer, or between adjacent hardware pieces.

Telecommunications manager The individual who is responsible for the acquisition, implementation, management, maintenance, and troubleshooting of computer networks throughout the organization.

Telecommuting The phenomenon of working from home or another remote location with the help of information technology, rather than performing the same tasks in the office.

Teleconferencing The ability to hold conferences with a number of other people who are all geographically remote from one another, via telecommunications devices.

Temporal method A currency translation method in which translation is viewed as a restatement of the financial statements. The foreign currency amounts are translated at the exchange rates in effect at the dates when those items were measured in the foreign currency.

Temporary accounts Revenue, expense, or income summary accounts that are periodically closed; nominal accounts.

Temporary current assets Current assets that fluctuate with seasonal or cyclical variations in a firm's business. The accumulation of inventory in anticipation of the peak selling season and the resulting receivables generated by the increased sales. This bulge then subsides as the firm passes through its peak selling season.

Temporary differences Differences between income before income tax and taxable income created by items that are recognized in one period for income statement purposes and in another period for tax purposes. Such differences reverse, or turn around, in later years.

Temporary investments Investments in securities that can be readily sold when cash is needed.

Tenor Time period of drafts.

"Tentative U.S. tax" The calculation of U.S. taxes on foreign source incomes to estimate U.S. tax payments.

Term loan A loan made with an initial maturity of more than one year.

Term repos Repurchase agreement that is arranged with a maturity of several days to several weeks, making them well-suited for the investor having an investment horizon longer than one day.

Term spread The component of a security's return that is necessary to induce investors to bear risks linked to maturity.

Term structure of interest rates The relationship between yields and maturities of securities.

Terminal cash flow The *net* cash flow that occurs at the end of the life of a project, including the cash flows associated with 1) the final disposal of the project and 2) returning the firm's operations to where they were before the project was accepted.

Terminal value The future value of a cash flow stream.

Terminal warehouse agreement Inventories pledged as collateral are moved to a public warehouse that is physically separated from the borrower's premises.

Terms of credit The payment conditions offered to credit customers; the terms include the length of the credit period and any cash discounts offered.

Territorial approach A national tax system that only taxes domestic income.

Terrorism Illegal and violent acts toward property and people.

Testimonial evidence Evidence based on querying techniques, such as interviewing, interrogation, and honesty testing.

Theft investigation methods Investigation methods that focus on the actual transfer of assets from the victim to the perpetrator; helps determine how the theft was committed and often includes methods such as surveillance and covert operations, invigilation, and the obtaining of physical evidence.

Theocracy A legal perspective based on religious practices and interpretations.

Theoretical capacity The maximum output capability, allowing no adjustments for preventive maintenance, unplanned downtime, shutdown, and so on.

Theoretical standards Standards that represent levels of performance that can be achieved only under perfect operating conditions.

Theory of comparative advantage Each country should produce only those goods and services that it can produce with relative efficiency.

Theory of constraints (TOC) 1: A management philosophy developed by Dr. Eliyahu M. Goldratt that can be viewed as three separate but interrelated areas—logistics, performance measurement, and logical thinking. Logistics include drum-buffer-rope scheduling, buffer management, and VAT analysis. Performance measurement includes throughput, inventory and operating expense, and the five focusing steps. Thinking process tools are important in identifying the root problem (current reality tree), identifying and expanding win-win solutions (evaporating cloud and future reality tree), and developing implementation plans (prerequisite tree and transition tree). *Syn:* constraint theory. **2:** A manufacturing strategy that attempts to remove the influence of bottlenecks (constraints) on a process.

Theory of dual entitlement Consumers believe there are terms in a transaction to which both consumers and sellers are "entitled" over time. Cost-driven price increases are believed to be fair because they allow sellers to maintain their profit entitlement. Demand-driven price increases are not believed to be fair, however, since they allow sellers to increase per-unit profit, while buyers receive nothing in return.

Theory of knowledge Belief that management is about prediction, and people learn not only from experience but also from theory. When people study a process and develop a theory, they can compare their predictions with their observations; profound learning results.

Theory T and Theory T+ Complementary theories based on Southeast Asian assumptions that work is a necessity but not a goal itself, people should find their rightful place in peace and harmony with their environment; absolute objectives exist only with God; in the world, persons in authority positions represent God, so their objectives should be followed; and people behave as members of a family and/or group, and those who do not are rejected by society.

Theory X and theory Y Theory developed by Douglas McGregor that maintains that there are two contrasting assumptions about people, each of which is based on the manager's view of human nature. Theory X managers take a negative view and assume that most employees do not like work and try to avoid it. Theory Y managers take a positive view and believe that employees want to work, will seek and accept responsibility, and can offer creative solutions to organizational problems.

Theory Z Coined by William G. Ouchi, refers to a Japanese style of management that is characterized by long-term employment, slow promotions, considerable job rotation, consensus-style decision making, and concern for the employee as a whole.

Thin capitalization The set of taxation issues from a host government's perspective, arising from the perceived imbalance between debt capital and equity capital when a foreign investor is financing a business operation in the country.

Thin client A computer without an external storage device.

Thin market One with little participation by buyers and/or sellers.

Third-country national 1: A citizen of one country, working in a second country, and employed by an organization headquartered in a third country. **2:** A resident of a country other than the home-country or host-country assigned to manage a firm's foreign subsidiary.

Third-generation languages (3GLs) Higher-level programming languages that let the programmer focus on a problem without being concerned with how the hardware will execute the program; but they require the programmer to detail a logical procedure to solve the problem.

Third-party information vendor An information service that receives deposit information from field offices and transmits that information to the appropriate concentration banks and to corporate headquarters.

Three-sixty-degree (360°) feedback process Evaluation method that provides feedback from the perspectives of self, peers, direct reports, superior, customers, and suppliers.

Throughput 1: The total volume of production through a facility (machine, work center, department, plant, or network of plants). **2:** In the theory of constraints, the rate at which the system (firm) generates money through sales. Throughput is a separate concept from output.

Throughput time Total time required (processing + queue) from concept to launch or from order received to delivery, or raw materials received to delivery to customer.

Tiered pricing The Fed has proposed this method where it reduces its charges to banks submitting large volumes of checks. This move to preserve its market share is seen as contradictory to the privatization initiative that the Fed officially espouses.

Time-based competition A strategy of competition based on the ability to deliver products and services faster than competitors.

Time bomb Rogue code that is installed in a computer system and starts destroying data files and applications at a preset time.

Time draft Involves a credit element, because the payment obligation agreed to by the drawee is designated as due at a specified future date. Time drafts are usually dated after verification of a shipment of goods.

Time equals money The perception of people in some cultures that time is a commodity and an asset and high importance is placed on it.

Time estimate *See:* Duration estimate.

Times-interest-earned (TIE) ratio A ratio that measures the firm's ability to meet its annual interest obligations; calculated by dividing earnings before interest and taxes by interest charges.

Time preferences for consumption The preferences of consumers for current consumption as opposed to saving for future consumption.

Time series A set of observations measured at successive points in time or over successive periods of time.

Time series models Models that examine series of historical data; sometimes used as a means of technical forecasting, by examining moving averages.

Time series regression A naive modeling approach in the sense that the mere passage of time generally does not cause the variable to change in value.

Time span The period of time that a set of data covers.

Time tickets The form on which the amount of time spent by each employee and the labor cost incurred for each individual job, or for factory overhead, are recorded.

Time to market The time between generating an idea for a product and completing a prototype that can be mass-manufactured. Also called *engineering lead time*.

Time value of money concept The concept that money invested today will earn income.

Time, place, and possession utilities Conditions that enable consumers and business users to have products available for use when and where they want them and to actually take possession of them.

Time-series analysis Analysis of relationships between two or more variables over periods of time.

Time-series techniques Forecasting methods which predict future movements in the forecast variable based on patterns revealed in historical movements of that same variable.

TL 9000 Series of standards pertaining to the telecommunications industry; ISO 9001 is embedded in the standard.

Token passing A telecommunications method whereby a computer that needs to send a message captures a "token," consisting of a small group of bytes, and releases the token with the message.

Tolerance design (Taguchi) Provides a rational grade limit for components of a system; determines which parts and processes need to be modified and to what degree it is necessary to increase their control capacity; a method for rationally determining tolerances.

Tolerance for ambiguity The psychological characteristic that allows a person to be untroubled by disorder and uncertainty.

Tolerance Variability of a parameter permitted and tolerated above or below a nominal value.

Top-down budgeting A budgeting process in which middle and lower-level managers set departmental budget targets in accordance with overall company revenues and expenditures specified by top management.

Top-down planning Planning that begins at the top level of an organization and focuses on clear objectives for the entire organization; also called *holistic planning*.

Top-management commitment Participation of the highest-level officials in their organization's quality improvement efforts. Their participation includes establishing and serving on a quality committee, establishing quality policies and goals, deploying those goals to lower levels of the organization, providing the resources and training that the lower levels need to achieve the goals, participating in quality improvement teams, reviewing progress organization-wide, recognizing those who have performed well, and revising the current reward system to reflect the importance of achieving the quality goals. Commitment is top management's visible, personal involvement as seen by others in the organization.

Top manager A manager who is at the top of the organizational hierarchy and is responsible for the entire organization.

Topology The physical layout of a network.

Total assets turnover ratio The ratio calculated by dividing sales by total assets.

Total budgeted cost (TBC) The portion of the entire project budget that is allocated to complete all of the activities and work associated with a particular work package.

Total cost approach Calculating the cost of a logistical system by addressing all of the costs of logistics together rather than individual costs taken separately, so as to minimize the total cost of logistics.

Total cost concept 1: A concept used in applying the cost-plus approach to product pricing in which all the costs of manufacturing the product plus the selling and administrative expenses are included in the cost amount to which the markup is added. **2:** A decision concept that uses cost as a basis for measurement in order to evaluate and optimize logistical activities.

Total cost of ownership Considers not only the purchase price but also an array of other factors such as complete life cycle.

Total factor productivity A measure of the productivity of a department, plant, strategic business unit, firm, and so on, that combines the individual productivities of all its resources including labor, capital, energy, material, and equipment. These individual factor productivities are often combined by weighting each according to its monetary value and then adding them. For example, if material accounts for 40 percent of the total cost of sales and labor 10 percent of the total cost of sales, and so on, total factor productivity = .4 (material productivity) + .1 (labor productivity) + and so on.

Total productive maintenance (TPM) Aimed at reducing and eventually eliminating equipment failure, setup and adjustment, minor stops, reduced speed, product rework, and scrap. Five Ss are relevant here. It is operator-oriented maintenance with the involvement of all qualified employees in all maintenance activities.

Total quality management (TQM) Term initially coined by the Naval Air Systems Command to describe its management approach to quality improvement. Total quality management (TQM) has taken on many meanings. Simply put, TQM is a management approach to long-term success through customer satisfaction. TQM is based on the participation of all members of an organization in improving processes, products, services, and the culture they work in. TQM benefits all organization members and society. The methods for implementing this approach are found in the teachings of such quality leaders as Philip B. Crosby, W. Edwards Deming, Armand V. Feigenbaum, Kaoru Ishikawa, J. M. Juran, and others. Four significant elements of TQM are employee involvement, focus on the customer, benchmarking, and continuous improvement.

Total slack (TS) Float. If it's a positive value, it's the amount of time that the activities on a particular path can be delayed without jeopardizing completion of the project by its required completion time. If it's a negative value, it's the amount of time that the activities on a particular path must be accelerated in order to complete the project by its required completion time.

Touch screen A computer monitor that serves both as input and output device. The user touches the areas of a certain menu item to select options, and the screen senses the selection at the point of the touch.

Tourism The economic benefit of money spent in a country or region by travelers from outside the area.

Traceability Ability to trace the history, application, or location of an item or activity and like items or activities by means of recorded identification.

Track pad A device used for clicking, logging, and dragging displayed information; the cursor is controlled by moving one's finger along a touch-sensitive pad.

Trackball A device similar to a mouse, used for clicking, locking, and dragging displayed information; in this case, the ball moves within the device rather than over a surface.

Tracking The capability of a shipper to track goods at any point during the shipment.

Trade acceptance Draft that allows the buyer to obtain merchandise prior to paying for it.

Trade allowances (trade deals) Offered to retailers simply for purchasing the manufacturer's brand or for performing activities in support of the manufacturer's brand.

Trade barriers Imposed by nations to limit or restrict competition.

Trade creation A benefit of economic integration; the benefit to a particular country when a group of countries trade a product freely among themselves but maintain common barriers to trade with nonmembers.

Trade credit Permission to delay payment which arises when goods are sold under delayed payment terms.

Trade discount 1: Percent reduction to quoted price offered to all customers, and not linked to early payment. This discount is typically offered to all customers, and the seller expects all customers to pay at the discounted price within the agreed-upon period. One example is a quantity discount, a price break given for a large purchase. **2:** Special discounts from published list prices offered by sellers to certain classes of buyers.

Trade diversion A cost of economic integration; the cost to a particular country when a group of countries trade a product freely among themselves but maintain common barriers to trade with nonmembers.

Trade draft A withdrawal document drawn against a company.

Trade-in allowance The amount a seller grants a buyer for a fixed asset that is traded in for a similar asset.

Tradeoff analysis Trading one variable against another variable such as time versus cost. Used in problem-solving and decision-making situations.

Trade-off concept A decision concept that recognizes linkages within the decision system.

Trade policy measures Mechanisms used to influence and alter trade relationships.

Trade promotion authority The right to negotiate, accept, or reject trade treaties and agreements with minimal amendments by other parties.

Trademark A name, term, or symbol used to identify a business and its products.

Traders Market participants which try to profit on anticipated interest rate or currency movements. They hold securities not as intermediaries, but as investors attempting to gain profits for their company's own account.

Trading blocs 1: Formed by agreements among countries to establish links through movement of goods, services, capital, and labor across borders. **2:** Free trade zones created by member countries through mutual agreements.

Trading company Marketing intermediary that undertakes exporting, importing, countertrading, investing, and manufacturing.

Trading security A debt or equity security that management intends to actively trade for profit.

Traditional organizations Those organizations not driven by customers and quality policies. Also refers to organizations managed primarily through functional units.

Tragedy of the commons Name given to the process in which individuals, pursuing their own self interest, overuse a common good to such an extent that the common good is destroyed.

Training Skills that employees need to learn in order to perform or improve the performances of their current job or tasks, or the process of providing those skills.

Training evaluation Techniques and tools used and the process of evaluating the effectiveness of training.

Training needs assessment Techniques and tools used and the process of determining an organization's training needs.

Traits Distinguishing personal characteristics, such as intelligence, values, and appearance.

Tramp service Ocean shipping via irregular routes, scheduled only on demand.

Transaction A business event. In an IS context, the record of a business event.

Transaction approach An approach to bank selecting in which there is a decoupling or "unbundling" of services, meaning the company will not necessarily borrow from the bank(s) it utilizes for cash management services. Increasingly prevalent, in this approach the treasurer selects the bank(s) that can best provide a specific service or can provide it at the best price.

Transaction-Based Information System (TBIS) Captures and analyzes all of the transactions between a company and its customers.

Transaction efficiency Designing marketing channels to minimize the number of contacts between producers and consumers.

Transaction exposure 1: Degree to which the value of future cash transactions can be affected by exchange rate fluctuations. **2:** The potential for losses or gains when a firm is engaged in a transaction denominated in a foreign currency.

Transaction motive Inventory held in relation to the level of operating activity expected by the firm.

Transaction Processing System (TPS) A type of operations information system that records and processes data resulting from routine business transactions such as sales, purchases, and payroll.

Transaction risk exposure A condition that is caused by the changes in the exchange rate between the transaction date and the settlement date.

Transaction sets A set of standards for EDI information flows developed by the ANSI X12 committee to facilitate the electronic communication between trading patterns.

Transactional leader A leader who clarifies subordinates' role and task requirements, initiates structure, provides rewards, and displays consideration for subordinates.

Transactional leadership Style of leading whereby the leader sees the work as being done through clear definitions of tasks and responsibilities and the provision of resources as needed.

Transactions balance A cash balance necessary for day-to-day operations; the balance associated with routine payments and collections.

Transceiver A communications device that can receive messages, amplify them, and retransmit them to their destination. Transceivers are used when the distance is long, and the signal may weaken on its way to the destination.

Transfer agent The financial institution that takes care of updating the records for the corporation's stock and registered bonds.

Transfer items Checks drawn on banks that do not participate in a bank's local clearing house or exchange; these are sometimes called "out-of-town" checks.

Transfer price The price one segment of a company charges another segment of the same company for the transfer of a good or a service.

Transfer pricing Policy for pricing goods sent by either the parent or a subsidiary to a subsidiary of an MNC.

Transfer risk The danger of having one's ability to transfer profits or products in and out of a country inhibited by governmental rules and regulations.

Transferable letter of credit Document that allows the first beneficiary on a standby letter of credit to transfer all or part of the original letter of credit to a third party.

Transformational leader A leader distinguished by a special ability to bring about innovation and change.

Transformational leadership Style of leading whereby the leader articulates the vision and values necessary for the organization to succeed.

Transformative technological innovations Replace traditional technologies (in farming, a tractor replaces the plow).

Transit items Are checks drawn on banks that do not participate in a deposit bank's local clearinghouse or exchange.

Transit routing number Also called the FRD/ABA (Federal Reserve District/American Banker's Association) bank ID number, a number imprinted on checks which identifies the payee's bank. This number is used by the deposit bank to determine how best to clear the check.

Transit time The period between departure and arrival of a carrier.

Transition stay bonus Extra payment for employees whose jobs are being eliminated, thereby motivating them to remain with the organization for a period of time.

Transition tree Technique used in applying Goldratt's Theory of Constraints.

Translation exposure Degree to which a firm's consolidated financial statements are exposed to fluctuations in exchange rates.

Transmission Rate The speed at which data are communicated over a channel.

Transnational corporation (TNC) The term favored by the United Nations as an alternative to the term multinational corporation.

Transnational strategy A strategy that combines global coordination to attain efficiency with flexibility to meet specific needs in various countries. *See:* global strategy.

Transparency A desired environment for the use of applications and telecommunication whereby the user is not exposed to the inner workings of the software or to the fact that information may actually come from different sources.

Transposition The erroneous arrangement of digits in a number, such as writing $542 as $524.

Trash investigation Searching through a person's trash for possible evidence in an investigation.

Treadway Commission National Commission on Fraudulent Financial Reporting that made recommendations on financial statement fraud and other matters in 1987.

Treasury management workstation A computer system that provides a means for the treasury manager to efficiently manage cash concentration, account balances at banks, cash transfers, and the short-term investment and borrowing portfolio. These are sold by banks and some specialized vendors.

Treasury stock A corporation's issued stock that has been reacquired.

Tree A network topology in which each computer (or other communications device) is connected to several other computers in a shape that resembles the breaches of a tree.

Tree diagram Management and planning tool that shows the complete range of subtasks required to achieve an objective. A problem-solving method can be identified from this analysis.

Trend 1: Consecutive points that show a nonrandom pattern. **2:** The long-run shift or movement in the time series observable over several periods of data.

Trend analysis 1: A financial analysis that provides intrafirm as well as interfirm comparisons for two or more periods or dates. **2:** An analysis of a firm's financial ratios over time, used to determine the improvement or deterioration in its financial situation. **3:** Charting of data over time to identify a tendency or direction.

Trial balance A summary listing of the titles and balances of the accounts in the ledger.

Trial impact Inducing nonusers to try a brand for the first time, or encouraging retrial by consumers who have not purchased the brand for an extended period.

Triangular arbitrage 1: Action to capitalize on a discrepancy where the quoted cross exchange rate is not equal to the rate that should exist at equilibrium. **2:** The exchange of one currency for a second currency, the second for a third, and the third for the first in order to make a profit.

Trigger mechanisms Specific acts or stimuli that set off reactions.

True and fair view A British concept of what financial statements ought to convey and an important feature of the Fourth Directive. The implementation of this concept means that companies may be required to disclose additional or different information. Each country determines, based on its own circumstances, how its corporations should comply with the true and fair view concept.

Trust receipt loans A financing arrangement where the collateralized inventory items are noted by serial number or some other readily identifiable mark.

Trust services Safekeeping, record keeping, and perhaps investing of corporate or individual pension or profit-sharing plans. For a corporate pension, the trustee institution receives the payments, invests them, maintains record for each of the employees, and pays the pensioners after they retire.

Trustee 1: An official who ensures that the bondholders' interests are protected and that the terms of the indenture are carried out. **2:** Individual or firm who collects a debtor's assets and distributes them to creditors.

Trustee under indenture The third-party financial institution charged by investors with the responsibility of monitoring the issuing corporation to ensure that it abides by all provisions of the bond agreement, called indenture.

Turnkey operation A specialized form of management contract between a customer and an organization to provide a complete operational system together with the skills needed for unassisted maintenance and operation.

Turnover Process in which employees leave the organization and have to be replaced.

Turnover ratios *See:* Efficiency ratios.

Twisted-pair-cable Traditional telephone wires, twisted in pairs to reduce electromagnetic interference.

Two-bin inventory system A type of fixed-order system in which inventory is carried in two bins. A replenishment quantity is ordered when the first bin (working) is empty. During the replenishment lead time, material is used from the second bin. When the material is received, the second bin (which contains a quantity to cover demand during lead time plus some safety stock) is refilled and the excess is put into the working bin. At this time, stock is drawn from the first bin until it is again exhausted. This term is also used loosely to describe any fixed-order system even when physical "bins" do not exist. *Syn:* bin reserve system. *See:* visual review system.

Two-card kanban system A kanban system where a move card and production card are employed. The move card authorizes the movement of a specific number of parts from a source to a point of use. The move card is attached to the standard container of parts during movement to the point of use of the parts. The production card authorizes the production of a given number of parts for use or replenishment. *Syn:* dual-card kanban system.

Two-column journal An all-purpose journal.

Two-transaction approach An approach used to translate foreign currency where any gains or losses are separately recorded as gains or losses from exchange rate exchanges.

Type A behavior Behavior pattern characterized by extreme competitiveness, impatience, aggressiveness, and devotion to work.

Type B behavior Behavior pattern that lacks Type A characteristics and includes a more balanced, relaxed lifestyle.

Type I error An incorrect decision to reject something (such as a statistical hypothesis or a lot of products) when it is acceptable. Also known as "producer's risk" and "alpha risk."

Type II error An incorrect decision to accept something when it is unacceptable. Also known as "consumer's risk" and "beta risk."

U

U chart Count per unit chart.

Ubuntu An African thought system that stresses a high degree of harmony and emphasizes unity of the whole, rather than its distinct parts.

Umbrella policy Policy issued to a bank or trading company to insure exports of an exporter and handle all administrative requirements.

Unattainable capability The portion of the production capability that cannot be attained. This is typically caused by factors such as equipment unavailability, suboptimal scheduling, or resource limitations.

Unbiased expectations hypothesis A theory of interest rate determination which posits that the prevailing yield curve is mathematically derived from the present short-term rate and expectations for rates that will exist at various points in time in the future.

Uncertainty Managers know what goal they wish to achieve, but information about alternatives and future events is incomplete.

Uncertainty acceptance The extent to which uncertainty is considered a normal part of life; feeling comfortable with ambiguity and unfamiliar risks.

Uncertainty avoidance 1: A value characterized by people's intolerance for uncertainty and ambiguity and resulting support for beliefs that promise certainty and conformity. **2:** Dimension of culture that refers to the preference of people in a country for structured rather than unstructured situations.

Uncollected balance percentages A proportional breakdown of the present accounts receivable balance, with the proportions based on the month the credit sales originated. The pitfalls of DSO, accounts receivable turnover, and the aging schedule have led to the development of this improved measure, in which the receivables balance is broken down, and the monthly components are divided by the credit sales in the month in which the receivables originated. Sometimes called the "payments pattern approach," the uncollected balance percentages accurately depict a company's collection experience, even when sales are changing.

Uncollectible accounts expense The operating expense incurred because of the failure to collect receivables.

Uncommitted lines of credit Short-term lending agreements which are not technically binding on the bank, although they are almost always honored. Uncommitted lines are usually renewable annually if both parties are agreeable. A less formal agreement than a committed line and the availability of funds may be in question if the general economic or bank internal liquidity position slips.

Unconditional guarantee Organizational policy of providing customers unquestioned remedy for any product or service deficiency.

Uncontrollable input The environmental factors or inputs that cannot be controlled by the decision maker.

Underapplied factory overhead The amount of actual factory overhead in excess of the factory overhead applied to production during a period.

Underwriter's spread The difference between the price at which the investment banking firm buys an issue from a company and the price at which the securities are sold in the primary market; it represents the investment banker's gross profit on the issue.

Underwriting syndicate A syndicate of investment firms formed to spread the risk associated with the purchase and distribution of a new issue of securities.

Underwritten arrangement Agreement for the sale of securities in which the investment bank guarantees the sale by purchasing the securities from the issuer, thus agreeing to bear any risks involved in the transaction.

Undistributed earnings The proportion of a firm's net income after taxes which is retained within the firm for internal purposes.

Undue hardship Significant difficulty or expense imposed on an employer when making an accommodation for individuals with disabilities.

Unearned revenues 1: Amounts that have been received from customers but for which performance of a service or sale of a product has not yet been made. **2:** The liability created by receiving cash in advance of providing goods or services.

Unethical What members of the society generally accept as being "wrong."

Uneven cash flow stream A series of cash flows in which the amount varies from one period to the next.

Unfreezing A stage of organizational development in which participants are made aware of problems in order to increase their willingness to change their behavior.

Uniform commercial code A system of standards that simplifies procedures for establishing loan security.

Uniform delivered pricing The seller charges all customers the same transportation cost regardless of their location.

Uniform Resource Locator (URL) The address of a Web site. Always starts with *http://*

Unilateral transfers Accounting for government and private gifts and grants.

Unintentional amoral management Results when managers are casual about, careless about, or inattentive to the fact that their decisions and actions may have negative or deleterious effects on others.

Uninterruptible power supply (UPS) A system that provides an alternative power supply as soon as a power network fails.

Unique visitor pages The number of different pages at a Web site that a single visitor accesses.

Unique visitors per month The number of people who visit a Web site each month; each person is counted only once, even if that person visits the site more than once during the month.

Unique ZIP code Used by banks to increase the efficiency of their lockbox operations.

Unit contribution margin The dollars available from each unit of sales to cover fixed costs and provide operating profits.

Unit labor cost Computed by dividing the average cost of workers by their average levels of output.

Unit of measure concept A concept of accounting that requires that economic data be recorded in dollars.

United Nations (UN) An organization representing governments of all countries in the world.

United States Foreign Corrupt Practices Act (FCPA) Makes it illegal for U.S. citizens and businesses to practice bribery in the conduct of business not only in the United States but in other countries as well, even when it is an acceptable or expected business practice there.

Units-of-production depreciation method A method of depreciation that provides for depreciation expense based on the expected productive capacity of an asset.

Unity of command Concept that a subordinate should be responsible to only one superior.

Universal *See:* Global.

Universal factors framework Identifies various universal situations and their impact on decision-making behavior.

Universal Product Code (UPC) Bar code on a product's package that provides information read by optical scanners.

Universalism A rigid global yardstick by which to measure all moral issues.

UNIX A popular operating system, versions of which run on machines from different manufacturers, and therefore make the software almost machine-independent.

Unrealized (holding) gains Gains that are not yet actually incurred, for example, as a result of a foreign currency translation.

Unrealized holding gain or loss The difference between the fair market values of the securities and their cost.

Unrealized (holding) losses Losses that are not yet actually incurred, for example, as a result of a foreign currency translation.

Unsecured Lending arrangement in which there is no collateral backing up the loan in the event of a default.

Unsolicited order An unplanned business opportunity that arises as a result of other activities.

Unstructured data Information collected for analysis with open-ended questions.

Unstructured problem A problem for whose solution there is no pretested set of steps, and with which the solver is not familiar—or is only slightly familiar—from previous experience.

Uploading Copying from one computer onto another computer.

Upper control limit (UCL) 1: Cash balance that triggers a purchase of securities large enough to reduce excess cash balances to a predetermined return point. **2:** Control limit for points above the central line in a control chart.

Upstream Used as a relative reference within a firm or supply chain to indicate moving in the direction of the raw material supplier.

Upward communication Messages transmitted from the lower to the higher level in the organization's hierarchy.

Usable funds The net proceeds the firm receives from the financing sources. This represents the amount borrowed less compensating balances, in the case of credit lines, and the bid-ask spread in the case of commercial paper.

Usage rate The daily rate of drawing down the inventory balance. Calculated by dividing the total inventory needs by the number of days in the production planning period.

Users Consumers who actually use the product.

Utilitarian approach The ethical concept that moral behaviors produce the greatest good for the greatest number.

Utilities Programs that provide help in routine user operations.

Utility A measure of the total worth of a consequence reflecting a decision maker's attitude toward considerations such as profit, loss, and risk.

Utility analysis Analysis in which economic or other statistical models are built to identify the costs and benefits associated with specific HR activities.

Utilization 1: A measure (usually expressed as a percentage) of how intensively a resource is being used to produce a good or service. Utilization compares actual time used to available time. Traditionally, utilization is the ratio of direct time charged (run time plus setup time) to the clock time available. Utilization is a percentage between 0 percent and 100 percent that is equal to 100 percent minus the percentage of time lost due to machine, tool, worker, and so on, unavailability. *See:* efficiency, lost time factor, productivity. **2:** In the theory of constraints, utilization is the ratio of the time the resource is needed to support the constraint to the time available for the resource, expressed as a percentage.

Utilization analysis An analysis that identifies the number of protected-class members employed and the types of jobs they hold in an organization.

Utilization review An audit and review of the services and costs billed by health-care providers.

V

Valence The value or attraction an individual has for an outcome.

Validation 1: Confirmation by examination of objective evidence that specific requirements and/or a specified intended use are met. **2:** The process of determining that a simulation model provides an accurate representation of a real system.

Validity 1: Ability of a feedback instrument to measure what it was intended to measure. **2:** The relationship between an applicant's score on a selection device and his or her future job performance.

Valuation approach Method of financial decision-making in which the anticipated shareholder value effect determines which alternative is chosen. The present values of cash inflows and outflows are compared for each alternative.

Valuation The determination of the present dollar value of a series of cash flows.

Value Refers to the usefulness, desirability, and worth of a product, object, or thing.

Value added 1: Value added equals total revenue minus the cost of goods, materials, and services purchased externally. **2:** Tasks or activities that convert resources into products or services consistent with customer requirements. The customer can be internal or external to the organization.

Value-added activities 1: The cost of activities that are needed to meet customer requirements. **2:** Activities that customers perceive as increasing the utility (usefulness) of the products or services they purchase.

Value-added lead time The time required to manufacture a unit of product or other output.

Value-added network (VAN) A computer system that receives EDI information from one firm in one format and transmits to another firm or bank in a different format. The system transmits messages and data from point of origination to prespecified endpoints, and which may offer one or more auxiliary services.

Value-added tax (VAT) A tax on the value added at each stage of the production and distribution process; a tax assessed in most European countries and also common among Latin American countries.

Value analysis Method of weighing the comparative value of materials, components, and manufacturing processes from the standpoint of their purpose, relative merit, and cost in order to uncover ways of improving products, lowering costs, or both.

Value analysis, value engineering, and value research Value analysis assumes that a process, procedure, product, or service is of no value unless proven otherwise. It assigns a price to every step of a process and then computes the worth-to-cost ratio of that step. VE points the way to elimination and reengineering. Value research, related to value engineering, for given features of the service/product, helps determine the customers' strongest "likes" and "dislikes" and those for which customers are neutral. Focuses attention on strong dislikes and enables identified "neutrals" to be considered for cost reductions.

Value at risk (VAR) Estimate of the risk of loss at various probability levels.

Value chain Activities in an organization are related to what is sometimes referred to as the *value chain:* inbound (receiving), operations (production or service), outbound (shipping), marketing, sales, and service. *See:* supply chain.

Value dating Involves forward movement of the amount of a deposited check and back dating of a presented check. This is a common practice by some European banks.

Value engineering and/or analysis A disciplined approach to the elimination of waste from products or processes through an investigative process that focuses on the functions to be performed and whether such functions add value to the good or service.

Value proposition Program of goods, services, ideas, and solutions that a business marketer offers to advance the performance goals of the customer organization.

Value stream The processes of creating, producing, and delivering a good or service to the market. For a good, the value stream encompasses the raw material supplier, the manufacture and assembly of the good, and the distribution network. For a service, the value stream consists of suppliers, support personnel and technology, the service "producer," and the distribution channel. The value stream may be controlled by a single business or a network of several businesses.

Value stream mapping Technique of mapping the value stream.

Values 1: A company's vision, objective, and philosophy as communicated to employees and the public worldwide. National values include good/evil, beautiful/ugly, normal/abnormal, and rational/irrational. Values vary from corporation to corporation, and national values vary from country to country. **2:** End-states or goals one lives for. **3:** Statements that clarify the behaviors that the organization expects in order to move toward its vision and mission. Values reflect an organization's personality and culture.

Variable cost 1: Expenses that increase or decrease with the level of production or sales, such as direct labor or raw materials. **2:** The portion of the total cost that is dependent on and varies with the volume.

Variable cost concept A concept used in applying the cost-plus approach to product pricing in which only the variable costs are included in the cost amount to which the markup is added.

Variable costing The concept that considers the cost of products manufactured to be composed only of those manufacturing costs that increase or decrease as the volume of production rises or falls (direct materials, direct labor, and variable factory overhead).

Variable data Data resulting from the measurement of a parameter or a variable. Control charts based on variables data include average ($\bar{x}$) chart, individuals (X) chart, range (R) chart, sample standard deviation (s) chart, and CUSUM chart.

Variable identification Involves determining what items need to be forecasted and how best to measure those items.

Variable pay Type of compensation linked to individual, team, or organizational performance.

Variable rate demand notes Medium-term debt instruments issued by municipalities, which are found in some corporate short-term investments portfolios because their interest rates are periodically reset.

Variable sampling plan Plan in which a sample is taken and a measurement of a specified quality characteristic is made on each unit. The measurements are summarized into a simple statistic, and the observed value is compared with an allowable value defined in the plan.

Variance 1: A measure of the dispersion, or spread, of a distribution from its expected value. **2:** The difference between actual performance and planned performance.

Variance, σ^2 The standard deviation squared. The amount by which the actual amount is over or under the forecasted or budgeted amount.

Variance analysis model Receivables control technique that builds on the decomposition model, and compares actual receivables performance to the budgeted amounts. If the budget captures the unique conditions and sales levels a company is experiencing, or is so adjusted after the period is over ("flexible budgeting") then one can discern the true reason(s) for changes in receivables levels.

Variation Change in data, a characteristic, or a function that is caused by one of four factors: special causes, common causes, tampering, or structural variation. *See:* individual entries.

VAT analysis In the theory of constraints, a procedure for determining the general flow of parts and products from raw materials to finished products (logical product structure). A V logical structure starts with one or a few raw materials, and the product expands into a number of different products as it flows through divergent points in its routings. The shape of an A logical structure is dominated by converging points. Many raw materials are fabricated and assembled into a few finished products. A T logical structure consists of numerous similar finished products assembled from common assemblies, subassemblies, and parts. Once the general parts flow is determined, the system control points (gating operations, convergent points, divergent points, constraints, and shipping points) can be identified and managed.

VAT concept A concept based on taxing each production activity or business activity that adds value to materials or goods purchased from other businesses.

Vendor fraud An overcharge for purchased goods, the shipment of inferior goods, or the nonshipment of goods even though payment is made.

Venture capital firm A group of companies or individuals that invests money in new or expanding businesses for ownership and potential profits.

Verification 1: Act of reviewing, inspecting, testing, checking, auditing, or otherwise establishing and documenting whether items, processes, services, or documents conform to specified requirements. **2:** The process of determining that a computer program implements a simulation model as it is intended.

Vertical analysis 1: An analysis that compares each item in a current statement with a total amount within the same statements. **2:** Tool that converts financial statement numbers to percentages so that they are easy to understand and analyze.

Vertical market A market in which the goods of one business are used as raw materials or components in the production or sale process of another business.

Vertical merger A merger between a firm and one of its suppliers or customers.

Vertical team A formal team composed of a manager and his or her subordinates in the organization's formal chain of command.

Vertically integrate To bring together more of the steps involved in producing a product in order to form a continuous chain owned by the same firm; typically involves taking on activities that were previously in the external portion of the supply chain.

Vesting The right of employees to receive benefits from their pension plans.

Victim The person or organization deceived by the perpetrator.

Videoconferencing A telecommunication system that allows people who are in different locations to meet via transmitted images and speech.

Virtual memory Storage space on a disk that is treated by the operating system as if it were part of the computer's RAM.

Virtual organization 1: An organization that has few full-time employees and temporarily hires outside specialists who form teams to work on specific opportunities, then disband when objectives are met. **2:** An organization that requires very little office space. Its employees telecommute, and services to customers are provided through telecommunications lines.

Virtual reality A set of hardware and software that creates images, sounds, and possibly the sensation of touch that give the user the feeling of a real environment and experience. In advanced VR systems, the user wears special goggles and gloves.

Virtual Reality Modeling Language (VRML) A standard programming language that supports three-dimensional presentation on the Web.

Virtual team A team that uses advanced information and telecommunications technologies so that geographically distant members can collaborate on projects and reach common goals.

Virus (computer virus) A rogue computer program that infects any computers it is entered into. It spreads in computers like a biological virus.

Visible pay inequity Visible pay inequity between the expatriates and their local peers could demoralize the foreign subsidiary's staff.

Vision 1: An attractive, ideal future that is credible yet not readily attainable. **2:** Statement that explains what the company wants to become and what it hopes to achieve.

Visual control Technique of positioning all tools, parts, production activities, and performance indicators so that the status of a process can be understood at a glance by everyone; provide visual clues: to aid the performer in correctly processing a step or series of steps, to reduce cycle time, to cut costs, to smooth flow of work, to improve quality.

Vital few, useful many Term used by J. M. Juran to describe his use of the Pareto principle, which he first defined in 1950. (The principle was used much earlier in economics and inventory control methodologies.) The principle suggests that most effects come from relatively few causes; that is, 80 percent of the effects come from 20 percent of the possible causes. The 20 percent of the possible causes are referred to as the "vital few"; the remaining causes are referred to as the "useful many." When Juran first defined this principle, he referred to the remaining causes as the "trivial many," but realizing that no problems are trivial in quality assurance, he changed it to "useful many."

Voice of the customer (VOC) Expression of the preferences, opinions, and motivations of the customer that need to be listened to by managers; a one-on-one interviewing process to elicit an in-depth set of customer needs.

Voice recognition Technology that enables computers to recognize human voice, translate it into program code, and act upon the voiced commands.

Voir dire Legal process of qualifying an expert witness.

Volatile memory Computer memory that cannot hold the original data when the machine is unplugged. Example: RAM.

Volume variance The difference between the budgeted fixed overhead at 100 percent of normal capacity and the standard fixed overhead for the actual production achieved during the period.

Voluntary restraint agreements Trade-restraint agreements resulting in self-imposed restrictions not covered by the GATT rules; used to manage or distort trade flows. For example, Japanese restraints on the export of cars to the United States.

Voucher A document that serves as evidence of authority to pay cash.

Voucher system Records, methods, and procedures used in verifying and recording liabilities and paying and recording cash payments.

Vroom-Jago model A model designed to help managers gauge the amount of subordinate participation in decision making.

Vulnerability chart Tool that coordinates the various elements of a fraud investigation to help identify possible suspects.

W

Wa A Japanese concept that necessitates that members of a group, be it in a work team, or a company, or a nation, cooperate with and trust each other.

Wage and salary surveys Surveys that show what other organizations pay incumbents in jobs that match a sample of "key" jobs selected by the organization.

Wages Payments directly calculated on the amount of time worked.

Wait states The clock-beat intervals during which a CPU sits idle.

Walk the talk Means not only talking about what one believes in but also being observed acting out those beliefs. Employees' buy-in of the TQM concept is more likely when management is seen involved in the process, every day.

Walkabout Visual, group technique used in resolving resource planning conflicts among organizational components.

WAN (Wide Area Network) A network of computers and other communications devices that extends over a large area, possibly comprising national territories. Example: the Internet.

Wants Desires to obtain more satisfaction than is absolutely necessary to improve an unsatisfactory condition.

Warehousing The management of distribution of products to a market by storing a product in a facility. Warehouses often include the following activities: consolidation (combining a large number of small shipments into a smaller number of large shipments, in order to gain transportation economies, by getting truckload rates); mixing (providing a mix of different items in a single shipment, using a "cross-dock" operation); service (making items available when needed, and reducing lead time for delivery); contingencies uncertainties (holding inventory in a warehouse as safety stock, in order to accommodate unpredictably high demand for a product); and smoothing (decoupling one entity from another in the supply chain—for example, decoupling the manufacturer from his supplier, or decoupling the manufacturer from his market).

Warrant 1: A long-term option issued by a corporation to buy a stated number of shares of common stock at a specified price. **2:** Order issued by a judge to arrest someone.

Warranty liabilities Obligation to perform service and repair items sold within a specific period of time and/or use after sale.

Waste Activities that consume resources but add no value; visible waste (for example, scrap, rework, downtime) and invisible waste (for example, inefficient setups, wait times of people and machines, inventory).

WCR/S Working capital requirements divided by sales.

Weak-form efficient Description of foreign exchange markets, implying that all historical and current exchange rate information is already reflected in prevailing spot exchange rates.

Web page A screenful of text, pictures, sounds, and animation that the user encounters when using a Web browser.

Web page authoring tools Software tools that make Web page composition easier and faster than writing code by providing icons and menus.

Web site The electronic presence of an organization or individual on the World Wide Web. The site is composed of Web pages and either shares a server with other sites or has a dedicated server.

Web-visit hijacking Mimicking another, similarly named Web site in order to trick or confuse e-mail and e-business users into sending information to a business other than the intended one.

Webb-Pomerene Act A 1918 statute that excludes from antitrust prosecution U.S. firms cooperating to develop foreign markets.

Webmaster The person who is in charge of constructing and maintaining the organization's Web site.

Weekend effect A concern in making cash transfers that takes into account weekend balances, since deposit accounts in the United States do not earn interest, and also considers weekend deposits that will be credited to the deposit account on Monday.

Weibull distribution Distribution of continuous data that can take on many different shapes and is used to describe a variety of patterns; used to define when the "infant mortality rate" has ended and a steady state has been reached (decreasing failure rate); relates to the "bathtub" curve.

Weighted moving averages A method of forecasting or smoothing a time series by computing a weighted average of past time series values. The sum of the weights must equal 1.

Weighted-average cost of capital (WACC) The summed product of the proportion of each type of capital used and the cost of that capital source, this "hurdle rate" for capital investments is usually based on a company's long-term financing sources.

Wellness programs Programs designed to maintain or improve employee health before problems arise.

Well-pay Extra pay for not taking sick leave.

What-if analysis 1: A trial-and-error approach to learning about the range of possible outputs for a model. Trial values are chosen for the model inputs (these are the what-ifs) and the value of the output(s) is computed. **2:** An analysis that is conducted to test the degree to which one variable affects another. Also called *sensitivity analysis*.

Wheel of retailing theory Pattern of competitive development in retailing which states that new types of retailers enter the market as low-status, low-margin, low-price operators. However, as they meet with success, these new retailers gradually acquire more sophisticated and elaborate facilities, thereby becoming less efficient and vulnerable to new types of low-margin retail competitors who progress through the same pattern.

Whistle-blowing The disclosure by an employee of illegal, immoral, or illegitimate practices by the organization.

Whitemail bribery Payments made to induce an official in a foreign country who is in a position of power to give favorable treatment where such treatment is either illegal or not warranted on an efficiency or economic benefit scale.

Wholesale lockbox system Special arrangement for collecting mailed payments, established for collecting relatively few large dollar remittances. Because the dollar amounts per check are larger (perhaps $1 million or more), the received checks are processed more often and checks are processed for deposit more rapidly by bank than by company personnel.

Wholesale market Investment supply and demand interaction for large dollar transactions between large investors (such as the money market).

Wholesalers Persons or establishments that sell to retailers and/or other organizational buyers for industrial, institutional, and commercial use, but do not sell in significant amounts to ultimate consumers.

Wholesaling Activities of persons or establishments that sell to retailers and/or other organizational buyers for industrial, institutional, and commercial use, but do not sell in significant amounts to final consumers.

Wholly owned foreign affiliate A foreign subsidiary over which an organization has complete control.

Wholly-owned subsidiary Enables an MNE to retain control and authority over all phases of operation. The firm establishes a subsidiary in a foreign country maintaining 100 percent ownership; unlike joint ventures, risks are not shared.

"Window dressing" techniques Techniques employed by firms to make their financial statements look better than they actually are.

Wire drawdowns Wire transfers that are initiated by the receiving party, instead of the sender or payor.

Wire transfers Are bookkeeping entries that simultaneously debit the payor's account and credit the payee's account. The best way to quickly move money from one place to another is with a wire transfer. A real-time transfer of account balances between banks.

Wireless access protocol (WAP) A protocol used in mobile communication (M-commerce).

Wireless communication Transmission of data as radio signals without wires or telephone jacks.

Wireless LAN A local area network that uses electromagnetic waves (radio or infrared light) as the medium of communication.

Wisdom Culmination of the continuum from data to information to knowledge to wisdom.

With recourse When the factor can demand funds returned for uncollected receivables.

Withholding taxes Taxes applied to the payment of dividends, interest, or royalties by firms.

Without recourse The seller is not liable for uncollected receivables.

Word (data word) The number of bits that the control unit of a computer fetches from the primary memory in one machine cycle. The larger the word, the faster the computer.

Work Effort directed toward producing or accomplishing results.

Work analysis Analysis, classification and study of the way work is done. Work may be categorized as value-added work (necessary work), non-value-added (rework, unnecessary work, idle). Collected data may be summarized on a Pareto chart, showing how people within the studied population work. The need for and value of all work is then questioned and opportunities for improvement identified. A Time Use Analysis may also be included in the study.

Work breakdown structure (WBS) 1: A hierarchical tree of work elements or items that will be accomplished or produced by the project team during the project. **2:** Project management technique by which a project is divided into tasks, subtasks, and units of work to be performed.

Work cycle A series of sequentially repeated activities involved in providing a service or creating a product.

Work group Group composed of people from one functional area who work together on a daily basis and whose goal is to improve the processes of their function.

Work in process (WIP) inventory 1: The direct materials costs, the direct labor costs, and the factory overhead costs that have entered into the manufacturing process, but are associated with products that have not been finished. **2:** Inventory composed of the materials that still are moving through the stages of the production process.

Work instruction Document which answers the question: How is the work to be done? *See:* procedure.

Work package The lowest-level item of any branch of a work breakdown structure.

Work redesign The altering of jobs to increase both the quality of employees' work experience and their productivity.

Work redesign programs Programs that alter jobs to both the quality of the work experience and productivity.

Work sample tests Tests that require an applicant to perform a simulated job task.

Work scheduling Preparing schedules of when and how long workers are at the workplace.

Work scope *See:* Project scope.

Work sheet A working paper used to summarize adjusting entries and assist in the preparation of financial statements.

Work specialization The degree to which organizational tasks are subdivided into individual jobs. Also called division of labor.

Workbook Collection of exercises, questions, or problems to be solved during training; a participant's repository for documents used in training (for example, handouts).

Worker efficiency A measure (usually computed as a percentage) of worker performance that compares the standard time allowed to complete a task to the actual worker time to complete it. *Syn:* labor efficiency.

Workers' compensation Benefits provided to persons injured on the job.

Workflow analysis A study of the way work (inputs, activities, and outputs) moves through an organization.

Workforce diversity Hiring people with different human qualities or who belong to various cultural groups.

Working capital 1: A firm's investment in short-term assets—cash, marketable securities, inventory, and accounts receivable. **2:** The excess of the current assets of a business over its current liabilities.

Working capital cycle The continual flow of resources through the various working capital accounts such as cash, accounts receivables, inventory, and payables.

Working Capital Guarantee Program Program conducted by Ex-Im Bank which encourages commercial banks to extend short-term export financing to eligible exporters; Ex-Im Bank provides a guarantee in the loan's principal and interest.

Working capital investment decision The proportion of total assets held in current asset accounts, with the outcome usually linked closely to the company's risk posture.

Working capital management The management of a firm's current assets (cash, accounts receivable, inventories) and current liabilities (accounts payable, short-term debt).

Working capital policy Decisions regarding 1) the target levels for each current asset account and 2) how current assets will be financed.

Working capital requirements The difference between current operating assets (receivables, inventory, and prepaids) and current operating liabilities (accounts payable and accruals).

Working capital turnover ratio Sales divided by average working capital; a measure of the amount of working capital used to generate revenues.

Works council Councils that provide labor a say in corporate decision making through a representative body that may consist entirely of workers or of a combination of managers and workers.

Workstation A powerful microcomputer providing high-speed processing and high-resolution graphics. Used primarily for scientific and engineering assignments.

World Bank Bank established in 1944 to enhance economic development by providing loans to countries.

World-class competitors Multinational firms that can compete globally with domestic products.

World-class quality Term used to indicate a standard of excellence: best of the best.

World Trade Organization (WTO) Institution that administers international trade and investment accords. It supplanted the General Agreement on Tariffs and Trade (GATT) in 1995.

World Wide Web (Web, WWW) 1: The application of the Internet that allows the posting and retrieval of text, pictures, sounds, and motion pictures. "Surfing" the Web is done by way of clicking on marked text and pictures to move to other pages at the same site or to a different site. **2:** A collection of central servers for accessing information on the Internet.

Worldwide approach A national tax system that subjects both domestic source and foreign source income to taxes.

WORM (Write Once, Read Many) A storage medium that is loaded with software by the manufacturer, and can never be overwritten. Example: CD-ROM.

Worm A rogue code that spreads in a computer network.

Worst-case scenario An analysis in which all of the input variables are set at their worst reasonably forecasted values.

Writer Seller of an option.

Written principles Those principles governing language and behavior that must be transmitted when sending a written message across cultures.

X

X-bar ($\bar{X}$) chart Average chart.

Y

Yankee stock offerings Offerings of stock by non–U.S. firms in the U.S. markets.

Yield 1: A measure of materials usage efficiency; it measures the ratio of the materials output quantity to the materials input quantity. Yields less than 1.0 are the result of materials losses in the process. **2:** Ratio between salable goods produced and the quantity of raw materials and/or components put in at the beginning of the process. **3:** The amount of good or acceptable material available after the completion of a process. Usually computed as the final amount divided by the initial amount converted to a decimal or percentage. In manufacturing planning and control systems, yield is usually related to specific routing steps or to the parent item to determine how many units should be scheduled to produce a specific number of finished goods. For example, if fifty units of a product are required by a customer and a yield of seventy percent is expected then seventy-two units (computed as fifty units divided by .7) should be started in the manufacturing process.

Yield curve A graph showing the relationship between yields and maturities of securities.

Yield ratios A comparison of the number of applicants at one stage of the recruiting process to the number at the next stage.

Yield spread The difference between two interest rates, expressed as a percentage difference.

Yield spread swap Exchange of one debt security for another, usually with the motivation of taking advantage of a mispriced security, based on the investor's study of historical interest rate differences.

Yield to maturity (YTM) The average rate of return earned on a bond if it is held to maturity.

Z

Zero coupon bond A bond that pays no annual interest but is sold at a discount below par, thus providing compensation to investors in the form of capital appreciation.

Zero defects Performance standard popularized by Philip B. Crosby to address a dual attitude in the workplace: People are willing to accept imperfection in some areas, while, in other areas, they expect the number of defects to be zero. This dual attitude had developed because of the conditioning that people are human and humans make mistakes. However, the zero-defects methodology states that if people commit themselves to watching details and avoiding errors, they can move closer to the goal of zero.

Zero-balance account (ZBA) A special checking account used for disbursements that has a balance equal to zero when there is no disbursement activity.

Zero-based budgeting A concept of budgeting that requires all levels of management to start from zero and estimate budget data as if there had been no previous activities in their unit.

Zero-growth stock A common stock whose future dividends are not expected to grow at all; that is, $g = 0$, and $\hat{D}_1 = \hat{D}_2 = \cdots = \hat{D}_\infty$.

Zero investment improvement Another term for a *kaizen blitz*.

Endnotes

1. Dean Foust with Gerry Khermouch, "Repairing the Coke Machine," *BusinessWeek* (March 19, 2001), 86–88.
2. John A. Byrne and Heather Timmons, "Tough Times for a New CEO," *BusinessWeek* (October 29, 2001), 64–70; and Patrick McGeehan, "Sailing into a Sea of Troubles," *The New York Times* (October 5, 2001), C1, C4.
3. Thomas Petzinger, Jr., *The New Pioneers: The Men and Women Who Are Transforming the Workplace and Marketplace* (New York: Simon & Schuster, 1999), 91–93; "In Search of the New World of Work," *Fast Company* (April 1999), 214–220+; Peter Katel, "Bordering on Chaos," *Wired* (July 1997), 98–107; and Oren Harari, "The Concrete Intangibles," *Management Review* (May 1999), 30–33.
4. Ian Wyle, "He is Belfast's Security Blanket," *Fast Company* (December 2001), 54–58.
5. Joe Ruff, "ConAgra CEO Finds Strength in Unity," Associated Press, *Johnson City Press* (May 5, 2000), 30, 32; Jack Neff, "The Biggest Nobody Really Knows," *Food Processing* (February 2001), 19; Brandon Copple, "Synergy in Ketchup?" *Forbes* (February 7, 2000), 68; and "ConAgra Attributes Acquisitions, Brands in Results," *Feedstuffs* (January 22, 2001), 6.
6. D. Michael Abrashoff, "Retention Through Redemption," *Harvard Business Review* (February 2001), 136–141; and Polly LaBarre, "The Most Important Thing a Captain Can Do Is to See the Ship from the Eyes of the Crew," *Fast Company* (April 1999), 115–126.
7. John Roemer, "A Hospital Is Reborn," *Management Review* (June 1999), 58–61.
8. David Whitford, "Before & After," *Inc.* (June 1995), 44–50.
9. Jean Kerr, "The Informers," *Inc.* (March 1995), 50–61.
10. Lori Hinnant, "Company Lowers HIV-Drug Prices for Africa, Others," Associated Press, *Johnson City Press* (March 8, 2001), 16.
11. Julia Lawlor, "Personality 2.0," *Red Herring* (April 1, 2001), 98–103.
12. Lucette Lagnado, "Strained Peace: Gerber Baby Food, Grilled by Greenpeace, Plans Swift Overhaul," *The Wall Street Journal* (July 30, 1999). A1, A6; and "Group Sows Seeds of Revolt Against Genetically Altered Foods in U.S.," *The Wall Street Journal* (October 12, 1999), B1, B4.
13. Roger O. Crockett, "A New Company Called Motorola," *BusinessWeek* (April 17, 2000), 86.
14. William J. Holstein, "Dump the Cookware," *Business2.com* (May 1, 2001), 68+; and Robert I. Sutton, "The Weird Rules of Creativity," *Harvard Business Review* (September 2001), 94–103.
15. Thomas Petzinger, Jr., *The New Pioneers: The Men and Women Who Are Transforming the Workplace and Marketplace* (New York, Simon & Schuster, 1999) 27–32.
16. Jonathan Friedland and Louise Lee, "The Wal-Mart Way Sometimes Gets Lost in Translation Overseas," *The Wall Street Journal* (October 8, 1997), A1, A12.
17. E. F. Harrison, *Policy, Strategy, and Managerial Action* (Boston: Houghton Mifflin, 1986), 43.
18. John Schorr, *Purchasing in the 21st Century* (New York: John Wiley & Sons, 1998).
19. B. Pine and J. Gilmore, "Welcome to the Experience Economy," *Harvard Business Review* (July–August 1998), 97–105.
20. B. Pine and J. Gilmore, *The Experience Economy* (Boston: Harvard Business School Press, 1999).
21. Discriminant analysis is used in marketing research and consumer predictive behavior, and interpretation and classification of data. Causal analysis can be used in marketing research to test cause-and-effect relationships.
22. See, for example, "The Three Factors of Fraud," by W. Steve Albrecht and G. Wernz, *Security Management*, July 1993, pp. 95–97.
23. Philip Kotler, *Marketing Management, The Millennium Edition*, Prentice-Hall, Copyright 2000, ISBN 0-13-012217-3; p. 698.
24. Kotler, pp. 404–405.
25. Anunpindi et al., *Managing Business Process Flows, 1E*, © 1999 by Prentice Hall, Inc., ISBN 0-13-907775-8.
26. Kotler, pp. 586–587.
27. Kotler, pp. 595–596.

28. Jackson and Sawyers, *Managerial Accounting*, Copyright 2001, ISBN 0-030-21092-5, p. 436.
29. J. S. Kim, *Manufacturing Futures Survey*. "Search for a New Manufacturing Paradigm," Research Report Series, Boston University, School of Management, October, 1996.
30. Berry and Parasuraman, *Marketing Services: Competing Through Quality*, Free Press, New York, Copyright 1991, pp. 136–142.
31. Terry J. Hill, *Manufacturing Strategy—Text and Cases*, Richard D. Irwin, Inc., 1994.
32. Kotler, pp. 234–236.
33. Ian C. MacMillan et al., *Global Gamesmanship*, Harvard Business Review, Cambridge, MA, May 2003, pp. 62–71.

Subject Index

A

Abandoned product ranges, G-1
ABC analysis, 49
ABC inventory classification system, 192, 199, G-1
Ability test, G-1
Abnormal demand, G-1
Absolute advantage, G-1
Absolute form of purchasing power parity, G-1
Absorption costing, 99–100, G-1
Accelerated depreciation method, G-1
Acceptance Quality Level (AQL), G-1
Acceptance sampling, G-1
Acceptance sampling plan, G-1
Access controls, 137, 146, G-1
Access newsgroups, 148
Account, G-1
Accountability, G-2
Account form, G-1
Accounting, G-2
   absorption costing method, 99–100
   auditing issues for global operations, 106–107
   controls over cash, 100–101
   controls over current liabilities, 104–105
   controls over fixed assets and intangible assets, 103–104
   controls over inventories, 102–103
   controls over receivables, 101–102
   cost, 90, 94–95
   cultural influences on, 105
   cycle, 91–92
   depreciation, 103
   development of principles, 90
   environmental, 90
   financial, 90
   financial statement analysis, 93–94
   information systems, 100
   international, 90
   managerial, 90
   measurement and disclosures, 106
   not-for-profit, 90
   operating budget, 97
   performance evaluation, 97–98
   product and service costing methods, 96–97
   profession of, 90
   relevant costs, 98–99
   role of, in business, 90
   social, 90
   statement of cash flows, 92
   strategies, 89–91
   tax, 90
   variable costing method, 99–100
   worldwide disclosures diversity and harmonization, 106
Accounting and Auditing Enforcement Release (AAER), G-2
Accounting anomalies, G-2
Accounting cycle, 91–92, G-2
   steps of, 91
Accounting diversity, G-2
Accounting equation, 90, G-2
Accounting exposures, G-2
Accounting information systems, 100
Accounting period concept, G-2
Accounting principles, G-2
Accounting Principles Board Opinion No. 15, G-2
Accounting profit, G-2
Accounting rate of return (ARR) method, 120, 179
Accounting standards, G-2
Accounting system, 90, G-2
Account parameters and records, G-1
Account receivable, G-1
Account reconciliation, G-2
Accounts payable, 111, G-2
Accounts payable/cost of goods sold ratio, 214
Accounts payable/inventory ratio, 214
Accounts payable/purchases ratio, 213
Accounts payable/total liabilities ratio, 214
Accounts receivable financing, 112, G-2
Accounts receivable turnover, G-2
Accounts receivable turnover ratio, 102, 206, G-2
Accreditation, G-2
Accrual, 111, G-2
Accrued expenses, G-2
Accrued liability, G-2
Accrued revenues, G-2
Acculturation, G-2
Accumulated depreciation account, G-2
Accuracy, G-2
ACH credit, G-2
ACH debit, G-2
Achievement culture, 222
Acid test, 128
Acid test ratio, G-102
Acid-test ratio, 205, 213, G-2
Acounting rules, related to leasing of fixed assets, 104
Acquired needs theory, 8
Acquisitions, 2, G-2
   cost of, 243
ACSI, G-2
Action plan, G-2
Active investment strategy, 110, G-2
Active listening, G-3
Active practice, G-3
ActiveX, 148, G-3
Activity, G-3
Activity analysis, G-3
Activity base, G-3
Activity-based cost accounting system, 231
Activity-based costing, 7, 74, 190, 242, G-3
Activity-bases management (ABM), G-3
Activity base usage, G-3
Activity cost pools, G-3
Activity in the box (AIB), 33, G-3
Activity method, 172
Activity network diagram (AND), G-3
Activity on the arrow (AOA), 33, G-3
Activity rates, G-3
Activity ratios, G-3
Act of state doctrine, 166, G-2
Actual cost, G-3
Actual demand, G-3
Actual (realized) rate of return, (k_s), G-3
Actual volume, G-3
Act utilitarianism, 10
Acumax, 136
Acute crisis stage, G-3
Adaptability culture, 222
Adaptability screening, G-3
Adaptable management, G-3
Adaptation, G-3
Adaptation problems, G-3
Adaptive transformative innovations, G-3
Additional funds needed (AFN), 116, G-3
Additional paid-in capital, G-3
Add-on interest, G-3
Ad hoc groups, G-3

I-1

Ad hoc reports, G-3
Adjourning, G-3
Adjustable pegged exchange-rate system, 165
Adjustable-rate preferred stock (ARPS), G-3
Adjusted r^2 hr., G-3
Adjusted trial balance, G-3
Adjusting entries, 91, G-3
Adjusting process, G-3
Administrative expenses (general expenses), G-3
Administrative model of decision making, 9, 221, G-3
Administrative principles, G-3
ADSL (Asynchronous DSL), G-3
Ad substantiation, 65
Adult learning principles, G-3
Ad valorem tariff, 163
Advanced determination ruling (ADR), G-4
Advance pricing agreement, G-4
Adverse selection, G-4
Advertising, 58, G-4
　analysis, 186–187
　effectiveness, 186
　reach and exposure, 186–187
　response analysis, 186
Advised line, G-4
Advising bank, G-4
Affidavit, G-4
Affiliate programs, G-4
Affinity diagram, 72, G-4
Affirmative action, 15, 84, 87, G-4
Affirmative action plans (AAPs), 87, G-4
Affirmative disclosure, 65
After-tax cost of debt, k_{dT}, G-4
Age discrimination, 88
Age Discrimination in Employment Act, 16, 88, 167
Agencies, G-4
Agency problem, G-4
Agent, G-4
Agent of change, G-4
Agents/brokers, G-4
Aggregate capacity planning, 47
Aggregate forecast, G-4
Aggregate plan, G-4
Aggregate planning, 47, G-4
Aggressive approach, G-4
Aggressive strategy, G-4
Agile approach or agility, G-4
Agility, G-4
Aging schedule, 110, G-4
Aging the receivables, G-4
Agreeableness, 223
Airfreight, G-4
Airway bill, G-4
Alcohol testing, 16
Algorithm, 139, G-4
Alliances, G-4

Allied Signal, 73
All-in-rate, G-4
Allocated item, G-4
Allocation mentality, G-4
Allowance account, 101
Allowance for doubtful accounts, G-5
Allowance for uncollectible assets as a percentage of receivables, G-5
Allowance method, G-5
Allowances for deferred income tax assets, G-5
Alpha risk, G-5
Alternative approaches to systems development, 143–144
Alternate transportation systems, 228
Alternative evaluation, G-5
Ambiguity, G-5
American-based leadership and motivation theories, G-5
American depository receipts (ADRs), 113, G-5
American Institute of Certified Public Accountants (AICPA), G-5
Americans with Disabilities Act (ADA) (1990), 16, 81, 87, 88, 167
American terms, G-5
Amoral management, 156
Amortization, 104, G-5
Amortized loan, 126, G-5
Analog model, G-5
Analog signal, G-5
Analogy, G-5
Analysis of means (ANOM), G-5
Analysis of variance (ANOVA), G-5
Analytical anomalies, G-5
Analytical thinking, G-5
Anchor stores, G-5
Andon board, G-5
Angel financing, G-5
Annual compounding, G-5
Annual percentage rate (APR), G-5
Annual report, 94, G-5
Annual sales, 197
Annuity, 124, G-5
Annuity due, G-5
ANOVA, G-5
ANSI, G-5
Antecedent, G-5
Anticipation, G-5
Antidumping, G-5
Antidumping laws, 163, G-5
Antiplanning, G-5
Antitrust laws, 13, 16, 166, G-5
Antivirus software, G-5
AOQ, G-5
AOQL, G-6
Appellate court, G-6
Applet, 148, G-6
Applicant pool, G-6
Applicant population, G-6
Application, G-6

Application controls, G-6
Application/Data Independence, G-6
Application form, 82, G-6
Application generator, G-6
Application service provider (ASP), G-6
Application-specific software, G-6
Appraisal costs, 214–215, G-6
Appreciation, G-6
Appropriation, G-6
AQL, G-6
Arbitrage, G-6
Arbitration, G-6
Arc elasticity, 63
Area expertise, G-6
Area structure, G-6
Area studies, G-6
Arithmetic analysis, 248
Arithmetic logic unit (ALU), G-6
Arm's length price, G-6
Arraignment, G-6
Arrow diagram, 72, G-6
Artificial intelligence, 141, G-6
Artificial vision, 141, G-6
AS-9100, G-6
ASCII, G-6
Asian dollar market, G-6
Asia-Pacific Economic Cooperation (APEC), G-6
Ask price, G-6
ASP, G-6
ASQ, G-6
Assembler, G-6
Assemble-to-order, G-6
Assembly languages, G-6
Assembly time, 184
Assessment, G-7
Assessment center, G-7
Asset-and-liability approach, G-7
Asset-based lending, G-7
Asset-based loans, G-7
Asset fraud, G-7
Asset information, 238
Asset management ratios, G-7
Asset misappropriations, G-7
Assets, G-7
　current, 91
　fixed, 91, 103
　plant, 91
　utilization, 206
　value, 131
Asset securitization, G-7
Asset swap, G-7
Asset turnover, 175, 190, 208, G-7
Assignable cause, G-7
Assignment of proceeds, G-7
Assignment problem, 246
Assistant-to positions, 83
Associated firms, G-7
Association of Certified Fraud Examiners (ACFE), G-7

Association of Southeast Asian Nations (ASEAN), G-7
Asymmetric information, G-7
Asymmetric key encryption, 137, G-7
Asynchronous communications, G-7
Atomic transactions, 137, 146, G-7
Attitudes, 23, G-7
Attitude survey, G-7
Attribute data, G-7
Attributions, G-7
Auction preferred stock (APS), G-7
Audit command language (ACL), G-7
Audit committee, G-7
Auditee, G-7
Auditing issues for global operations, 106–107
Auditor, G-7
Auditor's report, G-7
Audit program, G-7
Audits, G-7
  external, 107
  internal, 107
  trails, 137, 146
Audit team, G-7
Audit trail, G-7
Autarky, G-7
Authentication, G-7
Authoritarianism, 23, 223, G-7
Authoritative decision making, G-7
Authority, 5, G-7
Authority-compliance management, 6, 220
Autocratic leader, G-7
Autocratic management, G-7
Automated clearing house (ACH), G-8
Automated materials handling, 52
Automated storage/retrieval system (AS/RS), G-8
Automatic identification, 52
Automation, G-8
Autonomy, G-8
Autoregressive model, G-8
Availability, G-8
Availability analysis, G-8
Availability float, G-8
Availability schedule, G-8
Available-for-sale security, G-8
Available inventory, 191, G-8
Available (rated or calculated) capacity, 192
Available-to-promise (ATP), G-8
Average, G-8
Average chart, G-8
Average collection period, G-8
Average cost method, 102, 212, G-8
Average daily COGS, 197
Average daily sales, 133
Average flotation cost, 118
Average inventory, 134, 197, G-8
Average outgoing quality (AOQ), G-8

Average outgoing quality limit (AOQL), G-8
Average rate of return, G-8
Average tax rate, G-8
Avoidable costs, 203
Avoidance, G-8
Avoidance learning, 8

B

Backbone, 147, G-8
Backflush, G-8
Backflush costing, G-8
Background investigations, 82
Back scheduling, G-8
Backtranslation, G-8
Backup, 137, 146, G-8
Back value date, G-8
Backward chaining (backward reasoning), 77, G-8
Backward innovation, G-9
Bad debt expense, G-9
Badwill, G-9
Balanced scorecard, 74, 219, 242, G-9
Balanced tenancy, G-9
Balance fractions
  inventory, G-9
  payables, G-9
Balance-of-payments (BOPs), 126, 160, G-9
  international, 209
Balance-of-payments (BOPs) equilibrium, 161–162
Balance of payments deficit, G-9
Balance of payments surplus, G-9
Balance of the account, G-9
Balance of trade, G-9
Balance on goods and services, G-9
Balance reporting services, G-9
Balance sheet, 101, 106, G-9
  budgets for manufacturing business, 97
  presentation of receivables on, 102
Balance-sheet approach, G-9
Balance sheet recognition, G-9
Balancing operations, G-9
Balassa-Samuelson Theory, G-9
Baldrige, Malcolm, National Quality Award, 75, G-73
  Criteria for Performance Excellence, 72, 74
Bandwidth, G-9
Bank account, 101
Bank deposit notes, G-9
Bank draft, G-9
Banker's acceptance (BA), G-9
Bank for International Settlements (BIS), 162, G-9
Bank Holding Company Act (1956), G-9
Banking, international, 165
Banking Act, 1991, G-9

Bank Letter of Credit Policy, G-9
Bank loans, 111
Bank notes, G-9
Bank reconciliation, 101, G-9
Bank relationship policy, G-9
Bankruptcy, 113, G-9
Bankruptcy Code, G-9
Bankruptcy Courts, G-9
Bank selection process, G-9
Banner ad, G-9
Banners, G-9
Bar chart, G-9
Bar code, 52, G-10
Bar diagram, 245
Barometric price leadership, 22
Barriers, G-10
Barriers to entrants, 21, G-10
Barrier to exit, 21
Barrier to mobility, 21
Barter, 158, G-10
Baseband link, G-10
Base-case, 217, G-10
Base-case scenario, G-10
Base demand, G-10
Base inventory level, G-10
Basel accord, G-10
Baseline plan, G-10
Base pay, G-10
Base salary, G-10
Base stock system, 195, G-10
Basic income statement budgets for manufacturing business, 97
Batch processing, G-10
Bathtub curve, G-10
Baud, G-10
Bayes theorem, G-10
B2B marketplace, G-8
BCG matrix, G-10
Bearer bond, G-10
Behavioral interview, G-10
Behaviorally anchored rating scale (BARS), G-10
Behavioral rating approach, 84, G-10
Behavioral sciences approach, G-10
Behavior modeling, G-10
Behavior modification, G-10
Belonging needs, 8, 224
Benchmarking, 7, 74, 77, 78, 83, 144, 185, 249, G-10
Benchmark job, G-10
Benefit, G-10
Benefit concept, G-10
Benefit-cost analysis, G-10
Benefits needs analysis, G-10
Best and final offer (BAFO), G-10
Best-case scenario, 217, G-10
Best efforts arrangement, G-10
Best practices, 78, G-10
  in control, 150
  in information technology, 140
Beta coefficient, 123, G-11

Beta probability distribution, G-10–G-11
Beta risk, 121, 123, G-10, G-11
Beta site, G-11
Betterment, 103, G-11
Bhopal tragedy, 157
Bias, G-11
Biased expectations hypothesis, G-11
Biculturalism, G-11
Bid/ask spread, G-11
Bid/no-bid decision, 30, G-11
Bid price, G-11
Bid-rigging scheme, G-11
Big five, G-11
Big Five personality factors, G-11
Big Q, little q, G-11
Bilan Social (social report), G-11
Bilateral advance pricing agreement, G-11
Bilateral and multilateral netting systems, G-11
Bilateral contract, 19
Bilateral negotiations, G-11
Bilateral netting system, G-11
Billing scheme, G-11
Bill of batches, G-11
Bill of exchange (draft), G-11
Bill of labor, 48, G-11
Bill of lading, G-11
Bill of landing (uniform), G-11
Bill of material (BOM), G-11
Bill-of-material explosion, G-11
Bill of resources, G-11
Bill presentation, G-11
Binary number system, G-11
Binomial distribution, 153
Biometrics, 137, G-11
Bit, G-12
Bit map, G-12
Bits per second (bps), G-12
Black hole, G-12
Blackouts, G-12
Bleeding edge, G-12
Blemish, G-12
Block diagram, G-12
Blocked operation, G-12
Blue sky laws, G-12
Board of Governors, G-12
Body language, 40–41, G-12
Bona fide occupational qualification (BFOQ), 87, G-12
Bond anticipation notes, G-12
Bond indenture, G-12
Bonds, 113, 114, G-12
  value of, 114–115
  with warrants, 113
Bond-yield-plus-risk-premium approach, 117
Bonus, G-12
Book value, 202, G-12
Book value of the asset, G-12

Book value per share, 112, 129, 205, 207, 208, G-12
Boot, G-12
Boston Consulting Group (BCG) matrix, 2, 171
Bottleneck, 99, G-12
Bottom-up budgeting, 240, G-12
Bottom-up planning, 136, G-12
Bottom-up replanning, G-12
Boundaryless organization, G-12
Boundary-spanning roles, 24, G-12
Boundary systems, 243
Bounded rationality, G-12
Box-Jenkins model, G-12
Boycott, 16, G-12
BPR (business process reengineering), G-12
Brainstorming, G-12
Branch, G-12
Brand dilution, 173
Brand equity, 173, G-12
Brand extension, 173
Brand management analysis, 173
Brands, G-12
Breadth, G-12
Break-even analysis, 59, 177
Break-even point, 95, 173, 218, 240, 241, G-12
  for sales effort, 232
Break-even point analysis, 192
Break-even sales volume, 232
Break point (BP), G-13
Breakthrough, G-12–G-13
Bretton Woods Agreement (1944), 165, G-13
Bretton Woods system, breakdown of, 165
Bribery, 167, G-13
Bridge, G-13
Broadbanding, 86, G-13
Broadband link, G-13
Brokers, G-13
Brownouts, G-12
Browsers, 148, G-13
Browsing, G-13
Bucketed system, G-13
Bucketless system, G-13
Budget, G-13
Budgeting, 7
  computers in, 97
Budget performance report, G-13
Buffer, G-13
Buffer management, G-13
Buffer stock, G-13
Bug, G-13
Build cycle, G-13
Bulk service, G-13
Bullwhip effect, G-13
Bureaucratic control, 242, G-13
Bureaucratic culture, 222
Bureaucratic organizations, G-13

Bus, G-13
Business, G-13
  nature of, 90
  planning, 136
  policy, 10
  role of accounting in, 90
  uses of quantitative methods in, 42–43
Business continuity plan, G-13
Business cycle, 20
Business entity concept, 90, G-13
Business ethics, 10–11, G-13
  importance of, 90
Business ethics gap, G-13
Business ethics visibility gap, G-13
Business for Social Responsibility, 154
Business incubator, G-13
Business information systems, 146–147
Business-level strategy, 2, G-13
Business market, G-14
Business model, G-14
Business necessity, G-14
Business partnering, G-14
Business plan, G-14
Business planning, G-14
Business process change management, 78
Business process engineering, G-104
Business processes, G-14
Business process flows, 185
Business process improvement (BPI), 78, 185
Business process re-engineering principles, 78, 81, 185, 190–191
Business profit rates, 21
Business Recovery Plan (BRP), G-14
Business report, G-14
Business risks, 118, 234, G-14
Business stakeholder, 90, G-14
Business-to-business (B2B), 148, 149
  products, 57
  trading, 148
Business-to-consumer (B2C), 148, 149
Business transactions, 91, G-14
Business valuation analysis, 180–181
Business valuations, 181
Bustarella, G-14
Bustout, G-14
Buy-and-hold investment strategy, 110, G-14
Buy-back, G-14
Buyers, G-14
Buy hedge, G-14
Buying center, G-14
Buzzword, G-14
Bylaws, G-14
Bypass attack, 249
By-product, 65
Byte, G-14

C

Cache, G-14
CAD, G-14
Calibration, G-14
Call, G-14
Callback, G-14
Call option, 127, G-14
Call option on real assets, G-14
Call premium, 113, G-14
Call provision, G-14
CAM, G-14
Canonical analysis, 247, G-14
Can-order point, G-14
Capability ratio (Cp), G-14
Capable-to-promise (CTP), G-14
Capacity, G-14–15
Capacity control, G-15
Capacity management, 48, G-15
Capacity planning, 47, 53, 238, G-15
Capacity requirements planning (CRP), 48, G-15
Capacity strategy, G-15
Capital, cost of, 117–118, 207
Capital account, 126, 160, G-15
Capital asset, 122
Capital asset pricing model (CAPM), 117, G-15
Capital budget, 180, G-15
Capital budget analysis, 124, 179–180, 180, 240
Capital budgeting, 120–121, 132, 154, G-15
Capital component, G-15
Capital expenditures, 103, G-15
Capital expenditures budget, G-15
Capital flight, G-15
Capital gain (loss), 122, G-15
Capital gains yield, G-15
Capital investment analysis, G-15
Capitalization, 181, G-15
Capital lease, G-15
Capital loss, 122
Capital markets, G-15
Capital projects, 121
Capital rationing, 121, 180, G-15
Capital stock, G-15
Capital structure, 118–119, 133, 174, 207, G-15
Capital structure ratios, G-15
Captive finance companies, G-15
Captive finance subsidiary, G-15
Captive insurer, G-15
Capture theory of economic regulation, 13
Career, G-15
Careers and development, 83
Caribbean Basin Initiative (CBI), G-15
Carriage and insurance paid to (CIP), G-15

Carriage paid to (CPT), G-15
Carrier evaluation criteria, 229
Carryforwards, G-15
Carrying amount, G-15
Cartel, 22, G-16
Cascading training, G-16
CASE (Computer-Aided Software Engineering), G-16
Case study, G-16
CASE tools, 143
Cash, G-16
　bank account in controlling, 101
　control over, 100–101
　internal control over, 100
Cash and securities mix decision, G-16
Cash application, G-16
Cash basis, G-16
Cash break-even point (BEP), 240
Cash budget, G-16
　missing numbers in, 239
Cash collection system, G-16
Cash concentration, G-16
Cash conversion cycle, 108, G-16
Cash conversion period, G-16
Cash coverage ratios, 206
Cash cows, 171
Cash cycle, G-16
Cash discount, G-16
Cash dividend, G-16
Cash equivalents, G-16
Cash flow, G-16
　adequacy ratio, 212
　analysis, 212–213
　based on base-case, 212
　from financing activities, 213, G-16
　free, 92
　from investing activities, 213, G-16
　from operations, 212, 213, G-16
　types of activities, 92
Cash flow scenario analysis, 217
Cash forecasting, 117
　missing numbers in, 239
Cash inflows, G-16
Cash items, G-16
Cash letter, G-16
Cash management, 109–110, G-16
　international, 127–128, 235–236
Cash management systems, G-16
Cash outflows, G-16
Cash payback period, G-16
Cash pooling, G-16
Cash ratio, 205
Cash receipts, achieving internal control over, 100
Cash short and over account, G-16
Catchball, G-16
Categorical system, 215
Category killers, G-16
Category management, G-16
Category rating methods, 84
Cathode-ray tube, G-16

Causal analysis, 247, G-17
Causal distributions, G-17
Causal forecasting methods, G-17
Causal techniques, G-17
Cause-and-effect diagram, 73, G-17
Cause-related marketing, 58, G-17
CBT, G-17
C chart, G-14
CD-ROM (Compact Disc Read-Only Memory), G-17
Cease and desist order, 65
Cell, G-17
Cellular layout, G-17
Cellular manufacturing, G-17
Center of excellence, G-17
Central exchange rate, G-17
Central information systems (IS) management, 145, G-17
Centralization, 5, G-17
Centralized architecture, G-17
Centralized disbursing, G-17
Centralized internal audit model, G-17
Centralized multinational organizations, G-17
Centralized network, G-17
Centralized processing system, G-17
Centralized transfer initiation, G-17
Central plan, G-17
Central planning department, G-17
Central Processing Unit (CPU), G-17
Central tendency, G-17
Central tendency error, G-17
Certainty, G-17
Certificate of deposit (CD), G-17
Certification mark, 15
Certified Internal auditor (CIA), G-17
Certified public accountant (CPA), G-17
Certified suppliers, 176
Chain of command, 5, G-17
Chain of custody, G-17
Chaku-chaku, G-18
Champion, G-18
Chance event, 42, G-18
Chance nodes, G-18
Change agent, 225, G-18
Change management, 25–26, 78, 223
Changeover, G-18
Changing, G-18
Channel design, G-18
Channel intensity, G-18
Channel length, G-18
Channel (link, path), G-18
Channel richness, G-18
Channel strategy, G-18
Channel structure, G-18
Chapter 7 bankruptcy, G-18
Chapter 11 bankruptcy, G-18
Character, G-18
Characteristic, G-18
Chargeback, G-18
Charismatic leader, 6, G-18

SUBJECT INDEX　　　　I-5

Charter, G-18
Chart of accounts, G-18
Chase capacity approach, 183
Chase production method, G-18
Chase strategy, 183
Checklist, 123, G-18
Check processing float, G-18
Check sheet, 73, G-18
Check tampering, G-18
Check truncation, G-18
Chief Executive Officer (CEO), G-18
Chief knowledge officer, 145
Chief learning officer, 145, G-18
Child-care assistance, 85
Children, G-18
Chip, G-18
CHIPS, G-18
Chronic crisis stage, G-18
Chronic problem, G-18
CIO (Chief Information Officer), G-18
Ciphertext, G-18
Circuit switching, 146, G-18
Circular cultures, G-19
CISG, G-19
Cisis management, G-66
Civil law, G-19
Civil Rights Act (1964), 15–16, 87
  Title VII of, 167
Civil Rights Act (1991), 87
CKO (Chief Knowledge Officer), G-19
Clan culture, 222
Classical method, 245
Classical model of decision making, 9, 221, G-19
Classical perspective, 4, G-19
Classic system, G-19
Classified stock, G-19
Classroom courses, 83
Classroom training, 83
Clayton Act, 17
Clean Air Act, 18
Cleansing phase, G-19
Clean Water Act, 18
Clearing agent, G-19
Clearing bank(s), G-19
Clearing float, G-19
Clearing house, G-19
Click through, G-19
Clientele effect, 119, G-19
Client/server, G-19
Clipper, 138
Clock rate, G-19
Closed-loop MRP, G-19
Closed system, G-19
Closely held corporation, 112, G-19
Closeness ratings, 200–201
Closing entries, 91, G-19
Cluster analysis, 247, G-19
Clusters, G-19
Coaching, 83, G-19
Coalition, G-19

Coaxial cable, 146, G-19
COBIT model, 150
Cobranding, 173
CoCo model, 150
Code law, G-19
Code of ethics, G-19
Codetermination, G-19
Coding, G-19
Coefficient of determination, G-19
Coefficient of variation (CV), 153, 217, 245, G-19
Coercive power, 6, 220, G-19
Cofinancing agreements, G-19
Cognitive ability tests, G-19
Cognitive dissonance, G-19
Coin and currency services, G-20
Cold calling, G-20
Cold turkey conversion, G-20
Collaborative problem-solving strategy, G-20
Collected balance, G-20
Collection bank, G-20
Collection float, G-20
Collection policy, 110, G-20
Collection procedures, G-20
Collections float, techniques for speeding up, 109
Collective, G-20
Collective mark, 15
Collectivism, G-20
Collusion, 22, G-20
Comarketing agreement, G-20
Command team, 222
Comment cards, G-20
Commercial data-mining software, G-20
Commercial enterprises, G-20
Commercial/Industrial market, G-20
Commercial invoice, G-20
Commercial letter of credit, G-20
Commercial paper, 111, 112, G-20
Commercial service, G-20
Commission, G-20
Commitment, G-20
Commitment fee, G-20
Committed cost, G-20
Committed facility, G-20
Committed line, G-20
Committee, G-20
Committee assignments, 83
Committee of Sponsoring Organizations (COSO), G-20
Committee on Foreign Investments in the United States (CFIUS), G-20
Commodity analysis, G-20
Commodity price agreement, G-20
Commodity terms of trade, 162, 209
Common agricultural policy (CAP), G-20
Common causes, G-21
Common causes of variation, G-21

Common equity, G-21
  cost of, 117
Common Gateway Interface (CGI), 148, G-21
Common law, 18, G-21
Common market, G-21
Common-size financial statements, G-21
Common-size statements, 93, G-21
Common stock, 112–113, G-21
Common stockholders' equity (net worth), G-21
Communication, 9, 220–221, G-21
  crisis, 156
  oral, 161
  written, 161
Communications channel, G-21
Communication services, G-21
Communications gap, 69
Communications protocol, G-21
Community indifference curve, 162
Compact disc (CD), G-21
Company/brand sites, G-21
Company recapitalization, 207
Company-wide quality control (CWQC), G-21
Comparable worth, 16
Compa-ratio, G-21
Comparative advantage, G-21
Comparative methods, 84
Comparative negligence, 68
Comparative ratio analysis, G-21
Compensable factor, G-21
Compensating balances, 109, 111, G-21
Compensation, 158, G-21
  strategies, 85–86
Compensation committee, G-21
Compensatory Financing Facility (CFF), G-21
Compensatory justice, 224, G-21
Compensatory time off, G-21
Competence, G-21
Competencies, G-21
Competency-based training, G-21
Competitive advantage, 23, 72, G-21
Competitive analysis, 249–250, G-21
Competitive assessment, G-21
Competitive bids, G-21
Competitive environment, G-21
Competitive Equality Banking Act (1987), G-21
Competitive forces and strategies, 2
Competitively advantaged product, G-21
Competitive markets, 12
Competitive moves, 250
Competitive strategies, 21, 22–23
Competitive theories, 22–23
Compiler, G-22
Complaint, G-22
Complementary marketing, G-22
Complements, 64
Complete enumeration, G-22

Compliance, G-22
Compliance strategy, G-22
Components of internal control, G-22
Composite index, 20
Composite keys, 140, G-22
Composition of trade, G-22
Compounded interest, G-22
Compounding, 124, G-22
Compound tariff, 163
Comprehensive Environmental Response, Compensation and Liability Act (CERCLA), 18
Comprehensive financial analysis, 208
Comprehensive income, G-22
Comprehensive payables, G-22
Compresses workweek, G-22
Compression (data compression), G-22
Computer-aided design (CAD), 147, G-22
Computer controls, G-22
Computerized numeric control (CNC), G-22
Computer processing center, G-21
Computers in budgeting, 97
Computer virus (virus), G-22
Concealment investigative methods, G-22
Concentration account, G-22
Concentration bank, G-22
Concentration banking, G-22
Concentration ratios, 22
Concentration services, G-22
Concentration strategy, G-22
Concept, G-22
Conceptual skill, G-22
Conclusion, G-22
CONCT model, 150
Concurrent control, 242, G-22
Concurrent engineering, 76, G-22
Concurrent validity, G-22
Conditional probabilities, G-22
Conference training, 83
Confiscation, 159, 166, G-22
Conflict, 39–40, G-22
Conflict in marketing channels, G-22
Conflict resolution, G-22
Conformance, G-22
Confucianism, G-22
Congeneric merger, G-22
Conglomerate merger, 17, G-22
Conjoint analysis, 246
Conquest marketing, G-22
Conscientiousness, 223
Consensus, G-22
Consequence, G-22
Conservative approach to decision making, 237, G-22
Conservative strategy, G-23
Consideration, 6, G-23
Consigned stocks, G-23
Consignment, G-23

Consistency principle, G-23
Consistent norms, G-23
Consol, G-23
Consolidated financial statements, G-23
Consolidation, G-23
Constancy of purpose, G-23
Constant dollar accounting, G-23
Constant growth model, G-23
Constant monetary unit restatement, G-23
Constant payout ratio, 119, G-23
Constraint, 246, G-23
Constraint management, G-23
Construct, G-23
Construct validity, 88, G-23
Consultative, G-23
Consultative selling, G-23
Consult group style, 221
Consult individually style, 221
Consulting services, G-23
Consumer behavior, G-23
Consumer credit transactions, 66
Consumer decision making, 59, G-23
Consumer health and safety, 65–66
Consumer learning, 59
Consumer market customers, G-23
Consumer products, 57
Consumer Product Safety Act, 65
Consumer profiling, G-23
Consumer promotions, 58
Consumer right of rescission, 66
Consumer's risk, G-23
Consumers' surplus, 64
Consumption satiation, G-23
Container ships, G-23
Content analysis, 247, G-23
Content theories, G-23
Content validity, G-23
Contest, 250
Contingency, G-23
Contingency approach, 6, G-23
Contingency decision making, G-23
Contingency graph, G-23
Contingency plans, 4, G-23
Contingency theory, 220
Contingency view, 4, 225, G-23
Contingent liability, 105, G-23
Contingent workers, G-24
Continuous budgeting, G-24
Continuous compounding, G-24
Continuous improvement, 7, 45, G-24
Continuously compounding, G-24
Continuous probability distribution, G-24
Continuous process improvement, G-24
Continuous process production, 225
Continuous reinforcement schedule, G-24
Contra accounts, G-24
Contra asset, G-24
Contract, G-24

Contract analysis, 152
Contract enforcement, G-24
Contracting cost motive, G-24
Contractionary monetary policy, 162
Contraction defense, 249
Contract law, 18–19
Contract manufacturing, G-24
Contract rate, G-24
Contract review, G-24
Contracts
    classification of, 19
    requirements of, 18–19
Contractual alliances, 158, G-24
Contractual defenses, 67
Contractual hedging, G-24
Contrast error, G-24
Contribution margin (CM), 95, 173, 174, 187, 218, 241, G-24
Contribution margin (CM) analysis, 100, 203, G-24
Contribution margin (CM) per unit, 240–241
Contribution margin (CM) ratio, 95, 173, G-24
Contributor, G-24
Contributory negligence, 67, 68
Contributory plan, G-24
Control activities or procedures, G-24
Control analysis, 241–243
Control charts, 73, 216, G-24
    variable, 216
Control environment, G-24
Controllable costs, 202, G-25
Controllable expenses, G-25
Controllable input, G-25
Controllable variance, G-25
Controlled disbursement accounts (CDA), 109, G-25
Controller, 90, G-25
Control limits, G-24
Controlling account, G-25
Control models, 150
Control plan, G-24
Controls, 77, G-24, G-25
    best practices in, 150
    internal, 150
    management, 150
    in new workplace, 242
    operational, 150
    over cash, 100–101
    over current liabilities, 104–105
    over fixed assets, 103–104
    over intangible assets, 103–104
    over inventories, 102–103
    over receivables, 101–102
    risks and, 242–243
Control sample, G-24
Control Self-Assessment model, 150
Control systems, 2, G-24
Control unit, G-24

Convenience quota sample, G-25
Convenience translation, G-25
Conversational principles, G-25
Conversation analysis, 247, G-25
Conversion, G-25
Conversion costs, 203, G-25
Conversion ratio, CR, G-25
Conversion value, G-25
Convertible bond, G-25
Convertibles, 113
Convertible security, 114, G-25
Cookie, G-25
Cooperative programs, 83
Coordinated decentralization, G-25
Coordinated intervention, G-25
Coordination, G-25
Coordination costs, G-25
Co-payment, G-25
Copromotion agreement, G-25
Copyrights, 15, G-25
Core benefit proposition (CBP), G-25
Core competence, 249, G-25
Core competency, G-25
Core processes, G-25
Corporate agency services, G-25
Corporate annual reports, 94
Corporate charter, G-25
Corporate citizenship, G-25
Corporate citizenship and accountability, 154–155
Corporate control and governance, 150–157
   best practices in, 150
   citizenship and accountability, 154–155
   corporate governance, 157
   crisis management, 155–156
   ethics, 156
   fraud, 150–152
   international issues, 157
   issues management, 155
   management assurance, 156–157
   models, 150
   public policy and affairs, 155
   risk management, 152–154
   strategies, 150
Corporate control strategies, 150
Corporate culture, 78, 221–222, G-25
Corporate ethics, 156
Corporate fraud, 150–152
Corporate governance, 157, G-25
Corporate income tax, G-25
Corporate-level strategy, G-25
Corporate performance analysis, 204–205
Corporate public affairs and public affairs management, G-25
Corporate public policy, 155, G-26
Corporate risk, 121, G-26
Corporate risk management, 152–154
Corporate social performance model, G-26

Corporate social responsibility, 154–155, G-26
Corporate social responsiveness, G-26
Corporate sponsorships, G-26
Corporate strategies, 2
Corporate university, G-26
Corporation, 90, G-26
Corrective action, G-26
Corrective advertising, 65
Corrective control, G-26
Correlation, G-26
Correlation coefficient, G-26
Correspondent banks, G-26
Correspondent firms, G-26
Corruption, G-26
COSO model, 150
Cost, G-26
Cost, insurance, and freight (CIF), G-26
Cost accounting, 90, 231, G-26
Cost allocation, G-26
Cost analysis, 202–204
Cost and freight (CFR), G-26
Cost avoidance, 175
Cost-based approach, 59, 215
Cost-based transfer pricing, G-26
Cost behavior, 94, 240, G-26
Cost-benefit analysis, 10, 83, 238, G-26
Cost centers, 218, G-26
   responsibility accounting report for, 98
Cost changes, 175
Cost concepts, 90, 94–95, G-26
Cost containment, 175
Cost distortion, G-26
Cost driver, G-26
Cost driver analysis, G-26
Cost effectiveness measures, 175
Cost estimate, G-26
Cost estimate at completion (EAC), 210
Cost estimate to complete (ETC), 210
Cost improvements, 175, 190–191
Cost increase, 175
Cost-insurance-freight (CIF) measure, 163
Cost leadership, 171, 249, G-26
Costly trade credit, G-26
Cost method, 196, G-26
Cost object, G-26
Cost of acquisition, 243
Cost of capital, 117–118, 132–133, 207
Cost of carrying receivables, 134
Cost of communication, G-26
Cost of good solds budget, G-27
Cost of goods sold, 203, G-26
Cost of living allowance (COLA), G-26
Cost of lost customers, 243
Cost of merchandise sold, G-26
Cost of new common equity, k_e, G-27
Cost of poor quality (COPQ), G-27
Cost of preferred stock, k_{ps}, G-27
Cost of production report, 97, G-27

Cost of quality (COQ), G-27
Cost of quality report, G-27
Cost of retained earnings, k_s, G-27
Cost of risk, G-27
Cost per equivalent unit, G-27
Cost performance index (CPI), 36, 210, G-27
Cost per thousand (CPM), G-27
Cost planning and performance, 36–38
Cost-plus method, 177, G-27
Cost price approach, 178, G-27
   to transfer pricing, 98
Cost reduction, 175
Cost-reimbursement contract, G-27
Costs
   avoidable, 203
   characteristics of, 202
   conversion, 203
   of lost sales, 243
   markup percentage on, 178
   period, 203
   prime, 203
   product, 203
   relevant, 98–99
   unavoidable, 203
Cost savings, 190
Cost structure, 202
Cost variance, 36, 210, G-27
Cost-volume-profit analysis, 95, 240–241, G-27
Cost-volume-profit chart, 95, G-27
Council on Economic Priorities, 154
Council on Environmental Quality, 17
Count chart, G-27
Counterpurchase, 158, G-27
Countertrade, G-27
Countervailing power, 21
Count-per-unit chart, G-27
Country club management style, 6, 220
Country-related cultural factors framework, G-27
Country risk, 123–124, 165, G-27
Coupon-equivalent yield, G-27
Coupon interest rate, G-27
Coupon payment, G-27
Coupon security, G-27
Coups d'état, G-27
Coverage ratios, G-27
Covered interest arbitrage, G-27
Covert operations, G-27
Cp, G-27
Cpk, G-27
CQI, G-27
Crash cost, 211, G-27
Crashing project, 211
Crash time, 211, G-27
Crawford Slip Method, G-28
Crawling-peg exchange-rate system, 165
Creative problem-solving process, 73
Creativity, G-28

Credence attributes, G-28
Credit, G-28
Credit administration, G-28
Credit Card Fraud Act, 66
Credit decision process, G-28
Credit extension, G-28
Credit-granting decision, G-28
Credit interchange bureaus, G-28
Credit limit, G-28
Credit memorandum, G-28
Creditor, G-28
Creditors' remedies, 66
Credit period, G-28
Credit policy, G-28
Credit reporting agencies, G-28
Credit risk, 165
Credit scoring models, G-28
Credit standards, 110, G-28
Credit terms, 110, G-28
Criminal law, G-28
Crisis, G-28
Crisis communication, 156
Crisis management, 155–156
Crisis-management planning, 4–5
Crisis resolution stage, G-28
Criteria, G-28
Criteria for successful segmentation, G-28
Criterion, G-28
Criterion-related validity, G-28
Critical commodities list, G-28
Critical incident, G-28
Critical path, 210, G-28
Critical path method (CPM), G-28
Critical ratio, 191, G-28
Critical selection factors, 229
Critical success factors, 136, G-28
Crosby, Philip, 73, 74, 75
Cross-border factoring, G-28
Cross-cultural communication, 161, G-28
Cross-cultural message adjustment, G-28
Cross-cultural research, G-28
Cross-cultural social responsibility, G-28
Cross-currency swap, G-28
Cross exchange rate, G-29
Cross-functional team, G-29
Cross hedge, G-29
Cross-hedging, 235, G-29
Cross-marketing activities, G-29
Crossover rate, G-29
Cross rates, G-29
Cross-sectional analysis, G-29
Cross-subsidization, G-29
Cultural assimilator, G-29
Cultural barriers, G-29
Cultural briefing, G-29
Cultural contexts, G-29
Cultural convergence, G-29
Cultural differences, G-29

Cultural environment, G-29
Cultural fluency, G-29
Cultural imperialism, G-29
Cultural influences on accounting, 105
Cultural leader, G-29
Cultural relativism, 167, G-29
Cultural risk, G-29
Cultural-toughnesss dimension, G-29
Cultural universals, G-29
Culture, 221–222, G-29
Culture-free, G-29
Culture gap, G-29
Culture/people change, G-29
Culture shock, G-29
Culture shock phase, G-29
Culture-specific, G-29
Cumulative actual cost (CAC), G-29
Cumulative available-to-promise, G-29
Cumulative budgeted cost (CBC), 36, G-29
Cumulative dividends, G-29
Cumulative earned value (CEV), G-29
Cumulative lead time, G-29
Cumulative manufacturing lead time, G-30
Cumulative MRP, G-30
Cumulative preferred stock, G-30
Cumulative receipts, G-30
Cumulative sum control chart, G-30
Cumulative transaction adjustment (CTA), G-30
Cumulative trauma disorders (CTDs), G-30
Currency board, 164, G-30
Currency call option, 127, 235, G-30
Currency cocktail bond, G-30
Currency derivatives, 127, 234–235
Currency diversification, 235, G-30
Currency exchange rate, G-30
Currency flows, G-30
Currency futures contract, 127, G-30
Currency options, 127, 235, G-30
Currency options hedge, 235
Currency put options, 127, G-30
Currency risk, 165
Currency swap, 234, G-30
Current account, 126, 160, G-30
Current assets, 91, 109, G-30
Current cost accounting, G-30
Current employee referrals, 82
Current exchange rate, G-30
Current liabilities, 91, 105, G-30
  controls over, 104
  interpretation of ratio of cash to, 101
Current liquidity index, G-30
Currently attainable standards, G-30
Current maturity, G-30
Current-noncurrent method, G-30
Current position analysis, 205
Current purchasing power accounting, G-30

Current rate method, G-30
Current ratio, 128, 205–206, 213, G-30
Current reality tree, G-30
Current transfer, G-30
Current value accounting, G-30
Current yield, G-30
Custody account, G-30
Custom-designed software, G-31
Customer, G-31
  lifetime value of a, 243–244
Customer analysis, 243
Customer-centric companies, G-31
Customer council, G-31
Customer defection, 244
Customer delight, G-31
Customer fraud, G-31
Customer involvement, G-31
Customer loyalty/retention, 172, G-31
Customer needs identification, 29–30
Customer-oriented, G-31
Customer penetration, 172
Customer prototypes, G-31
Customer-related concepts, 244
Customer relationship management (CRM), 69, 244, G-31
Customer relationship management (CRM) software, 148
Customer relationship management (CRM) systems, G-31
Customer relationships, 3
Customer requirements, G-31
Customer retention, G-31
Customer satisfaction, G-31
Customer segmentation, G-31
Customer selectivity, 172
Customer service, 191, G-31
Customer structure, G-31
Customer-supplier partnership, G-31
Customer value, G-31
Customer value analysis and competition, 249
Customization, G-31
Customized application, G-31
Customs union, G-31
Cutoff time, G-31
Cybermall, G-31
Cybernetic system, G-31
Cycle, 184
Cycle counting, 192, G-31
Cycle stock, G-31
Cycle time, 184, 194, 249, G-31
  production, 194
Cycle time reduction, G-32
Cyclical component, G-32
Cyclical fluctuation, 20
Cyclical normal goods, 64

D

Daily NPV, G-32
Daily transfer rule, G-32

DASD (Direct Access Storage Device), G-32
Data, G-32
Database, G-32
Database administrator (DBA), G-32
Database approach, G-32
Database management, 140–141
Database management system (DBMS), 140
Database marketing, G-32
Database model, G-32
Data communication, G-32
Data definition language, 141, G-32
Data dictionary, 141, G-32
Data entry control, 146, G-32
Data envelopment analysis, 200
Data flow diagram, 143, G-32
Data hierarchy, 140
Data management module, G-32
Data manipulation language (DML), 141, G-32
Data mining, 141, G-32
Data privacy, G-32
Data processing, G-32
Data range, G-32
Data redundancy, G-32
Data store, G-32
Data theft, G-32
Data warehouse, G-32
Data warehousing, G-32
Daylight overdrafts, G-32
Days inventory held, G-32
Days of cost of goods sold invested in inventory, G-32
Days payables outstanding, G-32
Days purchases outstanding, G-32
Days sales outstanding (DSO), 108, 110, 128, 133, G-32
DBA (Database administrator), G-32
DBMS (Database Management System), G-32
Dealers, G-32
Debentures, 113, G-32
Debit, G-33
Debit cards, G-33
Debit memorandum, G-33
Debt buybacks, 165
Debt capital, G-33
Debt collection practices, 66
Debt-equity ratio, 207
Debt/equity swaps, 165
Debt financing, G-33
Debt-for-debt swaps, 165
Debtor, G-33
Debt ratio, 129, G-33
Debt rescheduling, 165
Debt-to-equity ratio, G-33
Debugging, G-33
Decentralization, 5, G-33
Decentralized architecture, 144
Decentralized control, 242, G-33

Decentralized disbursing, G-33
Decentralized internal audit model, G-33
Decentralized multinational organizations, G-33
Decentralized network, G-33
Decentralized operations, advantages and disadvantages of, 97–98
Decentralized planning, G-33
Decentralized processing system, G-33
Decentralized transfer initiation, G-33
Deception, 65
Decide style, 221
Decision, G-33
Decision analysis, 42–43, 237–238
Decision making, 9–10, 221, G-33
    differential analysis report for, 98
    information technology and, 139
    order cost information for, 96
    use of cost of production reports for, 97
    utility in, 43
Decision matrix, G-33
Decision nodes, G-33
Decision rules, 199
Decision strategy, G-33
Decision style, G-33
Decision support system (DSS), 52, 138, 139, G-33
Decision trees, 42, 176, 237, 238, G-33
Decision variable, 246, G-33
Declining-balance depreciation method, G-33
Decode, G-33
Decomposition method, G-33
Decoupling inventory, G-33
Dedicated capacity, G-33
Deductive fraud detection, G-33
Deemed exports, G-33
Default risk, G-33
Default risk premium (DRP), G-33
Defect, G-33
Defection rate, 243
Defensive merger, G-34
Deferred asset, G-34
Deferred expenses, G-34
Deferred income tax asset, G-34
Deferred income tax liability, G-34
Deferred revenues, G-34
Deficiency, G-34
Defined-benefit plan, G-34
Defined-contribution plan, G-34
Degree of financial leverage (DFL), 117, 118, 173, 174, G-34
Degree of individualism, G-34
Degree of operating leverage (DOL), 116, 118, 173, G-34
Degree of total leverage (DTL), 117, 118, 173, 174, G-34
Delay tactics, G-34
Delegation, G-34
Deliverables, G-34

Delivery duty paid (DDP), G-34
Delivery duty unpaid (DDU), G-34
Delivery gap, 69
Delphi method, 20, 123, 247, G-34
Delphi studies, G-34
Delphi technique, G-34
Demand, G-34
Demand deposit account (DDA), G-34
Demand during lead times, 193
Demand flow, G-34
Demand forecasting, 45
Demand management, 45, G-34
Demand pull, G-34
Demand relations, 63–64
Demand schedules, G-34
Demand-side market failure, G-34
Demerit chart, G-34
Deming, W. Edwards, 72, 74
Deming chain reaction, 75
Deming cycle, G-34
Deming Prize, 75, G-34
Democratic leader, G-34
Demodulation, G-34
Demographics, G-34
Demonstrated capacity, G-35
Denial of service (DoS), G-35
Denomination, G-35
Density, G-35
Deontology, 10
Departmentalization, 5, G-35
Departmental work sequence, 201
Dependability, G-35
Dependent demand, G-35
Dependent demand inventory, G-35
Dependent variable, 19, G-35
Depletion, G-35
Depletion accounting for natural resources, 104
Deployment, 71, G-35
Deposition, G-35
Depository Institution Deregulation and Monetary Control Act (1980), G-35
Depository transfer checks (DTC), G-35
Deposit reconciliation, G-35
Deposit reporting service, G-35
Depreciation, G-35
Depreciation accounting, 103
Depreciation expense, G-35
    reporting of, 104
Depth, G-35
Deregulation, G-35
Derivative, G-35
Derived demand, G-35
Descriptive, G-35
Descriptive ethics, G-35
Deseasonalized times series, 246, G-35
Design defect, 67
Design engineering, G-35
Design for environment (DFE), 76
Design for manufacturability, G-35

Design for manufacture and assembly, G-35
Design for quality, G-35
Designing in quality vs. inspecting in quality, G-35
Design of experiments (DOE), G-35
Design review, G-35
Desired quality, G-35
Desktop publishing, G-35
Detachable warrant, G-35
Detective control, G-35
Deterministic model, G-36
Devaluation, 164
Development, G-36
Deviation, G-36
Devil's advocate, G-36
DFD (Data Flow Diagram), G-36
Diagnosis, G-36
Diagnostic control systems, 243
Diagnostic journey and remedial journey, G-36
Dialog module, G-36
Dialogue, G-36
Differential analysis, 98, G-36
Differential cost, 202, G-36
Differential piece-rate system, G-36
Differential pricing, 200
Differential revenue, G-36
Differentiation, G-36
Differentiation strategy, 171, 249
Diffusion of innovation, G-36
Digital certificates, G-36
Digital signal, G-36
Digital signature, 137, G-36
Digital signatures and certificates, G-36
Digital Subscriber Line (DSL), 146, G-36
Digital technology, G-36
Dimensions of quality, G-36
Direct access, G-36
Direct cash bounties, 164
Direct controls, 161
Direct cost, 202
Direct demand, 63
Direct deposit, G-36
Direct exporting, G-36
Direct export sales, 167, G-36
Direct-financing lease, G-36
Direct foreign investment (DFI), 126, G-36
Direct format, G-36
Direct hedge, G-36
Direct intervention, G-36
Direct investing, G-36
Direct investment account, G-36
Direct involvement, G-36
Directive, G-37
Direct labor, 175
Direct labor cost, G-36
Direct labor rate variance, G-36
Direct labor time variance, G-37
Direct Loan Program, G-37

Direct materials, 175
Direct materials cost, G-37
Direct materials quantity variance, G-37
Direct method, G-37
  statement of cash flows using, 92
Direct presenting, G-37
Direct production subsidies, 164
Direct quotation, G-37
Direct taxes, G-37
Direct write-off method, G-37
Disabled person, G-37
Disassembly bill of material, G-37
Disaster recovery plan, G-37
Disbursement float, 109, G-37
Disbursement fraud, G-37
Disbursement policy, G-37
Disbursements, techniques for controlling, 109
Disbursements and receipts method (scheduling), G-37
Disbursement system, G-37
Disbursing bank, G-37
Disclaimer limitation, 66
Disclaimer of warranties, 67
Disclosure, 14, G-37
  requirements, 14
Disclosure fraud, G-37
Discontinued operations, G-37
Discount, G-37
Discount basis, G-37
Discount bond, G-37
Discounted cash flow (DCF) techniques, 118, G-37
Discounted payback, 120, G-37
Discounted payback period, 179
Discounting, 124, G-37
Discount interest loan, G-37
Discount rate, 128, G-37
Discount security, G-37
Discount yield, G-37
Discovery, G-37
Discovery sampling, G-37
Discrepancies between production and consumption, G-37
Discrete available-to-promise, G-37
Discrete-event simulation model, G-38
Discrete probability distribution, G-38
Discretionary responsibility, 12
Discriminant analysis, 247, G-38
Discrimination, 15, 84, G-38
Discriminatory governmental procurement practices, 163
Discriminatory regulations, G-38
Disequilibrium losses, 21
Disequilibrium profits, 21
Dishonored note receivable, G-38
Disillusionment phase, G-38
Disparate impact, 87, 88, G-38
Disparate treatment, 87, G-38
Displacement, G-38
Disposition, G-38

Disposition of nonconformity, G-38
Dissatisfiers, G-38
Distance learning, 83, G-38
Distributed architecture, 144
Distributed Denial of Service (DDoS), G-38
Distributed earnings, G-38
Distribution, G-38
Distribution capacity, 229
Distribution centers, inventory levels at, 228
Distribution method, G-38
Distribution requirements planning (DRP), G-38
Distribution resource planning, 229–230
Distributive justice, 11, G-38
Distributor, G-38
Distributorship, 167, G-38
Diversifiable, firm-specific, or unsystematic risk, 234
Diversifiable risk, G-50
Diversification, 153, G-38
Diversification strategy, G-38
Diversity, 87, G-38
  management, 84
  training, 84
Diversity awareness training, G-38
Diverting, G-38
Dividend capture strategy, G-38
Dividend growth model, 180–181
Dividend irrelevance theory, G-38
Dividend payout ratio, 206
Dividend policy, 119–120, 133
Dividend policy decision, G-38
Dividend reinvestment plan (DRIP), 119, G-38
Dividend relevance theory, G-38
Dividend roll, G-39
Dividends, G-39
Dividends per share (DPS), 206, 207, G-39
Dividend yield, 206, G-39
Division, G-39
Divisional performance analysis, 218–219
Divisional structure, G-39
Division of labor, G-39
DMAIC, G-39
Documentary collections, G-39
Documentary evidence, G-39
Document examiner, G-39
Documents against acceptance, G-39
Documents against payment, G-39
Documents and records, G-39
Dodge-Romig sampling plans, G-39
Dogs, 171
Dollar-day float, G-39
Dollarization, 164
Domain name, G-39
Domestication, 159, G-39
Domestic carrier evaluation, 229
Domestic content requirements, 163, 164

Domestic enterprises, G-39
Domestic environment, G-39
Dominant, G-39
Doomsday ratio, G-39
Dot-matrix printer, G-39
Double counting, G-39
Double-entry accounting, G-39
Double-entry bookkeeping, 160, G-39
Double taxation, G-39
Downloading, G-39
Downsizing, G-39
Downstream, G-39
Downward communication, 220, G-39
Draft, G-39
Draft (bill of exchange), G-39
Draw, G-39
Drawee bank, G-39
Drill down, G-39
Driver, G-39
Drivers of quality, G-39
Driving variable, G-39
Drug testing, 16, 82
Drum-buffer-rope, G-39
Dual balance, G-40
Dual branding, 173
Dual exchange rates, 165
Dual pricing, G-40
Dual role, G-40
Dual translation, G-40
Dual use items, G-40
Due date, G-40
Dummy activity, G-40
Dummy company, G-40
Dummy variables, G-40
Dumping, 164, 209, G-40
Duplication, 153
DuPont chart, G-40
DuPont equation, G-40
Duration, G-40
Duration estimate, G-40
Duty, G-40
DVD (Digital Video Disc), G-40
Dynamic feedback control, 185
Dynamic hedging, G-40
Dynamic IP number, G-40
Dynamic risks, G-40
Dynamic simulation model, G-40

E

Earliest finish time (EF), G-40
Earliest start time (ES), G-40
Early manufacturing involvement, G-40
Early supplier involvement (ESI), G-40
Earned value (EV), G-40
Earned value management method, 210
Earning power, 206
Earnings before interest and taxes (EBIT), 116, 182, 212
Earnings credit rate (ECR), G-40
Earnings flexibility, G-40

Earnings management strategy, 89
Earnings per share (EPS), 129, 180, 181, 206, 207, 208, G-40
Earnings per share (EPS) on common stock, G-40
EBCDIC (Extended Binary Coded Decimal Interchange Code), G-40
E-Business, G-40
E-commerce, 62, 148, G-40
Econometric methods, 20
Economic analysis, 211–212
Economic and monetary union (EMU), G-40
Economic cost concepts, 211–212
Economic environment, G-41
Economic exposure, 236, G-41
Economic extortion scheme, G-41
Economic feasibility study, G-41
Economic forces, G-41
Economic forecasting, 20–21
Economic infrastructure, G-41
Economic order quantity (EOQ), 134, G-41
  costs and, 198
Economic order quantity (EOQ) model, 110, 193
Economic profit, 204–205
Economic risk, G-41
Economics
  basic concepts, 19–20
  marketing and, 63–65
Economic security, G-41
Economic union, G-41
Economic-value-added (EVA) method, 7, 172, 204, 242, G-41
Economic value-added (EVA) system, G-41
Economic value (EV) method, 181–182
Economic values, 181–182
Economies of scale, 55, G-41
Economies of scope, G-41
ECU, G-41
Education, G-41
Education allowance, G-41
EEC, G-41
Effective annual rate (EAR), G-41
Effective financing rates, 209
Effective interest rate, G-41
Effective interest rate method, G-41
Effective internal control, G-41
Effectiveness, 248, G-41
Effective rate of interest, G-41
Effective tax rate, G-41
Effective yield, G-41
Efficiency, 192, 248, G-41
Efficiency markets, G-41
Efficiency ratios, G-42
Efficient consumer response system, 229
Efficient markets hypothesis (EMH), 115, G-41
Efficient retail stores, 200

The Eighth Directive, G-41
Eighty-twenty (80-20) rule, 199, G-41
Elasticity, 63
Elasticity of demand, G-42
Elder-care assistance, 85
E-learning, 83, G-42
Electronic agent, G-42
Electronic brochures, G-42
Electronic business data interchange (EBDI), G-42
Electronic check presentment, G-42
Electronic commerce, G-42
  information technology and, 147–148
  marketing and, 61–62
Electronic corporate trade payment, G-42
Electronic data interchange (EDI), 52, 149, G-42
Electronic depository transfer (EDT), G-42
Electronic funds transfer (EFT), 52, G-42
Electronic intermediary, G-42
Electronic lockbox, G-42
Electronic marketplace, 148
Electronic procurement, 52
Electronic spreadsheets, 139
Electronic superhighway, G-42
Electronic surveillance, G-42
Elements of fraud, G-42
Elements of internal control, G-42
E-mail (electronic mail), G-42
E-marketing, 62, G-42
Embargo, G-42
Embezzlement, G-42
Emotional intelligence, 23
Emotional/mental health concerns, 87
Emotional stability, 223
Emotions, G-42
Employee assistance programs (EAPs), 87, G-42
Employee benefits, 85
Employee earnings records, 105
Employee embezzlement, G-42
Employee fraud, G-42
Employee fringe benefits, journal entries for, 105
Employee involvement, G-42
Employee network groups, G-42
Employee performance and retention management, 80
Employee privacy, 16
Employee protection, 16
Employee Retirement Income Security Act (ERISA), 85
Employee's earnings record, G-42
Employee stock ownership plans (ESOPs), 8, 86, G-42
Employee termination at will, 16
Employee transition matrix, 226
Employee turnover rates and costs, 227

Employer liabilities for payroll, 105
Employment law, 15–16
Employment test, G-42
Empowered employees, 4
Empowerment, 71, G-42
Emptive right, 112
Encapsulated development, G-42
Encode, G-42
Encoding scheme, G-42
Encryption, 137, G-43
End users, G-43
Engineering, 54–55
Engineering change order, G-43
Engineering services, G-43
Engineer-to-order, G-43
Enterprise Application Systems, G-43
Enterprise-level strategy, G-43
Enterprise resource planning (ERP), 4, 52, G-43
Enterprise risk-management, 154, G-43
Entity, G-43
Entity relationship diagram, 141, G-43
Entrepreneurs, 109, G-43
Entrepreneurship, G-43
Entropy, G-43
Environmental accounting, 90
Environmental analysis, 155, G-43
Environmental contexts, G-43
Environmental impact statement, 17
Environmental law, 17–18
Environmental monitoring stage, G-43
Environmental protection, G-43
Environmental Protection Agency (EPA), 75–76
Environmental scanning, G-43
Environmental scanning stage, G-43
Environmental standards, 75–76
Environment-specific, G-43
EPA, G-43
E-P expectancy, G-43
EPS indifference point, G-43
Equal Employment Opportunity Commission (EEOC) (1970), 15, 88
Equal employment opportunity (EEO), 87, G-43
Equilibrium, G-43
Equilibrium exchange rate, G-43
Equity, G-43
Equity capital, G-43
Equity cost estimation, 118
Equity financing, G-43
Equity method, G-43
Equity multiplier, G-43
Equity reserves, 106, G-43
Equity security, G-43
Equity theory, 8, 224, G-43
Equivalent annual annuity (EAA) method, G-43
Equivalent annual costs (EACs), 188
Equivalent units of production, G-44

Ergonomics, 87, G-44
ERG theory, 8, G-44
Error distribution, G-44
Escalating commitment, G-44
Essential job functions, G-44
Esteem needs, 8, 224
Estimated start time, G-44
Ethernet, G-44
Ethical, G-44
Ethical decisions, 11–12
Ethical dilemma, G-44
Ethical fundamentalism, 10
Ethical impact statement, G-44
Ethical investing movement, G-114
Ethical relativism, 10, G-44
Ethical responsibilities, 11, G-44
Ethical standards in business, 11
Ethical values, G-44
Ethical vigilance, G-44
Ethics, 55, 69–70, G-44
  corporate, 156
  human resources and, 88
  international business and, 167
  managerial, 224
  marketing and, 62–63
Ethnocentric, G-44
Ethnocentric international strategy, 158
Ethnocentric staffing outlook, G-44
Ethnocentric strategy, G-44
Ethnocentrism, G-44
Ethnorelativism, G-44
Euro, G-44
Eurobanks, 165, G-44
Eurobond market, 126
Eurobonds, 113, G-44
Euro-clear, G-44
Euro-commercial paper, 113, G-44
Euro cp, G-44
Eurocredit loans, G-44
Eurocredit market, 126, G-44
Eurocredits, 113
Eurocurrency, 165, G-44
Eurocurrency market, 126, G-44
Eurodebt, G-44
Eurodebt market, 113
Eurodollar CDs, G-44
Eurodollars, 165, G-44
Euromarkets, G-44
Euronotes, 113, G-44
European Article Numbering (EAN) System, G-44
European Central Bank (ECB), G-44
European Confederation of Institutes of Internal Auditing, G-44
European Currency Unit (ECU), G-45
European Monetary System (EMS), G-45
European terms, G-45
European Union directives, G-45
European Union (EU), 44, 106, 107, 149, 166, G-45

Euro stock, 113
Evaluated receipt settlement, G-45
Evaluation criteria, G-45
Evaluative criteria, G-45
Event, G-45
Event-related marketing (ERM), G-45
Event risk, G-45
Every day low pricing (EDLP), G-45
Evidence square, G-45
Evidential matter, G-45
EVOP, G-45
Examples of hedging foreign transactions, 235–236
Exception reports, G-45
Excess capacity, G-45
Excess inventory, G-45
Exchange controls, 165, G-45
Exchange principle, G-45
Exchange rate, G-45
Exchange-rate adjustment, 161
Exchange rate exposure, 234–235
Exchange Rate Mechanism (ERM), G-45
Exchange rate risk, G-45
Exchange rate systems, 164–165
Exchange ratios, 181
Excited quality, G-45
Exclusive dealing, 17
Exclusive distribution, G-45
Ex-dividend date, G-45
Executed contract, 19
Execution education, G-45
Execution error, G-45
Execution information system (EIS), G-45
Executive compensation, 86
Executive information systems (EISs), 138, 139
Executive stock option, G-45
Executory contract, 19
Exempt employees, G-45
Exercise price (strike price), G-45
Exit interview, G-45
Exit measurement, G-45
Exogenous variables, 63
Expansionary fiscal policy, 162
Expansionary monetary policy, 162
Expansion decisions, G-45
Expansion project, G-45
Expatriate, G-45
Expatriation, G-46
Expatriation program, G-46
Expectancy theory, 224, G-46
Expectations theory, G-46
Expected demand during lead time (EDDLT), 193
Expected duration (t_e), 211, G-46
Expected quality, G-46
Expected rate of return, k_s, G-46
Expected return on an investment, 123
Expected return on a portfolio, k_p, G-46
Expected utility (EU), G-46

Expected value approach, G-46
Expected value (EV), 42, 176, 211, 217, 237, G-46
Expected value of perfect information (EVPI), G-46
Expected value of simple information (EVSI), G-46
Expedited check processing, G-46
Expedited Funds Availability Act of 1987, G-46
Expenditure-changing policies, 161
Expenditure-switching policies, 161
Expense budget, G-46
Expense liability reserves, G-46
Expenses, G-46
Expense scheme, G-46
Experience attributes, G-46
Experiential design, G-46
Experiential knowledge, G-46
Experimentation, G-46
Expertise, G-46
Expert power, 220, G-46
Expert system (ES), 138, 141, 142, G-46
Expert system shell, G-46
Expert witness, G-46
Explicit knowledge, G-46
Exponential distribution, G-46
Exponential smoothing, 20, 246, G-46
Export business, incremental analysis in, 209
Export complaint systems, G-46
Export controls, 159
Export-control system, G-46
Export-Import Bank (Ex-Im Bank), 127, G-46
Exporting, G-47
Export license, G-46
Export management companies (EMCs), G-46
Export quota, 163
Export trading company (ETC), G-46
Express contract, 19
Express warranty, 66, 67
Expropriation, 159, 166, G-47
Extended enterprise, G-47
Extensible Markup Language (EML), 148, G-47
External audits, 107
External collaboration, G-47
External cooperation, G-47
External customer, G-47
External data, G-47
External disparate impact, 226
External economies of scale, G-47
External failure of costs, 215, G-47
Externalities, 12, 121, G-47
External locus of control, G-47
External review, G-47
Extinction, 8
Extortion, G-47
Extraction phase, G-47

Extra dividend, G-47
Extranet, G-47
Extraordinary items, G-47
Extraordinary repairs, 103, G-47
Extraterritoriality, G-47
Extrinsic forecast, G-47
Extrinsic reward, G-47
Extroversion, 223
Ex-works (EXW), G-47

F

Face value, G-47
Facilitating payments, G-47
Facilitator, G-47
Facility planning, 47
Factor, G-47
Factor analysis, 247, G-47
Factoring, 112, G-47
Factor intensities, G-47
Factor mobility, G-47
Factor proportions theory, G-47
Factors of production, G-47
Factory overhead cost, G-47
Factual cultural knowledge, G-47
Failsafe work methods, G-47
Failure mode analysis (FMA), G-47
Failure mode effects analysis (FMEA), G-47
Failure mode effects and criticality analysis (FMECA), G-48
Failure to warn, 67
Fair credit reporting law, 66
Fair Debt Collection Practices Act, 66
Fair Labor Standards Act (FLSA), 16, 85, 87
Falsified identity (customer impersonation), G-48
Family and Medical Leave Act (FMLA) (1993), 16, 85, 87
Family-related benefits, 85
FASB Statement 95, G-48
Fatalism, G-48
Fault-tolerant computer system, G-48
Fault tree analysis, G-48
Fax capability, 146
Feasibility studies, G-48
Feasible solution, G-48
Features, G-48
Federal Advisory Council, G-48
Federal Contract Compliance Programs, Office of (OFCCP), 88
Federal Courts, G-48
Federal Deposit Insurance Corp. Improvement Act of 1991, G-48
Federal Insecticide, Fungicide, and Rodenticide Act (FIFRA), 18
Federal Open Market Committee (FOMC), G-48
Federal Reserve Act (1913), G-48
Federal Reserve member banks, G-48

Federal Reserve System (Fed), G-48
Federal Trade Commission (FTC), 65
Federal Trade Commission (FTC) Act, 17
Fed float, G-48
Fed funds rate, G-48
Fedwire, G-48
Feedback, G-48
Feedback control, 242, G-48
Feedback loops, G-48
Feedforward control, 241, G-48
Feigenbaum, A. V., 74, 75
Feint, 250
Femininity, G-48
FICA tax, G-48
Field, G-48
Field experience, G-48
Field selling, G-48
Field warehouse agreement, G-48
FIFO, G-48
File, G-48
File transfer protocol (ftp), 148, G-48
Fill rates, 226
Filters, G-48
Final assembly schedule (FAS), G-48
Final reports, 41
Finance
    capital budgeting, 120–121
    capital structure, 118–119
    cash forecasting, 117
    cost of capital, 117–118
    dividend policy, 119–120
    financial planning and control, 116–117
    financial risk management, 123–124
    international financial markets, 126
    international flow of funds, 126
    managing long-term financing, 112–115
    managing short-term assets, 109–111
    managing short-term financing, 111–112
    quantitative techniques and, 124–126
    strategies and role of finance and chief financial officer, 107–108
    working capital policy, 108–109
Finance lease, G-49
Financial accounting, 90, G-49
Financial Accounting Standards Board (FASB), 90, G-49
Financial Accounting Standards Board (FASB) Statement 95, G-49
Financial assets, valuation of, 114–115
Financial break-even analysis, 116, G-49
Financial break-even point, 116, 240, G-49
Financial condition, 205–206
Financial control, G-49
Financial EDI (FEDI), G-49
Financial engineering, 234, G-49
Financial flexibility, G-49

Financial incentives, G-49
Financial infrastructure, G-49
Financial Institution Buyer Credit Policy, G-49
Financial Institutions Reform, Recovery and Enforcement Act (1989), G-49
Financial instruments, 113
Financial intermediaries, G-49
Financial lease, 114, G-49
Financial leverage, 116, 118, 173, 174, 208, G-49
Financial management analysis, 205–208
Financial managers, 107
Financial markets, 122, G-49
   institutions and, 107
   international, 126
Financial motive, G-49
Financial planning, G-49
Financial planning and control, 116–117, 129–130
Financial ratio analysis, G-49
Financial restructuring, G-49
Financial risks, 234, G-49
   management of, 123–124
Financial sensitivity analysis, 218
Financial Services Modernization Act (1999), G-49
Financial shenanigans, G-49
Financial solvency, 92
Financial statement analysis, 93–94, 152, G-49
Financial statement fraud, 151, G-49
Financial statements, 91, G-49
   analysis of, 128
   impact of inventory errors on, 102
Financing activities, 213, G-49
   cash inflows from, 92
Financing analysis, 208
Financing cash flows, G-49
Financing feedbacks, G-49
Finding, G-49
Finished-goods inventory, G-49
Finished goods ledger, G-49
Finite forward scheduling, G-49
Finite loading, G-49
Finite scheduling, G-50
Firewall, G-50
Firm planned order (FPO), G-50
Firm-specific risk, G-50
First-come, first-served (FCPS) rule, 191
First-degree price discrimination, 64
First differencing, G-50
First generation languages (1GLs), G-50
First-in, first-out (FIFO) method, 102, 196, 197, G-50
   accounting for completed and partially completed units under, 96
First-line manager, G-50
Fiscal incentives, G-50
Fiscal policy, 161
   expansionary, 162

Fiscal year, 92, G-50
Fishbone diagram, G-50
Fisher effect, G-50
Fitness for particular purpose, 67
Fitness for use, G-50
Five C's of credit, G-50
Five focusing steps, G-50
Five (5)-Ss, G-50
Five stages of national economic development, G-50
Five whys, G-50
Fixed assets, 91, 103, G-50
   costs of, 103
   internal controls over, 104
   lease and accounting rules related to leasing of, 104
Fixed assets turnover ratio, 128, G-50
Fixed charge coverage ratio, 129, G-50
Fixed costs, 190, 212, 241, G-50
Fixed exchange rate, G-50
Fixed exchange-rate system, 161, 162, 164, G-50
Fixed-for-floating rate swap, G-50
Fixed-interval review system, G-50
Fixed order period model, 199
Fixed order quantity, G-50
Fixed point surveillance, G-50
Fixed-position layout, G-50
Fixed-price contract, G-50
Fixed rate currency, G-50
Fixed reorder cycle inventory model, G-50
Fixed reorder quantity inventory model, G-50
Fixed wireless service, 146
Flash memory, G-51
Flat structure, G-51
Flat yield curve, G-51
Flexible benefits plan, G-51
Flexible benefits systems, 85
Flexible budget, G-51
Flexible capacity, G-51
Flexible manufacturing system (FMS), G-51
Flexible spending account, G-51
Flexible staffing, G-51
Flexible work schedules, 8
Flextime, G-51
Float, G-51
Floating exchange rates, 161, 164, G-51
Floating lien, G-51
Floating rate bond, G-51
Floating rate currency, G-51
Floating rate debt, 113
Floating rate notes (FRNs), G-51
Floor planning, G-51
Flotation costs, G-51
Flowcharts, 73, 77, 143, 152, G-51
Flow of capital, 166, G-51
Flow of funds, international, 126
Flow of labor, 166, G-51

Flow of trade, 166, G-51
FOB (free on board) destination, G-51
FOB (free on board) shipping point, G-51
Focus, G-51
Focused factory, G-51
Focus group, G-51
Focus strategy, 171, 249
Footnote disclosure, G-52
Footnotes, G-52
Forced distribution, G-52
Force-field analysis, 26, G-52
Forecast, G-52
Forecast bias, G-52
Forecasted cost at completion (FCAC), 36–37, G-52
Forecast horizon, G-52
Forecasting, 246, G-52
Forecast interval, G-52
Forecast reliability, 20
Foreign agents, 167, G-52
Foreign availability, G-52
Foreign bond, G-52
Foreign Corrupt Practices Act (FCPA), G-128
Foreign Corrupt Practices Act (FCPA) (1977), 107, 167, G-52
Foreign currencies, 165
Foreign currency transactions, G-52
Foreign currency translation, G-52
Foreign debt, G-52
Foreign direct investment, G-52
Foreign environment, G-52
Foreign exchange market, 126, G-52
Foreign exchange rate, G-52
Foreign exchange risk, G-52
Foreign exchange risk management, G-52
Foreign investment, G-52
Foreign investment property, taking of, 166
Foreign investment risk matrix (FIRM), G-52
Foreign keys, 140, G-52
Foreign market opportunity analysis, G-52
Foreign policy, G-52
Foreign service premium, G-52
Foreign subsidiary, G-52
Foreign tax credit, G-52
Foreign trade zones, G-52
Forfaiting, G-52
Formal communication, G-52
Formal communication channel, G-52
Formalization, G-52
Formal team, G-52
Form utility, G-52
Fortress Europe, G-52
Forward buying (bridge buying), G-52
Forward chaining (forward reasoning), G-53

SUBJECT INDEX   I-15

Forward contracts, 127, 234, 235, G-53
Forward discount, G-53
Forward exchange contract, G-53
Forward exchange rates, 236
Forward premium, G-53
Forward pricing, G-53
Forward purchase contract, 236
Forward rate(s), G-53
Forwards, 236
Forward scheduling, G-53
Forward sell contract, 236
Forward value date, G-53
Founder's shares, G-53
4GLs, 144
401(k) plans, 85
Fourteen (14) points, G-53
Fourth Directive, 106, G-53
Fourth-generation languages (4GLs), G-53
Fraction defective chart (p chart), G-53
Franchise holding/loading, G-53
Franchising, 53, 158, G-53
Fraud, G-53
   corporate, 150–152
   financial statement, 151
   liability, asset, and inadequate disclosure, 151–152
   against organizations, 151
   revenue and inventory, 151
Fraud analysis, 213–214
Fraud losses, 213–214
Free alongside ship (FAS), G-53
Free carrier (FCA), G-53
Free cash flow hypothesis, G-53
Free cash flows, 92, 119, 212, G-53
Freely floating exchange rate system, G-54
Free market, 62
Free market economic system, G-53
Free on board (FOB), 163, G-53
Free on board (FOB) pricing, G-53
Free rider, G-53
Free slack (FS), G-53
Free trade area, G-53
Free Trade Area of the Americans (FTAA), G-53
Free-trade arguments, 163
Free trade credit, G-53
Freight forwarders, G-54
Fringe benefits, G-54
Frustration-regression principle, G-54
Fulfillment, G-54
Full compensation, G-54
Full-cost accounting, 231
Full disclosure, G-54
Full-duplex, G-54
Full reconciliation, G-54
Full-service merchant wholesalers, G-54
Functional approach, 5
Functional currency, G-54
Functional-level strategy, G-54

Functional manager, G-54
Functional organizations, 27, 28, G-54
   types of, 27–28
Functional organization structure, G-54
Functional structure, G-54
Functional team, 222
Fundamental attribution error, G-54
Fundamental forecasting, G-54
Funded debt, G-54
Funded retention, 153
Funnel experiment, G-54
Future reality tree, G-54
Futures, 236
Futures contracts, 127, 234, 235, G-54
Futures option, G-54
Futures rates, G-54
Future value (FV), G-54
   of an annuity of $1 per period for n periods, 257–258
   of $1 at the end of n periods, 255–256
Future value interest factor for an annuity (FVIFA), G-54
Future value interest factor for I and n (FVIF), G-54
Fuzzy logic, 142, G-54
FVAn, G-54
FVIFA(DUE)$_{i,n}$, G-54

G

Gainsharing, 8, 86, G-54
Gambit, 250
Game theory, 22, G-54
Gantt chart, G-54
Gap analysis, 171, G-54
Garnishment, 66, G-54
Garn-St. Germain Depository Institutions Act (1982), G-54
Gatekeeping, G-54
Gateway, G-54
Gauge repeatability and reproducibility (GR&R), G-54
Gearing adjustment, G-55
General adaptation syndrome (GAS), G-55
General Agreement on Tariffs and Trade (GATT), 166, G-55
General Agreement on Trade in Services (GATS), G-55
General Arrangements to Borrow, 165
General controls, G-55
General efficiency, 248
General Electric, 73
General environment, 24
General journal, 105
General ledger, G-55
Generally accepted accounting principles (GAAP), 90, 151, G-55
Generally accepted manufacturing practices (GAMP), G-55
General manager, G-55

General obligation, G-55
General price index, G-55
General price-level accounting, G-55
General purpose application software, G-55
General reserve, G-55
Genetic algorithms, G-55
Geocentric staffing outlook, G-55
Geodemographic information, G-55
Geographic Information Systems (GIS), 139, G-55
Geographic organization, G-55
Geometric dimensioning and tolerancing (GDT), G-55
Giro acceptance, G-55
GIRO systems, G-55
Glasnost, G-55
Glass ceiling, G-55
Global, G-55
Global account management, G-55
Global business strategies, 157–158
Global capital markets, G-55
Global corporate culture, G-56
Global corporations, G-56
Global international strategy, 158
Globalization, 2, 89, G-56
Global manager, G-56
Global mind-set, G-56
Global operation, auditing issues for, 106–107
Global organization, G-56
   structure and control, 159–160
Global outsourcing, G-56
Global positioning systems, 52
Global Reporting Initiative, G-56
Global strategy, G-56
Global teams, 26, G-56
Global village, G-56
Glocalization, G-56
Goal, G-56
Goal conflict, G-56
Goal formulation, 155
Going concern concept, G-56
Going public, 113, G-56
Golden parachute, G-56
Gold standard, G-56
Go/no-go, G-56
Good person theory, 11
Goods, 18, G-56
Goods trade, G-56
Goodwill, G-56
Government policies, G-56
Government regulation, G-56
Government units, G-56
Government warrant, G-56
Grade, G-56
Gramm-Leach-Bliley Act, G-56
Grand jury, G-56
Grand strategy, G-56
Grapevine, 9, G-56

Graphical evaluation and review technique (GERT), G-56
Graphical User Interface (GUI), G-56
Graphic rating scale, G-56
Gravity model, 200
Gray market, G-56
Gray marketing, G-56
Grease payments, G-56
Green-circled employee, G-56
Greenfield venture, G-57
Greenmail, G-57
Gross margin, 186, 197, 219
Gross margin amount, 197
Gross margin percentage, G-57
Gross pay, G-57
Gross profit, G-57
Gross profit margin, G-57
Gross profit method, 103, 196, G-57
Gross rating points (GRPs), 186, G-57
Gross requirements, 191, G-57
Group decision support system, G-57
Group decision-support systems (DSSs), 139
Group of Seven, 162
Group technology (GT), G-57
Groupware, G-57
Growth rate, g, G-57
Growth trend analysis, 20
Guerrilla campaign, 250
GUI tools, 144

H

Hacker, G-57
Half-duplex, G-57
Halo effect, 23, 223, G-57
Hand-held computers, G-57
Handling costs, G-57
Hands-on consumer research, G-57
Hard controls, G-57
Hard currencies, G-57
Hard disk, G-57
Hard sell, G-57
Hardship allowance, G-57
Hard skills, G-57
Harmonization, 106, G-57
Harvesting, 250
Hawthorne studies, G-57
Health, 86–87, G-57
Health-care benefits, 85
Health maintenance organization (HMO), G-57
Health promotion, 87, G-57
Hedge, G-57
Hedge inventory, G-57
Hedger, G-57
Hedging, 153, 236, G-57
  foreign transactions, 235, 236
Heinrich's domino theory, 153
Held-to-maturity securities, G-57
Help desk, G-57

Herfindahl Hirschmann Index (HHI), 22
Heterogeneity, G-57
Heuristics, 246, G-57
Hierarchical database, G-58
Hierarchy of needs theory, G-58
Hierarchy structure, G-58
High-beta stock, 123
High-context culture, G-58
High Dollar Group Sort, G-58
Higher trial courts, G-58
High liquidity strategy, G-58
High-low method, G-58
High performance work, G-58
High power distance culture, G-58
Histograms, 73, 245, G-58
Historical cost convention, G-58
Historical yield spread analysis, G-58
Holder-of-record date (date of record), G-58
Hold-harmless agreements, 153
Holding cost, G-58
Hold point, G-58
Holiday pay, 85
Holistic planning, G-58
Home page, 148, G-58
Horizontal analysis, 93, G-58
Horizontal communication, 221, G-58
Horizontal dependency, G-58
Horizontal information interchange, 149, G-58
Horizontal market, G-58
Horizontal merger, 13, 17, G-58
Horizontal privity, 67
Horizontal promotions, G-58
Horizontal restraints, 16
Horizontal structure, G-58
Horizontal team, G-58
Horizon value, 181
Hoshin kanri, 71–72, G-58
Hoshin planning, G-58
Host-country national, G-58
Hostile environment, 84, G-58
Hostile takeover, G-58
Household decision making, G-58
House of quality, 76, G-58
Housing allowance, G-58
HR audit, G-58
HR research, G-58
HR strategies, G-58
Human capital, G-58
Humanistic perspective, 4
Human relations movement, G-59
Human relations theory, G-59
Human relations training, 83
Human resource (HR) planning, 79, G-59
Human resource information system (HRIS), 80, G-59
Human resource management, 79–80
  analysis, 226–227

compensation strategies, 85–86
employee benefits, 85
employee performance and retention, 80
ethics and human resources, 88
health, safety, and security, 86–87
international issues, 89
law and human resources, 87–88
staffing, development, and employment practices, 81–84
strategies, 79–80
variable pay and executive compensation, 86
workforce diversity, 84
Human resource management (HRM), G-59
Human resources, 2, G-59
Human skill, G-59
Hurdle rate, G-106
Hybrid capacity approach, 183
Hybrid forms, 113
Hybrid production method, G-59
Hygiene factors, 8, 224, G-59
Hypergeometric distribution, G-59
Hypermedia, G-59
Hypernorms, G-59
Hypertext, G-59
Hypertext Markup Language (HTML), G-59
Hypertext Transfer Protocol (HTTP), 148, G-59

I

Iconic model, G-59
Idea champion, G-59
Idea incubator, G-59
Idle capacity, G-59
If-then rules, 142, G-59
Illegal gratuities, G-59
Illegitimate norms, G-59
Image reinforcements, G-59
Imaging, G-59
Immigration Reform and Control Acts, 88
Immoral management, 156, G-59
Impact printer, G-59
Imperfection, G-59
Imperfect market, G-59
Imperfect market theory, G-59
Implementation, G-59
Implementor, G-59
Implied in fact contract, 19
Implied in law contract, 19
Implied warranty, 66
  of fitness for particular purpose, 67
  of merchantability, 67
Implosion, G-59
Import/export letters of credit, G-59
Importing and exporting, G-59
Import quota, 163

Import substitution, G-59
Impoverished management style, 6, 220
Improper accumulation, G-59
Improvement, 78
Incentives, 86, G-59
Income analysis under variable costing and absorption costing, 99
Income bond, G-60
Income bonds, 113
Income elasticity of demand, 64, G-60
Income from operations (operating income), G-60
Income leveling, G-60
Income reconciliation ratio, 213
Income reporting under variable costing and absorption costing, 99
Income smoothing, G-60
Income statement, 106, G-60
Income summary, G-60
In-control process, G-60
Incorporation, 153
Incorrect reporting of liabilities, 214
Incoterms, G-60
Incremental analysis in export business, 209
Incremental cash flow, G-60
Incremental concept, 20
Incremental cost, 212
Incremental operating cash flows, G-60
Incremental utilization heuristic, 194
Indented bill of material, G-60
Indented where-used, G-60
Indenture, 113, G-60
Independent checks, G-60
Independent contractors, G-60
Independent demand, G-60
Independent demand item management models, G-60
Independent projects, G-60
Independent variable, 19, G-60
In-depth interviewing, 57
Indexed file, G-60
Indexed (purchasing power) bond, G-60
Indexed sequential organization, G-60
Index fund, G-60
Indicators of fraud, 213–214
Indirect costs, 202, G-60
Indirect exporting, G-60
Indirect format, G-60
Indirect investment, G-60
Indirect involvement, G-60
Indirect method, G-60
  statement of cash flows using, 92
Indirect quotation, G-60
Indirect taxes, G-60
Individual/adversarial external affairs strategy, G-60
Individual-centered career planning, G-60
Individual development, G-60
Individualism, 11, 224, G-61

Individualism approach, G-61
Individual retirement accounts (IRAs), 85, G-61
Inductive fraud detection, G-61
Inefficient targeting, G-61
Infeasible solution, G-61
Inference engine, G-61
Inflation, G-61
Inflation accounting, G-61
Inflation premium (IP), G-61
Inflow, G-61
Influence diagrams, 42, G-61
Influence peddling, G-61
Informal communication, G-61
Informal integration, G-61
Informal training, G-61
Information, 2, 4, G-61
Information-based services, G-61
Information center, G-61
Information content (signaling) hypothesis, G-61
Information management, leading practices for, 73
Information map, G-61
Information overload, G-61
Information reporting system, G-61
Information search, G-61
Information sites, G-61
Information system (IS), G-61
Information systems architecture, 144
Information systems auditor, G-61
Information systems infrastructure, 144
Information systems planning, 136
Information technology (IT), 135–149, 185, G-61
  alternative approaches to system acquisition, 143–144
  best practices in, 140
  business information systems, 147
  database management, 140–141
  decision making and, 139
  electronic commerce and, 147–148
  international issues, 149
  knowledge systems, 141–142
  managing, 138
  managing resources, 144–145
  quality in, 140
  risk management, 137–138
  systems development, 142–143
  systems planning, 136
  telecommunications, 145–146
Infrastructure, G-61
Infrastructure shortages, G-61
Infringement, 15
Inherent limitations, G-61
Inherent risks, G-61
Inheritance, 141
Inhwa, G-61
Initial investment, G-61
Initial investment outlay, G-62
Initial phase, G-62

Initial pleading, G-62
Initial public offering (IPO), 113, G-62
  analysis, 182
Initiating structure, G-62
Initiating structures, 6
Injury, 17
Ink-jet printer, G-62
Innovator, G-62
Input, G-62
Input device, G-62
Input-output analysis, G-62
Input price measurement, G-62
In-sample validation, G-62
Inseparability, G-62
Inside directors, G-62
Insiders, G-62
Insider trading liability, 14
Inside trading, G-62
Insourcing, 51, G-62
Inspection, 123, G-62
Instant messaging, 148, G-62
Institute of Internal Auditors (IIA), G-62
Institutional customers, G-62
Instrument, G-62
Insurance services, G-62
Intangibility, G-62
Intangible assets, G-62
  amortization accounting for, 104
  reporting of, 104
Integrated circuits, G-62
Integrated disability management programs, G-62
Integrated international operation, G-62
Integrated marketing communications (IMC), 58, G-62
Integrated risk management, G-62
Integrated services digital network (ISDN), 146
Integrated system, G-62
Integrative Social Contracts Theory, 157
Integrity, G-62
Integrity strategy, G-62
Intellectual property rights, G-62
Intelligence, G-62
Intelligent agents, 141–142, G-62
Intensive distribution, G-62
Intentional amoral management, G-62
Interactional justice, G-62
Interactive leadership, 6, G-62
Interactive multimedia, G-62
Interbank interest rates, G-63
Interbank market, G-63
Interdependence, G-63
Interdistrict Transportation System, G-63
Interest-bearing, G-63
Interest Equalization Tax (IET), G-63
Interest income, 122
Interest rate cap, G-63
Interest rate collar, G-63
Interest rate floor, G-63

Interest rate parity, 235, G-63
Interest rate parity (IRP) line, G-63
Interest rate parity theory, G-63
Interest rate price risk, 115, G-63
Interest rate reinvestment risk, G-63
Interest rate risk, G-63
Interest rate swap, G-63
Interface, G-63
Interlinking, 74
Intermediate customers, G-63
Intermodal movements, G-63
Internal audit, 107, G-63
Internal bank, G-63
Internal capability analysis, G-63
Internal collaboration, G-63
Internal control, 150, G-63
　achieving, over cash receipts, 100
　over cash, 100
Internal control structure, G-63
Internal control weakness, G-63
Internal cooperation, G-63
Internal customer, G-63
Internal data, G-63
Internal disparate impact, 226
Internal economies of scale, G-63
Internal failure costs, 215, G-63
Internalization, G-63
Internal locus of control, G-63
Internal memory, G-63
Internal rate of return (IRR), 118, 120, 179, 240, G-63
Internal rate of return method, G-63
Internal review, G-63
International, G-63
International accounting, 90, G-63
International Accounting Standards Committee (IASC), 106
International Accounting Standards (IAS), 106, G-64
International balance of payments, 209
International Bank for Reconstruction and Development (IBRD), G-64
International banking, 165
International bond, G-64
International business, 157–167
　banking, 165
　cultures and protocols, 161
　environment, 166
　equilibrium, 162
　ethics and, 167
　exchange rate systems, 164–165
　forms of, 158
　forms of multinational enterprises, 167
　global organization structure and control, 159–160
　global strategies, 157–158
　issues, 148–149, 167
　jurisdiction over actions of foreign governments, 166
　macroeconomic policy, 161–162

　marketing strategies, 158
　non-tariff trade barriers, 163–164
　payments, 160
　risks, 159
　tariff trade barriers, 163
　trade and investment, 160
　transacting business abroad, 166–167
International cash management, 127–128, 236
International competitiveness, G-64
International contracts, G-64
International corporation, G-64
International Court of Justice, 166, G-64
International cultures and protocols, 161
International debt financing costs, 209
International debt load, G-64
International Development Association (IDA), G-64
International distribution selection, 229
International division, G-64
International environment, G-64
International equilibrium, 162
International Federation of Accountants (IFAC), 107, G-64
International Financial Corporation (IFC), G-64
International financial markets, 126
International Fisher Effect (IFE) line, G-64
International flow of funds, 126
International human resource management function, G-64
International intermediaries, G-64
Internationalization, G-65
International labor relations, G-64
International law, G-64
International long-term financing, 128–134
International management, 44, G-64
International marketing, 70, G-64
　strategies of, 158
International Monetary Fund (IMF), 162, G-64
　drawing positions, 165
International mutual funds, G-64
International organizational structures, G-64
International Organization for Standardization (ISO), G-64
International Organization of Securities Commission (IOSCO), 107, G-64
International payments, 160
International pricing, 158, G-64
International product life cycle (IPLC), G-64
International promotions, 158
International purchases, 56
International relocation and orientation, G-64
International reserves, 165

International risks, 159
International short-term financing, 127
International sourcing, barriers to, 56
International Standards on Auditing (ISA), G-64
International Standards Organization (ISO) 9000, 75, 176
International Standards Organization (ISO) 14000, 76
International trade
　financing analysis and, 208–209
　financing, 127
　investment and, 160
International Trade Organization (ITO), G-64
International treaties, G-64
Internet, G-64
Internet domain, G-64
Internet hosts, G-64
Internet Protocol (IP) number, G-64
Internet recruiting, 82
Internet relay chat (IRC), 148, G-65
Internet servers, G-65
Internet Service Providers (ISPs), 147, G-65
Interorganizational context, G-65
Interorganizational information systems, G-65
Interorganizational partnerships, 24
Interpreter, G-65
Interpretive knowledge, G-65
Interrelationship diagraph, G-65
Interrelationship digraph, 72
Interrelationships between price and cost, 178
Interrogatory, G-65
Interstate Banking and Branching Efficiency Act (1994), G-65
Interval scale, G-65
Intervention, G-65
Intervention intensity, G-65
Interviews, 82, G-65
In-the-money options, G-65
Intracompany trade, G-65
Intra-industry trade, G-65
Intranets, 148, G-65
Intransit forecast method, G-65
Intransit lead time, G-65
Intransit reward, G-65
Intransit value, G-65
Intuition, 71, G-65
Intuitionism, 11
Intuitive-feeling, 23
Intuitive-thinking, 23
Inventory, G-65
　control over, 102–103
　cost of, 103
　　under periodic inventory system, 102
　　under perpetual inventory system, 102

Inventory, *cont.*
　cycle counting of, 192
　levels of
　　at distribution centers, 228
　　at work center, 191
Inventory blanket lien, 112
Inventory carrying costs, 183, G-65
Inventory control systems, G-65
Inventory conversion period, 108
Inventory cost flow assumptions, 102
Inventory errors, impact of, on financial statements, 102
Inventory financing, 112, G-65
Inventory investment, 175
Inventory management, 48–49, 199, G-65
Inventory ordering system, G-65
Inventory shrinkage, G-65
Inventory turnover, 197, G-65
Inventory turnover ratio (ITR), 103, 128, 175, 185, 197, 206, G-65
Inverted "abnormal" yield curve, G-66
Investing activities, 213, G-66
　cash inflows from, 92
Investment banker, 113, G-66
Investment centers, 218, G-66
Investment grade bonds, G-66
Investment income, G-66
Investment opportunity schedule (IOS), 118, G-66
Investment policy, G-66
Investments, 107, 158, G-66
　evaluation techniques, 179
　risks, 233
Investment scams, G-66
Investment turnover, G-66
Invigilation, G-66
Invoice, G-66
Involvement, G-66
IRR, G-66
Irregular component, G-66
Irrevocable letter of credit, G-66
IS architecture, G-66
ISDN (Integrated Services Digital Network), G-66
Ishikawa, Kaoru, 74, 75
Ishikawa diagram, G-66
IS infrastructure, G-66
ISO, G-66
ISO 9000, G-66
ISO 14000-series, G-66
ISO 9000 series standards, G-66
IS planning, G-66
IS subsidiaries, G-66
Issues management, 154, 155, G-66
Issuing bank, G-66

J

Jamaica Agreement, G-66
Java, 148, G-66
JavaScript, 148
J-curve effect, G-66
Jidoka, G-66
Job, G-66
Job aid, G-66
Job analysis, 81, G-66
Job anxiety, G-67
Job characteristics model, G-67
Job cost sheet, G-67
Job criteria, 83, G-67
Job description, 81, G-67
Job design, 81, G-67
Job enlargement, G-67
Job enrichment, G-67
Job evaluation, 86, G-67
Job order cost accounting system, 96, G-67
Job order cost system, 96, G-67
Job posting, 83, G-67
Job-related validation, 88
Job rotation, 83, G-67
Jobs, 81
　production scheduling, 191
Job satisfaction, G-67
Job simplification, G-67
Job specifications, 81, G-67
Join, G-67
Joint Application Development (JAD), G-67
Joint occurrence, G-67
Joint planning meetings, G-67
Joint probabilities, G-67
Joint Research and Development Act, G-67
Joint venture agreement, 158
Joint ventures, 2, 24, 158, 167, G-67
Journal, G-67
Journal entries, 101, G-67
　for direct write-off of uncollectible receivables, 102
　for disposal of fixed assets, 104
　for notes receivable transactions, 102
　for short-term notes payable, 104
Journalizing, G-67
Judgmental approach, G-67
Judicial limitations, 16
Junk bonds, 113, G-67
Juran, Joseph, 72, 74, 75
　quality improvement approach, 73
Juran's Trilogy, G-67
Jurisdiction, G-67
JUSE, G-67
Justice, 11
Justice approach, 224, G-67
Just-in-time (JIT), 229, G-67
Just-in-time (JIT) inventory, 190, G-67, G-68
Just-in-time (JIT) manufacturing, G-68
Just-in-time (JIT) operations, 45
Just-in-time (JIT) processing, 97, G-68
Just-in-time (JIT) production, 193
Just-in-time (JIT) systems, 110
Just-in-time (JIT) training, G-68

K

Kaikaku (Japanese), G-67
Kaizen approach, 45, 77, 185, G-67
Kaizen blitz/event, G-67
Kanban, 193, G-68
Kano model, G-68
KEE, 142
Keiretsu, G-68
Keogh plans, 85, G-68
Key, G-68
Key buying influentials, G-68
Kickback fraud, G-68
King model, 150
Kinked demand curve, 22
Kiting, G-68
KJ method, G-68
Knowledge, skills, and abilities (KSAs), 81
Knowledge base, G-68
Knowledge engineer, 142, G-68
Knowledge gap, 69
Knowledge management, 4, 79, 141, G-68
Knowledge management portal, G-68
Knowledge systems, 141–142
Knowledge worker, G-68
KonTrag model, 150
Kotler, Philip, 172, 173, 186, 249
　competitive strategies of, 249

L

Labeling, 66, G-68
Labor force population, G-68
Labor laws, 15, G-68
Labor-management relations, 89
Labor-Management Relations Act, 15
Labor-Management Reporting and Disclosure Act, 15
Labor markets, G-68
Labor productivity, 198, G-68
Labor specialization, G-68
Laddering, G-68
Lagged regression analysis, G-68
Lagging, 235, 236, G-68
Lag indicators, 219
Lags, G-68
Lambda, G-68
Land bridge, G-68
Language translator, G-68
Lanham Act, 15
LAN (Local Area Network), G-68
Lapping, G-68
Larceny, G-68
Large-batch and mass production, 225
Large-group interventions, 225, G-68
Large power distance culture, G-68

Laser printer, G-69
Last in, first out (LIFO) method, 102, 196, 197, G-69
Latest finish line (LF), G-69
Latest start time (LS), G-69
Law, 55
    human resources and, 87–88
    of large numbers, 153
    marketing and, 65
Law of effect, G-69
Law of one price, G-69
Leader, G-69
Leadership, 2, 3, 71, 171, G-69
    styles of, 220
Leadership concepts, 6–7
Leadership grip, G-69
Leadership traits, 6
Leading, 235, 236, G-69
Leads, G-69
Lead times, G-69
    demand during, 193
    service levels and, 193
Lead underwriter, G-69
Leaky bucket theory, G-69
Lean approach/lean thinking, G-69
Lean manufacturing, G-69
Lean production, G-69
Learner-controlled instruction, G-69
Learning, 23, G-69
Learning curve, 55, 248, G-69
Learning-curve tables, 248
Learning objectives, G-69
Learning organization, 24, G-69
Lease, G-69
Lease analysis cash flows, 114
Lease rules, related to leasing of fixed assets, 104
Lease versus purchase analysis, 208
Leasing, 113, 114
Least changeover cost rule, 191
Least preferred coworker (LPC) scale, 220
Leaves, G-69
Leaves of absence, 85
Ledger, G-69
Ledger balance, G-69
Legacy system, G-69
Legal environment, G-69
Legitimate power, 6, 220, G-69
Legitimation, G-69
Lemon Laws, 66
Leontief Paradox, G-69
Less-developed country (LDC), G-69
Lessee, G-70
Lessor, G-70
Letter of credit (L/C), 166, G-70
Level capacity approach, 183
Level capacity costs, 183
Level of detail, G-70
Level of equality, G-70
Level of service, G-70
Level production method, G-70

Level schedule, G-70
Leverage, 173, G-70
Leverage analysis, 173–174
Leveraged buyout analysis, 182
Leveraged buyout (LBO), 114, 182, G-70
Leverage ratios, G-70
Liabilities, 14, G-70
    current, 91
    incorrect reporting of, 214
    long-term, 91
    ratio of, to stockholders' equity, 91
Liabilities, asset, and inadequate disclosure frauds, 151–152
Liability frauds, G-70
Liability swap, G-70
Libertarians, 11
LIBOR, G-70
Licensing, 158, G-70
    multinational enterprise (MNE), 167
Licensing agreement, G-70
Licensing program, G-70
Lie detector tests, 16
Lien, G-70
Life cycle, G-70
Lifetime value of a customer, 243–244
LIFO, G-70
Limitations
    imposed by union contract, 16
    or modification of warranties, 67
Limited-service merchant wholesalers, G-70
Limiting operation, G-70
Line, G-70
Linear cultures, G-71
Linear programming, 246
Linear regression, G-71
Linear responsibility matrix, G-71
Linear trend analysis, 20
Line authority, G-70
Line balancing, G-70
Line efficiency, G-70
Line extensions, G-71
Line loading, G-71
Line of credit, 111, G-71
Liner service, G-71
Lingua franca, G-71
Link analysis, G-71
Liquid asset, G-71
Liquid crystal display (LCD), G-71
Liquidity, 205, G-71
    analysis, 205
Liquidity preference hypothesis, G-71
Liquidity preference theory, G-71
Liquidity premium (LP), G-71
Liquidity ratios, G-71
Liquidity risk, G-71
LISP, 142
Listening, 41, G-71
Listening post data, G-71
Little's law, 185, G-71
Load, 192, G-71

Load balancing, 192, G-71
Load-distance analysis, 201
Load leveling, G-71
Load participation, G-71
Lobbyist, G-71
Local area network (LAN), 146
Local content, G-71
Locational arbitrage, G-71
Location decision, G-71
Lockbox, 109, G-71
Lockbox arrangement, G-71
Lockbox collection system, G-71
Lockbox consortium, G-71
Lockbox optimization model, G-71
Lockbox services, G-71
Lockbox study, G-71
Lock out/tag out regulations, G-71
Locus of control, 23, 223, G-71
Logarithmic analysis, 248
Logical design, G-72
Logic bomb, G-72
Logistical management, 52–53
Logistical service standards, G-72
Logistics, 61, G-72
    analysis, 227–230
Logistics (or physical distribution), G-72
Logistics platform, G-72
Log-linear regression, G-71
London Interbank Offer Rate (LIBOR), G-72
Long-range planning, 47
Long-term debt, 113
Long-term financing
    international, 128–134
    managing, 112–115
Long-term forward contracts, G-72
Long-term goals, G-72
Long-term liabilities, 91, G-72
    interpretation of ratio of fixed assets to, 104
Long-term orientation, G-72
Long-term vision, 136
Loss control, 153, G-72
Loss exposure, G-72
Loss exposure checklists, 152, G-72
Loss from operations, G-72
Lost sales, cost of, 228, 243
Lot, G-72
Lot sizing decision rules, 45
Lottery, G-72
Lot tolerance percent defective (LTPD), G-72
Louvre Accord, 162, G-72
Lower control limit (LCL), G-72
Lower-of-cost-or-market (LCM) method, 196, G-72
Lower-of-cost-or-market value, 103
Lower trial courts, G-72
Low liquidity strategy, G-72
Low power distance culture, G-72

Low-regular-dividend-plus-extras policy, 119
Lubrication bribes, G-72
Lump-sum bonuses, 8
Lump-sum increase (LSI), G-72
Lumpy assets, G-72

M

Maastricht Treaty, G-72
Machiavellianism, 23, 223, G-72
Machine center, G-72
Machine language, G-72
Machine loading, G-72
Machine productivity, G-72
Machine selection, 187–188
Machine setup cost and time, 193
Machine utilization, G-73
MacOS, G-73
Macroassessment, G-73
Macroeconomic forecasting, 20
Macroeconomic level, G-73
Macroeconomic policy, 161–162
Macroenvironmental forces, 56
Macroenvironmental variables, 70
Macro processes, G-73
Magnetic disk, G-73
Magnetic Ink Character Recognition (MICR) line, G-73
Magnetic tape, G-73
Magnuson-Moss Warranty Act, 66, 67
Mail float, G-73
Mainframe, G-73
Maintainability, G-73
Maintenance, G-73
Maintenance margin, G-73
Make-or-buy analysis, 175
    manufacturing, 190
Make-to-order, G-73
Make-to-stock, G-73
Managed care, G-73
Managed earnings, G-73
Managed float, G-73
Management, 69–70, G-73
    nature of, 3
Management accounting, 90, G-74
Management assurance, 156–157
Management by exception, 138, G-73
Management by fact, G-73
Management by objectives (MBO), 84, 223–224, G-73
Management by policy, G-73
Management by walking around (MBWA), G-73
Management by wandering around (MBWA), 9, G-73
Management contracts, 158, G-73
Management controls, 150, G-73
Management Discussion and Analysis (MDA), G-73

Management fraud, G-73
Management information system (MIS), G-73
Management intervention, G-74
Management override, G-74
Management perspectives, 4
Management process, G-74
Management reserve, G-74
Management review, G-74
Management science perspective, 4, G-74
Management styles, G-74
Management theories, 4
Management training, G-74
Manager, G-74
Managerial commitment, G-74
Managerial ethics, 224
Managerial finance, 107
Managerial grid, G-74
Managing about a target rule, G-74
Managing for growth, 53
Mandated benefits, G-74
Manufacturability, G-74
Manufacturer's agents, G-74
Manufacturer's sales branches, G-74
Manufacturing balanced scorecard, 185
Manufacturing business, G-74
    balance sheet budgets for, 97
    basic income statement budgets for, 97
    master budget for, 97
Manufacturing cells, G-74
Manufacturing costs, 203
Manufacturing cycle efficiency, 184, G-74
Manufacturing defect, 67
Manufacturing environment, G-74
Manufacturing execution system, G-74
Manufacturing lead time, G-74
Manufacturing make-or-buy analysis, 190
Manufacturing management analysis, 187–188
Manufacturing margin, G-74
Manufacturing operations analysis, 190–194
Manufacturing organization, G-74
Manufacturing overhead, 203
Manufacturing performance measures, 184
Manufacturing planning, 47
Manufacturing process, G-74
Manufacturing Resource Planning (MRP II), G-74
Manufacturing strategy, G-75
Manufacturing volume strategy, G-75
Maquiladoras, G-75
Margin, G-75
Marginal cost, 212, G-75
Marginal cost method, G-75

Marginal cost of capital (MCC), 118, G-75
Marginal costs, G-75
Marginal functions, G-75
Marginal revenue, 20, G-75
Marginal tax rate, G-75
Margin call, G-75
Margin of safety, 95, 241, G-75
Margin requirement, G-75
Marked-to-market, G-75
Market
    methods, 177
    penetration, 57
    risks, 233
Marketable securities, 109, G-75
Market allocation, 16
Market audit, G-75
Market-based forecasting, G-75
Market-based scorecard measure, 219
Market-based transfer pricing, G-75
Market/book (M/B) ratio, 129, G-75
Market development, 57
Market-differentiated pricing, G-75
Market-driven approach, 59
Market entry strategy, G-75
Market failure, 12
Marketing, G-75
    concept, 56
    economics and, 63–65
    ethics and, 62–63
    law and, 65
    research, 60–61
    strategies, 56
Marketing channel, G-75
Marketing channel management, G-76
Marketing channel power, G-76
Marketing channel profitability analysis, 172
Marketing channels and distribution, 61
Marketing concept, G-76
Marketing environment, G-76
Marketing expense-to-sales ratio, 232
Marketing infrastructure, G-76
Marketing management analysis, 172–173
Marketing mix, 61, G-76
Marketing myopia, G-76
Marketing public relations, 58
    impact of, on sales, 187
Marketing strategy, G-76
Market interest rates, determinants of, 128
Market line, G-75
Market microstructure, G-75
Market niche, 22
Market-perceived quality, G-75
Market potential, G-75
Market price, 98, 178, G-75
Market price approach, G-75
Market (price) skimming, G-75

Market risk, 233, G-75
Market risk premium, RPM, G-75
Market segment, G-75
Market segmentation, 68
Market segmentation hypothesis, G-75
Market segmentation theory, G-75
Market-share, 171, 172
Market structure analysis, 21–22
Market-to-book (M/B) ratio, 205, 206, 207, 208
Market transparency, G-75
Market-value-added (MVA), 204–205
Market-value-added (MVA) analysis, 7, 205, 242
Market value-added (MVA) system, G-75
Market value and competition, 182
Market value measures, 206
Market value ratios, G-75
Marking the evidence, G-76
Markov analysis, 246
Markup, 177, G-75
Markup laws, G-76
Markup percentages, 99
 on cost, 178
 on selling price, 178
Markup pricing, 64
Masculinity, G-76
Masculinity/femininity, G-76
Maslow's hierarchy of needs theory, 8, 59, G-76
Mass customization, G-76
Massed practice, G-76
Master budget, 97, G-76
Master note, G-76
Master of destiny, G-76
Master operating budget, G-76
Master planning, G-76
Master planning of resources, G-76
Master production schedule, 47–48, 183, G-76
Matching achievement, G-75
Matching concept, G-76
Matching demand approach, 183
Matching demand costs, 183
Matching model, G-76
Matching possessions, G-76
Materiality concept, G-77
Material achievement, G-76
Material requirements planning (MRP), G-76
Materials inventory, G-77
Materials ledger, G-77
Materials management, 49, G-77
Materials requirement planning (MRP) system, 147, 191, 199, 230, G-77
Materials requisitions, G-77
Materials review board (MRB), G-77
Materials scheduling, 191–192
Material tracking, 52
Mathematical model, G-77

Mathematical tables, 251–258
Matrix approach, G-77
Matrix chart/diagram, G-77
Matrix data analysis, 72
Matrix diagram, 72
Matrix organization, G-77
Matrix organization structure, G-77
Matrix structure, 5, G-77
Matrix-type organization, 28
Maturity curve, G-77
Maturity date, G-77
Maturity extension swap, G-77
Maturity matching, G-77
Maturity risk premium (MRP), G-77
Maturity value, G-77
Maximization of shareholder value, G-77
MBO, G-77
McFadden Act (1927), G-77
M-commerce, 148, G-77
Mean, 153, 244, G-77
Mean absolute deviation, 45, 244, G-77
Mean absolute error (MAE), G-77
Means (in the hoshin planning usage), G-78
Mean squared error (MSE), 245, G-77
Mean square error, G-77
Mean time between failures (MTBF), 216, G-77
Measured (demonstrated) capacity, 192
Measurement, 51, G-78
Mechanistic organization, G-78
Median, 153, 244, G-77
Media strategy, G-77
Mediation, G-78
Mediators, G-78
Medical examinations, 82
Medium, G-78
Medium-Term Guarantee Program, G-78
Member banks, G-78
Mentor, G-78
Mentoring, 83, G-78
Mercantilism, G-78
Merchandise control, 195
Merchandise inventory, G-78
 balance sheet presentation of, 103
Merchandise planning, 195
Merchandise pricing, 194–195
Merchandise productivity, 198
Merchandise profitability analysis, 197
Merchandising businesses, G-78
Merchantability, 66
Merchant wholesalers, G-78
Mergers, 2, 13, 17, 24, G-78
 acquisition analysis and, 180–181
Message, G-78
Methods analysis, G-78
Metric, G-78
Metrology, G-78
Microassessment, G-78

Microcomputer, G-78
Microeconomic forecasting, 20
Microeconomic level, G-78
Micro managing, G-78
Micromarkets, G-78
Microprocesses, G-78
Microprocessor, G-78
Middle manager, G-78
Middle-of-the-road management, 6, 220
Midrange computer, G-78
Migration, G-78
Milestone, G-78
Milestone chart, G-78
Mill, John Stuart, 162
MIL-STD, G-78
Mind mapping, G-78
Minimax regret approach, 237, G-78
Mininationals, G-78
Minority interest, G-78
Minority participation, G-78
MIPS, G-78
Mirror, G-78
Miscellaneous fraud, G-78
Mission, G-78
Mission-critical applications, G-78
Mission-critical hardware or software, G-78
Mission statement, 136, G-78
Misuse or abuse of product, 68
Mixed aid credits, G-78
Mixed approach, G-78
Mixed cost, G-78
Mixed forecasting, G-78
Mixed instruments, G-78
Mixed-model production, G-78
Mixed structure, G-79
Mnaging underwriter, G-69
Mobile observation, G-79
Mode, 153, 244, G-79
Model, G-79
Model audit, G-79
Model estimation, G-79
Modeling, 83, G-79
Model management module, G-79
Modem (modulator/demodulator), G-79
Moderate current asset investment policy, G-79
Moderate liquidity strategy, G-79
Moderate strategy, G-79
Modified accrual technique, G-79
Modified buy-and-hold strategy, G-79
Modified IRR (MIRR), G-79
Modified rebuy, G-79
Modigliani and Miller (MM) trade-off theory, 119
Modular approach, G-79
Modular bill of material, G-79
Modulation, G-79
Moment-of-truth, G-79
Monetary barriers, G-79
Monetary gold stocks, 165

Monetary items, G-79
Monetary-nonmonetary method, G-79
Monetary policy, 161
    contractionary, 162
    expansionary, 162
Money market, G-79
Money market deposit accounts, G-79
Money market hedge, G-79
Money market hedge strategy, 235
Money market mutual fund, G-79
Monitoring receivables, 110
Monoculture, G-79
Monopolistic competition, 22
Monopolization, 17
Monopoly, 21
Monopsony, 21
Monte Carlo simulation, 121, G-79
Montreal Protocol, 18
Monument, G-79
Moods, G-79
Moral free space, G-79
Moral judgment, 156
Moral management, 156, G-79
Moral-rights approach, 11, 224, G-79
Mortgage, G-79
Mortgage bonds, 113, G-79
Most critical path, G-79
Most-Favored Nation (MFN), G-80
Most likely time estimate (*tm*), G-80
Motion, G-80
Motion for dismissal, G-80
Motivating channel members, G-80
Motivation, 8–9, 224, G-80
Motivational research, G-80
Motivators (satisfiers), 224, G-80
Motorola, 73
Moving averages, 45, G-80
Moving surveillance, G-80
Muda, G-80
Multiattribute evaluation, G-80
Multibuyer policy, G-80
Multicollinearity, G-80
Multicriteria decision problem, G-80
Multiculture centers, G-80
Multiculture team, G-80
Multidimensional development, G-80
Multidomestic approach, G-80
Multidomestic strategy, 158, G-80
Multilateral Investment Guarantee Agency (MIGA), G-80
Multilateral negotiations, G-80
Multilateral netting system, G-80
Multilevel bill of material, G-80
Multilevel master schedule, G-80
Multilevel where-used, G-80
Multimedia, 83, G-80
Multinational corporations (MNCs), 44, 108, 127, 128, 149, 157, 209, G-80
Multinational enterprises (MNEs), 167, G-80
    forms of, 167

Multinational firms, 109, 110
Multinational restructuring, G-80
Multiple-drawee checks, G-80
Multiple IRRs, G-80
Multiple processing centers, G-80
Multiple production department factory overhead rate method, G-81
Multiple product order, 65
Multiple regression, 245, G-81
Multiple-step income statement, G-81
Multiple-unit pricing strategies, 64
Multiplexer, G-81
Multiplicative time series model, G-81
Multiprocessing, G-81
Multiprogramming, G-81
Multitasking, G-81
Multivariate control chart, G-81
Multivariate models, G-81
Multivoting, G-81
Municipal obligations, G-81
Mutually exclusive projects, G-81
Mystery shopper, G-81

N

NACHA, G-81
Name-your-price auction, G-81
Narrative methods, 84
Narrow band, G-81
Nash equilibrium, 22
National Ambient Air Quality Standards (NAAQS), 18
National Crime Information Center (NCIC), G-81
National-culture scheme, G-81
National Environmental Policy Act (NEPA), 17
Nationalization, G-81
National Labor Relations Act (1935) (NLRA), 15
National Pollutant Discharge Elimination System (NPDES), 18
National security, G-81
National sovereignty, G-81
Native application, G-81
Natural business year, 92, G-81
Natural hedging, G-81
Natural language processors (NLPs), 141, G-81
Natural monopoly, 13, 21
Natural resources, depletion accounting for, 104
Natural team, G-81
NDE, G-81
Nearby contract, G-81
Needs, G-81
Need to achieve, G-81
Negative exposure, G-81
Negligence
    comparative, 68
    contributory, 68

Negotiable bill of lading, G-81
Negotiable certificate of deposit, G-81
Negotiated price approach, 178, G-81
    to transfer pricing, 98
Negotiated transfer pricing, G-81
Negotiation, G-81
Nemawashi, G-82
Nepotism, G-82
Net cash flows, 121
Net change MRP, G-82
Net errors and omissions account, G-82
Net float, 109, G-82
Net income, 212, 219, 238, G-82
Net income after taxes, 197
Net liquid balance, G-82
Net loss, G-82
Net operating loss carrybacks, G-82
Net operating loss carryforwards, G-82
Net pay, G-82
Net present value (NPV), 180, 181–182, 240, G-82
Net present value (NPV) method, 120, 179, G-82
Net present value (NPV) profile, G-82
Net realizable value, 103, G-82
Net requirements, 191, G-82
Net requirements schedule, 198
Netting, 236, G-82
Net transaction exposure, G-82
Network diagram, G-82
Network externality, 13
Net working capital (NWC), 108, 121, 205–206, G-82
Network model, G-82
Network planning, 32–33
Network protocol, G-82
Networks, 5, G-82
Network structure, G-82
Net worth method, G-82
Neural net, G-82
Neural networks, 141
Neutralizer, G-82
New economy, G-82
New products
    development, 57
    equity financing and, 231
    opportunity rating analysis, 230
    payback periods and, 231
    profit margins and, 231
Newsgroup, G-82
New-task buying situation, G-82
New-venture fund, G-82
New-venture team, G-82
Next operation as customer, G-82
Niche marketing, G-82
Node, G-82
Nolo contendere, G-82
Nominal group technique, G-82
Nominal interest rate, G-83
Nominal (quoted) risk-free rate, k_{RF}, G-83

Nominating committee, G-83
Nonbank banks, G-83
Noncallable, G-83
Non-cash activities, 213
Noncompetitive bid, G-83
Nonconformity, G-83
Nonconstant growth, G-83
Non-contributory plan, G-83
Noncontrollable costs, G-83
Noncyclical normal goods, 64
Nondeliverable Forward Contracts (NDFs), G-83
Nondestructive testing and evaluation (NDT), G-83
Nondirective interview, G-83
Non-exempt employees, G-83
Nonfinancial incentives, G-83
Nonfinancial measures, G-83
Nonimpact printer, G-83
Nonmonetary item, G-83
Nonparticipating preferred stock, G-83
Nonparticipator role, G-83
Nonpoint sources, 18
Nonprogrammed decision, G-83
Nonprogrammed decision making, G-83
Nonrecourse or participation bias, G-83
Nonroutine reports, G-83
Nonsampling risk, G-83
Nonsterilized intervention, G-83
Nontariff barriers, G-83
Non-tariff trade barriers, 163–164
Nonvalue-added, G-83
Nonvalue-added activities, G-83
Nonvalue-added lead time, G-83
Nonverbal communication, G-83
Nonverbal messages, 221
Nonvolatile memory, G-83
Norm, G-83
Normal (constant) growth, G-83
Normal cost, 211, G-83
Normal distribution, 153, G-83
Normal goods, 64
Normal probability distribution, G-84
Normal profits/rates of return, G-84
Normal time, G-84
Normal yield curve, G-84
Normative, G-84
Normative ethics, G-84
Normative integration, G-84
Norming, G-84
Norms, G-84
Norris-La Guardia Act, 15
North American Free Trade Agreement (NAFTA), 44, 106, G-84
Notebook computer, G-84
Notes receivable, G-84
 journal entries for, 102
Not-for-profit accounting, 90
Not-invented-here syndrome, G-84
Notional amount, G-84
NPV (net present value), G-84

N sample size, G-81
Nuisance, 17
Number of affected units chart (np chart), G-84
Number of days in receivables, G-84
Number of days of payables outstanding (DPO), G-84
Number of days' sales in inventory, G-84
Number of days' sales in receivables, G-84
Number of times the interest charges are earned, G-84

O

Object code, G-84
Objective, G-84
Objective evidence, G-84
Objective function, 246, G-84
Objective risks, 234, G-84
Objectivity concept, 90, G-84
Object linking and embedding (OLE), G-84
Object-oriented databases, 140–141
Object-oriented programming (OOP), G-84
Observation, G-84
Obsolescence costs, G-84
Occupational Safety and Health Act (OSHA), 16
Occupational Safety and Health Administration (OSHA), 87
Ocean bill of lading, G-84
Ocean shipping, G-84
OC (operating characteristic) curve, G-84
Off-balance-sheet financing, G-84
Offering price, G-84
Office automation systems, G-84
Official reserves account, G-84
Off-invoice allowance, G-84
Offshore banking, G-85
Off-target, G-84
Off-the-job training, G-84
OLAP (online analytical processing), G-85
Oligopoly, 22
Omitted variables, G-85
Omnibus surveys, G-85
One-stop logistics, G-85
One-to-one marketing, G-85
One-transaction approach, G-85
Ongoing validation, G-85
Online analytical processing (OLAP) applications, 141
Online processing, G-85
On-site inspections of property, 152
Onslaught, 250
On-the-job development methods, 83
On-the-job training (OJT), G-85
On-us, G-85

Open account, G-85
Open account transaction, G-85
Open-book management, 8, 242, G-85
Open communication, G-85
Open criticism, G-85
Open-ended questions, G-85
Openness to experience, 223
Open regionalism, G-85
Open source software, G-85
Open system, G-85
Open Systems Interconnection (OSI), G-85
Open-to-buy (OTB) approach, 195
Operating activities, 213, G-85
Operating break-even analysis, 116, G-85
Operating break-even point, 116, 240, G-85
Operating budgets, 97, 239–240
 analysis, 238–240
 linking, for consecutive years, 239
Operating cash flows, 212, G-85
Operating characteristic curve, G-85
Operating controls, 12
Operating cycle, G-85
Operating expenses, G-85
Operating income, 241
Operating leases, 114, G-85
Operating leverage, 95, 116, 173, G-85
Operating motive, G-85
Operating performance ratio, G-85
Operating profit, 197, 241
Operating risk, G-85
Operating system, G-85
Operational control, 150
Operational feasibility study, G-85
Operational goals, G-86
Operational managers, G-86
Operational plans, G-86
Operational restructuring, G-86
Operations, 54–55, G-86
Operations information system, G-86
Operations lead-times, 192–193
Operations management, G-86
Operations queuing models, 192
Operations scheduling, G-86
Operations sequence, G-86
Operations sequencing, G-86
Operations strategy, G-86
Operation start date, G-85
Opportunity, G-86
Opportunity cost, 121, 202, G-86
Opportunity cost per unit, G-86
Opportunity cost rate, G-86
Opportunity loss, or regret, G-86
Opportunity rating method, 230
Optical character recognition (OCR), G-86
Optical disc, G-86
Optical fiber, G-86
Optical tape, G-86
Optimal dividend policy, 119, G-86

SUBJECT INDEX

I-25

Optimal solution, G-86
Optimistic approach to decision
    making, 237, G-86
Optimistic time estimate (t_o), G-86
Optimization, G-86
Opting-out right, G-86
Option overplanning, G-86
Options, 236, G-86
Option securities, 113, 114
Oral communication, 40, 161
Order control, G-86–87
Order cycle time, G-87
Order getter, G-87
Order handling, G-87
Ordering costs, G-87
Order loser, G-87
Orderly marketing agreements, 163
Order management, G-87
Order point, 193, G-87
Order point (OP) decision rules, 45
Order point system, G-87
Order promising, G-87
Order qualifiers, 244, G-87
Order taker, G-87
Order winners, 244, G-87
Ordinary annuity, 125, G-87
Organic organization, G-87
Organization, G-87
    fraud against, 151
Organizational and general
        management analysis, 220–225
    change management, 223
    communication, 220–221
    corporate culture, 221–222
    decision making, 221
    design and structure, 225
    development, 225
    leadership styles, 220
    managerial ethics, 224
    motivation, 224
    new perspectives in, 225
    personality, behavior, and
        perception, 223
    planning, 223–224
    teamwork, 222
Organizational behavior, 23–24
Organizational budget, 242
Organizational change, 25, 223
Organizational controls, 7–8, 241–242
Organizational culture, 24
Organizational design and structure, 225
Organizational development (OD), 26,
    225, G-87
Organizational environments, 24
Organizational measurement, 7–8
Organizational socialization, G-87
Organizational structure, 24–25
Organization behavior, G-87
Organization-centered career
    planning, G-87
Organization change, G-87

Organization chart, G-87
Organization citizenship, G-87
Organization commitment, G-87
Organization control, G-87
Organization culture, G-87
Organization development (OD), G-87
Organization for Economic
    Cooperation and Development
    (OECD), 162, G-87
Organization structure, G-87
Organized exchanges, 122
Organized security exchange, G-87
Organizing, 5, G-88
Orientation, 83, G-88
Orientation program, G-88
Original maturity, G-88
Originating ACH, G-88
Originating depository financial
    institution (ODFI), G-88
Other expense, G-88
Other income, G-88
Outdoor training, 83
Outflow, G-88
Out-of-control process, G-88
Out-of-money option, G-88
Out of pocket expenses, G-88
Out-of-sample validation, G-88
Out of spec, G-88
Outpartnering, G-88
Output, G-88
Output devices, G-88
Output price measurement, G-88
Outside directors, G-88
Outsourcing, 51, 88, 110, 143, G-88
Outstanding stock, G-88
Overapplied factory overhead, G-88
Overbooking, 200
Over-capacity, 192
Overcentralization, G-88
Overdraft credit lines, G-88
Overdraft facility, G-88
Overhead, G-88
Overhead cost, G-88
Overhedging, G-88
Overseas Private Investment
    Corporation, 127
Over-the-counter (OTC) market,
    122, G-88
Owner's equity, G-88
Ownership risk, G-88
Ozone layer, 18

P

Pacifier-oriented leader, G-88
Packaged software, G-88
Packet, G-88
Packet switching, G-88
Paid-in capital, 112
Paid-only reconciliation, G-88
Paid time-off plan, G-89

Palm computer, G-89
Panel consensus method, 20
Panel interview, G-89
Panels, G-89
Panels of households, G-89
Par, G-89
Parallel bonds, G-89
Parallel conversion, G-89
Parallel loan, G-89
Parallel processing, G-89
Parallel structure, G-89
Parallel transmission, 146, G-89
Parameter design (Taguchi), G-89
Parameters, 139, G-89
Parent, G-89
Parent-child relationship, 140
Parent company, G-89
Parent/subsidiary relationship, G-89
Pareto chart, G-89
Pareto diagrams, 73
Pareto principle, 199, 244
Parity check, G-89
Partial compensation, G-89
Partial productivity, G-89
Partial reinforcement schedule, G-89
Participation, G-89
Participation decision making, G-89
Participative design/engineering, G-89
Participative management, G-89
Participatory design approach, G-89
Partnership, 90, G-89
Partnership/alliance, G-89
Partnership strategies, 2
Par value, G-89
Passive investment strategy, 110, G-89
Passwords, 137, G-89
Patent Cooperations Treaty
    (PCT), G-89
Patents, 15, G-89
Path-goal model, 6
Path-goal theory, G-89
Pax Americana, G-89
Payable deferral period, 108
Payables centralization, 109
Payables turnover ratio, G-90
Payable through draft (PTD), G-90
Payback period, 181, G-90
    new products and, 231
Payback period method, G-90
Pay compression, G-89
Pay equity, G-90
Payers, G-90
Pay for knowledge, 8
Pay-for-performance, 8, G-90
Pay grade, G-90
Paying agent, G-90
Payment, G-90
Payment date, G-90
Payoff analysis, 237
Payoffs, 237, G-90
Payoff tables, 42, 194, 237, 238, G-90

Payroll, G-90
   employer liabilities for, 105
Payroll fraud scheme, G-90
Payroll register, 105, G-90
Pay survey, G-90
P chart, G-88
PDSA cycle, G-90
Peer-to-peer LAN, G-90
Peer-to-peer (P2P) file sharing, G-90
Pegged exchange rate, G-90
Pegging, G-90
Penetration strategy, G-90
Pension liabilities, G-90
Pension plans, G-90
Pensions, 85, 105, G-90
People-processing services, G-90
Perceived opportunity, G-90
Perceived pressure, G-90
Percentage variation method, 195
Percent complete, G-90
Percent of sales, G-90
Perception, 223, G-90
Perceptual defense, 23, 223, G-90
Perceptual distortions, G-90
Perceptual mapping, G-90
Perceptual selectivity, G-90
Perfect competition, 21
Perfect forecast line, G-90
Performance, G-90
Performance analysis, work center, 192
Performance appraisal, 83, G-90
Performance-based incentives, 86
Performance-based pay, G-90
Performance consulting, G-90
Performance evaluation, 97–98
Performance gap, 223, G-90
Performance management and appraisal, 83–84
Performance management system, G-90
Performance measures, 46
Performance pay, G-91
Performance plan, G-91
Performance report, G-91
Performance shares, G-91
Performance standards, G-91
Performance test, G-91
Performing, G-91
Period costs, 203, G-91
Periodic inventory system, G-91
Periodic inventory system, cost of inventory under, 102
Periodic rate, G-91
Periodic replenishment, G-91
Period order quantity, G-91
Peripheral equipment, G-91
Perishability, G-91
Permanent current assets, G-91
Permanent differences, G-91
Permanent issues, G-91
Permanent teams, G-91
Perpetrator, G-91

Perpetual inventory system, G-91
   cost of inventory under, 102
Perpetuity, G-91
Perquisites (perks), G-91
Per se violations, 16
Personal communications, 40
Personal decision-support systems (DSSs), 139, G-91
Personal digital assistant (PDA), G-91
Personal efficiency, 248
Personal insight method, 20
Personality, 23, G-91
   behavior, and perception, 223
Personality test, G-91
Personal observation evidence, G-91
Personal power, 6
Personal selling, 69–70, 232, G-91
Person-job fit, G-91
Personnel competencies, G-91
Person-organization, G-91
PERT chart, G-91
Pessimistic time estimate (t_p), G-91
Petrodollars, G-91
Petty cash fund, 101, G-91
Phantom bill of material, G-91
Phased conversion, G-91
Phased retirement, G-91
Philanthropic responsibilities, G-91
Philanthropy, G-92
Physical ability tests, G-92
Physical design, G-92
Physical distribution, 61, G-92
Physical distribution management, G-92
Physical evidence, G-92
Physical inventory, G-92
Physical safeguards, G-92
Physiological needs, 224
Piggyback, G-92
Piloting, G-92
Pipeline stock, G-92
Pipelining, G-92
Pixel (picture element), G-92
Place, 61
Place/entry strategy, G-92
Placement, G-92
Plaintext, G-92
Plaintiff's conduct, 67
Plan, G-92
Plan-do-check-act cycle (PDCA), 73, G-92
Planned contraction, 249
Planned issue receipt, G-92
Planned obsolescence, G-92
Planned on hand (POH) data, 48
Planned order, G-92
Planned order receipt, 192, G-92
Planned order release, 192, G-92
Planning, 4–5, 223–224, G-92
Planning bill of material, G-92
Planning task force, G-92
Planning time fence, G-92

Plant assets, 91
Plant capacity and bottlenecks, 187
Plant close or open analysis, 188
Plant layout, 193–194
Plant operating efficiency, 191
Plant selection, 188
Platform, G-93
Plaza Accord, G-93
Plaza Agreement, 162, G-93
Pledging, 112
Pledging receivables, 112, G-93
Plug-and-play, G-93
Plug-ins, 148
Pluralism, G-93
PM theory of leadership, G-93
P-O expectancy, G-93
Point-counterpoint, G-93
Point elasticity, 63
Point estimate, G-93
Point of presence (POP), G-93
Point-of-purchase communication, G-93
Point-of-purchase (P-O-P) materials, 58
Point to point protocol (PPP), G-93
Poison pill, G-93
Poisson distribution, 153, G-93
Poka-yoke, 73, G-93
Policy, G-93
Political environment, G-93
Political forces, G-93
Political instability, G-93
Political model of decision making, 9, 221
Political risk, G-93
Political systems, G-93
Political union, G-93
Polling, G-93
Polycentric staffing outlook, G-93
Polygamous loyalty, G-93
PONC, G-93
Pooled interdependence, 25, 225
Pooling, G-93
Pooling-of-interests method, G-93
Poor quality costs, 214–215
Population, G-93
Population increase, G-93
Population stabilization, G-93
Port, G-93
Portability, G-93
Portal, G-93
Porter's competitive forces and strategies, 249
Portfolio analysis, G-93
Portfolio approach, G-93
Portfolio diversification, 233
Portfolio investment, 126, G-93
Portfolio models, G-93
Portfolio risk, G-93
Portfolio strategy, G-94
Ports, G-94
Position defense, 249
Positioning, G-94

Position power, 6
Positive adjustment phase, G-94
Positive exposure, G-94
Positive float, G-94
Positive pay, G-94
Positive reinforcement, 8
Possession-processing services, G-94
Postal inspectors, G-94
Post-audit, 120, G-94
Post-closing trial balance, 91, G-94
Posterior (revised) probabilities, G-94
Posting, G-94
Postpurchase behavior, G-94
Post-retirement benefits, G-94
Power, G-94
Power distance, G-94
Ppk, G-94
PPM, G-94
Practices, G-94
Preauthorized debits, 109, G-94
Preauthorized debit system, G-94
Preauthorized draft, G-94
Preauthorized payment, G-94
Precautionary balances, G-94
Precautionary motive, G-94
Precedence diagramming method (PDM), G-94
Precedential relationship, G-94
Precision, G-94
Pre-control, G-94
Predatory pricing, G-94
Predecessor event, G-94
Predetermined factory overhead rate, G-94
Predication, G-94
Predictive consistency, 20
Predictive validity, G-94
Preemptive right, G-94
Pre-expatriation program, G-94
Preferential policies, G-94
Preferred provider organization (PPO), G-94
Preferred stock, G-94
Preferred stocks, 113–114, 115
Preferred supplier arrangements, 2
Pregnancy discrimination, 87
Preliminary control, 241–242
Preliminary hearing, G-94
Preloss activities, G-95
Premium, G-95
Premium bond, G-95
Prepaid expenses, G-95
Prepayment, G-95
Prerequisite tree, G-95
Presale disclosure, 66
Presentation principles, G-95
Presentment, G-95
Present value, 217, G-95
Present value analysis, 154
Present value concept, G-95
Present value index, G-95

Present value interest factor for an annuity (PVIFA$_{i,n}$), G-95
Present value interest factor for i and n (PVIF$_{i,n}$), G-95
Present value of an annuity, 124–125, G-95
 of $1 per period for *n* periods, 253–254
Present value of $1 due at the end of *n* periods, 251–252
Pretest, G-95
Prevention costs, 214, G-95
Prevention vs. detection, G-95
Preventive action, G-95
Preventive control, 241–242, G-95
Preventive maintenance management, 194
Price, 61, G-95
Price controls, G-95
Price/cost analysis, G-95
Price discrimination, 17, 64, G-95
Price-earnings (P/E) ratio, 129, 180, 181, 206, 207, 208, G-95
Price-elastic, G-95
Price elasticity, 63–64, 172
Price escalation, G-95
Price factor, G-95
Price-fixing, 16, G-95
Price leadership, 22
Price promotions, G-95
Price response analysis, 172–173
Price response coefficients, 172
Price strategy, G-95
Price variance, 233
Pricing analysis, 177–178
Pricing market, G-95
Pricing methods, 177
Pricing motive, G-95
Pricing practices, 64–65
Pricing strategies, 59
Primacy effect, G-95
Primary, G-95
Primary audience, G-95
Primary data, G-95
Primary keys, 140, G-95
Primary market, G-95
Primary memory (primary storage, main memory, main storage), G-95
Primary research, G-95
Prime costs, 203
Prime rate, G-95
Principal, G-95
Principal amount, face value, maturity value, par value, G-95
Priorities matrix, G-96
Prior-period adjustments, G-96
Prior probabilities, G-96
Prisoner's Dilemma, 22
Privacy, G-96
Private Branch Exchange (PBX), G-96
Private Export Funding Corporation, 127

Private nuisance, 17
Private placement, G-96
Private Securities Litigation Reform Act (1995), G-96
Privatization, G-96
Privity of contract, 67
Proactive marketing public relations, 58, G-96
Probabilistic input, G-96
Probability, 211, G-96
Probability distribution, 152, G-96
Probability-impact matrix, G-96
Problem, 73, G-96
Problem recognition, G-96
Problem solving, 9–10, 23, G-96
 styles of, 223
Problem-solving meetings, 41
Problem-solving team, G-96
Procedural justice, 224, G-96
Procedure, G-96
Proceeds, G-96
Process, G-96
Process analysis, 184–186
Process capability, 186, G-96
Process capability index, 186, G-96
Process control system, G-96
Process costing systems, 96
Process cost system, G-96
Process decision program chart (PDPC), 72, G-96
Process improvement, 77, 185, G-96
Process improvement team (PIT), G-96
Processing float, G-97
Process layout, G-96
Process management, 76–77, G-96
Process manufacturers, G-96
Process mapping, G-96
Process organization, G-96
Process-oriented layout, G-96
Process owner, G-96
Process quality audit, G-96
Process-related needs, 57
Process structure, G-97
Process theories, 8, 224, G-97
Process time, 184
Process village, G-97
Procurement, G-97, G-100
Procurement costs, G-97
Prodromal crisis stage, G-97
Producer's risk, G-97
Product, 61
Product cost concept, G-97
Product costing, 96–97, G-97
Product costs, 99, 203, G-97
Product cycle theory, G-97
Product development, G-97
Product-development, 57
Product differentiation, G-97
Product-diversification strategies, 57
Product division structure, G-97
Production automation alternatives, 192

Production bottleneck, G-97
Production budget, G-97
Production capability, G-97
Production capacity expansion, 183
Production capacity levels, 183
Production cycle time, 194
Production forecast, G-97
Production job scheduling, 191
Production learning curve analysis, 188
Production management, G-98
Production opportunities, G-98
Production plan, G-98
Production planning, 47, G-98
Production planning analysis, 183
Production planning and control strategies, G-98
Production possibilities frontier, G-98
Production rules, G-98
Production scheduling, G-98
Production volume, 202
Productivity, 79, 248–249, G-98
Productivity analysis, 248–249
Product layout, G-97
Product life cycle, G-97
Product line, G-97
Product line profitability analysis, 231
Product load profile, G-97
Product management, 57, 231–232
Product management-product line profitability analysis, 231
Product mix, 57, G-97
Product organization, G-97
Product orientation, G-97
Product-oriented layout, G-97
Product positioning, G-97
Product quality audit, G-97
Products, G-98
Product/service liability, G-97
Product/service strategy, G-97
Product structure, 190–191, G-97
Product tree, 191, G-97
Product tree structure, 190–191
Product warranties, 105
Professional certification, 88
Professional development plan, G-98
Profit, 197, 237
Profitability, 206, G-98
Profitability analysis, 93–94, 206
Profitability index method, 120, 179
Profitability ratios, G-98
Profitable sales call, 200
Profit centers, 218, G-98
   responsibility accounting report for, 98
Profit margin, 64, 206, G-98
   on sales, 129
Profit margin analysis, 172
Profit maximization, G-98
Profit repatriation limitations, G-98
Profit sharing, G-98
Profit-sharing plans, 86

Profit-volume chart, 95, G-98
Pro forma balance sheet approach, G-96
Pro forma balance sheet method, 116
Profound knowledge, system of, G-99
Program, G-99
Program evaluation and review technique (PERT), G-99
Programmable problems, 139, G-99
Programmed decision, G-99
Programmed decision making, G-99
Programming, G-99
Programming languages, G-99
Progress reports, 41
Project, G-99
Project cash flows and risks, 121, 132
Project communication and documentation, 40–42
Project control, 34–35, G-99
Projected balance sheet method, 116, G-99
Project Finance Loan Program, G-99
Projection, 23, 223, G-99
Project life cycle, 28, 31–32, G-99
Project management, 28–29, 143, G-99
Project management analysis, 210–211
Project manager, 38–39, G-99
Project manufacturing, G-99
Project meetings, 41
Project operating cash flows, 212
Project organizations, 27–28
   types of, 27–28
Project organization structure, G-99
Project plan, 32–33, G-99
Project required rate of return, k_{proj}, G-99
Projects, 28, 31–32
   crashing, 211
   risks, 180, 234
   scheduling, 33–34
Project scope, G-99
Project selection, G-99
Project sensitivity analysis, 217
Project strategy (protocol), G-99
Project team, 39–40
Prolog, 142
Promissory estoppel, 19
Promissory notes, G-99
   nature and characteristics of, 102
Promotion, 58, 61
Promotional message, G-99
Promotion strategy, G-99
Property rights, 12
Proposal, G-99
Proposal for appropriation of retained earnings, G-99
Proposed solution, 30–31
Proprietorship, 90, G-99
Prospectus, G-99
Protected class, G-99
Protectionistic legislation, G-99
Protection of intellectual property, G-99
Protocol, 146, G-99

Prototype, G-99
Prototyping, 143, 144, G-100
Prox, G-100
Proxy, 112, G-100
Proxy flight, G-100
Proxy information, G-100
Proxy process, G-100
Proxy solicitations, 14
Prudence concept, 106, G-100
Psychocultural contexts, G-100
Psychographic customer characteristics, G-100
Psychographics, 59, G-100
Psychological contract, G-100
Psychomotor tests, G-100
Psychopath, G-100
Public affairs, 155
Public issues committee (public policy committee), G-100
Publicity, G-100
Public-key encryption, G-100
Publicly-owned corporation, G-100
Public nuisance, 17
Public offering analysis, initial, 182
Public-private key method, 137
Public relations, 58, G-100
Pull manufacturing, G-100
Pull strategy, G-100
Pull system, G-100
Punishment, 8
Punitive tariff, G-100
Purchase, G-100
Purchase method, G-100
Purchase order with payment voucher attached, G-100
Purchases discounts, G-100
Purchases returns and allowances, G-100
Purchase terms, G-100
Purchasing, 44, 55, 177, G-100
Purchasing and supply chain organization, 49–50
Purchasing cards, G-100
Purchasing learning-curve analysis, 176
Purchasing management, 49–52
Purchasing policies and procedures, 50
Purchasing power gain, G-100
Purchasing power (indexed) bonds, 113
Purchasing power loss, G-100
Purchasing Power Parity (PPP) line, G-100
Purchasing Power Parity (PPP) theory, G-100
Purchasing power risk, G-100
Purchasing process, 49
Pure play method, 121, G-101
Pure risk, G-101
Push manufacturing, G-101
Push strategy, G-101
Push system, G-101
Put, G-101
Putable bonds, 113, G-101

SUBJECT INDEX   I-29

Put option on real assets, G-101
Put options, 127, G-101
PVA_n, G-101
$PVIFA(DUE)_{i,n}$, G-101
Pyramid forecasting, G-101
Pyramid model, G-101

Q

Qualified sales leads, G-101
Qualitative analysis, 20, 247
Qualitative data, link between quantitative data, 247
Qualitative forecasting, 45, 233
Qualitative information, G-101
Quality, 72, G-101
   in information technology, 140
   service, 77
Quality adviser, G-101
Quality analysis, 214–216
Quality and financial statements, 215
Quality and process management, 71–78
   benchmarking, 78
   best practices, 78
   business process reengineering, 78
   change management, 78
   environmental standards, 75–76
   improvement, 78
   models and awards, 74–75
   organization, 78–79
   principles and practices, 72–73
   process-management practices, 76–77
   quality, costs, and profits, 73–74
   quality control, 76
   redesign, 78
   service quality, 77
   standards, 75
   statistics, 76
   strategies, 71–72
   tools and techniques, 73
Quality assessment, G-101
Quality assurance, 72
Quality assurance/quality control (QA/QC), G-101
Quality audit, G-101
Quality characteristics, G-101
Quality circles, 7, G-101
Quality control, 76
Quality cost programs, 74
Quality cost reports, G-101
Quality costs, G-101
Quality council, G-101
Quality culture, G-101
Quality engineering, G-101
Quality function, G-101
Quality function deployment (QFD), 76, G-101
Quality improvement, G-102
Quality level agreement (QLA), G-102

Quality loop, G-102
Quality loss function, G-102
Quality management, 51, G-102
Quality manual, G-102
Quality metrics, G-102
Quality models and awards, 74–75
Quality of life, G-102
Quality of work life, G-102
Quality organization, 78–79
Quality plan, G-102
Quality planning, 72, G-102
Quality policy, G-102
Quality principles, 72–73, G-102
Quality score chart (Q chart), G-102
Quality standards, 75
Quality strategies, 71–72
Quality system, G-102
Quality system audit, G-102
Quality tools and techniques, 73
Quality trilogy, 75, G-102
Quantitative analysis, 123
   assignment problem, 246
   basic probabilities, 245
   basic statistics, 244–245
   forecasting methods, 246
   linear programming, 246
   regression, 245
   sales seasonality and deseasonality, 246
   transportation problem, 246
   transshipment problem, 247
Quantitative approach, G-102
Quantitative data, link between qualitative data and, 247
Quantitative data variables, 247
Quantitative methods, 45, 229
   in business, 42–43
Quantitative techniques
   finance and, 124–126
   marketing and, 70
   operations and, 55
   of sales forecasting, 233
Quantity discounts, G-102
Quantity factor, 100, G-102
Quasi-contract, 19
Query, G-102
Question marks, 171
Questionnaires, G-102
Queue, 201
Queue processing, G-102
Queue time, G-102
Queuing theory, 201
Quick assets, G-102
Quick ratio, 105, 205, G-102
Quick response system, 228–229
Quick test, 128
Quid pro quo, 84, G-102
Quincunx, G-102
Quotas, G-102
quoted rate, G-113

R

Radar chart, G-102
RAID (Redundant Array of Independent Disks), G-102
Random Access Memory (RAM), G-102
Random number generator, G-102
Random sample, G-103
Random sampling, G-103
Range, G-103
Range chart (R chart), G-103
Range reconciliation, G-103
Ranking, G-103
Rapid Application Development (RAD), G-103
Rapid prototyping, G-103
Rate-based scheduling, G-103
Rated capacity, G-103
Rate earned on common stockholders' equity, G-103
Rate earned on stockholders' equity, G-103
Rate earned on total assets, G-103
Rate of return on investment (ROI), G-103
Rater bias, G-103
Ratio analysis, G-103
Rationalization, G-103
Rational subgroup, G-103
Ratio of fixed assets to long-term liabilities, G-103
Ratio of liabilities to stockholders' equity, G-103
Ratio of net sales to assets, G-103
Ratio scale, G-103
Raw and in process inventory, G-103
Raw material scarcity, G-103
Raw materials inventory, G-103
R chart, 216
Reach percentage, G-103
Reactive marketing public relations (MPR), 58
Reactive MPR, G-103
Read-Only Memory (ROM), G-103
Real accounts, G-103
Real cost of hedging, G-103
Real interest rate, G-103
Realistic job preview (RJP), G-103
Realized gains, G-103
Realized losses, G-103
Realized rate of return, G-103
Real options, G-103
Real risk-free rate of interest, G-103
Reasonable accommodation, 84, G-103
Reasonable assurance, G-103
Receipts and disbursements method, G-103
Receivables, G-103
   control over, 101–102
Receivables collection period, 108

Receivables control, G-103
Receivables investment, 134
Receivables monitoring, G-104
Receiving depository financial
    institution (RDFI), G-104
Receiving report, G-104
Recency effect, G-104
Reciprocal demand, theory of, 162
Reciprocal interdependence, 25, 225
Record, G-104
Recourse, G-104
Recruiting, 81–82, G-104
Recruiting yield ratios, 227
Recursive least squares (RLS), G-104
Red bead experiment, G-104
Red-circled employee, G-104
Redesign, 78
Red-line method, 110
Red-lining, G-104
Reduced cycle time, 7
Reengineering, 77, G-104
Reference group, G-104
Referent groups, G-104
Referent power, 220
Referrals, G-104
Refreezing, 225, G-104
Refunding, 113, G-104
Regiocentric staffing outlook, G-104
Regional audit staff internal audit
    model, G-104
Regional Check Processing Centers
    (RCPCs), G-104
Regional structure, G-104
Regional trade communities, G-104
Register, G-104
Register disbursement scheme, G-104
Registrar, G-104
Registration statement, G-104
Registration to standards, G-104
Regression analysis, 245, G-104
Regression coefficient, G-104
Regular reports, G-104
Regulation CC, G-104
Regulation Q, G-105
Reinforcement, G-105
Reinforcement rate risk, G-105
Reinforcement theory, 8, G-105
Reinvestment rate assumption, G-105
Reinvoicing, 236, G-105
Reinvoicing center, G-105
Relational database, G-105
Relational operation, G-105
Relationship approach, G-105
Relationship selling, G-105
Relative-aggregate-scores approach, 201
Relative form of purchasing power
    parity, G-105
Relative frequency method, 245
Relaxed current asset investment
    policy, G-105
Relevant cash flows, G-105

Relevant costs, 98–99
Relevant range, G-105
Relevant risk, 123, G-105
Reliability, G-105
Religion, G-105
Remanufacturing, G-105
Remedy, G-105
Remittance advice, G-105
Rental, G-105
Reorder point, 110, 134, G-105
Repair, G-105
Repatriation, G-105
Repatriation of earnings, G-105
Repatriation program, G-105
Repeatability and reproducibility
    (R &R), G-105
Repeater, G-105
Repetitive manufacturing, G-105
Replacement analysis, 121
Replacement chain approach, G-105
Replacement charts, 226
Replacement cost, G-106
Replacement decisions, G-106
Replication, G-106
Reportable condition, G-106
Report form, G-106
Reporting period, G-106
Representative firms, G-106
Representative office, G-106
Repurchase agreement (RP), G-106
Request for admission, G-106
Request for information (RFI), G-106
Request for proposal (RFP), 29, G-106
Required completion time, G-106
Required rate of return, G-106
Requirements explosion, G-106
Re-recruiting, 82
Research and development costs, G-106
Research and development (R&D), 189
Research collaboration, G-106
Reserve borrowing capacity, G-106
Resident staff and central reviewers
    internal audit model, G-106
Resident staff and regional and central
    reviewers internal auditing
    model, G-106
Resident staff and regional reviewers
    internal audit model, G-106
Residual dividend policy, 119,
    208, G-106
Residual income (RI), 218–219, G-106
Residual value, G-106
Resiliency, G-106
Resistance to change, 26, G-106
Resolution, G-106
Resource Conservation and Recovery
    Act (RCRA), 18
Resource considerations, 35–36
Resource leveling, 35, G-106
Resource-limited scheduling,
    35–36, G-106

Resource planning, 47
Resource profile, 48
Resource requirements matrix, G-106
Respect-oriented leadership, G-106
Responsibility, 5, G-107
Responsibility accounting, 218, G-107
Responsibility accounting report
    for cost center, 98
    for profit center, 98
Responsibility center, G-107
Responsibility matrix, 32, G-107
Restricted current asset investment
    policy, G-107
Restrictive covenant, G-107
Restructuring, G-107
Retailing, G-107
Retail inventory methods, 196, G-107
Retail inventory pricing systems, 196
Retail inventory turns and levels,
    197–198
Retail inventory valuation
    methods, 196
Retail life cycle, G-107
Retail lockbox, G-107
Retail lockbox system, G-107
Retail management analysis, 194–199
Retail market, G-107
Retail method, 103, 196
Retail mix, G-107
Retail stores
    efficient, 200
    forecasting sales, 200
    layout, 199
Retained earnings, 112, 238, G-107
    cost of, 117
Retained earnings forecast, 239
Retained earnings statement, G-107
Retaliation, G-107
Retention of employees, 80
Return items, G-107
Return on assets (ROA), 172, 174, 190,
    198, 206, 208, 219, G-107
Return on common equity (ROE),
    129, G-107
Return on equity (ROE), 21, 172, 174,
    206, 208, 219, G-107
Return on investment (ROI), 83, 175,
    204, 215, 218–219, 219, G-107
Return on net assets (RONA), G-107
Return on net worth, 174
Return on quality (ROQ), 74, 78,
    215, G-107
Return-on-sales (ROS), 190, 208
Return-on-sales (ROS) ratio, 172
Return on total assets (ROA), 129, G-107
Revaluation reserve, G-107
Revenue, G-107
Revenue and inventory frauds, 151
Revenue Anticipation Notes, G-107
Revenue budget, G-107
Revenue center, G-107

Revenue expenditures, 103, G-107
Revenue recognition, G-107
Revenue recognition concept, G-107
Revenue securities, G-107
Reverse auction, G-107
Reverse culture shock, G-107
Reverse discrimination, 15, G-107
Reverse distribution, G-107
Reverse engineering, G-107
Reverse positive pay, G-108
Reverse price analysis, 176
Reverse repo, G-108
Reversion to the mean, 21
Revised-case scenarios, 212
Revocable letter of credit, G-108
Revolving credit agreement, 111, G-108
Revolving (guaranteed) line of credit, G-108
Reward power, 6, 220, G-108
Rework, G-108
Ricardian trade theory, 162
Ricardo, David, 160
Riding the yield curve, G-108
Rightsizing, G-108
Right the first time, G-108
Right-to-sue letter, G-108
Ring, G-108
Ringi, G-108
RISC (Reduced Instruction Set Computer), G-108
Risk, G-108
Risk-adjusted discount rate, 121, G-108
Risk-adjusted return on capital (RAROC), G-108
Risk analysis, 217, 233–236, G-108
Risk arbitrage, G-108
Risk assessment, G-108
Risk assessment/management, G-108
Risk aversion, G-108
Risk avoidance, 153, G-108
Risk avoider, 237, G-108
Risk classes, G-108
Risk exposure, G-108
Risk-free rate, 122, G-108
Risk identification and evaluation, 152–153
Risk management, G-108
Risk management information system (RMIS), G-108
Risk management policy, G-108
Risk management process, G-108
Risk management techniques, 153 implementing, 153–154
Risk manager, G-108
Risk mapping, G-108
Risk neutral, G-108
Risk neutral person, 237
Risk premium, RP, G-108
Risk profile, 42, G-108
Risk profiling, G-108
Risk propensity, G-109

Risk reduction, G-109
Risk-related concepts, 233–234
Risk retention, 153, 154, G-109
Risk-return analysis, 110
Risks
  business, 234
  controls and, 242–243
  financial, 234
  fundamentals of, 152
  investment, 233
  market, 233
  objective, 234
  project, 234
  rates of return and, 130
  systematic, 233
Risk spread, G-109
Risk structure of interest rate, G-109
Risk taker, 237, G-109
Risk transfer, 153, 154, G-109
Robinson-Patman Act, 17
Robotics, G-109
Robots, 141
Robustness, G-109
ROI, G-109
Role, G-109
Role ambiguity, G-109
Role conflict, G-109
Role-playing, G-109
Roll-on-roll-off (RORO), G-109
Root cause analysis, G-109
Root mean square error, G-109
Rough-cut capacity plans (RCCP), 48, G-109
Routine reporting, G-109
Routing, G-109
Royalty, G-109
Rule of reason, 16
Rules of Professional Conduct, G-109
Rule utilitarianism, 10
Run, G-109
Run charts, 73, G-109

S

Sabbatical leaves, 83
Safety, 86–87, G-109
Safety capacity, 185, G-109
Safety inventory, 185
Safety lead time, G-109
Safety needs, 8
Safety stock, 193, G-109
Safety time, 185
Salaries, G-109
Sale-and-leaseback, 114, G-109
Sales, 18
  marketing public relations on, 187
  strategic management and, 232
Sales administration, 69–70
Sales agents, G-109
Sales analysis, 232–233
Sales budget, G-109

Sales call anxiety, G-109
Sales calls, cost of, 232
Sales discounts, G-109
Sales effort, break-even point for, 232
Sales force automation, G-110
Sales force structure, 232
Sales forecast, 233, G-110
Sales leveling, G-110
Sales method, 172
Sales mix, 241, G-110
Sales performance variance, 233
Sales potential, G-110
Sales promotion, 58, G-110
Sales return percentage (ratio), G-110
Sales return (sales returns and allowances), G-110
Sales seasonality and deseasonality, 246
Sales-type lease, G-110
Sales variance analysis, 232–233
Same-day settlement, G-110
Sample, G-110
Sample information, G-110
Sample size, G-110
Sample standard deviation chart (s chart), G-110
Sampling risk, G-110
Sanction, G-110
Satellite links, 146
Satisficing, G-110
Scalability, G-110
Scale of market entities, G-110
Scanner, G-110
Scanning system, G-110
Scatter diagrams, 73, 245, G-110
Scenario analysis, 121, 217–218, G-110
Scenario building, G-110
Scenario planning, G-110
Scenario writing, G-110
Schedule, G-110
Scheduled receipts, 191
Schedule of reinforcement, G-110
Schedule performance index (SPI), 210
Schedule variance (SV), 210
Schema, G-110
Scientific management, G-110
S corporation, 123, G-109
Scrambled merchandising, G-110
Scrap factor, G-110
Sea bridge, G-110
Search, G-110
Search attributes, G-110
Search warrant, G-110
Seasonal component, G-111
Seasonal dating, G-111
Seasonal index, 246, G-111
Seasonality, 20
Sea transport and freight restrictions, 163
Secondary audience, G-111
Secondary data, G-111
Secondary market, G-111
Secondary research, G-111

Secondary statement approach, G-111
Second-degree price discrimination, 64
Second generation languages (2GLs), G-111
Secured loan, G-111
Securities Act (1933), 13–14
Securities and Exchange Commission (SEC), G-111
Securities Exchange Act (1934), 14
Securities regulation, 13–14, 166, G-111
Securitization, G-111
Security, 86–87, G-111
Security audit, G-111
Security interest, 66
Security market line (SML), 123, G-111
Security markets, 113
Security measures, G-111
Segregation of duties, G-111
Select, G-111
Selection, 51, G-111
   placement and, 82
Selection criterion, G-111
Selection rate, G-111
Selection tests, 82
Selective distribution, G-111
Selective listening, G-111
Selective restatements, G-111
Self-actualization needs, 8, 224
Self-concept, G-111
Self-directed learning, G-111
Self-directed team, G-111
Self-efficacy, G-111
Self-inspection, G-111
Self-insurance, 153, 154
Self-liquidation approach, G-77
Self-managed team, G-111
Self-management, G-111
Self-reference criterion (SRC), G-111
Self-serving bias, G-111
Self-sustaining international operation, G-111
Self-understanding as leadership skill, 71
Sell-a-product-as-is-or-process-it-further analysis, 204
Sell company, G-40
Sell hedge, G-111
Selling expenses, G-111
Selling forward, G-111
Selling group, G-111
Selling price
   determining, 178
   markup percentage on, 178
Selling sites, G-111
Semantic, G-111
Semantic nets, G-111
Semiannual compounding, G-111
Semistrong-form efficient, G-111
Semistructured problem, G-111
Seniority, G-111
Sensation-feeling, 23
Sensation-thinking, 23

Sensitivity analysis, 42, 43, 47, 121, 139, 217–218, G-111
   project, 217
Sensitivity training, G-112
Separation, 153
Sequential access, G-112
Sequential interdependence, 25, 225
Sequential oral interpreters, G-112
Serial correlation, G-112
Serial port, G-112
Serial transmission, 146, G-112
Serious health condition, G-112
Servant leader, G-112
Server, G-112
Serviceability, G-112
Service blueprint, G-112
Service capacity, 53, G-112
Service capacity management, 54
Service consistency, G-112
Service costing methods, 96–97
Service department charges, G-112
Service experiences, managing, 54
Service facility layout, 200–201
Service gap, 69, G-112
Service heterogeneity, G-112
Service lease, G-85
Service level agreement (SLA), G-112
Service levels, lead times and, 193
Service management analysis, 200–201
Service mark, 14
Service organization, G-112
Service quality, 69, 77, G-112
Service recovery, G-112
Services, G-112
Services businesses, G-112
Servicescapes, G-112
Service sites, G-112
Services marketing, 69
Services trade, G-112
Service strategy, 53–54
Service technology, G-112
SERVQUAL, 77
Settlement, G-112
Settlement date, G-112
Settlement range, G-112
Setup, G-112
Setup time, G-112
Seven basic tools of quality, G-112
Seven management tools of quality, G-112
Seven QC Tools, 73
Seventh EU Company Law Directive, 106, G-112
Severance pay, G-112
Sex/gender discrimination, 87
Sexual harassment, 16, 84, 87, G-112
Shamrock team, G-112
Shape, G-113
Shareholder value maximization, G-113
Sharing, G-113

Shelf registration, G-113
Sherman Antitrust Act, 16, G-113
Shewhart cycle, G-113
Shingo's seven wastes, G-113
Shipper's order, G-113
Ship-to-stock program, G-113
Shop floor control, G-113
Shortest processing time (SPT) rule, 191
Short-term assets, managing, 109–111, 133–134
Short-term credit, 109, 111, G-113
Short-term financing
   alternatives, 112
   international, 127
   managing, 111–112
Short-term investment management, 110–111
Short-term liabilities, managing, 111–112, 134
Short-term notes payable, journal entries for, 104
Short-term orientation, G-113
Shrinkage, G-113
Sight draft, G-113
Sigma, G-113
Sign, G-113
Signal, G-113
Signal-to-noise ratio (S/N ratio), G-113
Signified, G-113
Signifier, G-113
Silo, G-113
Simple interest, G-113
Simple interest approximation formula, G-113
Simple interest loan, G-113
Simple linear regression, 245
Simple moving average method, 246
Simple (quoted) interest rate, G-113
Simple rate, G-113
Simple regression, G-113
Simplex, G-113
Simulation, 43, 83, G-113
   of equipment maintenance times, 238
   of stock prices, 237
Simulation experiment, G-113
Simultaneous engineering, 76
Simultaneous oral interpreters, G-113
Single-buyer policy, G-113
Single-criterion decision problem, G-114
Single European Act, G-113
Single-minute exchange of dies (SMED), G-114
Single-piece flow, G-114
Single plantwide factory overhead rate method, G-113
Single-source systems, G-114
Single-step income statements, G-114
Single-use plans, G-114
Sinking fund, 113, G-114
SIPOC, G-114
Site location, 201

SUBJECT INDEX   I-33

Situational ethics, 10
Situational theory, 6
Situation analysis, 2, 171, G-114
Situation ethics, G-114
Situation interview, G-114
Situation leadership, G-114
Situation scheme, G-114
Situation theory, G-114
Six-sigma, 7, 73, 214, G-114
Six-sigma quality, G-114
Skill variety, G-114
Skimming, G-114
Skip-level meeting, G-114
SKU, G-114
Skunkworks, G-114
Slack times, 210, G-114
Slary surveys, G-131
Slide, G-114
Small-batch and unit production, 225
Small business policy, G-114
Small power distance culture, G-114
Smith, Adam, 160
Smithsonian Agreement, 162, G-114
Smoking at work, 87
Smoot-Hawley Act, G-114
Smoothing, 35, G-114
Smoothing constant, 246, G-114
Snail mail, G-114
Snake, G-114
Social accounting, 90
Social altruism, G-114
Social audit, G-114
Social awareness, G-114
Social contract, 62
Social contribution, G-114
Social egalitarians, 11
Social ethics theories, 11
Social facilitation, G-114
Social forces, G-114
Social infrastructure, G-114
Social interaction paradigm, G-114
Socially conscious movement, G-115
Socially acceptable and unacceptable, G-115
Social regulations, 163
Social responsibility, 11, G-114
Social stratification, G-115
Sociocultural contexts, G-115
Socioemotional role, G-115
Soft controls, G-115
Soft currencies, G-115
Soft skills, G-115
Software, G-115
Software piracy, G-115
Sogoshosha, G-115
SOHO (Small Office/Home Office), G-115
Sole proprietorship, G-115
Solvency, 205, G-115
Solvency analysis, 93
Solvency ratios, G-115

Source code, G-115
Southeast Asian management, G-115
Sovereign immunity, 166, G-115
Spaced practice, G-115
Space productivity, 198, 199
Spaghetti chart, G-115
Spamming, 148
Span of control, G-115
Span of management, 5, G-115
Special causes, G-115
Special drawing rights (SDRs), 164, 165, G-115
Special economic zones, G-115
Specialization of division of labor, G-115
Special orders, 204
Special-purpose team, G-115
Special reports, G-115
Specie, G-115
Specification, G-115
Specific price index, G-115
Specific tariff, 163
Speculative balance, G-115
Speculative motive, G-115
Speculative risk, G-115
Speculator, G-115
Speech recognition, G-115
Speech synthesizing, G-115
Sponsorship marketing, G-115
Sponsorships, 58
Spontaneous financing, G-115
Spontaneously generated funds, G-115
Spoofing, G-115
Sporadic problem, G-115
Spot market, G-116
Spot rates, 236, G-116
Spreadsheets, 19
Spurious correlation, G-116
SQL (Structured Query Language), G-116
Square root law (SRL), 228, G-116
Stable, predictable dividends, G-116
Stable distribution, G-116
Staff authority, G-116
Staffing levels, 226
Stage-Gate process, G-116
Stage of subsidiary development, G-116
Stages of creativity, G-116
Stages of team growth, G-116
Stakeholder, G-116
Stakeholder audit, G-116
Stakeholder-based performance scorecard measurements, 219
Stakeholder environment, G-116
Stakeholder management, 154
Stakeholders, G-116
Stand-alone risk, 121, G-116
Standard, G-116
Standard check processing, G-116
Standard cost, G-116
Standard cost systems, G-116

Standard deviation, 153, 211, 245, G-116
Standardization, G-116
Standardized approach, G-116
Standard of living, G-116
Standards gap, 69
Standard worldwide pricing, G-116
Standby letter of credit, G-116
Standby machine, 194
Standby parts, 188
Standing plans, G-116
Star, G-116
Stars, 171
Stated value, G-116
Statement of cash flows, 92, G-116
Statement of Financial Accounting Standards No. 52, G-116
Statement of retained earnings, G-116
Statement of stockholder's equity, G-117
Statement of work (SOW), G-117
Statement on Auditing Standards (SAS), G-117
State-owned enterprise, G-117
States of nature, 42, G-117
Static budget, G-117
Static IP number, G-117
Static simulation model, G-117
Static surveillance, G-117
Stationary surveillance, G-117
Statistical analysis, 152, 154, G-117
Statistical confidence, G-117
Statistical decomposition, G-117
Statistical process control (SPC), G-117
Statistical quality control (SQC), G-117
Statistical thinking, G-117
Statistics, 76
Status review meeting, 41
Statute, G-117
Statutory (legal) reserve, G-117
Statutory limitations, 16
Statutory merger, G-117
Stepped-up exercise price, G-117
Stereotypes, G-117
Stereotyping, 23, 223, G-117
Sterilized intervention, G-117
Stochastic model, G-117
Stock, G-117
Stock dividend, 119, G-117
Stockholders, G-117
Stockholders' equity, 112
  ratio of liabilities to, 91
Stockholder wealth maximization, G-117
Stock market, 122
Stock option, G-117
Stockouts, costs of, 228
Stock prices, simulation of, 237
Stock split, 119, G-117
Stock-to-sales ratio method, 195
Stone model, G-117
Storage, G-117
Storage costs, G-117

Storage service provider (SSP), G-117
Store productivity and performance, 198
Storming, G-117
Storyboarding, G-117
Straddle, G-117
Straight bill of lading, G-117
Straight-line depreciation method, G-118
Straight piece-rate system, G-118
Straight rebuy, G-118
Strategic activities, G-118
Strategic advantage, G-118
Strategic alliance, G-118
Strategic analysis, 171
Strategic business partnering, 2
Strategic business unit (SBU), 171, G-118
Strategic control, 155
Strategic fit review, G-118
Strategic goals, 225, G-118
Strategic human resource management, G-118
Strategic information system, 135, G-118
Strategic leader, G-118
Strategic management, 2, 44, 155, G-118
Strategic management analysis, 171
Strategic managers, G-118
Strategic marketing concept, G-118
Strategic objectives, G-118
Strategic plan, G-118
Strategic planning, 71, G-118
Strategic plans, G-118
Strategic sourcing, G-118
Strategic supply chain, 46
Strategic withdrawal, 249
Strategy, G-118
Strategy development, 71
Strategy evaluation, 155
Strategy formulation, 2, 155, 171, G-118
Strategy implementation, 155, 171, G-118
Stratified random sampling, G-118
Strengths, weaknesses, opportunities, and threats (SWOT), 2, 171
Stress, 23–24, G-118
Stress interview, G-118
Stretch goals, G-118
Stretching accounts payable, G-118
Strict liability, 17, 67–68
Strike price, G-118
Striking price, G-118
Strong-form efficient, G-118
Structural Adjustment Loan Facility (SAL), G-118
Structural causes, G-118
Structural design, 2
Structural variation, G-118
Structured data, G-118
Structured interviews, 82, G-118
Structured problem, 139, G-118

Structured Query Language (SQL), 141, G-118
Stylus, G-118
Subjective method, 245
Subjective risk, G-119
Suboptimization, G-119
Subordinated debenture, G-119
Subscription, G-119
Subsidiary, G-119
Subsidiary company, G-119
Subsidiary ledger, G-119
Subsidies, 163, 164
Substance abuse, 87, G-119
Substitute, G-119
Substitutes-for-leadership concept, 6
Subsystem, G-119
Succession planning, 226, G-119
Successor event, G-119
Suggestion selling, G-119
Sugging, G-119
Suite, G-119
Sum-of-the-years-digits depreciation method, G-119
Sunk costs, 121, 202, G-119
Supercomputer, G-119
Super-NOW accounts, G-119
Superordinate goal, 27
Superordinate goalss, G-119
Supplier, G-119
Supplier audits, 176, G-119
Supplier base and supplier performance analysis, 176
Supplier break-even analysis, 177
Supplier certification, 176, G-119
Supplier credit, G-119
Supplier development, G-119
Supplier evaluation, 51, G-119
Supplier identification, G-119
Supplier integration, G-119
Supplier management, G-119
Supplier network, G-119
Supplier partnering, G-119
Supplier performance measurement, 215, G-119
Supplier quality assurance, G-119
Supplier quality evaluation, 215
Supplier quality management, 51
Supplier quality rating index (SQRI), 215
Supplier selection strategy and criteria, G-119
Supply and demand, 63
Supply chain, G-119
Supply chain inventory, managing, 46
Supply chain management, 44, 61, G-120
Supply chain management analysis, 175–177
Supply side market failure, G-120
Support processes, G-120
Support systems, G-120
Surfers, 147, G-120

Surplus, 63
Surveillance audit, G-120
Survey, G-120
Survey feedback, 225, G-120
Survey techniques, 20
Sustainable competitive advantage, G-120
Sustainable growth, G-120
Swaps, 165, 236, G-120
Swap strategies, G-120
Sweatshops, G-120
Sweep accounts, G-120
SWIFT, G-120
Switch, 158
Switching costs, G-120
Switching techniques, G-120
SWOT analysis, G-120
Symmetric encryption, G-120
Symmetric information, G-120
Symptom, G-120
Synchronized cash flows, G-120
Synchronized production, G-120
Syndicate, G-120
Syndicated Eurocredit loans, G-120
Synergy, G-121
Syntax error, G-121
Synthetic composite, G-121
System, G-121
System acquisition, alternative approaches to, 143–144
Systematic risk, 233, G-121
System clock, G-121
System of authorizations, G-121
System of profound knowledge (SoPK), G-121
System reliability and redundancy, 216
System requirements, G-121
Systems analysis, G-121
Systems approach to management, G-121
Systems concept, G-121
Systems concept of logistics, G-121
Systems design, G-121
Systems development, 142–143
Systems development led by users (SDLU), 143, G-121
Systems development life cycle (SDLC), 33, 142–143, G-121
Systems integration, G-121
Systems integrator, G-121
System software, G-121
Systems theory, 4, 225, G-121
Systems thinking, G-121

T

Tablet computer, G-121
T account, G-121
Tacit knowledge, G-121
Tactical activities, G-121
Tactical goals, G-121

Tactical managers, G-121
Tactical objectives, G-121
Tactical plans, G-121
Tactics, G-121
Taguchi, Genichi, 74, 75
  loss function of, 76
Taguchi loss function, G-121
Taguchi methods, G-121
Tailing, G-121
Takeover, G-121
Takt time, G-121
Tall structure, G-121
Tally sheet, G-121
Tampering, G-121
Target balance sheet, 116
Target costing, G-122
Target costs, 172, G-122
Targeting, G-122
Target marketing, G-122
Target markets, 68, G-122
Target (minimum) cash balance, G-122
Target (optimal) capital structure, G-122
Target profits, 172
Target returns, 172
Target zones, G-122
Tariff-rate quota, 163
Tariffs, 208, G-122
  ad valorem, 163
  compound, 163
  specific, 163
Tariffs and quotas, G-122
Tariff trade barriers, 163
Task, G-122
Task-based job analysis, 81
Task environment, 24
Task force, G-122
Task identity, G-122
Task significance, G-122
Task specialist role, G-122
Task specialists, 222
Taxable-equivalent yield, G-122
Taxable income, G-122
Taxable instruments, G-122
Tax accounting, 90
Tax-advantaged instruments, G-122
Tax anticipation notes, G-122
Tax concessions, 164
Tax courts, G-122
Tax credit, G-122
Tax equalization, G-122
Tax equalization plan, G-122
Tax-exempt commercial paper, G-122
Tax holiday, G-122
Tax loss carryback and carryover, G-122
Tax policy, G-122
TCP/IP (Transmission Control Protocol/Internet Protocol), G-122
Teaching services, G-122
Team, G-122
Team approach, 5

Team-based compensation, 8
Team-based structure, 4, G-122
Team building, 39, 225, G-122
Team cohesiveness, G-122
Team culture, G-122
Team dynamics, G-122
Team facilitation, G-122
Team interview, G-122
Team management, 6, 220
Team performance evaluation, rewards, and recognition, G-122
Team reward, 230
Team structure, G-122
Teamwork, 26–27, 222
Technical core, G-122
Technical design review meetings, 41
Technical feasibility study, G-122
Technical forecasting, G-123
Technical skill, G-123
Technology, G-123
Technology-driven workplace, 4
Technology transfer, G-123
Telecommunications, 145–146, G-123
Telecommunications manager, G-123
Telecommuting, G-123
Teleconferencing, G-123
Temporal method, G-123
Temporary accounts, G-123
Temporary current assets, G-123
Temporary differences, G-123
Temporary investments, G-123
Tender offers, 14
Tenor, G-123
"Tentative U.S. tax," G-123
Terminal cash flow, G-123
Terminal value, G-123
Terminal warehouse agreement, G-123
Term loan, 113, G-123
Term repos, G-123
Terms of credit, G-123
Term spread, G-123
Term structure of interest rates, G-123
Territorial approach, G-123
Terrorism, G-123
Testimonial evidence, G-123
Theft investigation methods, G-123
Theocracy, G-123
Theoretical capacity, G-123
Theoretical standards, G-123
Theory of comparative advantage, G-123
Theory of constraints (TOC), 187, G-123
Theory of dual entitlement, G-123
Theory of knowledge, G-123
Theory T and Theory T+, G-123
Theory X, 224, G-124
Theory Y, 224, G-124
Theory Z, 224, G-124
Thin capitalization, G-124

Thin client, G-124
Thin market, G-124
Third-country national, G-124
Third-degree price discrimination, 64
Third-generation languages (3GLs), G-124
Third-party information vendor, G-124
Three-sixty-degree (360) feedback process, G-124
Throughput, G-124
Throughput time, G-124
Tiered pricing, G-124
Time, place, and possession utilities, G-124
Time-based competition, G-124
Time bomb, G-124
Time draft, G-124
Time equals money, G-124
Time estimate, G-124
Time preferences for consumption, G-124
Time series, 246, G-124
Time-series analysis, 45, G-124
Time series decomposition, 45
Time series models, G-124
Time series regression, G-124
Time-series techniques, G-124
Times-interest-earned (TIE) ratio, 129, G-124
Time span, G-124
Time tickets, G-124
Time to market, G-124
Time value of money, 130–131, 181, G-124
Time value of money analysis, 124
Title, warranty of, 66, 67
TL 9000, G-124
T1 line, 146
T3 line, 146
Tobin's q ratio, 13
Token passing, G-124
Tolerance, G-124
Tolerance design (Taguchi), G-124
Tolerance for ambiguity, G-124
Top-down budgeting, 239–240, 242, G-124
Top-down planning, 136, G-124
Top-management commitment, G-124–125
Top manager, G-125
Topology, G-125
Total assets, 239
Total assets turnover, 174, 206
Total assets turnover ratio, 129, G-125
Total budgeted cost (TBC), 36, G-125
Total carrying cost, 134
Total (combined) leverage, 117
Total contribution margin, 173
Total cost, 211, G-125
Total cost concept, G-125
Total cost of ownership, G-125

Total debt ratio, 206
Total factor productivity, G-125
Total fixed costs, 202
Total inventory cost, 134
Total leverage, 173, 174
Total load, 192
Total manufacturing cycle time, 84
Total operating costs, 197
Total ordering cost, 134
Total productive maintenance (TPM), G-125
Total quality, 72, 78–79
Total quality control, 75
Total quality culture, 77
Total quality management (TQM), 4, 7, 44, 77, 225, 242, G-125
Total slack (TS), G-125
Total stocking cost (TSC), 198
Total throughput, 184–185
Total variable costs, 202
Touch screen, G-125
Tourism, G-125
Toxic Substances Control Act (TSCA), 18
Traceability, G-125
Trackball, G-125
Tracking, G-125
Track pad, G-125
Tradable emissions, 12
Trade, 158
Trade acceptance, G-125
Trade allowances (trade deals), G-125
Trade barriers, G-125
   non-tariff, 163–164
   tariff, 163
Trade creation, G-125
Trade credit, 111, G-125
Trade discount, G-125
Trade diversion, G-125
Trade draft, G-125
Trade-in allowance, G-125
Trademark, 14, G-125
Trade names, 15
Tradeoff analysis, 238, G-125
Trade-off concept, G-125
Trade policy measures, G-125
Trade promotion authority, G-125
Traders, G-125–126
Trade secrets, 14
Trade symbols, 14–15
Trading blocs, G-126
Trading company, G-126
Trading security, G-126
Traditional organization, G-126
Traditional payback period, 179
Tragedy of the commons, G-126
Training, 82–83, G-126
Training evaluation, G-126
Training needs assessment, G-126
Traits, G-126
Tramp service, G-126

Transaction, G-126
Transactional leader, G-126
Transactional leadership, G-126
Transaction approach, G-126
Transaction-Based Information System (TBIS), G-126
Transaction efficiency, G-126
Transaction exposure, G-126
Transaction motive, G-126
Transaction Processing System (TPS), 138, G-126
Transaction risk exposure, G-126
Transactions, 91
Transactions balance, 109, G-126
Transaction sets, G-126
Transactions exposure, 235
Transceiver, G-126
Transferable letter of credit, G-126
Transfer agent, G-126
Transfer items, G-126
Transfer price, G-126
Transfer pricing, 65, 98, 178, G-126
Transfer risk, G-126
Transformational leader, G-126
Transformational leadership, 6, G-126
Transformative technological innovations, G-126
Transition stay bonus, G-126
Transition tree, G-126
Transit items, G-126
Transit routing number, G-126
Transit times, G-126
Translation exposure, 236, G-126
Transmission rate, G-126
Transnational corporation (TNC), G-126
Transnational international strategy, 158
Transnational strategy, 2, G-126
Transparency, G-126–127
Transportation cost analysis, 228
Transportation problem, 246
Transposition, G-127
Transshipment problem, 247
Trash investigation, G-127
Treadway Commission, G-127
Treasury management workstation, G-127
Treasury stock, G-127
Tree, G-127
Tree diagram, 72, G-127
Trend, G-127
Trend analysis, 20, G-127
Trespass, 17
Trial-and-error analysis, 201
Trial balance, 91, G-127
Trial impact, G-127
Triangular arbitrage, G-127
Trigger mechanisms, G-127
True and fair view, 107, G-127
Trustee, G-127

Trustee under indenture, G-127
Trust receipt, 112
Trust receipt loans, G-127
Trust services, G-127
Truth-in-Lending Act, 66
T test, G-120
Turnbull model, 150
Turnkey operation, G-127
Turnover, 80, G-127
Turnover ratios, G-127
Twisted-pair-cable, G-127
Two-bin inventory system, G-127
Two-card kanban system, G-127
Two-column journal, G-127
Two-factor motivation theory, 8, 224
Two-transaction approach, G-127
Tying arrangement, 16, 17
Type A behavior, G-127
Type B behavior, G-127
Type I error, G-127
Type II error, G-127

U

Ubuntu, G-127
U chart, G-127
Umbrella policy, G-127
Unattainable capability, G-127
Unavoidable costs, 203
Unbiased expectations hypothesis, G-127–128
Uncertainty, G-128
Uncertainty acceptance, G-128
Uncertainty avoidance, G-128
Uncollected balance percentages, G-128
Uncollectible accounts expense, G-128
Uncollectible receivables, journal entries for direct write-off of, 102
Uncommitted lines of credit, G-128
Unconditional guarantee, G-128
Uncontrollable input, G-128
Underapplied factory overhead, G-128
Under-capacity, 192
Underpricing, 182
Underproduction, 21
Underwriter's spread, G-128
Underwriting syndicate, G-128
Underwritten arrangement, G-128
Undistributed earnings, G-128
Undue hardship, G-128
Unearned revenues, G-128
Unenforceable contract, 19
Unethical, G-128
Uneven cash flow stream, G-128
Unfairness, 65
Unfreezing, G-128
Uniform commercial code, G-128
Uniform Commercial Code (UCC), 18
Uniform delivered pricing, G-128
Uniform Guidelines on Employee Selection Procedures, 88

Uniform Resource Locator (URL), G-128
Unilateral contract, 19
Unilateral transfers, G-128
Unintentional amoral management, G-128
Uninterruptible power supply (UPS), G-128
Unique visitor pages, G-128
Unique visitors per month, G-128
Unique ZIP code, G-128
Unit contribution margin, 95, 241, G-128
Unit cost factor, 100
United Nations, G-128
United Nations Convention on Contracts for the International Sales of Goods (CISG), 166
Unit labor cost, G-128
Unit measure concept, G-128
Unit price, 100
Units-of-production depreciation method, G-128
Unity of command, G-128
Universal, G-128
Universal factors framework, G-128
Universalism, 167, G-128
Universal Product Code (UPC), G-128
UNIX, G-128
Unrealized (holding) gains, G-129
Unrealized (holding) losses, G-129
Unsecured, G-129
Unsolicited order, G-129
Unstructured data, G-129
Unstructured problem, 139, G-129
Uploading, G-129
Upper control limit (UCL), G-129
Upstream, G-129
Upward communication, 221, G-129
Usable funds, G-129
Usage rate, G-129
Users, G-129
Utilitarian approach, G-129
Utilitarianism, 10, 11, 224
Utilities, 237, G-129
    in decision making, 43
Utility analysis, G-129
Utilization, 192, 201, G-129
Utilization analysis, G-129
Utilization review, G-129

V

Vacation pay, 85, 105
Valence, G-129
Validation, G-129
Valid contract, 19
Validity, G-129
Valuation, G-129
Valuation approach, G-129
Value, G-129

Value added, G-129
Value-added activities, G-129
Value-added lead time, G-129
Value-added network (VAN), 149, G-129
Value-added tax (VAT), G-129
Value analysis, 177, 189–190, G-129
Value at risk (VAR), 153, G-129
Value chain, 189, G-130
Value congruence as leadership skill, 71
Value dating, G-130
Value engineering, 177, 189, 190, G-129, G-130
Value index, 189
Value offering analysis, 243
Value/price ratio, 243
Value proposition, G-130
Value research, G-129
Values, G-130
Values and lifestyles (VALS), 59
Value stream, G-130
Value stream mapping, G-130
Variable control charts, 216
Variable cost concept, G-130
Variable costing, 99–100, G-130
Variable costs, 99, 190, 202, G-130
Variable data, G-130
Variable identification, G-130
Variable overhead, 175
Variable pay, 86, G-130
Variable rate demand notes, G-130
Variable sampling plan, G-130
Variance, 153, 211, 245, G-130
Variance, σ^2, G-130
Variance analysis model, G-130
Variation, G-130
VAT analysis, G-130
VAT concept, G-130
Vendor analysis and selection, 176
Vendor capital firm, G-130
Vendor fraud, G-130
Verification, G-130
Vertical analysis, 93, G-130
Vertical information interchange, 149
Vertical integration, 65
Vertically integrate, G-130
Vertical market, G-130
Vertical merger, 17, G-130
Vertical privity, 67
Vertical restraints, 16
Vertical team, G-130
Vesting, G-131
Victim, G-131
Videoconferencing, 146, G-131
Video streaming, 83
Virtual approach, 5
Virtual memory, G-131
Virtual organization, 146, G-131
Virtual reality, 83, G-131
Virtual Reality Modeling Language (VRML), 148, G-131
Virtual teams, 26, G-131

Virus (computer virus), G-131
Visible pay inequity, G-131
Vision, G-131
Visionary leadership, 6, 71
Visual control, G-131
Vital few, useful many, G-131
Voice mail, 146
Voice of the customer (VOC), G-131
Voice recognition, G-131
Voidable contract, 19
Void contract, 19
Voir dire, G-131
Volatile memory, G-131
Volume variance, 233, G-131
Voluntary assumption, 67, 68
Voluntary restraint agreements, G-131
Voucher, G-131
Voucher system, 100, G-131
Vroom-Jago model, 221, G-131

W

Wa, G-131
Wage assignments, 66
Wages, G-131
Wage surveys, G-131
Waiting line management, 54, 201
Waiting line models, 201
Wait states, G-131
Walkabout, G-131
Walk the talk, G-131
Wants, G-131
WAN (Wide Area Network), G-131
Warehouse receipt financing, 112
Warehousing, G-131
Warrant, 114, G-131
Warranties, 66–67
    disclaimer of, 67
    express, 66, 67
    implied, 66
    limitation or modification of, 67
Warranty liabilities, G-132
Warranty of merchantability, implied, 67
Warranty of title, 66, 67
Waste, G-132
WCR/S, G-132
Weak-form efficient, G-132
Web-based applications, 52
Webb-Pomerene Act, G-132
Webmaster, G-132
Web page, G-132
Web page authoring tools, G-132
Web site, G-132
Web-visit hijacking, G-132
Weekend effect, G-132
Week's supply method, 195
Weibull distribution, G-132
Weighted average cost of capital (WACC), 118, 179, 207, G-132
Weighted moving averages, 246, G-132

Weighted-point system, 215
Wellness programs, 87, G-132
Well-pay, G-132
What-if analysis, 139, G-132
Wheel of retailing theory, G-132
Whistle-blowing, G-132
Whitemall bribery, G-132
Wholesale lockbox system, G-132
Wholesale market, G-132
Wholesalers, G-132
Wholly owned foreign affiliate, G-132
Wholly-owned subsidiaries, 158, 167, G-132
Wide area network (WAN), 146
Window dressing techniques, G-132
Winters' three-factor model, 45
Wire drawdowns, G-132
Wireless access protocol (WAP), G-132
Wireless communication, G-132
Wireless LAN, G-132
Wire transfers, G-132
Wisdom, G-132
Withholding taxes, G-132
Within-firm risk, 121
Without recourse, G-132
With recourse, G-132
Word (data word), G-132
Work, G-132
Work analysis, G-132–133
Workbook, G-133
Work breakdown structure (WBS), 32, G-133
Work center, inventory levels at, 191
Work center load balancing analysis, 192
Work center performance analysis, 192
Work cycle, G-133
Worker Adjustment and Retraining Notification (WARN), 16
Worker efficiency, G-133
Workers' compensation, 87, G-133
Workflow analysis, 81, G-133
Workflow interdependence, 25
Workforce diversity, G-133
Workforce diversity analysis, 226

Workforce diversity management, 84
Workforce forecasting, 226
Work group, G-133
Working capital, 108, 205–206, G-133
Working capital cycle, G-133
Working capital financing policy, 207
Working Capital Guarantee Program, G-133
Working capital investment decision, G-133
Working capital management, G-133
Working capital policy, 108–109, 133, G-133
Working capital requirements, G-133
Working capital turnover ratio, G-133
Work-in-process inventory, 203, G-133
Work instruction, G-133
Work measurement, 248
Work packages, 28, G-133
Workplace air quality, 87
Work redesign, G-133
Work redesign programs, G-133
Work sample tests, G-133
Work scheduling, G-133
Work scope, G-133
Works council, G-133
Work sheet, G-133
Work specialization, 5, G-133
Workstations, 194, G-133
World Bank, G-133
World-class competitors, G-133
World-class suppliers, 176
World-class supply base, 52
World Trade Center, attacks on, 157
World Trade Organization (WTO), 166, G-133
Worldwide approach, G-133
Worldwide disclosures diversity and harmonization, 106
World Wide Web (Web, WWW), G-133
Worm, G-133
WORM (Write Once, Read Many), G-133

Worst-case scenario, 217, G-133
Writer, G-133
Written communication, 41, 161
Written principles, G-133

X

X-bar chart, 216, G-133

Y

Yankee stock, 113, G-133
Yield, G-134
Yield curve, 122, G-134
Yield management, 54, 200
Yield ratios, G-134
  recruiting, 227
Yield spread, G-134
Yield spread swap, G-134
Yield to maturity (YTM), 115, G-134

Z

Zero-balance account, G-134
Zero-balance accounts, 109
Zero-based budgeting, G-134
Zero coupon bond, G-134
Zero defects, G-134
Zero-growth, 115
Zero-growth stock, G-134
Zero Investment Improvement, G-134
Zones of policy agreement, 162

Numbers

10-K, G-1
10-Q, G-1
360-degree feedback, G-1
40/30/30 rule, G-1
401(k) plan, G-1
4/5ths Rule, G-1
8-K, G-1